History of the Middle Temple

The history of the Middle Temple is a long and fascinating one. Templars held the estate of the Temple from the twelfth century until their suppression in the early fourteenth century; thereafter the lawyers came. The magnificent Tudor Hall of the Middle Temple was completed in 1574. By Elizabethan times the Inns of Court were known colloquially as the Third University of England. Many persons other than lawyers became members of Middle Temple—among them Sir Walter Raleigh, Elias Ashmole, Edward Hyde (Earl of Clarendon), William Congreve, Henry Fielding, Edmund Burke, William Cowper and William Makepeace Thackeray. Another Middle Templar and explorer was Bartholomew Gosnold, discoverer of Cape Cod, who named a nearby island Martha's Vineyard in honour of his six-year-old daughter. From those beginnings grew the thirteen American colonies, and in due course five Middle Templars signed the American Declaration of Independence on 4 July 1776. Moreover, the US Constitution was drafted by a committee chaired by yet another Middle Templar, John Rutledge, who, along with six other Middle Templars, was among its 39 original signatories.

The story of the Inn in modern times has seen it become one of the world's pre-eminent centres for legal education and practice.

This history of the Middle Temple, written by a team of eminent lawyers and legal historians, is the product of original research in the archives of the Middle Temple and will be a treasure trove of information about the Inn, its diverse history and influence.

History of the Middle Temple

Edited by

Richard O Havery

·HART·
PUBLISHING

OXFORD AND PORTLAND, OREGON
2011

Published in the United Kingdom by Hart Publishing Ltd
16C Worcester Place, Oxford, OX1 2JW
Telephone: +44 (0)1865 517530
Fax: +44 (0)1865 510710
E-mail: mail@hartpub.co.uk
Website: http://www.hartpub.co.uk

Published in North America (US and Canada) by
Hart Publishing
c/o International Specialized Book Services
920 NE 58th Avenue, Suite 300
Portland, OR 97213–3786
USA
Tel: +1 503 287 3093 or toll-free: (1) 800 944 6190
Fax: +1 503 280 8832
E-mail: orders@isbs.com
Website: http://www.isbs.com

British Library Cataloguing in Publication Data

Data Available

ISBN: 978-1-84113-421-5

Typeset by Columns Design XML Ltd, Reading
Printed and bound in Great Britain by
the MPG Books Group, UK

While every care has been taken to establish and acknowledge copyright, and to contact
copyright owners, the publishers apologise for any accidental infringement and would be
pleased to come to a suitable agreement with the rightful copyright owners in each case.

This book is dedicated to the memory of
Sir David Calcutt, QC, whose idea it was

Editor's Note

Lesley Whitelaw, the Archivist of the Middle Temple, has made a signal contribution to this book. Her familiarity and facility with the archives of the Inn, coupled with her historical and palaeographical knowledge, have been of invaluable help to me in the preparation of the book. She has made a particular contribution to the passages on the Molyneux Globes, and has been the source of numerous ideas in relation to the writing and illustration of the book.

Lesley's assistant, Hannah Baker, has used her skills in making up CDs of many of the illustrations. Celia Pilkington, the Archivist of the Inner Temple, has given freely of her time in helping me to find documents relating to the fate and replacement of the old Purbeck marble columns in the Temple church. Christopher Morcom Q.C. has advised me on copyright questions. Ian Garwood, the Director of Estates, and Ian Smith, the Surveyor of the Middle Temple, produced the diagrams relating to the construction of the double hammerbeam roof of Middle Temple Hall. One of the authors, Sir John Baker, has suggested, read and translated ancient documents. The opinion of Peter Barber, MA, FSA, FRHistSoc, Head of Map Collections at the British Library, that Ashley is a more likely source than James I for Middle Temple's Molyneux Globes, finds expression in the book. Kristine McGlothlin, head of bench administration at Middle Temple, has prepared publicity material for the book, in conjunction with Jo Ledger of Hart Publishing. Rachel Pydiah, the secretary of the Under-Treasurer of the Middle Temple, provided the typescript of the American appendix. I have had the pleasure of dealing with Richard Hart in many respects relating to the publication of the book, in particular in relation to the finding of authors and to the design of the book. Rachel Turner, his assistant, has been infinitely patient and businesslike in receiving the various drafts. Mel Hamill has tirelessly helped in the administration of the copy editing. The copy editor herself, Catherine Minahan, has proposed some felicitous amendments. Tom Adams has smoothed the way to the production of the printed copy. And it was Sir Louis Blom-Cooper, QC, who made the happy suggestion that I approach Hart Publishing to publish the book. To all of these people I am deeply grateful.

Dates given in the text are NS. References to Parliament are generally references to the Middle Temple Parliament, which is a general meeting of benchers of the Inn held regularly during the year as part of the governance of the Inn.

Finally, two small points. I have used the spelling Raleigh for Sir Walter notwithstanding that his name is spelt Rawley in the Middle Temple Admissions Register and is spelt Ralegh in the DNB and the ODNB. Raleigh is the common spelling and any other is likely to be distracting to the general reader. If necessary, I pray in aid Cardinal Wolsey, who, the DNB tells us, invariably signed his name Wulcy. And I use the plural Knights Templar in deference to modern usage.

Contents

Author Biographies

BAKER

Professor Sir John Baker QC, FBA, has since 1998 been Downing Professor of the Laws of England at Cambridge, where he is a Fellow of St Catharine's College. He is an Honorary Bencher of the Inner Temple, where he was called to the Bar in 1966, and an Honorary Queen's Counsel. For 30 years he has been Literary Director of the Selden Society. His books include *The Order of Serjeants at Law* (1984); *The Legal Profession and the Common Law* (1986); *Readers and Readings in the Inns of Court and Chancery* (2000); *The Common Law Tradition* (2000); *An Introduction to English Legal History* (4th edn, 2002); *volume VI of the Oxford History of the Laws of England*, covering the period 1483–1558 (2003), and *An Inner Temple Miscellany* (2004). In 2003 he was knighted for services to English legal history.

COCKS

Ray Cocks is a member of the Middle Temple and has taught law at various universities including the University of Keele where he was Head of the Law School and a Pro-Vice-Chancellor. Now a Professor Emeritus, he continues to teach and engage in research. In addition to articles in legal journals, his publications include *Foundations of the Modern Bar*, (1982); *Sir Henry Maine: a Study in Victorian Jurisprudence* (1988 and 2004); with F Cownie, *'A Great and Noble Occupation!': The History of the Society of Legal Scholars* (2009); and an analysis of Victorian statutory reforms in *The Oxford History of the Laws of England* (2010).

COLYER

John Colyer (His Honour John Colyer QC) was an Open History Scholar at Worcester College Oxford. Admitted to the Middle Temple in 1957, and called to the bar in1959, he took silk in 1976 and was made a bencher in 1983. He lived in the USA 1959–1961 when he was an Assistant Professor at the University of Pennsylvania Law School. He is an Honorary Member of the Luzerne County Bar Association, Pennsylvania. Now that he has retired from the Circuit Bench he has several times returned to the United States to talk upon legal history topics. He was a Reader at the Inns of Court School of Law, is a past Chairman of Middle Temple Estates and

Library Committees and a former Master of the Archives. For 15 years he was Chairman of Middle Temple Historical Society.

HAVERY

Barrister of Middle Temple 1962; QC 1980; Master of the Bench of the Middle Temple 1989; Official Referee 1993–1998; Judge of the Technology and Construction Court 1998–2007.

HILL

Richard Hill served for 40 years in the Royal Navy, including four tours in the Ministry of Defence, retiring in 1983 in the rank of rear admiral. He was Under Treasurer of the Middle Temple from 1983 to 1994 and is an Honorary Master of the Bench. He wrote and lectured on maritime subjects from 1970 onwards. His ten books include *Maritime Strategy for Medium Powers*, *The Prizes of War* and the *Oxford Illustrated History of the Royal Navy*, of which he is General Editor. He was Editor of *The Naval Review* from 1983 to 2002.

PREST

Wilfred Prest was born in Melbourne, where he took his first degree, followed by an Oxford D.Phil. Wilfrid Prest has spent most of his career teaching history at the University of Adelaide, where he is now Professor Emeritus in History and Law. His publications include books on the early modern bar and Inns of Court, an outline history of England 1660–1815, an historical encyclopaedia of South Australia, a biography of Sir William Blackstone and an anthology of essays *Blackstone and his Commentaries: Biography, Law, History* (2009).

RILEY-SMITH

Jonathan Riley-Smith was educated at Eton and Cambridge. His first university post was in the Department of Medieval History at the University of St Andrews in Scotland. In 1972 he returned to the Faculty of History in the University of Cambridge before being appointed Professor of History at Royal Holloway College, University of London in 1978. From 1994 to 2005 he was Dixie Professor of Ecclesiastical History in Cambridge. He is a Knight of Justice of The Most Venerable Order of St John and a Knight Grand Cross of Grace and Devotion of the Sovereign Military Order of Malta. His books include *The Knights of St John in Jerusalem and Cyprus, c1050–1310* (1967), *The Feudal Nobility and the Kingdom of Jerusalem, 1174–1277* (1973), *What Were the Crusades?* (1977, 4th edn 2009), *The First Crusade and the Idea of Crusading* (1986), *The Crusades: A History* (1987, 2nd edn 2005), *The First Crusaders, 1095–1131* (1997), *The Crusades, Christianity and Islam* (2008) and *Templars and Hospitallers as Professed Religious in the Holy Land* (2010).

STOCKDALE

Eric Stockdale, who is a Bencher, joined the Inn at the age of 17 in 1946 and was called to the Bar in 1950. From 1972 to 1994 he served as a Circuit judge. He obtained a PhD at the London School of Economics and has written, among others, four historical books. The last one, with Justice Randy Holland of the Supreme Court of Delaware as co-author, was *Middle Temple Lawyers and the American Revolution* (2007).

TOULMIN

His Honour John Toulmin CMG QC FKC. Called to the Bar, Middle Temple, 1965. QC 1980. Bencher 1986. Master Reader Lent 2008. Member of the Church Committee 1991–2010 (Chairman 2003). Trustee of Temple Music Trust 1991– , (Chairman 2002–). Worshipped at Temple Church with wife Carolyn since married there in 1967. Full time judge as Official Referee and Judge of the Technology and Construction Court 1997–2011, now independent mediator and arbitrator. President of CCBE (European Bar Council) 1993. Chairman of Trustees, European Law Academy (ERA) 1997–2010, now Honorary President. Council of King's College London 1997–2009. Fellow (FKC) 2006. Visiting Professor at King's College London teaching Dispute Resolution. Many legal publications in national and international journals. For his services to European Law he was made a Companion of the Order of St Michael and St George (CMG) and an Honorary Life Member of the Law Society of England and Wales in 1994 and, in 1995, he was awarded the decoration Das Grosse Ehrenzeichen für Verdienste (Great Decoration of Merit (Austria)). He died on 2nd July 2012.

WHITELAW

Lesley Whitelaw was born in 1958 and educated in South Africa and at St Andrews University (MA Hons 1981). Archivist to Royal College of Surgeons of Edinburgh and to Lothian Health Board 1981–1985. Held curatorial posts at The Scottish Record Office (now The National Archives of Scotland) until appointed Middle Temple Archivist in 1990.

WINSTON

Jessica Winston is an associate professor of English at Idaho State University. Her research interests focus on the literary culture of the Inns of Court, 1500–1640. Her recent publications include 'Lyric Poetry at the Inns of Court: Forming a Professional Community' in *The Intellectual and Cultural World of the Early Modern Inns of Court* (2010) and 'Drama of the Inns of Court' (with Alan H Nelson, first author) in *A New Companion to Renaissance Literature and Culture* (2010).

WOOLLEY

David Woolley was educated at Winchester College and Trinity Hall, Cambridge. Called to the Bar, 1962. Silk 1980. Bencher 1987. Practice specialising in Town Planning and Local Government. Member of the MCC and Swiss Alpine Club. Trials with Tottenham Hotspur FC 1962. His publications include *Town Hall and the Property Owner* (1967); (with others) *Environmental Law* (2000, 2nd edn 2009); articles in legal journals.

List of plates and illustrations

(All references are to records in Middle Temple Archive and to pictures in the Middle Temple collection unless otherwise stated)

PLATES 2 (BETWEEN PAGES 68 AND 69)

ILLUSTRATIONS

List of Abbreviations

A-G   Attorney-General

CB   Chief Baron [of the exchequer]

CJ   Chief Justice

CP   Common Pleas

GI   Gray's Inn

IT   Inner Temple

KB   King's Bench

LI   Lincoln's Inn

MR   Master of the Rolls

MT   Middle Temple

QB   Queen's Bench

Introduction

by the Lord Chief Justice
of England and Wales

The story of the Middle Temple, like that of the Inner Temple, is vivid and remarkable. It is interleaved with the history of England and nations beyond the seas. Sir David Calcutt QC, Treasurer in 1998, to whose memory the book is affectionately dedicated, believed that a new history of the Middle Temple was long overdue. The result would, I believe, have gladdened him.

The land on which the Middle and Inner Temples are situated belonged to the Order of the Knights Templar from the 12th century until the Order was cruelly suppressed in 1312. On the other side of what is now the Strand, on the site where the Royal Courts of Justice were built in the 19th century, the Knights indulged themselves in the remunerative but dangerous sport of jousting. At the same time they set about the creation of the wonderful Temple Church, which was consecrated by a rare visitor to England, the Patriarch Heraclius of Jerusalem, in 1185.

Parliaments were held in the Temple in 1272 and 1299, at a crucial stage in the development of Parliament after Simon de Montfort was slain at the battle of Evesham in 1265. Perhaps that provides the first indication of the link between lawyers and Parliament which has continued throughout our history. Certainly the researches by Sir John Baker have shown that lawyers moved in as tenants of the Knights Hospitaller, who succeeded to the land which formerly belonged to the Knights Templar, from about 1340, and the records demonstrate that the societies of the Inner Temple and Middle Temple, if not always distinct, were certainly so by 1388. At about the same time Wat Tyler and his rebels sacked the Temple, and not so very long afterwards, when Jack Cade and his rebels were wandering round London looking for something to do, they came upon the Temple, and Shakespeare created the memorable line, 'the first thing we do, let's kill all the lawyers'. By then, according to legend and Shakespeare, Richard of York had plucked a white rose and the Duke of Somerset a red rose, in a battle of words during an encounter in the Temple Gardens which culminated in the Wars of the Roses.

The Knights Hospitaller disappeared from England during the dissolution of the monasteries and the chantries. One Master of the Chapel was William Ermestede, who managed successfully to survive the changes to the religious establishment of the reigns of Henry VIII, Edward VI, Mary, and Elizabeth I herself. Presumably he was no theologian. Not long afterwards he was succeeded by Richard Hooker, author of the *Laws of Ecclesiastical Polity*, a true theologian, and a pillar of the Anglican faith. More recently, William Parry gave the tune for the great music in 'Jerusalem' to Walford Davies, the then Master of the Chapel, who secured the copyright not for the Temple Church or himself, but for Parry. Less fortunate was Ernest Lough, the treble in the Temple Church whose recording of 'Oh for the Wings of a Dove' was made into a record in 1927, but without any attempt to secure the royalties either for him or for the Temple Church. Lough stood with others and watched the church burning after bombs had been dropped in May 1941.

The History describes changes in the nature of the teaching of the law that has taken place in the Inn over the centuries. The earliest surviving Middle Temple reading contains a record of a debate from the 1430s between Chief Justice Newton (d 1448) and William Warbelton (d 1469). But the Middle Temple was not merely for the education of lawyers. It was reported that Henry VIII himself told a suitor 'he could not make him a gentleman, but bid him go to the Inns of Court, where an admission makes one a gentleman...' and John Evelyn went to the Middle Temple from Oxford 'as gentlemen of the best quality did, tho' with no intention to study the Law as a profession'.

Our wonderful Hall, with its double hammer beam roof, was built under the auspices of the great Edmund Plowden from about 1562–1574. It was built on what was still Crown land, evidently in the confidence that the land would not revert to the Crown. The confidence proved justified when James I granted the Temple lands to the Inner and Middle Temples in 1608. Plowden was a Roman Catholic, but he remained as a Bencher of the Inn until his death in 1585, presumably because Elizabeth I herself had no wish to 'open windows into men's souls'. Unfortunately, but inevitably, during the national crisis of the Armada in 1588 eight members of the Inn were expelled for failing to take Holy Communion in the Temple Church.

From these times of turbulence and excitement, the Middle Temple is linked with some of the greatest names in our maritime history. They include Raleigh, Hakluyt, Gilbert, Frobisher, Amadas, Richard Grenville, John Hawkins, and Francis Drake himself, who in the present book is said to have had much in common with the great Denis Compton, 'a notorious partygoer and often to the wrong party'. He was, I believe, rather less modest than the great hero of so many of our youths, whose modest, unassuming presence on a guest night will be an abiding memory.

The voyage of Bartholomew Gosnold, who discovered Cape Cod and Martha's Vineyard, along with Raleigh's settlement of Roanoake, were seminal moments in the history of what became the United States of America, and the first steps of the common law outside the shores of

England. Edward Sandys negotiated the great Virginia Charter of 1618 which gave all the colonists in Virginia 'the liberties, franchises and immunities of English subjects' and recognised freedom of speech, equality before the law and trial by jury as principles for the colonies. Sandys was later described as the 'Father of American Constitutionalism'. Some 150 years later, the rebel colonists, influenced by charters in similar terms among most of the then colonies, included many Middle Templars. Five Middle Templars signed the Declaration of Independence, and seven signed the Constitution of 1789. The terms of the surrender of Lord Cornwallis were negotiated by another Middle Templar, John Laurens. When he was called to the bench, the former President of the United States, then the Chief Justice, William Taft, said that he was 'strangely moved, finding myself sitting here in the home of Blackstone, in the very cradle of the common law of England and of America'. And the restoration of the Hall following bomb damage in World War II was financed in part by generous contributions from the American Bar Association and the Canadian Bar Association.

The Middle Temple is indeed linked with the development of the common law across the world. The links with Ireland are perhaps best embodied in Edmund Burke, who passionately defended the position taken by the colonists in North America, and encapsulated the principle of judicial independence when he spoke of disputes being submitted to the 'cold impartiality of the neutral judge'. John Dunning famously complained at the same time that 'the influence of the Crown has increased, is increasing and ought to be diminished'. William Wentworth was one of the first to cross the Blue Mountains in Australia in 1813, and according to the Australian dictionary of biography 'more than any other man he secured our fundamental liberties and nationhood'. Woomes Bonnerjee, a barrister in the High Court of Calcutta was the first President of the Indian National Congress, Francis Bell was the first native born person to become Prime Minister of New Zealand, and Jan Christian Smuts was a student member of the Inn from South Africa who fought against the British in the Boer War, but led South Africa to the side of the Allies in both World Wars. The Inn continues to maintain relationships based on respect and admiration with members of the Bar and the judiciary in many countries across the world.

The History highlights some of the Inn's literary connections, both among writers who were associated with or who were members of the Inn, and with literature, such as Shakespeare's Henry VI, in which the Temple forms an essential part of the story. Charles Dickens was 'entirely diverted from the pursuit of the law' when he became a 'writer of books'. Dickens was not the first, and we anticipate will not be the last member of the Inn to identify contemporary failings in the administration of justice, and to seek improvement by using unequivocal language. We shall surely each have our favourites among the writers who have been associated with Middle Temple. I wonder whether John Webster, whose characters undergo bizarre experiences and extremes of suffering may yet be accorded greater public recognition as the great dramatist he was. He might have had something to say about the proposal by Baron Auckland in 1799 that the law of adultery should be reformed so that those who 'engaged in an act of adultery could never marry each other'. And no writer could better convey the way in which the spirit of the law can enter into a man's soul, as the dying words of Chief Justice Abbott witnessed: 'Gentlemen of the jury, you are discharged'.

The records of the disciplinary processes of the Inn date back to the earliest days of the 16th century. The variety of issues is remarkable, and in their way, these records tell us a great deal about the social history not merely of the profession but of the country as a whole. Thus, for example, in 1570 a member was suspended for three months for speaking English in a suit heard by the Chief Justice at the Guildhall in London. In 1722 it was ordered that no member of the Inn should eat in Hall unless wearing '...a decent and complete gown, whole and untorn'. In 1914 there was a remarkable debate about whether dishonesty or impropriety committed otherwise than in pursuit of the profession may constitute professional misconduct by a barrister. And we find that a member of the Bar refused to pay a penny a day extra rent for the installation of what was then a new water closet because he was fearful of an epidemic of ill health breaking out in consequence. In October 1952 when a Nigerian student was unable to obtain a recommendation for the purposes of membership 'owing to his suspected pro-communist activities' it was resolved by Parliament that 'it has not been the practice of this Inn to refuse an applicant otherwise qualified for admission purely on grounds of his political views'.

It was not until the Sex Disqualification (Removal) Act 1919 that it became possible for women to join the Inns. The first woman to do so was Helena Normanton, who later took silk. The first woman to be called to the Bar was Ivy Williams. The processes were slow. In January 1920 a newspaper asked the question 'are the Benchers of Middle Temple, after all, a little frightened of the women law students they have admitted?'. This year our Treasurer is Professor Dawn Oliver and in 2007 one third of the 36 newly elected Benchers were women. Progress has been slow, but thank goodness that it has been persistent.

The Great Wars provided their own memorable moments. For example, In 1914 it was resolved that any permanent member of the staff should not suffer any loss of salary when serving in the forces, in effect so that the difference between his pay and his salary would be made up. It was also resolved that any members of the Belgian Bar present in England should become honorary members of the Inn with all the privileges of full membership. Special arrangements were made to allow exemptions from examinations following war service and injury. Captain Bennett, who had been awarded both the Victoria Cross and the Military Cross, was given leave to omit the part 1 examinations in 1921 and Airey Neave, the first British prisoner of war to return as an escapee from Colditz Castle, was granted exemption from his Bar Finals. The story of the saving of the east end of the Hall following bomb damage, when all the materials were collected together in some 200 sacks, tells of the devotion and commitment of those working in and for the Inns, no doubt defiantly replicated across London and the bombed cities of this country. The spirit was encapsulated in a letter following the damage to the Hall, 'it doesn't matter what we eat but it does matter that we should eat together'. When she was called to the Bench in 1944 Queen Elizabeth the Queen Mother wrote that it was 'most agreeable to be able to defy the Germans…'

For years, there have been debates about the future of the profession. They represent something of a microcosm of the social history of this country. Perhaps of particular interest to today's generation of students is the debate in the late 1970s and early 1980s between senior members of the Bench about the future of the Bar, and the differences of view between those who believed that the Bar should continue to remain a relatively small profession and those who believed that it should be significantly expanded. The consequences of the proposed changes to the arrangements for legal aid will bear very heavily on many members of the now much expanded profession.

The History of the Middle Temple is a monumental work, crafted by a number of different writers, with consequent different styles of writing, based on careful research into the records of the Inn which now date back for over 500 years. Between them, the contributors put the story of the Middle Temple into its context. It is a story of great fascination which will, I am sure, be of great interest not only to members of the Middle Temple itself, but to those in the wider community with an interest in one of this country's historic institutions.

IGOR JUDGE

Prologue: The Knights Templar

JONATHAN RILEY-SMITH

I. The Origins of the Order

THE ORDER OF the Temple was founded in 1119–20, when Hugh of Payns, a knight from Champagne, formed himself and eight companions into a regular community of lay brothers. They dedicated themselves to the defence of the pilgrim roads through Palestine to Jerusalem. The King of Jerusalem gave them part of the royal palace in the Temple enclosure, and St Bernard, the influential Cistercian Abbot of Clairvaux, persuaded a papal legate, two archbishops and ten bishops attending the Council of Troyes in 1129 to recognise them and to draw up a rule for them. Papal recognition was confirmed in the Bull *Omne datum optimum*, issued by Pope Innocent II in 1139. Divided into the classes of brother knights, brother sergeants and brother priests, the Templars were soon being endowed with properties all over Europe and were taking on major responsibilities in the defence of the Christian settlements in the Levant.

A. Commanderies

In the first half of the twelfth century the Temple was developing into an international religious order. A feature of this process was the establishment of local communities of brothers residing on the properties given by benefactors. These commanderies (or preceptories), at the same time conventual and administrative, provided the funds, *matériel* and men needed by the headquarters, which was based in Jerusalem until 1187, in Acre on the Palestinian coast from 1191 to 1291 and in Limassol in Cyprus from 1291 until the suppression of the order in 1312.[1] Commanderies could vary in size and economic function, although most in Europe

---

[1] See JSC Riley-Smith, 'The origins of the commandery in the Temple and the Hospital' in AT Luttrell and L Pressouyre (eds), *La commanderie. Institution des ordres militaires dans l'occident médiéval* (Paris, Ministère de l'éducation nationale, 2002), 9–26.

were agricultural. Among their heads, known as commanders (or precep-
tors), were to be found not only brother knights, but also brother priests
and brother sergeants. The brother sergeants came from a very wide
variety of backgrounds: they ranged from the treasurer of the Paris
Temple—the banker to the French Crown—to shepherds and labourers.
They constituted a much more important component of the Temple than
was the case in the other great international military order, the Hospital of
St John of Jerusalem, and many of the brother sergeants were engaged in
the kind of menial work for which the Hospital employed servants.[2]

Templar houses retained an independence that was a legacy of the way
they had been founded. In the first decade or so a few brothers had roamed
about western Europe picking up endowments and establishing isolated
houses which in time became centres of future development.[3] Early
Templar communities must often have been staffed by men with the
scantiest knowledge of their obligations. Perhaps advice was sought from
local religious, and this may have been responsible for the fact that,
whereas all Hospitaller houses, wherever they were, followed, as was
conventional, the liturgy of the original mother church of the order, the
Holy Sepulchre, the office heard in each Templar community seems to have
been that of the diocese in which it was situated.[4]

B.   *Baiuliae*

With the rapid extension of the Templars' landed estates in the middle of
the twelfth century, a kind of intermediate province, normally called by the
all-purpose word *baiulia*, grew up. The use of *baiuliae* was extended to
cover regions which were too small to justify the creation of full-scale
provinces, or too unwieldy or distant to be managed conveniently within
the existing provincial structure.[5] Britain itself, which seems to have been
at first subject to the French provincials,[6] probably started as a *baiulia*, and
it was not until the 1180s that the head of the Templars in Britain became

---

[2]   JSC Riley-Smith, *Templars and Hospitallers as Professed Religious in the Holy Land*
(Notre Dame, University of Notre dame Press, 2010), 38–39.

[3]   JSC Riley-Smith, 'The structures of the Orders of the Temple and the Hospital in c.
1291' in SJ Ridyard (ed), *The Medieval Crusade* (Woodbridge, Boydell, 2004), 127–28.

[4]   C Dondi, *The Liturgy of the Canons Regular of the Holy Sepulchre of Jerusalem*
(Tournout, Brepols, 2004), 41.

[5]   See Riley-Smith, above n 3, at 127; Riley-Smith, above n 1, at 14–15.

[6]   See BA Lees (ed), *Records of the Templars in England in the Twelfth Century* (London,
Oxford University Press for the British Academy, 1935), cxx, cxlv, 158–60, 208–09, 213–15,
226, 244–45.

a provincial in his own right.[7] The most likely date for this change of status is 1185, when Patriarch Heraclius of Jerusalem visited England to appeal to King Henry II for assistance. Heraclius was accompanied on his journey to Europe by the Masters of the Hospital and the Temple, although the latter, Arnald of Torroja, died in Italy on the way.[8] It can be no coincidence that the Hospitaller priory in England seems to have been established at the same time.[9] At any rate, the London house of the Templars (just outside the city proper), which had been the centre of the *baiulia*, now became one of between thirty-two and thirty-six commanderies in England—an important one, of course, but in institutional terms no different from the others.[10]

C. Provinces

Commanderies were collected into provinces, which the Templars called grand commanderies (or provincial masterships). A feature of these, at least when compared to their counterparts, the Hospitallers' priories, was that they were relatively large. The British Isles, for example, comprised a single Templar grand commandery (usually called the grand commandery of England), whereas the Hospitallers had separate priories of England (which included Scotland) and Ireland, probably because they preferred smaller units of senior management. The Templars, on the other hand, could always divide their commanderies into *baiuliae*[11]; by 1300, for example, Ireland and the archdiocese of York were *baiuliae* within the grand commandery of England.[12]

Templar grand commanders seem to have been usually appointed for terms of four years.[13] They supervised all the brothers in their provinces, over which they had disciplinary powers, and they presided over annual

---

[7] The Templar 'Inquest' of 1185 (*ibid*, at 1–135) may have been associated with this change in status, but may also have been part of a movement for systematisation to be found in the Temple and the Hospital. For early commandery cartularies, see P-A Armiger (ed), *Cartulaire de Trinquetaille* (Aix-en-Provence, Centre d'études des sociétés méditerranéennes, 1972); P Gérard and E Magnou (eds), *Cartulaires des Templiers de Douzens* (Paris, Bibliothèque Nationale, 1965); Marquis de Ripert-Montclar (ed), *Cartulaire de la Commanderie de Richerenches de l'ordre du Temple (1136–1214)* (Paris, Champion, 1907).

[8] M Barber, *The New Knighthood* (Cambridge, Cambridge University Press, 1994), 109.

[9] See KV Sinclair (ed), *The Hospitallers' Riwle* (London, Anglo-Norman Text Society, 1984), xlvii–viii.

[10] Lees, above n 6, at 169, fn 8. For the number of commanderies in 1307, see TW Parker, *The Knights Templars in England* (Tucson, University if Arizona Press, 1963), 126.

[11] Riley-Smith, above n 3, at 131–32.

[12] D Wilkins (ed), *Conciliae Magni Britanniae et Hiberniae*, 3 vols (London, R Gosling, F Gyles, T Woodward and C Davis, 1737), vol 2, 337, 378 (for Ireland) and 341–42, 362 (for York).

[13] AJ Forey, *The Templars in the Corona de Aragón* (London, Oxford University Press, 1973), 313–14.

provincial chapters. The last grand commander in the British Isles, William of la More, claimed to know personally every brother, except, he said, for two in Ireland.[14] Grand commanders received instructions on management from the grand master and his convent in the east,[15] whom they were expected to visit after their terms of office had ended.[16] They were, however, positively forbidden to leave their provinces without permission from the grand master and his chapter, not even for chapters-general, which were entirely the responsibility of the brothers in the east.[17] In Europe they were subject after 1250 to visitors-general, who had replaced the master *deça mer*, the original representative in Europe of the eastern headquarters.[18] One of these visitors had charge of France, England and Germany. It was said that when the visitor Hugues of Pairaud came to England in the absence of William of la More, who had gone to see the grand master in Cyprus, he dismissed some of the local commanders and put others in their place.[19]

D. Chapters

Chapters, regular meetings of all professed brothers, were essential elements in religious community life. Every Templar house, including the convent in the east, had one, meeting on a weekly basis and sometimes more often if the need arose.[20] All receptions were made in the chapter, many of them in commandery ones.[21] The chapter of a province met annually and dealt with a wide variety of business. There was an audit of the accounts of the commanderies, the heads of which were required to bring contributions, known as responsions, to the expenses of the order in the province and in the east. There was a review of appointments. There were disciplinary issues relating to brothers. There could also be land grants and tenancy agreements, and the naming of attorneys or procurators if a dispute with some other institution had arisen.[22]

Over and above provincial chapters were chapters-general. Those which met in the west were summoned by the visitors or by the grand masters on

---

[14] Wilkins, above n 12, vol 2, at 356.

[15] See K Schottmüller, *Der Untergang des Templer-Ordens*, 2 vols (Berlin, ES Mittler und Sohn, 1887), vol 2, 78, 97–98; H Finke, *Papsttum und Untergang des Templerordems*, 2 vols (Münster, Aschendorff, 1907), vol 2, 338; Forey, above n 13, at 419.

[16] Forey, above n 13, at 313.

[17] Riley-Smith, above n 2, at 51–52.

[18] Forey, above n 13, at 329; Barber, above n 8, at 245; Riley-Smith, above n 3, at 133–34.

[19] Wilkins, above n 12, vol 2, at 381.

[20] H de Curzon, *La Règle du Temple* (Paris, Librairie Renouard, 1886), 215. See also *ibid*, at 216–27, 248, 255–56, 287–89, 319–21.

[21] Riley-Smith, above n 3, at 134.

[22] *Ibid*, at 134–35.

visitation, and were attended by commanders and other brothers from more than one province. England, for example, would send its grand commander or his deputies to chapters-general convoked in Paris; and when chapters-general were held in England, brothers from France were disciplined at them. There is some evidence for these chapters being engaged in legislation, but it seems that they did so only when the grand master and members of his convent were present.[23] Otherwise, as the English sergeant Peter of Oteringham maintained, the grand commandery of England observed only those decrees issued 'in the great chapter in Cyprus'.[24]

II. LONDON

Hugh of Payns visited England and Scotland on a recruiting tour of western Europe in 1128, but it is not easy to find any evidence for endowments in England until the late 1130s, when King Stephen and his wife Matilda of Boulogne granted the Templars estates in Essex, Oxford-shire and possibly Lincolnshire.[25] The earliest charter relating to some of their property in London has been dated to around 1148,[26] but the date of the establishment of their first London house, 'the Old Temple', at Holborn, which was located east of the modern Southampton Buildings and south of High Holborn, was probably earlier. It is assumed, on no good evidence, to have been granted to Hugh of Payns in 1128, but the Templars must have occupied it before 1144, since the body of Geoffrey of Mandeville, who had died in that year, was later to be transferred from its church to the 'New Temple'.[27] Excavations, professional and otherwise, in 1704, 1876, 1905 and 2000 have established that the 'Old Temple' church had a round nave and a chancel.[28] Its ruins could still be seen in 1598, when they were described as being faced with Caen stone.[29]

The Templars sold the Old Temple to the Bishop of Lincoln in 1161. They must already have moved, because their sale was made 'at the New Temple' itself.[30] They began to construct a new church immediately, since visits to it were indulgenced from around 1160 onwards by successive

---

[23] *Ibid*, at 137–38.

[24] Wilkins, above n 12, vol 2, at 350–51.

[25] Parker, above n 10, at 15–16, 35.

[26] Lees, above n 6, at xlvii, 156.

[27] G Worley, *The Church of the Knights Templars in London*, 2nd edn (London, G Bell, 1911), 32; E Lord, *The Knights Templar in Britain* (Harlow, Longman, 2004), 30–33.

[28] A Telfer, 'Locating the first Knights Templar church' (2002) *London Archaeologist* 10. 1, 3–6.

[29] JB Williamson, *The History of the Temple, London* (London, J Murray, 1924), 8.

[30] Lees, above n 6, at liii, 158–61. It was transferred for 100 marks and carried a rent of 7 solidi (or 3 besants) a year.

Archbishops of Canterbury and an Archbishop of York.[31] One of the earliest Gothic buildings in England, it was consecrated by the Patriarch of Jerusalem in 1185 and still stands. Like its predecessor it features a round nave and a chancel. The latter began to be reconstructed in about 1220 and was consecrated twenty years later in the presence of King Henry III.[32] The church was very richly decorated and possessed a famous relic collection, which included a portion of the True Cross and a phial of the Precious Blood.[33]

The rest of the Templar buildings have disappeared, although elements were still visible as late as the nineteenth century. They stood on land still identified as Temple ground between Fleet Street and the Thames. There were also some outlying properties, including land across the river. Since thirteen houses were built near Fleet Street in around 1300 for renting to laymen, it is possible that the core of the Templars' estate, the enclosure necessary to separate them as professed religious from the rest of the site, which was occupied by pensioners, servants and tenants, was as clearly delineated, perhaps by a wall, as was the Hospitaller enclosure at Clerkenwell.[34] The main entrance to the Temple was a Great Gate on Fleet Street, where the Middle Temple Gateway now stands. From here a road led directly to the west end of the conventual church, beside which was a cemetery. To the south a range of buildings, connected to the church by cloisters, included a hall, which probably stood on the site of the modern hall of the Inner Temple Society, and presumably a chapter room. On the east side of the cloisters there was a chapel dedicated to St Anne, part of which survives underground. Adjoining the hall on the west was a chapel dedicated to the Blessed Virgin Mary, and additionally to St Thomas Becket, whose instrument of martyrdom—the sword which killed him— was one of the relics in the church. West of this chapel was another hall, on ground abutting Middle Temple Lane and now covered by parts of Pump and Elm Courts. It was described in the seventeenth century as being built in the same style as the round nave and must therefore have been erected in the twelfth century. West of the church itself was an imposing building, later described as the Inn of the Bishop of Ely. Within the complex there were also storehouses, a granary and a brewhouse, and by the Fleet and

---

[31] *Ibid*, at 162–64.
[32] See Worley, above n 27, at 15, 41ff; N Pevsner, *The Buildings of England. London I. The cities of London and Westminster*, 3rd edn (rev B Cherry) (Harmondsworth, Penguin, 1973), 313–16.
[33] Williamson, above n 29, at 73.
[34] B Sloane and G Malcolm, *Excavations at the priory of the Order of the Hospital of St John of Jerusalem, Clerkenwell, London* (London, Museum of London, 2004), 69ff. For other Templar properties in London and its neighbourhood, see Parker, above n 10, at 38; Lees, above n 6, at lxxxix–xcv. They were occupied by relatively well-to-do tenants.

down by the Thames were mills and landing stages.[35] Since, as we shall see, the Temple was regularly employed by the Crown and others as a place to store treasure, there may also have been a tower, not unlike those in the Paris Temple,[36] although the Hospitaller priory at Clerkenwell, which was also used as a depository, never had one.[37]

There can be no doubt that the New Temple comprised one of the most significant building complexes in the neighbourhood of the city. Recent analysis of stones which were removed during works at the Middle Temple provides evidence that already in the late twelfth century the conventual building was a sophisticated one.[38] By the later thirteenth century the site may have looked much more impressive than the Hospitaller priory at Clerkenwell, which took a long time to develop into the palace it became in the fourteenth century.[39] The New Temple was conveniently situated close to Westminster, and King Henry III occasionally heard petitioners there. A council was summoned to the Temple by Simon of Montfort to consider Henry's misgovernment in 1260, and parliaments were held there in 1272 and 1299. Between 1256 and 1299 the English clergy met there on at least nine occasions. Among these assemblies were provincial councils of the archdiocese of Canterbury in 1273 and in 1292, the second convoked, ironically enough, to discuss the union of the Templars and the Hospitallers.[40]

The Temple was used as a safe deposit. King Henry III's brother, Richard of Cornwall, stored in it the proceeds of vow-redemptions and legacies which in 1238 had been granted him for his crusade.[41] From the reign of King John it was regularly employed by the royal wardrobe as a treasure store; Brother Geoffrey of the Temple, the King's almoner from 1229, was also keeper of the wardrobe from 1236 to 1240. And the Exchequer regularly used it as a place to deposit the proceeds of taxation, although the influence of the order with the Crown began to decline in the later thirteenth century.[42]

---

[35] Williamson, above n 29, at 70–73; Parker, above n 10, at 24–25; Lord, above n 27, at 33–52; Pevsner, above n 32, at 315, 335–41.

[36] H de Curzon, *La maison du Temple de Paris* (Paris, Hachette, 1888), 114–28.

[37] Sloane and Malcolm, above n 34, at 202–03.

[38] TP Smith, 'Report on Worked Stones Recovered from Middle Temple, Fleet Street, London' (Museum of London Archaeology Service Report 2001), 1–3. I have to thank Sophie Jackson of the Museum of London Archaeology Service for providing a copy of this report.

[39] Sloane and Malcolm, above n 34, at 200–03.

[40] Parker, above n 10, at 49. For the provincial council of 1292, see FM Powicke and CR Cheney (eds), *Councils and Synods with other documents relating to the English Church AD 1205–1313* (Oxford, Oxford University Press, 1964), vol 2, at 1097–1113.

[41] C Tyerman, *England and the Crusades, 1095–1588* (Chicago and London, University of Chicago Press, 1988), 193.

[42] A Sandys, 'The Financial and Administrative Importance of the London Temple in the thirteenth century' in AG Little and FM Powicke (eds), *Essays in Medieval History presented to Thomas Frederick Tout* (Manchester, Manchester University Press, 1925), 147–62.

It has been estimated that at the time of the arrest of the Templars in England in 1308, thirteen brothers were living in the New Temple.[43] This would have made it one of the larger communities in Europe, but it could house many more, because at the time the grand commander William of la More was also staying there, together with Humbert Blanc, the grand commander of Auvergne, and these great officers doubtless had retinues.[44] But the New Temple was never a provincial headquarters in the generally understood sense of that term. Templar provincials did not usually have a single place of residence but were constantly on the move from house to house within their bailiwicks. This was certainly the practice of the English grand commanders.[45] And although many early chapters met in the New Temple,[46] they did not all do so.[47] By the late thirteenth century, in fact, the British chapters were being commonly assembled elsewhere, particularly at Temple Dinsley in Hertfordshire.[48] Templar provincial chapters were always held in houses with the capacity to put up large numbers of commanders and brothers at the same time.[49] The New Temple must have been capacious enough, but it was perhaps more convenient for the commanders and their retinues, including, of course, those from Ireland and Scotland, to meet elsewhere.

When the order was suppressed in 1312, its properties were granted by the Pope to the Hospital of St John. The Templar London estate was a valuable asset, the rents from which were estimated to be £155 18s 4d at the time of the dissolution of the Hospital in 1540, although it is not known whether other properties had been added to it in the interim. The New Temple itself was valued at £162 11s in 1535.[50] It returned £20 per annum, because the Inner and Middle Temple were let to their respective societies for £10 each, although one should note that the annual rent from the largest of six public houses belonging to the Temple estate, Le Hande in Fleet Street, was as much at £12 and that the Temple site itself accounted for only 13 per cent of the total value of rents from the associated

---

[43]   H Reddan, 'The Temple' in W Page (ed), *The Victoria History of the Counties of England. London 1* (London, University of London, 1909, repr 1974), 488. See now Caroline Barron and Matthew Davis (eds), *The Religious Homes of London and Middlesex* (London, University of London, 2007), 101–07.

[44]   Williamson, above n 29, at 50. For other grandees staying with their entourages, see *ibid*, at 28.

[45]   Forey, above n 13, at 315–17; Lees, above n 6, at lxv.

[46]   Lees, above n 6, at 165–66, 169–70, 205–06, 208–09, 217, 248–49.

[47]   Lees, above n 6, at 249–50 (at Cowley).

[48]   Schottmüller, above n 15, vol 2, 83, 94; Wilkins, above n 12, vol 2, 335, 337, 342, 343, 348, 360, 362, 381, 383. Also at other locations in England: see Wilkins, above n 12, vol 2, 345–46, 380.

[49]   In Aragon at Miravet, Monzón or Gardeny, in Castile at Zamora, in Germany at Lietzen, in France at Paris, in Lombardy at Piacenza or Bologna, in Poitou at Auzon, in Portugal at Tomar, in Provence at Ste Eulalie, St Gilles or Montpellier.

[50]   Reddan, above n 43, at 489.

properties.[51] The Crown's first reaction to the suppression of the Templars was to treat the New Temple as though it was its own. The London estate was granted to favourites and supporters, and it took the Hospitallers several decades to achieve actual possession. The New Temple itself was conveyed to them only in 1338. They had no use for the buildings since they already had their headquarters in Clerkenwell, and so they rented them out, eventually to lawyers, who were occupying at least part of the site by 1346.[52]

---

[51] Information provided by Dr Gregory O'Malley, the author of *The Knights Hospitaller of the English Langue 1460–1565* (Oxford, Oxford University Press, 2005).

[52] Williamson, above n 29, at 83–92. There is evidence that fairly soon after their occupation the lawyers substantially altered at least some of the structures they inherited. See Smith, above n 38, at 4; also Pevsner, above n 32, at 339.

The Temple Church

JOHN TOULMIN

T HE ROUND CHURCH was built by the Knights Templar and was consecrated by Heraclius, Patriarch of Jerusalem, on 10 February 1185. It was modelled on the Church of the Holy Sepulchre in Jerusalem, built over the traditional site of the crucifixion and burial of Christ. When you entered the Round of the Temple Church you were entering the most holy place.

The building of the Round Church was followed by the building of the chancel. The columns of both were made of Purbeck marble. The quarries had to be re-visited centuries later to quarry the marble needed to restore columns damaged by fire and war.

The grand consecration of the chancel took place on Ascension Day, 24 May 1240. The following account of the ceremony was given by Matthew Paris[1]:

> About the same time was consecrated the noble church of the New Temple at London[2] an edifice worthy to be seen, in the presence of the King and much of the nobility of the kingdom who ... after the solemnities of the consecration had been royally feasted at a most magnificent banquet prepared at the expense of the Hospitallers.

King Henry III and his wife Eleanor of Provence had chosen the Temple Church as their place of burial. In the event the King changed his mind and was buried in Westminster Abbey, built over the shrine of Edward the Confessor and dedicated in 1269.

On 13 October 1307, the leaders of the Knights Templar in France were arrested on largely trumped-up charges. They were interrogated under torture[3] and burnt at the stake. In England, the master of the Temple was

---

[1] Quoted in D Lewer and R Dark, *The Temple Church in London* (Historical Publications, 1997) at 47. Referred to in Master J Bruce Williamson, *The History of the Temple, London*, 2nd edn (John Murray, 1925), 22; *Chronicle of Matthew Paris*, Chron Maj (RS) IV, 11.

[2] Called the 'New Temple' to distinguish it from the 'Old Temple', north of Holborn.

[3] Williamson, above n 1, at 46, 47.

arrested and the New Temple was seized for the Crown. The Templars themselves were treated more mercifully than their French counterparts and the church was spared.

On the suppression of the Knights Templar,[4] the Pope granted their property to the Knights Hospitaller, the Order of St John of Jerusalem. In England, King Edward II ignored the Pope's grant and initially granted the land and the church to various favourites. Eventually, in 1324, the New Temple was granted to the Order of St John by the statute *De Terris Templariorum.*[5]

It would appear that by about 1340 apprentices of the law had settled in the New Temple as tenants of the Order of St John. The Temple Church became, by usage, the lawyer's chapel. It is not clear what form the service took, but the Sherriff's return of 1308 includes 28 copes, four little copes for the choristers and 'two pair of organs'.[6] There is an entry in Inner Temple records that on 30 January 1519, Inner Temple ordered a levy on its members to raise a sum of 70 shillings for new organs in the church.[7]

In 1540 the Order of St John was in its turn suppressed by King Henry VIII. The Master and his two chaplains remained. The church was unmolested. There were the first glimmerings of a church committee, in that two church wardens were appointed annually, one from each of the two Inns.[8]

In 1540 there is a reference to singing at Divine Service. In 1554 both Inns record an assessment of members to provide for the wages of singing men and to provide books for those singing in the choir: 'In the Middle Temple 12d from every Bencher and 4d from other members of the House.'[9] It appears that singing men disappeared in the 1580s and did not reappear until much later.

William Ermestede was appointed Master before 1540 and survived the political and religious vicissitudes of the next 20 years. He lived through the reigns of King Edward VI and Queen Mary, and into the reign of Queen Elizabeth I, through the introduction of Cranmer's Prayer Book, its suppression under Queen Mary and its reintroduction. He died in 1559. His successor, Dr Alvey, was appointed by letters patent from the Crown and took office, as the Master does now, without any induction from the Bishop.[10]

The degree of tolerance, by the standards of its day, shown in religious matters in England was exhibited towards Edmund Plowden who, apart

---

[4]   The order was suppressed by the Papal Bull *Vox in Excelso*, March–April 1312.
[5]   D Silsoe, *The Peculiarities of the Temple*, 14.
[6]   Williamson, above n 1, at 73.
[7]   Lewer and Dark, above n 1, at 56; Williamson, above n 1, at 126.
[8]   Lewer and Dark, above n 1, at 56.
[9]   *Ibid*, at 57.
[10]   *Ibid*, citing Sir William Dugdale, *Origines Juridiciales*, 3rd edn (1680).

from masterminding the building of Middle Temple Hall, was also the author of famous law reports which continued to be printed until the 19th century.[11] He remained faithful to Rome and is reputed to have written to Queen Elizabeth, in response to her invitation to become Lord Chancellor,

> Hold me dread sovereign excused ... I should not have in charge Your Majesty's conscience one week before I should incur your displeasure.[12]

Despite his Roman Catholicism, he was, as he wished, buried in the Temple Church. His is one of only two substantial memorials that remain in the church.

In 1584 Dr Alvey died. His successor was Dr Richard Hooker.[13] The religious spectrum in the church had moved so far away from Rome that Hooker, who preached his moderate and scholarly views on a Sunday morning, was answered from the pulpit on Sunday afternoon by Walter Travers, a Calvinist who believed that everything could be settled by biblical texts.[14] As Fuller[15] put it:

> The worst was, these two preachers, though joined in affinity (their nearest kindred being married together) acted with different principles ... so that what Mr Hooker delivered in the forenoon, Mr Travers confuted in the afternoon. At the building of Solomon's Temple (1 Kings V1 7) 'neither hammer, nor axe, nor tool of iron was heard therein' whereas alas! in this Temple not only much knocking was heard but (which was the worst) the nails and pins which one master-builder drave in were driven out by the other.

After he left the Temple in 1591, successful but exhausted by dispute, Hooker published his *Laws of Ecclesiastical Polity*, a cornerstone of the Anglican faith.

By 1603 the church had a Master and four stipendiary priests and a clerk.[16] These had stipends out of the revenues of the suppressed Order of St John of Jerusalem.

From the time of the dissolution of the Order of St John until 1608, the Middle and Inner Temples held their lands as tenants of the Crown. On 13 August 1608, King James I granted a Charter to the two Inns which, subject to a 'fee farm rent' of £20 a year payable by each Society, granted

---

[11] Williamson, above n 1, at 229–33; *Master Serjeant Sullivan's Reading* (Oxford, Oxford University Press, 1952), 7 (cited hereafter as 'Sullivan').

[12] Sullivan, above n 11, at 20, citing C Woolrych, *Laws of Eminent Serjeants* (1869), vol I, 115.

[13] Appointed 1585, see Williamson, above n 1, at 195.

[14] *Ibid*, at 200, 201.

[15] Lewer and Dark, above n 1, at 60.

[16] Stow, *A Survey of London* (1603), cited in D Lewer, *A Spiritual Song* (London, Templars' Union, 1981). David Lewer was a chorister 1931–33. When he died in 2008, he left a bequest to the Temple Church which enabled a stained glass window to be placed in the Round Church.

the land to the two Inns and the church in perpetuity 'for the entertainment and education of the students and professors of the laws aforesaid residing in the same Inns for ever'.[17] In addition the Inns were required to provide 'for the celebration of divine service and the sacraments and sacramental offices and ecclesiastical rites whatsoever henceforth for ever as is befitting and hitherto accustomed'[18] They were also responsible for assigning a 'convenient mansion or house' near the Church as a residence for the Master and for providing a stipend of £17 6s 8d per annum for the Master and for the upkeep of the church. In 1673, Middle Temple commuted the fee farm rent for a single payment and in 1675 Inner Temple did the same.[19]

On two occasions Masters of the Temple have tried to claim an authority superior to the benchers of the two Inns. The first was in 1628, when Dr Micklethwaite, on arrival as Master of the Temple, laid claim to be Master over the two Inns and to take precedence over all others at Bench Table. The Benchers of the two Inns proved that his jurisdiction was, under the Charter, confined to the church. Dr Micklethwaite's claim was rejected by the then Attorney-General.[20] In fact the Master of the Temple has no formal jurisdiction in the church since the management and care of the building and the ordering of the services are in the hands of the Benchers of the two Inns. Dr Micklethwaite continued unsuccessfully to petition the Privy Council until his death in 1639.

Soon after the Restoration in 1660 a new house was built on the north side of the garden of the Temple Church to be held by the then Master in accordance with the Charter.[21]

The year 1665 was the year of the Great Plague. John Evelyn recorded in his diary that on 16 July 1665 there were 1,100 dead of the plague that week. In the week of 15 August 1665, 5,000 died. The Great Fire of London started on 2 September 1666 at a baker's shop in Pudding Lane. On the third day of the fire the wind dropped. The fire continued for a further day before it burnt out, having destroyed Serjeant's Inn and the chambers in Kings Bench Walk.[22] The Church was spared, but the Master's House, so recently built, was burnt down and had to be re-built.[23] The fire known as the Great Temple Fire of 1679 stopped short of doing serious damage to the Church.

After the Restoration in 1660, the Temple became a centre for the musical life of the country. Around the Temple Church were a number of

---

[17] Williamson, above n 1, at 266.
[18] Williamson, above n 1, at 267.
[19] Lewer and Dark, above n 1, at 62.
[20] MT.15/TAM 55–80; Williamson, above n 1, at 385–95.
[21] Williamson, above n 1, at 504.
[22] *Ibid*, at 505–07; *Diary of John Evelyn* (1818 edn); Lewer and Dark, above n 1, at 65.
[23] Williamson, above n 1, at 504, 510, 512.

shops. In one of these, in the porch of the church, John Playford set up his shop.[24] He and his son Henry could be said to have been among the first music publishers. They published Henry Purcell's music.[25] When John Playford died in 1686, Purcell set to music Nahum Tate's *Elegy on my Friend, Mr John Playford*. When Purcell himself died in 1695, Henry Playford published John Blow's setting of Dryden's *Ode on the Death of Mr Henry Purcell*.[26]

The Purcell connection was important in what became known as the 'battle of the organs'.[27] The two Inns decided to install a new organ in the Temple Church. Middle Temple favoured an organ built by Bernhardt Schmidt, known to posterity as Father Smith; Inner Temple favoured one built by Renatus Harris, an acquaintance of Sir Thomas Robinson, Treasurer of Inner Temple. By 1684 the two organs had been set up in the church. Master John North of Middle Temple was a friend of Henry Purcell, and he engaged the famous court composers John Blow and Henry Purcell, who had succeeded Blow as Organist at Westminster Abbey[28] and, like Blow, was one of the three organists at the Chapel Royal, to demonstrate the Smith organ. Inner Temple engaged a well-known Catholic organist, Giovanni Battista Dragio, to demonstrate the Harris organ. On 2 June 1685, Middle Temple Parliament declared the Smith organ to be their choice 'both for sweetness and fullness of sound (besides the extraordinary stops quarter notes and other rarityes therein)'.[29] On 24 June 1685, Inner Temple Bench expressed its dissatisfaction with the Middle Temple's decision and 'desired masters of music' to arbitrate the dispute. There was skulduggery on both sides. On the night preceding the last trial of the reed stops, the bellows of the Smith organ were cut so that when the time came for playing the organ, no wind would be conveyed into the wind chest.[30] The dispute rumbled on, and finally it was agreed that the Lord Keeper, Lord Guilford (Sir Francis North), should make the final decision. He died before doing so, and it was left to his successor, Judge Jeffreys of Inner Temple, to decide in favour of the Smith organ. The

---

[24] S Sadie (ed), *New Grove Dictionary of Music and Musicians* (London, Macmillan, 1980), entries for John Playford and Henry Playford; Lewer and Dark, above n 1, at 67–69. John Playford was Clerk of the Temple Church 1653–86.

[25] Sadie (ed), above n 24; J Keates, *Henry Purcell 'A Biography'* (London, Bodley Head, 1995 (new edn 2010)); M Duffy, *Henry Purcell* (London, Fourth Estate, 1994).

[26] Lewer and Dark, above n 1, at 69; Sadie (ed), entries under 'Playford', 'Henry Purcell' and 'Blow'.

[27] MT.15/TAM 98–107; Williamson, above n 1, at 546–50; Lewer, above n 16, at 51–64; Lewer and Dark, above n 1, at 73–75.

[28] Blow was again appointed Organist at Westminster Abbey after the death of Purcell in 1695.

[29] MT.15/TAM 99.

[30] Burney and Charles, *History of Music*, vol III, 437 (1776–89).

organ was much modified in the following 250 years before being destroyed in the bombing of the church on 10 May 1941.

On 25 May 1688, Francis Piggott was appointed by the two Inns as Organist of the Temple Church as from 25 December 1687.[31] He was succeeded in 1704 by his son Thomas, who was Organist for the Middle Temple until 1734. In 1729, Inner Temple, tired of the frequent absences of Thomas Piggott, appointed its own organist. This arrangement was formalised, and from 1729 until 1814 there were two organists, one appointed by each Inn, who played on alternate Sundays.

In about 1707 the position of Reader was regularised. Previously the Master had appointed his own Reader.[32] From that date the Inns alternately would make the appointment. From 1724 the same method of appointment was applied to the Virger.[33]

For the Reader, this has recently been more a matter of form than substance, since there has been general agreement on the appointment of the last two outstanding Readers. The first, Prebendary WD Kennedy-Bell[34] (1955–95), who was the Head of Religious Broadcasting at the BBC and a noted amateur musician, was introduced by Dr George Thalben-Ball. His successor, the present Reader, the Reverend Hugh Mead, a distinguished master at St Paul's School, was introduced by the then Master of the Temple, Canon Joseph Robinson. In addition to their other duties, both have acted as Master during the interregnum between the departure of one Master and the arrival of his successor.

The Temple Church had a close connection with Handel. In 1727 the Reverend Thomas Broughton was appointed Reader. He was a writer of poetry and supplied Handel with the libretto for the musical drama *Hercules*.[35] A better-known connection is Handel's friendship with the blind organist John Stanley, appointed by Inner Temple in 1734, who was Organist until 1786. It was Stanley who taught Handel how to conduct after the latter had gone blind. Handel (and many other organists) frequently heard Stanley's organ voluntaries in the Temple Church.[36] A further link appears from a note in the Middle Temple archive for 1749, which shows that one Stephen Philpot, applying unsuccessfully for the post of Middle Temple Organist, claimed in support of his application that for five years he had received frequent instruction from Handel.[37]

Two organists appointed by Middle Temple during this period should be noted. John Jones, Organist from 1749 to 1796, was also Organist of

[31]   MT.15/TAM 108.
[32]   MT.15/TAM 125s.
[33]   MT.15/TAM 136.
[34]   Known in the Temple as 'K-B'.
[35]   *Middle Temple Bench Book* (1937), 309.
[36]   Sadie (ed), above n 24, entry for 'Stanley'.
[37]   MT.15/TAM 173.

St Paul's Cathedral from 1755 to 1796. He and Stanley played on alternate Sundays. Boswell noted in his diary that

> 3 September 1769 I went to the Temple Church, the idea of the Knights Templars lying in the church was solemn and pleasing. The noble music raised my sole to heaven though it was not Stanley's day, who officiates as organist every other Sunday.[38]

It must have been John Jones who was playing. In 2008, the Temple Players performed one of his compositions. This was probably the first time a work of his had been played in the church for 200 years.

The other Organist was Emily Dowding. She was appointed by Middle Temple in 1796 and dismissed in 1814 for appointing a deputy and not personally attending.[39]

During the period from 1684 to 1753 the Masters of the Temple were William Sherlock (1684–1704), Dean of St Paul's from 1691, and his son Dr Thomas Sherlock (1704–53). They were both distinguished preachers and prominent in church affairs. Thomas Sherlock was appointed when he was 26 years old. In 1724 the benchers requested that his sermons 'in defence of the Christian religion' should be printed. From 1728, whilst remaining Master of the Temple, he held the Bishoprics of Bangor and Salisbury, and, from 1748, the Bishopric of London. He gave a great deal to the Temple and obviously received a great deal in return. On 5 November 1753 he wrote to the Treasurer and Masters of the Bench that he regarded his relationship to the two Inns as 'the great happiness of my life as it introduced me to the acquaintance of some of the greatest men of the age'.[40]

There were five more Masters of the Temple before 1826, of whom Thomas Thurlow (1772–87) also became Bishop of Lincoln and Dean of St Paul's; William Pearce (1787–91) became Dean of Ely; and Thomas Rennell (1797–1826) was from 1805 also Dean of Winchester.

George Warne, appointed Organist of both Inns in 1826, was the second blind organist of the church. He remained until 1843 (although there was an acting organist in 1842) and was responsible for the reintroduction of the rudiments of a choir. On 13 February 1828, on Warne's recommendation, the female singers Mrs Taylor and Miss Elizabeth Flower were to receive 14 guineas per annum, and after the Easter term Miss Flower was to be replaced by a male singer.[41] On 21 May 1828, the minutes of the Standing Committee of both Houses recommended that both female singers should continue and, in addition, a male singer should be employed.[42]

---

[38] Boswell's London Journal, 10 April 1763, quoted in Lewer and Dark, above n 1, at 83.
[39] *Middle Temple Bench Book* (1937), 327.
[40] MT.15/TAM 179.
[41] MT.15/TAM 258.
[42] MT.15/TAM 259.

The Benchers of the Inns thought that the time had come for change and renewal. The refurbishment of the Church in the florid Victorian Gothic style was not to everyone's taste.

It is clear from a report of 26 October 1840 that extensive repairs to the Church were needed.[43] They were carried out over the following two years. The result was, according to taste, a most beautiful and embellished church or "the greatest vandalism of all", so described by WJ Loftie in 1893 in his history of the Inns.[44]

At this time there was much criticism of the banality of the Anglican Parish Church Service. The sentiment, if not the phrase, 'jingles and ditties', was much expressed.[45] The alternative was a 'Cathedral Service' with a surpliced choir. On 29 September 1841, Lincoln's Inn established a surpliced choir. On 25 August 1842, Middle and Inner Temple announced that a choir of about 14, including six boys, had been engaged to perform the regular Cathedral Service. On 20 November 1842, the church reopened with a choir of six boys, two altos, a tenor and a bass.[46] On 20 November 1842, the Middle Temple Bench recommended that a permanent choir be established.[47] Inner Temple Bench required two more meetings before agreeing.

In May 1840 the Benchers of the two Inns had set up a joint committee to oversee the repair and restoration of the Temple Church. In late 1843, the Inns were concerned that the management of the choir could not be left in the hands of John Calvert, who had been appointed master of the choir in February 1843, and it was resolved to set up a permanent Joint Choir Committee 'to have the superintendence and regulation of the choir of the Temple Church'.[48]

The Cathedral Service (with the Book of Common Prayer, used to this day) was a great success. It became necessary to issue tickets for the Temple Church services. Unfortunately the Master of the Temple, the Reverend Christopher Benson, appointed in 1826, did not approve of the refurbishment or of the new choir. He described admission by ticket to the church as admission to 'the painted Church as if it were a painted theatre'. He hoped that 'music would become a subordinate or chastened part of the service'.[49]

---

[43]   MT.15/TAM 266 *et seq*; Lewer and Dark, above n 1, at 94 *et seq*.

[44]   WJ Loftie, *The Inns and Courts of Chancery* (London, Seeley & Co, 1893).

[45]   Phrase coined by the late Master Leonard, Bishop of London, of uninspiring music at parish services in the 1980s.

[46]   Lewer and Dark, above n 1, at 107; Lewer, above n 16, at 106 *et seq*.

[47]   MT.15/TAM 291. On 7 May 1844 the benchers resolved to set up the Joint Committee, see Lewer and Dark, above n 1, at 109.

[48]   Lewer, above n 16, at 128. There had previously been a joint committee of the two Inns to supervise the extensive work on the Temple Church; see text to nn 43 and 44 above.

[49]   Benson was on the evangelical wing of the church.

The introduction of 'Cathedral Service', with a full choir, has attracted worshippers to the Temple Church ever since and has earned the Inns an extraordinary debt of public gratitude, in addition to that earned by their service to the law.

In an echo of the claim of Dr Micklethwaite, the Master said that 'the authority to regulate the spiritual services of the Temple Church must vest in some person or persons and I believe it to vest in myself as Rector of the Church'.[50] He was told by the Inns that was not so and that the Benchers regulated the services 'with a due regard to the wishes of the Master'. In 1845 Christopher Benson resigned the mastership. He lived for another 23 years and died in 1868 aged 79.

The Temple choir was directed from 1843 to 1898 by EJ Hopkins. He was 25 when he was appointed. He first played the organ in the church on 2 May 1843 and was appointed as Organist on the departure of John Calvert later in that year. Despite the setting up of the Choir Committee, Hopkins was requested 'that you will carry out your duties in a manner that seems best to yourself'.[51] Grove describes the music under his stewardship as 'a model for church services that were rapidly becoming established throughout the country'. His chant for the Venite, 'O come let us sing unto the Lord', is still sung regularly at Morning Service. He was one of the founders of the Royal College of Organists in 1869. He also edited an edition of Purcell's music for Novellos.

In 1866 the Reader's duties were extended. From that date he would not only preach on Sunday evening, but also sing the Sunday morning service. The Reverend Alfred Ainger was appointed at the age of 29. He remained Reader until 1892. In 1894 he was appointed Master. He retired in 1904.[52] He was also a Canon of Bristol Cathedral from 1886. The period seems to have been a settled one where the outstanding service of Master, Reader and organist was thoroughly appreciated.

Canon Ainger summed up Hopkins's legacy in a letter to him on the 50th anniversary of his first service at the Temple Church (8 May 1893). He said 'no living man has done more to raise the standing of all that is revered and beautiful in the conduct of divine worship than he has done'.[53]

Ainger said that Hopkins created the reputation of the Temple service musically and 'composed lovely services and hymns'.[54] Hopkins's last service was on 8 May 1898, the 55th anniversary of his first service in the

---

[50]   Lewer and Dark, above n 1, at 106,109.
[51]   C Pearce, *Life and Works of EJ Hopkins* (London, The Vincent Music Co Ltd, 1903), 27.
[52]   E Sichell, *Life and Letters of Alfred Ainger* (London, Archibald Constable & Co, 1906).
[53]   Lewer, above n 16, at 200, 201.
[54]   Sichell, above n 52, at 299.

Temple Church. Master the Prince of Wales (later King Edward VII) often came to services in the Temple Church at this time.[55]

It was again time for renewal. A treble of the time, Henry Humm, said of the music that by 1890 that very little was new, and nothing was ambitious, but much of it was beautiful.[56]

Walford Davies, then aged 28, was appointed on 25 February 1898 to succeed Hopkins. He was appointed by Middle Temple. Of the 100 candidates, three were invited to take choir practice and to play the organ. Walford Davies had impressive references and was a likely appointment, despite being much younger than the other two candidates. The boys thought that they had made the decision themselves. They preferred Walford Davies and said that they sang much better for him than for the other two candidates.[57] His letter of appointment made it clear that he was 'to act generally under the direction of the Church Committee'.[58]

The verdict of Kenneth Long in his *History of Music of the English Church* was that Walford Davies at the Temple Church 'created a legendary choir'.[59] The quality of the music was much appreciated not only by Canon Ainger,[60] but also by his successors. The combination of excellent preaching and excellent music put the Temple Church at the centre of Anglican worship and of the musical life of London.

From the setting up of the choir until 1900, the boys attended the Inns' choir school and from 1872 the Stationers' school. Since 1900 the Inns have paid for scholarships for the boys in the choir, mostly at the City of London School.[61] Originally the Inns paid full fees. Now they pay two-thirds of the fees for the 18 boys. Efforts have been made, with the assistance of a most generous benefaction from a member of the congregation, to provide a fund to ensure that no boy of sufficient musical talent will be unable to join the choir for want of financial resources.

As had happened with Stanley over 100 years before, young organists came to the Temple Church eager to learn from Walford Davies. On 10 March 1902, Leopold Stokowski, a former pupil, later the celebrated conductor of the Philadelphia Orchestra from 1913 to 1936, was then aged 20. He wrote to Walford Davies to tell him of his appointment as Organist of St James's Church, Piccadilly:

---

[55] Lewer, above n 16, at 171, noting a recollection of a chorister, Henry Humm, who left the choir in about 1890; Lewer and Dark, above n 1, at 130.

[56] Lewer and Dark, above n 1, 130.

[57] HC Colles, *Walford Davies* (Oxford, Oxford University Press, 1942), 46.

[58] *Ibid*, at 47.

[59] K Long, *History of Music of the English Church* (London, Hodder & Stoughton, 1972, repr 1991), 413; Lewer, above n 16, at 166–67.

[60] Letter to Mrs Andrew Lang, 2 February 1901, two days before he died: quoted in Sichell, above n 52.

[61] Lewer, above n 16, at 224.

I can never of course repay in any way your kindnesses to me. I can only hope to have an opportunity of passing them on to another,

Your affectionate pupil,

Leopold Stokowski[62]

Walford Davies opened up the church to performances outside the services. In 1900 the events for the year included two performances of the *St Matthew Passion*, the Brahms *German Requiem*, and the traditional performances of the *Christmas Oratorio*, Parts 1 and 2. Davies composed oratorios, founded the London Church Choir drawn from churches all over London and became conductor of the Bach Choir.[63]

Walford Davies was a friend of Sir Hubert Parry and helped him with the technical aspects of Parry's sets of *Choral Preludes for Organ*.[64] In June 1915 Parry gave him a tune that he had composed: 'Do what you like with it,' he said. Walford Davies took it to Curwen's for publication, scrupulously insisting on securing the copyright for the composer (not for himself or the Inns). The song was sung during the First World War at meetings of the Fight for Right Movement. It is now known as *Jerusalem*.[65]

In 1919 Walford Davies was offered the Chair of Music at the University of Aberystwyth. He wanted to play his part in promoting music in his native Wales. He attempted to combine the two posts by appointing an Assistant, George Thalben-Ball, then aged 23. He became Organist in 1923 on the resignation of Walford Davies, and remained until 1981.[66]

That was the start of the era of electrical recording. In 1922 Walford Davies had attempted to record the choir but the results were unsatisfactory. With some trepidation, the Choir Committee commissioned a recording of Mendelssohn's *Hear My Prayer* ('O for the Wings of a Dove') by a 14-year-old boy treble, Ernest Lough.[67] The unworldly Choir Committee made no attempt to secure royalties either for the Church or for Ernest Lough, or for Dr Thalben-Ball. To everyone's surprise the recording was an

---

[62] Colles, above n 57, at 49.

[63] *Ibid*, at 58.

[64] *Ibid*, at 68. Parry came frequently to the Temple Church at this time.

[65] *Ibid*, at 108–09. *Jerusalem* was sung in the Royal Albert Hall in March 1918 to celebrate votes for women over 30, see PA Scholes, *Oxford Companion to Music*, 9th edn (Oxford, Oxford University Press, 1955).

[66] J Rennert, *George Thalben-Ball* (Newton Abbot, London and North Pomfret (Vt), David & Charles, 1979), 51 *et seq*.

[67] Lewer, above n 16, at 349–52, with an Appendix which contains a list of all choir recordings to 1960; Rennert, above n 66, at 61–63; Lewer and Dark, above n 1, at 140. In CD CDH 7638272 many recordings of Thalben-Ball were included by EMI as *Great Recordings of the Century*. Another 'Great Recording of the Century', recently recommended as the 'Best Recording', is Sir John Barbirolli's recording of Vaughan Williams's *Fantasia on a Theme of Thomas Tallis* (EMI 5672402), made in the Temple Church on 17 May 1962: see BBC, *Music Magazine*, December 2010.

instantaneous success. The shell of the first recording on 5 April 1927 wore out after six months and the music had to be re-recorded.[68] Until 1929 tickets had to be issued for Sunday services at the Temple Church. The recording has never been out of the catalogue, and in 1962 both Ernest Lough and Thalben-Ball received golden discs after 1 million copies had been sold. It has now sold well over 5 million copies. In 2005 both recordings of *Hear my Prayer*, together with other Ernest Lough recordings, were issued as a CD on the Naxos label.[69]

This was another golden age for the church. Canon Draper, appointed Master of the Temple in 1920, Dr Carpenter, appointed in 1930, and Canon Anson, appointed in 1935, in conjunction with the choir, provided wonderful services. Thalben-Ball started a series of organ recitals which continue to this day. There were also monthly recitals of cantatas, and new works were introduced. The choir made a succession of successful recordings between 1926 and 1939, a number of which have subsequently been re-issued.[70]

The choir sang at the coronation of King George VI and Queen Elizabeth in 1937, and since then have worn the red cassocks of a royal choir. Soon after, there was the shadow of war. *The Templar* magazine of April 1939 noted that 'the Munich Agreement came just in time to prevent trenches being dug in the gardens. They were all pegged out in readiness'.[71] As we know, Munich merely delayed the inevitable. In the summer of 1939 the choristers were evacuated to Marlborough and could sing in the Temple Church only in the holidays. Other services were conducted with men's voices only.[72]

The Second World War saw the virtual destruction of the church as generations had known it. On 15 October 1940, at the height of the Blitz, a mine landed in Elm Court and brought down the Hall's east wall and the screen. Windows in the church were blown out, but services at Christmas 1940 and Easter 1941 took place as normal.

On the night of 10 May 1941 an incendiary bomb landed on the roof of the church at the south-east angle of the chancel.[73] The fire spread to the vestries and to the organ. Within half an hour the fire was out of control. The water pressure was too low to put it out and the roof fell in. One of the fire watchers, powerless to help, was Ernest Lough. The wooden roof

---

[68]   In March 1928.

[69]   Naxos 8.120832.

[70]   Few recordings of the choir were made after the War. A recording was made in 1979 sponsored by the Temple Music Trust. The next recording made by the choir on its own was released in November 2010.

[71]   Lewer and Dark, above n 1, at 145.

[72]   *Ibid.*

[73]   Anonymous, *Middle Temple Ordeal* (London, Middle Temple)32, 33; Lewer and Dark, above n 1, at 146–48.

of the Round caved in and fell on the effigies of the Knights below. Father Smith's organ was reduced to ash and solidifying trickles of molten metal. Father Smith's pipes were to have been removed later that month to a place of safety, but now it was too late.[74]

The story of the devotion of the Reverend AJ MacDonald, the Rector of St Dunstan's in the West (and from 1950 Acting Master, owing to the illness of Canon Anson), Thalben-Ball and the Temple choristers is told elsewhere.[75] They kept services going during the war in the ruins of the church and at St Dunstan's. There was a Christmas Carol service in the roofless ruins of the church on 28 December 1941.

The restoration work was undertaken by the firm of Carden and Godfrey, Architects. In 1949 the work of rebuilding began. Dove Brothers of Islington (Builders) had carried out the restoration of Middle Temple Hall. They now undertook the restoration of the Temple Church, overseen on behalf of the two Inns by Master Kenneth Carpmael, Master of the House at Middle Temple. The quarries at Purbeck were revisited to provide the marble columns which were needed to replace those that had been damaged.

Soon after the destruction of the 'Father Smith' organ, Thalben-Ball started the search for a new organ. In February 1950, Master Lord Glentanar offered to give the church an organ built by Harrison & Harrison in 1927/28.[76] Thalben-Ball described it as better than anything that could be obtained new at that time, and in many respects as equal and in a few respects as superior to the old organ.[77]

The new organ was brought down from Scotland in 1953 and reassembled in the Temple Church. The work took six months, in fact a very short time for such an instrument. It had to be ready for the service of rededication of the chancel on 23 March 1954, in the presence of Master Her Majesty Queen Elizabeth the Queen Mother.

Canon Anson, devoted to the Temple Church, lived just long enough to know of the rededication of the chancel. He died on 31 March 1954. In his book of reflections he said:

> I can only say that with most loyal and friendly cooperation of the Reader at the Temple, the Treasurers and Masters of the Bench, the Organist, choir and the surveyors I have never had so happy a post or one which gives greater opportunities to anyone ready to take account both of its limitations and its openings.[78]

---

[74] Lewer and Dark, above n 1, at 149.
[75] Lewer, above n 16, ch XV; Lewer and Dark, above n 1, at 152.
[76] MT.15/FIL No 16.
[77] Rennert, above n 66, at 108; Lewer and Dark, above n 1, at 157; MT.15/FIL No 19 contains a letter from Thalben-Ball urging the Choir Committee to accept the gift as 'a noble successor to the famous "Father Smith" Church Organ'.
[78] H Anson, *Looking Forward* (London, Heinemann, 1938), 282.

This quotation encapsulates the traditional view of the church centred around the Benchers of the Inns, which continued until the late 1990s.

The Round Church and Triforium were rededicated on 7 November 1958 in the presence of the Queen, the Duke of Edinburgh and Master Her Majesty Queen Elizabeth the Queen Mother.

Regular Sunday morning services had started again in January 1955. The boys sang again with the choirmen for the first time on 30 October 1955, when the choir included Ernest Lough as a baritone and his son Robin as a treble. His other two sons also sang as boy choristers. Ernest Lough died in 2000, and his and his wife's ashes rest in the Triforium.

One of the earliest choristers after the war was Ian le Grice, who became a chorister in 1957. He has given virtually unbroken service to the Temple Church since that date. After acting as unofficial assistant organist to Dr Thalben-Ball, he was formally appointed Assistant Organist in 1982. In 2007 he was presented with a scroll of appreciation by the two Inns to mark his 50 years of service to the Inns and to the church. To celebrate the event, he composed a setting for Holy Communion which is much appreciated.

Canon Firth (1954–57),[79] Canon Milford (1958–68), Dean Milburn (1968–80) and Canon Joseph Robinson (1980–99) all gave devoted service to the Temple Church. It will be remembered that authority for the conduct of church affairs rested with the Church Committee, who were not enthusiastic about change. The Masters of the Temple presided over the traditional activities, services on a Sunday, weddings and memorial services of benchers, and the annual carol service. They visited the sick and cared for those who lived in the Inns. In an unusual and well-merited mark of his service, Canon Robinson was elected an Honorary Bencher of Inner Temple. The author remembers Dean Milburn's sermons set in the context appropriate to an eminent ecclesiastical historian,[80] and Canon Robinson's wonderful Lenten Addresses and his sermons debunking the radical views of the then Bishop of Durham, Dr David Jenkins.

Dr Thalben-Ball continued as Organist until 1981 when, at the age of 85, he retired. He had been made an Honorary Bencher of Inner Temple[81] and was knighted in 1982. He was succeeded by Dr John Birch, Organist of the Royal Philharmonic Orchestra and formerly Organist of Chichester Cathedral. On his retirement in 1997, he became an Honorary Bencher of Middle Temple.

---

[79] Canon Firth died in September in 1957. The Rev WD Kennedy-Bell, as Reader, was acting Master until the arrival of Canon Milford.

[80] Dean Milburn's speech in October 1973 to celebrate the 50th anniversary of Dr Thalben-Ball's appointment as Organist of the Church is in File Treasury Ref 1108.

[81] For a list of his recordings, see Rennert, above n 66, at 151.

By the early 1990s, it was apparent to the author and others that unless we did something to renew the spirit of the Temple Church it would gradually fade away as an institution. On reflection there were a number of problems. The church was regarded too much as a preserve of the Benchers of the two Inns. At Sunday Services the whole of the area between the choir and the altar on both sides was set aside for Benchers even though, except on special occasions, relatively few attended. From the 1970s, the vast expansion of the Bar meant that residential chambers in the Inns had to be converted into professional chambers, and the church lost a significant part of its congregation. The congregation rarely included children or young persons and was growing ever more elderly.[82]

There was a further problem over taking new initiatives. While the troubles in Ireland were continuing, security in the Inns was of the greatest importance. It had been tightened in the 1970s. There was a risk in encouraging new people to come into the area of the Temple Church. While Master Diplock was alive, there was a constant reminder of the security problem. Master Diplock, founder of the Diplock Courts in Northern Ireland, sat in Middle Temple Benchers' pews for Sunday morning services. Opposite him, on the Inner Temple side, was an armed security guard. This security threat had become less acute by the mid-1990s.

The church needed a new focus, one where it was made evident that it was there primarily to serve the members and staff of the two Inns and their families, and not merely the Benchers. A start was made in the mid-1990s. Master Butler-Sloss of Inner Temple and the author formed a sub-committee with the Master to review those who could be married or have memorial services in the church, or whose children could be baptised in the church. Canon Robinson was enthusiastic about relaxing some of the limitations confining these privileges to benchers and their families, and some modest changes were made with the assistance of the Under and Sub Treasurers of the two Inns who have also done much to support the Church.

When Dr Birch decided to retire in 1997, the interviewing committee, comprising representatives of the two Inns, together with the distinguished organist and choirmaster Christopher Robinson as adviser, wanted to create a new tradition which took account of the developments in choral music in the last 70 years. Some of the candidates, however, thought that the committee would want to try to recreate the time of Ernest Lough and George Thalben-Ball in their heyday. In the view of the committee that was in any event an impossible task. Stephen Layton, Assistant Organist at

---

[82] The author and his wife, also a Middle Templar, have worshipped regularly in the Temple Church since 1967. Frequently, theirs were the only children in the church.

Southwark Cathedral, the youngest candidate, was appointed by the Inns on the recommendation of the Committee. It is interesting to note that Stanley, Hopkins, Walford Davies, Thalben-Ball, Layton and subsequently James Vivian, were all appointed Organist when under 30 years of age.

Immediately after his appointment, Layton recruited James Vivian, recently down from Cambridge, as Assistant Organist. When Layton left for Trinity College Cambridge in 2006, having been elected an Honorary Bencher of Middle Temple, Vivian succeeded him as Director of the Choir. Although each has his own distinctive style, this made for an easy transition. They have indeed created the new tradition which the Church Committee had hoped to achieve. Greg Morris from Blackburn Cathedral was appointed as Associate Organist to succeed Vivian.

In 1998 Canon Robinson became seriously ill. It was agreed at Christmas 1998 that he would formally retire and become Master Emeritus, although he would continue to reside in the Master's House and perform such duties as he could. The Reader, Hugh Mead, was appointed acting Master. Canon Robinson's last service was in May 1999; he died five weeks later.[83] Master Ian Kennedy provided considerable support as Chairman of the Church Committee.

In 1998 the status of the church was called into question by an opinion that the Temple Church was not a Royal Peculiar. The historical position was vigorously asserted by Master Boydell, an eminent ecclesiastical lawyer and former Treasurer. The matter was happily resolved.[84] The Queen confirmed that the appointment of Canon Robinson's successor would be a Royal appointment, and she decided to confer her Visitorial powers on the Dean of the Chapels Royal. The present Dean, Master Chartres, is, of course, also Bishop of London (who as such has no jurisdiction over the Temple Church) and an Honorary Bencher. The Church is much indebted to him for his great support and, not least, for conducting inspiring services of Baptism and Confirmation on the last Sunday in July.

The Choir Committee decided to look for someone younger to be Master. The thinking was that he could relate more easily to the problems of those starting at the Bar and in mid-career, and in this way the pastoral duties of the Master could be widened. The Choir Committee (with the Dean of St Paul's as adviser) was permitted to interview two candidates, and Her Majesty was then graciously pleased to appoint the Reverend Robin Griffith Jones as Master for 10 years from 1 September 1999. (His term has since been extended.) The new Master's father had been Master Reader of Middle Temple. The Master had been brought up in the Middle

---

[83] It is a pity that Canon Robinson's last sermons were not preserved and published.
[84] MT.15/FIL55.

Temple and was a student member of the Inn. Although he has pursued a very different career, he has the Temple in his bones.

On appointment the Master was aged 43. It is a measure of his success that he has been elected an Honorary Bencher by both Middle and Inner Temples. His extraordinary skill, energy and enthusiasm have enabled him to reach far beyond those who come to services on a Sunday morning. He has fulfilled the hope that pastoral duties would be extended to younger members of the Inns. He has helped to forge links with Middle and Inner Temple lawyers in other Common Law jurisdictions. This furthers the claim that the Temple Church should be regarded as the Mother Church of the Common Law.

The Master has written scholarly books on the Four Gospels, St Paul's Journeys and Mary Magdalene. In 2002, Dan Brown wrote the world best-seller *The Da Vinci Code*, which features the Temple Church. The Master has given many lectures on the Code to admiring audiences from this country and around the world, and his book on the subject—not flattering to Dan Brown's thesis—has also been a best-seller. In 2010, with David Park, he edited an important book, *The Temple Church: History, Architecture and Art*. In 2008 he promoted an important series of lectures on Islam, including a thought-provoking lecture by Dr Rowan Williams, Archbishop of Canterbury, in the Great Hall of the Royal Courts of Justice. In the lecture, entitled *Civil and Religious Law in England: A Religious Perspective*, the Archbishop discussed a number of topics, including the place of religious courts in the English legal system.

An important innovation in 1999 was the establishment of a Sunday school during morning service. The Temple Church owes a great deal to the Chartres family. They had two sons in the Temple Choir, and it was Master Chartres's wife, Caroline, who established the Sunday school and ran it for a number of years. This meant that families could come and enjoy the service. Children could offer the results of their labours at the altar. The choir parents have made a significant contribution, not only in relation to their own children but also in relation to the well-being of the choristers as a whole. They have been supported for many years by Liz Clarke, the parents' coordinator.

The words, the music and the more inclusive family atmosphere have combined to increase very substantially the congregation in the Temple Church, both at Sunday services and at the additional services of Evensong, supported by the Temple Music Trust.[85] It has been necessary once again to issue tickets for the annual Christmas Carol Services, now three in number. At the great festivals the church is full. For other services the average congregation now numbers over 150. With the encouragement of

[85] See text to n 91 below.

the Choir Committee, the Master has instituted bi-annual celebrations of baptisms and marriages, and for families who have held memorial services in the Church, followed by an informal lunch.

Layton and Vivian, supported by the Master, have transformed not just the musical life of the Temple Church but also the musical life of the Inns. Two Middle Temple Benchers have also had pivotal roles. Master Christopher Clarke was Chairman of the Church Committee from January 2005 to January 2011, and Master Richard Aikens has been the Chairman of the Temple Music Foundation since its launch in 2002. The Temple Music Foundation has promoted concerts by the choir and the newly-formed Temple Players in the Temple Church, as well as other concerts in the Church and song recitals in Middle Temple Hall by internationally-known singers accompanied by Julius Drake.

Since 1999 the choir has also taken part in a performance of *The Dream of Gerontius* with the London Philharmonic Orchestra, the boys have provided backing for the film *Gormenghast*, and the choir has toured Brazil for the British Council. In 2009 the choir recorded for Signum Records a successful CD,[86] *The Majesty of Thy Glory*, which was launched in 2010. This was the first recording by the choir alone since 1979. Also in 2010, James Vivian made a recording, *English Organ Music from the Temple Church*.[87] The men of the choir are singers in the front rank of the profession and include a number with international solo careers. The boys' singing and musicianship has steadily improved with additional teaching supported by the Temple Music Trust. The choir is now acknowledged as one of the three best in London.

In addition, a number of visiting choirs have given concerts, in particular Layton's two choirs, Polyphony and the Holst Singers, and Canticum, conducted by Mark Forkgen, a former head chorister. The church has been used regularly for classical recordings. The boys sang at the Lord Mayor's Banquet when Master Gavyn Arthur became Lord Mayor of London, and the Master was his Chaplain for the year.

Perhaps the most remarkable musical event has been the commissioning and performance of *The Veil of the Temple* by Sir John Tavener.[88] Tavener was recording another of his works, *Eternity's Sunrise*, in the church in June 2000. He was invited with Layton and others to tea in the Master's House. The author was among those present. Tavener suddenly mused, 'It is a pity that this is 2000 and not the year 1900. The Temple Church would be a

---

[86] SIGCD225.

[87] On Signum Classics, *English Organ Music from the Temple Church*, SIGCD 223. The recording was released in November 2010. See reviews in the *The Gramophone*, April 2011, at p 88 and *The Organ*, March 2011.

[88] See also D Dudgeon, *Lifting the Veil, a biography of Sir John Tavener* (London, Portrait, an imprint of Judy Piatkus Publishers Ltd, 2003).

wonderful place for an all-night vigil.' The idea was taken up immediately. Layton expressed the hope that the choir of the Temple Church might have the opportunity to recover the stature that it had had in the 1920s. The Master hoped that such a piece would bring the sanctity of the Round Church to life. What we had in mind was a relatively simple project of music and readings throughout the night. What Stephen Layton received in March 2002 was one of Sir John Tavener's greatest works, *The Veil of the Temple*, which provided unforeseen challenges in its length and complexity. The Vigil would last from 10 pm until 5 am, and the music would be continuous. It would cost substantially more to stage than had been budgeted.

It required the dedication of Layton, Vivian and the Master to bring the project to fruition. In addition to soloists, the performance required a choir of 140 drawn from the Temple Church choir, Polyphony and the Holst Singers, and organ, Indian harmonium, duduk, a Tibetan horn 5 feet in length, Tibetan temple bowls, tubular bells, a tam-tam and brass. There were two all-night performances on 27 June and 4 July 2003, and a shortened evening performance on 1 July 2003. The performances used the whole of the church, including the Round and the Triforium, and received excellent reviews and publicity for the choir and the Inns.[89] Thereafter the shortened version of *The Veil*[90] was performed at the Proms and, in the following year, the full version at the Lincoln Centre, New York. In New York, breakfast was served at the end of the performance.

A large part of *The Veil* was recorded successfully on to two compact discs. None of this could have been achieved without the most generous financial support from Middle and Inner Temple, the JC Baker Family Trust and the Temple Music Trust, which had been set up by members of the two Inns in 1979 to promote Temple music.[91] There were many others whose financial and practical support was vital. Penny Jonas has been responsible for coordinating the finances and raising the necessary support for *The Veil of the Temple*, and for many subsequent musical projects connected with the church and with Middle Temple through 'Temple Music Foundation'.

Since then there have been many highlights. The year 2008 was a year-long celebration in words and music of the 400th Anniversary of the granting of the Charter, led by the two Treasurers, Master Michael Blair of Middle Temple and Master Anthony May of Inner Temple. The two Inns

[89]   Richard Morrison's review of 30 June 2003 is available at <http://www.timesonline.co. uk/tol/comment/columnist/richard_morrison/article11465>. In the course of a review full of superlatives, he said that 'It was wonderfully and generously eccentric of the usually hard-nosed lawyers of Inner and Middle Temple to raise nearly half a million quid to get it commissioned, rehearsed and performed'.

[90]   The shortened version of *The Veil* was issued on two CDs, RCA 82876661542; it was an 'Editor's Choice' of *The Gramophone* magazine.

[91]   See Rennert, above n 66, at 173, for the setting up of the Trust.

achieved a degree of amity which has by no means always been evident throughout their history. The Anniversary was marked by a commemorative window on the south side of the church, the first since the church was re-built after the Second World War.

The church has, over the years, had remarkable support from the Royal Family. In most recent times the Prince of Wales acted as patron for *The Veil of the Temple*. Her Majesty the Queen and the Duke of Edinburgh attended a service in 2008 for the rededication of the two Inns and the presentation of a new Charter, and in 2009 Master HRH Prince William of Wales attended evensong in the church before being called to become Middle Temple's most recent royal bencher.[92]

There have been major changes in the appearance of the church since 1997. Ian Garwood, employed by Middle Temple since 1978 and currently the Director of Estates, has been responsible for many years on behalf of the two Inns for supervising the substantial works of renovation and renewal. Among the many changes in the last 10 years, in 2001 and 2002 the outside of the church was cleaned, clearing away the grime of war. In 2003 and 2004 the vaulted ceiling of the church was redecorated. In 2008, after many difficulties, the lighting of the church was transformed. The gloomy chandeliers were removed. The new lighting shows off the wonderful colours of the stone. The current task of refurbishing the organ, which has had only minor repairs since it was hastily installed in 1954, is a considerable current challenge for the Inns and their members.

Canon Alfred Ainger, then Reader of the Temple Church and subsequently Master, at the celebration of the 700th anniversary of the consecration of the Round Church on 10 February 1885, said in his sermon:

> The Templars have bequeathed us, as a legacy, this lesson which we must not forget in the hour when we would fain recall the days of their grandeur and fresh enthusiasm: there is no promise of continuance for any institute, any party, any church, any creed, out of which the Spirit shall have departed ... after 700 years the truth remains unchanged for all who pass to worship through the nobly beautiful building that, on this day, was consecrated.[93]

Looking back over the history of the Church, one can only echo the wise words of Canon Ainger, devoted servant of the Church and of the Inns, that any institution needs regular renewals of the spirit, otherwise it will die. One of the most remarkable public contributions of the Middle and Inner Temple is their continuing and generous support for the Temple Church which has enabled this to happen. They have amply fulfilled their obligations under the Royal Charter of 1608 and have received a remarkable heritage in return.

---

[92]   Also in 2011. Master Her Royal Highness Princess Anne is Master Treasurer of Inner Temple.

[93]   Lewer and Dark, above n 1, at 9.

1

The First Two Centuries

JOHN BAKER

I.   THE ORIGINS OF THE INNS OF COURT AND CHANCERY

T HE PRECISE ORIGINS of the Inns of Court and Chancery are lost to posterity and unlikely ever to be discovered. We can, nevertheless, date most of them with reasonable confidence to the second quarter of the fourteenth century, and on a balance of probabilities to the 1340s.[1] It is unlikely that the lawyers could have been in occupation of the Temple—except perhaps for a few in-house advisers or individual tenants—before the eviction of the Knights Templar in 1308. When the Temple was vacated by the Templars it was still not certain that the King's central courts would always remain at Westminster, for they had been at York for several years under Edward I and would go there again in the 1330s. During such periods the lawyers following the courts would leave London, presumably to take lodgings in York, an exodus which cost the Fleet Street shopkeepers a considerable loss of revenue.[2]

While such uncertainty prevailed as to the location of their usual place of work, the legal profession cannot have been much inclined to associate in order to acquire permanent accommodation; and it is noteworthy that, in a contract of 1323 to support a law student, the terms are not that he should be sent to some fixed institution or place but that he should be found for four years among the apprentices 'at our lord the king's court of Common

---

[1]   The first part of what follows is largely based on 'Learning in the Early Inns of Court' (1990) 105 *Selden Society* xxv–xxx; 'The Third University of England' (Selden Society lecture, 1990), repr in JH Baker, *The Common Law Tradition* (2000), 1–28; 'The Division of the Temple' (1987) *Inner Temple Yearbook* 1987, 17–23, repr in *The Common Law Tradition*, 29–36; and (with revisions) in J Baker, *An Inner Temple Miscellany* (2004), 24–31. There is a useful survey by Sir Ronald Roxburgh of what is known about the fourteenth-century Temple in 'Lawyers in the New Temple' (1972) 88 *LQR* 414.

[2]   See the inquisition of 1337 printed in AR Ingpen (ed), *Master Worsley's Book on the History and Constitution of the Middle Temple* (1910), 226–28.

Bench, wherever the said Bench should be in England'.[3] It is hardly surprising, then, that the early arrangements for lodging in the Temple should be so obscure. No one at the time would have seen any significance in them, and they may well have been informal.[4]

There is a specific reason for thinking that the Inns of Court probably date from around 1340, which is that the courts and the legal profession returned in 1339 to Westminster and the suburbs of London after a long spell in York.[5] Already by March 1339 some of the 'apprentices of court' had a servant, John le Wyse, who is remembered for having killed someone near the Temple and having then fled into Temple Church. The record does not explicitly link his employers with the Temple, but it does prove that there was a community of apprentices large enough to hire servants as a body, and it seems a likely inference that the community was in the Temple.[6] On a Sunday evening in the following June, four apprentices of the Bench—men from parts as distant as Somerset and Cumberland—were involved in a fatal battle with two Chancery clerks opposite the house rented by Serjeant Thomas de Lincoln in Holborn: a possible first reference to Lincoln's Inn, though not to the present premises.[7] The King's Bench rolls reveal that an appeal of murder was subsequently brought against someone who had received the apprentices in their flight; and this provides the additional information that they fled to the house of one John Davy or Tavy, the very house which later became Thavies Inn. Tavy's will (made in 1348) mentions that his inn had previously been let to apprentices. Clifford's Inn may well belong to the same decade: in 1344 it was let, perhaps for the first time, to apprentices of the Bench. Another bloodletting in Holborn, on Sunday, 25 February 1341, introduces us to a John of Cornwall, 'maniple', whose house faced that of the Bishop of Lincoln.

The word 'maniple' is itself of considerable evidential significance. It was an academical term, doubtless borrowed from Oxford, and indicated stewardship of a hall of residence with collegiate features—perhaps, in Cornwall's case, a nascent Gray's Inn. The term was never used for private stewards. A search through legal records of this period reveals the names of other maniples frequenting the western suburbs of London, and it is evident that their duties were sufficiently extensive to require

---

[3]   MJ Bennett, 'Provincial Gentlefolk and Legal Education' (1984) 57 *Bulletin of the Institute of Historical Research* 203, at 207.

[4]   Even in later times, the Inns of Court and Chancery tended to eschew formal leases and rely on trusts: see JH Baker, *The Legal Profession and the Common Law* (1986), 56–59.

[5]   For this paragraph, see Baker, *The Common Law Tradition*, above n 1, at 9–18.

[6]   City of London Record office [CLRO], Coroners Roll G, no 20; RR Sharpe (ed), *Calendar of Coroners' Rolls of the City of London* (1913), 214.

[7]   There is no direct reference to Lincoln's Inn as a legal society before 1419. By that date it was almost certainly on its present site, the former inn of the Bishop of Chichester in Chancery Lane, which (like the Temple) was part of the estate of the Knights Templar.

under-servants; it may be deduced that their masters formed substantial communities. This was a whole generation before Chaucer's 'gentle manciple ... of a temple' had 'masters ... more than thrice ten, that were of law expert and curious'; he at any rate was clearly employed by a well-established legal society, perhaps the Inner Temple, where Chaucer may have been a member. Now, these servants are of far greater interest to us than as providing glosses on Chaucer, or footnotes to the history of the stewards and under-treasurers of the Inns of Court; for it so happens that their appearance in the legal quarter in the 1340s and 1350s affords some of the best evidence we are likely to find for the establishment of collegiate legal communities at that period, communities perhaps consciously modelled on the colleges of Oxford and Cambridge. The previous half-century had been the most active period of college foundation at both universities, and also in Paris. And it is from the same generation that we find evidence of complex pleading exercises, and lectures on statutes, which later grew into the familiar educational routine of moots and readings.[8] The Temple, which was sacked by Wat Tyler and his rebels in 1381, was by that date firmly associated in the popular mind with the upper levels of the legal profession, the *apprenticii juris nobiliores*, who kept trunks full of their clients' papers and muniments in the church.[9]

II.   THE 'INNER AND MIDDLE INNS' OF THE TEMPLE

Whether the lawyer tenants of the Knights Hospitaller[10] in the Temple were always divided into two societies, or were created by fission from what was once a single body, has been a matter of debate for over three centuries. There was an old tradition that 'They were at the prime and in their original but one entire foundation and body, but in process of time

---

[8]   JH Baker (ed), 'Readings and Moots at the Inns of Court in the Fifteenth Century', ii ('Moots and Readers' Cases') (1990) 105 *Selden Society* xxii–xlv.

[9]   Thomas of Walsingham, *Historia Anglicana* (Rolls Series), i. 457: '*Etiam locum qui vocatur Temple Barre in quo apprenticii juris morabantur nobiliores diruerunt*' ('They also pulled down the place called Temple Bar, where dwelt the more distinguished apprentices of the law'). It is curious that Walsingham seems to have confused the area called the Temple with the bar across Fleet Street which separated the city of London from Middlesex; but casual passers-by might well have associated the Temple with this public landmark near its entrance, and indeed there exists a letter written in 1426 to the men of court '*demorans en lostel du Templebar*': J Gairdner (ed), *Paston Letters* (1872–75), i. 23, no 6.

[10]   The Hospitallers were successors in title to the Knights Templar, but did not require the Temple for their own occupation: see Jonathan Riley-Smith, Prologue, above, p 9. Lincoln's Inn was already let to the Bishop of Chichester when the freehold came to the Hospitallers; at some point before 1420 the Bishop sub-let the inn to a legal society (above n 7) which may have brought the name Lincoln with it from elsewhere.

became divided'.[11] A seventeenth-century manuscript in the Inner Temple placed the division in Henry VI's time:

> By what time they were so multiplied and grown into so great a bulk as could not conveniently be regulated into one society, neither was the old hall capable of so great a number, whereupon they were forced to divide themselves. A new hall was then erected, which is now the Inner Temple hall.[12]

No authority for this is cited, but

> That they were at first but one is apparent by all the records of that time, which make mention only of the Temple in the singular number without any addition or distinction.

Sir William Dugdale, in the same vein, said that

> notwithstanding the spoil of the Temple by the rebels, the students of the law so increased there that at length they divided into two bodies.[13]

William Downing, steward of the Middle Temple, wrote in 1739 that the matter was settled:

> I think it admits of no dispute that those now two flourishing Societies were originally one, voluntarily associated, ... but the time when or reason why they separated I nowhere find.[14]

He proceeded to offer some conjectures. He thought it must have been a voluntary separation, and that (as earlier writers had suggested) it arose from 'the Society superabounding with numbers too great to be contained in one Dining Hall'. He then embarked on a consideration of the Middle Temple's claim to seniority, which had been a matter of sharp controversy since 1736 as a result of a dispute over the order of procession at the call of serjeants in that year.[15] He based this partly on topographical grounds and partly on the arms of the Inn. The older writers on the Inner Temple, from

---

[11] Tract of about 1620, which circulated widely in manuscript and was printed in J Carter, *Honor Redivivus* (1673 edn); quotation *ibid*, at 325. (All quotations in this chapter have been rendered into modern spelling and repunctuated.)

[12] Printed (from Inner Temple Library MS Petyt 538.17, fo 400) in JB Williamson, *History of the Temple, London*, 3rd edn (1925), 84, fn 3; and see Anon, *Treatise on the History and Division of the Temples*, Inner Temple Library MS ITR Misc 32, fo 1. See also FA Inderwick, *The Inner Temple: its early history, as illustrated by its records, 1505–1603* (1896) [hereafter Inner Temple Records], xvii–xviii; 88 *LQR* 426.

[13] W Dugdale, *Origines Juridiciales*, 3rd edn (1680), 145.

[14] W Downing, *Observations on the Constitution, Customs and Usage of the Middle Temple* (1739), ed CH Hopwood (1896), at 6 (and see *ibid*, at 10–11); Ingpen (ed), above n 2, at 91.

[15] See JH Baker, *The Order of Serjeants at Law* (5 Selden Society Supplementary Series, 1984), 424. Precedence was awarded to the Inner Temple, because they had had it at the last call, saving any right of the Middle Temple; but it 'was agreed on both sides that they were originally one society'.

Daines Barrington[16] to Inderwick,[17] similarly accepted the notion of a split occurring in the fifteenth century, though Inderwick was inclined to hedge his bets by describing the split as 'gradual'.

Some of the old traditions are compatible with the few known facts, and therefore might just be correct; but such were the standards of historical scholarship in previous centuries that they might equally be the result of mere speculation over the dinner table. What does seem unlikely is that the seventeenth-century writers were making use of written evidence now lost. Had such evidence been available at the time when the traditions were set down, it would almost certainly have been cited and discussed in detail. Maybe the fission theory was no more than a deduction from the absence of known references to the Inner or Middle Temple before Henry VI's time. Perhaps it was just a misinterpretation of Sir George Buc's remark in 1615 that 'although they came to be divided into three several houses, yet they were at the first all but one house'.[18] Buc's 'one house', however, referred to the occupation by the Knights Templar, not by the lawyers: he placed the advent of the 'reverend, ancient professors of the law' in the reign of Edward III, which as we have seen is probably correct. By the third house he did not intend a legal society either: we shall return to it in section III.

In the twentieth century, our domestic historians have generally become more sceptical about 'ancient tradition'. Hutchinson argued in 1904, against the traditional view, that there had always been two societies, the first wave of lawyers coming in the time of the Earl of Lancaster (1315–22) and the other by migration from Thavies Inn between 1327 and 1348.[19] He criticised reliance on vague seventeenth-century traditions, and argued that the division of a single Inn of Court into two was an inherently unlikely phenomenon. But he himself depended on old traditions, because there is no firm historical evidence for either of the settlements which he supposed. Indeed, he admitted that both views were based on 'what are little better than pure speculations'. Master Bruce Williamson, in his excellent history of the Temple, chose to remain agnostic.[20]

Hutchinson and Williamson both agreed with Inderwick that the first clear references to the two Inns were not to be found until the 1440s—the Inner Temple being mentioned in the *Paston Letters* in 1440, the Middle Temple in the *Black Books of Lincoln's Inn* in 1442—and this view has often been repeated since then. In 1908, however, Bolland discovered a reference to one Robert, manciple of the Middle Temple, in a will of

---

[16] 9 *Archaeologia* 130 *et seq.*

[17] Inner Temple Records, above n 12, intro, xiii–xviii.

[18] 'The Third Universitie of England' appended to J Stow, *Annales* (1615 edn), col 968.

[19] *Minutes of Parliament of the Middle Temple*, ed CT Martin (as part of *Middle Temple Records*, ed CH Hopwood) [hereafter *MTR*], i., 4–15.

[20] Williamson, above n 12, at 83–92.

1404[21]; and this seemed to carry the division back at least 40 years, certainly well before the time of Fortescue, who wrote in mid-century that there were four Inns of Court (without naming them).[22] Manciples, as we have seen, offer us some important evidence about the emergence of the Inns; but they also feature more specifically in the early history of the Temple. There has been much discussion of Chaucer's manciple—was he the manciple of 'the Temple' or of 'a Temple'? The unified Temple school of thought supported the definite-article reading, and could also point to a record of 1356 referring to the killing of a servant of the—or is it 'a'?—'manciple of the New Temple'.[23] But we should be wary of reading too much into such fleeting references. Indeed, it is quite likely that our Middle Temple manciple Robert (of 1404) is the same person as one Robert 'Maunsipul del Temple' mentioned in 1395 without distinction of house.[24]

The topographical evidence is no more conclusive than that afforded by tradition, but it is nevertheless strongly supportive of the thesis that there were two societies from the outset. It is known that there were already two halls in existence in the time of the knights.[25] One of them was connected with the church by a cloister, and was therefore evidently on the site of the present Inner Temple hall. The Inner Temple hall which was demolished in 1868 was perhaps only of 14th or 15th-century date, but it was built on the foundations of a still earlier building, some of which—or rather, foundations belonging to the same range of buildings, which included a chapel—can still be seen exposed opposite the south end of the cloisters. The original Middle Temple hall, which stood on the east side of Middle Temple Lane and extended as far as the old Vine Court on the east,[26] was converted into chambers when the Elizabethan hall was built, and then demolished in 1639[27]; but some medieval foundations apparently coeval

[21]   24 *LQR* 402; PCC 8 Marche (a bequest by John Bownt of Bristol, '*Roberto mancipio Medii Templi*').

[22]   J Fortescue, *De Laudibus Legum Anglie*, ed SB Chrimes (Cambridge, 1942), 118, line 32 ('*maiora hospicii studii illius, que hospicia curie appellantur ... Quorum maiorum quatuor sunt in numero ...*').

[23]   *Calendar of Patent Rolls 1354–58*, 377. The record being in Latin, there is of course no article.

[24]   Indictment of 1395, abstracted in E Williams, *Early Holborn* (1927), para 1398.

[25]   AR Ingpen, introduction to *Master Worsley's Book* (1910), pp. 53–55; Williamson, above n 12, at 70–71.

[26]   It seems to have been on the site now occupied by the south range of Pump Court. But possibly it was further south, where Elm Court now stands, which would have placed it on the same latitude as the Inner Temple hall.

[27]   Serjeant Chauncy (*History of Hertfordshire*, cited by Ingpen) recollected that the building was 'after the form of the Round Walk in the Temple Church', presumably meaning that it was supported on round arches.

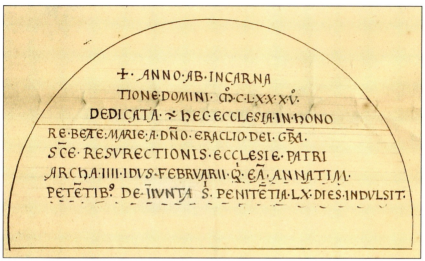

1 – 1   Heraclius inscription

The Latin inscription was in the tympanum over a doorway (of which all trace has disappeared) from the Round to the cloisters, two bays to the south of the west door; a copy now surmounts the west door itself. In translation, it reads:

In the year from the Incarnation of our Lord 1185, this church was consecrated in honour of the Blessed Mary by the Lord Heraclius, Patriarch of the Church of the Holy Resurrection, on 10th February. And he has granted to anyone who visits it an indulgence of sixty days, once in any year, from any penance imposed on him.

The inscription was defaced in 1656, restored in May 1671 and within a few days defaced again; it was destroyed by accident in repairs undertaken in 1695.

1 – 2   Bust by Alfred Gatley of Richard Hooker, Master of the Temple 1584-1591, destroyed in the Blitz, 1941

1 – 3   Drawing of Sir Thomas Elyot by Holbein. From a print in the collection of Sir John Baker

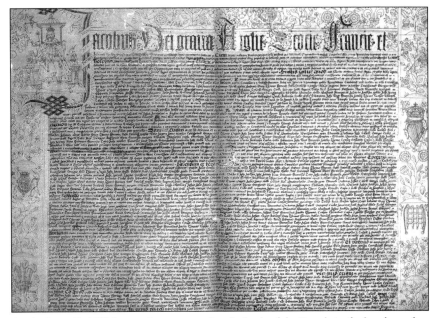

1 – 4   James I's 1608 Letters Patent conveying the lands of the Temple to the benchers of the Inner and Middle Temple. Photographic image of 1896 before the parchment suffered damage in mid-20th century

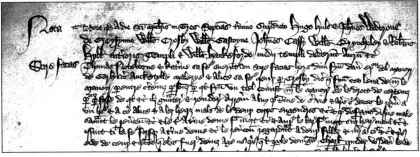

1 – 5   Extract from Year Book 12 Ric 2: note of the call of the eight serjeants, 1388

Transcript and translation of extract from Year Book 12 Ric 2

Nota quod a die Sancti Michaelis in tres septimanas termino supradicto Hugo Huls et Johannes Woderove de Greysynne, Willelmus Crosby, Willelmus Gascoyne, Johannes Cassy, Willelmus Bryncheley et Robertus Hyll interioris Templi, et Willelmus Hankeforde medii templi, dederunt aurum etc.

[Translation]
Note that three weeks after Michaelmas day in the above-mentioned term [Michaelmas 1388] Hugh Huls and John Woderove of Gray's Inn, William Crosby, William Gascoyne, John Cassy, William Bryncheley and Robert Hyll of the Inner Temple, and William Hankeforde of the Middle Temple, gave gold etc.

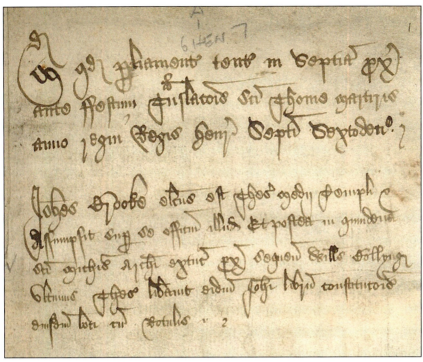

1 – 6   *First entry in the Minutes of Parliament, 1501*

Records of the Middle Temple Parliament

Memorandum quod [ad] parliamentum tentum in septimana proxima ante festum
Translationis Sancti Thome Martiris anno regni Regis Henrici Septimi sextodecimo

Johannes Brooke electus est thesaurarius Medii Templi et assumpsit super se officium
illud. Et postea in quindena Sancti Michaelis Archangeli extunc proxima sequenti
Willelmus Bollyng ultimus thesaurarius liberavit eidem Johanni librum constitutionis
ejusdem loci cum rotulis.

[Translation]
Be it remembered that [at] the parliament held in the week next before the feast
of the Translation of St Thomas the Martyr in the sixteenth year of the reign of
King Henry the Seventh:

John Brooke is elected treasurer of the Middle Temple and has taken upon himself that
office. And afterwards, on the quindene of St Michael the Archangel then next following,
William Bollyng, the last treasurer, delivered to the same John the book of the constitution
[*sic*] of the same place, with the rolls.

(Pencil annotation at top shows incorrect regnal year)

1 – 7 *Memorandum concerning Sir Francis Drake's visit to Middle Temple, 1586* *

1 – 8 *Effigy of Edmund Plowden in the Temple Church*

* *[Translation]*
Memorandum, Thursday, 4th August, in the year of our Lord 1586, in the 28th year of the reign of our lady Queen Elizabeth. Francis Drake, knight, one of the society of the Middle Temple, after his voyage undertaken the previous year and through the goodness of almighty God successfully completed came into the Middle Temple Hall at dinner time, and acknowledged to John Savile, esq., then Reader, Matthew Dale, Thomas Bowyer, John Agmondesham and Thomas Hanham, Masters of the Bench, and others there present, his old familiarity and friendship with the Society of gentlemen of the Middle Temple aforesaid, all those present unanimously congratulating him on his happy return with great joy. Signed Jo. Savile, Lector, Matthew Dale, Th. Bowyer, Jhon Agmondesham, Tho. Hanam.

1 – 9   Grant of the Temple by the Knights Hospitaller to Hugh le Despenser, 1324

Sciant presentes et futuri quod nos, frater Thomas Larchier, sancte Domus Hospitalis
Sancti Johannis Jerusalemitani prior humilis in Anglia, ex concessu totius capituli nostri,
dedimus, concessimus et hac presenti carta nostra confirmavimus pro nobis et successoribus
nostris nobili viro Domino Hugoni le Despenser, filio Domini Hugonis le Despenser,
comitis Wyntonie, totum mesuagium nostrum vocatum Novum Templum, London',
jacens inter hospicium venerabilis patris Exonie Episcopi versus occidentem et hospicium
Domini Hugonis de Courteneye militis versus orientem, et inter viam regiam ducentem de
Westmonasterio versus Sanctum Paulum in uno latere et aquam Thamisie ex altero latere,
et sex libras tresdecim solidos et quatuor denarios annui redditus in civitate et suburbio
London' redditibus que quondam fuerunt magistri militie Templi et fratrum ordinis
ejusdem, percipiendo annuatim de tenentibus infrascriptis, ac etiam omnia alia servicia
tenentium eorundem, videlicet, de Episcopo Cicestrie pro hospicio suo in parochia Sancti
Dunstani triginta solidos, de Magistro Willelmo le Dorturier pro domibus suis in eadem
parochia viginti solidos, de Johanne le Bray pro domibus suis in eadem parochia tresdecim
solidos et quatuor denarios, de Magistro Ricardo de Gloucestre pro duobus tenementis suis
in eadem parochia septem solidos, de Reginaldo de Thorpe de tenementis suis in parochia
Sancte Brigide quadraginta et quatuor solidos, de Thoma le Mirurier pro tenemento suo in
eadem parochia tresdecim solidos et quatuor denarios, de tenementis Ventrier in Fridaistrete
tresdecim solidos et quatuor denarios, habendum et tenendum totum illud mesuagium per
metas et bundas prenominatas et sex libros tresdecim solidos et quatuor denarios annui
redditus antedicti percipiendi de tenementis suprascriptis, ac etiam alia servicia eorundem
debita de dictis tenementis, prefato Domino Hugoni filio dicti comitis, heredibus et assignatis
suis, de domino rege et heredibus suis pro servicia inde debita imperpetuum, salvis nobis
et successoribus nostris libere ingressu et egressu per quandam viam a regia strata usque
ad magnam capellam sitam infra dictum mesuagium, videlicet per eandem viam per quam
vicini de visneto illo intrare solebant ad eandem capellam, pro omnibus capellanis quos
invenire tenemur ad celebrandum in eadem pro animabus illorum qui diversas terras et
tenementa dederunt Templariis ad cantarias in dicta capella perpetuo sustinendas, qui
quidem capellani possint ibidem licite intrare et morari ad divina ibidem de die celebranda

absque impedimento seu contradictione prefati Domini Hugonis filii dicte comitis, heredum seu assignatorum suorum. Et sciendum est quod nos prior et fratres predicti pro nobis et successoribus nostris liberavimus predicto Domino Hugoni filio dicti comitis seisinam dicti mesuagii sub forma et modo superius expressis. Et nos prior et fratres predicti pro nobis et successoribus nostris concessimus warantizare totum mesuagium predictum, redditus et servicia tenementorum predictorum prefato Domino Hugoni filio dicti comitis, heredibus et assignatis suis in forma supradicta dum terras et tenementa que fuerunt dictorum Templariorum in Anglia in manibus nostris habuerimus. In cujus rei testimonium sigillum domus nostre commune ac sigillum dicti Domini Hugonis filii dicti comitis huic carte indentate alternatim sunt appensa. Datum in celebratione capituli nostri London' die Jovis in vigilia Appostolorum Petri et Pauli, Anno Domini millesimo tricesimo vicesimo quarto et regni Regis Edwardi filii Regis Edwardi decimo septimo.

[Translation]

Know all men present and in the future that we, brother Thomas Larchier, humble prior in England of the hallowed House of the Hospital of Saint John of Jerusalem, by the concession of our whole chapter, have given, granted and by this our present charter confirmed for us and our successors unto the noble Lord Hugh le Despenser, son of Lord Hugh le Despenser, earl of Winchester, our whole messuage called the New Temple, London, lying between the inn of the venerable father the Bishop of Exeter on the west and the inn of the Lord Hugh de Courteneye, knight, on the east, and between the royal highway leading from Westminster to St Paul's on one side and the River Thames on the other side, and £6. 13s. 4d. rent in the city and suburb of London which once belonged to the master of the Knights of the Temple, and the brethren of the same order, to be received annually from the tenants written below, and also all other service of the same tenants, namely, from the Bishop of Chichester for his inn in the parish of St Dunstan 30s., from Master William le Dorturier for his houses in the same parish 20s., from John le Bray for his houses in the same parish 13s. 4d., from Master Richard of Gloucester for his two tenements in the same parish 7s., from Reynold de Thorpe for his tenements in the parish of St Bride 44s., from Thomas le Mirurier for his tenement in the same parish 13s. 4d., from the tenements of the Vintry in Friday Street 13s. 4d., to have and to hold all that messuage, by the metes and bounds aforementioned, and the £6. 13s. 4d. of annual rent aforesaid, to be taken from the above-mentioned tenements, and also all the services of the same due from the said tenements, unto the said Lord Hugh, son of the said earl, his heirs and assigns, of the lord king and his heirs, for the services due therefrom, for ever, saving to ourselves and our successors free entry and egress by a certain way from the royal street to the great chapel situated within the said messuage, namely by the same way to the same chapel through which the neighbours of that vicinity are accustomed to enter, for all the chaplains which we are bound to find to celebrate therein for the souls of those who have given various lands and tenements to the Templars to maintain chantries in the said chapel in perpetuity, which same chaplains may lawfully enter and remain in order to celebrate divine services there daily without hindrance or gainsaying from the said Lord Hugh, son of the said earl, his heirs or assigns. And it is to be known that we the prior and brethren aforesaid, for ourselves and our successors, have delivered seisin of the said messuage to the said Lord Hugh, son of the said earl, in the manner and form expressed above. And we the aforesaid prior and brethren, for ourselves and our successors, have granted to warrant the whole messuage aforesaid, and the rents and services of the aforesaid tenements, unto the said Lord Hugh, son of the said earl, his heirs and assigns, in form aforesaid, so long as we shall have in our hands the lands and tenements which belonged to the said Templars in England. In witness whereof the common seal of our house, and the seal of the said Lord Hugh, son of the said earl, are appended to this indented charter. Given at the meeting of our chapter in London on Thursday in the vigil of the Apostles Peter and Paul in the year of Our Lord 1324 and in the seventeenth year of the reign of King Edward, son of King Edward.

INTERIOR OF THE TEMPLE CHURCH.

1 – 10 *Temple Church by C. Knight, 1846, showing the decoration following the Victorian restoration*

with the Round of the Church were discovered on the site in 1735.[28] This was very much in the 'middle' of the Temple, and would account for a name which now seems less geographically apt. The existence of two halls would have provided a natural reason for forming two communities, since the principal communal activities of eating and learning both centred on hall. And it is highly probable that the geographical division of the Temple had preceded the coming of the lawyers, since the Inner Temple portion seems to correspond with the consecrated inner precinct, and its hall with the refectory of the priests, the Middle Temple with the unconsecrated remainder which had belonged to the secular knights and was let off separately by the Hospitallers. There is evidence that this division had already been made in 1324.[29] There were therefore effectively two Inns to let in the Temple when the legal profession returned from York in 1339. Both parts were leased from the same landlord—the Priory of the Hospital of St John of Jerusalem, as successor in title to the Knights Templar—but separate rents were paid until the dissolution of the Priory in the time of Henry VIII.[30] It seems inherently unlikely that this state of affairs could have come about through a partition negotiated with the landlord, given that the demarcation had already occurred before the initial letting and would probably have been forgotten about if the Temple had ever been let to lawyers in its entirety.

The most concrete piece of evidence to have emerged from the fourteenth century occurs in a Bodleian Library manuscript of the yearbook 12 Richard II, where, in noting the call of eight serjeants in Michaelmas term 1388, the reporter named their inns.[31] Two of the new serjeants were from 'Greysynne', five from the Inner Temple ('*interioris Templi*') and one from the Middle Temple ('*medii Templi*'). Besides being the earliest known reference to all three Inns as legal societies, this little note is of interest on two other counts. First, it shows that the Inns of Court, whether or not they were already so known, and whether or not Lincoln's Inn was then in

---

[28] Ingpen (ed), above n 2, at 54–55; Williamson, above n 12, at 71–72, 234. Recent work beneath the present Middle Temple hall has revealed dressed stones with mouldings possibly dating from the 12th century; they had been broken up as rubble and may have been moved from the old hall.

[29] See Williams, above n 24, paras 1382–83, where he concludes that the Temple was formally divided, for purposes of letting, by 1336. In his note to para 1382 he says that the division occurred in 1324, when the Knights Hospitaller reserved to themselves the church and the consecrated portion of the Temple, and the remainder was let at farm to William de Langeford. The rent of the consecrated portion in 1336 was £12 4s 1d, which is not far short of the customary uncertain rent of about twenty marks (£13 6s 8d) paid by the Inner Temple to the Prior of St John's until 1521.

[30] The Temple then passed to the Crown, under which the two societies occupied until the purchase of the freehold in 1608. No written leases have been found.

[31] Bodleian Library, MS Bodley 189, fo 32v; Baker, above n 15, at 256; Baker, above n 4, at 3–6. The note does not occur in the other manuscripts of this year, and was overlooked by the Ames Foundation editor.

being as a fourth, by 1388 possessed a superior status in providing candidates for the coif. And, secondly, it shows that there were two societies in the Temple having that status and bearing the names which they still bear. This discovery does not, of course, disprove the possibility of a split having occurred slightly earlier, but it does establish beyond doubt that there were two societies within 50 or 60 years of the first coming of the lawyers to the Temple. The strong likelihood, therefore, is that the lawyers had from the outset taken separate leases of the two pre-existing portions of the Temple and had always formed two distinct societies.

The late-medieval name of the Middle Temple in Latin was *Medium Templum* or *Hospitium Medii Templi*.[32] This might seem to be a solecism, if the Temple is considered to be a unity, since the Latin suggests that each inn was considered a separate Temple.[33] Too much should not be read into this, however, since the Temple as a whole retained its unitary character in common parlance. In the early sixteenth century, for instance, we sometimes find lawyers described simply as being 'of the Temple'.[34] The name *Medium Templum* was, nevertheless, routinely used; it is found in the yearbooks reporting the serjeants' calls in 1388 and 1425,[35] in the will of 1404 mentioned above, on an inscription of 1470 formerly in Temple Church,[36] in actions brought by the treasurer in 1479 and 1486,[37] and frequently thereafter. In English the Inn was sometimes, in the fifteenth century, known as 'the Middle Inn' of the Temple,[38] and it has been

---

[32] For the latter see, eg, the 15th-century inscription in a register of writs now in Kent County Archives, U522/Z3 ('*Liber Nich. Goderiche hospic. medii templi*'); MS *Black Books of Lincoln's Inn*, I, fo 44v ('*hospicium medii templi*', 1442); the 1498 suit for dues cited above; and a Chancery mainprise of 1506, C244/156/62 ('*de hospicio medii Templi*').

[33] The editor of *Black Books of Lincoln's Inn*, i., 45, uses the expression 'both the Temples' where the original manuscript (fo 149) reads '*ex duobus hospicii templi*' (the two inns of the Temple). However, in 1530 we find 'the ij Templez' in English: *ibid*, at 229. Note also 'the said Temple' (meaning the Middle Temple) in 1517: *MTR*, i., 32–33 ('*in dicto Templo*' in the manuscript).

[34] Eg PRO, REQ 1/3, fo 205 (John Butler '*de Templo*', 1505); YB Mich 12 Hen VIII, fo 11, pl 5; 119 *Selden Society* 48 ('Browne del Temple', 1520); REQ 1/104, fo 74v (James Randolphe '*de le Temple*', 1521); DL 5/5, fo 265v (Blount 'of the Temple', 1526).

[35] Baker, above n 15, at 256 ('*Willelmus Hankeforde medii Templi*', 1388), 260 ('*Ricardus Newton de medio templo*', 1425).

[36] J Weever, *Ancient Funeral Monuments* (1767 edn), 225 ('*Jacobus Bayle medio templo sociatus*').

[37] *Poulet v Marmeyn and others* (1479) CP 40/870, m 440; *Copley v Royton and others* (1486) CP 40/895, m 252 ('*thesaurarius Medii Templi*'). (The class CP 40 in the PRO contains the plea rolls of the Common Bench, or Court of Common Pleas.)

[38] Gairdner, above n 9, i. 159 ('Mydle Inne'), 186 ('Mydill Inne', 1451); Baker, above n 15, at 263 ('Yong de Bristowe de Middel Inne', 1463); 105 *Selden Society* 280 ('un companyon dell Middell In', 1493). Cf *The Plumpton Correspondence*, ed T Stapleton (1839), 12 (letter from Brian Roclyffe, 'Written in hast in the Middle Temple', 1464); CP 40/930, m 38 ('*Johannes Thornton de le Middill Tempill in Fletstret gentylman*', defendant in 1494). For examples of the 'Inner Inn', see *Inner Temple Miscellany*, above n 1, 29.

suggested that such names as the Inner and Middle Inns 'were originally nothing but a description of their respective shares of the area of the New Temple allocated to them'.[39] No doubt the prime meaning of 'Inn' (*hospicium*) is the house itself rather than the society which occupies it. But the use of this name does not itself establish whether the house or the society came first.

III. THE OUTER TEMPLE

The name 'Middle' Temple seems to imply a tripartite division, and the Outer Temple—or Outward Temple, as Buc called it—was either a third portion of the New Temple or, more probably, an area adjoining but just outside it. Old tradition identified the Outer Temple as the site of the medieval Exeter Place (later Essex House),[40] which occupied the north-west corner between the Middle Temple, Milford Lane and the Strand, where Essex Street now runs.[41] Until recently, the few early references to the Outer Temple were taken to indicate premises not in the occupation of a legal society. A recent discovery in the plea rolls, however, shows that in 1448 it was regarded as 'an inn of men of court'.[42] It did not survive as a distinct Inn, perhaps because it did not possess a hall suitable for communal purposes such as learning exercises, and the place somehow came under the control of the two neighbouring Inns. In the early sixteenth century, the Inner Temple assigned chambers in a tower or 'bastelle' in the Outer Temple, but no one is very sure what this was or what interest the Inner Temple had in it. In 1517 complaint was made to the Middle Temple that a latrine in 'le utter Inne' was a nuisance to the Inner Temple members there, which shows that the Middle Temple also had control over at least part of the place. But it also shows that in 1517 the lawyer inhabitants of the Outer Temple were members of the other Inns rather than a distinct society.[43] There are no references to it in the

[39] Sir Ronald Roxburgh, above n 1, at 429.

[40] So named after Robert Devereux, Earl of Essex, who made it his London residence in the time of Elizabeth I. It was demolished in the 1670s. The grant of the Temple in 1324 shows that the Bishop of Exeter's inn was adjacent to but outside the Temple. (The reference in Williams, above n 24, ii., 1370, to the Bishop of Oxford (*Oxoniensis*) should be to the Bishop of Exeter (*Exoniensis*); it is correctly indexed at 1851.)

[41] Buc, in Stow, above n 18, col 971; Carter, 326; Barrington, above n 16; Ingpen (ed), above n 2, 78, fn 3, referring (somewhat inadequately) to MS Petyt 538. The text referred to by Ingpen must be MS Petyt 538.17, fo 400, in the Inner Temple Library; this text is also the source of the first part of a treatise on the history and division of the Temple societies in ITR Misc 32.

[42] *Tew v Catesby* (1448) KB 27/750, m 105; 'The Inn of the Outer Temple' (2008) 124 LQR 384–87.

[43] Anthony Wood (d 1554), described in 1535 as '*de exteriori Templo gentilman*' and 'of thutter Temple Gentylman' (CP 40/1086, m 507), was in fact a member—and later a bencher—of the Middle Temple.

Inner Temple records after 1521,[44] and there seem to be none in the Middle Temple records.[45] It seems safe to conclude, as was suggested above, that the Middle Temple was not so named because it was half-way between two societies called the Inner and Outer Temples, but because its hall was situated in the very middle of the Old Temple.

IV.   EARLY RECORDS OF THE MIDDLE TEMPLE

The Inn possesses no domestic records prior to 1501, when the first book of memoranda and minutes of the Inn's parliament commences.[46] It is clear that a considerable part of that volume, which is uniformly written in court hand, is not an exactly contemporaneous minute of business but a transcript of some rougher record; and it contains errors and inaccuracies which are attributable to a copyist. It was formerly lettered A and numbered 1, on a label thought to date from the eighteenth or earlier nineteenth century, but the label was unfortunately destroyed when the volume was rebound in 1926. It was certainly the earliest surviving volume at the time when Dugdale wrote on the Inns of Court in the mid-seventeenth century. But the first entry in that book records the election of John Brooke as treasurer and the delivery to him of '*librum constitutionis ejusdem loci cum rotulis*' ('the book of the constitution of the same place, together with the rolls'). Presumably this constitution-book was a written book rather than the blank volume in which the entry was written. Since the Inns of Court did not have written constitutions, like those of the Inns of Chancery, the likelihood is that the word *constitutionis* was a mistranscription of *constitutionum*: in other words, it was an earlier book of constitutions or ad hoc decisions, similar in nature to the new one. As it happens, the earliest volume of minutes of the Inner Temple parliaments begins in 1505 and also contains internal evidence of the existence of an earlier volume.[47] The mention of rolls reminds us that the financial affairs of the Middle Temple, as of the other Inns, were chiefly managed on nominal rolls, such as the pension rolls and commons rolls,[48] and an occasional subsidy roll—such as a serjeants' roll for levying the customary present to members who left the society on taking the coif.[49] Neither society now possesses any rolls from this period. It has been suggested that

---

[44]   For all these references see *Inner Temple Miscellany*, above n 1, 29–30.

[45]   Note, however, an obscure reference in 1552 to chambers within 'lez rentes' and those without (*MTR*, i. 84).

[46]   Middle Temple Archives, MPA 1.

[47]   *Inner Temple Miscellany*, above n 1, 198.

[48]   In 1507 there is mention of a commons book: *MTR*, i., 22.

[49]   For Inns of Court rolls, see *Inner Temple Miscellany*, above n 1, 197–98. Serjeants' rolls are mentioned in 1507 and 1521 (*MTR*, i., 19, 20, 65). The serjeants of 1503 were given 20 marks 'as was customary': *MTR*, i., 8.

this coincidental loss of all pre-1500 records by both societies may have resulted from an early fire[50], but it may simply be that they were considered too ephemeral to preserve beyond their working life.

Rolls were ephemeral, but it was important to keep a more permanent record of members, the better to enforce their financial obligations, and most (though not quite all) of the admissions were entered in the treasurers' minute-books, with details of any special undertakings or exemptions. By order of the parliament of 23 November 1522, the name of any member admitted in hall had to be recorded by the chief butler in a book kept in the buttery,[51] from which he was to inform the treasurer, presumably so that an entry could be made in the treasurer's book.

The first minute-book ends on 3 February 1525, and there is then a hiatus of a quarter of a century before the next volume commences on 14 February 1551. This second volume was formerly lettered D and numbered 4, which shows not only that two volumes are missing but that they were still in existence in the eighteenth century—unless the label merely copied an earlier marking when the book was rebound.[52] The contents of the surviving volumes were very accurately calendared at the beginning of the twentieth century by Charles Trice Martin, author of *The Record Interpreter* and an experienced editor of medieval texts.[53] However, the loss of all but one of the pre-1551 volumes leaves us with a formal record for only twenty-five years out of the first two centuries of the Inn's history. Fortunately, some of the deficiency may be made good from other sources.

V.   MEMBERSHIP

An examination of the serjeants' calls in the fifteenth and sixteenth centuries—and, indeed, that of 1388—suggests that the Middle Temple was then the smallest of the Inns; at any rate, it produced far fewer serjeants than the others. Part of the reason may have been its narrow catchment area. From the very beginning, the Middle Temple had a strong

---

[50]   This was Hutchinson's suggestion: *MTR*, i,, intro, 14.

[51]   *MTR*, i., 72. The original text reads (fo 43): '*quandocumque aliquis socius seu clericus admissus est in aula quod capitalis pincerna vocetur pro intratione nominis in libro in promptuario cum admissione*'.

[52]   The missing volumes were certainly available to Dugdale around 1660.

[53]   Very few errors have been noticed. The principal are: at 7 ('Hasy' should read 'Husy'); at 30 ('signorum' is translated as 'swans' but should read 'cognizances' or 'badges': see below, n 169); at 39 ('Bythe More' should read 'Bythemore', though it was apparently altered from More); at 45 ('Breket' should read 'Broket'); at 65 ('for teaching' should read 'for building', the Latin word being *edificatione*'). The word 'unsyttyng' (at 39) is the original copyist's error for 'unfyttyng'.

west-country bias in its admissions, as did its satellite New Inn.[54] The first known member, William Hankford, who became a serjeant in 1388 and was later Chief Justice of the King's Bench (d 1422), was from Devon. The 1404 testator was from Bristol. The next known member, Richard Newton, another future Chief Justice (but of the Common Pleas), who was called serjeant from the Middle Temple in 1425,[55] was also from Bristol and nearby Yatton in Somerset.[56] Four other fifteenth-century serjeants known or thought to have emanated from the Middle Temple—John Hody (another Chief Justice of the King's Bench), Richard Choke, Thomas Young and Thomas Tremayle—were all from the same county. But the membership was not exclusively from those parts. A colourful fifteenth-century alumnus was Sir Thomas Thorpe, Speaker of the Commons in 1453, a man from Northamptonshire, who rose from being a minor Exchequer official to Baron of the Exchequer and finally Chancellor of the Exchequer before losing his life in the Wars of the Roses. As Speaker he was imprisoned for drawing articles against Edward, Duke of York, and unsuccessfully claimed privilege of Parliament. He is said to have escaped from the battle of St Albans in 1455, the year in which he was briefly Chancellor, and was knighted in the field at Northampton in 1460 before being captured and imprisoned in the Marshalsea; he attempted to escape disguised as a monk, but was beheaded by a London mob at Harringay in 1461.[57]

From 1479, a good number of names of rank-and-file members may be collected from the plea rolls, because the Inn's authorities (like those of the other inns) were always having to sue members for unpaid dues. The first suit of this nature was brought in 1479 by William Poulet, as '*thesaurarius Medii Templi*', against 45 men, claiming £10 from each of them.[58] Poulet (or Paulet) is probably the younger Somerset justice of that name, who was seated at Goathurst. A similar action was brought in 1486 by William Copley as treasurer against one knight, two esquires, two clerks and 62 gentlemen, mostly of London, for £10 each.[59] A third action, in 1498, was brought by Andrew Dymmok, '*secundus baro Scaccarii domini regis*', Richard Empson and Thomas 'Inglefeld', the three governors of the Inn

---

[54] New Inn became attached to the Middle Temple before 1540 (see section VI below), perhaps in the fifteenth century. In 1503 two members were admitted to the Middle Temple but each was allowed to remain in commons ('*ut commensalis*') in New Inn until sufficiently learned in the law (*MTR*, i., 5, 13; MS, ff 3, 7).

[55] Baker, above n 15, 260.

[56] His effigy (*c* 1448), in judicial robes, may still be seen in Yatton church. It is the earliest portrait of a known Middle Templar, Hankford's brass (at Monkleigh, Devon) having disappeared before 1800.

[57] HCG Matthew and B Harrison (ed) *Oxford Dictionary of National Biography* (Oxford, 2004) [hereafter*ODNB*]. His membership of the Inn is disclosed in the address of a letter sent to him from Calais in 1460: 37 *English Historical Review* 544.

[58] CP 40/870, m 440 (continued at m 530); exigent in CP 40/871, m 477.

[59] CP 40/895, m 252 (continued at m 255); exigent in CP 40/896, m 181d.

('*gubernatores hospicii Medii Templi*'), and Henry Harman as treasurer ('*thesaurarius ejusdem hospicii*'), against five knights, four esquires and 11 gentlemen, of various places, for £10 each.[60] Empson was perhaps the most famous Middle Templar of Henry VII's reign. He was at this time Attorney-General of the Duchy of Lancaster, Privy Councillor and soon to become notorious for his ruthless money-raising activities on behalf of his royal master; after his conviction on a more or less fabricated charge of treason, he was—together with his equally notorious associate Edmund Dudley, bencher of Gray's Inn—executed on Tower Hill in 1510. Englefield (later Sir Thomas Englefield) was also a leading figure in public affairs, since he was Speaker of the House of Commons and would become, with Empson, one of the King's executors; but he survived the accession of Henry VIII and died naturally in 1514.[61] Their fellow benchers included Sir John Mordaunt, another Privy Councillor and sometime Speaker of the Commons, who was Attorney-General to Prince Arthur and was appointed Chancellor of the Duchy of Lancaster just before his death in 1504; his son John, admitted to the Inn not long before his father's death, was created Lord Mordaunt of Turvey in 1532; and Lord Mordaunt's son, the second baron, was also a member of the Inn. Another bencher ennobled by Henry VIII was Sir Andrew Windsor, created Lord Windsor of Stanwell in 1529.[62] Sir John Russell, admitted in 1514 (but not, it seems, a bencher) became Lord Russell of Chenies in 1539 and first Earl of Bedford in 1550. Other members raised to the peerage—in mid-century—were Henry, Lord Stafford, whose chamber in the new buildings was designated a Bench chamber in 1553,[63] and Richard Bridges, created Lord Chandos of Sudeley in 1554.

These senior members, distinguished in the upper reaches of law and politics, were mostly not from the west country; and yet the plea-roll lists show that Somerset and Dorset were nevertheless the chief recruitment areas for the rank and file. The 1498 action is particularly interesting in that connection. The benchers who brought the action were not west countrymen: Empson was from Northamptonshire, Englefield from Berkshire, Mr Baron Dymmok from Lincolnshire and Harman (Clerk of the Crown in the King's Bench) from Kent. On the other hand, four of the five knights and one of the esquires were from Somerset[64]: Sir John Byconell of

---

[60]   CP 40/946, m 543; exigent in CP 40/947, m 201d.

[61]   He was also a Justice (later Chief Justice) of Chester. His son, also Sir Thomas and a bencher of the Middle Temple, was a Justice of the Common Pleas 1526–37; an indent of his brass figure in judicial robes may still be seen at Englefield in Berkshire.

[62]   Biography in ST Bindoff (ed), *History of Parliament: The House of Commons 1509–58*, iii., 633–36.

[63]   *MTR*, i., 93. He was born in 1501, and so was probably admitted in the 1530s; but it does not appear whether he was elected to the Bench.

[64]   The fifth was merely 'of London'. Speke and Wadham are also in the 1486 action, as gentlemen.

North Perrott; Sir Hugh Luttrell of Dunster; Sir John Speke of White Lackington; Sir John Wadham of Merrifield; and Thomas Malet of Currypool. Other Somerset names in the list include John Wyndham of Orchard (knighted in 1487 after the Battle of Stoke), who was executed for treason after the Earl of Suffolk's conspiracy in 1502. In the 1486 suit we also find Robert Hill, esquire, of Somerset, Sir John Paulet, knight, and Amyas Paulet, esquire—who was knighted with Wyndham in 1487 and (as Sir Amyas) was still being pursued by the Inn for his debts in 1504 and 1516.[65] This Sir Amyas Paulet (1457–1538) became an important figure in the history of the Inn, for in 1520 he served as treasurer and at his own costs rebuilt the gate-house in Fleet Street, which he caused to be decorated with the arms and cardinal's hat of Thomas Wolsey. According to Wolsey's biographer, this was an attempt to appease the mighty Lord Chancellor, who had supposedly placed Paulet under house-arrest in the Temple[66]: a story which, if true, might explain why an elderly knight should have taken upon himself an office normally reserved in those times for lawyers of lower rank. The building contained a large upper room which was used as a parliament chamber before the new hall was built in the early years of Elizabeth I.[67] The gate-house stood until 1684, when it was replaced by the present edifice. Sir Amyas's son, Sir Hugh Paulet (d 1573), who became Governor of Jersey, was also a member of the Inn and contributed to the building of the hall, where his arms may still be seen. The Paulets exemplify the influence of family connections as well as geography in the membership of an inn.

These knights were not lawyers. The evidence shows that fewer than 10 per cent of Inns of Court men in the fifteenth and sixteenth centuries even thought of the legal profession as a career. Indeed, a commentator of around 1539 complained that the 'learners' in the Middle Temple were much troubled by the noise made by 'them that be no learners'.[68] This was a university in the modern sense, a place to grow up, to learn about life, to make useful contacts, even to misbehave a bit; and a considerable part of the gentry of England went through the system, if only for a brief spell of residence. It seems from these actions for dues that the Middle Temple was, apart from everything else, a club for the landed families of Somerset. But that did not detract from its role as a law school. The Somerset connection

---

[65]   CP 40/970, m 381d (1504); CP 40/1015, m 392d (1516).

[66]   Williamson, above n 12, at 139–40, citing Cavendish's *Life of Wolsey*; *ODNB*, which errs in stating that Paulet was admitted to the Middle Temple around 1513.

[67]   *MTR*, i., 169, 178.

[68]   'State of the Fellowship of the Middle Temple' (*c* 1539) British Library [hereafter 'BL'] Cotton MS Vitellius C.9, ff 319–323v (badly damaged), printed in Dugdale, above n 13, at 193–97 (including words now lost); this passage is at 195. There is a modern edition by RM Fisher (1977) in 14 *Journal of the Society of Public Teachers of Law* at 111–17. References here are to Dugdale.

continued into the sixteenth century, and the county produced its fair share of eminent lawyers, including four chiefs: Sir William Hody CB, Sir John Fitzjames CJ, Sir William Portman CJ and Sir James Dyer CJ. Even a century later (1590–1639), one-third of entrants to the Inn came from the six western counties of Cornwall, Devon, Dorset, Gloucestershire, Somerset and Wiltshire. The Inn also admitted more members from Northampton-shire and Warwickshire than any of the others.[69] It was, however, reportedly the only Inn of Court which closed its doors completely to Irishmen.[70]

Membership of the Inns of Court was by no means confined to the upper gentry, though there was a polite fiction that the inns (unlike the universities) were for those of gentle origins. Sir John Fortescue, whose memory of the Inns stretched back to the 1420s, wrote 50 years later that all the members of the Inns were the sons of *nobiles*, and said that

> In these inns ... there is, besides the law school, a kind of academy of all the manners which inform *nobiles*. They learn to sing and practise all kinds of music; they also engage in dancing, and sports suitable for *nobiles*, just like those brought up in the king's household.[71]

This Latin word *nobiles*, though sometimes mistranslated as 'noblemen', clearly did not refer to nobility in the later sense but to that *nobilitas* which in English would be called gentility or gentlemanliness.[72] There is only one clear example in the fifteenth century of a peer's son being admitted to an Inn: William Herbert, fourth son of the Earl of Pembroke, who was admitted to Lincoln's Inn in 1468 and was subsequently created Earl of Pembroke. But even the association with established gentry is open to question. There was certainly a view that the Inns ought to be limited to the gentry, and an attempt was made to re-enforce this by legislation in 1559, on the grounds that they were the class most fitted to govern.[73] In the 1580s, John Ferne—who was admitted to the Inner Temple in 1576 and called to the Bar in 1587—wrote that in ancient times no one could be admitted but a 'gentleman of blood':

---

[69] WR Prest, *The Inns of Court 1590–1640* (1972), 33. The Warwickshire connections went back to Henry VII's time, with such members as John Rastell and Christopher St German (noted below). The Northamptonshire connections may also have been long-established: we have noticed above the membership of Thomas Thorpe (murdered 1461) and Sir Richard Empson (executed 1510).

[70] *Letters & Papers of Henry VIII*, xvii., 722 (complaint from the Council in Ireland 1542).

[71] SB Chrimes (ed), *De Laudibus Legum Anglie* (Cambridge, 1942), 118, ch 49 (retrans).

[72] For the equivalence of nobility and gentry as concepts in medieval times, see GR Sitwell, 'The English Gentleman' (1902) 1 *The Ancestor* 58, esp at 69–71.

[73] *MSS of the Most Hon the Marquis of Salisbury, preserved at Hatfield House*, i., 587, no 9: 'That none study the laws, temporal or civil, except he be immediately descended from a nobleman or gentleman, for they are the entries to rule and government, and generation is the chiefest foundation of inclination.' Cf below, ch 2 by Prest at p 90 for a similar attempt under James I.

And that this may seeme a truth, I my selfe have seene a kalender of all those which were together in the societie of one of the same houses about the last yeere of King Henry the fifth [1422] with the armes of theyr house and familie, marshalled by theyr names; and I assure you, the selfesame monument doth both approve them all to be gentlemen of perfect discents and also the number of them much lesse then now it is, beeing at that time in one house scarcely threescore ...[74]

This interesting document may well have existed, and it might even have emanated from the Middle Temple,[75] but there was at that date no College of Arms to control the use of armorial bearings, and the evidence was in any case skewed by the fact that membership of an Inn was considered ipso facto to confer gentle status. This may even have become a principle of law, for in 1522 the outlawry of a yeoman was set aside on information being given that he was a member of Lincoln's Inn and therefore a gentleman.[76] It seems likely that a good many members of the Inns were in reality the first armigerous members of their families; certainly they often head the recorded pedigrees. Ferne himself acknowledged that those qualified to practise at the Bar were entitled to arms,[77] and indeed his own grant of arms was obtained just before call.

It was, of course, necessary to have funds to maintain a student in decent state in London. In 1495 Mr Baron Rouclyff left his nephew Guy Palmes (later a serjeant) as much as £20 a year to study in the Middle Temple, and in 1523 an exhibition of £10 a year was considered on the low side.[78] That level of support would in practice have excluded the poorer classes, unless they caught the attention of a local benefactor. Some may have started their educational career at university, as in later times. The average age on admission to an Inn of Court between 1450 and 1550 was around 21, so that the usual age of admission to an Inn of Chancery was around 18, and that would have been the university leaving-age for anyone not intended for the Church. The evidence of actual residence at university is thin because intending law students would not usually have stayed long enough to graduate and records of undergraduates are sparse: one of the exceptions was Mr Justice Kingsmill (d 1509), who became a fellow of New College, Oxford, before proceeding to the Middle Temple around 1480.[79]

---

[74] J Ferne, *The Blazon of Gentrie* (1586), pt i: 'The glorie of generositie', at 24 (punctuation adjusted).

[75] It seems unlikely that the other Inns were so small. But Lincoln's Inn is a possible candidate, since 1422 is the year when its *Black Books* commence and may have marked some change in the course of its history.

[76] CP 40/1035, m 112.

[77] Ferne, above n 74, at 38.

[78] J Baker, *Oxford History of the Laws of England* (2003), vol vi [hereafter '*OHLE*, vi'], 449.

[79] *Ibid*, at 447. A good few wills provide for sons or nephews to be sent to 'school' or 'the schools' (ie Oxford or Cambridge) before going to 'court' (the Inns of Court).

But university did not of itself improve the financial circumstances of a poor scholar. One can only speculate as to how the poorer entrants managed to gain a foothold in the Inns, in the absence of endowed scholarships; but it was undoubtedly possible to rise from little or nothing to the highest positions in the law. Of the 53 serjeants at law created between 1463 and 1510, only half came from a social background of any consequence, and all those called in 1486 were of obscure origin.[80] It was said that no less a person than Chief Justice Hody (d 1441) had been born a villein and freed through the influence of his uncle, a canon of Wells Cathedral. Whether true or not, the story must have reflected what was considered possible, if unusual.[81]

Sir William Hody, son of the Chief Justice, was a Middle Templar and served as Chief Baron of the Exchequer for a remarkably lengthy period: in fact, substantially the whole of the reign of Henry VII and half that of Henry VIII (1486–1524). He was a judicial colleague for two years of Brian Rouclyff (d 1495), also of the Middle Temple, a junior baron from 1452 to 1488, and for eight years a colleague of the ill-fated Thomas Thorpe (d 1461). Their influence may explain why the Middle Temple seems to have enjoyed the fellowship of a disproportionate number of junior barons in the reign of Henry VII: Andrew Dymmok (mentioned above), William Elys, William Bollyng and Bartholomew Westby.[82] As a matter of bare conjecture, it is possible that the barons were brought in as associate benchers to boost numbers in an otherwise rather small society. There was also at that time a substantial representation of clerks of the central courts of common law, who kept their offices in the Inn[83]: for the whole of Henry VII's reign, the Chief Prothonotary of the Common Pleas (William Copley 1468–90,[84] followed by William Mordaunt 1490–1518) and the Chief Clerk of the King's Bench (Henry Harman 1480–1502, followed by John Mervyn 1502–09) were members of the Middle

---

[80]   EW Ives, *The Common Lawyers of pre-Reformation England* (1983), 449–50. There were only two Middle Templars in the 1486 call: John Fisher and Thomas Wode, both of whom became judges in the Common Pleas.

[81]   See HC Maxwell-Lyte, 'The Hody Family' (1925) 18 *Somerset & Dorset Notes & Queries* 127; *History of Parliament: the House of Commons 1386–1419*, iii., 384–6 (and Dr H Kleineke's draft entry for 1422–1504 volume). John's younger brother Alexander was a member of the Middle Temple in 1460 (KB 9/941/4).

[82]   Mr Baron Wolseley may also have been a Middle Templar.

[83]   Muscote's office was in the Middle Temple in the 1490s: *OHLE*, vi., 340. Harman, as noted above, was treasurer of the Inn in 1498; Mervyn succeeded to his chamber (*MTR*, i., 26).

[84]   A William Copley served as treasurer of the Inn in 1486; but this may have been the Chief Prothonotary's nephew: see JH Baker, *Readers and Readings in the Inns of Court and Chancery* (13 *Selden Soc Supplementary Series*, 2000), 146; Baker, above n 86 375, fn 7.

Temple—presumably benchers or associate benchers.[85] The Common Pleas Office moved to Lincoln's Inn on Mordaunt's death in 1518, but returned to the Middle Temple around 1557 under William Wheteley and remained there until 1590.[86] The office of Second Prothonotary was situated in the Inn from at least 1498 until the death of John Jenour in 1542.[87] Jenour happens to be the first recorded pupil-master, and is known to have taken in a succession of young members of the Inn as clerks to learn the intricacies of pleading—among them no fewer than four future Chief Justices (Brooke, Browne, Catlyn and Dyer).[88] The office of Third Prothonotary usually belonged to Inner Templars, but from 1539 to 1558 it was in the Middle Temple.[89] Another important court office kept in the Inn during the early sixteenth century was that of the Custos Brevium of the Common Pleas.[90] The Temple was therefore not merely full of students and practitioners, but also housed the offices through which much of the country's litigation was conducted.

The Middle Temple of the early Tudor period was particularly distinguished for the legal editing which went on within its walls. It may be an accident of historical evidence, but almost our only information about the men who edited law books for the press at this period relate to Middle Templars. A lawsuit involving the printer Richard Pynson, whose shop 'The George' faced the Temple on the north side of Fleet Street, shows that his printed abridgment of statutes (1499) was prepared for the press by a committee of three barrister members of the Inn, including Christopher St German.[91] It therefore seems possible that editing was St German's principal occupation in the mysterious years before he became a successful writer in the 1520s. The first part of his own great work, *Doctor and Student*, was printed in 1528 by John Rastell, a contemporary member of the Middle Temple who (like St German) hailed from Warwickshire.

---

[85] Note also Robert Lytton, Lord Treasurer's Remembrancer of the Exchequer 1485–1505, who was admitted late in his career (in 1503) but is not described as a bencher. Most of the senior Exchequer officials were Inner Templars, though Sir Richard Pollard (King's Remembrancer 1535–42) was a bencher of the Middle Temple.

[86] *OHLE*, vi., 127, fn 19. Wheteley's successor John Forde (1575–83) moved the office into the north part of the old hall, and his own successor William Nelson (1583–90) continued there: *MTR*, i., 213, 218, 266. For these dates of office, see Baker (ed), *The Reports of Sir John Spelman* (94 *Selden Society*, 1978), 375–78.

[87] The sequence was: John Muscote 1498–1512, John Jenour 1512–42. Muscote's predecessor, William Wylkes (1487–98), may also have been a member of the Inn; he is not recorded as having been in any of the others.

[88] *OHLE*, vi., 452; *ODNB*.

[89] Ie in the time of John Reymond (1539–52) and John Poley (1552–58). Poley's former office is mentioned in 1559: *MTR*, i., 123.

[90] Ie during the tenure of Richard Decons or Dycons, 1501–21. His former office is mentioned in 1521: *MTR*, i., 67. The Officer of Exigenter for London and Middlesex was in the Middle Temple some time before 1572: *ibid*, at 187.

[91] HR Plomer, 'Two Lawsuits of Richard Pynson' (1909) 10 *The Library* (2nd series) 115–33; *Boweryng and St German v Pynson* (1506) CP 40/978, m 617; *OHLE*, vi., 500.

Rastell was a true Renaissance man: lawyer, publisher, playwright, explorer and pioneer of the use of English.[92] He printed the first English edition of Littleton, and the first English law dictionary (*Expositiones Terminorum*, later known as *Les Termes de la Ley*). But his principal achievement in the history of printing was the publication of Mr Serjeant Fitzherbert's *Graunde Abridgement* (completed in 1516/17), which comprised 13,845 entries digested from the yearbooks, filling 2,252 folio pages. Its production is thought to have consumed a quarter of a million large sheets of paper.[93] One of the editors who worked on the manuscript was William Owen of the Middle Temple, who also edited under his own name a revised abridgment of statutes (1521) and was an anonymous editor of the old *Natura Brevium*.[94] This last was an ancient student primer—overtaken by Fitzherbert's *Novel Natura Brevium* in 1538—and it is worthy of note that a version was reprinted in the 1490s, 'at the instaunce of my maistres of the company of Stronde Inne', one of the satellites of the Middle Temple. This is the only known example of a law book being commissioned by one of the Inns.

Law reporting went on in all the Inns of Court, but the printed reports (the yearbooks) were almost all anonymous. The first volume of reports printed under the author's own name was Plowden's *Commentaries* (1571), written and edited in the Middle Temple by one of its greatest members during the 1550s and 1560s. The second, published posthumously, was Dyer's *Ascun Novel Cases* (1585/6), the work of a former Middle Templar,[95] containing cases dating back to his days at the Bar in the 1530s—including what seems to be the only citation in the English reports of a reading in the Middle Temple.[96] By this period, all books of the common law were printed by Richard Tottell, who had a monopoly granted him by letters patent; Tottell's shop, 'The Hand and Star', was adjacent to the great gate of the Middle Temple.

The membership of the Inn grew steadily in the sixteenth century, to the point where a grand new hall was needed in the 1560s, and new

---

[92] See JH Baker, 'John Rastell and the Terms of the Law' in M Robinson (ed), *Language and the Law* (Buffalo, NY, 2003), 15–30; R Ross, 'The Commoning of the Common Law: the Renaissance Debate over Printing English Law, 1520–1640' (1998) 146 *University of Pennsylvania Law Review* 323, at 330–42.

[93] HJ Graham, 'The Rastells and the Printed English Law Book of the Renaissance' (1954) 47 *Law Library Journal* 6, at 17. See also HJ Graham and JW Heckel, 'The Book that "Made" the Common Law' (1958) 51 *Law Library Journal* 100; FL Boersma, *An Introduction to Fitzherbert's Abridgement* (1981). The case-count is Dr Boersma's.

[94] *OHLE*, vi., 500.

[95] Dyer had, of course, left the Inn on becoming a serjeant at law in 1552.

[96] Dyer, fo 56a ('*Et puis le case fuit argue in lectura More quadragesima post et semble a luy et a Brooke, Hadley, Fortescue et Brown Justice ...*'). This is a reference to John More's reading in Lent 1544, which was attended by Humphrey Browne J; Robert Brooke, John Hadley and Lewis Fortescue were benchers. Cf *ibid*, fo 67b ('*Ideo quaere, quia contra opinionem multorum in Templo*').

buildings.[97] Unfortunately, little is known of the physical development of the site, since ranges of chambers were rarely paid for by the Inn and therefore came into existence without notice in the records.[98] But there certainly arose more of 'those bricky towers' which characterised the Elizabethan Temple.[99] In the year 1560 admissions peaked at 69.[100] Like the other Inns of Court, the Middle Temple could now afford to be more selective in its admissions and (in common with the other societies) to proclaim the exclusion of common attorneys,[101] though in reality the exclusion was far from complete.[102] The size of the Inn is reflected in the actions for dues. When such a suit was brought in 1552, there were no fewer than 338 defendants—including 34 knights and 74 esquires—whose names conveniently fill in many of the gaps in the Middle Temple admissions for the preceding quarter-century.[103] By 1574, when the new hall was completed, there were 92 sets of chambers in the Inn, accommodating 130 members.[104] The hall itself, 100 feet in length, was far larger than any of the other halls in the legal university.[105] Indeed, it was a masterpiece of Elizabethan architecture, and its double hammer-beam roof of eight trusses is said to be the finest in the country.[106] It is still one of the principal surviving wonders of Tudor London, retaining much of the

[97]   The New Buildings frequently mentioned in *MTR* in the 1550s evidently contained a substantial number of chambers. There is an earlier reference to new buildings in 1523 (*MTR*, i., 73), perhaps those built by John Danyell (cf *ibid*, at 67).

[98]   As in the other Inns, building chambers was largely a matter of private enterprise, the entrepreneur retaining a property interest for a time for himself and his family. See, eg, *MTR*, i., 105, 167, for Thomas Danyell's part in erecting new brick buildings in the 1550s.

[99]   E Spenser, *Prothalamion* (1596), lines 32–35 ('Those bricky towers / The which on Thames broad aged back doth ride / Where now the studious lawyers have their bowers / And whilom wont the Templar knights to bide ...').

[100]   Prest, above n 69, at 243.

[101]   *MTR*, i., 104, 111 (1555–57); cf Inderwick, above n 12, i., 190 (1557). Attorneys had often been admitted earlier in the century, and in 1552 attorney members were expressly excused from moots (*MTR*, i., 86); four years later, refusing to study in order to practise attorneyship was cause for dismissal from the society (*ibid*, at 104).

[102]   Eg the under-treasurer himself, at the time when the order was made, was a practising attorney of the Common Pleas (John Garnons), and he continued to practise in the next decade. Attorneys were taxed at the same rate as barristers for the new hall in 1571: *MTR*, i., 176. See further ch 2 below by Prest at pp 90, 91.

[103]   CP 40/1150, m 811a–c; CP 40/1151, m 497 and mm 281–284 (exigent); *MTR*, i., 93. This is the last such action by the Inn to have so far come to light; but the writer has not searched the rolls after 1565. There are no recorded Middle Temple admissions between 1525 and 1551, the records having been lost.

[104]   Inderwick, above n 12, i., 469. Lincoln's Inn had the same number of chambers, but the other two Inns of Court had more.

[105]   Gray's Inn had rebuilt its hall in the 1550s, Lincoln's Inn in the 1490s. The Inner Temple had the smallest hall of all, dating (probably) from the fourteenth century, but it was not replaced until 1868–70.

[106]   For the architectural history of the hall, see now MG Murray, *Middle Temple Hall: An Architectural Appreciation*, ed R Hill (2000).

armorial glass inserted in the 1570s to commemorate the chief contributors.[107] Its erection was a remarkable expression of confidence in the future of the Inn and of the great academy of law to which it belonged, especially since the freehold still belonged to the Crown. The membership did indeed continue to grow, and by the end of the century the Middle Temple was second in size only to Gray's Inn.[108]

VI. THE 'THIRD UNIVERSITY'

The most interesting of the members, albeit the minority, were the lawyers. The Inns were first and foremost a law school, colloquially known by Elizabethan times as the Third University of England.[109] In this role they were greatly admired by contemporaries as models of academical discipline. Sir Thomas Elyot, a product of the Middle Temple, went so far as to claim in 1531 that the exercises were perfect if unconscious revivals of classical rhetoric.[110] In the later 1530s, prompted by humanist thinking such as Elyot's, there was a project to found a new secular royal academy for selected mature students, modelled closely on the Inns of Court but with 'all good sciences and knowledges' on the curriculum, for the purpose of improving the education of the upper classes. It probably foundered only because of the sudden downfall and execution of Thomas Cromwell in 1540.[111] But in preparation for the committee's report a paper was written describing the organisation and educational system in the Middle Temple, and it is the earliest detailed description of any of the Inns and their usages.[112] It may have been written by Robert Cary (d 1587), a member of the Inn who helped in the preparation of a more detailed report on the Inns of Court soon afterwards.[113] The paper on the Middle Temple will be much relied upon in the following pages. Although it can only be taken as sure evidence of the domestic routine of the 1530s, the regime it

---

[107] Only 13 have been lost. Well over 100 panels have been added since 1574, with the arms of judges and serjeants who were formerly members of the Inn; 160 shields were engraved in Dugdale, *Origines Juridiciales* (1666). A list of the shields in 1925 was printed by JB Williamson, *Roll of Honour: Including the Names of all who are commemorated in the Windows of the Hall of ... the Middle Temple* (1925). They were photographed by the Royal Commission on Historical Monuments, and the Middle Temple Library also has a pictorial record.

[108] Prest, above n 69, at 11.

[109] Baker, *The Common Law Tradition*, above n 1, at 3.

[110] *The Boke named the Governour* (1531), fo 56.

[111] RM Fisher, 'Thomas Cromwell, Humanism and Educational Reform 1530–1540' (1977) 50 *BIHR* 151.

[112] 'State of the Middle Temple' (*c* 1539), above n 68.

[113] Below, text to n 186. Robert Cary, of Clovelly, Devon, was admitted to the Inn in the 1530s and was later a justice of the peace for Devon (1547–87), recorder of Barnstaple, and Member of Parliament for Barnstaple (1553); he died of gaol fever in 1587: Bindoff (ed), above n 62, i., 583–84.

describes is consistent with what is known of the Middle Temple and the other Inns in the later fifteenth century as well.

Unlike the universities and their colleges, the Inns of Court were unincorporated, and this enabled their constitutions to evolve over time. There were no written codes of statutes as there were for the Inns of Chancery.[114] Their original constitution was apparently independent of the degree system which grew up during the fifteenth century.[115] All the members—including those in clerks' commons[116]—were regarded as members of the *societas* or fellowship, and were described in the sixteenth century as fellows (or *socii*).[117] Even on a formal monumental inscription, it was appropriate to describe a bencher merely as 'one of the fellowship of the Middle Temple',[118] while as late as 1660 a young student could be described likewise as a 'fellow of the Middle Temple'.[119] As in the other Inns, this fellowship was divided into two 'companies', known as Clerks' Commons and Masters' Commons,[120] alluding to their separate tables in hall.[121] 'Clerks' in this context were newly-admitted students, who paid lower dues and had cheaper commons (food rations) in return for waiting on the masters in hall, like sizars at Cambridge. They remained in this station for about two years,[122] until they were themselves 'called' to Masters' Commons by the benchers. The masters were

---

[114] 'State of the Middle Temple' (*c* 1539), above n 68, at 196, says there was no certain punishment for offences, which rules out the kind of statutes made for the Inns of Chancery. For the *'liber constitutionis'* (probably meaning *'liber constitutionum'*), see section IV, above. A reference in 1503 to the constitutions and decrees of the house (*MTR*, i., 5) should no doubt be taken in the same way.

[115] For the other Inns, see AWB Simpson, 'The Early Constitution of the Inns of Court' [1970] *Cambridge Law Journal* 241; 'The Early Constitution of Gray's Inn' [1975] *Cambridge Law Journal* 131; both reprinted in *Legal Theory and Legal History* (1987), 17–52; JH Baker, 'The Old Constitution of Gray's Inn' (1977) 81 *Graya* 15, reprinted in Baker, above n 4, at 39–43.

[116] Even clerks were said to be admitted as a fellow (*ut socius*): the first such entry reads, '*Johannes Mervyn admissus est ut socius et intravit ut clericus*' (1502). In 1506, Robert Moreton was admitted as a fellow '*ad communes clericorum*'. These entries are calendared in *MTR*, i., 2, 17.

[117] Eg in actions for defamation: *Nicholas Vaus v Serle* (1540) KB 27/1116, m 110 ('*unusque sociorum medii templi*'); *Edmund Pyle v Ascue* (1541) CP 40/1108, m 632 ('*in lege terre eruditus unusque sociorum de Medio Templo London*'); *Clement Tusser v Rede* (1553) KB 27/1167, m 179 ('*in lege terre hujus regni eruditus ... ac unus sociorum Medii Templi*'). None of these 'fellows' was a bencher; Vaus and Tusser were clerks of the central courts.

[118] Inscription formerly in Temple Church for '*Johannes Portman quondam unus societatis Medii Templi*' (1521): Dugdale, above n 13, 173. Portman was reader in 1509 and 1515, and the father of Chief Justice Portman: see Baker, above n 84 150.

[119] Monument formerly in Temple Church for Edward Barnard, who died aged 22 in 1660: Dugdale, above n 13, at 174 ('*socius*'). There is an example of 1655 on the same page.

[120] The first reference in 1503 (calendared in *MTR*, i., 5), when Chamberleyne was admitted '*ut socius ad communes magistrorum*'.

[121] What follows is based on 'State of the Middle Temple' (*c* 1539), above n 68, at 193–94, and therefore describes the position as it was in the 1530s. There were also Servants' Commons, or Yeomen's Commons; but the servants were not members of the society.

[122] This could be lengthened by agreement. In 1514, William Owen was admitted to clerks' commons for five years, if he should so please: *MTR*, i., 46.

divided into benchers (or Masters of the Bench), utter-barristers (or Masters of the Utter Bar), and 'no utter-barristers' (or Masters of the Inner Bar[123]); it was only in more recent times that the title 'Master' came to denote benchers.[124]

Each Inn was self-governing, in the sense that the whole society made orders for its regulation, and once a year elected three or four governors to act as an executive governing body for the next twelve months. The assembly of the society was known in Lincoln's Inn as the council. But in each of the Temple societies there was a 'parliament', and, as noticed above, we have records of the Middle Temple parliaments from 1501 onwards. Decisions of the Middle Temple parliaments, at any rate until 1525,[125] were recorded as having been made by the 'company' (*comitiva*) or 'fellowship' (*societas*) rather than by the Bench. Already by the 1480s each Inn had a treasurer, presumably elected by the fellowship. We have already noticed William Paulet as the first known treasurer of the Middle Temple (1479), and it is evident from the Common Pleas suits for dues that the treasurer was closely associated with the governors and helped them to administer the society. In the report of 1539 the treasurer is described as the 'head officer'. But the office did not necessarily have the presidential connotations of later times; it was sometimes held by a relatively junior fellow, not necessarily even a bencher, and might be renewed for several successive years. As the title implies, the treasurer was primarily concerned with the finances of the Inn, collecting the chamber-rents and the 3s 4d due by way of 'pensions' from each fellow in Masters' Commons, and making disbursements for wages and necessaries; but he also had authority to admit new members and to allocate chambers, perhaps because such decisions also had financial implications.[126] Admissions, indeed, as in the other Inns, were a matter of careful negotiation: a new member could be excused the holding of offices, or permitted to be in or out of commons at his pleasure, in return for a substantial fine (such as 40s, or a pipe of good wine). The first known under-treasurer is mentioned in 1556,[127] though there were doubtless informal arrangements before then: as early as 1523 John Sedley (a professional auditor) was excused from being Christmas butler in return for

---

[123]   This expression is found in 1552: *MTR*, i., 84 (ordered that they are to plead at the Inner Bar at moots). Cf *ibid*, at 86 for Masters of the Utter Bar.

[124]   Note, however, a petition of 1507 from the 'whole body or company' of the Middle Temple to the 'masters or rulers' of the same: *MTR*, i., 20. It is probable that this indicates a petition from the clerks to the masters as a whole, but it might be taken to indicate a shift in authority towards the more senior members of Masters' Commons.

[125]   There is then a hiatus in the records until 1550.

[126]   'State of the Middle Temple' (*c* 1539), above n 68, at 193. The prerogative of the treasurer in respect of admissions was confirmed in *MTR*, i., 28, 68, 98, but it was apparently transferred to the benchers in 1557 (*MTR*, i., 110).

[127]   *MTR*, i., 107 (John Garnons, an attorney member of the Inn).

assisting the treasurer with his accounts.[128] These early under-treasurers and assistants were all members of the society rather than employees. The principal employed officer in early days had been the manciple, whose position had disappeared by 1501; his functions had by Tudor times been distributed between the steward and the chief butler.[129] The steward and butler are not to be confused with the Christmas officers of the same name, more frequently mentioned in the records, who were members of the Inn and acted only temporarily during the festive season. The other principal employees mentioned in the records were the under-butler, the cook and under-cook, the pannierman (responsible for buying provisions), the gardener and the minstrel.[130] There was probably also a porter.

In the course of the early Tudor period, the government of the Inns gradually passed from the fellowship at large, and their elected governors, to the Masters of the Bench: that is, those masters who had graduated from the Utter Bar to the Bench of the society. Our 1539 report on the state of the Middle Temple nevertheless informs us that the parliament was still a general assembly of the benchers 'and utter barristers', and this is borne out by the records: as late as 1551, it was held that utter-barristers of the Middle Temple could be amerced 3s 4d for not attending a parliament.[131] It does not follow that barristers were still part of the governing body, with a vote, since it is known that by 1615 they were summonable solely for the purpose of being informed what the benchers had decided.[132] As with the national Parliament, such constitutional changes are invisible on the face of the record. At any rate, it is plain that matters of day-to-day control, including call to Masters' Commons, to the Utter Bar[133] and to the Bench, and the imposition of routine punishments, belonged by 1540 to the 'elders' or benchers. And in 1559 it was ordained that admissions also belonged to 'the whole council of masters of the bench', rather than the treasurer alone.[134] Governors were still elected in some of the Inns until the time of Elizabeth I,[135] but there is no mention of them at all in the Middle Temple parliament records: indeed, the only known mention of governors of the Middle Temple is in the 1498 plea roll mentioned in section V above.

---

[128]   *MTR*, i., 77.

[129]   The steward is mentioned in 1502 (*MTR*, i., 2). The same steward (John Hasell) sued 11 members as '*senescallus hospicii Medii Templi*' for 40s each in 1500: CP 40/953, m 67d.

[130]   See *MTR*, i., 88, 91, 108 (gardener). The minstrel received annual wages: *ibid*, at 84 (1551).

[131]   *MTR*, i., 80. For an example of such a fine being imposed in 1502, see *MTR*, i., 2.

[132]   Williamson, above n 12, at 297.

[133]   Readers formerly claimed the prerogative of calling to the Bar during their readings, but after 1565 they could do so only with the permission of the Bench: *MTR*, i., 150 (order of 1565), 160, 163, 164, 189 (reader expelled for breach of order). In 1574 the Privy Council ordered that calls should take place only in term-time: *ibid*, at 200.

[134]   *MTR*, i., 110.

[135]   The last governors of the Inner Temple were elected in 1566.

We have noted that the 'learners' were but a minority of the younger members, and it follows that the educational system—though sophisticated and demanding—was not compulsory, any more than it was (for example) in early Victorian Cambridge. The principal sanction was self-qualification. No one was obliged to attend an Inn of Chancery, though he might find it more difficult or expensive to join an Inn of Court if he did not,[136] and he might be daunted by the lack of elementary preparation if he intended to pursue the law. No one was obliged to join an Inn of Court, but he could not advance in the law beyond the status of an attorney unless he did so; and if he meddled in litigation without being a member of an Inn he was probably guilty of the offence of maintenance.[137] No one who joined an Inn was obliged to attend its learning exercises, provided he was prepared to pay a fine or find a substitute[138]; but he could not become a barrister or a bencher without doing so, and indeed in 1568 the Middle Temple went so far as to decree that benchers who were elected without having read were to have no voice or place in parliaments.[139] The unwritten incentives were enough of a sanction for those intending to live from the law, and the new serjeants of 1503 were doubtless sincere in praising the Inn for 'binding them to study by the good rules ordained by the company, which restrained them in their youth from their disinclination to study'.[140] The compulsory side of discipline was primarily directed to the payment of commons and dues, and to the preservation of good order. Defaulters who owed money to the society were proclaimed at the cupboard[141]; if they still failed to settle their debt they could lose their chambers[142] and—as the plea rolls show—be sued in the courts as far as outlawry.[143]

Social order was enforced by fines or by temporary expulsion from commons, the last resort of permanent expulsion being rare.[144] All members were expected to behave like gentlemen, to treat each other with

---

[136] The records contain several examples of increased admission fines for new members who had not been at an Inn of Chancery: eg *MTR*, i., 136 (1562), 159, 161 (1567). For orders on the subject, see *MTR*, i., 164 (1568), 171, 176 (1570).

[137] Baker, above n 4, at 109–11, 135–49.

[138] In 1574, however, the Privy Council ordered that no one should be in chambers or commons in the Inns of Court unless he took part in moots within three years of admission: *MTR*, i., 200.

[139] *MTR*, i., 166.

[140] Baker, above n 15, at 267; *MTR*, i., 8.

[141] See *MTR*, i., 56, 67. The steward was himself chargeable with what he failed to proclaim: *MTR*, i., 91 (1553). For the cupboard, see below, n 155.

[142] 'State of the Middle Temple' (c 1539), above n 68, at 197, which says that anyone paying the debt instead of the defaulter could take over his chamber. See also *MTR*, i., 146–47, 192, 214.

[143] There is mention of this in *MTR*, i., 93 (new writs of proclamation to be made for the debts of the house, 1553).

[144] An example is found in 1503, when a member was expelled on grounds of poverty and inability to pay his dues: *MTR*, i., 5.

courtesy,[145] outside the Inn was well as inside,[146] and to wear suitable dress—which was assumed to be the ankle-length robe or gown of a gentleman. In Tudor times the colourful parti-coloured robes of the 15th century gave way to the plain open gown of a dark colour, though our 1539 description states that there was

> no order for their apparel, but every man may go as him listeth, so that his apparel pretend no lightness or wantonness in the wearer.[147]

Study gowns are mentioned in 1557, when it was ordered that they should not be worn beyond the Savoy to the west, Fleet Bridge to the east, or Holborn bridge to the north.[148] It was only towards the end of the sixteenth century that utter-barristers acquired their distinctive bar gown, decorated with black velvet facings and two vertical bands of black velvet on the upper arm[149]; benchers were then distinguished by more elaborate gowns, with black lace and tufts. The earlier dress had been plain, as may be seen on monumental effigies.[150]

Study facilities were minimal: there had once been a small library, according to the 1539 report, 'in which were not many books besides the law', but it had been 'robbed and spoiled of all the books in it'.[151] Members of the Inns had to rely on small private libraries, containing manuscript as well as printed books, and to make good the deficiencies by loan or exchange.[152] The only communal meeting place, apart from the

---

[145] Slandering a fellow member was said in 1523 to be dishonourable and against the laudable customs of the society: *MTR*, i., 73; MS, fo 44 ('*contra honestatem et laudabiles consuetudines societatis*'). Members were not to be of counsel in lawsuits against other members: *MTR*, i., 122 (1559), 174 (1570).

[146] In 1570 a barrister was put out of commons for 'using English' against William Fletewoode in a King's Bench trial at the Guildhall, though he was readmitted in 1571: see *MTR*, i., 173, 175. This is one of the earliest references to professional discipline, though the context is domestic harmony rather than the public interest.

[147] 'State of the Middle Temple' (*c* 1539), above n 68, at 197.

[148] *MTR*, i., 110, 111 (the first specific dress regulations, made for all the inns: Middle Temple Records, above n 12, 192; *Black Books*, i., 320); see also *ibid*, at 116. By way of concession to recent fashion, knights—but only knights—were allowed beards above three weeks' growth: *ibid*, at 112.

[149] Clearly depicted on the effigy of John Saunders (d 1638), barrister of the Middle Temple, at Uffington, Berkshire: illustrated in *Inner Temple Miscellany*, above n 1, 74, fig 14.

[150] Eg the kneeling figure of Humphrey Cavell (bencher, d 1558) on his brass at Acton, Middlesex; and the effigy of Edmund Plowden (bencher, d 1585) in Temple Church. Earlier Middle Templars depicted on brasses, in long open gowns, are John Muscote (Prothonotary, d 1512) at Earls Barton, Northants, and John Sedley (Auditor of the Exchequer, d 1532) at Southfleet, Kent (reported stolen in 1988).

[151] 'State of the Middle Temple' (*c* 1539), above n 68, at 197. It used to be thought that a 15th-century manuscript register of writs, inscribed '*hospicii medii templi*', might have belonged to the Inn; but the full inscription (now very faded) appears to read '*Liber Nich. Goderiche hospic. medii templi*': Centre for Kentish Studies, Maidstone, Dalison MSS, U522/Z3. (Goderiche was nominated constable of the Tower for the Inn's Christmas festivities in 1501 and 1504.)

[152] *OHLE*, vi., 491–93.

Round of Temple Church[153] or the garden,[154] was the hall. Nothing much is known of the old hall, which was doubtless of similarly modest dimensions to the old Inner Temple hall which survived until 1868. As in its much grander Elizabethan successor, its focal point seems to have been the 'cupboard'.[155] There were in addition five separate 'boards' at which the members sat, according to their rank in the society: the first for the benchers (the 'high board'[156] or 'high table'[157]), the second for the utter-barristers,[158] the third for the inner-barristers, the fourth for the youngest students (in Clerks' Commons), who sat below the cupboard,[159] and the fifth for the members' servants (in Yeomen's Commons), presumably the lowest table of all. Commons were probably served on wooden trenchers,[160] with green earthenware pots for beverages.[161]

A surprisingly large proportion of the entries in the Inn's records relate to Christmas, though in this respect they were no different from those of the other societies. The maintenance of the courtly traditions of Christmas was taken very seriously, and the customs were closely similar in all the Inns.[162] Attendance seems originally to have been compulsory, since new entrants were sometimes willing to pay for exemption. Special Christmas officers were elected each year from among the fellowship. Many were the defaults of those elected and heavy the fines,[163] though some found the

[153] 'Item, they have no place to walk in, and talk and confer their learning, but in the Church; which place all the term-times hath in it no more quietness than the parvise of [St] Paul's, by occasion of the confluence of such as are suitors in the law': 'State of the Middle Temple' (*c* 1539), above n 68, at 195.

[154] In 1506 the Prior of St John's as landlord was to be approached to allow a necessary way through the great gate to the garden (*'pro via necessaria per magnam portam ad gardinam'*): *MTR*, i., 17; MS, fo 9. The meaning is not entirely clear. By 1556 there was a gardener: *MTR*, i., 108.

[155] Mentioned on the occasion of the serjeants' farewell in 1503, when all the fellows in town assembled around the cupboard: Baker, above n 15, at 266. (The original text reads, *'convenerunt in aula circa le cubbord omnes socii in villa'*.) The word did not, of course, denote a closet but a table on which plate was laid out.

[156] *MTR*, i., 39. In 1556 two aldermen of London gave a new table for 'lez seignors benchers': *MTR*, i., 106.

[157] It is *'alta tabula'* in 1503 (text calendared in *MTR*, i., 9).

[158] In 1559 it was ordered that none but utter-barristers could sit at their board: *MTR*, i., 122.

[159] See *MTR*, i., 133 (1561).

[160] The pewter 'dishes' mentioned in *MTR*, i., 18, 24, are *'vasa'* in the Latin text and seem rather to have been cooking vats or large vessels for use in the kitchen.

[161] Several such pots have been unearthed in and around the Inns of Court and Chancery: *Inner Temple Miscellany*, above n 1, at 136–37, fn 2.

[162] See *ibid, at* 41–47; Baker, above n 86, 130–31.

[163] In 1551, no fewer than eighteen members refused the stewardship and ten the marshalcy, and likewise the other offices, so that Christmas was not in the event kept: *MTR*, i., 82, 84.

duties more agreeable than remaining at home with their wives.[164] The custom was to elect a steward and butler, three masters of the revels, a marshal and a constable of the Tower. The last office seems to have been peculiar to the Middle Temple, and was evidently associated with the mock government of the youthful 'king' who presided over the festive season,[165] perhaps with the role of taking the 'lord of misrule' into his custody as a traitor.[166] From 1519 a marshal's constable was also elected.[167] In Gray's Inn, the constable was a mock lord high constable and held court as such. The marshal there was responsible for leading the company to church, having first given each of them a silver badge (*'un conusanz de argent'*), and was entitled to take the profits of the gambling with cards and dice which was allowed at Christmas.[168] According to a cryptic note in the minutes, it was the masters of the revels who gave out badges (*signi*) in the Middle Temple.[169] The significance of these badges, and the form they took, does not appear. The masters of the revels were also responsible for engaging the services of harpists or minstrels.[170] And this was not the only entertainment, for, besides music, the revels included 'disguisings' and other shows.[171] The steward and butler oversaw the provision of the Christmas fare, which might include a boar[172]; those attending paid an agreed rate for commons, but exceedings could be charged to the society.[173] Part of the festivities included 'meetings' with the Inner Temple.[174] Another courtly activity, distinct from Christmas, in which the Inns were

[164] See R Beadle and C Richmond (eds), *Paston Letters and Papers of the Fifteenth Century* (2007), iii, 118: 'Ulveston is styward of the Mydill Inne, and Isley of the Inner Inne, be cause thei wold have officez for excuse for dwellyng this tyme from her wyves' (1451). John Ulveston, of Debenham, Suffolk, was MP for Yarmouth 1447–50.

[165] In Gray's Inn the 'king' was chosen by the clerks of the third table, ie the most junior students.

[166] A lord of misrule is mentioned in the Middle Temple in 1560: *MTR*, i., 126.

[167] *MTR*, i., 60 (original reads 'constabular. Turris marescalli').

[168] For John Spelman's account of Christmas in Gray's Inn (*c* 1500), see 93 *Selden Society* 233–34. When the floor-boards of the present Middle Temple hall were taken up around 1764, nearly 100 pairs of dice were found: *Inner Temple Miscellany*, above n 1, at 46, fn 28.

[169] *MTR*, i. 30, where the word 'signorum' is understandably rendered as 'swans' (ie 'cygnorum'); but it would have made no sense for the masters of the revels to distribute swans. The Latin reads, '*pro eorum allocatione ad cust[agium] signorum per eos datorum*'.

[170] *MTR*, i., 18, 30, 75. The word used is 'citherator'. By the 1550s a 'minstrel of the Temple' received annual wages whether or not Christmas was solemnly kept: *ibid*, at 84.

[171] John Husee wrote to Lord Lisle in 1534 that the Inns of Court had kept Christmas 1533 'with such disguisings and pastimes as hath not been seen': M Byrne (ed), *Lisle Letters* (Chicago, 1981), i. 20, no 108.

[172] *MTR*, i., 74.

[173] The surplus costs were known as 'apparels': *MTR*, i., 64, 68, 75. Cf Williamson, above n 12, at 559.

[174] *Inner Temple Miscellany*, above n 1, at 44. Cf 'le metyng nyght' (1521), which is not explained: *MTR*, i., 66.

involved was attendance at royal jousts.[175] These old-style celebrations waned in the Elizabethan period, though a solemn Christmas was revived in 1596.[176] Members of the Elizabethan Inns nevertheless continued to nurture the accomplishments of gentlemen, nicely summarised in verse by a woman on quitting London around 1570:

> And also leave I at each inn / of court or chancery
> Of gentlemen a youthful root, / full of activity:
> For whom I store of books have left / at each bookbinder's stall
> And part of all that London hath, / to furnish them withall.
> And when they are with study closed, / to recreate their mind
> Of tennis courts, of dancing schools, / and fence they store shall find …[177]

The heavy emphasis on Christmas in the records was a reflection of the difficulty of enforcing its traditions rather than of its relative importance. Seldom do we find any mention of the academical routine of the Inn, apart from the election of readers, although legal education was much more central to its purpose than revelling. The system of learning exercises in the Inns of Court was inherited from the lectures and disputations of the thirteenth-century school for apprentices of the Common Bench, about which only a little is known. The division of exercises into lectures, called readings, and disputed cases, called moots, evidently reflected the educational system in the universities, and it resulted in a parallel graduation system. Utter-barristers, corresponding with bachelors, were those who took part in disputations by arguing cases in hall as if at the bar of a court, that is, outside the bar[178]; and for centuries a barrister could only take that degree at a moot. That the process of self-graduation, by performing an exercise, was more significant than the 'call' which authorised it, may be deduced from the absence of any formal record of the making of utter-barristers until 1574.[179] Benchers, corresponding to masters or doctors, were those who had delivered a course of lectures and thereafter sat on the bench at moots. Since the election of a reader belonged to the whole company, it was recorded in the parliament books from the beginning.

---

[175] Eg that held to celebrate the arrival of Katharine of Aragon in 1501: *MTR*, i., 2. Each member paid 12d towards a stand. Likewise for the great tournament of 1511: *ibid*, at 36.

[176] Williamson, above n 12, at 208 (who says no solemn Christmas was held in the Middle Temple between 1559 and 1596).

[177] Isabella Whitney, 'Wyll and Testament' in *A Sweet Nosgay, or Pleasant Posye* (1573), sig e (spelling modernised).

[178] It might be supposed that inner-barristers sat within the Bar, like officers of the court; but an order of 1552 says that they pleaded 'at the inner bar' at moots (*MTR*, i., 84).

[179] *MTR*, i., 202. By the seventeenth century, however, it was the call that mattered. In 1634 a plaintiff in slander pleaded his call to the Bar by the Middle Temple (in 1611) without mentioning any moot: *Franklyn v Boteler* (1634) KB 27/1611, m 463 ('*ad gradum et officium causidici anglice* an utterbarrister *in eadem societate debito modo electus et vocatus fuit et licenciatus juris in eadem hospicio*').

The readings were not given in term-time but in the two 'grand' vacations—or 'learning vacations'[180]—during Lent and the early autumn (August).[181] These were the chief events in the educational cycle, and were regularly attended by those judges and serjeants who were former benchers of the Inn. Each course originally lasted about four weeks, though readings became shorter in later centuries. They were always given on statutory texts, and in the fourteenth and early fifteenth centuries it seems to have been the custom to proceed through the *statuta vetera* from Magna Carta until the reign of Edward I, each reader beginning where his predecessor left off. Our earliest Middle Temple reading is unattributed but contains a debate between Chief Justice Newton (d 1448) and William Warbelton (d 1469) in the 1430s; we also have fragmentary discussions involving Chief Justice Hody (d 1441/2) and Thomas Cokayne, who was Recorder of London from 1438 until his death in 1440.[182] The earliest identified reading from the Inn is that which Thomas Young (later a judge) gave on the Statute of Merton around 1440.[183] The manuscript containing Young's lectures also contains a series of lectures by Richard Pygot on Westminster II, cc 45–50; *De mercatoribus*; *De defencione juris*; *De finibus*; and the Statutes of Lincoln and York.[184] Although *Quia emptores* is inexplicably missing, it looks as though Pygot's turn had come at the end of the statutory cycle; his successor would have gone back to Magna Carta, c 1. Pygot and Young both became serjeants at law in 1463.

In early Tudor times we find some readers breaking away from the old cycle, in order to make a mark and impress the Crown with their usefulness: the earliest known example is Edmund Dudley's reading in Gray's Inn on *Quo warranto*, around 1485. The first reading of that type which we have from the Middle Temple is Edmund Knightley's reading of 1523 on the 1484 Statute of Uses, and we also know from Sir Robert Brooke's *Graunde Abridgment* that the younger John Fitzjames lectured on *Prerogativa Regis* in 1537. Once readers had a free choice, they were able to introduce an element of practical usefulness into a course which was still necessarily random in its coverage. After 1530, it was not at all unusual to expound the statutes of Henry VIII, including those concerned with technical matters. Dyer, for instance, read on the Statute of Wills. Brooke

---

[180]   The term is used in 1517: *MTR*, i., 51.

[181]   For what follows, see Baker, *Readers and Readings*, above n 84.

[182]   Bodleian Library MS Rawlinson C.294, fo 154; BL MS Harley 7536, fo 33v; MS Lansdowne 465, fo 61; Cambridge University Library MS Ee.5.22, fo 291; MS Hh.2.8, fo 58v (all Newton and Warbelton); MS Ee.5.22, fo 60v (Cokayne, Hody); MS Hh.3.6, fo 27v (Hody); Baker, above n 84 144.

[183]   'Merton secundum Yong', BL MS Lansdowne 1138, ff 19–23v; Baker, above n 84, at 145.

[184]   MS Lansdowne 1138, ff 105–18.

was really up-to-date, since he lectured in 1542 on a statute passed as recently as 1540.[185]

The readings, like *lecturae ordinariae* in the universities, consisted of textual exposition followed by disputation. The reader read out a clause of his statute each day, commented upon it, and then explained its operation with the aid of a spectrum of illustrative cases. The 15th-century tradition was to gloss each phrase in the statute seriatim, and this method was still followed by some readers in the earlier Tudor period. But the new form of reading introduced by Dudley and his contemporaries laid more emphasis on the analytical treatment of a topic, ranging if need be far away from the wording of the set text. Both the old and the new traditions recognised the importance of interactive exercises, and the most intellectually testing part of the reading was the disputation of the readers' 'cases'.

Each day a few of the put-cases were challenged for argument by the barristers, benchers, serjeants and judges who were present. The process is described in our report of 1539 or thereabouts[186]:

> Furthermore, in the same grand vacations [Lent and Summer], when that one of the elders do read and expound [a statute],[187] such utter-barristers as are of long continuance do stand in a place together, whereas they rehearse some one opinion or saying of him that readeth, and by all ways of learning and reason that can be invented do impugn it; and some other do approve it; and all the rest of the house give ear unto their disputations; and at last the reader doth confute all their sayings and confirmeth his opinion. Also in the same grand vacations, every day at night (except Sunday, Saturday, or some feast of nine lessons), before three of the elders or benchers at the least, is pleaded and declared in homely law French by such as are young learners some doubtful matter or question in the law, which afterwards an utter-barrister doth rehearse and doth reason and argue to it in the law French; and after him another utter-barrister doth reason in the contrary part; and then do the three benchers declare their minds in English: and this is what they call mooting. And the same manner is observed in the term-time.

An expanded version of this description was embodied in the report on all the Inns of Court, written by Thomas Denton, Nicholas Bacon and Robert Cary in 1540[188]:

---

[185] 'Lectura Magistri Roberti Brooke tempore autumpnali anno 34 H. 8. super statutum de lymitation anno 32 H. 8', BL MS Add 28607, ff 21–28v; Baker, above n 84 157, 606. The reading was on the Statute of Limitations 1540, 32 Hen VIII, c 2. An abridged version was printed in 1647.

[186] 'State of the Middle Temple' (*c* 1539), above n 68, at 194.

[187] Reads 'and an Estatute'.

[188] E Waterhous, *Fortescutus Illustratus* (1663), at 544–45. This is the only surviving text. There are modern editions in CH Williams (ed), *English Historical Documents* (1971), at 563–73; and DS Bland, 'Henry VIII's Royal Commission on the Inns of Court' (1969) 10 *Journal of the Society of Public Teachers of Law* 178–94. For its date and context, see RM Fisher, 'Thomas Cromwell, the Dissolution of the Monasteries, and the Inns of Court, 1534–40 (1973) 14 *Journal of the Society of Public Teachers of Law* 103 at 108.

[The reader], openly in the hall before all the company, shall read from one such act or statute as shall please him to ground his whole reading on for all that vacation; and that done doth declare such inconveniences and mischiefs as were unprovided for, and now by the same statute be [remedied], and then reciteth certain doubts and questions which he hath devised that may grow upon the said statute, and declareth his judgment therein; that done, one of the younger utter barristers rehearseth one question propounded by the reader, and doth by way of argument labour to prove the reader's opinion to be against the law; and after him the rest of the utter barristers and readers one after another in their ancienties do declare their opinions and judgments in the same; and then the reader who did put the case endeavoureth himself to confute objections laid against him, and to confirm his own opinion; after whom the judges and serjeants, if any be present, declare their opinions; and after they have done the youngest utter barrister again rehearseth another case, which is ordered as the other was. Thus the reading ends for that day: and this manner of reading and disputations continues daily two hours, or thereabouts ... And besides this daily, in some houses, after dinner, one at the reader's board before they rise propoundeth another of his cases to him, put the same day at his reading, which case is debated by them in like form as the cases are used to be argued at his reading; and like order is observed at every mess at the other tables; and the same manner always observed at supper, when they have no moots.

Four collections of notes have been found which report discussions of this nature in the Middle Temple in the 1530s, 1540s and 1550s.[189] They have not as yet been edited for publication.

These disputations in the course of readings have sometimes been confused with moots,[190] but they were an entirely different exercise.[191] Moots were primarily vocational pleading exercises, founded upon sets of facts provided to the students for the purpose, like examination questions. The problems were mostly taken from moot-books of considerable antiquity, in which some of them are given mnemonic names such as Jacob and Esau, The Rod (*Le virge*), The Rose between Thorns (*Rosa inter spinas*), The Sparrowhawk (*Lesperver*) and The Little Rose (*Parva rosa*). Unlike moots in the Inns of Chancery, those in the Inns of Court were extremely complex. The object was not to thrash out a contested point of law in a single sitting but to practise the art of pleading, and incidentally of oral argument, in an exercise divided up into manageable instalments. The first task would be to draw a writ in Latin, and then suitably elaborate

---

[189]   Harvard Law School MS 125, nos 1–77, 115–43, 150–66, 172–73; Bodleian Library MS Rawlinson C.707; CUL MS Gg.5.2, ff 1–40; BL MS Add 35939, ff 209v–349v (mixed with some from Gray's Inn).

[190]   The term 'mooting' is indeed used rather ambiguously in the report of *c* 1539, quoted above, though not in the more carefully written report of 1540.

[191]   For what follows, see the introduction to Baker, above n 8.

pleadings in law French bringing out all the questions in the case, recited orally and with argued exceptions at each stage. This could occupy many days, or even a whole vacation.

Whatever the non-reading men might get up to, law school was not for the idle but was intended as a gruelling preparation for an exacting profession. Discussion of moots could even continue after the formal exercise, for we find a member of Gray's Inn noting what he heard Nevill and Tingleden saying in the Fields about a moot-case, and a Middle Templar jotting down what Maudlen said in his room. A range of less formal exercises are first encountered in the sixteenth century, such as library and chapel moots,[192] Clerks' Commons cases, cases put 'at the fire' in hall[193] and discussions 'at the cupboard'.

The daily commitment to learning was not supposed to end with call to the bar or bench. The utter-barrister was expected to participate in some of the exercises,[194] and to read in due course in one of the Inns of Chancery. The Middle Temple by 1540 was responsible for providing readers at two of these societies, New Inn and Strand Inn,[195] though Strand Inn was lost when the building was demolished in 1549 to make way for Somerset House.[196] New Inn naturally sent many students to the Middle Temple in due course, but it was unnecessary for entry to the latter to have been at any particular Inn of Chancery.[197] Readers in chancery, as they were called, had to read in term-time as well as the grand vacations during their year of office; the earliest identifiable New Inn reading is that given by Edmund Plowden on *De donis* in 1550, eight years before he became a bencher of the Middle Temple.[198] Barristers of still greater seniority were appointed to attend on the reader of the Middle Temple, and then to 'read in court'[199] themselves. Although the term was not much used within the Inns of

---

[192] Chapel moots, presumably held in one of the chapels appurtenant to Temple Church, took place in the 'mesne vacations' (ie periods which were neither term nor grand vacations): 'State of the Middle Temple' (*c* 1539), above n 68, at 195. In 1559 they were held three times a week: *MTR*, i., 121, 124.

[193] CUL MS Ii.5.15, fo 309 ('al fyer in Temple Hall', *c* 1600).

[194] In 1574 the Privy Council ordered that no one should continue an utter-barrister unless he took part in moots for three years after call: *MTR*, i., 201.

[195] 'State of the Middle Temple' (*c* 1539), above n 68, at 195.

[196] Its society was thereupon dissolved: *OHLE*, vi., 453. An attempt by the Middle Temple in 1561 to acquire Lyon's Inn, one of the Inner Temple's three Inns of Chancery, in order to achieve a more equitable distribution, was thwarted through the intervention of Robert Dudley: Middle Temple Records, above n 12, 178, 215–18. New Inn continued to exist until the site was compulsorily purchased by the LCC in 1902 in order to build the Aldwych.

[197] Eg, in the year 1580 (new style), 33 were admitted from New Inn and 33 from other inns (11 from Clement's Inn, 10 from Clifford's Inn, 6 from Staple Inn, 4 from Lyon's Inn and 2 from Furnival's Inn): *Middle Temple Admissions Register*, i., 45–48.

[198] 'Les lectures de Edmund Plo. de Medio Templo Lector de Newe Inne fait sur lestatut de W. 2. comensant termino Pasche anno 4 Regis Edwardi sexti', BL MS Hargrave 89, ff 38–47.

[199] Ie in their Inn of Court.

Court,[200] the bencher remained an 'apprentice of the law' until he took the coif, and even after becoming a serjeant was expected by custom to participate in the readings in his old Inn.[201] Plowden himself, reckoned one of the most learned lawyers of his day, described himself as an 'apprentice' on the title-page of his *Commentaries* (1571). No doubt the benchers were in a way still learning, since lawyers never stop doing so; but they had a public form of continuing education, besides the readings at which they assisted, since cases could be moved at 'the board' or 'the board's end' (the high table in hall). Benchers sometimes moved their own real cases for discussion. Sir James Dyer recalled in 1558 that, when he was a bencher of the Middle Temple (some time between 1538 and 1546), Sewster[202] had asked a question concerning his own ward; moreover, Dyer treated the answer as authoritative. We also find, in one reported case, a statement about the 'opinion of the Middle Temple' on a disputed point: an opinion presumably expressed by the benchers at a learning exercise.[203]

The readings underwent something of a decline in the sixteenth century. There is telling evidence of this in the notebook of a Middle Temple student, now in the British Library.[204] After attending Henry Archer's reading in 1580, the student noted that everyone rejoiced when the reader had finished, because he was the worst reader that ever was or ever would be, both for learning and good cheer, and was derided by everyone. (This implies, of course, that the standard was usually much better.) And the student may have been unduly influenced by the lack of 'good cheer', because later in the same year he praised John Boys as a reader in that every day he had provided such liberal and exceeding good cheer as had never been seen before in the memory of any of the utter-barristers. The reader's feast would indeed become the last vestige of the system, as the educational content diminished. But perhaps the greatest days of the Inn as an academical institution were already over by 1580. The graduation system continued, because the degree of the utter bar had become a *sine qua non* for practice as a 'counsellor',[205] and the rank of bencher, besides having professional consequences, had become associated with the government of the Inns. But the educational system was stuck in the 14th century,

---

[200]   For an exception of 1562 (where it seems to equate with bencher), see *MTR*, i., 138; Williamson, above n 12, at 114–15. See also *OHLE*, vi., 426–27.

[201]   For early regulations as to attendance of benchers at readings, see *MTR*, i., 21. Benchers were excused if they were knights, Barons of the Exchequer, Irish judges or over 60 years of age.

[202]   John Sewster became a bencher in 1538 and died in 1545: Baker, above n 84, at 156.

[203]   Baker, *The Common Law Tradition*, above n 1, at 50–51.

[204]   BL MS Add 16169, ff 198v, 237; printed in Baker, above n 84, at 353, 354.

[205]   See 'Rights of Audience' in *OHLE*, vi., 426–30; *Inner Temple Miscellany*, above n 1, at 85–87. Call to the Bar was never an admission to practice as such. In 1552 members of the Utter Bar who were 'counsellors' were excused mooting (*MTR*, i., 86), an indication that there were other members of the Utter Bar who were not in practice.

there were no incentives to improve it, and the common law was increasingly coming to be associated with judicial pronouncements rather than with the 'old common learning' of the Inns of Court. Sixty years later the system would collapse amidst the clash of arms, never to be revived in its original vigour.

Buildings of the Middle Temple[1]

RICHARD O HAVERY

WILLIAMSON DESCRIBES THE buildings of the Temple when it was occupied by the Templars. He says[2] that in trying to reconstruct the scene, it is necessary to obliterate all landmarks now existing except the church, then surrounded by cemetery ground in which many benefactors and Brethren of the Order lay buried. On the outlying part of the ground next to Fleet Street, 13 houses had been built at the wish of the Master and Brethren of the Temple by one Roger Blome, the Nuntius (messenger) of the Temple, to be let to tenants to secure an income for the upkeep of the lights and ornaments of the church.[3] On the south side of the cemetery was a hall connected to the church by cloisters. The hall had a chamber above it which may have been used as a dormitory. The hall appears to have been pulled down and rebuilt after the suppression of the Templars, since no later reference to the hall alludes to such a chamber. Adjoining the hall on the west was a chapel dedicated to St Thomas à Becket. All the foregoing, including the houses next to Fleet Street, were on consecrated ground. West of the chapel of St Thomas, at an uncertain location on ground adjacent to Middle Temple Lane, now covered partly by Elm Court and partly by Pump Court, stood another hall.[4] Williamson suggests that that hall may have been the hall of the military knights, the hall on consecrated ground being the refectory of the priests of the Order.

There was a great gate with five chambers, kitchens and stables on the site of the present Middle Temple gateway at the top of Middle Temple Lane. It was the main entrance to the New Temple from Fleet Street and is described in documents dating from 1337.[5] The old gatehouse was rebuilt

---

[1] For this article the author is indebted particularly to S Bradley and N Pevsner, *The Buildings of England, London 1: The City of London* (London, Penguin, 1997), 344 to 350; and to JB Williamson, *The History of the Temple*, 2nd edn (London, John Murray, 1925) and JB Williamson, *Notes on the Middle Temple in the Nineteenth Century* (hereafter Williamson C19). He has also been greatly assisted by Lesley Whitelaw, archivist of the Middle Temple.

[2] Williamson, *The History of the Temple*, above n 1, at 70, 71.

[3] TNA C145/129, item no 11, m 3. See Plate 2–6.

[4] See ch 1 at p 36.

[5] Williamson, *The History of the Temple*, above n 1, at 72.

at his own expense by the Treasurer of the Middle Temple, Sir Amyas Paulet, in 1520.[6] It was again rebuilt, by Roger North, in 1684 and 1685.[7] That gatehouse still stands.

The location of the original Middle Temple Hall, and the conversion of the old hall into chambers which were demolished in 1639, are described above.[8] Part of a map of London of *c* 1561, traditionally attributed to Ralph Agas, may been seen in Plate 2–7.[9] Middle Temple Lane can be seen descending from the gatehouse in Fleet Street to the Temple stairs. The Temple church is identified on it. A section of Leake's Survey of the Post-Fire City of London, published in 1667, is reproduced in Plate 2–8.[10]

The western boundary of the Great Fire of 1666 is shown by the red line on Plate 2–9[11]. The fire consumed some buildings of the Inner Temple, and the Master's house, but the only Middle Temple building[12] destroyed was a building in the South Churchyard on the site of the old (1667–1941) Lamb Building.[13]

The layout of the courts and buildings of the Temple shortly after the Great Fire and before the Great Temple Fire of 1679[14] is shown in a map of 1677.[15] Comparison of the maps of 1677 and pre-1940[16] shows that the layout of the buildings in the Middle Temple was substantially the same immediately after the fire of 1679 as before, apart from the extension of Pump Court and the concomitant disappearance of Vine Court.

[6] See ch 1 above at p 44. Williamson, *The History of the Temple*, London above n 1, at 139, 140, tells us that Paulet resided in the Middle Temple for five or six years in consequence of an injunction from Wolsey to attend upon the Council. He lodged in the gatehouse, 'which he re-edified very sumptuously garnishing the same on the outside thereof with Cardinal's hats and arms, badges and cognizances of the Cardinal, with divers other devices in so glorious a sort, that he thought thereby to have appeased his old unkind displeasure' (Cavendish). What had displeased Wolsey was that when Wolsey was a young man, Paulet had put him in the stocks.

[7] Williamson, *The History of the Temple*, above n 1, at 536, 537. See also ch 3 below, p 238.

[8] See ch 1 p 36.

[9] It is more likely that the author of the map was Gyles Godhed, a printer and purveyor of woodcuts, whose 'Carde of London' was entered in the Stationers' Register in 1562–63. It was published *c* 1603. See City of London, London Metropolitan Archives, RC 23.

[10] The survey was done by Jennings, William Marr, William Leyburn, Thomas Streete and Richard Shortgrave in December 1666: *ibid*.

[11] See Plate Section 2.

[12] If it was a Middle Temple building: see below, n 69.

[13] For the site of the old Lamb Building, see Plates 2–10 and 2–12. A drawing of its predecessor, showing the names of its occupants, is at Plate 2–3.

[14] As to the fire, see ch 3 below, at p 205. The approximate bounds of the fire are shown by the green line on Plate 2–9.

[15] Plate 2–9.

[16] Plate 2–10.

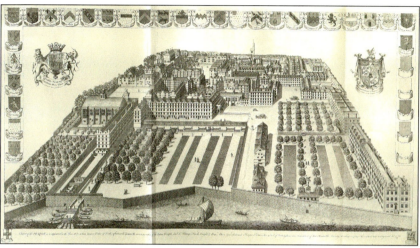

2 – 1 *View of the Temple (1671) [according to the caption, which states that it was re-engraved in 1770]*

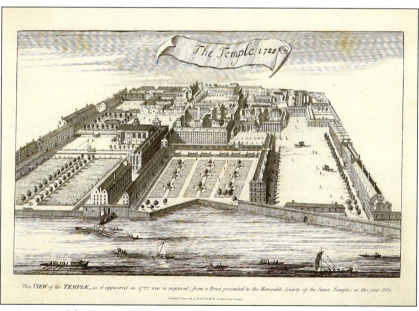

2 – 2 *View of the Temple (1722) [as re-engraved in 1831]*

2 – 3   Lamb Building (or Caesar's Buildings) before the Great Fire of 1666. For inhabitants, etc., shown see Annex, pp 79-80.

This is a drawing of Caesar's Buildings, possibly also known as Lamb Building, which was burnt down in the Great Fire of London in 1666.

On the back of the drawing there is a note in a hand which appears to date from the middle to late seventeenth century which says "A plott of the Anntient Lambs building both ground & inhabitants". It appears to have been prepared for the purpose of the enquiry ordered by Parliament on 30th October 1666 (see footnote 70 on p 76).

The inhabitants are listed in the annex to the 'Buildings' article (See pp 79-80).

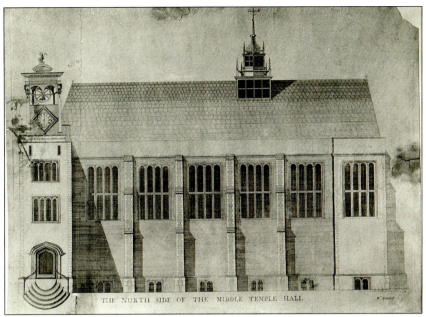

2 – 4   *The north side of the Middle Temple Hall by Emmet c. 1698*

2 – 5   *Middle Temple Hall, showing Plowden Buildings and entrance tower as executed by James Savage, 1832*

Plates 2

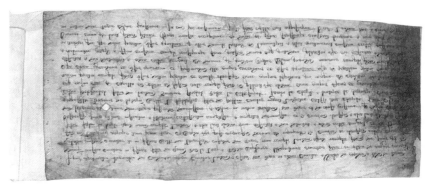

2 – 6 *Inquisition of 1336*

Abbreviations and contractions have been extended; punctuation and capitalisation have been adjusted in accordance with modern usage. A | has been inserted between lines.

Inquisitio capta coram Reginaldo de Conductu, maiore civitatis London' et escaetore domini Regis in eadem civitate, et Waltero de Mordon et Radulpho de Upton, | vicecomitibus ejusdem civitatis, in presencia Johannis de Oxonia, Ricardi le Lacer et Ricardo de Berkyngg, aldermannorum civitatis predicte, et Thome de Maryns, camerario | Gyhalde ejusdem civitatis, ac in presencia Willelmi de Langeford, custodis domini Regis novi Templi London', apud Templum predictum die Jovis proxime ante | festum Sancti Laurencii Martiris anno regni Regis Edwardi tercii post conquestum decimo, ad inquirendum si cimiterium ac claustrum ecclesie prioris Sancti | Johannis Jerusalem' in Anglia apud novum Templum London' et alia loca ibidem sint sanctificata et Deo dedicata et eidem ecclesia annexa, et si Hugo le | Despenser junior ea contra justiciam et libertatem ecclesiasticam occupasset et occupata detinuisset, et si cimiterium, claustrum et alia loca predicta per forisfacturam dicti Hugonis ad manus domini Regis postmodum devenissent et adhuc in manu ejusdem domini Regis ea de causa existunt, per sacramentum Willelmi de | Toppesfeld, Hugonis de Ardern', Walteri le Arblaster, Johannis de Pelham coteler juxta Ludgate, Galfridi atte Cherche, Johannis Elys, | Roberti Pekfychel, Johannis de Hendon, Simonis Nichol, Roberti le Goldsmyth, Jacobi le Clerk et Andree le Hornere, qui dicunt | super sacramentum suum quod capella Sancti Thome ad hostium aule Templi predicti cum placea terre ibidem sicut murus terreus se extendit usque ad | veterem portam Templi predicti versus viam regiam et similiter claustrum sicut murus lapideus qui incipit ad cameram vocatam Camera | Episcopi Eliensis extendens se versus orientem et postmodum ille murus extendens se versus aquilonem usque ad regalem viam sunt loca | sanctificata et Deo dedicata et eidem ecclesie annexa. Et dicunt quod quidam Rogerus Blom quondam nuncius Templi predicti de assensu et | voluntate magistri et fratrum ejusdem Templi construere fecit quasdam domos super quandam placeam terre sic sanctificate et Deo dedicate | in anteriori parte prope viam regiam versus aquilonem pro illis domibus locandis ad luminaria et alia ornamenta ejusdem ecclesie sustinenda.[1] Dicunt enim quod loca predicta predictus Hugo injuste occupavit, et dicunt quod ratione forisfacture ejusdem Hugonis et non alia de causa | in manu domini Regis adhuc existunt. In cujus rei testimonium juratores predicti <huic inquisitioni>[2] sigilla sua apposuerunt. Datum London' die et anno supradictis.

[1] *Reads sustinendend*
[2] *Interlined*

Translation of the inquisition of 1336

[Surnames modernised]

An inquest taken before Reginald of the Conduit, mayor of the city of London and the lord king's escheator in the same city, and Walter of Morden and Ralph of Upton, sheriffs of the same city, in the presence of John of Oxford, Richard the Lacer and Richard of Barking, aldermen of the aforesaid city, and Thomas de Maryns, chamberlain of the Guildhall of the same city, and in the presence of William of Langford, the lord king's keeper of the New Temple, London, at the aforesaid Temple, on the Thursday [6 Aug. 1336] next before the feast of St Lawrence the Martyr in the tenth year of the reign of King Edward the third after the conquest, for the purpose of inquiring whether the cemetery and cloister of the church of the prior of St John of Jerusalem in England at the New Temple, London, and the other places there, are sanctified and dedicated to God, and annexed to the same church, and whether Hugh the Dispenser, junior, had occupied them and detained the things so occupied against justice and ecclesiastical liberty, and whether the cemetery, cloister and other aforesaid places afterwards came to the lord king's hand by the forfeiture of the said Hugh and are still in the same lord king's hand, by the oath of William of Toppesfield, Hugh of Arden, Walter the Arblaster, John of Pelham (the cutler next Ludgate), Geoffrey at the Church, John Ellis, Robert Pekfychel, John of Hendon, Simon Nichol, Robert the Goldsmith, James the Clerk, and Andrew the Horner, who say upon their oath that the chapel of St Thomas at the door of the hall of the aforesaid Temple, with a piece of land there just where the earthen wall runs towards the old gate of the aforesaid Temple against the highway, and likewise the cloister just where the stone wall which begins at the chamber called the Bishop of Ely's Chamber runs towards the east and then to the north as far as the highway, are places sanctified and dedicated to God and annexed to the same church. And they say that a certain Roger Blom, formerly messenger of the aforesaid Temple, with the consent and will of the master and brethren of the same Temple caused certain houses to be built upon a certain piece of the land so sanctified and dedicated to God, on the front side near the highway towards the north, in order to let those houses for the maintenance of the lights and other ornaments of the same church, and they say that indeed the aforesaid Hugh occupied the aforesaid places unjustly. And they say that by reason of the forfeiture of the same Hugh, and for no other cause, they are still in the lord king's hand. In witness whereof the aforesaid jurors have set their seals to this inquisition. Given at London on the day and in the year above stated.

2 – 7   Agas Map, Civitas Londinum (c 1562) (Detail)

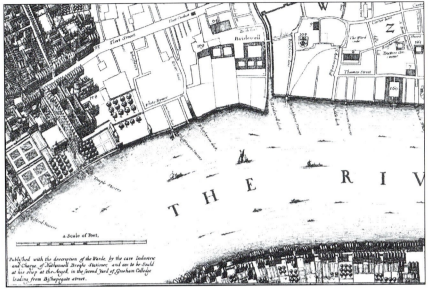

2 – 8   *Leake's Survey of the City of London after the Great Fire (1667) (Detail)*

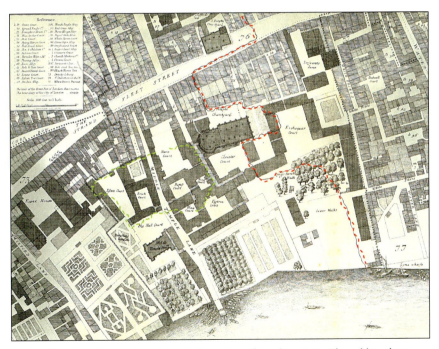

2 – 9   *Plan of the Temple from John Ogilby's Map of London, 1677. The red line shows the western extent of the Great Fire of London of 1666; the green line shows the extent of the Temple fire of 1679*

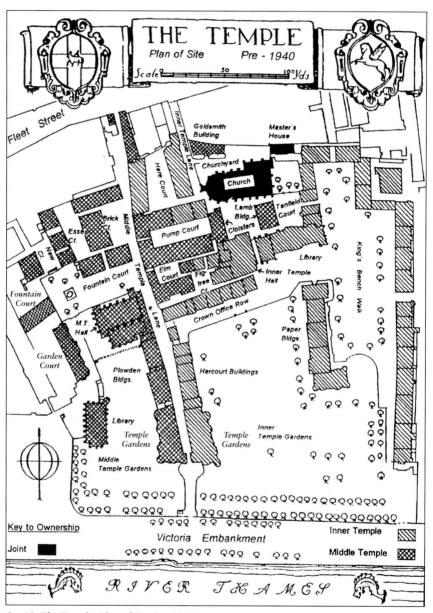

2 – 10 The Temple: Plan of Site Pre-1940

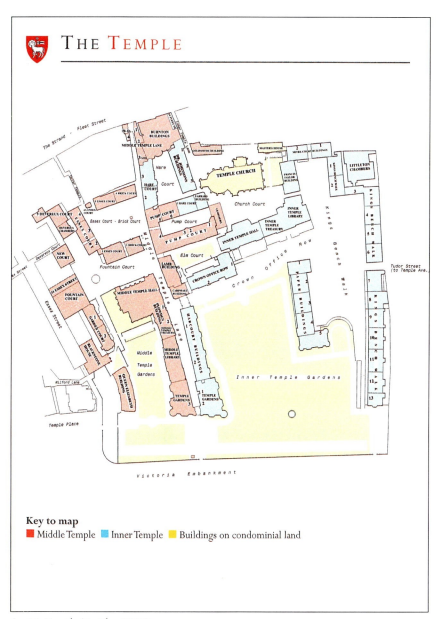

2 – 11 Temple Site Plan (2008)

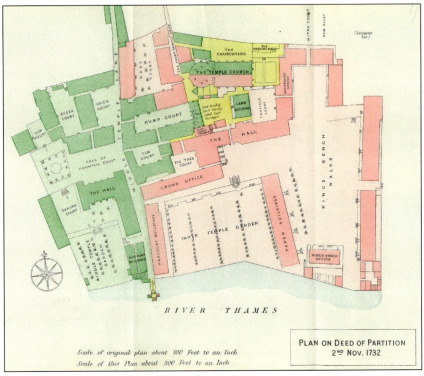

2 – 12 *Plan on deed of partition, 2 November 1732*

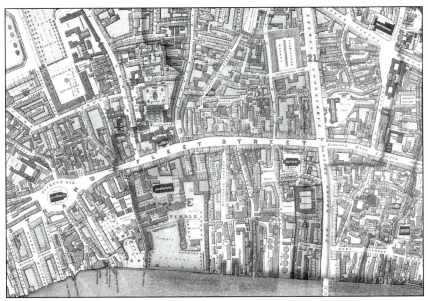

2 – 13 *The Temple, from Wyld's Plan of the City, 1845*

2 – 14 Middle Temple Hall in the 1820s (engraver, J Hinchliff)

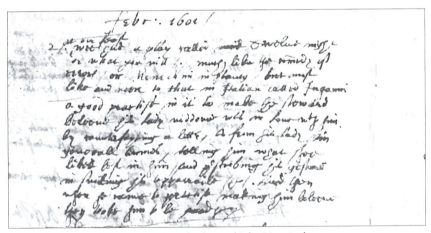

2 – 15 Entry of 2nd February 1602 in the diary of John Manningham

at our feast wee had a play called Twelve night or what you will much like the commedy of errors or Menechmi in plautus but most like and neere to that in Italian called Inganni a good practise in it to make the Steward beleeve his Lady widdowe was in Love with him by countarfeyting a letter as from his Lady in generall tearmes, telling him what shee liked best in him and prescribing his gesture in smiling, his apparaile &c. And then when he came to practise make him beleeve they tooke him to be mad.

Image reproduced from the British Library collection.

Transcript reproduced from Diary of John Manningham, ed J Bruce, the Camden Society, London 1868, from Anthony Arlidge, Shakespeare and the Prince of Love, London 2000 *[Giles de la Mare Publishers Ltd]*

2 – 16 *View of North America with Arms of Elizabeth I*

2 – 17 *Detail of Solomon Islands on the Molyneux terrestrial globe with information supplied by Pedro di Sarmiento*

2 – 18 Inscription next to William Sanderson's arms on the Molyneux terrestrial globe

[Transcripts]

Guill[emus] Sanderson S[alutem dicit] Spectori Candido

Non me suscepit gremio divina Mathesis,

Nec studiis (agnosco dolens) stellisve vacavi:

Dum tamen hinc artes illinc virtutis honores

Suspicit admirans mea mens & fixa tenetur,

Sumptibus ecce meis cernis revolubile caelum

Cernis & immensos tractus terraeque marisque,

Ut patriae, utque orbi, prosim [prosum?], claraeque Mathesi,

Quo possint Angli factis extendere fama[m]

Visere & externas gentes, terrasque, repostas

Haec ego perfeci, quae toti consecro mundo.

Ore faveto precor, caeptis & mente faveto

Ut Virtus artesque suo decorentur honore

Quod si quis meliora potest, impartiat [i]lle

Sumptibus haud parcam, studiis modo c[on]sulo doctis

William Sanderson to [Th]e Gentle Reader

Not in the lappe of learned skill I ever was upbrought

Nor in the study of the starres, (w[i]th griefe I graunt) was taught

Yet whilst on this side arts, on that syde vertues honor

My minde admiring viewd, & rested fixt upon her

Soo at my charge thou seest the ever whirling Sphere

The endles reaches of the land, & sea in sight appeare

For co[u]ntries good, for worlds behoofe, for learnings fourtherance

Wherby our vertuos englishmen, their actions may adva[n]ce

To visite forraine landes, where farthest coastes do lye

I have these worldes thus formd; & to worldes good apply

W[i]th word I pray you favor them, [& further] them with will

That arts & vertue may be deckt, w[i]th their due honor still

But yf that any better have, let them the better shewe

For lernings sake, I will not spare [th]e charges to bestowe

2 – 19 Plasterer's bill of 1682, showing amounts allowed by Sir Christopher Wren*

2 – 20 Library catalogue 1684, showing the Ortelius atlas (item 2) and Ashley's Mariners' Mirrors (item 10).

* Transcript of Sir C Wren's revision on the plasterer's bill

John Phillips's bill for £23 4s 11d for plasterer's work in Temple Church was revised downwards by Wren whose annotation reads:

"I have perused this Bill, & find it may be allowed as followeth

For whiting stopping sizing & colouring 797 yards upon stone worke in part & part upon rendering at 2d per yard	£6 12s 10d
For making the scaffolds	£7 0 0
For the use of the Scaffolding	£1 5 0
For new rendring 60 yards that were fallen down as the workmen assert	£1 10 0
	£16 7s 10d

In all for all demands for the Middle Temple sixteen pounds seaven shillings & ten pence
Chr. Wren
Aug. 11th 1682"

Endorsed by the Treasurer:
Aug. 29. Lett this bill be p[ai]d according to the allowance of S[i]r Xpher Wren
(Signed) Fran. Wythens

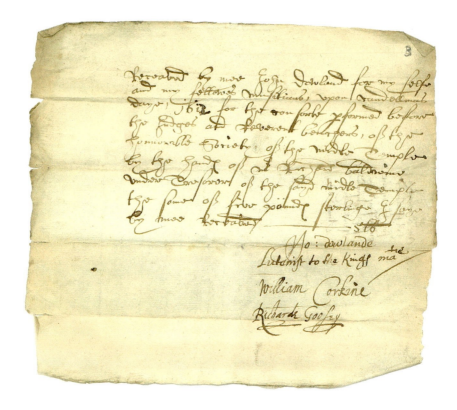

2 – 21 *Receipt signed by John Dowland. It reads as follows:*

'Receaved by mee John Dowland for my selfe and my fellowes musicians, upon Candlemas Daye, 1612 for the conserte performed before the Judges and Reverend Benchers, of the Honnorable Society of the Middle Temple by the hands of Mr Richard Baldwine Under Tresoror of the sayd middle Temple the some of five pounds Sterlinge I saye by mee Received ——————————5 lib

(Signed)   Jo. Dowlande

Lutanist to the Kings Ma[jes]tie

William Corkine

Richarde Goofey'

Comparison of the map of 1677 with a perspective drawing of the Temple made in 1671[17] shows that some building work had been carried out in the interval on the west side of Middle Temple Lane at the south end. A plan dated 2 November 1732[18] identifies the building then on that site, evidently a different building, as Barbom's [*sic*] Buildings.[19] That building is illustrated in a view of the Temple taken in 1722.[20] At that date the south end of the building was at the riverside, next to the watergate. But in 1770 a river embankment was built. Wyld's Plan of the City[21] of 1845 shows the effect of that on the location of the riverside. Barbon's Buildings had been rebuilt in one block shortly after 1732.[22] Soon after Plowden Buildings were built in 1830, the building formerly called Barbon's Buildings was also given the name Plowden Buildings, its staircases being designated numbers 3, 4, 5 and 6. In 1849 the south end was rebuilt and the west front repaired; the east front was refaced in 1906.[23]

Wyld's Plan of the City may be compared with the plan of the Temple pre-1940.[24] The latter shows the Victoria Embankment, the relevant section of which was opened in 1870. The former shows Middle Temple Library in Middle Temple Lane adjacent to the Hall, whereas the latter shows the new library (nowadays referred to as the old library) built in 1858–61. The latter plan, unlike the former, also shows Temple Gardens. That building extends further south than the old watergate.

Plate 2–11 shows the buildings of the Middle Temple as of 2010.

The Hall was begun probably in 1562 and completed in 1574.[25] Edmund Plowden, the Treasurer, summoned Sir John Thynne's chief carpenter, John Lewis from Longleat. Lewis returned there by 1565. A single hammerbeam roof at Longleat has detailing similar to that of Middle Temple Hall, suggesting that he designed both roofs.[26] An entrance tower was added in 1667[27] and replaced in 1745. Its appearance in the

---

[17] Plate 2–1.

[18] Plate 2–12.

[19] See ch 3 below, at p 210. Bradley and Pevsner, above n 1, give the date of the new building as 1687. HHL Bellot, *The Temple*, 3rd edn (London, Methuen, 1925), 160, says that Barbon's Buildings may have been the 'good fair fabrick' erected in 1653, apparently quoting from a letter of 1689. That is clearly not so, since Barbon first treated with the Middle Temple in 1675 (Williamson, *The History of the Temple*, above n 1, at 520). But the building shown in the drawing of 1671 may have been built in 1653. Barbon (Dr Nicholas Barbon, MD) was the son of Praisegod Barebone, who was briefly an MP and after whom the Barebones Parliament was named: DNB, ODNB.

[20] Plate 2–2.

[21] Plate 2–13.

[22] Bellot, above n 19, at 183

[23] *Ibid*.

[24] Plate 2–10.

[25] See ch 1 above at p 50.

[26] Bradley and Pevsner, above n 1, at 348.

[27] Superseding two chambers: Williamson, *The History of the Temple*, above n 1, at 233.

1820s can be seen by reference to Plate 2–14. James Savage rebuilt the entrance tower to a neo-Tudor design in 1832. The lower stage of that tower was reconstructed in 1930 by Maurice Webb and survived the war. Sir Edward Maufe rebuilt the upper part of the tower damaged in the Blitz and provided the semi-circular entrance steps.[28]

The shop or shops that appear against the west end of the Hall in the 1722 print were built in 1684. By 1758 there were three shops of two storeys. In that year the shops were demolished. Repairs were carried out for the preservation of the Hall in 1745. Those repairs did not affect the original design of the interior, but the north wall was partly rebuilt and was surmounted by a crenellated parapet in stone. At the same time, the original semi-circular steps were replaced by straight steps.[29]

Buttresses on the west wall of the Hall were thickened and adorned with stone dressings and pinnacles in 1757[30] by the mason Christopher Horsnaile Jun. The original louvre or lantern, allowing smoke from the fire to escape, gave place in 1732 to a new cupola with a vane.[31] That was replaced by a gothic louvered cupola designed by Henry Hakewill in about 1826, though the old open hearth in the Hall was removed in the 1830s. Hakewill's original cupola was destroyed in an air raid on 25 March 1941. It was restored after the war by Maufe, the work being completed in 1950.

Construction of a new two-storey building against the south side of the Hall to the design of Henry Hakewill was started in 1822 and completed in 1824. The upper storey was level with the Hall floor and contained a new library and the Parliament Chamber. Access to the new library was by way of a staircase from the garden.

The building to the north of Barbon's Buildings appearing on the drawings of 1671 and 1722, which extended from the east end of the Hall some distance down Middle Temple Lane, was built in 1626 and was known as 1 and 2 Garden Court. It contained the Parliament Chamber, kitchen and library[31a] (founded in 1641 by a bequest of Robert Ashley), as well as many sets of chambers. That building was taken down in July 1830

---

[28] Four in number. The Hall originally had five semi-circular entrance steps, according to Emmett's drawing (see Plate 2–4). Subsequently the steps were rectangular.

[29] MT.2/TRB/103, 55.

[30] MG Murray, 'Middle Temple Hall: An Architectural Appreciation' R Hill (ed), Middle Temple, (2000), 9; MT.2/TRB/117, 13.

[31] Bellot, above n 19, at 147.

[31a] There was a library in the time of Henry VIII. "They" [the Fellowship of the Middle Temple] "had a simple library, in which were not many bookes besides the law, and that library by meanes that it stood allways open, and that the learners had not each of them a key unto it, it was the [sic] last robbed of all the bookes in it": "A Description of the Form and Manner, how and by what Orders and Customes the State of the Fellowship of the Middle Temple (one of the Houses of the Court) is maintained; and what Ways they have to attaine unto Learning (temp. Reg. Hen. VIII)" quoted in Herbert's Inns of Court London 1804, p.222; see also Williamson, The History of the Temple, above n.1, p.106.

to make way for a new structure comprising a new kitchen, offices and 13 sets of new chambers. The new structure, designed by James Savage[32] (though largely to the design of Hakewill, who had died) and completed in 1831, was named Plowden Buildings, in so far as it lay south of the Hall, with staircases numbered 1 and 2. Adjacent to the east end of the Hall, the structure (called by Bradley and Pevsner a forebuilding) was two storeys high. In Plowden Buildings, the Treasury doorcase was added in 1896, probably by HJ Wadling. An oriel window at the west side of the building, by Sir Reginald Blomfield, was added in 1905–06. A further alteration, the north doorcase, by Sir Aston Webb, was made in 1913.[33]

After 1 and 2 Garden Court were taken down in 1830, the building known as numbers 3 and 4 Garden Court, situated on the west side of the garden, was renumbered 1 and 2 Garden Court. That building was acquired by the Inn from Barbon in 1676. It had been built on land formerly part of Essex House garden. It was rebuilt in red brick in 1884 and 1885 to the design of St Aubyn, the surveyor to the Inn. The earlier building is visible through the window of the Parliament Chamber in Plate 3–14.

The 1824 Hakewill library on the south side of the Hall rapidly became inadequate to accommodate the increasing number of books it had to contain. A gallery was erected on iron supports around three sides of the room. That was at best a temporary expedient. Land had to be found for a new library without sacrificing existing chambers. In consequence, land known as 'Essex Wharf and premises' was purchased, on the river frontage immediately south of Garden Court chambers. The new library was built on that land to the designs of Henry Robert Abraham and completed in 1861.[34] It consisted of a single room, 96 feet long, 42 feet wide and 70 feet high. The architecture had an ecclesiastical flavour. The building was decorated with glass showing the arms of princes from Richard I to Edward VII when Prince of Wales.[35]

The former library became a second parliament chamber, and St Aubyn inserted a bow window on the west side of the room, overlooking the garden and Garden Court. Hakewill's original Parliament Chamber is now known as the Queen's Room. The plasterwork in the Parliament Chamber and the Queen's Room is by Maufe and dates from 1947 to 1949. It is described by Bradley and Pevsner[36] as 'excellent fleshy plasterwork . . . exactly capturing the charm of provincial heraldic work of c. 1600'. The benchers' smoking room (renamed the Prince's Room after the call to the

---

[32] For these buildings of Savage, see Plate 2–5.
[33] Bradley and Pevsner, above n 1, at 349.
[34] See Plate 2–10.
[35] Bellot, above n 19, at 162.
[36] Above n 1, at 348.

Bench of Prince William of Wales in 2009) is by Sir Aston Webb & Son, 1929, with neo-Jacobean plasterwork by Laurence Turner. The door (sometimes inappropriately called the watergate[37]) between the hall and the benchers' apartments is contemporaneous with the hall.[38]

The building of the Victoria Embankment afforded space for chambers south of the existing buildings in Middle Temple Lane (Plowden Buildings on the west side and Harcourt Buildings, belonging to the Inner Temple, on the east side). The two Inns collaborated in the construction of Temple Gardens, mentioned above, which occupies both sides of Middle Temple Lane and at its south end straddles the lane over an arch. It was designed by EM Barry (consultant St Aubyn) and built in 1878–79. Middle Temple Lane was extended to the Embankment road and a single storey lodge[39] built in 1880 beside a new gateway.

The library was so severely damaged by a landmine on the night of 5 December 1940 that it had to be demolished after the war (the books, however, were salvaged). In its place a new set of chambers by Maufe, Queen Elizabeth Building, was constructed. It was completed in 1956. A new library, neo-Georgian, also by Maufe, was built on the site of 3 to 6 Plowden Buildings, also destroyed in the Blitz.

The following is a summary of the principal damage (other than the damage to the old library) caused to the buildings of the Inn by the Blitz of 1940–41.[40] On the night of 15 October 1940, a landmine destroyed Elm Court, blowing the masonry through the east gable end of the Hall, smashing the minstrels' gallery and reducing the Elizabethan screen to rubble. The shattered oak remains were gathered into 200 sacks and stored until they were painstakingly reassembled after the war.[41] Fortunately drawings had been made of the detailed designs on the screen. The forebuilding was also destroyed. It was rebuilt by Maufe as a three-storey building using the original bricks or bricks contemporary with those bricks. On 10 May 1941, Temple Church and the Master's House were burnt out, and Lamb Building, Cloisters, numbers 1, 2 and 3 Pump Court, numbers 2 and 3 Brick Court and numbers 3 to 6 Plowden Buildings were destroyed. On the night of 25 March 1941 about 140 incendiary bombs fell on the Inn. Fortunately, fire fighters were able to save the Hall, though the cupola was destroyed.

Barbon began his development of Essex House and its garden in 1674. He conveyed Garden Court and New Court to the Middle Temple in 1676. The date 1667 over the door of New Court is not the date of the building.

[37] Murray, above n 30, at 20, 21.
[38] Expert opinion of Dr Mark Girouard, FSA. See also above, n 37.
[39] Described by Bradley and Pevsner, above n 1, as a 'dainty pedimented lodge'.
[40] See Plate 2–10 for the situation before the bombing.
[41] *Middle Temple: A Guide*, 36.

The building was erected in 1676 from designs by Sir Christopher Wren[42] and survives to this day. The Little Gate, which gives access to Devereux Court, was constructed at the same time.

Adjacent to 1 Brick Court is 1 Essex Court, dating from about 1680. In 1655 leave was granted to Mr Agar to build on the plot of ground in Essex Court next to 'the tavern'.[43] The tavern was evidently the Palsgrave's Head. Until 1687, when it was pulled down, it occupied the site later occupied by Lloyd's Bank. Numbers 2 and 3 on the west side of Essex Court were reconstructed by Barbon in 1677, joined with Agar's buildings. The new buildings extended a distance of 7 feet further west than before, into New Court. A passageway from Essex Court into New Court was introduced at the same time.[44] Number 4 Essex Court dates from 1717.[45]

As can be seen from the map of 1677, before the fire of 1679 Brick Court was divided into two courts, north and south. The eastern part of Brick Court abutted Middle Temple Lane continuously. There was a garden in the northern court.[46] In April 1704 a fire occurred in the west range of Brick Court requiring the repair of the staircase later known as number 3.[47] The repair was effected the same year.[48] The west range survived until it was demolished by a bomb on the night of 10 May 1941. It has not been replaced. The south side of Brick Court, number 1, was rebuilt apparently about 1708.[49] In 1908, it was found to be unsafe and was rebuilt in 1909 and 1910 in late seventeenth-century style by Aston Webb. At its east side it contains a covered walkway running down the edge of Middle Temple Lane.

---

[42]   Bellot, above n 19, at 171.

[43]   Minutes of Parliament 22.6.1655, iii 1081; Bellot, above n 19, at 88.

[44]   Williamson, *The History of the Temple*, above n 1, at 521.

[45]   Williamson, ibid, 606, tells us that there was a passage from Palsgrave's Head Court to Essex Court. In 1692 the benchers ordered that a candle be hung up there on the usual nights for 'enlightening the said passage out of Essex Court'. The passage was evidently blocked up later. The following information comes from Ian Garwood, Director of Estates of the Middle Temple. In April 1985 the Inn carried out some preliminary investigation works in connection with a proposal to refurbish rooms on the ground floor of 4 Essex Court. When a section of wall in the North East corner room adjoining the Outer Temple was opened up, the remains of Palsgrave Passage were discovered. They presented something of a time warp with half burnt candles still in their wall brackets, rough plastered walls yellowed with age and the original worn stone slab floor with fragments of clay pipes. The decision was taken to seal the passage and leave it in an untouched condition for future generations.

[46]   See also Bellot, above n 19, at 62.

[47]   Williamson, *The History of the Temple*, above n 1, at 642.

[48]   Commemorated by an inscription: 'Phoenicis instar revivisco Martino Ryder Thesaurario An° 1704'. Bellot, above n 19, says that almost the whole of Brick Court was destroyed by fire in 1703, and that the west side, numbers 2 and 3, was rebuilt in 1704. However, the Minutes of Parliament make reference to the repair of only one staircase: MT1/MPA7 (12 May 1704). And Bradley and Pevsner, above n 1, at 347, describe what can be identified as the west side of Brick Court as 'a late seventeenth century range destroyed in the war'.

[49]   In 1708, £410 was paid by the Inn to Michael Noble for chambers erected on the south side of Brick Court: Bellot, above n 19.

The north range of Brick Court and Essex Court, built after the fire of 1679,[50] survived until it was rebuilt in 1882 and 1883 to the design of St Aubyn, when a passage through the Outer Temple was constructed.[51] The replacement building, known as 5 Essex Court and 4 Brick Court,[52] survived the war, though not unscathed. A further storey was added to it about 1950.

On the east side of Middle Temple Lane, at the north end of the lane, number 1 Middle Temple Lane is part of the gatehouse. Numbers 2 and 3 date from 1693 to 1694. The map of 1677 shows buildings in the same location. Number 3 occupies the site of Luther's Building, erected by Anthony Luther, an Utter-barrister of the Middle temple, in 1614.[53] Number 2 is the site of a brick building erected by Sir Walter Cope and Sir Arthur Gorges, which was so flimsily built that in 1629 it was ordered to be pulled down and rebuilt.[54] Number 4, on the west side of Middle Temple Lane, dates from the eighteenth century.[55]

Elm Court is first mentioned in the records of the Inn in 1620.[56] Reference is made to repair of 'dark and noisome ways' from Elm Court and Pump Court toward the church. Two new single chambers (one between Pump Court and Vine Court) and two shops in the 'new entry' at the foot of the steps leading to Pump Court were built at the same time. The chambers on the south side of Elm Court, towards Middle Temple Lane, were taken down and rebuilt by 1634 pursuant to an order made in 1632.[57] The buildings at the south side of Elm Court, which survived the fire of 1679, also survived contemporaneous attempts to blow them up to prevent spread of the fire. In a dilapidated condition, they were replaced in 1880 by a new building designed by St Aubyn. That building was destroyed by the landmine of 15 November 1940, as was number 1 Elm Court, forming part of the south block of Pump Court, which was rebuilt by Barbon after the fire of 1679.

---

[50]   The chambers ordered 'to be set more northwards' in 1679: *ibid*, at 63.

[51]   In 1881, Middle Temple Parliament considered building a subway from the north end of Middle Temple Lane (on the west side) to the east wing of the new Royal Courts of Justice. The subway was to be 7 ft wide and 8 ft 6 in high, with 28 steps at each end; the depth from the street to the paving of the subway was to be 14 ft: MT1/MPA 19. The project was abandoned in 1883. The advantage of a subway can be seen from the fact that as long before as 1850, 2,969 omnibuses passed and re-passed along Fleet Street every day: *Bradshaw's General (Monthly) Railway and Steam Navigation Guide*, no 200, 1 March 1850, at vii, advertisement for Clifford's Inn Coffee and Chop House.

[52]   Williamson C19, p 16, writing in 1936. They appear to have been known earlier as 4 and 5 Brick Court: Bellot, above n 19, at 63.

[53]   Bellot, above n 19, at 158; Williamson, 291, says 1615.

[54]   Bellot, above n 19, at 158.

[55]   Bradley and Pevsner, above n 1, at 346, 347.

[56]   Bellot, above n 19, at 84.

[57]   Williamson, *The History of the Temple*, above n 1, at 375; Bellot, above n 19, at 84.

After the war, the buildings in Fig Tree Court and on the south side of Elm Court were not rebuilt. Fig Tree Court was thereby merged with Elm Court and lost its separate identity. The building on the west side of Elm Court was replaced by a new building by Maufe. That building was named Lamb Building, perpetuating the name of the building south of the church that was destroyed in the war.

South of the new Lamb Building, a new building, Carpmael Building, was built at the west end of Crown Office Row on land provided by the Inner Temple. Carpmael Building is connected to the Inner Temple's rebuilt Harcourt Buildings by an arch.

At the west end of Pump Court, on the north and west sides of the court, the chambers date from a time shortly after the fire of 1679. Earlier buildings on the north side were ordered in 1627 to be pulled down by reason of decay and rebuilt. The new chambers were completed in 1628, and destroyed in the fire of 1679.[58] On the west side, a brick building dating from 1630 was destroyed in that fire, as were chambers built in 1637 on the south side. The south side of Pump Court, numbers 1, 2 and 3, was demolished in the air raid on the night of 10 May 1941. Those chambers were rebuilt by Maufe from 1951 to 1953.

The Cloisters, at the east end of Pump Court, are on the site of the Cloisters erected by the Templars and destroyed by fire in 1679.[59] Chambers three storeys high were built over the Cloisters in 1612.[60] However, there were chambers over the Cloisters before then, for in 1526 a Mr Grenfeld was 'admitted to a chamber over the Cloisters'.[61] After the fire, a plan for rebuilding the Cloisters was prepared by Sir Christopher Wren,[62] but the matter went to arbitration and the award, which was complied with, departed to some extent from Wren's plan. The new building again included chambers three storeys high over the Cloisters. The Cloisters were double their former width, but they no longer extended to the wall of the church. Their northern extremity was close to the corner of what is now Farrar's Building. Access to the chambers above the Cloisters was gained by a staircase projecting eastwards from the north end of the building into South Churchyard Court. In 1825, the Chapel of St Anne, adjacent to the Round Church on its south side, was removed, and the staircase was moved to give an entrance to the north face of the Cloisters, thus blocking one of two arches. The Wren Cloisters were damaged in the air raid on the night of 10 May 1941.[63] They were rebuilt to Maufe's

---

[58] Bellot, above n 19, at 177, 178.
[59] Bradley and Pevsner, above n 1, at 350.
[60] Williamson, *The History of the Temple*, above n 1, at 530.
[61] Bellot, above n 19, at 69.
[62] Williamson C19, 21.
[63] Anon, 'Middle Temple Ordeal' Middle Temple (1948), 33, 43.

designs from 1949 to 1952. They were one bay shorter than before the war, in accordance with Wren's original design.[64]

The building in South Church Court, known (from 1683 at any rate) as Lamb Building[65] from the lamb and flag coat of arms over the entrance,[66] was 'a fine example of Stuart architecture'.[67] It was on the site of an earlier building containing fifteen chambers, which was burnt down in the Great Fire of 1666. An illustration of the earlier building, showing the names of the occupiers, appears at Plate 2–3. It was known as Caesar's Buildings, having been built by Sir Julius Caesar, MR, and was erected in 1596.[68] It originally belonged to the Inner Temple.[69]

There was a dispute between the Middle and Inner Temples in relation to Lamb Building which led to litigation in 1679.[70] Inner Temple petitioned[71] the Lord Chancellor on the ground that Middle Temple was refusing to admit to chambers in the building Inner Templars who had been inhabitants before the fire. It may be that the drawing the subject of

---

[64]   Bradley and Pevsner, above n 1, at 350; and see ch 5 p 402.
[65]   Williamson, *The History of the Temple*, above n 1, at 517 ('Lamb Buildings').
[66]   Bellot, above n 19, at 138.
[67]   *Ibid.*
[68]   *Ibid*, at 137.
[69]   Bellot, *ibid*, at 138, says that the change of ownership probably took place after the Great Fire of London of 1666. On the other hand, the occupants of the old building, probably at the time of the fire, were largely Middle Templars: see Plate 2–3. But given that the old building was built by Sir Julius Caesar, it may well have belonged to Inner Temple before the fire.
[70]   Lamb Building certainly belonged to the Middle Temple by 1732: see Plate 2–12. Bellot relies on a tradition that Middle Temple purchased Lamb Building from Inner Temple after the Great Fire: Bellot, *ibid*, at 138. However, its ownership appears to have been derived from the fact that it was largely or entirely Middle Templars, and the Inn itself, who paid for the rebuilding. On 30 October 1666 Middle Temple Parliament ordered that there be an enquiry as to what interest any person had in the building lately burnt down, and how the interest of the House might be separated from that of Inner Temple in rebuilding. On 23 November 1666, on a petition from gentlemen whose chambers had been burnt down to have leave to rebuild, two persons were appointed to treat with the Master of the Temple and the benchers of Inner Temple for assigning ground for them to build on. On 3 May 1667 proposals to rebuild in brick were referred to Sir Peter Ball and Messrs Hervey, Constantine Mundy, Bramston and Lechmere, or any two, to settle, so that the building might be forthwith put in hand. They were desired to take care that the House lose none of its ground, but that there be fifteen chambers or parts of chambers as before. The House was to join in the building and bear some of the charge. On 22 May the committee were empowered to enlarge the building six or eight feet in front if they saw cause. It was ordered that the chambers were to be disposed of as follows: to the House, which would bear a proportion of the charge, three; to Thomas Walcott, Alexander Denton, Sir Nicholas Crispe, Thomas Gape, Richard Ruddiard, Richard Hall, Thomas Vesey, George Bradbury, Robert Merrett, William Noyse, one each; and Edward Palmer, two, as he held before a double chamber containing three storeys. All should bear their portion of the charge according to the goodness of their chambers. On 12 February 1668 allotments and values of the chambers and the cellar were specified, and rents were reserved apportioned to the chambers. [MT.1/MPA/6, 105–108, 112–114, 120–127]. As to the historic practice of the Middle Temple to allow its members to build chambers see ch 2 p 85.
[71]   MT temporary reference Box 57, bundle 1, no 3.

Plate 2–3[72] relates to that litigation. Most of the names written on the drawing can be identified as Middle Templars. The only identifiable Inner Templar is described as such.[73]

As can be seen from the map of 1677, at that time there were buildings adjacent to the Round Church on the north, west and south sides. The plan of 1732 shows the ownership of the various buildings. The northernmost building in Churchyard Court was 1 and 2 Churchyard Court, a building of the Middle Temple. It comprised a row of timber-framed houses probably erected in 1608, replacing buildings on the same site referred to in the Rent Roll of the Middle Temple of 1567.[74] Numbers 1 and 2 Churchyard Court were taken down and replaced in 1861[75] by a new building by St Aubyn which was named Goldsmith Building after Oliver Goldsmith, who had lived at 2 Brick Court.[76] The Temple porch was surmounted by three floors of chambers. In 1857 the rooms which for more than 200 years had rested on the porch, together with the adjoining block of buildings, were taken down and not rebuilt.[77]

The original chambers building known as Fountain Court dates from 1881. It was built on the site of a house at 33 Essex Street, which was purchased by the Inn in 1871.[78] The original building on that site was by Barbon. It had been rebuilt in the 19th century. The adjacent properties, numbers 32 and 34 Essex Street, by Barbon, were purchased by the Inn in 1975 and combined to form a larger chambers building under the same name, Fountain Court. Number 35 Essex Street was acquired in 1992 and linked internally with number 34 in 2009, thus enlarging the chambers at Fountain Court.[79] The fountain itself is said to have been the first permanent fountain in London. The circular basin was made in 1681.[80]

The Inn purchased 24 to 27 Essex Street[81] in 1996. Those buildings were converted into chambers and opened in 1998 as Blackstone House.

To the north of New Court, Devereux Chambers and 9, Devereux Court were bought by the Inn in 1975.[82]

The properties at 7 to 15 Fleet Street were purchased in 2000 and converted to chambers (retaining a shop) in 2004. The building has

---

[72] MT temporary reference Box 60, bundle 1, no 1.
[73] For a list of identifications, some tentative, see Annex to this chapter.
[74] Bellot, above n 19, at 99. Bellot speculates that these buildings, or their immediate predecessors, were some of the buildings built by Roger Blome, the Nuncius of the Temple. (See above p 67, text to n 3.)
[75] Bellot, *ibid*, at 99.
[76] See 'Literary Associations of the Middle Temple' by Jessica Winston below at p 158.
[77] Williamson C19, 22, 23.
[78] Essex Street is outside the Temple.
[79] See ch 5 below at p 457.
[80] Bradley and Pevsner, above n 1.
[81] See ch 5 below, at pp 467, 468.
[82] See ch 5 below at p 457.

entrances both from Fleet Street and from Hare Court. It was named Burnton Buildings, in recognition of the signal service to the Inn rendered by the Chairman of the Estates Committee, Master Burnton, in relation to the acquisition and refurbishment of the building.

Annex
INHABITANTS OF LAMB BUILDING

Name or other legend	Tentative identification
Mr W[illegible]	Richard Wallop, adm 1638, called 1646, bencher 1666.
Mr Bradbury	George Bradbury, adm 1660, called 1667, bencher 1690.
Curate	
Sir Nicholas Crispe	Sir Nicholas Crisp (1599?-1666). His mother's second husband was Sir Walter Pye (1571–1635), a barrister of the Middle Temple and from 1621 attorney-general of the court of wards.
Mr Rudyard	Richard Rudyard, adm 1648.
Turnspitt of the Inner Temple	
Mr Pleydwell	Charles Playdwell, adm 1663.
Mr Merrett	Robert Merrett, adm 1663, called 1672.
Mr Bradborne	John Bradborne, adm 1656.
Mr Walcott	Thomas Walcot, adm 1647, called 1653, bencher 1671, Reader Lent 1677.
Mr Gape	Thomas Gape, adm 1648, called of grace 1667.
Mr Vesey	Thomas Vesey, adm 1645.
Mr Beare	John Beare, adm 1641, or his brother George Beare, adm 1655, sons of George Beare, adm 1605, called 1613, bencher 1632, Lent Reader 1632; or Balthazar Beare, adm 1633, called 1640, Reader.
Mr Denton 3 storys backward	Alexander Denton, adm 1653, called 1660.
Mr Stoner Inner Temple	Angel Stoner adm Inner Temple 1651.

Mr Noyse & Mr Hall	William Noyes, adm 1630; or William Noyes, adm. 1650. Richard Hall, adm. 1651.
Mr Palmer 3 storys backwards	Edward Palmer, adm 1660, called of grace 1664, son of Sir Geoffrey Palmer, Attorney-General and one of the Masters of the Bench.
Inner Temple Bench Chamber	

2

Conflict, Change and Continuity: Elizabeth I to the Great Temple Fire

WILFRID PREST

BETWEEN THE ACCESSION of the last Tudor monarch and the destruction of much of the Temple by fire (and fire-fighters) in 1679, the cultural, politico-religious and social prominence of the Inns of Court was far greater than ever before, or since. The main reasons were their mushroom growth as 'Seminaries and Nurseries wherein the Gentrie of the Kingdome and such as serve ... the Common Wealth are bredd and trayned upp', together with the high salience of the common law and its practitioners in an era of constitutional crisis and hyper-litigiousness.[1] Probably the smallest of the four medieval Inns, the Middle Temple had emerged as the largest player in the legal quartet by the 1670s. Yet that same decade also saw the last of the formal readings, or law lectures, which had constituted the high point of the old aural learning-exercise system, signalling the abandonment of any serious institutional commitment to legal education, by the Middle Temple and the other three houses, for some two centuries.

I. NUMBERS

Although the Middle Temple's admissions records between 1524 and 1551 do not survive, figures from the other three houses point to a steady

---

[1] *Acts of the Privy Council of England 1629 May–1631 May* (London, HMSO, 1960), 145. This chapter draws on my *The Inns of Court under Elizabeth I and the Early Stuarts 1590–1640* (London, Longman, 1972), and *The Rise of the Barristers: A Social History of the English Bar 1590–1640* (Oxford, Clarendon Press, corrected edn, 1991) [hereafter '*Inns of Court*' and '*Barristers*', respectively].

growth in numbers admitted, beginning around 1530 and accelerating markedly at mid-century. This upward trend, sustained throughout Elizabeth's reign and into the early Stuart era, was part of what has been termed[2] an 'Educational Revolution', a cultural and social movement which boosted enrolments at schools, academies and universities throughout Western Europe. The five years 1551–56 saw an annual average of some 150 members admitted to the four Inns; by the first decade of the following century their intake had nearly doubled. In the 1650s, notwithstanding the disruptions of civil war, regicide and republic, the four Inns were still admitting some 250 to 290 new members every year.

The Middle Temple itself made no extraordinary contribution to this Elizabethan–early Stuart admissions boom. Although its intake grew more or less in line with the overall expansion, for most of the century after 1550 the house actually registered less than its strictly proportionate share of entrants. Recorded enrolments at each Inn fluctuated sharply and more or less unpredictably from year to year. But generally speaking Gray's Inn took the lion's share, with the Middle Temple very much among the also rans, except for a brief period from the mid-1590s to the end of the following decade, when its average annual admissions slightly exceeded one-quarter of the combined total for the four houses. So although the Middle Temple's catchment area had broadened considerably since medieval times, with entrants from London, Gloucestershire, Northamptonshire and Warwickshire now featuring strongly alongside the traditional West Country[3] cohort, it was certainly not the most fashionable or best-favoured Inn, at least before Charles II's restoration in 1660. Thereafter, however, its relative popularity grew by leaps and bounds. Indeed, by the late 1670s the house was attracting nearly one-third of all new entrants admitted to the Inns (well over 200 a year out of a somewhat smaller aggregate total than earlier in the century). As we shall see in chapter three, this numerical dominance continued and become even more pronounced in the succeeding century.

It is true that the enrolment statistics may not tell the whole story, for the simple reason that mere membership of an Inn of Court did not necessarily imply residence or any other form of engagement with that house. A small proportion (perhaps 5 per cent under Elizabeth and the early Stuarts) of all recorded admissions were purely honorific, typically given gratis as a reader's ex-officio perquisite and prerogative. Thus the Duke of Buckingham, James I's unpopular favourite, together with his brother Edward Villiers, was admitted a member of the Middle Temple on 1 March 1618 by Walter Pye, the Lent Reader; on subsequent days the same honour was

---

[2]   By Lawrence Stone in his article 'The Educational Revolution in England, 1540–1640' (1964) 28 *Past and Present* 41.

[3]   Cornwall, Devon, Somerset and Dorset.

conferred on Sir Lionel Cranfield and several other courtiers. Like the recipients of university degrees *honoris causa*, such notables might or might not add lustre to the society's public image, but there was no expectation that they would take any further part in its activities.

While frequently likened to colleges (and even termed 'our sister University' by an Oxford don in 1630[4]), the early modern Inns of Court and Chancery differed from the two English universities in important respects. Above all, as voluntary societies, not corporate bodies, they lacked founding charters or statutes which prescribed teaching and learning as their prime function and raison d'être. True, the preamble to James I's conveyance of title in fee simple to the benchers of the two Temples in 1608 characterised their societies as 'two of the four Colleges the most famous of all Europe as always abounding with persons dedicated to the study' of the law, while the actual grant of lands, buildings and the Temple Church was said to be 'for the accommodation and education of the students and professors of the laws'.[5] But even if this document, which cost the benchers a gold cup to the value of £666 13s 4d (not an unreasonable price in the circumstances), might be said to represent their conscious aspirations at that point of time, its terms did not privilege education before accommodation, nor provide any means of monitoring or regulating performance in either capacity.

So notwithstanding the considerable practical benefits of securing their freehold title against the potential threat posed by predatory Scots and other courtiers, in educational terms James I's charter was of merely rhetorical significance. After paying the usual admission fees, entrants were neither required to come into residence, nor to undertake any course of study if and when they did arrive in London. Lacking the landed endowments enjoyed by the colleges of Oxford and Cambridge, the early modern Inns drew their working income largely from members' fees and fines. Hence they faced a constant temptation to commute academic obligations under the learning-exercise system into cash payments. The earliest surviving Middle Temple records suggest that those who joined between 1501 and 1525 were not usually charged anything at all, except for a minority who sought exemption from attendance at learning exercises or other customary obligations. But by the middle of the sixteenth century two types of fee-paying admission had come into existence. General admissions carried no exemption from learning exercises or residential requirements; however the special admission was 'a little the dearer, yet

⁴ FS Boas (ed), *The Diary of Thomas Crosfield* (London, Oxford University Press for Royal Society for Literature,1935), 44.
⁵ FA Inderwick (ed), *A Calendar of the Inner Temple Records* (London, Inner Temple,1898), vol II, xiii–xix; JH Baker, *An Inner Temple Miscellany* (London, Inner Temple, 2004), 2n.

doth it leave a man free'.[6] By the 1620s, when this considered advice was offered by the young Puritan barrister Simonds D'Ewes to his Suffolk correspondent Sir Martin Stuteville (whose second son's back-dated and *in absentia* admission D'Ewes was about to arrange), nine out of 10 entrants to the Middle Temple chose to be specially admitted, thereby escaping all requirements for attendance, or participation in learning exercises, unless and until they sought call to the Bar.[7]

Nearly 500 non-honorific entrants joined the Middle Temple over that same decade; fewer than half appear ever to have been admitted to chambers. A judges' order of 1574, 'that no more in number be admitted from henceforth, than the Chambers of the Houses will receive, after two to a Chamber', clearly fell on deaf ears, despite being repeated in 1584 and 1591.[8] While private sales or subleases of chambers were strictly forbidden, they certainly did occur, so the proportion of Middle Templars living on site may have been higher than the official record suggests. On the other hand, formal possession of a chamber and occupation of it were two different things, as Simonds D'Ewes himself could well attest. For in July 1611, aged 8 years and 6 months, he had been admitted simultaneously to membership of the Middle Temple and to a house chamber previously held by his father, an important official in the Court of Chancery. Reaching London fresh from Cambridge University in October 1620 to commence his legal studies, Simonds was mortified (as he later recalled) to discover that 'the chamber to which I had been admitted near upon nine years before' had been 'sold to a stranger'. He was accordingly obliged to be 'pestered with other company' at his father's lodgings in Chancery Lane, since 'I could not recover the possession' for more than a year.[9]

D'Ewes was certainly unlucky, and possibly disingenuous in his telling of this tale, since despite the formal requirement for those possessing house chambers to remain in residence at least two months of every year (reduced

[6] JB Williamson, *The History of the Temple*, 2nd edn (London, John Murray, 1925), 110–11, 149; JO Halliwell (ed), *The Autobiography and Correspondence of Sir Simonds D'Ewes* (London, R. Bentley, 1845), vol 2, 82; *Register of Admissions to the Honourable Society of the Middle Temple from the Fifteenth Century to the year 1944*, comp. H A C Sturgess, vol 1, 1501–1781 (London, Middle Temple, 1949), i., 117.

[7] Prest, *Inns of Court*, above n 1, at 15.

[8] W Dugdale, *Origines Juridiciales* (London, F and T Warren, 1666), 312, 316; RJ Fletcher (ed), *The Pension Book of Gray's Inn (Records of the Honourable Society) 1569–1669* (London, Gray's Inn, 1901), 61.

[9] D'Ewes, *Autobiography*, n 6 above at i. 149. In point of fact D'Ewes's original admission (by the 1611 summer reader John Strode, presumably as a favour to his legal-bureaucrat father), had been revoked after protests from the chamber's other occupants, although D'Ewes was subsequently given a reversionary interest; see *Middle Temple Records*, ed. C H Hopwood and C T Martin, 3 vols (London, Middle Temple, 1904–5) (hereafter *MTR*), ii.,538, 541, 546, 551, 653, 659, 660, 663, 667, 669, 676.

to six weeks by the 1630s),[10] little notice seems often to have been taken of less than a year's absence, or even longer periods, especially when demand for on-site accommodation slackened. Thus in 1619, a father and his sons lost their chambers because they had not used the rooms for 16 years; but two years later the benchers ordered that

> Mr Roger Burgoine, notwithstandinge his absence and discontinuance from this howse for thirty years and upwards shall yet hold his parte in one upper Chamber or Garrett ...[11]

By now pressure on chambers had somewhat eased. Enrolments at the Middle Temple peaked early in James I's reign, while additions to and renovation of the existing building stock continued. In 1574, amid government unease about the unregulated growth of the Inns, and the threat of catholic missionary activity among their membership, a survey commissioned by the Privy Council noted that at the Middle Temple 92 chambers were occupied by 130 members, with a further 60 'havinge no chambers'.[12] The judges' orders of that same year prohibited erecting new accommodation and the admission of any more members than could be currently housed on site, although the Middle Templars were expressly permitted to convert their old hall into a maximum of 10 new chambers. Yet only 12 years later Attorney-General John Popham, speaker of the House of Commons as well as Treasurer of the Middle Temple and future Chief Justice of King's Bench, reported that the supply of chambers had increased by half, to 138. Unforthcoming about the distribution of these rooms among the fellowship, Popham estimated that some 200 members were 'ordynarily in Commons in the Terme tyme', about half that number during readings and 'in the somer vacacon not passyng fyfty'.[13]

Unlike construction of the society's magnificent new hall, chamber building or renovation was still undertaken as a private venture by members (and occasional outsiders) under licence from the house, to which the premises reverted after the builders had recouped their costs from the initial occupants; Popham himself constructed a block of chambers in 1582.[14] But in 1615, perhaps emboldened by improving finances and hopes of future gains, as well as weary of recurrent disputes about

---

[10] *MTR*, ii., 644 (an earlier order of 1568 required only four weeks a year in commons: *ibid*, i., 166); Dugdale, above n 8, at 202 ('Brerewood ms').

[11] *MTR*, ii., 638, 663; MT1/MPA/4, 11 May 1621. In 1614, however, a member evidently thought it prudent to seek permission to keep his chamber despite a year's absence due to sickness: *MTR*, ii., 590; see also *ibid*, at 597, 600, 602, 609, 610, 620, 641.

[12] FA Inderwick (ed), *The Inner Temple: its early history as illustrated by its records, 1505–1603* (London, Inner Temple, 1896), 468–69.

[13] BL Lansdowne MS 106, fo. 95; cf JD Walker (ed), *Records of the Honourable Society of Lincoln's Inn The Black Books* (1897), vol I, 460–62.

[14] *MTR*, i., 257–58; the recorded admissions suggest that Popham's building consisted of three storeys, with three chambers on each floor.

occupancy and title, the Bench outlawed all private building initiatives, resolving that any new structures were henceforth to be erected at the expense of the house itself, 'and the howse to have the disposing of the chambers'.[15] Like many other parliament orders, this edict turned out to be more aspirational than absolute, since private building operations continued in Brick Court, Middle Temple Lane, Pump Court, Elm Court and elsewhere over the next 30 years. The most ambitious project, a large brick structure of 'six spacious floors ... which never were in any other buildinge of the house', cost the huge sum of £4,668 in the late 1630s; this was paid partly by individual 'Gentlemen that were Builders', with the balance coming 'out of the Treasury, which did put the House much in Debt'.[16] A detailed but seemingly incomplete survey of chambers and shops in 1654, doubtless an initiative of the newly-appointed under-treasurer William Jones, enumerated no fewer than 210 chambers, together with space occupied by a cobbler, 'Mr Browne the barber', 'Mr Jocelyn, stationer', and the buttery, library, 'Parliament Chamber' and 'music room' (formerly the steward's chamber).[17]

As all but benchers were supposed to share their chambers with at least one other member, this might suggest a resident population at mid-century mark not much below 400 persons, both members and 'strangers', the latter including for most of the 1650s the wives, female servants and children of such notables as the Lord Commissioners John Lisle and Bulstrode Whitelocke. A more persistent problem, identified by the judges' orders of 1614 (repeated in 1630) was the use of the Inns for 'the lodging or abode of Gentlemen of the Country', whether 'foreiner or discontinuer'; the Middle Temple parliament had already legislated on this issue in 1612, threatening those who lodged strangers with loss of their chamber.[18] But having no systematic means of monitoring the occupants of chambers, none of the houses kept records of residents as such, although the Middle Temple's butler maintained a roll of those taking commons in hall, from which the steward compiled his weekly accounts. Indeed 'residence' is a potentially misleading concept in this context. Members' obligations and qualifications were generally expressed in terms of 'continuance in commons', which implied eating communal meals (especially midday dinner and supper) in hall, but not necessarily living on the premises, as distinct from neighbourhood lodgings or taverns. Since the Inn's catering arrangements depended upon sufficient numbers being in commons to keep the costs of providing and serving meals at an acceptable level, the benchers

[15]   Williamson, above n 6, at 292.
[16]   *Ibid*, at 292, 373–76; Dugdale, above n 8, at 188–90; MT.2/TRB/4 (Parker's accounts, Bayliffe's response, fo 14).
[17]   MT5/CSL/2.
[18]   Williamson, above n 6, at 424–27; Dugdale, above n 8, at 192, 317, 320.

naturally attached considerable importance to 'the holding together in commons of the companie of this Fellowship in their publique hall', without which (as they claimed) 'a companie so voluntarilie gathered together to live under government could hardly be termed a Society'.[19] Commons were provided and charged for on a weekly basis, with 'half-commons' for those requiring less than a full week's meals, and 'repasts' ('being one Meal in the Hall, and of which two and no more are allowed').[20] Such a system was well suited to the needs of a diverse, fluid and transient population of lawyers, students and young gentleman, whose movements were not primarily dictated by the cycle of an academic calendar, although they might well reflect the rhythms of law term and vacation. These demographic characteristics plainly make it difficult to estimate the size of the early modern Middle Temple as a residential institution. According to James Whitelocke, father of Bulstrode, writing at the beginning of the seventeenth century, 'there are not at this time any more in commons amongst us, when there are most, than 200, or 10 or 11 score, which is very seldom'; Whitelocke glossed Fortescue's assertion some 130 years before that each Inn then had at least 200 members to mean 'only those that at that time were as residents and students in those houses *at some times or others*'[21] (emphasis added).

Although no commons rolls for this period have survived, the miscellaneous domestic records in the Middle Temple archives include a series of receipts for payments towards the stipends of two lecturers or preachers, William Crashawe and his successor Abraham Gibson, employed by the two Temple societies between 1605 and 1618 to deliver sermons in the Temple Church. Every member of the house in commons at any time during the four law terms was levied at the appropriate rate according to his rank (bencher, utter-barrister or inner-barrister); payments were collected on a 'preacher's roll', one of which was made up for each term, and evidently re-circulated in subsequent terms until all those due to pay had done so or been otherwise accounted for. It seems that the total active (or at least paying) membership of the Middle Temple in Easter term 1605 comprised 221 individuals: 20 benchers, 98 barristers and 103 inner-barristers, gentlemen under the Bar or students; although only 18 benchers, 72 barristers and 68 students contributed when the roll was first sent around. Numbers rose to a peak of 290 for Michaelmas term 1605, thereafter settling to a slightly lower level in the 260 to 279 range, before dropping sharply to 203 for Hilary term 1608, when Crashawe's relations with his Middle Temple congregation took a serious turn for the worse.

---

[19] Prest, *Inns of Court*, above n 1, at 11–12 (where this quotation is misdated to 1611).
[20] Dugdale, above n 8, at 198.
[21] Prest, *Inns of Court*, above n 1, 7–8; DX Powell, *Sir James Whitelocke's Liber Famelicus 1570–1632* (New York, Peter Lang, 2000), 62.

The record of payments in support of Gibson covers only five terms (Easter 1614 to Trinity 1615); contributors ranged between 158 (Hilary 1615) to 279–80 (Easter and Trinity 1614). How far these figures may have been distorted by the popularity or otherwise of the respective preachers is unclear.[22]

Taken together with Whitelocke's earlier testimony, and the statement of the Middle Temple Benchers that there were nearly 260 members in commons at the middle of Trinity term 1609,[23] the evidence points to expansion continuing quite strongly into the second decade of the seventeenth century. If admissions provide a reliable guide to the relative size of the four Inns, at that point the Middle Temple was slightly larger than Lincoln's Inn and comfortably ahead of the Inner Temple, but well behind Gray's Inn, and indeed falling further back over the next 30 years or so. There is no obvious explanation for these differences, nor for the remarkable turnaround after the Interregnum, when the Middle Temple's share of admissions rose first from one-fifth to a quarter, then reached nearly one-third of the total by the late 1670s. But a good part of the answer involves the contraction of Gray's Inn, easily the largest of the four houses under Elizabeth and the early Stuarts, where enrolments nearly halved between the 1650s and the first decade of Charles II's reign, continuing to decline thereafter. The massive swing of sentiment underlying this collapse almost certainly had a political dimension. Some of the most prominent republicans and regicides were Gray's Inn men, among them John Bradshaw, who presided at the trial of Charles I, and the King's prosecutor, John Cooke. By contrast, the former MP turned royalist politician who returned in 1660 with Charles II as Lord Chancellor and de facto Chief Minister was Edward Hyde, Earl of Clarendon, a Middle Templar from south-west England, like many members of his extended family.

II. LAW AND LEARNING

In the later fifteenth century Fortescue had emphasised the dual pedagogical mission of the Inns: courtly academies as well as law schools, they attracted not only would-be lawyers, but also well-born young men with no ambitions for a legal career. Some fathers may have enrolled their sons at the Inns on the off-chance that they would take to the law. But during the fifteenth century perhaps no more than one in five of those admitted to Lincoln's Inn, Fortescue's own house, are later identifiable as professional

---

[22]   MT.15/TAM/3, 25. RM Fisher, 'The Predicament of William Crashawe Preacher at the Temple, 1605–1613', (1974) 25 *Journal of Ecclesiastical History* 269–71.
[23]   *MTR*, ii., 509.

lawyers, even if some more may have practised in provincial obscurity.[24] By the second half of the sixteenth century, when call to the bar of an Inn of Court had become the prerequisite qualification for would-be advocates in Westminster Hall, the proportion of Middle Temple entrants who became barristers seems to have been slightly lower, averaging around 15 per cent of all entrants. This ratio increased a little after 1650, perhaps as part of a reaction against the educational fashion of the previous century and more, which had strongly encouraged use of the Inns as finishing schools for gentlemen. At the end of the century the diarist John Evelyn would look back to the 1630s as a far distant epoch, when both he and his elder brother went on to the Middle Temple from Oxford 'as gent[lemen] of the best quality did, tho' with no intention to study the Law as a Profession'. Yet notwithstanding his use of the past tense, abandonment of the Middle Temple and other Inns of Court by such well-born youths was a more protracted process than Evelyn's comment would imply.[25]

Among the minority later called to the Bar at the Tudor and early-Stuart Middle Temple, there seem to have been rather more men from commercial, professional, yeomanry and lesser gentry backgrounds, and fewer sons of peers or knights, than among the whole body of entrants. True, the information provided about the parentage of each newly-admitted member in the record of his admission was not always wholly complete or conclusive. Thus the poet and successful barrister John Davies (who died in 1626, the night before he was to be installed as Chief Justice), and the celebrated antiquary Elias Ashmole, their fathers respectively a tanner and a saddler, appear as gentlemen's sons in the records of their respective admissions to the Middle Temple.[26] Moreover the early modern social hierarchy was ambiguous, fluid and ill-defined at best. Edward Machen, described on his admission as a younger son of Thomas Machen esquire, of Gloucester, entered the house in October 1604 and was called to the Bar seven years later. But Edward's father was in fact a wealthy alderman, three times mayor of Gloucester, who also owned a large estate 14 miles outside that city; hence we might well wonder whether his son should be classified as of commercial/mercantile or landed gentry stock.[27]

But if deconstructing the social composition of the Middle Temple's membership is hampered by such difficulties of definition and evidence, the

---

[24] JH Baker, 'The English Legal Profession, 1450–1550' in W Prest (ed), *Lawyers in Early Modern Europe and America* (London, Croom Helm, 1981), 33.

[25] Calculation based on calls noted in *MTR*, i. See Stone, above n 2; ES De Beer (ed), *The Diary of John Evelyn* (Oxford, Oxford University Press,1955), v., at 357–58; also ch 3 of this book.

[26] *Oxford Dictionary of National Biography (ODNB)*; *MTR*, i., 296, iii.,1113.

[27] *MTR*, ii., 448; HA Machen, 'The Machen Family of Gloucester' (1944 for 1943) 64 *Bristol and Gloucestershire Archaeological Society Transactions* 96; R Atkyns, *The Ancient and Present State of Glocestershire* (London, W. Herbert, second edition, 1768), 145.

increased emphasis during the later 16th and early 17th centuries on the society's elite status and collegiate role is unmistakable. Insistence that the Inns of Court were truly 'honourable societies' ensured that entrants' fathers were never explicitly described by the admission records as 'plebeian', in sharp contrast to the practice at both Oxford and Cambridge Universities. James I commanded early in his reign that only sons of gentlemen by descent be admitted to membership of the four Inns, but this royal edict carried neither legal nor practical force. A more realistic assessment was encapsulated in Bulstrode Whitelocke's anecdote about Henry VIII telling a suitor 'he could not make him a gentleman, [but] bid him goe to the Innes of Court, where an admission makes one a gentleman'.[28] It is true that, apart from Clerks' Commons, an institution which seems to have been falling into gradual disuse during this period, there was no formal provision for poor mens' sons to work their way to the Bar, as with the servitors or sizars of Oxford and Cambridge colleges whose menial labour paid for their board and tuition. On the other hand, complaints like those by Sir George Buck about dilution of the social quality of the Inns by the 'sons of graziers, farmers, merchants, tradesmen and artificers'[29] underline a distinct gap between rhetoric and reality.

Asserting the elevated status of the Inns of Court and their members was one way of responding to contemporary sneers at 'hireling, mercenary barristers'.[30] In 1561 the Middle Temple benchers proclaimed that any member retained in service would lose his chamber; in 1614 all those who served or attended upon 'any man except noblemen and gentlemen of worth' were threatened with expulsion.[31] Yet three years later a student petition accused the benchers themselves of admitting to membership 'their owne livery servants ... to the utter dishonor of this societie and the name of an Inne of Courtman'.[32] While long-serving butlers and other house servants had been customarily enrolled since at least the later sixteenth century, the 1617 petitioners were apparently objecting to the admission of law clerks and personal servants, like the future barrister Richard Oakley, who entered James Whitelocke's service in 1609 and was admitted to the house four years later.[33] They also lamented the dimming of the Middle

---

[28]   Prest, *Barristers*, above n 1, at 87–88; BL Additional MS 53726, fo 27.

[29]   Buc[k] was himself a Middle Templar; see his 1615 supplement to John Stow's *Survey of London*, cited in Prest, *Inns of Court*, above n 1, at 25.

[30]   Cf Prest, *Barristers*, above n 1, at 90, 287–89.

[31]   *MTR*, i.,131, ii., 582.

[32]   MT.3/MEM: 'Articles exhibited on the behalf of the gentlemen of the Middle Temple whereof they desire reforma[ti]on for the societie', 20 June 1617.

[33]   Williamson, above n 6, at 222–23; Powell, above n 21, at 157; *MTR*, ii., 574–75; cf *ibid*, at 640, reference to proposed demolition of 'Clerk's house' by the Temple Church in 1619.

Temple's 'glorye' by the 'swarmes of Attorneys w[hi]ch are nowe admytted', contrary to 'the auncient fundamentall institu[ti]ons of this Kingdome'. For the Inns of Court

> were erected and have so continued till of late tymes, nurseries for the gentrie (and w[hi]ch ys more for the nobilitie of this lande) in the studdye of the Lawes, and other laudable sciences ...

with the smaller and less prestigious Inns of Chancery reserved for attorneys 'and those of meaner esteeme in the profession'. In reality the first of many half-hearted attempts to exclude attorneys and solicitors from membership of the Middle Temple went back only to the mid-sixteenth century, although growing insistence on the academic and social exclusiveness of the Inns of Court, and the functional differentiation of the upper and lower branches of the legal profession, ensured that this campaign would continue throughout the following century and beyond.[34]

While the 59 signatories to the 1617 petition were all students under the Bar, or inner barristers, no fewer than 25 later became barristers. Three eventually joined the Bench themselves: Sir Peter Ball, Attorney-General to Queen Henrietta Maria and long-time Recorder of Exeter, the Parliamentarian puritan MP John 'Century' White, and Job D(e)ighton, who was associated to the Bench in 1645 and served as treasurer in 1654. (Associates enjoyed the privileges of full benchers, other than a voice in the government of the house, without having previously performed a reading.) Their formal protest appears to have been precipitated by attempts to enforce the dress regulations introduced at the Middle Temple and the other three houses in the mid-sixteenth century, and most recently reiterated by the 1614 judges' orders, which required the wearing of student caps and gowns, primarily with a view to maintaining the benchers' authority and containing 'young men within the bounds of Civility and Order'.[35] The petitioners also made accusations of domestic mismanagement, or worse (failure to check the 'dishonest behaviour' of house servants, and the provision of subsidised commons for benchers' clerks, 'whereby Com[m]ons growe to soe high a rate that gent[lemen] find yt better cheape to lyve owt of Com[m]ons').

A further grievance concerned 'the exercises and disports of gent[l]emen, wherewith the Courts of our former princes have not disdained to be

---

[34] CW Brooks, *Pettyfoggers and Vipers of the Commonwealth: The 'Lower Branch' of the Legal Profession in Early Modern England* (Cambridge, Cambridge University Press, 1986), 161–62; Williamson, above n 6, at 157–58, 492–93; M Birks, *Gentlemen of the Law* (London, Stevens and Sons, 1960), 101, 103–05, 107–08.

[35] See text to n 18; see also above, p 56; below, p 345; Dugdale, above n 8, at 319.

entertayned', and for which 'this societye . . . hath bynn famous'. According to the petitioners, in the past those who participated in such activities had been

> crowned ... with the garlands of the profession, by being called to the barre as the most serious students both in honor of those com[men]da ble qualities, as allsoe to encorage the succeeding posteritye.

But now 'those who by their [the benchers'] earnest request have bestowed theire charges in these exercises to the honour of the howse' received no such recognition. On the contrary, with 'others both to the dishonour of the howse and contempt of the profession . . . advanced to that degree', *they* were

> onely remembred by waye of penaltye, yf they doe butt weare a hatt, boots or a yellowe band, habits in other societies esteemed indifferent ... .

These claims and protests doubtless involved an element of self-serving mythology. But they also point to a vision widely shared among the junior members of the early-Stuart Middle Temple. Future lawyers and laymen alike saw their Inn as an elite academy, devoted to the cultivation of gentlemanly accomplishments and liberal studies, no less than to the common law—very much the image first promulgated by Fortescue, with perhaps a subsequent dash of Renaissance humanism. The 'exercises and disports' to which the petitioners referred were the revels, with dancing, music, feasting, interludes, masques and other entertainments, particularly associated with the keeping of Christmas and, to a lesser extent, the Grand Days at Allhallows or All Saints (1 November) and Candlemas (2 February). They may also have had in mind two specific recent events: the 'Barriers', a display of martial arts with dramatic accompaniment presented by 'fortie worthie Gentlemen of the Noble Societies of Innes of Court, being tenne of each House' at the celebration of Prince Charles's installation as Prince of Wales in November 1616, and the masque at which the Middle Templars entertained Buckingham in January 1617.[36]

The benchers for their part regarded such activities with a mixture of approval and apprehension. Introducing his reading in 1619, James Whitelocke lamented that 'the glory of our Society . . . of late hath beene impayred in the exercises of the younger gentlemen which touch Gentry and Honour'; neither does he seem to have objected to the involvement of his son Bulstrode as elected Master of the Revels 10 years later. Among Bulstrode's fellow revellers was young Edward Hyde, whose bencher uncle

---

[36] J Nichols (ed), *The Progresses, Processions and Magnificent Festivities of King James the First* (London, pp, 1828), iii., 213–14; Williamson, above n 6, at 276–77; Prest, *Inns of Court*, above n 1, at 224; NE McClure (ed), *The Letters of John Chamberlain* (Philadelphia, PA, American Philosophical Society, 1939), ii., 49; DS Bland, *Three Revels from the Inns of Court* (Amersham, Avebury Publishing Company, 1984), 47–67.

urged Edward's father to provide for his nephew 'a suit of satin for a revelling suit to accompany those divers sober fine gentlemen that are students and yet revellers'.[37] Bulstrode's own recollections, which were admittedly compiled for his children many years later, emphasised the positively wholesome nature of these proceedings, with the claim that under his leadership 'instead of drinking, which they contemned', the revellers, when not practising their dances, were accustomed 'sometimes to putt cases, to inquire of publique affayres, and to intermix discourses of some kind of learning'. However, he also revealed that the Saturday night 'post revels' over the long Christmas vacation, at which they danced a mixture of 'old measures', galliards, corantoes, French and country dances, attracted numerous spectators, including ladies from the royal Court. The presence of 'forraine men or women' was one of 'divers Innovacions' censured by Parliament in 1632, when those in Christmas commons were specifically forbidden 'To bring downe the Ladies and Gentlewomen and daunce with them in the Hall when the Benche are gone'.[38]

Some also deplored the decline of the traditional dances, supposedly degenerated into 'Bare walkinge' by the 1630s. For in the early seventeenth century the typical Inns of Court Christmas was being transformed from a mandatory and inclusive communal experience designed to provide training in courtly manners as well as entertainment, to an elective gathering of junior members, dominated by gaming at cards and dice. Following outbreaks of disorder associated with a Christmas lord of misrule in the later sixteenth century, attendance at Christmas commons in the Middle Temple became voluntary, while gambling was expressly permitted by the 1614 judges' orders, so long as only members took part. Thereafter conflicts between students, barristers and the Bench over the keeping of Christmas intensified, leading to sequential outbreaks of defiance, 'great disorders' and 'insufferable misdemeanours' during the 1630s. The climax came in 1639, when 'divers gentlemen of this societie with their swords drawne in a contemptuous and riotous manner' forced open the locked hall and kitchen in order to hold Christmas commons; they were dislodged only after the intervention of Chief Justice Sir John Bramston (a Middle Templar himself) at the King's command.[39]

While Christmas celebrations as such ceased during and after the civil wars, in the 1650s revels with music, dancing and plays were held in Michaelmas and Hilary terms and the intervening vacation. A newsletter reported in December 1651

[37] MT Library, Rare Books Room, 'Lectura Jacobi Whitelocke Armig. in Medio Templo', fo 3; G Davies, 'The Date of Clarendon's First Marriage' (1917) 32 *English Historical Review* 407.
[38] BL MS Additional 53726, fos 45–45v. MT.1/MPA/5, p. 102; *MTR*, ii., 802–03.
[39] Prest, *Inns of Court*, above n 1, at 108–09.

a masque in the Middle Temple . . . before it began the Benchers or ancients of the house were in the Hall and singing the hundred Psalm, which being ended every man drank a cup of Hippocras, and so departed to their Chambers, then the young Gentlemen of that Society began to recreate themselves with civil danceings and melodious musick . . .[40]

The monarchy's return in 1660 brought a resumption of Christmas gaming, and renewed confrontations between benchers and junior members over attempts to prohibit or regulate Christmas commons, with a Lord of Misrule elected, possibly for the last time, in 1661. On New Year's Day 1668, notwithstanding the Middle Temple parliament's previous order for commons to break up over Christmas, Samuel Pepys

coming from the playhouse stepped into the two Temple halls, and there saw the dirty prentices and idle people playing—wherein I was mistaken in thinking to have seen gentlemen of quality playing there, as I think it was when I was a little child . . .[41]

A week later Sir John Evelyn, having viewed with disgust the gamesters at the King's court, went on 'to see the Revells at the Middle Temple, which is also an old, but riotous Costome, and has relation to neither Virtue nor policy'.[42] As moral, prudential and social objections gained further ground, precautionary orders against keeping a grand, gaming, or indeed any Christmas commons continued until and beyond the end of the century. No serious breach or disturbance is recorded after 1683–84, pointing to the effective extinction in the later seventeenth century of what had become at last a degraded remnant of the Middle Temple's former corporate life.[43]

The courts of the mock lords or princes associated with Christmas revels at the Tudor Inns were fertile settings for dramatic and musical performances. Gray's Inn and the Inner Temple took the lead in staging productions written and presented by their own members, but in 1597–98, 1617, 1621, and 1634 the Middle Temple put on its own masques (the last attended by Queen Henrietta Maria disguised as a citizen's wife); others possibly left no record.[44] A masque in honour of the marriage of James I's daughter, Princess Elizabeth, was jointly staged with Lincoln's Inn in 1613. Bulstrode Whitelocke and Edward Hyde served as the Middle Temple's

---

[40]   Williamson, above n 6, at 441.

[41]   *Ibid*, at 498; *MTR*, iii., 1222; R Latham and W Matthews (eds) *The Diary of Samuel Pepys* (London, Bell,1976), ix., 2–3.

[42]   De Beer (ed), above n 25, iii., at 504.

[43]   Williamson, above n 6, at 498; *MTR*, iii., 1198–1499 *passim*.

[44]   AW Green, *The Inns of Court and Early English Drama* (New Haven, CT, Yale University Press, 1931), chs 6–8; DS Bland (ed), *Gesta Grayorum* (Liverpool, Liverpool University Press, 1968), xvi–xxv; PJ Finkelpearl, *John Marston of the Middle Temple* (Cambridge, MA, Harvard University Press, 1969), chs 3–4.

representatives on the committee which managed the performance of the great 'Royall Masque' jointly presented by all four Inns before the King and Queen in the new Banqueting House at Whitehall in 1634.[45] If only an affluent minority of presentable young gentleman students took an active part in these more elaborate productions, 'service and attendance' over Christmas on the elected 'Prince D'Amour' in his 'Pallace of the Middle Temple' was more inclusive.[46] Such occasions also provided an ideal forum for the poets and wits who flourished in and around the late-Elizabethan Middle Temple, notably John Hoskyns, Benjamin Rudyerd, Henry Wotton, John Davies, Richard Martin, John Marston, Edward Sharpham, Thomas Overbury and John Ford.[47]

In the following century the cultural ambience of the Inns of Court lost some creative edge, as their members increasingly became consumers rather than producers of drama, poetry and the arts in general. The Middle Temple continued to patronise players and playwrights, most famously William Shakespeare (whose *Twelfth Night*, performed 'At our feast' on 2 February 1602, was noted appreciatively by the student and future barrister John Manningham[48]). A few years later William Crashawe, father of the poet and himself a scholarly bibliophile, editor and theological controversialist, described the two Temples as 'the most comfortable and delightfull company for a Scholler, that (out of the Vniuersities) this kingdome yeelds'.[49] Among Crashawe's congregation at the Temple Church, where he was employed as lecturer or preacher from 1605–13, Middle Templars included the verbose essayist Anthony Benn, later recorder of London, to whom Ben Jonson dedicated a poetical epigram; William Martin, later Recorder of Exeter and author of a popular *Historie . . . of the Kings of England* (1615); and the polyglot translator and bibliophile Robert Ashley, best known as founder of the present Middle Temple Library. In 1641 Ashley bequeathed to the house his personal library of some 5,000 volumes (having 'addicted myselfe to the general studdy of the great booke of the world, wherin all the glorious workes of God are comprehended'), plus an endowment for a library keeper.[50] Most of Crashawe's extensive collection of books and manuscripts was dispersed when he reluctantly left the Temple. But he may

[45] R Spalding (ed), *The Diary of Bulstrode Whitelocke 1605–1675* (Oxford, British Academy, 1990), 73–76.

[46] Bodl, MS Ashmole 826, fo 52 is a summons from 'Richard Pr de l'amour' for the attendance of 'o[u]r trusty and well beloud servant Mr John Jarrett', 'Given under o[u]r Privy Seale the xxvith day of december Anno D[o]m[i]ni 1635 And of our Dominion the first'. Cf PG Pizzorno, *The Ways of Paradox from Lando to Donne* (Florence, Olschki, 2007), 116–20.

[47] See further Jessica Winston, Literary Associations of the Middle Temple, below, p 147.

[48] R P Sorlien (ed), *The Diary of John Manningham of the Middle Templle, 1602-1603* (Hanover, NH, University of Rhode Island, 1976), 48.

[49] W Crashawe, *Romish Forgeries and Falsifications* (London, M. Lownes and R Field, 1606), sig 3.

[50] *ODNB*; *MTR*, ii., 917–18; Prest, *Barristers*, above n 1, at 198–201.

be the source of the Inn's two large Molyneux Globes, now the sole surviving pair of the first globes designed and published in England, since he had offered to sell to the house 'one of the fairest paire of globes in England'.[51]

Various autobiographical sources amply confirm the possibilities for cultural exchange and stimulus available to members of the Middle Temple throughout this period. Edward Hyde's acquaintance 'whilst he was only a student of the law' included the great names of Ben Jonson and John Selden, among other poets, playwrights and scholars; as the antiquary and biographer John Aubrey put it, recalling his student days at Oxford and 'the Middle Temple (off and on)' just after the first civil war, 'I (for the most part) enjoyed the greatest felicity of life (ingeniose youths, like Rosebudds, imbibe the morning dew'.[52] Yet religious and political tensions increasingly absorbed energies previously devoted to the arts and scholarship. Although the ideal of the gentleman virtuoso-lawyer with a serious interest in 'polite learning and history' continued to be exemplified by men like Hyde himself, and Francis North, later Lord Keeper, the latter's brother and biographer Roger was careful to deny that Francis had ever 'frequented either dancing or fencing scools; which are rendezvouzes not only expencive, but also dangerous to unexperienced youth in London'.[53] A narrower professional orientation is also apparent in the advice of the aged bencher Sir John Strode (d 1642) for his eldest son to 'get Learning' in Latin and the laws of England ('next after the lawes of God'):

> hebrewe & greeke, the french and Italian . . . leave them to others, whose study and travayle requires to be conversant with strange tongues ... .[54]

Study of the common law was now primarily a matter of reading and summarising case notes, formularies and treatises, both printed and manuscript, combined with attendance at sittings of the courts. The traditional learning exercises served a useful supplementary educational purpose. Case-putting, or the argument of hypothetical scenarios and complex points of law in moots, at readings and more informally over dinner in hall, provided a particularly valuable training in advocacy and argument. As 'Iron whetteth Iron, conversation ripeneth man's Judgment' declared Anthony Benn; according to Francis North, 'a man could scarce be a good lawyer unless he were a good put-case'.[55] In the later sixteenth

---

[51] RM Fisher, 'William Crashawe and the Middle Temple Globes 1605–15' (1974) 140 *The Geographical Journal* 105–12.

[52] [E Hyde], *The Life of Edward, Earl of Clarendon* (Oxford, Oxford Universiy Press, 1759), 59–61; OL Dick (ed), *Aubrey's Brief Lives* (Harmondsworth, Penguin, 1962), 27.

[53] *ODNB*; M Chan (ed), *The Life of the Lord Keeper North by Roger North* (Lewiston, E Mellen Press, 1995), 14.

[54] Prest, *Barristers*, above n 1, at 205.

[55] Cambridge University Library, MS D.d.5.14, fo. 8; Chan (ed), above n 53, at 16.

and early seventeenth century there are occasional recorded instances of failure to observe the complex pattern of term and vacation exercises laid down by long usage, and overseen by a servant known as the 'Exercise Butler', who had the duty of entering in his 'moot book' and then filing the paper cases drafted by students.[56] But such defaults were by no means unprecedented, while surviving books of case notes, such as those 'collect per moy John Barton in le Hale de Middle Temple M[ichaelemas] 13° Caroli 1637 & apres', suggest that students and barristers alike continued to value and benefit from the performance of case-argument exercises.[57] More serious problems affected the twice-yearly readings or lectures, the most elaborate, prestigious and prolonged form of learning exercise. At the Middle Temple, alone among the four Inns, full membership of the Bench was reserved until the 1640s for those who had previously delivered a reading in the house. But by the end of the previous century so many barristers had chosen to pay a fine rather than undertake this costly and intellectually demanding task that a new rank of membership between bencher and barrister was created. 'Ancients' sat at a separate table in hall and were freed from participation in learning exercises: in the 1630s it was deemed 'no disgrace for any man to be removed hither, for by reason of the great and excessive charge of readings' many learned and prosperous practitioners had taken that option. Recurrent attempts to restrain the competitive expenditure of readers on the drinking and feasting which had always accompanied such lectures points to their ineffectiveness.[58]

Multiple surviving manuscript copies of some early seventeenth century Middle Temple readings, such as those of Francis Moore on charitable uses and James Whitelocke on benefices, testify to their wide circulation. Yet the jurisprudential value of such discourses was in decline, for the growing authority attributed to reported judicial decisions tended to marginalise the common learning of the profession, in so far as this was embodied in arguments and opinions delivered at readings. And since individual readers were free to lecture upon whatever statute they liked, it could hardly be claimed that even an extended sequence of readings constituted anything like a comprehensive introduction to the legislative component of English law. Nor did readers always place the instruction of students before their own professional preoccupations (hence the 'Hazard of Reputation' which James Whitelocke identified as part of a reader's 'Burden'). Peter Ball maintained that 'Ostentation & Exercise of his owne Witt & Learning,

---

[56] Inner Temple Archives, Miscellaneous MS XXIV, fo 35: 'The Manner of doeing Exercise in ye Midd: Temple as I was informed by Mr Thomas Seingoe ye Exercise Butler'.

[57] Lincoln's Inn, Bevir MS, 'Bacons Law Maxims Etc' (Cupboard CIV), unfoliated; cf Cambridge University Library, D.d.5.14 (Thomas Wateridge's notes of Middle Temple moots and readings, 1611–14).

[58] Prest, *Inns of Court*, above n 1, at 60–63.

meere quiddities and curious questions' were the stock-in-trade of 'our usual Readers'.[59] When Ball wrote these words, readings had been suspended since the outbreak of civil war between King and Parliament in August 1642. They did not resume again until 1661. In the 1630s a Middle Temple bencher lamented that '[h]eretofore the Readings contynued by the space of a Month, Afterwards three weekes, and now latelie not a fortnight'; during their brief revival in the 1660s and 1670s, few readings lasted more than a week.[60]

Once Ball had delivered his own lectures on the first chapter of Magna Carta in 1641 he remained an active bencher for the next 35 years. Appointment the previous year as King's Counsel and Queen's Attorney-General had not sufficed to win him this promotion, although he had been 'associated' to the Bench since 1636 on becoming Solicitor-General to the Queen. The latter office seems to have determined Ball's allegiance during the civil war, when he followed the royal couple to Oxford, where he was both knighted and awarded an honorary Doctorate of Civil Law. But by 1647 Ball was back again at the Middle Temple, and understandably anxious to redeem his fortunes from 'the ill condition whereinto the publike deluge hath involved me'. So he wrote in 1649 to Bulstrode Whitelocke, a fellow Middle Templar, by far his junior in years and professional standing, but now, as one of the Lords Commissioners of the Great Seal of the Commonwealth of England, potentially capable of furthering a project which might save both Ball's own career and the law itself from what he termed that 'ignorance, calumny and ruine, which now much menace it'.[61]

Ball sought to address what he believed to be the root cause of hostility, both among the population at large and many leading figures in the new republican regime, towards the common law, and its practitioners. This was the impenetrability of the law's 'vast & indigested Chaos', not just to the general public, but also to students and practitioners. So besides 'divulging the Laws in English, that all persons, that will or shall bee capable, may read & understand them', it was necessary to reduce their complexities

> into one entire body & scientificall method, by extracting out of all those particulars, such generalls, as may Comprehend all the particulars related in our bookes, & all others that may happen.

---

[59] 'Whitelocke's Reading', fos 3, 4v; BL MS Additional 32096, fo 178; W Prest, 'Law reform and legal education in Interregnum England' (2002) 57 *Historical Research* 112, at 121.

[60] Brerewood MS, at 20.

[61] *ODNB*; Prest, above n 59, at 117–18.

Ball claimed to have invented a 'method' which would enable both common law and statute to be abbreviated into a manageably small compass, as also to have 'fully and methodically perfected and reduced, out of vast volumes of all sortes of authors, into 5 or 6 quire of paper', what he termed the 'Precognitions' or philosophical fundamentals of 'Generall Jurisprudence divine, ecclesiastical and civil'.[62]

That the common law could and should be 'methodised' in a rational, systematic fashion for learning and teaching purposes was not a novel claim. Ball's originality lay rather in propounding adoption of his scheme as the basis for a wholesale reform of legal education. Instead of 'students studying itt in the Chaos of our bookes, without a guide or tutor', the State should establish 'a publicke Lecture[r] & Reader of the Lawe'. Equipped with the author's method, this person would expound his entire subject over the space of three years, giving three lectures a week 'one houre at the least, in the morning, between ten and eleven through the whole year' (except for spring and summer vacations), and 'arguing cases, by the Students, upon each lecture the same day'. The Middle Temple hall ('as most indifferent to all the Innes of Court & most capable & co[m]modious') would serve as lecture theatre and moot court, with 'the Library designed in the Middle Temple . . . forthwith prepared & furnished with bookes fitted for his & all students' use'.[63]

Needless to say, this far-sighted proposal for something like an Inns of Court Law School—plainly written by Ball on his own behalf, at least so far as the specified qualifications and terms of employment of the proposed reader were concerned—went no further. Establishing a single readership to serve all four Inns would have been more practicable than instituting the 'two professors of the law to direct young students' whom John Cooke had urged each society to appoint some years before.[64] But given the extent of antagonism towards the legal profession among the victorious Parliament and its army, not to mention their more radical supporters, such a project had no chance of gaining official support, with or without Whitelocke's backing. So law students continued to struggle as best they could, sometimes joining together for mutual support and assistance, as with the group of Middle Templars and others who 'usually met at appointed times and by turnes did read upon the Writs in Fitzherbert's *Natura Brevium* and lent each other their readings' in the late 1650s.[65]

The Middle Temple benchers showed themselves anxious to revive and maintain the traditional learning exercises, up to a point. Thus during the 1650s they made orders for keeping up moots and other exercises in

---

[62] Prest, above n 59, at 120–21.
[63] *Ibid*, at 120–22.
[64] Prest, *Inns of Court*, above n 1, at 170–73.
[65] British Library, MS Lansdowne 1169, fo 1.

traditional form, insisting that benchers themselves must participate, that barristers should formulate pleadings to moot cases, and that such cases must be argued *viva voce*, not read. (This last provision may well indicate that the aural learning exercises were becoming perfunctory rituals, performed solely in order to fulfil prescribed qualifications for call to the Bar.) But there is no evidence of any attempt to restore the twice-yearly lectures until after the return of the monarchy in 1660, when external pressure from the judges and Lord Chancellor Clarendon eventually spurred all four houses to action.[66] Then the problem was to find barristers willing to shoulder the financial and intellectual burden of a reading. As we have seen, this was not a novel difficulty, and the long cessation of readings had created a considerable backlog of potential readers. But these men were now aged in their early sixties, rather than (as before the civil war) their late forties.[67] The professional advantages of undertaking a reading in order to become a full bencher were also less compelling than before. That became starkly apparent when the 41-year-old Francis North was made King's Counsel in 1668. The Middle Temple's benchers refused to add him to their number, 'alledging that if yong men, by favour so preferred, came up strait to the bench . . . it might in time destroy the government of the society'. North simply reported that fact to the Chief Justices, who then refused to allow any Middle Temple bencher to plead before them, until 'they had done their duty in calling Mr North to their bench'.[68]

Three years later North staged his 'publique reading in the Midle Temple Hall', a famously extravagant occasion. According to his brother-biographer, while

> some might attend the exercises, where learned men argued pro and con upon the reader's cases, yet more attended at the festivall dinners, which were very sumptuous and expensive

in this case amounting to 'at least £1000, in pure feasting', accompanied by riotous disorder during the serving of the food.[69] Readings nevertheless continued to be delivered at the Middle Temple over the next few years. If rising expectations of the hospitality readers felt obliged to provide at ever-increasing expense were among the causes of their eventual cessation, it must nevertheless be said that the provision of excessive hospitality by readers had provoked complaints as far back as the early sixteenth century.

---

[66]   *MTR*, iii., 1019, 1028, 1030, 1050, 1105, 1114, 1152, 1153, 1159.

[67]   Prest, *Inns of Court*, above n 1, 60, 112; cf letters in MT.3/MEM from William Lane (7 January 1662), Anthony Barker (10 May 1662) and Balthazar Beare (6 May 1667), citing their advanced years among other reasons for declining to read.

[68]   Chan (ed), above n 53, at 177; *MTR*, iii., 1229. However, the assumption that King's Counsel became benchers *ipso facto* was not universally accepted thereafter; see ch 3 of this book at p 220.

[69]   Chan (ed), above n 53, at 41–42.

Other disincentives were not in short supply either. The growing variety of printed legal literature made the traditional learning exercises seem ever more marginal to the business of learning the law, while recurrent financial crises in the 1660s and 1670s placed the Inn's rulers under enormous pressure to commute formal academic obligations into cash fines. The final blow may well have been the devastating Temple fire of 26–27 January 1679 (which Parliament cited to justify releasing that summer's elected reader from any obligation to read, while nevertheless according him the full status of bencher on payment of £300).[70] The disruptive effects of the fire must have been exacerbated by the prolonged political crisis which had followed Titus Oates's sensational revelations of a supposed popish conspiracy to murder the King and subjugate his loyal Protestant subjects. After several conferences between October 1679 and February 1680 with the judges, about readings and the seniority of benchers who had not read, in June 1680 North's close political ally Sir Francis Wythens was chosen Autumn reader. Wythens was licensed to read for one, two or three days, or not at all, and accorded all the rights of a reader on paying the sum of £200, with the same conditions applying to all subsequent readers over the next four years.[71] Such an arrangement did nothing to prevent and may well have encouraged the final degeneration of moots and other case-argument exercises into largely meaningless rituals, revenue raisers for the Inn rather than instructional resources for its students.

III.   GOVERNMENT AND BELIEF, POWER AND IDEOLOGY

Notwithstanding their extra-parochial autonomy and unincorporated status, the early modern Inns of Court could hardly escape the central government's gaze and direction. State surveillance and supervision increased markedly during the second half of the sixteenth century, driven largely by fears that the Inns might constitute receptive sanctuaries and recruiting grounds for opponents of the new Protestant state church formally established at the beginning of Elizabeth's reign. When Reformation confronted Counter-Reformation, religion was no mere subjective matter of personal choice and belief, but rather a crucial aspect of State policy and national security. Hence the surveys which reported to Elizabeth's Privy Council not only membership and accommodation statistics,

---

[70] *MTR*, iii., 1321. For the fire and its consequences, see ch 3 pp 205–206, 210 of this book.

[71] *MTR*, iii., 1321, 1333. Readers had continued to be appointed regularly at the first Michaelmas parliament before the fire, and were again nominated in October 1679 for the following Lent and Summer readings: *MTR*, iii., 1306, 1314, 1323. Prof Baker's list of post-1662 MT readings (*Readers and Readings in the Inns of Court and Chancery* (2000) 13 *Selden Society Supplementary Series*, 182–83) includes only those for which there is manuscript or other evidence that the reading was actually performed.

but also religious alignments within each house. While less prominent in these returns than Gray's Inn, the Middle Temple was the society of Edmund Plowden, the most distinguished of all Elizabethan Roman Catholic lawyers, who had been elected a bencher in the last year of Mary Tudor's brief reign, but remained a member of the governing body until his death in 1585, when he was buried in the Temple Church. Plowden and his co-religionist Thomas Pagitt (said to owe his post as under-treasurer to Plowden's influence) were accused in 1580 of being primarily responsible for the fact that 'the Middle Temple is pestred with papistes'.[72] During the following decade various individuals expelled on suspicion of their Catholic sympathies were restored only on certifying their 'detestation in writing of Popish religion'.[73] Three Essex families of recusant gentry well represented at the Middle Temple, the Brownes, the Petres and the Wisemans, were joined in 1594 by a trio of aristocratic Catholics—Henry Percy, ninth Earl of Northumberland, and his brother Charles, together with that 'great captain' of the papists, Anthony Browne, Viscount Montague.[74] Another eminent Middle Temple bencher, best known as inventor of the lease and release conveyancing technique, was Francis Moore, leader of the Chancery Bar under Lord Keeper Ellesmere (himself a lapsed Catholic), who numbered the Percy family among his clients; Moore's wife was a reputed papist, his daughter had married into a Catholic family, and he himself appointed a notorious recusant as overseer of his will.[75] Catholics still frequented the Middle Temple in the early 1620s; on the evening of 2 January 1622, Simonds D'Ewes casually noted 'some discourse with two or three papists in our buttries'.[76]

But what does the association of individual Catholics with the Middle Temple tell us about the society's overall religious complexion? Searching for any such thing might seem futile, given the Inn's comparatively loose-knit institutional structure and sheer lack of evidence about the religious—or indeed, political—views of the majority of its members. But the attitudes, beliefs and ideology of at least the benchers as a group, and occasionally other members as well, may sometimes be inferred from their dealings with the lecturers, preachers or 'readers of divinity' chosen to deliver sermons in the Temple Church. While the clergymen appointed to

---

[72]   G de C Parmiter, 'Elizabethan Popish Recusancy in the Inns of Court', *Bulletin of the Institute of Historical Research*, Special Supplement No 11 (1976), 27–29, 46–47; N Jones, *The English Reformation Religion and Cultural Adaptation* (Oxford, Blackwell, 2002), 124–25, 127–28.

[73]   *Ibid*, 30–31. CH Hopwood (ed), *A Calendar of Middle Temple Records* (London, Middle Temple, 1903), 25.

[74]   Prest, *Inns of Court*, above n 1, at 179.

[75]   Prest, *Barristers*, above n 1, at 212–13; ODNB.

[76]   E Bourcier (ed), *The Diary of Sir Simonds D'Ewes 1622–1624* (Paris, Didier, 1974), 56.

the mastership of the Temple by the Crown might preach occasionally, zealous Protestants hungry for pulpit expositions of God's word were not to be satisfied with a single Sunday sermon. It was also argued that a diet of evangelical preaching would help insulate the Inn's young gentlemen from Catholic proselytising. However, the appointment of Antony de Corro, a converted Spanish Jew and former Hieronymite monk, as first reader of divinity at the Temple Church (or at any Inn of Court) in 1571 preceded the initial post-Reformation Catholic missionary campaign in England. Despite powerful friends at court and in the episcopate, Corro's personality and his theology both brought him into conflict with Richard Alvey, a middle-aged Marian exile who had been master of the Temple since 1560. Alvey's orthodox Calvinism may well have been offended by Corro's unconventional doctrinal views, 'and speaking not wisely of predestination', which also disturbed some members of his Temple Church congregation. But it was not until 1578, when Corro was about to obtain a university lectureship at Oxford, that the Middle Temple benchers agreed their preacher should be 'licensed to depart without contribution or reward'.[77]

Corro's immediate successor was one 'Mr Chatterton', possibly Laurence Chaderton, the influential founding master of Emmanuel College, Cambridge. His brief and undocumented sojourn was followed by the engagement of a leading Presbyterian activist, Walter Travers, chosen by the now ailing Alvey and three members of the Ecclesiastical High Commission (an arm's-length arrangement approved by the benchers of both Temple societies). Travers worked energetically with Alvey to establish a more godly reformed discipline in the two Temple societies, including the Genevan-style appointment of 'such as he can persuade' to act as deacons and elders monitoring attendance at and conduct during church services, a plan seemingly accepted more readily by the Middle Temple Bench than their counterparts at the other house. But on Alvey's death in 1584 Travers was blocked from succeeding him by Archbishop Whitgift, who claimed that 'the greater and better number of both the Temples' disapproved of the liturgical innovations Travers had introduced. It seems possible that Travers enjoyed more support from the Middle than the Inner house, for on Richard Hooker's appointment to the mastership the Inner Temple parliament agreed to inform Travers that his services were no longer required. The Middle Temple made no such order, and indeed the same parliament which endorsed the levying of identical termly contributions for Hooker as Alvey had received also permitted Travers to keep his servant at Clerks' Commons with the benchers' men.[78]

---

[77] *ODNB*; Prest, *Inns of Court*, above n 1, at 190–91.
[78] Prest, *Inns of Court*, above n 1, at 193–94; *MTR*, i., 279.

Travers stayed on at the Temple for another two years, even after Whitgift had banned him from preaching, thereby ending his celebrated Temple Church debate with Hooker, who had sought to maintain that even papists might ultimately find salvation.[79] Thereafter no lecturer was appointed to supplement the master's sermons at the Temple Church for nearly 20 years, perhaps partly owing to difficulty in finding a candidate acceptable to both houses, as well as the changed ecclesiastical and political climate, now much less open to using puritan preachers as a weapon against popery. Yet Travers might not have been too disappointed by the man eventually agreed upon in 1605 as his successor. William Crashawe was an effective and prolific preacher, a committed anti-Romanist and editor of the works of the great Cambridge puritan theologian William Perkins. Despite Crashawe's later claim to have been appointed 'by the mutuall act of both the houses', the Inner Temple was now the active partner, taking the lead both in protracted negotiations about re-establishing a lectureship and Crashawe's eventual nomination 'for the better instruction of the gentlemen of this house'. From the start Crashawe enjoyed less support within the Middle Temple, judging by the difficulty with which levies were collected there towards his annual stipend. When in November 1609 the Bench responded to Crashawe's complaints by more than doubling the rate, ostensibly to ensure a minimum of £10 was raised every term, some 60 barristers signed a petition of protest expressing their 'generall dislike'. They pointed out ('w[i]thout offence') that as Crashawe held a benefice in Yorkshire, it was 'fitt [he] should attend elsewhere'. Moreover, the proposed new 'tax' was three times that charged for Dr Thomas Masters, who had been master of the Temple since 1601: 'o[u]r owne Pastor, whome wee esteeeme learned and industrious and resideth amonge us all the Yeare'.[80]

Relations with the Middle Temple were not improved by Crashawe's bluntness of manner, unauthorised building activities, financial imprudence (as a profligate collector of rare books and manuscripts) and censure by convocation for 'some points that hath fallen from his Pen and Tongue'.[81] Religious non-conformity seems not to have been the key issue, since besides some identifiable anti-puritans among the petitioners—for example, the diarist John Manningham, his friend Edward Curll and the poet John Hoskyns—their number included various godly brethren, such as Thomas Greene and Thomas Trist. What sealed Crashawe's fate was the

---

[79] Travers was still in residence and receiving payments from the Middle Temple as late as November 1586: *MTR*, i., 287; *ODNB*. See Jones, above n 72, at 129–30.

[80] MT.15/TAM 6, 'The utterbarresters peticon ... concerning Mr Crashawe'. The *ODNB* (*sv* W Crashawe) mistakenly attributes this protest to the Inner Temple.

[81] RM Fisher, 'The Predicament of William Crashawe Preacher at the Temple, 1605–1613' (1974) 25 *Journal of Ecclesiastical History* 268.

large number of discontented barristers (a clear majority of the Middle Temple Bar) and the evident absence from the Middle Temple Bench of any such influential and 'beloued friends' as the future judges George Croke and John Walter, both still Inner Templars.[82]

Hence despite a vigorous delaying campaign, and claims that 'the great number of the younger gents' at the Middle Temple wished him to stay, Crashawe failed to persuade the rulers of that house to continue his stipend.[83] When at last it became clear in 1613 that his departure was imminent, King James himself wrote to both houses recommending one Alexander Simpson, a Glasgow graduate, for the vacancy. Given the strength of anti-Scottish xenophobia,[84] not least among common lawyers, this proposal understandably aroused little enthusiasm, and may well have encouraged the Middle Temple benchers' decision that Crashawe's successor should be nominated by the master of the Temple.[85] Dr Masters's diplomatic choice fell upon Abraham Gibson, a rising young royal chaplain, whose good relations with the Middle house were evidenced by the benchers' cash gift when he took the degree of Bachelor of Divinity at Cambridge University in 1617. On Gibson's departure the following year, Thomas Chafin, chaplain to the courtier Earl of Pembroke, replaced him. More than 20 years on, when Chafin was accused in the Long Parliament of preaching High Church sermons, Simonds D'Ewes recalled him as 'never . . . deepe scholler but to say noe worst of him a sociable man'.[86]

So their backing of the Presbyterian Walter Travers scarcely presaged further support by the Middle Temple's rulers for puritan preachers at the Temple Church. Indeed, under James and Charles I the Middle Temple was anything but a hotbed of constitutionalist or religious opposition. Apart from John Hoskyns and James Whitelocke, who both adopted a more guarded stance after youthful indiscretions, John Pym's sponsor William

---

[82] Cf the dedication to four named Inner Temple benchers of Crashawe's translation *Querela sive Dialogus Animae et Corporis Damnati* (London, 1613), sig A3. Crashawe's publicity efforts on behalf of the Virginia Company were evidently insufficient to galvanise on his behalf the Middle Temple benchers and fellow investors William Gibbes, Henry Montague and Thomas Stephens: *ODNB*; TK Rabb, *Enterprise and Empire* (Cambridge, MA, Harvard University Press, 1967), 273, 298, 344, 383.

[83] Fisher, above n 81, at 273–74.

[84] North, in *Notes of Me The Autobiography of Roger North*, ed P Millard (Toronto, University of Toronto Press, 2000), at 118, writing with reference to James I's grant of 1608, said 'It has bin wondered that there was not such a grant before, but that the lawyers should buy and sell chambers, and be all that while precarious to the crowne (whose scite it was) for the whole. But it seems in that reigne the greediness of the Scotchmen was such that, the lawyers then were afraid that they should be granted (as Midle-Row in Holborne, and other such places had bin) to them, which would have flead them to the quick'.

[85] *MTR*, ii, 985, 565.

[86] Prest, *Inns of Court*, above n 1, at 198–99. As a Middle Temple student D'Ewes had himself socialised with Chafin and frequently attended his sermons: Bourcier (ed), above n 76, 60, 62 *et passim*.

Whitaker, and John Winthrop's business adviser John White, vocal spokes-
men for English liberties are hard to find among the senior ranks of Middle
Templars during the four decades before the Long Parliament met. (The
Inner Temple, by contrast, produced three leading parliamentary-political
activists of the 1620s in Edward Coke, Edward Littleton and John Selden.)
At the Middle Temple clients of Buckingham and other office holders
under the Crown were very well represented: among them Peter Ball,
Anthony Benn, Robert Henley, Nicholas Hyde, Richard Lane, the Montague brothers Henry and Sidney, Walter Pye and James Whitelocke. And
while it is possible to identify a few godly Middle Temple puritan
benchers—such as Henry Haule, John Puleston, Robert Tanfield and John
White again—we can also point to their opposites, men who might well
have been ill-disposed to Crashawe. William Bastard, for example, specified that his funeral sermon should be delivered by a minister who 'shall
live orderly submitting himself to the government of the church'; William
Gibbes claimed to 'detest and abhor' puritanism, while John Strode urged
his son to 'Reverence the Priests . . . intercessors between God and us',
whatever their personal failings.[87]

Of course this is not to say that politico-religious discontent and
dissidence were entirely absent from the Middle Temple, especially during
the 1620s and 1630s. Evidence to the contrary comes in various forms: the
scattering of 'libels' (handwritten attacks on measures and ministers), diary
and other records of political gossip and rumour, and occasional public
demonstrations, like the toast drunk to the exiled[88] Protestant heroine
Elizabeth of Bohemia at the Middle Temple Christmas of 1621, implicitly
critical of England's non-intervention in the Thirty Years War. Yet even if
the King was impelled to warn members of the Inns against discussing
'state matters' in 1623, these were all relatively peripheral issues so far as
the Middle Temple's rulers were concerned.[89]

Charles I's accession saw a notable intensification of official efforts to
supervise and regulate the Inns of Court. But there was no overt resistance
to the tide of governmental admonition and instruction. In view of the
difficulties experienced with the holding of unauthorised Christmas commons during the 1630s, 'to the disturbance of government and increase
and maintenance of disorder', the Middle Temple benchers probably
welcomed attempts by the Crown and judges to reinforce their internal
authority over barristers and students. So far as they were concerned, the
most sensitive matter addressed by Charles I's Government was the

---

[87] See Prest, *Barristers*, above n 1, App E, for further biographical details.
[88] James I's daughter Elizabeth and her husband Frederick, Elector Palatine, were forced
to flee their kingdom of Bohemia following the victory of imperial Catholic forces at the
battle of Prague in 1621.
[89] Prest, *Inns of Court*, above n 1, at 222.

long-running dispute between the two Temple societies and Dr Paul Micklethwaite, a former Cambridge don appointed master of the Temple in 1628 after having impressed 'the whole body of both our societies' with his sermons.[90] Unfortunately Micklethwaite seems to have taken his new title rather too literally, leasing out part of the church yard and demanding precedence in the halls of both Inns, while claiming episcopal jurisdiction and the right to 10 per cent of the lawyers' earnings as his tithe. If these extraordinary assertions of clerical rights were encouraged by the new Arminian ecclesiastical dispensation, they did not win support from the various arbitrators to whom the dispute was referred. Nevertheless Micklethwaite received the King's assent that the Temple Church might be disposed as a chapel royal, with railed altar, candles and restricted access except at times of divine service.

The benchers of both societies had good reason to treat Micklethwaite's incursions and pretensions very seriously, although the Middle Temple rejected a proposal from the Inner house to bring a joint action of trespass, 'supposing it would render us much to obloquy'.[91] But by 1640 Micklethwaite himself was dead, Scotland was in rebellion against Archbishop Laud's attempt to impose the English *Book of Common Prayer*, and financial crisis was about to terminate 11 years of non-parliamentary government. In these circumstances the Middle Temple's Lent reading by the Northamptonshire Calvinist Edward Bagshaw on the statute *Pro Clero*—concerning the temporal powers of the clergy—understandably struck the Archbishop as ill-timed. In an unprecedented intervention Bagshaw was ordered to cease lecturing. The silenced reader became a minor celebrity: '[S]carce any reader ever before was ever attended out of town with such a number of gentlemen of the same house'.[92]

If Bagshaw and the Middle Temple thereby contributed to the unpopularity of Laud and his ecclesiastical regime, dissatisfaction with the King and his ministers was now widespread. Lacking formal parliamentary representation (unlike the two universities), the Inns of Court took no direct part in the Long Parliament's proceedings. They also scarcely figured in its debates, unlike the much-criticised universities, even though slightly more MPs had Inns of Court experience than were Oxford or Cambridge alumni. Commons' committees continued to meet in the Middle Temple hall as they had long been accustomed to do, and Middle Templars were among the 500 armed men who marched from Holborn to Whitehall in the political crisis of late December 1641, offering their services to the King. But in response to warning messages from the House a few days later, the

---

[90] *ODNB*; Prest, *Inns of Court*, above n 1, at 199–201.
[91] Inner Temple Archives, *Miscellanea*, XXXI, 'A Treatise on the Duties of the Officers and Members', at 9.
[92] Prest, *Inns of Court*, above n 1, at 214–15; *ODNB*.

Inns protested their loyalty to both King and Parliament, the Middle Templars adding that 'their intention to defend the king's person was no more than they were therunto bound by the oathes of allegiance and supremacie'.[93]

In the months immediately preceding the outbreak of war, the Middle Temple benchers abandoned attempts to reach agreement with the Inner house on the choice of a lecturer for the Temple Church to supplement the preaching of Dr John Littleton, recently installed as master of the Temple. Their unilateral choice fell on Hugh Cressy, at a loose end in London after the politically-motivated trial and execution of Thomas Wentworth, Earl of Strafford and formerly Lord Deputy in Ireland, whose chaplain he had been. Recommended by James Ussher, the eirenical archibishop of Armagh, Cressy was also part of the Great Tew group associated with Lucius Cary, Viscount Falkland and his friend Edward Hyde, now a leading voice for moderate conservative opinion in Parliament and the nation. Cressy however joined the King (and Littleton) at Oxford early in 1643, subsequently converting to Catholicism and joining the Benedictine order.[94] Nothing is known of his time at the Temple Church.

Neither do the surviving Bench Minutes hint at the impending cataclysm, although the treasurer's accounts (which survive from 1637 onwards) record expenditure in October 1641 to repair muskets and acquire ammunition.[95] The 1642 summer reading was apparently held as usual, but no parliament met at the Middle Temple between June and November of that year, and only one in 1643. Its brief record endorsed the watch kept by two servants every night, noting the abandonment of commons in 'these hard and troublous times'.[96] Parliament's requisition 'upon the publique faith' of silver plate and candlesticks from the Temple Church that summer goes unmentioned, although subsequent entries for 1644 and 1645 provide partial glimpses of the wholesale confiscation of chambers held by 'delinquents and Papists'. Personal ties sometimes helped soften that blow; when Bulstrode Whitelocke gained possession of the Bench chamber formerly held by the royalist Richard Lane, 'he tooke care to preserve the writings, bookes, & manuscripts there belonging to Mr Lane, who was his friend'.[97] The eminent Puritan minister George Newton, exiled from his Taunton vicarage by a royalist army of occupation, was installed in Cressy's place by order of the House of Commons, while the learned Anabaptist John Tombes became master of the Temple. Neither

---

[93] Prest, *Inns of Court*, above n 1, at 223, 234–36.
[94] *MTR*, ii., 920–21; *ODNB* (which does not mention Cressy's Middle Temple connection).
[95] Hopwood (ed), above n 73, 156.
[96] *MTR*, ii., 929.
[97] MT.15/TAM/80a; MT.1/MIS; *MTR*, ii., 930–41; Spalding (ed), above n 45, at 150.

lasted long, nor made much impression on his congregation; after Tombes had returned to his native Worcestershire in 1646, the Middle Temple agreed to pay him a parting gift—but as for 'his preaching in the House, it is altogether denied him'.[98] His successor as both master and preacher was the more conformable and discreet Richard Johnson, whose lack of qualms about infant baptism later enabled him to christen Bulstrode Whitelocke's son in what had become the family's 'Temple Lodgings'.[99]

For reasons that are unclear—and probably in the last analysis unfathomable—the Middle Temple's ruling body seems to have been somewhat more evenly divided between parliamentarians and royalists than was the case at the other three houses.[100] The relative strength of Middle Temple royalism—if indeed the benchers were in this respect representative of the society's active membership—may have reflected a distinctive tradition of moderate episcopalian churchmanship and constitutionalism, as exemplified by the later earl of Clarendon. That the law courts remained in London after the outbreak of hostilities predisposed many senior practitioners to the anti-royalist side, except perhaps Crown law officers, who were well represented among the Middle Temple benchers. Their small and declining numbers 'by reason of these unnaturall civil warres' led to a major break with tradition; in October 1645, four senior barristers were associated to the Bench, on the understanding that they would later read in their turn. A still more ominous departure from previous practice occurred three years later, when Bulstrode Whitelocke, following his appointment as one of the Parliamentary Commissioners for the Great Seal, was first associated but then 'called to sit with the Masters of the Bench in Parliament'.[101]

Yet throughout the late 1640s and 1650s, the Middle Temple gradually resumed something like its pre-war pattern of existence, as admissions to the house and to chambers rebounded and exercises (other than readings) revived. In 1654, barristers and students petitioned for a further return to the status quo ante by ridding the Inn of women and children, while in 1657 the Bench insisted that gowns be worn in the Temple Church.[102] Following Richard Johnston's retirement in 1658, the Inner and Middle house jointly agreed to invite Dr Ralph Brownrigg, consecrated bishop of Exeter and deposed master of St Catharine's College, Cambridge, to become preacher. Brownrigg's sermons attracted overflow congregations;

[98] *ODNB*; MT Bench Book, 301–02, 309; *MTR*, ii., 945.
[99] Spalding (ed), above n 45, at 202.
[100] Cf Prest, *Inns of Court*, above n 1, at 237, which overstates the numbers of neutral/unknowns among the Middle Templars.
[101] *MTR*, ii., 935, 962, 959.
[102] *MTR*, iii., 1060, 1104.

his denial of the subject's right of resistance to a Christian ruler obviously struck a responsive chord. On his death less than a year later, Brownrigg was buried in the Temple Church, where his funeral sermon was preached by his successor and biographer John Gauden, who fully shared the bishop's theological and political principles, besides succeeding him in his diocese when the monarchy returned in May 1660.[103]

So despite the serious fears held by its depleted ruling body in the early 1650s for the very existence of the Inn (to say nothing of the common law and the legal profession), the Middle Temple had survived the greatest political and social upheaval in English history. Unsurprisingly, those now chosen as preachers in the Temple Church were solid Church-and-King men; from 1661–65 Dr Matthew Griffith, a former chaplain to Charles I and a hardened sufferer throughout the Interregnum, and then until 1685 James Buck, who had preached before the House of Lords at the Westminster Abbey thanksgiving service immediately following Charles II's arrival in London.[104] They would hardly have clashed with the new master of the Temple, Dr Richard Ball, a royal chaplain whose sole published sermon castigated Presbyterians, the Solemn League and Covenant, and all those 'who think that Obedience is due only unto God and vertuous Kings'.[105]

Yet the Middle Temple, like the other Inns, was not under the sway of a single head or ruler. Its treasurers were elected annually by a self-perpetuating oligarchy of senior members, with administrative power and responsibility resting in the hands of the salaried under-treasurer (from 1658 until 1711 the barrister and preacher's son James Buck, whose attempt to resign in 1703, after a mere 44 years' service, was rebuffed by the offer of additional assistance). Such a low-key administrative structure provided scope for individual initiative and varying levels of participation. It helped the society manage the disruptive impact of plague and other disease epidemics, destructive fires and floods, high levels of public violence and politico-religious conflict, in short the notably uncertain context of everyday life in early modern England. Unfortunately it was quite unsuited to reform or renovate the Inn's role as a school of law.

---

[103]   *ODNB*. The Middle Temple sought one 'Mr Buck' as preacher in November 1659, but then acquiesced in Gauden's appointment: *MTR*, iii., 1131, 1140, 1141–42, 1145. Johnson, Brownrigg and Gauden did not hold letters-patent as masters of the Temple, contrary to J B Williamson, *The Middle Temple Bench Book* 2nd edition (London, Middle Temple, 1937) 302: cf *ITR*, ii., cxxiv.

[104]   *ODNB*; J Buck, *St Paul's Thanksgiving* (London, John Playford, 1660).

[105]   R Ball, *The True Christian-man's Duty Both to God and the King* (London, John Playford, 1682), at 10.

The Maritime Connection

RICHARD HILL

T HE MIDDLE TEMPLE has tended to regard itself as the Inn of Court holding the strongest links with the maritime activities of Britain. Most of this belief is founded on the history of the Inn in the age of Queen Elizabeth I, and it is perpetuated in several publications of which Williamson's work[1] is the most celebrated.

On examination, some of the evidence—or assumptions—on which the claim is based turn out to be of doubtful validity; but other facts, not generally known, considerably strengthen it. On balance, as this article will seek to show, the claim is credible, even though some extrapolation from the known evidence is involved. Moreover, the Middle Temple continued to be concerned, sporadically and sometimes fortuitously, in the maritime life of the nation from that day to this.

I. SIR FRANCIS DRAKE

It is necessary to deal first with the most frequently cited claim: the link to the Inn of Sir Francis Drake. The Minutes of the Middle Temple parliament[2] record that on 4 August 1586 Drake came into Middle Temple Hall during dinner, was welcomed 'with great joy' by the reader and four named benchers, and spoke of his affection for the Inn ('*antiquam familiaritatem et amicitiam cum consortio generosum Medii Templi praedict*'). He was described, in that Minute of Parliament, as '*unus de Consortio Medii Templi*'.

This has been held[3] by HAC Sturgess, Librarian of the Inn in the mid-twentieth century and compiler of the admissions record, to be evidence that Drake was a member of the society. However, there is no

---

[1] JB Williamson, *The History of the Temple, London* (London, John Murray, 1924).
[2] *Middle Temple, Records (MTR)*, vol I, 285–86.
[3] Middle Temple, *Register of Admissions* (1949), vol I, 14, fn 4.

record of his admission. The Admissions Book[4] gets round this by postulating that Drake must have been admitted in the period before 1550, when there is a gap in the admission records. Yet this supposition is scarcely tenable. Though there is no firm documentation of Drake's birth date, and speculation on it ranges from 1538 to 1546, most authorities place it in 1541 or thereabouts. With great respect to those postulating Drake's membership, it seems most unlikely that a country family in Devon would have taken all the initiatives necessary to enter a boy short of his teens in one of the university-level teaching institutions of London.

Moreover, it is known that Drake was (much later) admitted a member of the Inner Temple, in fact on 28 January 1582.[5] This would have been a special admission, *honoris causa*, such as was accorded by individual Inns of Court, as we shall see, to other maritime adventurers in the 1580s and 1590s. But that fact makes the visit of Drake to Middle Temple Hall in 1586 more rather than less mysterious. There is no record of a visit by him to Inner Temple in that or any other year.[6] He was certainly at a height of fame and popularity, having recently returned from a highly profitable buccaneering expedition on the Spanish Main, and would have been sure of a welcome anywhere. Moreover, at the end of that expedition he had been instrumental in rescuing a large number of the first Roanoke settlers and bringing them back to Britain; and as we shall see in section II. below, Raleigh—a member of the Middle Temple—was the prime mover of that project, so was in his debt. This could have been the reason for an invitation to Middle Temple[7]; but there is no record of Raleigh's being present on the occasion.

There are other possibilities, all speculative. Was the Middle Temple trying to steal a march on Inner Temple by inviting Drake? Had he fallen out with Inner Temple in some way? Inner Temple records, and tradition, hold no clue[8]. Or (the writer confesses to being influenced by a recent biography of the cricketer Denis Compton, a notorious partygoer and often to the wrong party) did Drake go to the Middle Temple by mistake and then bluff it out? This is far-fetched of course.

As for Drake's being of the '*Consortio Medii Templi*', the word '*consortio*' could have interpretations other than formal membership; indeed, were it not for its use in the other Latin phrase quoted above

---

[4]   HAC Sturgess (ed), *Middle Temple Register of Admissions, vol 1, Years 1501–1781*.
[5]   FA Inderwick (ed), *A Calendar of the Inner Temple Records: vol I 1505–1603* (London, Inner Temple, 1896), lxxxviii and 318.
[6]   Conversation with Dr Clare Rider, Archivist of the Inner Temple, 9 May 2003.
[7]   LA Whitelaw, *The Molyneux Globes and the Middle Temple* (unpublished monograph, Middle Temple, London, 2003), 23. I am deeply indebted to this excellent work, on which much of this article is based.
[8]   Rider, above n 6.

('*amicitiam cum consortio generosum Medii Templi praedict*')[9] it could quickly be dismissed as implying Drake was simply a companion—boon-companion, indeed—of the Middle Temple. But the use of the word '*consortio*' in two places, one applying to Drake and the other to the society as a whole, does give one pause. Could the wording be stretched to imply a kind of honorary admittance on the occasion of that evening in 1586? If so, it was never formally endorsed by Parliament. The safer view is that Francis Drake was not a member of the Middle Temple but had strong social links with the Inn.

There remains the very strong oral tradition of Drake's Table. The story goes[10] that long after his death a deputation from the Inn went down to Deptford where the *Golden Hind* was lying, waiting to be broken up, and requested that they might take away the main hatch cover. This was made into a table which is now the Cupboard, the centrepiece of all formal activity in the Inn; lectures in Hall are given from it, and the Register of Calls is placed upon it when members are called to the Degree of the Utter Bar.

Though there is no original documentation to support this tradition, it is of great antiquity and has not, so far as is known, been seriously challenged. The other alleged material links with Drake are probably derivative. The lantern which hangs in the ante-Hall, said to be of the pattern of the *Golden Hind*'s stern lantern, is a recent replacement[10a] for an earlier one destroyed in the World War II bombing; but the origins even of that are unknown.[11] A chair in the Bodleian Library is claimed to be of *Golden Hind* material, and is the only other artefact for which such a claim is made.[12]

The foregoing discussion covers the most frequently publicised links between the Middle Temple and the Elizabethan world of maritime adventure. References abound in prospectuses, pamphlets and tourist information.[13] As has been shown, some of the claims are robust, while others rest on fairly insubstantial evidence. Fortunately there is further material, much of it well-documented, to help produce a better-rounded picture, and it is to this that we now turn.

---

[9] Friendship with the honourable society of the Middle Temple aforesaid.

[10] Sir Lynden Macassey, *The Middle Temple's Contribution to National Life*, a Reading on 13 November 1930, (London, Solicitors' Law Stationery Society, 1930) at 23. See also MG Murray, *Middle Temple Hall: an Architectural Appreciation* (London, Middle Temple, 1991), at 16.

[10a] See below p 410.

[11] Williamson, above n 1, at 233.

[12] *Drake 400 Catalogue*, City Museum and Art Gallery, Plymouth, Item 192.

[13] T Daniell, *A Literary Excursion to the Inns of Court* (London, Wildy, 1971); B Weinreb and C Hibbert (eds), *The London Encyclopaedia* (1983), 513.

II.   SIR WALTER RALEIGH AND THE ELIZABETHAN ADVENTURERS

A.   Raleigh and the Middle Temple

The first and most prominent, as well as the most colourful and celebrated, person involved is Sir Walter Raleigh. Of his membership there is, indeed, no doubt. He was admitted on 27 February 1574–75, described as 'late of Lyons Inn, gent, son of Walter Raleigh of Budleigh'.[14] In spite of his entry from an Inn of Chancery, he seems to have had no serious intention of studying the law; during his trial in 1603 he claimed that he had 'never read a word of law or statutes'.[15] It can be guessed that his ambitions already lay in the adventurous field of foreign enterprises and the work of a courtier necessary to implement them, and that his membership of the Inn would help him in networking with influential people. His later setting up his London headquarters at Durham House, not far to the west of the Middle Temple, suggests that he found the proximity useful.

As to why Raleigh chose Middle Temple rather than any other Inn of Court, the answer again probably lies in the Elizabethan network system. Much of this was based on family connections, and the Devon network to which Raleigh belonged was one of the most intricate of all. Humphrey and Adrian Gilbert were his half-brothers; Humphrey was not a member of the Middle Temple, but Adrian was, having been admitted on 11 November 1562.[16] Four other members of the Gilbert family have been identified as members of the Inn with admission dates between 1593/94 and 1633,[17] and we shall meet at least one of them later in this narrative. Other more or less close relatives of Raleigh figure extensively in the Middle Temple registers around this time, Champernownes and Carews particularly.

The contacts Raleigh made during his early years as a member of the Middle Temple were not confined to Devon men, however. The elder Richard Hakluyt, with his lifelong interest in exploration (carried on with even greater distinction by his younger kinsman of the same name) was not only a member of the Inn, but was also one of the first to be honoured with the status of associate bencher (12 May 1585).[18] It has

---

[14]   Middle Temple, *Admissions Register*, vol 1, 39, where the spelling is 'Rawley'. All admissions were entered in Latin until 1853.

[15]   JB Williamson, *Sir Walter Raleigh and his Trial*, a Reading at Middle Temple, 13 November 1935 (London, Pitman,1936), at 17.

[16]   Middle Temple, *Admissions Register*, vol 1, 27.

[17]   Whitelaw, above n 7, at 8.

[18]   JB Williamson, *The Middle Temple Bench Book*, 2nd edn (London, Middle Temple, 1937), 84. Williamson explains (*ibid*, at xxix) that the original order which introduced associates to the Bench was limited to cases where a fine had been paid for refusing to read. He says that the office of reader, though a position of honour, must, while it lasted, have

been suggested[19] that his chambers were close to those of Adrian Gilbert, when in the 1570s he was adviser to the Muscovy Company; in any case, it is likely that these men of similar interests, including Raleigh, must have met on many occasions, some of them probably within the Inn.

Sometimes, perhaps, the circle may even at this stage have been widened to include others who had—belatedly in comparison with much of the rest of Europe—begun to look over the horizons of the known world. John Dee, the 'magus' who, amongst his astronomical, astrological, metallurgical and magical visions, had first coined the phrase 'British Empire'[20]; Thomas Hariot, with his equally powerful but more analytical mind, with whom Raleigh had probably come into contact during his time at Oriel College, Oxford[21]; and Martin Frobisher, sea captain and explorer, heavily involved in the search for the North West Passage: all may have been of the company. Dee and Hariot were never members of the Middle Temple; Frobisher was, as we shall see, admitted later, *honoris causa*. Certainly they must have met; whether it was within the confines of the Inn must be a matter of speculation, but it should be noted that Raleigh did not acquire Durham House until 1582, so the Middle Temple is a plausible candidate for a meeting place before that time.

B.   Expeditions to the Americas

All this activity and lively discussion must have fired Raleigh to action, and an opportunity was presented by Humphrey Gilbert's projected expedition to the Americas in 1578. Raleigh was given command of the *Falcon*, a 70-foot vessel which belonged to the Queen. The expedition as a whole was a failure—not a catastrophic one, simply because it got no further than the coast of Ireland before being beaten back by weather, desertions and ill-found ships.[22] But Raleigh stayed out for six months, reaching the Cape Verde Islands and returning with very little to show for his pains and the casualties his ship and her company had suffered.

From 1580 to 1582, Raleigh was in Ireland, where he earned a reputation for courage in action but also for ruthlessness on occasion, as at the massacre at Smerwick.[23] There is no record of any contact between him

---

seriously interrupted the practice of a busy member of the Bar, and having regard to the expenses it entailed it is not surprising that those nominated for it often preferred to submit to a fine for refusing the office than incur the liability it entailed. There is no record that Hakluyt had been fined for not taking on the office of reader.

[19]   Whitelaw, above n 7, at 8.
[20]   R Trevelyan, *Sir Walter Raleigh* (London, Allen Lane, 2002), 20.
[21]   *Ibid*, at 17.
[22]   G Milton, *Big Chief Elizabeth* (London, Sceptre, 2000), 17.
[23]   Trevelyan, above n 20, at 38–40.

and the Middle Temple during that time. His networking had a different focus; his correspondence with Francis Walsingham (whose association with Gray's Inn is close and well-known) was extensive, and directed quite as much to his own personal advancement as to the more efficient conduct of the campaign.

But when he returned to England in 1582, one part of Raleigh's vision (he had many irons in the fire) focused on the planting of the eastern seaboard of North America. This would not only have the effect of directly increasing England's power and influence, but would serve to check Spanish and Portuguese ambitions in the western hemisphere. As has been suggested, this interest probably had its origin in his discussions in the mid- to late 1570s, but now, with Raleigh's rapidly increasing influence at court, it came to a sharper point. Significantly, Thomas Hariot joined Raleigh's household in 1582,[24] and his extraordinary skills were at once directed towards the questions that abounded concerning North America.

Raleigh was closely involved in Humphrey Gilbert's final ill-fated venture, the first attempted plantation, in 1582–83. He contributed a ship, the *Bark Raleigh*, and £2,000; and there is evidence that he interceded with the Queen to overcome her misgivings and allow Gilbert to go.[25] The history of the expedition, which started with such lofty ideas, is a sad one. They found the coast of Newfoundland inhospitable, and the land further west scarcely less so; supplies ran low and it was decided to return. Gilbert himself drowned in the foundered *Squirrel* on a stormy return passage.

Adrian Gilbert quickly renewed the patent for the venture. But very soon afterwards, Raleigh himself secured a patent,[26] 'to plant a colony and hold it for ever'[27], provided that the land it occupied was not 'actually possessed by any Christian prince nor inhabited by Christian people'. Whether this new and very broad patent caused friction between Raleigh and Adrian Gilbert is unclear; Adrian's interest was moving more and more in the direction of the North West Passage, and he may well have relinquished any commitment to the eastern seaboard of America with relief. What is certain is that in April 1584, Raleigh dispatched a reconnaissance to the east coast by Arthur Barlowe and Philip Amadas.

Barlowe was not a member of Middle Temple, but Amadas was, having been admitted in 1582, 'late of New Inn, gent, son and heir of John Amadas of Plymouth'. This particular admission is one of the most intriguing in the story of the Inn's maritime links. All that is known of

---

[24] *Ibid*, at 17.

[25] M Waldman, *Sir Walter Raleigh* (Oxford, The Bodley Head, 1928), 33.

[26] The patent was signed by John Popham, Attorney-General: DW Rice, *The Life and Achievements of Sir John Popham 1531–1607* (Madison, NJ, Fairleigh Dickinson Univeristy Press, 2005), 66 [Ed]. See pp 131 ff below.

[27] Waldman, above n 25, at 36.

Amadas suggests a fiery little sea-captain, a real man of action in the Elizabethan mould. Why on earth had he entered this college of legal learning (and, what is more, from an Inn of Chancery)? The most likely explanation is that he had been influenced to do so by Raleigh himself, and for the same reasons as had caused Raleigh to come in by the same route: networking based upon Devon family connections.

The preparation and fitting out of the expedition, reconnaissance though it was, required extensive funding. Here Raleigh's contacts paid off handsomely. The principal financier was William Sanderson, a rich city merchant who had a hand in many ventures over the Elizabethan period and was distantly related by marriage to Raleigh. He was Raleigh's backer and agent in several other of Raleigh's businesses and monopolies at that time. Other backers of the North America reconnaissance were even closer to the Devonian nexus: the names of Richard Grenville, George Carey, George Carew and William Camden have been suggested with authority.[28] Of these, only George Carew (Carye) is recorded as a member of the Middle Temple, having been admitted on 3 February 1577; he was indeed called to the Bar on 17 June 1586, one of the few Middle Templars in this article to have acquired such a status.[29]

Amadas and Barlowe were almost certainly accompanied, amongst the hundred or so of their company which necessarily included a high proportion of soldiers as well as seamen, by Hariot, and probably also by John White, artist and cartographer. White was exceptionally talented in this field; as will be seen, he was subsequently found to be less effective in others. A John White, late of New Inn, son and heir of Hugh White of Standish, Lancashire, was admitted in 1573,[30] but no reliable connection can be found between that individual and the Durham House circle.

The reconnaissance returned in September 1584 with a glowing report of the potential of the coast of what is now North Carolina. The natives, it said, were friendly, the land fertile, the climate excellent. The explorers brought back not only their report—in the form of a *Discourse* by Barlowe, backed up by superb illustrations (probably by White) and a wide range of analysis, including outstanding linguistic study, by Hariot—but two native Americans, Manteo and Wanchese, who could serve as subjects for study in England and guides for future expeditions.

If, as has been suggested, the *Discourse* was designed to generate enthusiasm for a further enterprise, including settlement, which was already in the advanced planning stage,[31] then it was effective. Those who know the Cape Hatteras and Pamlico Sound areas would not now be

---

[28] Trevelyan, above n 20, at 70.
[29] Whitelaw, above n 7, at 9. Carye was made an associate bencher in 1602.
[30] Middle Temple, *Admissions Register*, vol I, 37.
[31] Trevelyan, above n 20, at 72.

inclined to describe them in such paradisical terms. Perhaps Barlowe and his party were singularly lucky with the weather; or perhaps, as the critics say, they were good at propaganda.

Raleigh was quick to build on this apparent success. Richard Hakluyt the Younger, whose visits to his elder kinsman in Middle Temple are well documented,[32] was enlisted to reinforce Barlowe's work with one of his own, *A Discourse on Western Planting*, which set out in detail not only the objectives of settlement in America—which may be summarised as economic expansion and a check to Spanish ambition—but also many of the practical requirements, including the provision of suitable tradesmen and materials. Hakluyt's *Discourse* was dedicated to Walsingham and clearly intended for the Queen's eyes.

Plans for a permanent settlement were already in hand. The expedition to what was still named Wingandacoa, which was to follow next year, would include several key figures: Sir Richard Grenville in charge of the squadron, Amadas in charge of the small craft, Thomas Cavendish as accompanying freebooter, Sir Ralph Lane as the Governor-designate, Thomas Hariot as principal researcher and linguistic adviser, and John White as cartographer and artist. Of these, Grenville, Hariot and Cavendish can be identified with certainty as non-members of the Middle Temple. Cavendish, indeed, had been a member of Gray's Inn since 1577.[33] The membership of Amadas, and possible membership of White, have already been discussed. Lane, however, bears further consideration.

A Ralph Lane was admitted to the Middle Temple in 1554, 'second son of Ralph Lane of Hogshawe, Bucks, knight'. In the *Dictionary of National Biography* [34] Governor Lane is said to be the second son of Sir Ralph Lane of Horton, Northants. Horton is the southernmost village in Northamptonshire, very close to the Buckinghamshire border; Hogshawe, a village now lost, was a dozen miles away to the south.[35] Enquiries of the County Archivists of Buckinghamshire and Northamptonshire have established that Robert Lane, first son of the elder Ralph, held the manors of both Horton and Hogshawe at the relevant time in the sixteenth century. It therefore is beyond reasonable doubt that the Ralph Lane who joined Middle Temple in 1554 and Governor Lane of Virginia in 1585 were one and the same person. The date of admission in 1554 is, indeed, early and

---

[32] Whitelaw, above n 7, at 19.

[33] Letter from Theresa Thom, Librarian, Gray's Inn, 26 March 2003.

[34] Hereafter 'DNB', vol XI, 518. In the *Oxford Dictionary of National Biography* ('ODNB') it is stated that Lane was of unknown parentage and education, that nineteenth-century scholars believed he came from Horton, Northants, but that these presumptions lack the sanction of unimpeachable evidence. On the evidence here presented, we disagree with that conclusion.

[35] Letters dated 12 June 2003 from the Assistant Archivist, Buckinghamshire CC, and 12 June 2003 from the County Archivist, Northamptonshire CC.

would probably put Lane in his fifties at the time of the 1585 expedition, but all the evidence is that he was at that time a highly experienced soldier of middle age.[36]

Lane's membership of Middle Temple, thus established, can lead to all kinds of speculation. It pre-dates that of Raleigh by 20 years. Did it have anything to do with Raleigh's choice of Middle Temple as an Inn? The two probably met when soldiering in France, Flanders or Ireland. Later on, did it have anything to do with the Queen's choice—no doubt on Raleigh's advice—of Lane as Governor-designate? No answer can so far be found to these questions.

Raleigh's search for backers, an essential part of any Elizabethan adventure, was largely successful, Sanderson again playing a leading part. The Queen herself put up no money but contributed the flagship, the *Tiger*, and a supply of gunpowder, and consented to the ultimate flattery of having her status commemorated in the name given to the projected plantation: Virginia. Preparations for the voyage were thorough and comprehensive. Five ships in all were involved, with a complement of 300 or so men. They were stored with supplies not only for the voyage but for subsistence covering the first few months of settlement, until the seeds— which had also been embarked—should have germinated and provided the first harvest.[37]

The outward voyage, begun from Plymouth on 9 April 1585, was by way of the West Indies and was generally successful, though the squadron was split up and did not finally reunite until the coast of America was reached in June. Then, however, misjudgement struck. The Portuguese pilot, Fernandez, recommended an inlet to Pamlico Sound that was too shallow for the *Tiger*; she grounded, was badly beaten and holed in a subsequent storm, and most of the precious stores, including the essential seeds, were destroyed when water entered the ship.[38]

C.   The Roanoke Island colony

The subsequent settlement of Roanoke Island was thus dependent on the goodwill of the indigenous people. Even though Manteo and Wanchese had been brought along, and Hariot contributed his unique knowledge, negotiation was never easy; and relations worsened as fall and winter set in. Morale in the colony, never high after the prospect of self-sufficiency had been destroyed, became increasingly brittle. The fleet (including the rebuilt *Tiger*) departed for England in the late summer, increasing the sense

---

[36]   Milton, above n 22, at 88.
[37]   Trevelyan, above n 20, at 81.
[38]   *Ibid*, at 109.

of isolation. Lane's instincts and tastes were more those of the soldier than the administrator or diplomat; when, finally, it came to open warfare with the local tribe he was successful, but some way from the high hopes and ideals with which the colony had been set up.[39] These were typified in a set of liberal ground-rules for dealing with the indigenous population, drafted by Raleigh himself,[40] which ordered, among other things, that 'no souldier do violat any woman; that no Indian be forced to labour unwillingly; that non shall stryke or misuse any Indian'.

Back in England, Raleigh had not been idle. Grenville was re-equipped to fulfil the promise, which the settlers had been given, that further supplies would be sent to them by Easter 1586.[41] But Grenville was diverted, some say by the prospect of easy prizes in the Atlantic, and by early June he had not appeared and the colonists despaired of any relief from England.[42] They were thus delighted when a squadron of English ships appeared off the coast on 8 June 1586. It was not, indeed, Sir Richard Grenville, but Drake, near the end of his marauding expedition on the Spanish Main. His arrival was not fortuitous; he had heard rumours of a planned Spanish attack on the Virginia settlement,[43] and since his route home passed up the eastern seaboard, no significant diversion was needed. Moreover, he had already taken some pre-emptive action against the bases further south, from which the Spaniards would have had to launch any assault.

The first discussions between Lane and Drake were on the basis that Drake would take home the weaker and more disaffected members of the settlement and reinforce it with experienced hands, supplies and several suitable vessels, so that the plantation could continue. These optimistic plans were frustrated only a few days later, when a sudden storm disabled much of the fleet and particularly the most substantial ship that was to be left for Lane's use. In the wake of the storm the underlying situation was all too plainly dire, and with great reluctance Lane requested that Drake should give passage to all the settlers back to England.[44]

Drake returned to England in late July 1586. The glittering success of his marauding was what the public wanted, and the relative failure of Lane's settlement was not. What was more, the detailed records kept by Lane and Hariot, and the larger part of White's superb drawings and charts, all of which might have been vastly interesting to the discerning, had been lost in the hurried departure from Roanoke.[45] To cap it all, on their return to

[39] Milton, above n 22, at134.
[40] *Ibid*, at 114.
[41] Trevelyan, above n 20, at 110.
[42] *Ibid*.
[43] Milton, above n 22, at 164.
[44] *Ibid*, at 167.
[45] *Ibid*, at 170.

England some of the settlers vented their disappointment in strong terms and were inclined to blame Lane for all that had gone wrong. That was scarcely just. Lane had been faced with problem after problem, nearly all outwith his own or anyone else's experience, most beyond his control and many extending beyond what could have been foreseen by the most prescient. He had dealt with them in the fashion of a good soldier, mostly with sound judgement, sometimes not. But in that astonishingly risky enterprise, lasting a full year, he had lost only four men. There it is: command is a hard taskmistress.[46]

Raleigh was not content to give up the idea of a plantation. He was moreover encouraged by the fact that Grenville's relief squadron had eventually made the coast near Roanoke—only a fortnight after the colonists' departure, in fact—and had left there a small garrison of 15 men, hardy and resourceful soldiers.[47] Consequently, it was thought reasonable to project another expedition for 1587. But who was to lead it? Lane was, however unjustly, discredited; Hariot was not inclined to join the expedition; Amadas and Barlowe were, it is to be presumed, not available. Clearly it was necessary to choose someone who had been in the previous party and had local knowledge. Raleigh's choice fell upon John White.

White started quite well in the planning stage. He had conducted an extended voyage into Chesapeake Bay, to the north of Roanoke, during the previous expedition and proposed, quite rightly, that that vast inlet offered great advantages for settlement: better access, shelter and deep water for ships, more fertile ground and more settled weather. Landing there was one of the basic assumptions, and it was a sound one. White's second assumption was far-reaching: the settlement, if it proved viable, was to be permanent, so the party would include women. Indeed White included his own daughter, with her husband Ananias Dare.

Leaving in April 1587, the ships made their way by the usual southern route to the Caribbean, and it was here that White's shortcomings as a commander began to show. He allowed himself to be overridden by the pilot Fernandez on several occasions, each more serious than the last, and by the time the ships arrived off Cape Hatteras his authority was much diminished. Here he was dealt the worst blow so far. Fernandez refused to take the squadron on into the Chesapeake: it was back to Roanoke or nothing. The situation was made worse by the fact that the small garrison left by Grenville had disappeared after a desperate fight against the local tribe,[48] so that the armed force available to White was very weak. White

---

[46] For harsher judgments on Lane, see AL Rowse, *The Elizabethans and America* (London, Macmillan, 1959), 52; P Fraser Tytler, *Life of Sir Walter Raleigh* (London, Nelson, 1851), 52.

[47] R Lacey, *Sir Walter Raleigh* (London, Weidenfeld & Nicholson, 1973), 86.

[48] Milton, above n 22, at 140.

did his best, with the help of Manteo who had accompanied the party, to establish good relations with the inhabitants of the neighbouring island of Croatoan, but this went disastrously wrong when the English attacked some of this tribe by mistake in a night engagement.

By mid-August the mood of the settlers was brittle. Morale had been raised by the elevation of Manteo to high office among his tribe, by the unexpected arrival of supplies in a hitherto missing fly-boat and by the birth of a daughter to Eleanor Dare—the first Virginian, and appropriately named Virginia.[49] But there was deep underlying unease about further support from England, which had been predicated on settlement in the Chesapeake and might therefore arrive—if at all—in the wrong place, and about relations with the indigenous people whose mood, as had been demonstrated, could change with great suddenness.

In consequence White himself was deputed to return to England to report the situation. He accepted, characteristically, after indecision and with reluctance, and after making inadequate arrangements for command and control in his absence, which was bound to last for several months. He nearly did not make it back to England at all, but after a harrowing, storm-tossed voyage finally arrived in late October 1587. There he found that because of the threat from Spain, which was to culminate next year in the Armada campaign, all transatlantic shipping had been stayed by order of the Queen.

After some fruitless attempts to get the ban lifted to take substantial aid to the settlers, Raleigh eventually dispatched two small craft loaded with supplies, and accompanied by White, in April 1588. But these were intercepted by French pirates, who pillaged the supplies and sent the ships back to England. The Armada intervened, and it was not until March 1590 that White was again able to sail for Roanoke. The two ships, *Hopewell* and *Moonlight* under Captain Cocke, arrived in August, but after hopes had been raised by the sight of smoke, the settlement was found in ruins and deserted. The only clue was the word 'CROATOAN' carved on a tree.[50] White had left instructions that this method was to be used to indicate where the settlers had gone, if they left the settlement. He was heartened by the fact that no cross, agreed as a sign of danger, accompanied the carving.

But further efforts to find the colonists came to nothing. Storms blew up, and Cocke, who in spite of his own heroic efforts had already lost a boat and several men in the surf and sandbanks, was unwilling to make the passage to Croatoan. White was never to see his daughter and

---

[49] Virginia Dare is generally acknowledged to have been the first person of European descent to have been born in North America.

[50] CW Porter III, *Fort Raleigh National Historic Site* (US National Park Service Handbook No16, 1952), 26.

granddaughter again; indeed no firm evidence of the fate of the colony was ever found, though rumour and speculation have continued from that day to this.[51] White returned to England a broken man.[52] He had proved quite inadequate as a governor or a commander of any sort. Certainly he had had bad luck, but it is not too harsh a judgement to say he deserved it. It had been a great mistake on Raleigh's part to select this talented, sensitive, indecisive man for a difficult command.

D.   The pursuit of knowledge and the Molyneux Globes

The setbacks and tragedies of the half-decade from 1585 to 1590 might have soured the Middle Temple's attitude to maritime adventure for some time to come. Moreover, their chief protagonist Raleigh was soon in trouble for other reasons, notably his supersession in the Queen's favour by Robert Devereux, Earl of Essex, and his clandestine marriage with Bess Throckmorton.[53] But there is ample evidence that over the period from 1590 to 1595 the Middle Temple's maritime links were carried on and in some ways strengthened.

In February 1593, Sir Martin Frobisher, Sir Thomas Norris and Sir Francis Vere ('Veer' in the parliament minutes) were all admitted 'specially' and gratis. These clearly were admissions *honoris causa*, probably at the instance of Raleigh; all were adventurers, though Norris and Vere were at that time more prominent in land warfare than by sea. Frobisher was, of course, celebrated for his attempts on the North West Passage and had been one of Howard's Vice Admirals against the Armada, though in the former enterprise the dominant force was John Davis. Davis was by many accounts yet another member of the Durham House set that coalesced round Raleigh and was financed by Sanderson; he was not a member of the Middle Temple, but his voyages were covered by the patent[54] granted to Adrian Gilbert, a Middle Templar.

In 1594 the Middle Temple acquired an even more prestigious member *honoris causa* in Sir John Hawkins, still Treasurer of the Navy after 15 incident-packed and sometimes scandal-ridden years. It was ironic that in 1573 Hawkins had been stabbed, almost to death, by a member of Middle Temple, one Peter Burchett[55]; but perhaps in hindsight he was mollified by

---

[51]   Milton, above n 22, at 379–82, puts forward the theory that the colony resettled in the Chesapeake area, survived until 1607 and was then—just before the first permanent settlement was established at Jamestown—massacred by the orders of Powhatan. The evidence is confined to circumstance and hearsay.

[52]   *Ibid*, at 269.

[53]   Trevelyan, above n 20, at 169–204.

[54]   *Ibid*, at 67.

[55]   *DNB; ODNB*.

Burchett's explanation, which was that he had mistaken Hawkins for Sir Christopher Hatton. Burchett was hanged anyway. In fact, by the mid-1590s Hawkins's power was on the wane, and naval administration was beginning to fall into the lamentable state inherited (and exacerbated) by James I.

In some ways a more significant admission, on 9 February 1593, was Bartholomew Gosnold of Grunsborough, Suffolk.[56] In common with many of the 'maritime' admissions, he is recorded as 'late of New Inn'; though of course he never was called to, or practised at, the Bar. He was encouraged by Richard Hakluyt, who was a neighbour in Suffolk, and almost certainly by Raleigh himself, to overseas ventures. In 1602 Gosnold set sail for North America in his ship *Concord* and landed in what is today New England. He named Cape Cod after the large quantities of cod to be found in the vicinity. He discovered an island 'abounding in strawberries, grapes and other fruit'[57] and named it Martha's Vineyard.[58] That voyage was to have significant results throughout the century and beyond; and Gosnold was to provide a link, as will be seen subsequently, with the first permanent settlements of North America later in the decade.

By the early 1590s Raleigh's imagination was increasingly caught by the prospect of Guiana and the fable of El Dorado, and no doubt he also saw a successful exploration there, if it could be achieved, as a means of restoring his fortunes at court.[59] There had already been four Spanish explorations of the Orinoco, from 1530 onwards; none had found any significant riches, but the myth endured, and was fostered by the report of Captain Whiddon, whom Raleigh sent on reconnaissance in 1594. The report was based on hearsay—Whiddon got no further than Trinidad—but it was enough for Raleigh, who this time went west himself, leaving on 6 February 1595. Of the captains who accompanied him, only one, Laurence Keymis (or Kemys) has a possible connection with the Middle Temple.[60]

The Guiana expedition, which returned in August 1595, has been held to be a success in that it lost only one man and penetrated many miles inland, establishing good relations with the inhabitants and checking Spanish influence in the region. But it had little lasting result and certainly did not bring in the quantities of treasure, particularly gold ore, that had been dreamed of. Neither did it ultimately live up to Raleigh's vision of a land fit for settlement; and later forays by Kemys in 1596 and Mace in

---

[56] Gosnold's significance is such that it might be said that without his achievement, North America could have become part of the Spanish Empire: Whitelaw, above n 7, at 23.

[57] *DNB*, sub nom Gosnold, Bartholomew.

[58] Gosnold also named another island Martha's Vineyard. It is that island which now bears this name. Martha was the name of his mother-in-law and of his young daughter: *ODNB*.

[59] Waldman, above n 25, at 93–94.

[60] An Arthur Kemis was admitted on 14 June 1588; no further evidence can be found.

1602 did no better on any of the potential counts. This narrative will come later to Raleigh's final, sad attempt with Kemys in 1617.

One result of Raleigh's first Guiana expedition was his magisterial work *The Discoverie of Guiana*, often held out as a model of travel writing. It has been pointed out that the more far-fetched tales, of which there are plenty in the book, are always presented by Raleigh as hearsay, while much of his actual experience as reported can be corroborated by subsequent evidence.[61] The *Discoverie* was an important contribution to the world's knowledge of itself.

But it was at about this time, the period 1592–96, that two artifacts of literally global significance, subsequently to have the closest of links with the Middle Temple, first saw the light of day. These were, and are, the Molyneux Globes, one terrestrial and one celestial, still in the possession of the Inn. A fine piece of research by Lesley Whitelaw,[62] the Archivist of the Middle Temple, in 2003 has been the basis for the discussion in the following paragraphs.

The Molyneux Globes are two of the few survivors (and the only surviving pair) of a large number[63] of terrestrial and celestial globes created by Emery Molyneux of Lambeth from 1592. They were the first globes made by an Englishman and the first globes made in England. The Inn's terrestrial globe was a revised edition made in 1603, showing discoveries made up to 1602. Like its predecessors, it contains an inscription dedicating the globes to Queen Elizabeth. The royal arms are emblazoned across North America, signifying the assertion of Elizabeth's claims to those lands. While little detail is known about the life of their maker Emery Molyneux, he was the foremost globe-maker of his time. His globes were described as 'the first soe published in Christendome' and were intended for 'Scholars, Gentrye and Marriners'. The publication of Molyneux's Globes caused a sensation in 1592. That was partly because the terrestrial globe showed the very latest discoveries of English and foreign navigators, and partly because Molyneux's Globes were much larger and better than earlier ones produced by Mercator. The evocative title-page of Wagenhaer's great work of a decade before, showing learned

---

[61] Waldman, above n 25, at 109.

[62] Whitelaw, above n 7; her article under the same title in *The Middle Templar* (Hilary 2004).

[63] At the time Molyneux Globes appear to have been quite widely available; the plates were held by the engraver Hondius, and there does not seem to have been any bar to their use for production. As late as 1656 Sanderson's son, Sir William Sanderson, wrote (in 'An Answer to a Scurrilous Pamphlet') that many of the Molyneux Globes of which his father had been financier 'are yet in being, great and small ones, Celestiall and Terrestrial, in both our Universities (here and beyond the Seas)'. None of the small ones have survived. Of all those Globes in Britain and abroad, the Middle Temple is unique in having preserved a pair with such care over the centuries, with specialist repairs undertaken and recorded in the 18th, 19th and 20th centuries.

men poring over a great globe—perpetuated to this day by every cover of the quarterly *Mariner's Mirror*[64]—is a powerful reminder of the hold that scientific enquiry into geography, in its broadest sense, exerted over the best minds of the time. The interest created both in England and abroad by Molyneux's Globes spawned a succession of books by English mathematicians and geographers such as Hues, Harriot, Blundeville and Hood, which ran to numerous editions in several languages. In the production of his Globes, Molyneux used the Flemish engraver Jodocus Hondius, who had emigrated to London. But Molyneux followed Hondius to Amsterdam shortly after Hondius took up residence there in 1594.

As was usual in work of this sort, the opportunity was taken to record the generosity of the sponsor and to make any other statement that might be considered appropriate. Thus, the arms of William Sanderson, who financed them,[65] appear prominently on both Globes. Moreover, a statement in Latin placed just off the eastern seaboard of North America proclaims, in a rough translation, 'Virginia, first settled and planted by the English under the supervision of Sir Walter Raleigh'. It is said that at Sanderson's house a pair was presented to the Queen, at which she said 'The whole earth, a present for a Prince', adding wryly if diplomatically, 'but with the Spanish king's leave'.

Among the wealth of new information on the terrestrial globes which was based on recent discoveries, some, such as information about the discovery of the Solomon Islands, clearly came directly from Raleigh.[66] That he was closely involved in the whole enterprise of Molyneux's Globes is hardly surprising given the relationship between him and Sanderson: Sanderson's wife was the daughter of Raleigh's half-sister, Mary Snedall (*née* Raleigh). And Emery Molyneux was one of the coterie of intellectuals, soldiers and mariners with whom Raleigh had surrounded himself in his[67] sumptuous home, Durham House, just a very short distance up the Thames from Temple Stairs. We may conclude that in the production of the terrestrial globes there were inputs from Raleigh, Sanderson, Davis, Hues,

[64] The first edition of the *Mariner's Mirror* was by Sir Antony Ashley, Bt, who, like his brothers Robert and Sir Francis, was a member of Middle Temple.

[65] The Latin dedication to Queen Elizabeth on the terrestrial globe refers to the great expense of the patron, William Sanderson (*'cum magnis suis sumptibus'*) and the industry of the creator, Emery Molyneux (*'indefessa Emerii Mollineuxi opera'*).

[66] On the terrestrial globe there is, in the Pacific Ocean, a legend in Spanish: *'Islas Istas descubrio Pedro Sermiento de Gamboa por la corona de Castilla y Leon des de el anno 1568 llamolas Islas de Jesus annq[ue] vulgarmente las llamá Islas de Salomon'*. Clements Markham has told us that Pedro de Sarmiento was the officer sent to fortify the Straits of Magellan after Drake had passed through. He was taken prisoner by an English ship on his way to Spain, and was the guest of Raleigh in London for several weeks. The fact that the statement is in Spanish strongly suggests that it was made to Raleigh by Sarmiento and passed on by Raleigh to Molyneux.

[67] Raleigh occupied Durham House at the Queen's pleasure: Trevelyan, above n 20, at 294.

Hakluyt, Hariot and Molyneux himself, and quite likely occasional inter-positions from other savants. All were habitués of Durham House, Hakluyt certainly of the Middle Temple as well. Hakluyt's *Principall Navigations* foreshadowed the production of the globes in 1589[68].

The terrestrial globe is the more significant for the purposes of this article. Not only does it delineate, with great accuracy for latitude but understandably less for longitude, the known world at the time, it traces in often intriguing detail the great English voyages of discovery: Drake's and Cavendish's circumnavigations, and Davis's three attempts to find the North West Passage. It is by no means alone in postulating a great southern continent; such a *terra incognita* was still widely believed to exist up to the time that James Cook, on his second voyage in 1772–75, disproved its existence.

How did the Middle Temple come to own its Globes? The Middle Temple's own records are inconclusive. The series of treasurers' annual account and receipt books is complete only from late 1637. Thus, if the Inn paid for the Globes they were probably acquired before 1637. Purchases or presentations, even important ones, were not necessarily mentioned in the records of parliament at the time. The first certain evidence of their being held in the Middle Temple is in March 1717, when repairs were under-taken, paid for and recorded in the account books. In view of Raleigh's close association with the production of the Globes, and of his eminence as a member of the Inn whose coat of arms was among those emblazoned in the heraldic glass of Hall at the time the Globes were made, there must be at least a possibility that the Inn acquired the Globes, if not from him, then through his influence.

Raleigh does appear to have had a pair of the Globes. When he was imprisoned in 1603, it would have been logical to move them to his quarters in the Tower of London where he was imprisoned, for no significant check was put upon his historical or geographical studies. Moreover, his fellow-prisoner, the ninth Earl of Northumberland, was an ardent enquirer after knowledge, and indeed one of the only other surviving Molyneux Globes, the Petworth Globe, can be traced back to his family. Moreover, after Raleigh's execution in 1618, a Royal Warrant directed that 'all the globes and instruments' then in his possession should be 'delivered to the King'. James I had notoriously little interest in the wider reaches of geography, and if the Molyneux Globes were amongst those involved, it would have been a sensible move on his part to assign them to the Middle Temple. But whether he did so is mere speculation.[69] There are stronger grounds for thinking that the Globes may have come to

---

[68]   Whitelaw, above n 7, p 14.
[69]   Another possibility is that the Globes came from William Crashawe: See ch 2, p 96.

the Inn from Robert Ashley. Robert Ashley's interest in travel and geometry suggests an active interest in maps and globes which could only have been increased by his close association (despite occasional tiffs) with his older brother Sir Anthony Ashley, the translator and sponsor of *The Mariner's Mirrour* (1588) and, as Clerk to the Privy Council, a person closely associated with the court and with Raleigh. The Globes may have come to the Inn as undocumented contents of Robert Ashley's library, which he left to the Inn in 1641.[70]

The pursuit of knowledge was not the only thing that occupied Raleigh in the last half-decade of the sixteenth century. He was still unwelcome at court, and his way back into Elizabeth's good books was barred by a new favourite, the Earl of Essex. But in 1596 a way seemed to open through this impasse. Spanish antagonism persisted and the perception of real menace was sharpened by coastal raids on England. These could not go without riposte, and an expedition to Cadiz was planned. Here was an opportunity for Raleigh to recoup his reputation, so long as he went in partnership with Essex under the overall command of Lord Howard of Effingham. Sir Francis Vere—probably on Raleigh's advice, and recalling his Middle Temple membership—was brought from the Low Countries to help with the land operations.[71]

The expedition as a whole comes into the category of 'Could Have Done Better'. Though surprise was achieved (aided by some strokes of luck as well as good security[72]), once the force was established off Cadiz there were arguments about which set of targets should first be attacked, ships or shore; and then, reprehensibly, about precedence and the 'honour' of being first into the attack. Raleigh and Vere had a public row about who commanded what[73]; so much, on this occasion, for Middle Temple fellowship. In consequence, far less booty was gathered than might have been; and on the way home the force, which might have intercepted the richly-laden Spanish *Flota* had it had better intelligence and more patience, missed its opportunity.

An even less productive venture the next year was an expedition to the Azores with, once more, the *Flota* in mind. The team, if it could be called a team, was much the same, but poor intelligence, bad weather, lack of

---

[70] Referring to the 'glorious workes of God', Ashley's will continued: 'For the attayning of some knowledge whereof, I have not spared any labour or expence in procuring the principall writers in their severall languages, espetially such as had opportunitie to be acquainted with the moste remote and unknowne partes. These, with all the residue of my library ... I doe therefore leave and bequeath to this noble society of the Middle Temple' (*MTR*, ii, 917).

[71] Trevelyan, above n 20, at 269.

[72] M Oppenheim (ed), *The Naval Tracts of Sir William Monson* (London, Navy Records Society, 1902), vol 1, 346.

[73] *Ibid*, at 375.

planning and a split force ensured that the results were minimal, and relations between Raleigh and Essex, always touchy, became badly strained. The Queen was not pleased by the expedition's lack of success, and it took some skilful court diplomacy, and clever (some say fanciful) eulogies of Essex's conduct by Sir Francis Vere,[74] to keep the principals from disgrace.

The great days of Elizabethan maritime adventure were on the wane. Drake and Hawkins had both died on their final foray on the Spanish Main in 1595–96, and with that ageing pair of swashbucklers had gone much of the glamour, though the urge for gold remained. More thoughtful projects, taking a longer view of permanent settlement, were coming to the fore, and indeed Raleigh and Hakluyt had a prominent part in them. It is quite likely that Gosnold too was a part of this movement, as was George Popham—not a middle Templar, but a previous associate of Raleigh and a nephew of a Middle Temple notable, Sir John Popham.

E.   Sir John Popham and the trial of Raleigh

John Popham[75] enters this narrative in 1603. Before that date he had, of course, been prominent in Inn affairs, having been called to the Bench as early as 1568 and held the office of treasurer for no fewer than eight years,

---

[74]   Trevelyan, above n 20, at 308.

[75]   Sir John Popham, Lord Chief Justice of the King's Bench, was severe on thieves and robbers, though he had been a highwayman in his youth. Lord Campbell tells us (Campbell, *Lives of the Chief Justices* (London, John Murray, 1849), vol 1, 210), with reference to Popham's time as a student at the Middle Temple, 'It seems to stand on undoubted testimony, that at this period of his life, besides being given to drinking and gaming ... he frequently sallied forth at night from a hostel in Southwark, with a band of desperate characters, and that, planting themselves in ambush on Shooters' Hill, or taking other positions favourable for attack and escape, they stopped travellers, and took from them not only their money, but any valuable commodities which they carried with them,—boasting that they were always civil and generous, and that, to avoid serious consequences, they went in such numbers as to render resistance impossible. We must remember that this calling was not then by any means so discreditable as it became afterwards; that a statute was made during Popham's youth by which, on a first conviction for robbery, a peer of the realm or lord of Parliament was entitled to benefit of clergy *'though he cannot read'* ... The extraordinary and almost incredible circumstance is, that Popham is supposed to have continued in these courses after he had been called to the bar, and when, being of mature age, he was married to a respectable woman. At last, a sudden change was produced by her unhappiness, and the birth of a child, for whom he felt attachment'. However, Popham was admitted to the Middle Temple before 1551 and, according to Rice (above n 26, at 21), he was married by 1550. Campbell continues (*ibid*, at 229) that Popham was much commended in his own time for the number of thieves and robbers he convicted and executed, and it was observed by Aubrey that 'if he was the death of a few scores of such gentry, he preserved the lives and livelihoods of more thousands of travellers, who owed their safety to this Judge's severity'. And the *DNB* quotes Fuller's *Worthies*, ii, 284, to the effect that Popham is said to have advised James I to be more sparing of his pardons to highwaymen and cutpurses. [Ed.]

from 1580–88.[76] But in 1603 he was, as Chief Justice, a player in an altogether darker episode: the trial of Sir Walter Raleigh. James I, on succession to the throne, was deeply suspicious of Raleigh on both personal and policy grounds. In terms of personality, Raleigh was still stylish and glamorous, a relic of the old regime, not popular but with great wealth and influence amongst a host of notable people. In terms of policy, his forward and generally bellicose foreign initiatives were anathema to James, who wished to discourage such adventures. Added to this, James, who was not at all certain how robust his claim to the succession might turn out to be, was suspicious of anyone who was in a position to advance the claims of a rival to the throne; and his doubts of Raleigh as such a person had been assiduously fed by advisers such as Henry Howard in the run-up to the accession.

The consequence was the trial[77] of Raleigh on charges of treason, memorably chronicled by Master Williamson in a Reading at the Middle Temple on 13 November 1935 and described by Williamson elsewhere[78] as 'that discreditable proceeding'. The principal result is well known: Raleigh was sentenced to death, but the sentence was not carried out for another

---

[76] *Middle Temple Bench Book*, 2nd edn (1937), 76.

[77] In a trial which was unacceptable by modern standards, and at the time was considered unfair by many, Raleigh was convicted of treason.

Of the indictment as summarised by Williamson, the first count was that Raleigh had conspired with Lord Cobham to put Arabella Stuart on the throne in place of her cousin James I, that Cobham would obtain money for the purpose from the Archduke of Austria and the King of Spain, and that The Lady Arabella would establish a firm peace between England and Spain; the fifth count alleged that Raleigh had instigated Cobham to correspond with the Spanish ambassador from The Netherlands to obtain from him money (600,000 crowns) and himself agreed to accept 8,000 crowns of it.

Prosecuting counsel, the A-G Sir Edward Coke, made vituperative and prejudicial statements about Raleigh. Most of the counts of the indictment were not supported by sworn evidence. The only oral testimony was that of a pilot who had recently made a journey towards Spain, who told the court that at Lisbon a Portuguese gentleman had told him that the new King of England would never be crowned, for Don Cobham and Don Raleigh would cut his throat before he came to be crowned.

However, that is not to say that Raleigh was not guilty of treason. A statement from Cobham was before the court to the effect that Raleigh was to have a pension of £1,500 for supplying intelligence (ie to Spain) about any action against Spain or the Indies. Raleigh did not deny that money had been offered to him by Cobham. On his way to the trial at Winchester, Raleigh had written a letter to Cobham asking for his help and saying 'You know that you offered me the money bona fide for the peace'. In his opening address to the court, Coke said that Raleigh had been prepared to accept money 'for the peace', but he was not a fit man to take so much money for procuring a lawful peace. Raleigh said 'I thought it was one of his [ie Cobham's] idle conceits and paid no heed to it'. Popham asked Raleigh what he said of the pension of £1,500 per annum. Raleigh's reply was that Cobham was a base, dishonourable, poor soul. Popham observed: 'I perceive you are not so clear a man, as you have protested all this while; for you should have discovered these matters to the king': Williamson, above n 15, at 15, 16, 20–23; Rice, above n 26, at 181,186. [Ed.]

[78] Williamson, above n 15.

15 years, for most of which Raleigh was confined to the Tower of London under conditions which were generally civilised by the standards of the time.

But there was another consequence of the trial which more concerns us here. Sir John Popham, presiding as Chief Justice, had not distinguished himself by a demonstration of impartiality, and had notably failed to check the ranting and bullying of Attorney Coke. Even recalling that treason trials at that time followed rules somewhat different from normal legal processes, it was by any standard a sorry proceeding and had the effect of bringing public opinion firmly into line behind Raleigh. Popham was not by all accounts a man too sensitive to what the public thought of him, but he cannot have been impervious to it. He may well have thought it time to move into a more populist field.

III. THE STUART ERA

A. The Virginia Charter

What is certain is that between 1603 and 1606, Sir John Popham[79] became the prime mover in another Virginia settlement,[80] the first indeed that became permanent. He may have been thinking about it before Raleigh's trial, having been in contact with Gosnold[81] and with his nephew George Popham. He may have discussed it with no fewer than three members of the Sandys family—all Middle Temple members—who will appear later in this narrative. He may also have consulted Sir Stephen Powle, a Middle Templar from 1574 and Raleigh's 'bedfellow' in their early days in the Inn[82]; Powle had had a career in public service, was at that time a Clerk of Chancery and was to become a member of the Council of the Virginia Company. But did Popham's confrontations with Raleigh during the trial not act as a catalyst for an initiative that was, on the face of it, uncharacteristic of this 'huge, heavie, ugly man', to quote the gossip John Aubrey?[83] The question must be left open.

John Popham moved with deliberation, but with determination too. This new enterprise was to be better prepared, more solidly financed and more

---

[79] Sir John Popham held many early meetings in connection with the formation of the Virginia Chartered Company in the Middle Temple. In the 1580s, when he was Speaker of the House of Commons, he set a precedent for using Middle Temple Hall for meetings of House of Commons Committees, something which continued well into Jacobean times: Whitelaw, above n 7, at 25.

[80] Milton, above n 22, at 293.

[81] See text to n 56 above.

[82] Whitelaw, above n 7, at 10.

[83] Also a member of Middle Temple (admitted April 1646).

legally well-founded than previous ventures. Edwin Sandys, by then in his forties and a Middle Temple member of 15 years' standing, was enlisted to draft the Virginia Charter which appeared in 1606; it 'conferred upon the colonists "all the liberties, franchises and immunities of English subjects', but no political powers'.[84] Edwin Sandys was to be closely associated with the Virginia Company for many years. His brother George (admitted seven years later than Edwin, in 1596) took a management part as treasurer of the Company in the 1620s, and was himself a settler for some considerable time. Their uncle, Miles Sandys, had been treasurer of the Inn from 1588 to 1596, and it is scarcely credible that his advice and encouragement had been absent from John Popham's counsels.

The Charter of 10 April 1606 provided for two separate ventures, the London Company and the Plymouth Company. The former was allocated rights from 34 to 41 degrees north latitude, the latter from 38 to 45 degrees north; the overlap zone from 38 to 41 degrees was to be claimed by the colony that emerged the stronger.[85]

The northern colony was something of a Popham family affair. Designated as President was George Popham, John Popham's nephew, quite probably by then already in his fifties. Francis Popham, his cousin and Sir John's son, was treasurer. The 'Admiral', in charge of the maritime side of the expedition, was Raleigh Gilbert, son of Sir Humphrey and half-nephew of Sir Walter Raleigh. Here was yet another Middle Temple connection.

The expedition set out from Plymouth in May 1607 in two vessels and arrived at the mouth of what is now the Kennebec River on 16 August. It was late in the year for all they had to do. They did succeed in constructing a substantial storehouse and some dwellings; a plan exists of a far more elaborate fortified settlement. Excavation on the site in the early 2000s has confirmed that at least part of this was carried into execution.[86]

But the winter proved, like all New England winters, a harsh one. Quite probably the settlers had not anticipated it; after all, the latitude was five degrees further south than that of Devon. George Popham died in February 1607–08, and though his was the only known fatality, the morale of the colonists suffered. There was little prospect they could see in agriculture, and the expected trade in furs was less than had been planned. Re-supply had been arranged from England and duly arrived in the summer of 1608, but with it came the news of the death of Raleigh Gilbert's brother. Raleigh Gilbert had inherited his lands, and now wished to return to England; the coherence of the colony could not withstand this loss of leadership. In September all the settlers sailed for the home country in their surviving

---

[84] Whitelaw, above n 7, at 25.
[85] JP Brain, 'The Popham Colony: An Historical and Archaeological Brief', 43 *The Maine Archaeological Society Bulletin* (Spring 2003) 2.
[86] *Ibid*, at 8ff.

vessel from England, the *Mary and John*, and a pinnace they had built in the colony, appropriately named the *Virginia* and the first ship constructed in the plantations of North America.

Planning of the practicalities for the southern colony was if anything more deliberate. Hakluyt's work, particularly the *Principall Navigations*, was vastly influential, not least in the choice of a place for settlement, which unremarkably was Chesapeake Bay; the Hatteras area was of bad omen. The work of the 1580s plantations, tragic though it had often turned out to be, was not in vain; all Hariot's and much of White's accumulated knowledge was put to use. So, even, was some Elizabethan equipment; many of the armament stores were of that vintage, the King having no inclination to provide new gear.[87] Similarly, lessons had been learned from the sometimes capricious financing of previous expeditions, for the Virginia Company was broadly based in the City and elsewhere.

In the actual composition of the first party of planters, the Middle Temple was represented by at least two men: Bartholomew Gosnold, already prominent as the discoverer of Martha's Vineyard much farther to the north, and George Percy. The Percys, of the family of the Earls of Northumberland, had joined the Middle Temple in numbers in the 1590s.[88] Henry, who became the ninth Percy Earl, is mentioned above as Raleigh's fellow-prisoner in the Tower.[89] Charles and Alan, his brothers, have no known connection with the maritime scene. But George, the seventh son of the eighth Percy Earl, was prominent amongst the 1607 settlers, published a *Discourse* concerning their early years that is still one of the most valuable primary sources on the history of the early plantations and became Deputy Governor of Virginia in 1609.[90]

The Deputy Governorship of Virginia, or even the governorship itself, might have devolved upon Bartholomew Gosnold had he not fallen prey to the great sickness that afflicted the settlers at the newly-named Jamestown in the autumn of 1607. Gosnold was a member of the nominated seven-man council, and clearly a man not only of experience and substance[91] but of learning too. His loss was a considerable one. However, the mantle of leadership passed to the shrewd and charismatic John Smith, with results that are well chronicled but outside the scope of this article.

---

[87] Milton, above n 22, at 295.

[88] Henry, Earl of Northumberland, and Charles Percy, his brother, were admitted in May 1594. Alan Percy and George Percy, respectively fifth and seventh sons of Henry, 'late Earl of Northumberland', and brothers of Henry, 'now Earl', were admitted in May 1597.

[89] See text to n 69 above.

[90] Whitelaw, above n 7, at 24.

[91] *Ibid*, at 23.

B.   Raleigh resurgent

Meanwhile, back in the Tower of London, Sir Walter Raleigh languished under suspended sentence of death by hanging, disembowelling and quartering. The regime there was, however, far from draconian, particularly in the early years under a complaisant Lieutenant of the Tower,[92] and Raleigh had scope to pursue many lines of study: experiments in chemistry, historical discourses (resulting in his famous *History of the World)* and a continuing interest in exploration.

In the Tower, Raleigh's life was enlivened after a few years by the arrival of the ninth Earl of Northumberland, under heavy suspicion after the Gunpowder Plot of 1605, when some of his kinsmen were involved. Henry Percy was a singular character. Known as 'the Wizard Earl', he had a reputation as a free-thinker, dabbler in all kinds of sciences and arts, suspected atheist, one of the Odd. He had been known to Raleigh for many years and was one of the Durham House set. He was a patron of Hariot. While he was not a proponent of seafaring or adventure as such, his fertile mind could act as a catalyst for a hundred speculations.

However congenial the company in the Tower, Raleigh would not have been Raleigh had he been content with confinement for the rest of his life. Moreover, he still dreamed of a spectacular success with which to crown a life of adventure and reinstate himself in the royal favour. To him, the most obvious possibility was to return to the place that had caught his imagination from the early 1590s onwards: Guiana.

It was a catastrophic misjudgement. Any British foray into the basin of the Orinoco was bound to run across the Kingdom of Spain, which claimed at least an absolute *droit de regard* if not actual sovereignty; and not only was Spain now on terms of reasonable amity with England, she was represented by an ambassador at the Court of King James, the Count Godomar, who wielded exceptional influence.[93] Raleigh did not help himself a bit by intriguing with the French, nor by surrounding himself with advisers and potential members of his party of doubtful character, people indeed in the old freebooting mode which was now so much less fashionable. The only thing that could have saved a Guiana expedition was the discovery of immense wealth, in fact a gold mine, that English enterprise could exploit.

Raleigh was convinced that such a mine existed, and he managed to persuade some people in power in England that an expedition had a chance of success. Whether James I himself was persuaded is a matter for

---

[92] Trevelyan, above n 20, at 398. The Lieutenant of the Tower was Sir George Harvey: *ibid*, at 400.
[93] *Ibid*, at 462–64.

speculation; some commentators[94] believe that James expected the voyage to fail, indeed half hoped it would as a means of discrediting Raleigh and bringing about his final downfall; and he certainly abetted the transmission of Raleigh's plans to the Spanish Government. However, the fact is that James gave a commission in August 1616 to Raleigh to command an expedition to Guiana, reserving to himself one-fifth of the proceeds.[95]

It was a melancholy characteristic of voyages of this kind, needing careful planning—not least financial planning—and assembling of the necessary people, vessels and supplies, that they nearly always started later in the year than they ought, and even then suffered disruption and difficulty in both material and personal fields. Added to that, the summer of 1617 was a singularly stormy one. The convoy of a dozen ships carrying a thousand men finally left England, after several false starts, on 19 August.

The expedition took the southern route, to catch the trade winds, as did nearly all such ventures. But the Canaries, which lay on the route and where ships tended to stop in order to water and re-victual, were unwelcoming, the Spanish authorities having been warned of Raleigh's approach. There were clashes: one of Raleigh's captains, Bailey, deserted with his ship and returned to England; and it was only with difficulty that they completed with a full supply of water, no food being forthcoming. Then the ships were becalmed in the doldrum belt for over a month, with sickness increasing daily. It was a bitter landfall on 11 October at one of the many mouths of the Orinoco. By then Raleigh was himself ill, with an unidentified fever after a fall on deck.

Inaction was not an option. It was imperative that the expedition should have a positive result, and since Spain was not an enemy *de jure*, the objectives narrowed down to finding a gold mine outside, or arguably outside, Spanish jurisdiction; or making a capture of Spanish booty that could be held to have been acquired in the course of an act of self-defence. Neither of these would have been out of the question in the days of Elizabeth I, but they offered far less firm ground in the reign of her successor. To make matters worse, Raleigh was immobilised by his illness and had to delegate responsibility for the sharp end of the business, which in the first instance had to be to search for the reputed mine.

He nominated Laurence Keymis for the task. Keymis had been a loyal supporter of Raleigh for over 20 years. He had led one follow-up Guiana expedition—albeit unsuccessful—in 1596 and knew much of the geography and some of the indigenous inhabitants. But he was set in the old Elizabethan mould of distrust amounting to enmity against Spain, and

---

[94] Waldman, above n 25, at 197.
[95] Trevelyan, above n 20, at 465.

possessed neither flexibility nor diplomatic skills. Nor was he well served by his subordinates. Wat Raleigh, Sir Walter's son, was immature and headstrong; George, Sir Walter's nephew, somewhat steadier; the five captains of ships and five company commanders were a motley lot, deeply motivated by the prospect of profit.

Raleigh wrote instructions for Keymis[96] that sought to cover the more likely eventualities, but they were many. There were at least two possible locations for the supposed mine, and the Spaniards' settlements, and their state of development and fortification, were only vaguely known. In the event, Keymis made a series of blunders. He approached the small Spanish settlement of San Thomé, thinking it less well fortified than it turned out to be. Spanish and English accounts differ about who fired the first shot,[97] but the certainty is that during late December and January 1617–18 there was a high level of conflict, occupation and reoccupation of the town, and the killing of several senior officers on either side, including the Spanish Governor Palomeque and Wat Raleigh. The English looted many Spanish goods but eventually withdrew. Keymis did not continue to search for the mine, taking refuge in evasions and excuses. He returned to rendezvous with Raleigh at Porto Gallo on 2 March.

Raleigh was appalled at Keymis's news. The death of Wat was the worst personal blow, but failure to find any worthwhile return for the venture was the most fatal for the mission as a whole and for Raleigh in particular, while the damage done to Spain was a diplomatic blunder of the first order. Raleigh told Keymis that he 'had undone' him; Keymis, totally cast down, left Raleigh's cabin and committed suicide.[98]

From that time forward, Raleigh was doomed, and he must have known it. This did not stop him from returning to England—when he might indeed have remained in self-imposed exile, probably in France—and conducting a more or less vigorous campaign on his own behalf, including one ill-conceived attempt at escape across the Channel. His chief minder Lewis Stukeley played a double game, probably on instructions from the King or his advisers. In the background stalked the Spanish ambassador Gondomar, demanding that Raleigh should be extradited to Spain for piracy and threatening the direst punishments for him when he got there.

James at least did not go that far in overseeing Raleigh's fate. Indeed, legally he was in some difficulty in compassing Raleigh's execution; it was scarcely possible to arraign him for failing in Guiana when his mission there—endorsed by Royal patent—had been so vaguely expressed and was, moreover, so potentially damaging to Spain. The Committee appointed to

---

[96]   *Ibid*, at 489.
[97]   *Ibid*, at 495.
[98]   *Ibid*, at 477–505.

examine the case[99] was packed with Raleigh's opponents, including Francis Bacon, the Earl of Worcester, and Sir Edward Coke. The most impartial member was probably Sir Julius Caesar, the Master of the Rolls; he was a member of Inner Temple and had been Treasurer of that Inn when the Temples had been awarded their Royal Charter in 1608. He had, moreover, been the Judge of the Admiralty Court in his time so was qualified to rule on questions of piracy and prize.[100]

Eventually Raleigh was condemned, not on any ground connected with the Guiana expedition but on his previous conviction in 1603. His execution, chronicled in many accounts, was the last occasion for a display of what can only be described as his star quality: a final poem that has gone into every worthwhile anthology since, a speech from the scaffold that was a model of dignified self-justification and a demonstration of calm courage at the end.

Thus ended the Middle Temple's most distinguished proponent of the maritime expansion of England in the decades spanning the 16th and 17th centuries. But, as has been shown, there were many other players, an extraordinary number of whom were members of the Inn, who had a place in the story that eventually led to the establishment of permanent settlement in North America and the perpetuation of British language and culture there—a story in which, in subsequent centuries, Middle Templars had a central role.

IV. DEFINING THE MIDDLE TEMPLE'S MARITIME LINKS

A. The 16th and 17th centuries

On analysis, the Middle Temple's links with maritime expansion in the 16th and 17th centuries can be better defined. There was a nexus around Raleigh in the 1580s and early 1590s, and another around Popham and the Sandyses from the later 1600s onwards. Apart from these principals may be recalled the presence, as members of the Middle Temple, of many of the principal operators on the ground or at sea: Adrian Gilbert, Philip Amadas, Ralph Lane, Bartholomew Gosnold, George Percy, Stephen Powle, even without the more speculative additions of White and Keymis. More generally, the Inn thought it right to honour Frobisher, Vere, Norris

---

[99] *Ibid*, at 531.
[100] 1585–1606: see RG Marsden (ed), *Law and Custom of the Sea* (London, Navy Records Society, 1915) vol I, 242ff.

and Hawkins, adventurers all. And Richard Hakluyt, kinsman and close associate of the contemporary chronicler, was made an associate bencher in 1585.

To some extent one nexus merged into the other. The link men were Gosnold, the Percys and the younger Hakluyt. But the two groups differed markedly in character, reflecting the spirit of the periods in which they flourished. The Raleigh nexus was individualistic, idealistic, speculative; although based upon reconnaissance and research, it had to make many assumptions about both climate and indigenous inhabitants, some of which turned out to be unfounded or over-optimistic. Its finances were too narrowly based to withstand the reverses that such an enterprise might face, and its leaders on the ground turned out not to be ruthless enough to cope with the problems they encountered.

By contrast, the Popham nexus was a good deal more hard-headed. It prepared more thoroughly, financed itself more comprehensively, gave itself a firm legal basis, sought to ensure a succession of strong leaders with sufficient reserves to make up for losses, and provided machinery for consultation, both on the ground and back in England, that by and large stood the test of time. Naturally too it sought to learn from the mistakes of the previous attempts. For all that, it had to withstand as many reverses as had the earlier expeditions—the Virginia epidemic of 1607, and the 'starving time'[101] later in the decade, were at least as potentially cata-strophic as the storms of 1585–86—but it overcame them by applying large resources to large problems.

There is little doubt, in the writer's view, about which of these two approaches was the more appropriate to the conditions of the early settlements on the eastern seaboard. Yet, such is the lure of the romantic, Raleigh and Durham are two of the principal cities of North Carolina, while Virginia has no Popham, no Sandys, no Percy. Maine has the tiny settlement of Popham Beach with its small State Park.

An exclusive Middle Temple claim cannot be read into any of the foregoing. All the other Inns have some connection with the mariners, adventurers and entrepreneurs of that age amongst their membership. Only three examples are Drake at Inner Temple, Cavendish at Gray's Inn, and a strong de la Warr connection at Lincoln's. But it does seem that the weight of association rests with the Middle Temple; and the presence of the Molyneux Globes in the Library is a powerful physical reminder of the great voyages of that time.

---

[101] This refers to the dreadful winter of 1608–09, when the colony was in real risk of extinction: Milton, above n 22, at 334.

B.   The Eighteenth century onwards: Sir William Scott and other jurists

No such close connection between the Middle Temple and the maritime life of the nation can be identified for the next century and a half. The peculiar ethos of the Elizabethan and early Jacobean age, where people of great individuality, ruthless energy and networked influence up to the highest level flourished, and where the Inns were some of their principal social milieux, gave place to a more complex structure of power in which commercial and financial enterprises, clubs and coffee houses, newspapers and pamphlets, landed and overseas estates all played a major part. In all these the sea was a pervasive factor: the East India Company was increasingly the most important enterprise in the country, the Royal Navy was Britain's largest single material undertaking, and the triangular trade to West Africa and the Indies—trade goods, slaves and sugar—the most profitable as well as the most reprehensible. But the Inns of Court were only peripherally involved in any of them.

However, in 1762 an individual joined the Middle Temple who was to have a marked impact on the maritime life of the nation, and indeed of the world, during the next 60 years. This was William Scott, son of a Newcastle coal merchant and at that time only 17 years old. There was a certain romance about his origins and education; he was born in the County of Durham, his mother having moved there hurriedly to escape the dangers of the 1745 rebellion, and this had enabled him to take up in 1761 a scholarship to Corpus Christi College, Oxford, reserved for Durham men.[102] He turned his academic abilities to account with distinction for the next decade and a half, teaching at Oxford and being made Camden Reader in Ancient History in 1774.

But his longer-term plan was clearly to follow the law. He began to keep terms at Middle Temple in 1777, obtained his Doctorate of Law in 1779 and was called to the Bar in 1780.[103] Thereupon he joined Doctors' Commons and, after the customary 'year of silence',[104] began a practice largely in the field of maritime prize—a busy area because the War of American Independence was still in progress. He quickly established a reputation in this specialised court, which was conducted in an atmosphere different from the rough-and-tumble of the common law: as its name implied, all the advocates held doctorates in law and were called 'civilians'

---

[102]   R Hill, *The Prizes of War* (Stroud, Glos, Sutton, 1998), 15.

[103]   *Bench Book*, above n 76, at 193.

[104]   GD Squibb (in *Doctors' Commons—A History of the College of Advocates and Doctors of Law* (Oxford, Clarendon Press, 1977), 32) mentions the 'year of silence'. He does not in terms describe its purpose, but the inference is that it was a reading-in period, and he points out that it was a real impediment to starting in practice, particularly as most of the new members would by then be 30 or thereabouts, having spent so much time acquiring their qualifications.

because the civil law was practised there, and much of the work was based upon documentary rather than witness evidence. Indeed, so far as prize was concerned it was the Law of Nations, rather than municipal law, that was primarily in issue.

Scott was well placed for advancement. The other significant names in Doctors' Commons—John Nicholl, James Henry Arnold, French Laurence, Maurice Swabey, Christopher Robinson, none of them incidentally Middle Templars—had all joined after Scott, which made him a natural choice for the post of King's Advocate in 1787 and elevation to the High Court of Admiralty in succession to Sir James Marriott in 1798.

For the next 30 years Sir William Scott, later Lord Stowell (1821), exercised massive authority at the Admiralty Court and delivered judgments of significance that have, fortunately, been recorded by good reporters throughout the period.[105] The accuracy of the reports was aided by the fact that Scott, by all accounts no orator himself,[106] was in the habit of writing out his own judgments; they are models of clarity, as are those items of his correspondence that survive, notably in the Doctors' Commons files in the Public Record Office.[107]

Naturally enough, considering that his period as judge covered the greater part of the most comprehensive maritime war fought by Britain up to that date, Scott's reported judgments cover the whole gamut of prize law as it stood and developed. The breadth of his work is forcibly indicated by a very full survey conducted in the early 1990s by Lynne Townley (herself a member of Middle Temple),[108] to which this part of the article must pay tribute.

In his earlier years Scott was heavily concerned with questions of neutrality. To be condemned as lawful prize, a captured ship had to be either of enemy character or in enemy service—which many so-called neutrals were. The captured ship's officers had by law to answer, to the captor's agent, a series of Standing Interrogatories that would, if honestly answered, establish the facts on these points; but Scott had frequently to deal with 'colourable' papers and statements. The nationality of the owner, master and any special circumstances all came into the matter, and in Scott's very first reported case, *The Vigilantia*,[109] he set out the factors

---

[105] C Robinson, *Reports of Cases heard in the High Court of Admiralty under Sir William Scott* (6 vols, 1798–1808); T Edwards, ditto (1 vol, 1809–12); J Dodson, ditto (2 vols, 1813–28) (hereafter 'CRob', 'TEdw', 'JDods' respectively).

[106] HJ Bourguignon, *Sir William Scott, Lord Stowell* (Cambridge, Cambridge University Press, 1987), at 50.

[107] ADM 1/3894–3903.

[108] L Townley, *Sir William Scott, Lord Stowell and the Development of Prize Law in the High Court of Admiralty 1798–1828, with Particular Reference to the Rights of Belligerents* (unpublished thesis, University of Birmingham, 1994).

[109] 1 CRob 1 (1798).

clearly. If there turned out to be an enemy connection with regard to the cargo, questions of contraband had still to be considered; here Scott (who by no means made law 'on the hoof') went deeply into precedent from the time of Sir Leoline Jenkins[110] onwards in deciding whether materials destined for the enemy were of a nature warlike enough to condemn them.

A further neutrality question, of critical importance to naval commanders, was the belligerent right of visit and search. This was disputed by some neutrals in cases where their merchantmen were formed in convoys escorted by one or more of their own warships. Scott's judgment in one such case, *The Maria*,[111] was one of the most important of his career. He founded his condemnation of the ships of a Swedish convoy, whose escort had offered token resistance to a superior British force, on numerous authorities from the *Black Book of Admiralty* onwards, including French, Swiss and Spanish writers and at least one Swede, Puffendorf. *The Maria* was also notable for Scott's statement of principle which must stand as a model for jurists of international law and is worth quoting in full:

> I consider myself as stationed here, not to deliver occasional and shifting opinions to serve present purposes of particular national interest, but to administer with indifference that justice which the law of nations holds out without distinction to independent states.

High-principled this might have been, but Scott's judgment was not accepted by many neutrals, particularly those who adopted the dictum of 'free ships, free goods'; and it was left to the force of arms, notably at the Battle of Copenhagen (1801), to put an end to the armed neutrality that followed on from *The Maria* and similar incidents.[112]

A further device of economic warfare was blockade: the total interdiction by a belligerent of traffic into and out of a port or area. Here, in the many blockade cases that came before him, there was plenty of precedent for Scott to work on, and up to 1806 he applied the classic tests: Had a blockade been notified by proper authority? Was it being effectively enforced? And had an attempt to break it actually been made? His judgments, eminently fair and not infrequently resulting in restoration of ship and/or cargo, rested on these factors, but that is not to say the facts always made them easy to resolve. In *The Juffrouw Maria Schroeder*, for example,[113] the effectiveness of the blockade of Le Havre was in question; the ship had been allowed in but was captured on her way out. Evidence was brought that Evan Nepean, the Secretary of the Admiralty, had remonstrated with the commanders of the

---

[110] 1625–85. Judge of the Court of Admiralty 1668–85: *ODNB* sub nom Jenkins, Sir Leoline and Exton, John.

[111] 1 CRob 340 (1799).

[112] WL Clowes, *The Royal Navy: A History from the Earliest Times to 1900* (London, Chatham, 1997), vol 4, at 427.

[113] 3 CRob 147 (1800).

blockading forces about the laxity of the blockade. Scott came to a conclusion that reads a little oddly now; he condemned the cargo on the ground that the shippers must have known of the blockade and were taking a risk unjustifiable in law, but restored the ship because she had come (in ballast, presumably) from a port where the existence of the blockade might not have been known. He added a rider that was severe on the Royal Navy: 'It is in vain for governments to impose blockades if those employed on that service will not enforce them ...'

More light-hearted was the matter of *The Shepherdess*.[114] The ship had been intercepted on course for Le Havre, and the master claimed that he had been drunk at the time and had no idea where he was going. Indeed, he added, he was generally in a state of intoxication. Few judges, then or now, could resist such an opportunity and Scott was no exception:

> [I]f such an excuse could be admitted there would be eternal carousings in every instance of violation of blockade. The master cannot, on any principle of law, be permitted to stultify himself ... The owners of the vessel have appointed him their agent, and they must in law be bound by his imprudence.

That was in 1804, and within two years the practice of blockade as a method of economic warfare was to change radically. By 1806 Napoleon was the effective master of Europe. Nominally sovereign and neutral States were subject to the decrees of the Empire, and British commercial, as well as warlike, interests were severely affected. In May 1806, therefore, Britain issued a proclamation imposing a blockade from the Elbe to Brest—a coastline of well over a thousand miles—with some concessions for neutrals not carrying enemy goods or contraband of war. Escalation followed with Napoleon's Berlin Decree (November 1806), the first British Order in Council (January 1807), the second such Order (November 1807) and the Milan Decree (December 1807). Effectively, the result from 1808 onwards was Napoleon's Continental System, seeking to cut off all intercourse between Britain and Europe, and a British-run licensing system that sought to circumvent the obstacles to trade under the protection of the Royal Navy's maritime dominance.

Sir William Scott was in the middle of this hugely complex situation, which cut across many of the principles of and tests for blockade that had grown over the centuries. For example, it was quite clear that rigorous enforcement over such a long coastline simply was not possible. Notification there had been, but it was shaded by the multitude of concessions and modifications that issued from the British authorities almost weekly.[115] Finally, evidence of attempts to break the blockade would boil down to a

---

[114]   5 CRob 262 (1804).
[115]   *Notifications, Orders and Instructions relating to Prize Subjects during the Present War* (Strahan, for Butterworth and White, 1810), *passim.*

new kind of test: licence or no licence. The practice of the Admiralty Court changed radically; from 1808 it was awash with licence cases.[116]

But it was the law that was most disputable in principle, and in particular whether the law as enunciated by the British Orders in Council was in accordance with the Law of Nations. Lord Erskine, in a severe speech in the House of Lords on 8 March 1808,[117] 'arraigned' the Orders as a violation of the Law of Nations and of the law of the land, arguing that a nation purporting to be the world's guardian against tyranny must safeguard the rights of neutrals. Even though Erskine's proposed resolutions did not pass, it is surprising that no challenge on the point of principle was made in the Prize Court until 1809. In this case, *The Fox*,[118] it was submitted that the Orders were indeed contrary to the Law of Nations. Scott's judgment was frank: the Order was

> doubtless a great and signal departure from the ordinary administration of justice in the ordinary state of the exercise of public hostility, but was justified by that extraordinary deviation from the common exercise of hostility in the conduct of the enemy.

The system, therefore, rumbled on, with knotty problems at sea, in the ports and in the courts. The Orders were repealed in June 1812, too late to prevent the outbreak of war with the United States (for which they were a prime *casus belli*), but their residue lingered to the middle of the decade. It can be argued, though, that they had done their work as an instrument of economic warfare; reaction to them in northern Europe and particularly Russia did much to undermine Napoleon's hold on the Empire and move him to his disastrous eastern enterprise in 1812.

Scott's work in the Admiralty Court was not confined to questions of neutrality, blockade and licensing. He gave massive judgments in matters of belligerent rights in neutral waters,[119] national sovereignty over low tide elevations,[120] recapture and salvage,[121] and droits of Admiralty where the time or place of a capture brought that principle into issue.[122]

He also had to rule frequently on a distasteful aspect of prize warfare, squabbles (sometimes between senior officers) about which units of a force were entitled to the proceeds of a prize. The general rule, of being 'in sight' at the moment of capture, was subject to all kinds of argument and gloss, centring on the principle (enunciated by Scott[123]) of 'constructive assistance',

---

[116] Hill, above n 102, at 50ff.
[117] Townley, above n 108, at 349n.
[118] JEdw 311 (1809).
[119] *The Twee Gebroeders*, 3 CRob 162 (1800) and 336 (1801), with Appendices XI–XII.
[120] *The Anna*, 5 CRob 373 (1805).
[121] *The Santa Cruz*, 1 CRob 49 (1798).
[122] *The Rebeckah*, 1 CRob 227 (1799).
[123] *La Flore*, 5 CRob 268 (1804); *l'Amitié*, 6 CRob 261 (1805); *The Odin*, 4 CRob 318 (1803).

and cases sometimes went on for years. In *The Guillaume Tell* [124] indeed, Scott gave a blast to all parties for the self-imposed delay: it was richly deserved, for most of the protagonists, including Troubridge the prime mover of the dispute, were long dead.

Not only was Sir William Scott the only Admiralty Judge in England, he was also the administrator of the whole Admiralty and Prize system. On foreign stations this was exercised through Vice Admiralty Courts, each formally established with its principal officers approved by London. While Scott's Court in Doctors' Commons was subject to accusations of cosy practices, deliberate delays and overcharging, these allegations failed to stick at the time and have been found, on analysis, [125] to be generally unfounded; in general, captors stood to receive about 80 per cent of the value of a prize, after court and agents' fees, incidental costs and statutory contributions to Greenwich Hospital were deducted.

The situation was more variable in the Vice Admiralty Courts. Some, in particular those in Bermuda, Halifax and Jamaica, measured up pretty well to the standard set in London. Others had a poor name either among captors or among the merchants of nations most subject to capture; Tortola was described as 'rascally' by an outraged American captain. [126] Malta can be singled out as the most disliked and, probably, the most corrupt; Thomas Cochrane, Earl of Dundonald's campaign against the administration of this court is well documented. [127]

Scott was, on all the evidence, a reluctant administrator. It is clear from the files in the National Archive concerned with the conduct of Doctors' Commons that he was slow to be drawn in to change of any description. He opposed any proliferation of Vice Admiralty Courts; it might be thought that this was for the very good reason that there were not enough competent (and honest) practitioners to go round, but it certainly slowed down business. He clearly disliked disputes about court fees and practices, and it was not until 1811 that he consented to a searching review of the conduct of the Vice Admiralty Courts. When this did occur, it was thoroughly conducted by a high-level commission and the scale of (reduced) fees was accepted with only one demur. [128]

Nevertheless, it must lie to the charge of Scott that, deeply conservative as he was, he could and should have done more to mitigate the principal evil of what was basically a sound system: delay in captors' coming to what was, by the *mores* of the time, their just reward. For merchant ship

---

[124]   1 JDods 359 (1813).
[125]   Hill, above n 102, at 181.
[126]   Clowes, above n 112, vol 6, at 13.
[127]   (1813) XXV *The Naval Chronicle* 300. See also Thomas Cochrane, Earl of Dundonald, *Autobiography of a Seaman* (London, Constable, 1995 edn), vol II, at 170, for his own account.
[128]   PRO ADM 1/3900.

captures adjudicated in the Admiralty Court, only 53 per cent settled within two years of capture; the figures for warship and privateer captures was higher at 65 per cent, and for recaptures higher still, at 84 per cent,[129] but it was still a long wait for the captors' people. It is unclear whether Scott was ever put under pressure to establish more Admiralty Courts in England with a jurisdiction in prize; had he done so, such delays must surely have been much reduced.

It may be said that Sir William Scott operated in a field of law that has long passed into history, even though some prize cases came to court in the First and Second World Wars, and questions concerning war booty arose as late as The Falklands conflict in 1982.[130] Nevertheless Scott's influence on British operation, and indeed strategy, during that critical war that ended in 1815 and ushered in the period still called *Pax Britannica*, was profound. He was, moreover, fully prepared to do his duty by the Inn. He was called to the Bench in 1794, was Lent Reader in 1799 and treasurer in 1807.[131] While the responsibilities may not have been particularly onerous during this period, it is extraordinary that Scott undertook them when he was at his busiest in Doctors' Commons. He also bequeathed £200 to the Inn, which was applied to the purchase of books for the Library. A fine portrait of him by Thomas Phillips, RA, hangs in the Bench corridor. Lastly, a unique memento of Scott exists in the Rare Books Room of the Inn: three notebooks concerned with prize law, which, although probably not compiled by him, were in his possession while he held office and were passed by him to the Admiralty Judges 'in succession'. They were donated to the Inn in 1918 by John F Lewis. Their provenance and coverage have been fully discussed by Townley.[132]

Later in the nineteenth century the distinguished Admiralty Judge Sir Robert Phillimore was of the Middle Temple; while in the twentieth century, the distinguished publicist C John Colombos and the historian ES Roscoe both made unique contributions to the scholarship of international law. Towards the end of the twentieth century Masters Sheen, Darling and Clarke[133] carried on the tradition of the Middle Temple's service to the maritime interests of the nation.

---

[129] Hill, above n 102, at 213.

[130] Conversation Richard Hill/Judge David Anderson (ex FCO Deputy Legal Adviser), *c* 1998.

[131] *Bench Book*, above n 76, at 193.

[132] Townley, above n 108, at 14–24.

[133] (1) Sir Barry Sheen (1918–2005), Judge of the Queen's Bench Division (Admiralty Court) 1978–93; Middle Temple Reader 1990. (2) Gerald Ralph Auchinleck Darling QC (1921–96) Judge of the Admiralty Court of the Cinque Ports 1979–96; treasurer of the Middle Temple 1991. (3) Lord Clarke of Stone-cum-Ebony, Admiralty Judge of the Queen's Bench Division 1993–98.

Literary Associations of the Middle Temple

JESSICA WINSTON[*]

A S FAR BACK as the Greek philosopher Plato (427–347 BC) and Roman poet Ovid (43 BC–AD 17), law and literature have been viewed as largely incompatible. In his *Republic* (*c* 375 BC), Plato banished most poets from his ideal commonwealth, suggesting that their fabrications could corrupt youth. Ovid neglected his legal studies, writing that he was unfit for the 'toil' of law (and a related political career) and more drawn to poetry.[1] Given such ancient incompatibility, readers may wonder why, over the centuries, an extraordinary number of literary authors studied, lived or worked at the English legal institutions, the Inns of Court or their affiliated Inns of Chancery. These authors include the poet John Donne (1572–1631, adm LI 1592), the playwright John Marston (bap 1576, d 1634, adm MT 1592), the playwright Francis Beaumont (1584/85–1616, adm IT 1600), the playwright William Congreve (1670–1729, adm MT 1690 or 1691), the novelist Henry Fielding (1707–54, adm MT 1737), the poet Thomas Gray (1716–71, adm IT 1735), the novelist Charles Dickens (1812–70, adm MT 1839), the novelist Wilkie Collins (1824–89, adm LI 1846), as well as, more recently, the playwright and screenwriter Anthony Shaffer (1926–2001, adm MT 1949) and the mystery writer Sarah Caudwell (1939–2000, adm MT 1962).[2]

[*] The research for this article was funded by Grant No 1013 from the Faculty Research Committee, Idaho State University (ISU) and by a Research Fellowship from the Idaho Humanities Council (IHC). The views expressed here do not necessarily represent those of Idaho State University, the IHC or the IHC's parent organisation, the National Endowment for the Humanities. Ms D Kimbro, an ISU MA student, assisted with the research. L Whitelaw, the archivist at the Middle Temple, provided invaluable help, answering queries and providing specific details on Middle Temple authors (see esp n 43 and n 79 below). W Prest and M O'Callaghan also offered helpful feedback.
[1] Ovid, *Tristia*, AL Wheeler (trans), Loeb Classical Library (Cambridge, Cambridge University Press, 1953), 4.10.
[2] This article follows authors' names with dates and dates of admission ('adm') to the Inns of Court. The names of the four Inns are abbreviated as follows: Lincoln's Inn (LI), Gray's Inn (GI), Inner Temple (IT), and Middle Temple (MT). Life dates are as given in the

Judging from Plato's and Ovid's sentiments, we might suppose that the literary associations of the Inns result from the longstanding opposition between literature and law, or so this thinking might go: law is tedious, a profession befitting a 'mercenary drudge' (in the words of Christopher Marlowe[3]), but literature is an amusing pastime, so much so that students have routinely rejected law in favour of literary pursuits. The idea has some merit (as we shall see further below), but it assumes that the Inns have been solely legal communities throughout their history. Michelle O'Callaghan observes of the Inns in the Renaissance (*c* 1485–1640):

> The Inns of Court were a meeting place for a range of early modern communities—legal, intellectual, parliamentary—and constituted an important social space for intellectual exchange.[4]

This is no less true for later periods. Historically, the Inns have been part of broader intellectual communities, attracting bright, well-educated men, and in the twentieth century women too, who in their time at the Inns have connected with members of any number of professions, including politics, journalism, medicine, religion and the arts, as well as law. Members also often pursued careers other than law (or they combined other careers with a legal practice during their lives). As one author noted in the mid-eighteenth century: 'there have been lawyers that were orators, philosophers, historians', not to mention novelists, poets, and playwrights.[5] When viewed as part of a broader group of intellectual and social activities, the Inns' literary associations make more sense. The social environment there encouraged and fostered literary endeavours of members through the centuries.

A look at the literary associations of any one or all of the Inns could illustrate this point, especially since members of the four frequently interacted socially and inspired each others' literary, legal and other work. This article focuses on the Middle Temple, a substantive topic in its own right and the subject of this volume. Hugh Bellot, John Gover and Blake Odgers have documented these associations in chronological surveys of

---

Oxford Dictionary of National Biography, HCG Matthew and B Harrison (eds), 60 vols (Oxford, Oxford University Press, 2004), referred to throughout as *ODNB*. The symbol 'x', as in '1578x80', indicates a range where the precise date is not known. I have modernised the spelling of all quotations and amended archaic or missing punctuation. While Caudwell was a member of the Middle Temple, she had chambers in Lincoln's Inn, an important setting in her novels.

[3] C Marlowe, *Dr Faustus* in F Romany and R Lindsey (eds), *The Complete Plays* (London, Penguin Books, 2003), 1.1.34.
[4] M O'Callaghan, 'Literary Commonwealths: A 1614 Print Community, *The Shepheards Pipe* and *Shepherds Hunting*' (1998) 13 *The Seventeenth Century* 104.
[5] H St John, 'Of the Study of History' in *Philosophical Works*, 5 vol (London, D Mallet, 1754), 2.353.

authors connected to the Inns.[6] This article also mentions many individual authors, but the main issue is why so many writers were members of the Inns, and the examples are drawn mainly (but not exclusively) from the period of the Renaissance, an era in which various literary groups thrived at the Middle Temple. The period provides a clear illustration of the way that the intellectual communities at and connected with Middle Temple, and the Inns of Court more generally, fostered the talents and stirred the imaginations of so many major and minor dramatists, poets and novelists.

I. LAW V LITERATURE

It is easy to assume that law and literature are incompatible and, more than this, that law students turned to the pleasures of literature to escape the tedium of legal studies. The assumption makes some sense if one looks back to the Renaissance, arguably the period when the most literary activity occurred at the Inns. Then, legal training was very difficult, since the Inns had no classes or professional teachers and learning the law involved a significant amount of independent reading, which could be dull, if not entirely baffling.[7] Writing in his diary, Simonds D'Ewes (1602–50), a student at the Middle Temple (adm 1620), complained about his legal studies, noting that they made him 'perplexed' and 'puzzled' to the point where, 'I prostrated myself before my good God' and prayed for better 'apprehension and judgment'.[8] D'Ewes persevered, becoming a successful lawyer, but faced with the same puzzlement many of his contemporaries abandoned their studies to read novels, write poetry and attend plays. When the future playwright John Marston, also a student at the Middle

---

[6] HHL Bellot, *The Inner and Middle Temple: Legal, Literary, and Historic Associations* (London, Methuen, 1902); JM Gover, *Literary Associations with the Middle Temple: A Reading Delivered before the Honourable Society of the Middle Temple* (London, Pitman, 1935); WB Odgers, 'Literary Men Connected with the Inns of Court and of Chancery' in WB Odgers (ed) *Six Lectures on the Inns of Court and Chancery: Delivered in the Middle Temple Hall during Easter and Trinity Terms, 1912* (London, Macmillan, 1912). Instead of broad surveys, more recent discussions of the literary associations of the Inns profile individual authors, but these do not explore why the Inns were such important literary or intellectual communities. See 'Music and Recreation' in C Rider and V Horsler (eds), *The Inner Temple: A Community of Communities* (London, Third Millenium, 2007), 150–65 and 'Poets, Playwrights, and Novelists' in A Holdsworth (ed), *A Portrait of Lincoln's Inn* (London, Third Millenium, 2007), 70–83.

[7] PJ Finkelpearl, *John Marston of the Middle Temple: An Elizabethan Dramatist in His Social Setting* (Cambridge, Harvard University Press, 1969) 8; W Prest, 'Legal Education and the Gentry at the Inns of Court, 1560–1640' (1967) 8 *Past and Present* 20; L Knafla, 'The Studies of an Elizabethan Law Student' (1969) 32 *Huntington Library Quarterly* 21.

[8] E Bourcier (ed), *Diary of Sir Simonds D'Ewes (1622–1624)* (Paris, Didier, 1974) 77. Legal education was always difficult. As JH Baker writes, from the earliest times, 'the Inns of Court were nominally institutions of learning but were clearly not institutions for teaching … [T]he accepted method of legal education before the last century was self-help': *An Introduction to English Legal History* (London, Butterworths, 1971), 76.

Temple, did just this, his father grumbled that he 'hoped that [his] son would have profited in the study of the law', but he took 'delight in plays and vain studies and fooleries'.[9]

The tendency of law students to neglect their studies in favour of literary pursuits (and other 'vain fooleries') resulted in the stereotype of the dilettante, even debauched, Inns of Court man in the satirical poetry and drama of the period. In 1592, Thomas Nashe (bap 1567, died *c* 1601) disparaged Inns of Court men who 'do wholly bestow themselves upon pleasure, and that pleasure they divide ... either into gaming, following of harlots, drinking, or seeing a play'. Another author described the 'inns of court man' who has 'heard one mooting, and seen two plays'. Yet another contemporary reiterated the contrast, stating that the Inns of Court man 'reads not *Littleton*, / But *Don Quixote* or else *The Knight o' th' Sun*' and 'Instead of Perkins peddlers' French, he says / He better loves Ben Jonson's book of plays'.[10] In other words, the Inns of Court man avoids those classic books on land law (originally written in law French) by Thomas Littleton (died 1481; adm IT, date not known) and John Perkins (died 1545?; adm IT *c* 1518) and reads instead romances and the plays of Ben Jonson (1572–1637).

This seemingly negative correlation between legal and literary activities at the Inns continued in later periods, and is a minor theme in the lives of famous members of the Middle Temple in the *Oxford Dictionary of National Biography*. Concerning the editor and playwright Nicholas Rowe (1674–1718, adm MT 1691) one finds he

> did not take to the law ... and having, even as a youth, read greatly, especially in classical and modern dramatic literature, he tried his hand as a dramatist. On his father's death in 1692 ... he was free to follow his inclinations.[11]

About the same time, William Congreve did likewise:

> He was evidently able to put his knowledge of the law to good use later [in his writing], but ... his inclinations were decidedly towards the theatre and poetry, and he was never called to the bar.[12]

In later centuries, the novelist William Makepeace Thackeray (1811–63, adm MT 1831)

---

[9]   Quoted in the *Oxford Dictionary of National Biography* (ODNB), 36:895.

[10]   T Nashe, 'Pierce Penniless His Supplication to the Devil' in FP Wilson (ed), *The Works of Thomas Nashe*, 5 vols (New York, Barnes and Noble, 1966), 1.212; T Overbury, 'Characters' in EE Rimbault (ed), *Miscellaneous Works in Prose and Verse* (London, Reeves and Turner, 1890), 103; F Lenton, *The Young Gallants Whirligigg: or Youths Reakes* (London, MF for Robert Bostocke, 1629), sig B2v.

[11]   *ODNB*, 47:1001.

[12]   *ODNB*, 12:934. The same was true for several of Congreve's contemporaries. The playwrights George Etherege (1636–1691/92, adm Clement's Inn 1659) and William Wycherley (bap 1641, d 1716, adm IT 1659), as well as the poet and playwright Thomas Shadwell (*c* 1640–92, adm MT 1658).

read law, clerked, attended dinners, and disparaged his work in letters home … He remained in this routine for nearly a year, during which his passion for the theatre and for reading fiction and history were developed more assiduously than the law.[13]

For the prolific (if minor) playwright Henry James Byron (1835–84; adm MT 1858), 'The aspiring barrister was quickly swallowed by the practising playwright who, over the next twenty-five years, would produce upwards of 150 dramatic pieces'.[14] More recently, Anthony Shaffer 'read law, but took considerably more pleasure in editing *Granta*', a literary journal.[15]

Despite such examples, the seeming tedium of law and joy of literature cannot explain the numerous literary associations of the Inns in general or the Middle Temple specifically. Why then did many men continue to study law, even when exposed to literary diversions? And why did some authors pursue literary careers alongside legal ones, notably the lawyer and poet Stephen Harvey (1655–1707, adm MT 1673) or the magistrate and novelist Henry Fielding, or the lawyer and playwright Thomas Talfourd (1795–1854, adm MT 1813), or Talfourd's son Frank (1828–62, adm MT 1848), a barrister and playwright, who 'occasionally went on [the legal] circuit, but was chiefly known as the writer of a series of burlesques and extravaganzas'.[16] And why did so many men go on to other professions altogether, especially in journalism, the arts or the Church?

Some students attended an Inn of Court because their parents wanted them to learn the law. Examples are John Marston and the poet Thomas Carew (1594/95–1640, adm MT 1612), whose fathers were themselves members of the Middle Temple. Such students chose new professions while at the Inn because that was the point when they had reached an age (and level of independence) to choose another field. Yet the number of writers at the Middle Temple cannot be mere coincidence or coming-of-age.

Another possible, but only partial, answer is signalled by some work in the academic field of law and literature. Scholars have traced numerous connections between the disciplines, arguing, for instance, that reading literature deepens the ethical sensibilities of lawyers and sharpens their skills in interpretation and argumentation; that works of literature filter (and shape) our interpretation of legal concepts; and that legal ideas and cases influence literary plots.[17] The idea that both fields share an interest in

---

[13]   *ODNB*, 54:194.

[14]   *ODNB*, 9:362

[15]   K McCarron, 'Shaffer, Anthony Joshua (1926–2001)', *ODNB* (online edn) (Oxford, Oxford University Press, Jan 2005), available at <www.oxforddnb.com/view/article/76427>, accessed 19 November 2008, para 2.

[16]   *ODNB*, 53:735.

[17]   For some recent examples, see R Weisberg, 'Wigmore and the Law and Literature Movement' (2009) 21 *Law and Literature* 129–47; B Cormack, *A Power to Do Justice: Jurisdiction, English Literature, and the Rise of Common Law, 1509–1625* (Chicago,

narrative and rhetoric is promising, since some Inns of Court authors themselves recognised the connection. The poet Sir Philip Sidney (1554–86, adm GI 1567) compares the poet to the lawyer in his *Apology for Poetry* (1595) because both are skilled in the art of persuasion.[18] And another writer-lawyer, John Hoskins (1566–1638), while studying at the Middle Temple (adm 1593), wrote *Directions for Speech and Style* (*c* 1599), an elaborate treatise on rhetoric aimed in part at lawyers, which draws most examples from Sidney's own prose romance *Arcadia* (*c* late 1570s). Yet the fact that the fields require attention to rhetoric, storytelling and interpretation is at best a partial explanation: while it might account for the substantial and sustained overlap between law and literature at the Inns, it also leads one to expect that more Inns of Court men would have become writers (if both lawyers and authors are skilled in rhetoric, why would not more apply their expertise in one field to the other?). At the same time, this idea does not account for the imbrication of legal study and the endeavours of Inns of Court men in so many other fields.

Wilfrid Prest offers a better theory, suggesting that—at least in the Renaissance—the very fact that the Inns were not very effective as law teaching institutions made them especially conducive environments for literary and creative activities. Even as the Inns gave students opportunities to develop in their legal knowledge, the culture fostered by their 'laissez-faire' educational system tended to encourage extra-legal pursuits.[19] While it is necessary to recognise that legal learning was an important part of life at the Inns, this article builds from Prest's insight, looking more precisely at how the social milieu of the Inns fostered literary and other intellectual interests in the Renaissance and later.

The Inns traditionally have admitted bright, well-educated and ambitious students. Some (such as Simonds D'Ewes) came to study law, but many others came to make social contacts and acquire an urban sophistication that would help them to advance in elite circles. Like residential colleges and universities today, the institutions provided men with opportunities to eat, study, work and play together. Since so much of the legal training was not scheduled and formalised, daily life at the Inns also involved extracurricular pursuits, including privately-contracted lessons in socially-advantageous skills (such as, depending on the period, dancing, singing, fencing). In the centuries before radio and television, recreation often centred on the enjoyment of language and letters: witty and satirical

University of Chicago Press, 2007); and L Hutson, *Invention and Suspicion: Law and Mimesis in Shakespeare and Renaissance Drama* (Oxford, Oxford University Press, 2008).

[18] P Sidney, 'Defence of Poesy' in M Payne and J Hunter (eds), *Renaissance Literature: An Anthology* (Oxford, Blackwell, 2003), 506, 517.
[19] W Prest, *The Inns of Court under Elizabeth I and the Early Stuarts, 1590–1640* (London, Longman, 1972), 168.

conversation, play-going and storytelling. In many cases, groups from outside the Inns furnished entertainment. For instance, professional actors performed Shakespeare's *The Comedy of Errors* at Gray's Inn (1594) and *Twelfth Night* at the Middle Temple (1602). But it was common for members to develop pastimes too, to write and perform plays, share their own poetry and tell their own stories. Thus, in 1560, Jasper Heywood (1535–98), a future member of Gray's Inn (adm 1561), observed that the Inns were places where 'Minerva's men and finest wits do swarm' and the poet Thomas Churchyard (1523?–1604) wrote that there 'sages' and 'muses' dwell and 'wit & knowledge flows'.[20] Far more recently (if still some time ago), in 1955, a group of Middle Temple barristers formed an acting troupe, presumably for their own entertainment and to create an intellectual and artistic outlet for themselves.[21]

Over the centuries many authors linked their writing directly to the Inns of Court milieu. In one early instance, Thomas Lodge (1558–1625), a member of Lincoln's Inn (adm 1578), dedicated his *Alarum Against Usurers* (1584) to 'my courteous friends, the Gentlemen of the Inns of Court' and his *Scilla's Metamorphoses* (1590) to 'his most entire well-willers, the Gentlemen of the Inns of Court and Chancery'.[22] The satirist and soldier William Goddard (d 1624/25, adm MT 1565) dedicated his book of satires *The Mastif Whelp* (*c* 1614) to several 'loving friends ... of the Inner Temple'.[23] In the same vein, poet Roger Lort (1607/08–64, adm MT 1627) indicates that the Middle Temple inspired many of his poems, when he notes in his *Epigrammatum* (1646) that he was 'lately of the society of the Middle Temple' ('*nuper de societate Medii Templi*') and writes several poems to members of the society as well as one 'to the fellows of the Middle and Inner Temple' ('*Ad socios medii et interioris templi*').[24]

In later periods: the lawyer and aspiring playwright, Henry Lucas (*c* 1740–1802, adm MT 1763) identified himself with the Inn, noting on the title page of his historical drama the *Earl of Somerset* (1777) that he was a 'student of the Middle Temple'.[25] The poet William Cowper (1731–1800, adm MT 1748, adm IT 1757) likewise allied himself and his work with the Inns, publishing his first collection under the title *Poems by William Cowper, of the Inner Temple, Esq* (1782). Such claims are intended to confer a type of

---

[20] J Heywood, 'Preface' in *The Seconde Tragedie of Seneca Entituled Thyestes* (London, Thomas Berthelette, 1560), sig *7v; T Churchyard, *A Light Bondell of Lively Discourses Called Churchyards Charge* (London, John Kyngston, 1580), sig D4r.

[21] L Whitelaw, 'Fifty Years Ago: The Middle Temple in 1955' (2005) 38 *The Middle Templar* 39.

[22] T Lodge, *Alarum Against Usurers Containing Tryed Experiences Against Wordly Abuses* (London, T Este for Sampson Clarke, 1584), sig A2r and *Scillaes Metamorphosis Enterlaced with the Unfortunate Love of Glaucus* (London, Richard Jones, 1590), sig *1r.

[23] W Goddard, *A Mastif Whelp* (Dordrecht, George Waters, 1616?), sig A1v.

[24] R Lort, *Epigrammatum* (London, John Langley, 1646), title page and sigs B3r–B4v.

[25] *ODNB*, 34:679.

prestige on their authors by associating them with elite cultural institutions. Yet they also begin to suggest that something in the affiliation with the Inns themselves might have energised the wits and fostered the literary talents of many, many amateur and professional authors.

II.   THE MIDDLE TEMPLE IN LITERATURE

The idea that Inns of Court are social and intellectual communities (rather than strictly legal ones) may come as news to those unfamiliar with the history of the Inns of Court. For many, the first encounter with the Inns comes through literature, and from the sixteenth century to the present, the institutions have only rarely been represented as an important intellectual hub (and then only in works that are not widely known today, such as those cited in section I. above by Jasper Heywood and Thomas Church-yard). And it appears that Middle Temple has never been represented in this way. In the words of Wilfrid Prest, 'barristers were prominent in the cultural and intellectual life of Elizabethan and early Stuart England', but 'that fact seems to have failed to register on their public image, then or later'.[26] Before discussing Middle Temple writers specifically, it is instructive to examine some influential images of this Inn in literature, since such representations have shaped the popular perception of the Middle Temple (and the Inns of Court generally) and help to set off the portrait of the intellectual communities at the Inn that we shall see later.

The Middle Temple (or the area of the Inner and Middle Temple, simply called the Temple) appears frequently in poetry, novels and plays, and perhaps more so than Gray's Inn or Lincoln's Inn, since the Temple gardens and church are open to the public and serve as an important meeting place in London, and thus also figure in literary works set in the city. In these, the Temple is usually portrayed as a setting for solitary activities or for private meetings, where the cloistered walks, gardens and chambers allow characters to engage in personal, social, political, romantic—and sometimes illicit—conversation and activities.

English literature is peppered with characters who hail from in and around the Middle Temple. The earliest appears in Chaucer's *Canterbury Tales* (1381), which describes a 'gentil manciple ... of a temple'.[27] Many of the legal figures in Dickens are associated with the Temple as well (which is not surprising since Dickens was a member of the Middle Temple and lived at Furnival's Inn for many years). In *Barnaby Rudge* (1841), the villainous

---

[26] *The Rise of the Barristers: A Social History of the English Bar, 1590–1640* (Oxford, Clarendon Press, 1986), 184.

[27] G Chaucer, 'General Prologue' in LD Benson (ed), *The Riverside Chaucer* (New York, Houghton Mifflin, 1987), line 567.

Sir John Chester has chambers in Paper Buildings in the Temple, as does the lawyer Stryver, the barrister who defends Charles Darnay in *A Tale of Two Cities* (1859), as well as the young solicitor Mortimer Lightwood in *Our Mutual Friend* (1865). In *Martin Chuzzlewit* (1844), Tom Pinch works for a mysterious employer at the Temple too. In addition, the doctor-turned-barrister, Dr Thorndyke, the detective in the mysteries of Austin Freeman (1862–1943), lives at 6A King's Bench Walk (Inner Temple), and the Temple appears incidentally in the novels (for instance, the Temple bell rings intermittently in the first Thorndyke novel, *The Red Thumb Mark*, 1907).

Most frequently the Temple appears as a setting, and more specifically as a cloistered place, full of history as well as mystery. Thus in *Barnaby Rudge*, Dickens mordantly describes the 'clerkly monkish atmosphere, which public offices of law have not disturbed, and even legal firms have failed to scare away'.[28] In *Martin Chuzzlewit*, the Inn is even more foreboding: there is a 'ghostly air' and 'ghostly mist' about the 'dusty office[s]' where the character Tom Pinch goes about his 'solitary labours'.[29] Also, in Thackeray's *Pendennis* (1850), a visitor to the Inn finds it 'a rather shy place' where 'the lawyers live', and more enigmatically as a place full of 'dark alleys', 'various melancholy archways' and 'courts each more dismal than the other'.[30] In Herman Melville's short story, 'A Paradise of Bachelors' (1855), a visitor approaches the Temple through a 'dim, monastic way flanked by dark, sedate, and solemn piles' where one can 'give the whole care-worn world the slip, and, disentangled, stand beneath the quiet cloisters of the Paradise of Bachelors'.[31] In these works, the Middle Temple seems to exist outside time; it is a gendered space (populated by monk-like lawyer bachelors), which, in its association with solemnity and order, lies beyond the hubbub of the world.

Not surprisingly, because of its association with the legal profession, the Middle Temple is also linked with the preservation of law. In Christopher Marlowe's *Edward II* (c 1592), a disgruntled peer, Warwick, and the Archbishop arrange a meeting 'at the New Temple' to plan to bring complaints to an unresponsive king.[32] Here, the ostensibly unlawful assembly is designed to reinstitute the law and thus occurs in a place associated with its defence. In a similar way, in Shakespeare's *1 Henry IV* (c 1596), Prince Hal tells his roguish friend Falstaff to meet him 'in the Temple Hall'

---

[28] C Dickens, *Barnaby Rudge*, GK Chesterton (ed) (1906, rpt New York, EP Dutton, 1966), 111.

[29] C Dickens, *Martin Chuzzlewit*, Margaret Cardwell (ed) (Oxford, Clarendon, 1982), 618.

[30] WM Thackeray, *Pendennis*, 2 vols (New York, EP Dutton, 1910), 1:288–9.

[31] H Melville, 'The Paradise of Bachelors and the Tartarus of Maids' in John Bryant (ed), *Tales, Poems, and Other Writings* (New York, Modern Library, 2001), 147.

[32] C Marlowe, *Edward II* in Romany and Lindsey (eds), above n 3, scene 2, line 75.

to learn his 'charge' in the coming war.[33] As in *Edward II*, the location is associated with law, suggesting that the meeting is Falstaff's opportunity to reform, to turn himself from criminality to lawfulness and respectability.

Authors sometimes rely on the Temple's connection with law, setting disruptive, even criminal, activities there in order to highlight the disturbance such events pose to the normal order. One example is Shakespeare's *1 Henry VI* (1592), which deals with the outbreak of the Wars of the Roses (1453–85). In one scene, the enemies Richard Plantagenet and Somerset heatedly debate the law in the Temple Garden, upsetting its normal serenity and thus drawing our attention to the developing danger of the scene, while also underscoring its irony: in the secluded garden of a legal institution, a civil war begins.[34] Dickens's *Great Expectations* (1861) develops a similar contrast. At the end of part 2, Pip moves into chambers at Garden Court, Middle Temple, where the ex-convict Magwich visits him, revealing that he is Pip's mysterious benefactor.[35] Like *1 Henry VI*, the setting underscores the irony of the meeting: Pip's seemingly respectable life in the heart of London's legal quarter has been supported by criminal activities.

Other references play up a different sort of opposition, between the Inn's official existence as a serious legal institution and its function as a public, often romantic, meeting place. The opening of the novel *The Temple Beau* (1754) describes this role:

> The Temple Church is the place of rendezvous of many of the petit maitres and belles of that quarter of the town, as whoever goes there on a Sunday must see, not worshipping the God of heaven and earth, but the little droll Cupid with a fervent zeal.[36]

Here the usually monastic world of God (and law), the 'paradise of bachelors', becomes a romantic locale, overseen by the 'little droll Cupid'.

Indeed, in literature, women at the Middle Temple are a transformative force, vivifying an otherwise fossilised world. In *Martin Chuzzlewit*, Dickens sets several scenes in the Middle Temple's Fountain Court, contrasting the grey and lifeless Inn with the joyful ebullience of the 'brightest and purest-hearted' Ruth Pinch, who comes to the Temple to visit her brother. Ruth is 'a delicate little figure' who 'passed like a smile from the grimy old houses'. Comparing her to the fountain itself, Dickens describes her as a 'sparkling' young woman, who livens 'the dry and dusty

---

[33] W Shakespeare, *The First Part of King Henry the Fourth* in S Orgel and AR Braunmuller (eds), *The Complete Pelican Shakespeare* (New York, Penguin Putnam, 2002), 3.3.199–201.

[34] W Shakespeare, *The First Part of Henry the Sixth* in *The Complete Pelican Shakespeare*, above n 33, act 2, scene 4.

[35] C Dickens, *Great Expectations*, A Calder (ed) (New York, Penguin Books, 1965), ch 39, 330–42.

[36] Anon, *Temple Beau, or The Town Coquets: A Novel* (London, W Owen and E Baker, 1754), 2–3.

channels of the law'.[37] Something similar happens in Austin Freeman's mystery *The Red Thumb Mark*, notably in a romantic final scene, which is also set in Fountain Court. The narrator, a melancholy Dr Jervis, delightedly discovers that the lady in the case, Miss Gibson, returns his affections. At the beginning of the scene he is in 'low spirits', but as Miss Gibson happily 'tripped up the steps leading to Fountain Court', he 'followed cheerfully'. An older Templar looks on with approval, remembering his 'spring-time and giving ... his blessing'.[38] Like Ruth Pinch, Miss Gibson enlivens the scene.

Other authors play with and reverse these associations, such as JS Fletcher in his mystery *The Middle Temple Murder* (1919). Fletcher presents the Middle Temple as a masculine, orderly and secluded place, which is disrupted when a crime occurs. The mystery follows the newspaper reporter, Spargo, who investigates the murder of an unidentified man in a dark alley of the Middle Temple late one night. As Spargo probes the incident various suspects emerge, each with a connection to the Inn. The first, a Member of Parliament, Mr Stephen Aylmore, rents an office in the Middle Temple. The second, the lawyer Mr Elphick, lives and works in the Middle Temple. A third, Mr Cardlestone, also resides there. All three are quiet and respectable, and two of the men, Aylmore and Elphick, work in legal fields. Yet as the plot progresses, Fletcher contrasts the Middle Temple as a place of respectability and law with the illicit activities of its residents, revealing each man to have had a shady if not criminal past that connects him to the victim. This contrast creates some scepticism in the reader, leading one to expect that each one of the men is guilty. Yet Spargo discovers that each man is innocent; the true villain is the victim's sister-in-law, a woman who instead of enlivening the Temple commits a murder there.[39]

The Middle Temple comes up elsewhere in literature, as the setting, for instance, in Henry Fielding's play *The Temple Beau* (written in 1730 before he had any personal involvement with the Middle Temple), where the title character Young Wilding conceals his rakish life under the apparently respectable study of law at the Temple.[40] The Middle Temple also appears in Walter Scott's *The Fortunes of Nigel* (1822), which is set in the reign of King James I (1603–25) and mentions the foppish, witty and hot-tempered students of the Temple in that period: they are men who wear 'flowing ringlets' as a sign 'of superiority and of gentility', and are 'wild youngsters'

---

[37] Dickens, above n 29, at 684.
[38] RA Freeman, *The Red Thumb Mark* (1907, rpt New York, Dover Publications, 1986), 298, 302, 304.
[39] JS Fletcher, *The Middle Temple Murder* (New York, Alfred A Knopf, 1919).
[40] H Fielding, *The Temple Beau* in T Lockwood (ed), *Henry Fielding: Plays, Vol 1 1728–1731* (Oxford, Clarendon Press, 2004), 109–84.

and 'tip-top revellers of the Temple' who want the latest 'ruffs, cuffs, and bands'.[41]

Of course, many of these references reflect and appeal to public perceptions of the Middle Temple (and the Inns more broadly), and the Inns have certainly had their share of bachelors, prodigals, romancers, rakes and fops. Yet the members of the Middle Temple have also fostered broader social and intellectual communities at the Inns of Court, as many of the authors listed above would have known, since they lived, studied or worked in the Temple. One wonders why such writers seemingly never represented the Middle Temple in this other way. Perhaps when writing for a broader play-going or reading public, they wanted or needed to appeal to such public perceptions. Whatever the case, it is back to those writers who were members of the Inn that this article now turns.

III.   MIDDLE TEMPLE WRITERS

While over the centuries many writers studied, lived and worked in the Middle Temple, precisely how many is difficult to know. A search in the online *ODNB* yields names of over 200 authors who were associated with the Middle Temple.[42] And Lesley Whitelaw, the Middle Temple archivist, has compiled a list of over 350 'Literary Middle Templars' through the ages, including many who do not appear in the *ODNB*.[43] These compilations include authors who wrote only non-literary works (some theatre critics and political pamphleteers), as well as authors who had only informal links with the institution, like the playwright Oliver Goldsmith (1728?–74) who was not a member but lived in rooms at 2 Brick Court. Obviously, such searches illustrate that a great number of accomplished men and women spent at least some time at the Inn, and support the idea that it was a place of real intellectual importance.

This section looks at members of the Middle Temple who wrote imaginative fiction (poetry, prose and drama, as well as translations of them from other languages) and who wrote while in residence at the Middle Temple, or who explicitly linked themselves and their writing to this milieu, or who maintained a lifelong connection with the Inn. While these limitations reduce the number greatly, a chronological survey of even these authors would be little more than a prose list, and so this section addresses the communities of writers that appeared at the Middle Temple

---

[41]   W Scott, *Fortunes of Nigel* (Boston, Houghton Mifflin, 1913), 16, 17, 38.

[42]   This involved a keyword search for 'Middle Temple', with a limitation to the subject area of 'literature, journalism, and publishing'. Some hits were eliminated because the author in the end had no direct connection with the Middle Temple.

[43]   See L Whitelaw's appendix 'Men of Letters Associated with the Middle Temple', below p 173. I am very grateful to Ms Whitelaw for sharing this list with me in manuscript.

in the Renaissance and especially in the 1590s, since this decade provides the earliest and clearest example of the pattern that exists through the centuries. The culture of the Inn (rather than the study of law *per se*) promoted the work of individual writers and the development of literary circles and communities there.

As we consider these early literary circles, it is important to keep two points in mind. The first is that literary studies were not part of the educational training at the Inns, and thus such writing was an extracurricular activity, part of the entertainments and pastimes of members. Even so, such literary and dramatic pastimes were part of the customs of members of the societies and, as such, they were central to the intellectual development of members and the creation of community at each Inn. Michelle O'Callaghan observes that the

> professional rituals and institutional practices of the Inns thus deeply ingrained habits of *communitas*, of sharing space, of conversation, and of entering into contracts, ranging from friendships and informal fellowships to more formal obligations.[44]

Given such habits, it is tempting to romanticise the Inns as high-minded salons, where men studied and dined together, discussing literary, legal and cultural issues into the night. Yet, and this is the second point, it is helpful to resist this sort of idealisation. While members and non-members alike sometimes described the Inns in laudatory and idealistic ways (as we saw in section I. above, they were full of 'sages' and 'Minerva's men'), members were also often competitive and sometimes disgruntled with each other, and used their wit to engage in a kind of competitive verbal sparring, which confirmed their belonging in the community, even as it threatened to disrupt the community itself.[45] Wit could be used to ridicule (even to humiliate) colleagues, as well as to entertain and connect with them.

While the history of the Middle Temple goes back to the fourteenth century, the first literary men appear in the Renaissance, with the printer-lawyer John Rastell (*c* 1475–1536, adm MT before 1501), the author and literary critic, George Puttenham (1529–90/91, adm MT 1556), and the translator William Bavand (*fl* 1559, adm MT 1557).[46] It is difficult to know why the Middle Temple emerged as a literary centre in this century and not earlier, but it is like the other Inns of Court in this respect. One possibility is that there was a community, but before this time members wrote and circulated their works in ephemeral manuscripts, which have

---

[44]   M O'Callaghan, *The English Wits: Literature and Sociability in Early Modern London* (Cambridge, Cambridge University Press, 2007), 11.

[45]   O'Callaghan develops this point in *The English Wits*, esp ch 1 on 'Gentleman Laywers at the Inns of Court' (at 10–34).

[46]   William Bavand was part of a literary community that mainly involved members of Gray's Inn and the Inner Temple in the 1560s.

since been lost. Another possibility has to do with the influence of humanism in England—that is, the Renaissance educational movement that emphasised the classics and Latin language training. Following humanist principles, in the sixteenth-century grammar schools and universities emphasised reading and writing poetry, and consequently more men who attended the Inns were trained in, and thus predisposed to pursue, literary endeavours.[47]

Whatever the case, the first substantial group of writers coalesced at the Middle Temple in the 1590s. An extended discussion of this circle shows how the intellectual atmosphere created by the men in it promoted literary production. The community involved many important poets, playwrights and aspiring public officials of the day: the poet and lawyer Sir John Davies (bap 1569, d 1626, adm MT 1588), the poet and politician Benjamin Rudyerd (1572–1658, adm MT 1590), the poet and playwright John Marston, the poet Charles Best (*fl* 1592–1611, adm MT 1592), the poet and judge John Hoskins (1566–1638, adm MT 1593), the writer and diplomat Henry Wotton (1568–1639, adm MT 1595), the playwright and pamphleteer Edward Sharpham (bap 1576, d 1608, adm MT 1594); the courtier and author Thomas Overbury (bap 1581, d 1613, adm MT 1598); the lawyer and diarist John Manningham (*c* 1575–1622, adm MT 1598), the playwright and poet John Webster (1578 × 80–1638?, adm MT 1598), and the playwright John Ford (bap 1586, d 1639 × 53?, adm MT 1602), as well as prospective civic leaders, such as the future judge James Whitelocke (1570–1632, adm MT 1593) and the wit, and later barrister and politician, Richard Martin (1570–1618, adm MT 1590). This group developed because the personalities and social interactions of members provoked and refined their literary interests and abilities.

The group was relatively homogeneous. Philip Finkelpearl observes:

> To a remarkable degree, these Middle Temple wits came from the same background, pursued the same course in life, shared the same tastes and preferences, and often tended to act in very similar ways.[48]

They were serious students, serious enough at least to pursue legal careers (and some, such as John Davies, were highly successful). Moreover, they had a similar fondness for witty, biting satire and they had similar personalities, often characterised by volatile tempers as well as an intellectual and egotistical discontentedness with society and the follies of others.[49]

---

[47] On poetry in the English grammar schools, see RF Watson, *The English Grammar Schools to 1660: Their Curriculum and Practice* (Cambridge, Cambridge University Press, 1908), esp ch 19 on 'Verse Making' (at 468–86).

[48] PJ Finkelpearl, John Marston of the Middle Temple: *An Elizabethan Dramatist in His Social Setting* (Cambridge, Harvard University Press, 1969), 46–47.

[49] Ibid, at 47; RW Ingram, *John Marston* (Boston, MA, Twayne, 1978), 25–28.

The diary of John Manningham, one of the men connected with this group, provides some examples of the personalities and characteristics of the men associated with it. Manningham's *Diary* is known today mainly for the description of the performance of Shakespeare's *Twelfth Night* at the Middle Temple Hall in 1602, which he observed was a 'good practise' and 'much like the *Comedy of Errors*, or *Menaechmi* in Plautus'.[50] Beyond this record, the diary is full of colourful vignettes that capture the nature of the life and men at the Inns at the turn of the seventeenth century. For instance, in November 1602, Manningham records an incident involving his colleague John Marston:

> John Marston the last Christmas when he danced with Alderman Mores wife's daughter, a Spaniard born, fell into a strange commendation of her wit and beauty. When he had done, she thought to pay him home, and told him she thought he was a poet. 'Tis true,' said he, 'for poets fain and lie, and so did I when I commended your beauty, for you are exceeding foul'.[51]

Manningham recalls Marston's quick and mean-spirited comeback to the compliment that he is a 'poet', in which Marston turns the praise of his rhetorical ability into statement of his distaste for those who use such skills ('poets fain and lie'). Yet even as he criticises poets, his response shows his ingenuity and verbal dexterity: He employs an internal rhyme ('lie' and 'I') as well as some opposition and balance, ending one clause with 'beauty' and the next with an opposite, the word 'foul'.

Marston's behaviour seems exceptional, but it is typical. The men in this group were similarly able skilfully and colourfully to ridicule those within their circle as well as outside it. According to Manningham, Benjamin Rudyerd and Thomas Overbury complained of their fellow Templar John Davies: 'Davies goes waddling with his arse out behind as though he were about to make every one that he meets a wall to piss against.'[52] Likewise, Richard Martin wittily and meanly characterised Davies. Playing with the interchangeable i/j and u/v in Renaissance writing, Martin noted that 'Davies' (pronounced 'Davis' and spelled d-a-u-i-s) is an anagram for 'Judas' (i-u-d-a-s).[53]

These Middle Temple wits were clever as well as malicious, and their aggressiveness sometimes spilled over into physical altercations. Martin and Davies are the most well-known example. The two were expelled in 1591 for disruptive behaviour and, in a famous incident in 1598, Davies cudgelled Martin on the head in the Middle Temple hall, which resulted in his expulsion from the Inn (he was readmitted in 1602). One might wonder

---

[50] RP Sorlien (ed), *Diary of John Manningham of the Middle Temple, 1602–1603* (Hanover, University Press of New England, 1976), 48.
[51] *Ibid*, at 133.
[52] *Ibid*, at 238.
[53] *Ibid*, at 48.

about the source of such latent and overt aggression. As Arthur Marotti has detailed, men at all four Inns used the law schools as stepping stones to further their social ambitions and careers, and this made the atmosphere 'heatedly competitive'.[54] Nonetheless, this close and combative environment promoted literary talents. Even as the men ridiculed each other, their verbal sparring exercised their faculties, prompting them to invent literary and ingenious, if malicious, quips and sayings, and to hone their expressive abilities.

The poetry and plays that emerged from Middle Temple register the friendships and antipathies of the men there. Several works satirise specific types of men at the schools as well as individuals. In *The Fleire* (1606), the playwright Edward Sharpham, who describes himself on the title page as 'of the Middle Temple, Gentleman', jibes at the sexual exploits of Inns of Court men when two characters debate whether one 'born and begotten in an Inns Court' is as much a gentleman as one admitted there.[55] Similarly, in *Cupid's Whirligig* (1607), Sharpham parodies the sometimes self-important display of legal learning of law students in the character of the laughable Master Exhibition (described as an 'inns-of-court man' in the opening list of 'Actors' Names'), who woos a lady in legal terms, attempting to lease the lady's love for a term of life.[56] In the same vein, in his book of *Characters* (1614), Thomas Overbury describes the vanity of a typical Inns of Court man of this time:

> His very essence he placeth in his outside, and his chiefest prayer is that his revenues may hold out for taffeta cloaks in the summer, and velvet in the winter.[57]

Other works ridicule specific people. In *Metamorphoses of Pygmalion's Image and Certain Satires* (1598), John Marston attacks John Davies, giving him the pseudonym Ruscus.[58] Thus, in addition to the personalities of members of the Inn in the 1590s, the events and types of people at the Middle Temple (and the Inns in general) sparked literary production.

The work of the oft-maligned John Davies is especially grounded in this milieu. He gravitated toward genres that were popular at the Middle Temple: brief epigram and satire in works like *Epigrams* (c 1595) and *Gulling Sonnets* (1596), as well as acrostics like *Hymns to Astrea* (1599), 26 poems formed around the letters in 'Elisabetha Regina'.[59] Moreover, like Sharpham and Marston, his works ridicule (and praise) types of men

---

[54] AF Marotti, *John Donne: Coterie Poet* (Madison, University of Wisconsin Press, 1986), 26.
[55] E Sharpham, *The Fleire* (London, FB, 1607), sig B3r.
[56] E Sharpham, *Cupid's Whirligig* (London, E Allde, 1607), sig I1r.
[57] Overbury, above n 10, at 104.
[58] Finkelpearl, above n 48, at 86–88.
[59] *Ibid*, at 76.

familiar to him at the Inns.[60] In one poem, he mentions the 'clamorous fry' (ie children or spawn) of the 'inns of court', in another he depicts 'a student at common law' who for 'filthy sports his books forsakes', and in another he portrays a lawyer who 'the known dishonest cause … never did defend, / Nor spun out suits at length'.[61] In addition, he uses imagery drawn from his legal training. In the *Gulling Sonnets* (c 1594), he describes Cupid who goes 'into the Middle Temple of my hart' and stands before Reason 'that old Bencher'. In others he uses extensive legal conceits.[62]

A fuller example of a poem indebted to the Middle Temple context is Davies's *Orchestra, or a Poem of Dancing* (1596). Initially, the topic of the poem may seem unrelated, since it comes from the Greek myth concerning Odysseus, and attempts on the part of his wife Penelope to fend off suitors while he battles in the Trojan War. In *Orchestra*, Penelope's primary suitor, Antinous, asks her to dance, and when she refuses he offers a lengthy defence, arguing that dancing, in its association with harmony, is essential to all creation. Despite the mythological remove, the environment at the Middle Temple influenced the poem. Davies dedicates it to his sometime friend and fellow Middle Templar, Richard Martin, noting that Martin himself inspired the verse: he is 'first mover and sole cause of it' as well as his 'own-selves better half, my dearest friend'.[63] Even the form—a disputation—is indebted to the context. As Krueger writes:

> Disputation was a principal source of entertainment and instruction at the Inns of Court; cases and points of law were argued in the hall before the assembled members of the Inn.'

For this reason, Kreuger suggests:

> 'A poem combining the activities of dancing and argument, both part of life at an Inn of Court, may well have been written for a public entertainment there.[64]

Finkelpearl suggests that *Orchestra* was performed at the Middle Temple revels of 1597–98, with Richard Martin reciting some of the lines. Sanderson observes, 'Such a speculation is purely hypothetical', even as he acknowledges that 'the tone of *Orchestra* and its amusingly learned wit would certainly be appropriate to such a Saturnalian occasion and audience'.[65]

Whatever the initial occasion, *Orchestra* and Davies's other poems were certainly written to appeal to an audience at the Inns. Sanderson argues

---

[60] JL Sanderson, *Sir John Davies* (Boston, MA, Twayne, 1975), 45.
[61] R Krueger (ed), *The Poems of Sir John Davies* (Oxford, Clarendon Press, 1975), 130, 148–50, 226.
[62] *Ibid*, at 166, 167.
[63] *Ibid*, at 89, lines 3–4.
[64] *Ibid*, at 359.
[65] Finkelpearl, above n 48, at 77; Sanderson, above n 59, at 69–70.

that 'The principal target' of Davies's *Epigrams*, his 'laughing rimes', are 'the pretenses and follies of London dandies and Inns of Court wastrels those whom Davies groups under the rubric of "gulls"'. Krueger observes that the Middle Temple wits were the primary audience for the *Gulling Sonnets*.[66] The poems were indeed read by such men. Lewiston Fitzjames, a student at the Middle Temple (adm 1594), copied *Orchestra* and several other of Davies's works into his commonplace book, which still exists in manuscript.[67] Other contemporaries were familiar with *Orchestra*, since they responded to it in their own works. John Marston satirises Davies as a lover of flattery: 'Praise but *Orchestra*, and the skipping art, / You shall command him, faith you have his heart'; and another colleague, John Hoskins, refers to *Orchestra* in his *Directions for Speech and Style* (1599) as an illustration of the rhetorical device 'Division'.[68]

Davies's poems were firmly tied to the Middle Temple milieu, and his works indicate how the social atmosphere there prompted members to create literary works while influencing the form, tone and topics of their writings. That said, this literary community extended beyond the Middle Temple. It included others at the Inns of Court, such as the poet (and later Dean of St Paul's) John Donne, who was at Lincoln's Inn at the time. Like the Middle Temple wits, Donne adopted the persona of the 'Inns-of-Court wit' and a style that was 'congenial to his immediate audience of Inns gentlemen'.[69] Donne also ridiculed gulls and lawyers, for instance in his first verse satire on an Inns-of-Court-type 'gull' and his second about an avaricious lawyer.[70]

Admittedly, such a large literary group never again coalesced at the Middle Temple, but important authors as well as smaller literary communities appear over the centuries. Even more so than in the 1590s, these later groups also intersected with broader intellectual networks at the Inns or in London.

In the 1610s, a literary circle centred on the Inns (although this time the Inner Temple and Lincoln's Inn) and involved important political figures and authors, including William Browne (1590/91–1645?, adm IT 1612) and Christopher Brooke (c 1570–1628, adm LI 1587), as well as George Wither (1588–1667, adm LI 1615), who wrote numerous works, including

[66]   Sanderson, above n 59, at 45; Kreuger (ed), above n 60, at 391.
[67]   Sanderson, above n 59, at 67; Krueger (ed), above n 60, at 378.
[68]   J Marston, *The Scourge of Villanie: Corrected with the Addition of Newe Satyres* (London, IR, 1599), sig H3r; J Hoskins, *Directions for Speech and Style*, HH Hudson (ed) (Princeton, NJ, Princeton University Press, 1935), 23.
[69]   Marotti, above n 53, at 35.
[70]   J Donne, *The Complete English Poems*, CA Patrides (ed) (New York, Alfred A Knopf, 1991), 214–24.

Abuses Stript and Whipt (1613), for which he was imprisoned.[71] Wither's poetry show how such works grew out of an Inns-of-Court context. Wither contributed a commendatory poem to Brooke's *The Ghost of Richard III* (1614) and Browne's *Britannia's Pastorals* (1613). Browne's next collection of eclogues *The Shepheard's Pipe* (1614) was published with 'Other Eclogues: by Mr. Brooke, Mr. Wither, and Mr. Davies', and Brooke, Browne and Wither appear throughout the eclogues under the pseudonyms Cuddy, Willy and Roget respectively.[72] Moreover, Wither created a sequel to Browne's *The Shepheard's Pipe*, *The Shepherd's Hunting* (1615), in which Cuddy (Brooke) and Willy (Browne) appear as his visitors in prison.[73] Yet much as Wither's work developed out of this circle of Inns-of-Court men, it also was inspired by broader intellectual conversations in the period, involving the wits and politicians who gathered at the 'Mitre' and 'Mermaid' taverns, near the Temple. They included the poet and playwright Ben Jonson (1572–1637), who seems to have been especially energised by his connection with the Inns, dedicating his play *Every Man Out of His Humour* to the Inns of Court, 'the noblest nurseries of humanity and liberty in the kingdom', and his play *Poetaster* to Richard Martin.[74] Other members of this group were the architect and theatre designer Inigo Jones (1573–1652), the traveller and writer Thomas Coryate (1577?–1617), the merchant, financier and government minister Lionel Cranfield (1575–1645), the landowner, courtier and Middle Templar Sir Henry Goodere (bap 1571, d 1627, adm MT 1589), as well as other Members of Parliament and political writers.[75]

In other words, the literary associations of the Middle Temple in the 1610s were part and product of broader intellectual and political communities. That is true also in the 1640s, when a group of royalist-leaning literary, political and religious figures gathered around the poet Thomas Stanley (1625–78, adm MT 1664) who, according to Nicholas McDowell, aimed to turn 'his Middle Temple rooms into a refuge for writers impoverished by the civil war and the dissolution of the court patronage system'.[76] This circle included the translator and poet Edward Sherburne (bap 1616, d 1702), who lived in the Middle Temple for some time, the

---

[71] The most recent article in the *ODNB* indicates that Wither was a member of the Middle Temple (59:873), but he was member of Lincoln's Inn (adm 1615), and appears in the *Admissions Record* of that Inn.

[72] *ODNB*, 8:223.

[73] *ODNB*, 59:873.

[74] *The Workes of Benjamin Jonson* (London, Will Stansby, 1616), 81 and 273.

[75] O'Callaghan, above n 4, at 110; M O'Callaghan, 'Tavern Societies, the Inns of Court, and the Culture of Conviviality in Early Seventeenth-Century London' in A Smyth (ed), *A Pleasing Sinne: Drink and Conviviality in Seventeenth-Century England* (Cambridge, Brewer, 2004), 37–51.

[76] N McDowell, *Poetry and Allegiance in the English Civil Wars: Marvell and the Cause of Wit* (Oxford, Oxford University Press, 2008), 16.

poet and dramatist James Shirley (bap 1596, d 1666, adm GI 1634), the poet John Hall (bap 1627, d 1656, adm GI 1647), the poet and lawyer Alexander Brome (1620–66, adm GI 1648, adm LI 1659), and the poet and army officer Richard Lovelace (1617–57).[77] Following studies of the Inns of Court authors of the 1590s and the 1610s, Stella Revard observes that the men in this group 'shared similar literary interests and tastes; all of them were involved in translation of some sort, from Greek, or from the Romance languages.' She continues,

> So interconnected were their literary interests and their political allegiances that it is sometimes difficult to disengage the two or to pronounce positively whether the poets in Stanley's circle were more bound together by devotion to poetic pursuits or to the waning royalist cause.[78]

In either case, this group is another example of a broader intellectual circle that encompassed the Middle Temple and fostered literary activities.

After the middle of the seventeenth century, a steady line of authors emerge from the Middle Temple, including (to list just a dozen or so authors who have not yet been mentioned): the poet and playwright Thomas Shadwell (c 1640–92, adm MT 1658), the poet and lawyer Henry Higden (bap 1645, adm MT 1665), the playwright Edward Ravenscroft (*fl* 1659–97, adm IT 1659, adm MT 1667), and the playwright and translator William Burnaby (1673–1706, adm MT 1693). In later centuries, there is the barrister and poet Francis Chute (1697–1745, adm MT 1712), the romance writer Robert Paltock (1697–1767, adm MT 1719, adm Clement's Inn 1722), the playwright Richard Sheridan (1751–1816, adm MT 1773), the biographer and playwright James Boaden (1762–1839, adm MT 1793), the essayist Thomas de Quincey (1785–1859, adm MT 1812), the novelist Sir Anthony Hope Hawkins (1863–1933, adm MT 1887), and the novelist and publisher (and later Governor General of Canada) John Buchan (1875–1940, adm MT 1897).

It is notable that the literary associations of the Middle Temple decline in the twentieth century, something that might be attributed to many factors, although the Middle Temple is no different from the other Inns in this respect. One factor could be the advent of radio and television, which may have mitigated the need for members to invent their own entertainments. Another factor might lie in changes in legal education, the main responsibilities for which passed to institutions outside the Inns of Court in the late nineteenth century. With those changes, the Inns began mainly to attract people aiming to obtain a qualification to

---

[77] SP Revard, 'Thomas Stanley and "A Register of Friends"' in CJ Summers and T-L Pebworth (eds), *Literary Circles and Cultural Communities in Renaissance England* (Columbia, University of Missouri Press, 2000), 148.

[78] *Ibid*, at 149.

practise at the Bar, or for use in employment; consequently, fewer of those men and women who became members were drawn to pursue other lines of work after joining.

Yet even without addressing the twentieth century, there is not enough space here to discuss each of the authors above individually, or even to list exhaustively the numerous writers who have not yet been named. Even so, like their counterparts in earlier eras, such authors and playwrights were most probably influenced by a similar web of intellectual, legal and social affiliations that encompassed them at the Inns, and more specifically the Middle Temple. For instance, there was an intellectual circle surrounding the eighteenth-century poet William Cowper, a member of the Middle Temple (adm 1748), who later moved to the Inner Temple (adm 1757). In his time at the Inns, Cowper made many friends and acquaintances, including the writer and poet William Hayley (1745–1820, adm MT 1766) and Edward Thurlow (1731–1806, adm IT 1752), who became Lord Chancellor in 1778. He also kept up with friends from his Westminster School days, such as George Colman (bap 1731, d 1794, adm LI 1755), the future playwright and theatre manager, with whom Cowper formed the Nonsense Club, a literary dining group that met weekly through the 1750s and early 1760s.[79]

Tracing such connections is difficult in the case of minor authors: What intellectual and social interests prompted a group of barristers in 1955 to form a theatrical group?[80] Yet it is tricky to track such alliances for even the most canonical writers. For instance, a literary biography of Henry Fielding describes his studies at the Middle Temple, but does not mention the friendships the author made there.[81] Nevertheless, his legal affiliations certainly influenced his literature. For example, in his depiction of the legal system in *Tom Jones*, there is an episode where the title character is found guilty of a murder he did not commit. According to one critic, that shows 'Fielding's mastery of the law and his scorn for those who misuse it'.[82] Moreover, Fielding was probably part of at least a small literary circle, since an anonymous poem by someone who must have been a fellow Inns of Court man describes his study habits. The author complains of Fielding:

> While others feel the drowsy pow'r of Coke,
> Thy antidote shall be some well-timed joke.
> And what to some shall seem Herculean pain,
> Shall only be th' amusement of thy brain.

---

[79] C Rider, 'William Cowper of the Inner Temple', *Inner Temple Historical Articles*, available at <www.innertemple.org.uk/archive/cowper.html>, accessed 5 January 2009, para 2.

[80] Whitelaw, above n 21, at 39.

[81] R Paulson, *The Life of Henry Fielding: A Critical Biography* (Oxford, Blackwell, 2000), 105–08.

[82] FL Alfandary, 'An Odd Sort of Author: Henry Fielding, Writer and Magistrate' (1994) 43 *Columbia Library Journal* 29.

Canst thou behold the statutes' monstrous size,
And feel no ludicrous emotion rise?
Canst thou look forward to a hundred year,
Compute their growth, and yet the smile forbear?[83]

The poet grumbles that while others find that law books have a 'drowsy pow'r', Fielding thinks them a source of 'amusement' and he 'smiles' as he computes the growth of the statute law. The easy familiarity of this portrait suggests that it was written by a close acquaintance, and thus points to the existence of a social and literary circle surrounding Fielding at the Middle Temple or the Inns more broadly.

More attention should be paid to the relationship between the experiences of authors at the Middle Temple and their writing, especially in the case of Fielding who went on to pursue legal and literary careers. Yet it is important to acknowledge that some members felt the incompatibility between the fields. Thus in 1751, a 'Gentleman of the Middle Temple' wrote a poem on 'The Northern Circuit', which begins with an address to the muse, Clio: 'Clio forbear—Admit my plea, / what has Law to do with thee?'[84]

Moreover, unlike Fielding or the 'Northern Circuit' author, most Middle Templars could not combine law and literature, which is why so many authors ultimately left the Middle Temple to pursue writing full time. Most famously, Charles Dickens resigned his membership with the Middle Temple when novel writing became his principal profession. In a petition dated 1855 (16 years after his initial admission), Dickens writes to the Middle Temple Treasurer that 'years ago' he 'entered himself a student ... with the intention of keeping the requisite number of terms and being called to the Bar'. Even then, he admits, he was a 'writer of books' but he 'did not foresee that literature as a profession would so entirely engross his time and become the business of his life, as it has since done and now does'. Consequently he was 'entirely diverted from the pursuit of the law'.[85] (For a copy of the petition, see Figure 1 and transcription below.)

Such documents—the poem on Fielding, the 'Northern Circuit' poem and Dickens's petition—return us to (and reinforce) the assumption that this article has attempted to resist, that law and literature are, by their very nature, incompatible. Admittedly, the poem on Fielding affirms that legal study is very dull; Dickens admits that his novels 'diverted' him from law; the 'Northern Circuit' author asks what law has to do with poetry. Yet all

---

[83] *Young Senator, a Satyr Together with An Epistle to Mr. Fielding, On His Studying the Law* (London, David Jones, 1738), 17.

[84] *A Northern Circuit: Described in a Letter to a Friend: A Poetical Essay ... By a Gentleman of the Middle Temple* (London, 1751).

[85] 'To The Worshipful The Treasurer and the rest of the Masters of the Bench of The Honourable Society of the Middle Temple' The letter is in the Middle Temple Archives MT.3/MEM/(1855). I am grateful to L Whitelaw for drawing my attention to this petition and for making a transcription of it for me.

three cases also suggest points of compatibility between the professions. The verses on Fielding and the 'Northern Circuit' show that the law and literature can be combined (for instance, in poem about law), while suggesting that law can be a source of amusement and delight, and even poetry. Moreover, despite the fact that Dickens was forced to give up his legal career, he does not complain that it was the nature of the law that 'diverted' him. The opposite was the case: he was unarguably spurred to write by the community that surrounded him at the Middle Temple. While there, he became friends with the playwright and fellow Middle Templar Thomas Talfourd, the model for Tommy Traddles, the idealistic law student in *David Copperfield* (1850).[86] Moreover, the environment influenced his subject matter and characters, shaping the numerous scenes in the Temple and the Inns, and his representation of the dozens of lawyers that appear in his novels.

It is true that most members of the Inns were not (and never or rarely tried their hands at being) poets, dramatist or novelists, and it is also true that literature and law demand different kinds of skill, as well as different intellectual and professional inclinations. Nonetheless, what Wilfrid Prest observes of the Inns in the Renaissance is relevant for later periods too:

> By ability, training, and calling, lawyers were literate, articulate, wordy, as well as worldly, men; their work brought them into contact with a large cross-section of humanity, and to London's uniquely rich cultural milieu, where the inns of court occupied a strategically favoured position ....[87]

This background and milieu made it likely that some men at the Inns would develop interests beyond the law, not the least in literature.

In 1748, a letter writer in one London newspaper assumed an odd fit between the law and literature, calling Henry Fielding 'an odd sort of author', 'a kind of jack-of-all-trades! A would-be humorist, a farce maker, a journal scribbler, a mock lawyer, a novel framer'.[88] Yet it would be wrong to concur with these sentiments, to assume that law and literature, or law and journalism, or law and any number of other fields are a necessarily peculiar mix. The literary associations of the Middle Temple show that law and literature, and indeed many other fields too, exist as part of the broader intellectual and social endeavours of members of this Inn of Court.

---

[86] *ODNB*, 53:736.
[87] Prest, above n 26, at 207.
[88] *Old England* (no 226, Sept 3, 1748) 1.

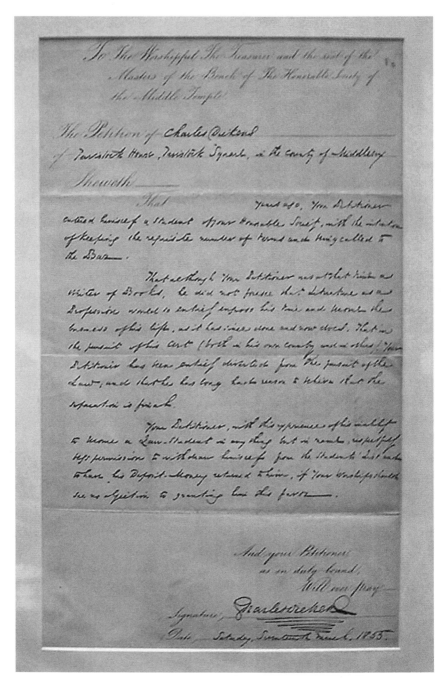

Figure 1: Petition of Charles Dickens to withdraw from the Inn

Transcript of Dickens's letter

To The Worshipful The Treasurer and the rest of the Masters of the Bench of The Honorable Society of the Middle Temple

The Petition of Charles Dickens

Of Tavistock House, Tavistock Square, in the county of Middlesex

Sheweth

That [space] years ago your Petitioner entered himself a student of your Honorable Society, with the intention of keeping the requisite number of terms and being called to the Bar.

That although your Petitioner was at that time a Writer of Books, he did not foresee that Literature as a Profession would so entirely engross his time and become the business of his life, as it has since done and now does. That in the pursuit of his Art (both in his own country and in others), Your Petitioner has been entirely diverted from the pursuit of the Law, and that he has long had reason to believe that the separation is final.

Your Petitioner, with this experience of his inability to become a Law-Student in any thing but in name, respectfully begs permission to withdraw himself from the Students' List and to have his Deposit-Money returned to him, if your Worships should see no objection to granting him this favor.

And Your Petitioner
as in duty bound,
Will ever Pray

Signature: Charles Dickens
Date: Saturday, Seventeenth March, 1855

Appendix
Men of Letters Associated with the Middle Temple

LESLEY WHITELAW

FOR FIVE CENTURIES the writings of Middle Templars have influenced most aspects of English life. Many members found fame—some in their own lifetimes and some more lastingly, transcending the fashions of their age—as playwrights, poets, novelists, essayists, diarists, literary scholars and editors. Although it includes many eminent men (and two women) of letters, this list attempts to widen the scope beyond those of literary distinction and to encompass deceased members whose writings on a range of non-legal topics may be regarded as being of national or international importance. They include classicists; translators; historians; writers on philosophy, politics and religion; topographers and county historians; antiquaries; writers on heraldry and genealogy, on architecture and music, and on military history and sport; travellers and colonial writers; orientalists and a lesser number of scientists, mathematicians, botanists, ornithologists and economists. Chronologically the list extends from the age of astrologers and alchemists to the modern world of journalists and newspaper editors and proprietors.

The list has been arranged alphabetically to facilitate checking names, but the dates of admission to (or, in a small number of cases, association with) the Middle Temple are also given as indicators of possible mutual influences and acquaintanceships, and also to show patterns of interest of the writers over many generations.

Those members whose published fame rests entirely on their law reporting and works relating to the law—even the great Plowden and Blackstone—have been excluded.

Some of the decisions on inclusion or exclusion of members have necessarily been subjective and there are doubtless many unintentional oversights, but it is hoped that this may nevertheless be a useful tool for researchers.

The main sources for the list are: HAC Sturgess, *The Register of Admissions of the Middle Temple from the Fifteenth Century to 1944* (London, Butterworth & Co, 1949); *The Middle Temple Bench Book*, vols 1–4; *The Oxford Dictionary of National Biography*; J Hutchinson, *Notable Middle Templars* (London, Butterworth, 1902); EA Jones, *American Members of the Inns of Court* (London, The Saint Catherine Press, 1924); Middle Temple's archival records of admission; rent books and leases.

Name and dates*	Genre	Date of admission/ Association
Edward Strutt Abdy (1792–1846)	Traveller and author of *Journal of a Residence and Tour in the United States, 1833–34*	19 June 1813
Anthony Allen [Allin] (d 1754)	Lawyer and antiquary; author of 5-volume biographical account of members of Eton; collected material for dictionary of obsolete words	26 October 1704
Christopher Anstey (1724–1805)	Poet	22 December 1746
Thomas Chisholm Anstey (1816–73)	Legal and political writer; author of *A Guide to the Laws Affecting Roman Catholics*	6 June 1835
John Anstis (1669–1744)	Heraldic writer	31 January 1690
William Archer (1830–97)	Theatre critic and journalist	2 November 1878
Sir Joseph Arnould (1813–86)	Judge and author of *Law of Marine Insurance; Memoir of Lord Denman*	10 November 1836
John Asgill (1659–1738)	Author	4 May 1686
Sir Anthony Ashley, Bt (1552–1628)	Politician and translator of *The Mariners Mirrour*	27 January 1575
Robert Ashley (1565–1641)	Scholar, translator of numerous published works and book collector	8 October 1588
Elias Ashmole (1617–92)	Author on antiquities and heraldry	9 November 1657

*   The dates are dates of admission to the Inn except in those cases where in the first column it is stated that the individual was not a member.

John Aubrey (1626–1697)	Antiquary and biographer	18 April 1646
Anthony Babington (1920–2004)	Judge; author of *For the Sake of Example*; *Shell Shock*; *An Uncertain Voyage*	19 December 1946
Montagu Bacon (1688–1749)	Scholar and critic	29 March 1704
Edward Bagshaw [Bagshawe] (1584–1662)	Lawyer and writer on political and religious controversies	25 November 1608
David Bristow Baker (1803–52)	Religious writer	17 June 1824
John Ball (1818–89)	Scientist, traveller and writer for *Alpine Guide* and scientific journals	18 April 1837
John Evelyn Barlas (*pseud* Evelyn Douglas) (1860–1914)	Poet, anarchist and communist	20 April 1882
Eaton Stannard Barrett (1786–1820)	Poet and satirist	14 November 1805
William Battie (1704–76)	Physician; published classical orations and a work on madness	27 January 1743
William Battine (1764–1836)	Lawyer and poet	19 May 1773
William Bavand [Bavande](*fl* 1559)	Translator of *A Woorke of Joannes Ferranius Montanus Touchynge the Goode Orderynge of a Commonweale*	14 August 1557
Ernest Belfort Bax (1854–1926)	Marxist theoretician and activist, journalist	5 December 1890

Sir Edward Clive Bayley[1] (1821–84)	Administrator in India; antiquary, numismatist, contributor to journals of Bengal Asiatic Society and Royal Asiatic Society; author of *Journal of a Diplomat's Three Years in Persia*	25 January 1855
Roger Baynes (1546–1623)	Author and administrator	24 November 1565
Dabridgecourt Belchier (bap 1581, d 1621)	Playwright	29 June 1601
Beaupré Bell (1704–45)	Antiquary and contributor to journal of Spalding Club and to *Archaeologia*	2 July 1722
Not a member Jeremy Bentham (1748–1832)	Philosopher, jurist, reformer	Lincolns Inn, but sometime chambers in Middle Temple
Richard Bentley (1708–82)	Author	16 August 1720
Sir William Berkeley (d 1677)	Colonial Governor and playwright (*The Lost Lady*)	3 May 1624
Charles Best (*fl* 1592–1611)	Poet; referred to in Rudyard's *Le Prince d'Amour*	22 April 1592
James Ebenezer Bicheno (1785–1851)	Author and colonial official	29 November 1816
Richard Doddridge Blackmore (1825–1900)	Novelist and fruit farmer	27 January 1849
William Blandy/ Blandie (*fl* 1563–81)	Author	27 November 1571
Thomas Blore (1764–1818)	County Historian	17 November 1792
James Boaden (1762–1839)	Biographer and playwright	25 January 1793

---

[1] Professor Raymond Cocks: "The Middle Temple in the Nineteenth Century", below p 331.

Sir William Bolland (1772–1840)	Judge, bibliophile and poet; a founder of the Roxburghe Club	25 January 1792
Edmund Borlase (d c 1682)	Historian and physician; writer on the Irish rebellion of 1641	27 August 1638
William Boscawen (1752–1811)	Author and translator of Horace into English verse	2 February 1769
Not a member James Boswell (1778–1822)	Barrister and literary scholar	Lived at 3 Garden Court
Andrew Kennedy Hutchison Boyd (1825–99)	Church of Scotland minister and author (*Recreations of a Country Parson*)	25 April 1842
Hugh Boyd (1746–94)	Essayist	10 October 1771
James Bramston (1694?–1743)	Poet and Church of England clergyman	20 May 1718
Sir John Bramston the younger (1611–1700)	Politician and autobiographer	26 October 1597
Edward Atkyns Bray (1778–1857)	Poet and writer	21 January 1801
Sir Robert Brerewood (1588–1654)	Publisher of works of Edward Brerewood	21 October 1607
John Bridges (1666–1724)	Material he collected was published in *History of Northamptonshire* compiled by Peter Whalley nearly 70 years after Bridges's death	23 April 1684
Henry Brooke (1703–83)	Author, poet, translator and playwright	27 October 1725
Not a member Thomas Broughton (1704–74)	Church of England clergyman and author	Appointed Reader at Temple Church1727
Sir Samuel Egerton Brydges Bt, 13th Baron Chandos (1762–1837)	Writer and genealogist	2 May 1782

John Buchan, 1st Baron Tweedsmuir (1875–1940)	Author, publisher and Governor-General of Canada	20 March 1897
Sir George Buc(k) (1560–1622)	Master of the Revels, historian, author of *Eclog* dedicated to James I	16 April 1585
Edmund Burke (1730–97)	Statesman and man of letters	23 April 1747
Sir John Bernard Burke (1814–92)	Genealogist and author; *Peerage* editor	30 December 1835
William Burke (1728–98)	Political writer and administrator	26 May 1750
Ulick Ralph Burke (1814–95)	Spanish scholar; author of histories and novels	28 January 1865
William Burnaby (1673–1706)	Playwright and translator	17 May 1693
Hans Busk (1815–82)	Educationalist and writer	16 April 1834
William Byrd (1674–1744)	Virginian landowner and diarist	25 April 1692
Henry James Byron (1834–84)	Dramatist and actor	14 January 1858
Thomas Caldecotte (1744–1833)	Barrister and literary editor	29 May 1767
George Canning (d 1771)	Poet and miscellaneous writer	23 June 1752
Edward Capell (1713–81)	Literary scholar	9 May 1730
Richard Carew (1555–1620)	Antiquary and poet	5 February 1574
Thomas Carew (1595–1640)	Poet	6 August 1612
Sir John Carr (1772–1832)	Travel writer	18 April 1806
Donald Carswell (1882–1940)	Journalist and author	10 November 1906
Stephen Hyde Cassan (1789–1841)	Biographer	24 October 1811
Anthony Champion (1725–1801)	Poet and politician	5 July 1739
Not a member George Chapman (1560–1634)	Poet and playwright	Wrote MT/LI masque 1613

Henry Samuel Chapman (1803–81)	Journalist and colonial judge	17 March 1837
Sir Henry Chauncy (1632–1719)	Topographer and author of *The Historical Antiquities of Hertfordshire*	6 February 1650
Thomas Morris Chester[2] (1834–92)	Afro-American lawyer, abolitionist, colonizationist and editor of *Star of Liberia*	8 June 1867
Walter Chetwynd (1633–93)	County historian and author	2 December 1651
Hugh Chisholm (1866–1924)	Journalist and editor of *Encyclopaedia Britannica*	16 November 1888
Francis Chute (1697–1745)	Barrister and poet	25 November 1712
George Thomas Clark (1809–98)	Engineer and archaeologist; author of *Medieval Military Architecture of England*; *Land of Morgan*	22 January 1842
Frederick Clifford (1828–1904)	Journalist and legal writer	3 November 1856
Sarah Caudwell Cockburn [*pseud* Sarah Caudwell] (1939–2000)	Barrister and novelist	5 February 1962
Sir Richard Cocks, 2nd Bt (*c* 1659–1726)	Parliamentary diarist and religious controversialist	1 November 1667
Henry Nelson Coleridge (1798–1843)	Author; editor of works of uncle, Samuel Taylor Coleridge	16 June 1821
Sir John Taylor Coleridge (1790–1876)	Judge; editor of *Quarterly Review*; published an edition of *Blackstone's Commentaries* and memoir of John Keble	5 November 1812
Steven William Buchan Coleridge (1854–1936)	Author and anti-vivisectionist	8 July 1875; re-admitted 5 May 1882

---

[2] Professor Raymond Cocks: "The Middle Temple in the Nineteenth Century", below p 320.

John Payne Collier (1789–1883)	Shakespearian critic, literary editor and literary forger	31 July 1811
Anthony Collins (1676–1729)	Theological writer	24 November 1694
William Congreve (1670–1729)	Playwright and poet	17 March 1691
Sir Harry Coningsby (*fl* 1633–65)	Translator of Boethius's *Consolation of Philosophy*	5 February 1633
George Wingrove Cooke (1814–65)	Legal and historical writer and biographer; *Times* correspondent in China	5 February 1830
William Cooke (d 1824)	Writer and poet	23 June 1770
Walter Arthur Copinger (1847–1910)	Author on law (copyright), bibliography (first President of the Bibliographical Society), genealogy, heraldry, manorial history, Suffolk	12 April 1866
Sir Charles Cornwallis (d 1629)	Diplomatist; author of discourse on Henry, Prince of Wales	20 February 1611
William Courthope (1808–66)	Herald; author of genealogical and biographical treatises	29 January 1848
William Cowper (1731–1800)	Poet and letter-writer	29 April 1748
Edward William Cox (1809–79)	Lawyer and publisher	30 April 1840
Irwin Edward Bainbridge Cox (pseud IEBC) (1838–1922)	Barrister, politician, proprietor of *The Field*, author, editor of the annual *Angler's Diary*	3 June 1861
Wilfred Joseph Cripps (1841–1903)	Writer on silver; antiquary	14 January 1840
Richard Crompton (*c* 1529–99 or later)	Lawyer; editor and writer on legal subjects; author of *The Mansion of Magnanimitie*	19 April 1553
Sir Thomas Culpeper (1578–1662)	Political writer	15 May 1594

Sir Thomas Culpeper (1626–97)	Political writer	1 December 1647
Timothy Cunningham (d 1789)	Legal antiquary	22 August 1754
Sir David Dalrymple, Lord Hailes (1726–92)	Scottish judge, historian, author of learned treatises and *Annals of Scotland*	8 August 1744
John D'Alton (1792–1867)	Historian of Ireland and essayist	3 May 1811
Sir George Webbe Dasent (1817–96)	Scandinavian scholar and writer	30 May 1844
John Morrison Davidson (1843–1916)	Radical and journalist	12 November 1874
Not a member William Davenant (1606–68)	Poet, playwright, theatre manager	Author of 1636 Middle Temple masque *The Triumph of the Prince d'Amour*
Sir John Davies (1569–1626)	Lawyer and poet	10 February 1587
Sir Robin Day (1923–2000)	Journalist and broadcaster	9 October 1947
Thomas Day (1748–89)	Political campaigner; author of *Sandford and Merton* and *The Dying Negro*	12 February 1765
John Thadeus Delane (1817–79)	Journalist and editor of *The Times*	15 January 1839
Sir Edward Dering [Deering] 1st Bt (1598–1644)	Antiquary, politician and author of *The Four Cardinal Virtues of a Carmelite Friar*; *Discourse of Proper Sacrifice*	23 October 1617
Sir Simonds D'Ewes, 1st Bt (1602–50)	Diarist and antiquary	2 July 1611
John Thomas Dibdin (1771–1841)	Actor and dramatist	6 November 1793
Charles Dickens (1812–70)	Novelist	6 December 1839

John Dickinson (1732–1808)	Revolutionary and political writer in America	21 December 1753
Sir Charles Wentworth Dilke (1843–1911)	Writer and politician	19 December 1862
Wentworth Dillon, 4th Earl of Roscommon (1637–85)	Poet and translator	9 February 1683
John Disney (1746–1816)	Unitarian writer	11 November 1762
Henry Hall Dixon [*pseud* The Druid, General Chasse] (1822–70)	Sporting writer	27 January 1848
Sir John Doderidge [Doddridge] (1555–1628)	Legal antiquary and judge	29 November 1577
Michael Dodson (1732–99)	Jurist, author of Admiralty reports, translator, essayist and biographer	31 August 1754
Alfred Domett (1811–87)	Colonial statesman and poet; Robert Browning marked their friendship with the poem *Waring*	7 November 1835
Frank Lewis Dowling (1823–67)	Newspaper editor	24 May 1845
George Duckett (1684–1732)	Author	14 January 1703
Sir Henry Bate Dudley (1745–1824)	Journalist; Editor of *Morning Post* and originator of *Morning Herald*	21 November 1776
Bartholomew Thomas Duhigg (*c* 1750–1813)	Legal antiquary and author of *History of King's Inns*	6 November 1771
Richard Duppa (1768–1831)	Writer on artistic subjects and botany; draughtsman	7 February 1810
Romesh Chunder Dutt (1848–1909)	Administrator in India and author	11 November 1868

Sir Fortunatus William Lilley Dwarris (1786–1860)	Lawyer and writer on law, archaeology, literature; author of plays and short stories	18 May 1803
Edward Backhouse Eastwick (1814–83)	Orientalist; author of *Handbooks for India*, Persian translations and Hindustani grammar	8 January 1858
Richard Lovell Edgeworth (1744–1817)	Author and essayist	14 September 1762
Sir Clement Edmondes [Edmonds] (c 1564–1622)	Clerk of the Council and author of learned military histories	11th August 1614
Sir Thomas Elyot (c 1490–1546)	Humanist and diplomat; author of *The Boke Named the Governour*; Latin-English dictionary; *Castel of Helth*	7 November 1510
Christopher Temple Emmet (1761–88)	Lawyer and poet	5 January 1779
George Ensor (1769–1843)	Political writer	26 October 1787
John Evelyn (1620–1706)	Diarist and writer	18 February 1637
Sir Francis Fane (d c 1689)	Dramatist	18 December 1667
Richard Fenton (1747–1821)	Topographical writer and antiquary; poet	24 August 1774
Henry Fielding (1707–54)	Author and magistrate	1 November 1737
William Francis Finlason (1818–95)	Legal writer and journalist	6 January 1841
Joseph Robert Fisher (1855–1939)	Journalist	1 May 1876
Thomas Fitzherbert [Fitzharbert] (1552–1640)	Jesuit writer	10 November 1571
Albany William Fonblanque (1793–1872)	Journalist	27 January 1814

John Ford (1586–1639)	Playwright	16 November 1602
William Fowler (1561–1612)	Scottish poet	4 August 1604
Sir James George Frazer (1854–1941)	Social anthropologist, classical scholar, author of *The Golden Bough*	24 October 1878
Sir Ralph Freeman (d 1667)	Governmental official dramatist and translator of Seneca	18 November 1606
William Freke (1662–1744)	Theological and mystical writer	20 November 1677
Philip Frowde (1679–1738)	Poet	19 January 1698
John Fry (1609–57)	Puritan politician and writer	11 November 1631
John Gibbon (1629–1718)	Heraldic writer	22 November 1656
Sir Ambrose Harding Giffard (1771–1827)	Colonial judge and poet	24 April 1790
Stanley Lees Giffard (1788–1858)	Editor of newspaper *The Standard*	21 November 1807
Alexander Gilchrist (1828–61)	Biographer	29 April 1847
John Allen Giles (1808–84)	Classical scholar, writer and translator of Old English Chronicles	22 November 1828
Laurence Ginnell[3] (1852–1923)	Lawyer, Irish republican and political pamphleteer; one of the founders of the Irish Literary Society	19 November 1890
William Goddard [Godderde] (d 1624)	Satirist, soldier and poet	Probably the same WG as was admitted 30 June 1565
Not a member Oliver Goldsmith (1728?–74)	Author	Lived at Garden Court and later 2 Brick Court
Richard Graham (*fl* 1695–1727)	Author	30 January 1683

[3] Professor Raymond Cocks: "The Middle Temple in the Nineteenth Century", below p 328.

William Greatrakes (c 1723–81)	Barrister and supposed author of the *Letters of Junius*	19 March 1751
Canon William Greenwell (1820–1918)	Antiquary, archaelogist, angler and author of works on British barrows, numismatics, Durham Cathedral Library; editor of the *Boldon Buke*	12 November 1840
Fulke Greville, 1st Baron Brooke (1554–1628)	Courtier, poet and author of *Life of Sir Philip Sidney*	11 February 1581
Archer Thompson Gurney (1820–87)	Anglican clergyman and hymn writer	29 April 1842
William Gwavas [Guavas] (1676–1741)	Author of *History of Cornwall*	31 March 1696
Richard Gwinnett (1675–1717)	Playwright	22 June 1697
Not a member Sir Henry Rider Haggard (1856–1925)	Novelist	Lincoln's Inn, but guarantor of chambers at No 1 Cloisters 1888
Thomas Gordon Hake (1809–95)	Physician and poet	2 July 1828
Not a member Richard Hakluyt (1552?–1616)	Geographer, editor, translator; most noted work, *The Principall Navigations* (1589) gave advance notice of publication of Molyneux Globes; supported Raleigh's settlement in "Discourse on Western Planting"	Introduced as a boy to an interest in navigation and exploration by "bookes of cosmologie" and "an universal map" in Middle Temple chambers of his cousin and guardian, the elder Richard Hakluyt, a Bencher of the Inn
James Hammond (1710–-1742)	Politician and poet	14 January 1724
George Hardinge (1743–1816)	Judge, poet and essayist	15 May 1764
Nicholas Hardinge [Harding] (1699–1758)	Classical scholar and antiquary; author of *Poems, Latin, Greek and English*	12 October 1721

Francis Hardy (1751–1812)	Politician and biographer	27 January 1772
Harold Sidney Harmsworth, 1st Viscount Rothermere (1868–1940)	Newspaper proprietor	Honorary Bencher 3 May 1928
James Harrington [Harington] (1611–77)	Political writer and author of *Oceana*	27 October 1631
Not a member Thomas Harriot (c. 1560–1621)	Mathematician, natural philosopher, author of *A Brief and True Report of the New Found Land of Virginia*	15 March 1582 stood surety for Philip Amadas in his admission bond to the Middle Temple; associate of Middle Templar colonizers, explorers and navigators
George Harris (1809–90)	Author	4 December 1839
Walter Harris (1686–1761)	Irish historian	31 May 1708
Stephen Harvey (1655–1707)	Lawyer and poet	21 May 1673
Sir Henry Havelock (1795–1857)	General; author of *A Narrative of the War in Afghanistan*	14 May 1813
Sir Anthony Hope Hawkins [*pseud* Anthony Hope] (1863–1933)	Novelist	6 January 1883
William Hay (1695–1755)	Political and philosophical writer	24 May 1715
William Hayley (1745–1820)	Poet and biographer	13 June 1766
Abraham Hayward (1801–84)	Essayist; translator of *Faust*	14 July 1830
Benjamin Heath (1704–66)	Literary scholar, critic and book collector	28 June 1721
Thomas Henshaw (1618–1700)	Alchemist, scientific writer, translator and editor	21 April 1638

Sir William Herbert [Harbert] (d 1593)	Astrologer, politician and poet	20 June 1589
Richard Hey (1745–1835)	Essayist and mathematician	7 November 1768
Henry Higden (bap 1645)	Author and lawyer	27 April 1665
Bevill Higgons (1670–1736)	Historian and poet	12 November 1687
Sir Thomas Higgons (1624–91)	Politician and author	4 February 1640
John Hoadly (1711–76)	Poet and playwright	1 November 1726
John Baptist Cashel Hoey [*psdeuds* C.h., D.F.B., U-Ulad] (1828–92)	Journalist; husband of Frances Sarah Johnson (1830–1908), novelist	25 January 1859
Thomas Jefferson Hogg (1792–1862)	Biographer of Percy Bysshe Shelley	5 November 1812
Francis Ludlow Holt [Holte] (1780–1844)	Author of legal works and of a comedy *The Land we Live in*	11 December 1801
Sir Robert Honywood [Honiwood] (1601–86)	Politician and translator of Nani's *History of the Affairs of Europe*	21 June 1620
Not a member Richard Hooker (1554–1600)	Author of theological works including *Of the Lawes of Ecclesiasticall Politie*	Master of the Temple 1585–91
Nicholas Hookes (1628–1712)	Poet	24 June 1654
Charles Hopkins (1671–1700)	Poet and playwright	17 August 1695
Richard Hopkins (b *c* 1546; d in or before 1596)	Roman Catholic writer and translator of Spanish theological works	24 May 1561
Arthur Hopton (*c* 1588–1614)	Mathematician and author on mathematical subjects	11 November 1609
Samuel Horsley (1733–1806)	Theologian and author of religious and scientific works	25 January 1755

John Hosack (d 1887)	Police magistrate and author of legal and historical works	26 January 1838
John Hoskins (1566–1638)	Poet and judge	13 March 1593
Durant Hotham (1617–91)	Biographer	25 January 1641
Edward Hyde, 1st Earl of Clarendon (1609–74)	Lord Chancellor, politician, historian and author of *History of the Rebellion*	1 February 1626
Alexander Kennedy Isbister (1822–83)	Headmaster, writer of text books and critic of the Hudson's Bay Company	8 January 1862
Arthur Mason Tippetts Jackson (1866–1909)	Sanskrit scholar, Indian Civil Service; superintendent of revision of *Imperial Gazetteer*	17 November 1885
David Jardine (1794–1860)	Historical and legal writer	17 April 1817
George Jeffreys (1678–1755)	Poet and dramatist	3 November 1694
Edward Jenks (1861–1939)	Jurist and writer on legal and historical subjects	3 January 1884
Not a member Charles Johnson (1679?–1748)	Playwright and poet	Wrote play *Love and Liberty* in Middle Temple
Ernest Charles Jones (1819–69)	Radical and writer and author of political songs	8 March 1841
Inigo Jones (1573–1652)	Architect and masque and theatre designer; with George Chapman designer of the Middle Temple & Lincoln's Inn Whitehall masque of February 1613	21 February 1613
John Matthew Jones (*fl* 1850–78)	Author of *The Naturalist in Bermuda* and *Contributions to Natural History of Bermuda*	1 June 1850
Sir William Jones (1746–94)	Linguist, orientalist, judge and author	19 November 1770
Richard John Kelly (1866–1931)	Journalist	3 November 1884

Thomas Kelly (1769–1855)	Hymn writer and founder of Kellyites	4 July 1786
(William) Charles Mark Kent [*pseud* Mark Rochester] (1823–1902)	Writer and journalist	17 November 1856
Richard Brinsley Knowles (1820–82)	Journalist	14 November 1839
Rowley Lascelles (1771–1841)	Writer, antiquary, archivist and editor of *Liber Munerum Publicorum Hiberniae*	9 February 1788
Frederick Lawrence (1821–67)	Barrister and journalist	5 November 1846
Charlwood Lawton (1660–1721)	Writer	23 November 1676
William Leach (*fl* 1631–55)	Attorney and pamphleteer	25 January 1632
Arthur Lee (1740–92)	American politician and author of *Monitor's Letters* and *Junius Americanus*	15 November 1773
Edward Leigh (1603–1761)	Writer	30 October 1624
Sir George Cornewall Lewis, 2nd Bt (1806–63)	Politician, author and contributor to literary reviews	21 June 1828
Sir Lewes Lewknor (1560–1627)	Courtier and translator; author of *The Commonwealth and Government of Venice*	12 October 1579
Not a member (Barnaby) Bernard Lintot[t] (1675–1736)	Literary bookseller and publisher of plays	Occupied premises in Middle Temple Gate 1700–05
William Livingstone [*pseud* The American Whig] (1723–90)	Lawyer, political writer and colonial governor; author of poem *Philosophical Solitude*	29 October 1742
Capell Lofft (1806–73)	Classical scholar, poet and writer	15 April 1831
Michael Lok [Locke] (b *c* 1530)	Traveller; translator of *Historie of the West Indies*	28 February 1585

Sir Roger Lort [Lorte], 1st Bt (1608–64)	Latin poet	23 May 1627
Not a member Richard Lovelace (1618–57)	Poet and army officer	Frequented Stanley's MT chambers
Edward Lovibund (1724–75)	Poet	25 January 1738
Moses Lowman (1679–1752)	Non-conformist minister and theological writer; author of *Dissertation on the Civil Government of the Hebrews*	14 March 1698
Frederick Lucas (1812–55)	Journalist and politician	8 March 1831
Henry Lucas (*c* 1740–1802)	Writer and lawyer	28 September 1763
Sir Humphrey Lynde [Lynd] (1549–1636)	Puritan writer	12 June 1601
Edward Lysaght (1763–1811)	Poet and wit	17 March 1784
James Carlile McCoan (1829–1904)	Politician and journalist	15 November 1851
Charles McCormick (*c* 1755–1807)	Historian and biographer	27 June 1783
Alexander Mackay (1808–52)	Journalist	8 August 1843
(Maurice) Harold Macmillan, 1st Earl of Stockton (1894–1986)	Prime Minister, publisher, author of *Winds of Change; Tides of Fortune*	Hon Bencher 13 November 1958
Leonard Macnally (1752–1820)	Playwright and political informer	8 June 1774
Spencer Madan (1758–1836)	Poet and translator	12 April 1776
Thomas Madox (1666–1727)	Legal antiquary and author	17 May 1705
Thomas Manley (1638–*c* 1690)	Author of religious works, a translation of Grotius's *De Rebus Belgicis* and a treatise on *The Present State of Europe*	6 February 1655

Edward Manlove (bap 1615, d 1671)	Lawyer and poet	12 May 1635
John Manningham (*c* 1575–1622)	Lawyer and diarist	16 March 1598
John Marston (bap 1576, d 1634)	Poet and playwright	2 August 1592
Richard Martin (1570–1618)	Barrister, politician and one of the 'Mitre' circle of poets	7 November 1587
Henry Martyn (bap 1665, d 1721)	Essayist	12 December 1684
George Mason (1735–1806)	Writer and book collector	5 June 1752
John Monck Mason (1726?–1809)	Literary scholar and politician	4 March 1745
Thomas Erskine May, Baron Farnborough (1815–86)	Constitutional historian and author	20 January 1834
Not a member Francis Meres (1566–1647)	Writer and translator	Dedicated books to Middle Templars William Sammes and Thomas Eliot
William Minto (1845–93)	Critic (*Characteristics of English Poets* and *English Literature under the Georges*)	12 November 1874
William Mitford (1744–1827)	Historian and author of works on harmony in languages, history of Greece, the Corn Laws and military force	11 January 1763
Charles Molloy (d 1767)	Playwright and journalist	28 May 1716
William Molyneux (1656–98)	Philosopher and author of *Sciothricum Telescopium*; *Dioptrica Nova*; *The Case of Ireland's being bound by Acts of Parliament in England Stated*	23 June 1675
The Hon Ewen Edward Samuel Montagu (1901–85)	Judge and intelligence officer; author of *The Man Who Never Was* and *Beyond Top Secret*	22 November 1920

Thomas Moore (1779–1852)	Poet	19 November 1795
Macnamara Morgan (c 1720–62)	Playwright	20 June 1744
William Hook Morley (1815–60)	Orientalist and lawyer; editor for the Society of Oriental Texts; author of *Digest of Cases decided in the Supreme Court of India*	17 August 1833
John Moultrie (1799–1874)	Church of England clergyman and poet	24 January 1822
Walter Moyle (1672–1721)	Writer on politics, theology and literature	26 January 1691
Arthur Murphy (1727–1805)	Playwright and actor	20 January 1757
Sir David Murray (1567–1629)	Poet; author of *Sophonisba* and *Caelia*	16 March 1609
Sir Richard Musgrave (c 1757–1818)	Political writer and author of *Memoirs of the different Rebellions in Ireland*	25 September 1765
William Johnstoune Nelson Neale (1812–93)	Lawyer and novelist	4 November 1836
Thomas Newenham (1762–1831)	Writer on Ireland	14 October 1782
Arthur Newman (fl 1614–19)	Poet and essayist	19 October 1616
John Noble (1827–92)	Writer on politics and finance	2 May 1861
Helena Florence Normanton (1882–1957)	Barrister, feminist campaigner, author and novelist (under *pseud* Cowdray Browne)	24 December 1919
Francis North, 1st Baron Guilford (1636–85)	Lord Chancellor; author of treatises on music and scientific subjects	27 November 1655
Roger North (1651–1734)	Lawyer, politician, historian, biographer and writer on architecture	21 April 1669

John Northleigh (1657–1705)	Physician, pamphleteer and author of philosophical and political treatises, eg *Parliamentum Pacificum*	8 November 1682
Richard Barry O'Brien (1847–1918)	Irish nationalist, barrister, journalist, biographer, writer on the Irish Land Question, founder and chairman of Irish Literary Society of London	12 November 1878
Sir John Oglander (1585–1655)	Diarist	31 October 1604
John Ormsby (1829–95)	Writer and translator	3 May 1850
Sir Thomas Overbury (1581–1613)	Poet, philosopher and courtier	30 July 1597
Richardson Pack [Packe] (1682–1728)	Soldier and poet	5 January 1699
John Paget (1811–98)	Police magistrate and author; contributor of historical and biographical articles to *Blackwood's Edinburgh Magazine*	16 October 1835
Justinian Pagitt (1612–68)	Lawyer and diarist	11 October 1628
Edward Henry Palmer (1840–82)	Orientalist, translator, author of *The Desert of the Exodus* and a Persian–English Dictionary	8 June 1869
Robert Paltock (1697–1767)	Romance writer and author of *The Life and Adventures of Peter Wilkins*	13 January 1716
Sir Edward Abbott Parry (1863–1943)	Judge, dramatist and author; autobiography *My Own Way*	18 January 1882

John Humffreys Parry (1786–1825)	Antiquary; established *Cambro-Briton* magazine of Welsh history and antiquities, and edited *Transactions of the Cymmrodorion Society*	1 May 1806
Sir Edwin Pears (1835–1919)	Barrister, publicist and historian	12 November 1867
Samuel Pegge (1733–1800)	Antiquary and writer; author of *Curialia* and *Anecdotes of the English Language*	20 November 1754
George Percy (1580–1632)	Colonist and author of *Discourse of the Plantation* and *A True Relation of the ... Occurrents in Virginia*	12 May 1597
Walter Copland Perry (1814–1911)	Writer and collector of casts	12 January 1844
Sir Peter Pett (1630–56)	Lawyer and author of *Discourse of Liberty of Conscience* and of political tracts	18 May 1656
William Petyt [Petitt] (1636–1707)	Antiquary, keeper and cataloguer of the Tower Records, donor of extensive manuscript collection to Inner Temple	8 June 1660
Fabian Philipps (1601–90)	Author	17 June 1628
Charles Phillips (*c* 1787–1859)	Poet and miscellaneous writer, author of *The Consolations of Erin*	30 October 1807
Sir Francis Taylor Piggott (*pseud* Hope Dawlish) (1852–1925)	Jurist, novelist and writer on Japanese arts	10 June 1873
Not a member John Playford (1623–87)	Music publisher	Clerk to Temple Church; leased shop in porch of Temple Church with son Henry Playford

Winthrop Mackworth Praed (1802–39)	Poet and politician	19 November 1825
John Patrick Prendergast (1808–93)	Historian and genealogist; author of *The Cromwellian Settlement* and *The Tory War in Ulster*	14 November 1828
William Preston (1750–1807)	Poet and playwright	25 July 1775
Richard Price (1790–1833)	Literary scholar	29 May 1823
George Puttenham (1529–91)	Writer and literary critic	11 August 1556
John Pym (1554–1643)	Republican statesman and publisher of his speeches and *Vindication of Himself in Parliament of the Accusation of High Treason*	23 April 1602
Thomas Penson de Quincey (1785–1859)	Essayist	12 June 1812
Sir Walter Raleigh (1554–1618)	Courtier, explorer, poet and author	27 February 1575
John Rastell (*c* 1475–1536)	Lawyer and printer	Before 1501
Edward Ravenscroft (*fl* 1659–97)	Playwright	2 April 1667
Thomas Rawlinson (1681–1725)	Bibliophile; supposedly Addison's 'Tom Folio'; poet	7 January 1697
Henry Reeve (1813–95)	Journalist and man of letters	14 January 1832
John Reeves (1752–1829)	Barrister and writer on legal, political and religious subjects	11 May 1776
Carew Reynell (1636–90)	Economist and poet; author of *The Fortunate Change* and *The True English Interest*	13 November 1654
Frederick Reynolds (1764–1841)	Playwright	5 January 1781

Joseph Richardson (1755–1803)	Writer and politician	24 March 1781
William Roberts (1767–1849)	Barrister and writer; editor of *British Review* and author of *Life of Hannah More*	2 November 1793
James Burton Robertson (1800–77)	Historian, translator and poet	8 November 1819
Henry Crabb Robinson (1775–1867)	Diarist, journalist and author of *Memoirs*	18 February 1808
William Robinson (1777–1848)	Topographer and law writer	1 May 1822
William Caldwell Roscoe (1823–59)	Poet and essayist; contributor to *National Review*	16 December 1843
Francis Rous (1581–1659)	Puritan writer and politician	5 May 1601
Nicholas Rowe (1674–1718)	Poet and playwright	4 August 1691
Daniel Rowland (1778–1859)	Antiquary; author of an account of the Nevill family; editor of Blakeway's *Sheriffs of Shropshire*	31 August 1820
Sir Benjamin Rudyerd (1572–1658)	Politician and poet	18 April 1590
Sir William Howard Russell (1820–1907)	Journalist; *The Times* correspondent in the Crimea and India	2 May 1846
John St John (1746–93)	Author and playright (*Mary Queen of Scots* and *The Island of St Marguirite* were produced at Drury Lane)	15 May 1767
Samuel Salt (d 1792)	Lawyer and benefactor of Charles Lamb	4 August 1741
Thomas Salmon (1679–1767)	Historian and geographer, author of *A Review of the History of England*	27 June 1694

George Sandys (1578–1644)	Writer and traveller; translator of *Ovid's Metamorphoses* into English verse; wrote *Paraphrase of the Psalms and Hymns of the Old Testament*	11 February 1590
Alexander MacCallum Scott (1874–1928)	Politician and author of *The Truth About Tibet*; *Through Finland to St Petersburg*; *Beyond the Baltic*	28 October 1901
Denis Scully (1773–1830)	Political writer and author of *Statement of the Penal Laws*; *An Irish Catholic's Advice to his Brethren*	25 October 1793
James Sedgwick (1775–1851)	Writer of legal and political articles and pamphlets	25 August 1795
Frederick Seebohm (1833–1912)	Historian and banker; his writing, strongly influenced by Maine's Middle Temple lectures, includes *The English Village Community*, works on emancipation in America and Christianity	17 January 1854
Edmund Selous (1857–1934)	Ornithologist and author of *Bird Watching* and *Evolution and Habit in Birds*	18 November 1878
William Senior (1861–1937)	Contributor of legal, maritime and historical articles to *Cornhill Magazine*, *Mariner's Mirror* and *Punch*	23 November 1895
Thomas Shadwell (*c* 1640–92)	Playwright and poet	7 July 1658
Anthony Joshua Shaffer (1926–2001)	Playwright and screenwriter	4 March 1949
Not a member William Shakespeare (1564–1616)	Playwright and poet	Candlemas 1602 performance of *Twelfth Night* in Middle Temple Hall

Edward Sharpham (bap 1576, d 1608)	Playwright and pamphleteer	9 October 1594
Thomas Shaw, 1st Baron Craigmyle (1850–1937)	Lawyer and politician (Lord of Appeal in Ordinary under title Lord Shaw of Dunfermline); Scottish biographer; author of *Letters to Isabel*; *The Other Bundle*; *The Law of the Kinsmen*; and of the plays *Darnley* and *Leicester*	Hon Bencher 18 April 1910
Not a member Sir Edward Sherburne (bap 1616, d 1702)	Translator and poet	Lived in MT chambers of John Povey
Richard Brinsley Sheridan (1751–1816)	Playwright and politician	6 April 1773
Thomas Sheridan (1646–1712)	Government official and Jacobite pamphleteer	29 June 1670
Not a member Thomas Sherlock (1678–1761), Bishop of London	Author of *Discourses at the Temple Church* and *Trial of the Witnesses of the Resurrection of Jesus*	Master of the Temple 1705–53
Sir Christopher Sibthorp (d 1633)	Lawyer and pamphleteer	14 June 1584
Henry James Slack (1818–96)	Journalist, editor and proprietor of the *Atlas*; author of treatise on aesthetics	17 April 1850
Sir Edward Smirke (1795–1875)	Lawyer, antiquary, archaeologist, and prolific author of papers on charters and history of mining in Duchy of Cornwall	2 August 1816
Sir Thomas Smith (1513–77)	Statesman, ambassador, scholar; author of *De Republica Anglorum*	[between 1524 and 1551]

William Henry Smith (1808–72)	Writer and philosopher; author of *The Conflict of Opinions* and *Thoughts on Good and Evil*	2 November 1838
Jan Christiaan Smuts (1870–1950)	Prime Minister of South Africa, army officer, writer	7 May 1892
John Smyth (1567–1641)	Antiquary and genealogist; author of *Lives of the Lords of Berkeley from the Conquest down to 1628*	17 August 1594
Thomas Solly (1816–75)	Philosophical writer; author of *Syllabus of Logic* and *Will Divine and Human*	4 November 1841
William Somervile [Somerville] (1675–1742)	Poet	3 October 1696
Henry Southern (1799–1853)	Journalist and diplomatist	23 January 1822
Thomas Southerne (1660–1746)	Playwright	15 July 1680
Robert Spearman [Speareman] (1703–61)	Theologian and biographer of John Hutchinson; author of *An Enquiry after Philosophy and Theology*	19 May 1720
Richard Stafford (bap 1663, d 1703)	Jacobite pamphleteer; author of *The Printed Sayings of Richard Stafford, prisoner in Bedlam*	14 May 1680
Thomas Stanley (1625–78)	Poet and classical scholar	27 May 1664
Abraham Stanyan (c.1669–1732)	Diplomat, merchant, lord of Admiralty, member of the Kit-Kat Club, author of an *Account of Switzerland*	20 January 1691
Sir George Thomas Staunton (1781–1859)	Orientalist; a founder of the Royal Asiatic Society; author of *Miscellaneous Notices Relating to China*	21 October 1796

Alexander Stephens (1757–1821)	Biographer (*Life of John Horne Tooke*) and producer of periodical *The Templar*	9 January 1786
Robert Stephens (1665–1732)	Historiographer Royal; literary editor and publisher of *Letters of Sir Francis Bacon*	21 November 1681
William Stephens (1672–1753)	Historian of State of Georgia	25 November 1691
Edward Sterling (1773–1847)	Journalist and co-proprietor of *The Times*	6 April 1791
Henry Sewell Stokes (1808–95)	Cornish poet (*The Lay of the Desert*; *The Song of Albion*)	27 May 1829
Graham Storey (1920–2005)	Literary scholar and editor	7 October 1946
James Stuart (1764–1842)	Historian and journalist	19 January 1790
Robert Surtees (1779–1834)	Antiquary and historian of Durham	20 May 1800
Theophilus Swift (1746–1815)	Poet	22 June 1764
Jelinger Cookson Symons (1809–60)	Author and pamphleteer on social, political, legal and educational subjects	5 June 1839
Francis [Frank] Talfourd (1828–62)	Playwright (*The Millar and his Men*)	5 May 1848
Sir Thomas Noon Talfourd (1795–1854)	Writer, judge and politician	5 May 1813
Francis Tate (1560–1616)	Lawyer and antiquary; essays published in *Gutch's Collectanea Curiosa* and *Hearne's Discourses*	2 June 1579
William Tayler (1808–92)	Commissioner of Patna; author of *Thirty-Eight Years in Patna*	31 January 1828
John Sydney Taylor (1795–1841)	Journalist	8 April 1815

William Johnston Temple (bap 1739, d 1796)	Church of England clergyman and essayist	2 May 1759
William Makepeace Thackeray (1811–63)	Novelist	3 June 1831
William Marcus Thompson (1857–1907)	Journalist and barrister	6 April 1877
Richard Tickell (1751–93)	Playwright and satirist	8 November 1768
Theobald Wolfe Tone (1763–98)	Irish nationalist and political writer	3 February 1787
Sir John Salusbury Salusbury-Trelawny, 9th Bt (1816–85)	Politician and diarist	1 May 1841
Thomas Anthony Trollope (1774–1835)	Barrister and author of *Encyclopaedia Ecclesiastic*; husband and father respectively of novelists Frances and Anthony	20 April 1799
John Bernard Trotter (1775–1818)	Author of *Memoirs* of Charles James Fox	3 November 1797
Robert Turner (b 1620, d in or after 1664)	Writer and translator of occult and medical works	27 October 1648
Thomas Tyers (1724/25–1787)	Writer and essayist; depicted by Dr Johnson as 'Tom Restless' in the *Idler*	19 March 1753
Thomas Tyrwhitt (1730–86)	Literary editor and critic	28 April 1749
Robert Studley Vidal (1770–1841)	Antiquary; translator of *Affairs of the Christians before the time of Constantine*	22 August 1795
Clement Walker [*pseud* Thodorus Verax] (d 1651)	Political pamphleteer	18 October 1611
Robert Wallace (1831–99)	Divine, politician and writer on ecclesiastical subjects	22 January 1881
John Edward Walsh (1816–69)	Judge and author of *Ireland Sixty Years Ago*	19 January 1838

William Walsh (bap 1662, d 1708)	Poet	6 December 1679
Gervase Warmestry (1604–41)	Poet	18 November 1628
Thomas Watson (1556–92)	Poet and translator	Probably the TW adm. 30 November 1581
Philip Carteret Webb (1700–70)	Antiquary and author of treatises on Domesday, Danegeld and the political status of Jews in England	18 December 1727
John Webster (1578x80–1638?)	Poet and playwright	1 August 1598
William Weir (1802–58)	Journalist	2 March 1840
Charles Richard Weld (1813–69)	Author	6 November 1841
Thomas Whately (1726–72)	Political pamphleteer and author of *Some of Shakespeare's Characters*	19 June 1742
Sir George Wheler [Wheeler] (1650–1723)	Traveller and author of *A Journey into Greece*	4 July 1671
John White (1590–1645)	Puritan lawyer and writer	6 November 1610
Bulstrode Whitlocke [Whitelocke] (1605–75)	Lawyer and statesman; author of political, legal and historical treatises	5 August 1619
Sir James Whitelocke [Whitlock] (1570–1632)	Judge and scholar; writer on heraldry, genealogy, history and classics	2 March 1593
James Wills (1790–1868)	Poet, Church of Ireland clergyman and biographer	14 November 1814
Richard Windeyer[4] (1806–47)	Lawyer, journalist, Australian statesman and Hunter Valley wine pioneer	15 May 1829

---

[4] Professor Raymond Cocks: "The Middle Temple in the Nineteenth Century", below p 302.

Robert Wood (*c* 1717–71)	Traveller and politician; author of *The Ruins of Palmyra* and *The Ruins of Balbec*	16 November 1736
Sir Henry Wotton (1568–1639)	Scholar, diplomat, writer and poet	12 August 1595
Christopher Wren (1675–1747)	Son of the architect; antiquary; author of *Numismatum Antiquorum Sylloge*	6 February 1694
James Wright (1644–1717)	Antiquary, poet and author of *A History of the English Stage*	14 November 1670
William Wynne (1692–1765)	Serjeant-at-Law and author of historical treatises	12 December 1712
Not a member William Butler Yeats (1865–1939)	Poet	Lived in Fountain Court chambers 1895–96[5]
Walter Yonge (bap 1579, d 1649)	Politician and diarist of the Long Parliament	26 October 1600
Bartholomew Young (1560–1612)	Translator of *Diana* and *The Civile Conversation of M Stephen Guazzo*	19 May 1582
Charles Yorke (1722–70)	Lord Chancellor; essayist and contributor to *Athenian Letters*	1 December 1735
Philip Yorke 2nd Earl of Hardwicke (1720–90)	Contributor to *Athenian Letters*, diarist, editor of *Carleton Letters* and *Miscellaneous State Papers*	28 October 1729

[5] Michael Ashe QC, 'Yeats, Fleet Street and Fountain Court', *The Middle Templar* Issue 49, Winter 2010.

3

The Unreformed Middle Temple

WILFRID PREST

T HE MOST DESTRUCTIVE single event in the Middle Temple's long history began about 10 o'clock on a bitterly cold Saturday evening in late January 1679. The young barrister Roger North

heard the cry of fire. I went out and perceived a light in a chamber 3 pair of staires, next the lane, out of Pump Court; this light was too fierce for anything but fire, which made me run up to see what the matter was; at the door I found such an evaporation, as forct me back. And I was no sooner come downe, but the court was as light as day, all the smoak being turned to flame, and breathing out at the windoes, as from a furnace.[1]

Not until noon next day was the blaze at last extinguished, using gunpowder to demolish buildings in its path, since 'water froze in carrying and choakt the engines with the ice' (some resourceful students substituted beer instead). By then much of the Inn had been burned to the ground:

[A]n area of great extent bounded by the Middle Temple hall and part of Elme Court southwards, the Palsgrave buildings in old Essex Court westward, the [Fleet Street] tavernes and Hare Court northwards, and the church and Inner Temple buildings eastwards, all which places lay in view of one, and another.[2]

Yet destruction was not total; the hall itself was saved, 'which burnt had bin an irreparable loss, almost to dissolve the society'. Except for part of John Tradescant's famous collection of books, coins and medals in the chambers of the antiquarian attorney Elias Ashmole near where the fire began, North considered the losses 'not great'; the buildings destroyed

---

[1] *Notes of Me The Autobiography of Roger North*, ed P Millard (Toronto, University of Toronto Press, 2000) [hereafter '*Notes of Me*'], 110. North's description indicates that the destruction caused by the fire was more total and covered a wider area than that inflicted over a longer period during the Blitz, even if the latter did not leave the hall unscathed.

[2] *Ibid*, at 115.

being 'for the most part ... ragged deformed stuff'.[3] And despite the inevitable difficulty of obtaining agreement on a detailed rebuilding plan, reconstruction of Brick, Essex, Pump and Elm Courts began only a few months later. North then observed 'a decrepit old woman, who trudging thro the Temple ... stopt and lookt around', before remarking 'well, I see ill weeds will grow fast'.[4]

I.   RESURGENCE AND DECLINE

The Civil War and Interregnum may have inflicted more long-term damage on the Inns of Court than on any other English institution.[5] The trauma of those turbulent years saw not only the suspension of readings and other learning exercises, but an end to the education boom of the sixteenth and early seventeenth centuries. Between the Stuart restoration in 1660 and the accession of George III a hundred years later, annual enrolments at the four Inns contracted, as they did also at the two English universities. While the Middle Temple did not entirely escape this overall downturn, during the half-century 1680–1730 its intake of new members remained comfortably above the levels reached for most of the 40 years before the Long Parliament (see Fig 1 below).[6]

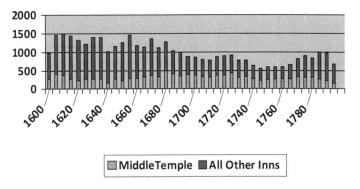

Admission to the Inns of Court*, 1600–1799 (quinqennial totals)

□ MiddleTemple   ■ All Other Inns

*Gray's Inn, Lincoln's Inn, Inner Temple and Middle Temple

Figure 1

---

[3] *Ibid*, at 112, 116. North makes no mention of the loss of literary manuscripts collected by the barrister, translator and historian James Wright (1644–1717); here and below in this chapter otherwise unattributed biographical information comes from the *Oxford Dictionary of National Biography (ODNB)*.

[4] *Notes of Me*, above n 1, at 115.

[5] I owe this suggestion to Prof CW Brooks.

[6] DF Lemmings, *Gentlemen and Barristers: The Inns of Court and the English Bar 1680–1730* (Oxford, Clarendon Press, 1990), 10. My thanks to Prof Lemmings for the data plotted in Fig [1], and much else besides.

This experience contrasted markedly with that of the other three societies, especially Gray's Inn and the Inner Temple. Indeed Lincoln's Inn was unique among the four houses in recording slightly more admissions during the 1720s than the 1680s. But nearly 80 new entrants still joined the Middle Temple every year between 1720 and 1729, as against a mere 30 odd at Lincoln's Inn. The Middle Temple's overwhelming numerical predominance for most of the period *circa* 1680 to 1800 may be gauged from the fact that not until the 1790s did the house contribute less than a quarter of all admissions recorded by the four societies. Otherwise the Middle Temple's share rose to as high as 43 per cent of the total in the 1720s (and up to 46 per cent in the five years 1725–29), remaining above four-tenths until the 1770s, when for the first time Lincoln's Inn gained over one-third of all entrants to the four Inns of Court.[7] While admissions fell away during the middle decades of the eighteenth century, the drop was less precipitous at the Middle Temple than elsewhere. However, the recovery of the 1760s was also less marked, and was rapidly outstripped by the booming popularity of Lincoln's Inn, which in the last quarter of the eighteenth century effectively took over the Middle Temple's former numerical leadership.

Why was the Middle house insulated from the worst effects of the general collapse of admissions to the Inns of Court before the 1760s? And why did the house thereafter forfeit its popularity with potential Inns of Court entrants? In chapter two we saw that the major expansion in Middle Temple admissions after 1660 was largely attributable to a commensurate drop in entrants to Gray's Inn, a reversal possibly reflecting the perceived politico-religious coloration of the two houses. In the later 1670s and early 1680s, with tensions over the anticipated accession of Charles II's Roman Catholic younger brother James threatening renewed civil war, the Middle Temple evidently continued to be regarded as a royalist bastion, not least by some of its own members. Yet opinion within the house was actually split between Church-and-King Tories, and Whig supporters of 'exclusion'. Thus in June 1681 attempts by some 65 'Gentlemen of the Middle Temple' to promote a loyal address drafted at the Devil Tavern in Fleet Street were fiercely resisted by 'about seventy-two of the Barristers and a great number of the Students'. This group then proceeded to compose their own 'Declaration', which disowned any such document purporting to be 'made or done with the consent of this Society', and apparently secured the

---

[7] Slightly different figures are provided by P Lucas, 'A Collective Biography of Students and Barristers of Lincoln's Inn, 1680–1804: A Study of the "Aristocratic Resurgence of the 18th Century"' (1974) 46 *Journal of Modern History* 245, and my own *The Inns of Court under Elizabeth and the Early Stuarts 1590–1640)* (London, Longman, 1972) [hereafter '*Inns of Court*'], 6, 241–45, but these minor variations, attributable to counting errors, do not affect the argument.

benchers' unqualified endorsement of their actions at a parliament meeting held on 17 June. Notwithstanding the governing body's condemnation of the would-be addressers' 'disorderly and irregular proceedings', the next issue of the semi-official *London Gazette* reported that a 'Humble Address of the Loyal Society of the Middle Temple' had been presented to King Charles on 22 June, expressing 'zeal for your Majesties Person and Government, both in Church and State, by Law established …'.[8]

Internal dissension was further highlighted early next year, when 'Edmund Saunders, Esq. Counsellor at Law, and several other Gentlemen of the Middle Temple' presented at Whitehall a 'Declaration, Signed by the Gentlemen of the said Society'. This document asserted as a matter of expert opinion ('conceiving our selves, by reason of our profession, more obliged than others of your Majesties Subjects'), that a London grand jury's recent refusal to indict the Whig leader Shaftesbury had 'in a high measure perverted the Laws'.[9] Saunders, 'one of the prime' pleaders of his time and a notable law reporter, had yet to be raised to the Middle Temple Bench, and was almost certainly acting on his own initiative (albeit with an unknown number of colleagues). Within less than a year he was successively appointed King's Counsel, knighted and promoted Chief Justice of King's Bench.[10]

Yet foremost among those who organised the packing of Shaftesbury's Old Bailey jury with Dissenters and Whigs was that 'pestilent attorney' Richard Goodenough, who had joined the Middle from the Inner Temple in 1679. Goodenough and other radical Whig conspirators met in the Middle Temple chambers of the barrister Robert West, with his younger colleague Nathaniel Wade.[11] Disclosure in June 1683 of their abortive 'Rye House' plot against the King and his brother prompted yet another loyal address, purportedly from 'the SOCIETY of the Middle-Temple'. This appeared both in the *London Gazette* and as a separate broadsheet signed by John Bernard, another relatively junior barrister, who seems to have been the elected speaker of a vacation parliament of barristers and

---

[8] Anon, *The Lawyers Demurrer to the Addresses in Fashion. Or the Several Declarations and Orders of the Honourable Societies of the Middle Temple and Gray's Inn* (London, R Janeway, 1681), 1; Anon, *An Impartial Account of the Nature and Tendency of the late Addresses* (London, R Baldwin, 1681), 4; Anon [John Bernard?], *A Vindication of Addresses in general, And of the Middle Temple Address and Proceedings in particular … By a Barrester of the Middle Temple* (London, N Thompson, 1681), 4–5; *London Gazette* no 1627 (20–23 June 1681), 3.

[9] *London Gazette*, 19 February 1682; cf *Observator in Dialogue*, 2 March 1682.

[10] *Notes of Me*, above n 1, at 160–06; WS Holdsworth, *A History of English Law* (London, Methuen, 1924), vi., 563–67; Lemmings, above n 6, at, 134, 161, 271.

[11] RL Greaves and R Zaller (eds), *Biographical Dictionary of British Radicals in the Seventeenth Century* (Hassocks, Harvester,1982–84), ii., 13–14, iii., 275–76, 302–04; M Zook, *Radical Whigs and Conspiratorial Politics in Late Stuart England* (University Park PA, Pennsylvania State University Press, 1999), 24–26.

students.[12] In condemning 'the *late hellish Conspiracy* begun and carried on by *desperate persons* of Fanatical, Atheistical *and* Republican *Principles*', Bernard and his associates emphasised that 'this Society has been eminent for its Loyalty and early Tokens of Duty and Affection', an assertion slightly at odds with their following pledge 'to bring the Villains to Justice, especially those of this Society'.[13] The Middle Temple's rulers did not formally expel Goodenough, Wade and West until the first parliament of Michaelmas term some three months later, when they also noted the likely involvement of the radical Wiltshire MP John Trenchard, and other members.[14]

The political polarisation of the later 1670s and 1680s must have had some impact on the society's previous loyalist credentials. (In January 1683 the *London Gazette* reported Charles II's knighting of the Tory barrister Humphrey Mackworth, 'as a mark of his Royal Favour to the *Loyal Society of the Middle Temple*'; this partisan characterisation did not become standard usage.)[15] Internal divisions continued to be on display during the short reign of James II, as when that monarch's initial Declaration of Indulgence, suspending the operation of penal laws against both Catholics and Dissenters, elicited an approving address from no more than 'several Benchers and Barristers of the Middle Temple'. Shortly after James's accession a florid yet purportedly 'unanimous Address of the Barristers and Students of the Middle Temple in Parliament Assembled'—presumably again a vacation parliament, with no benchers present—had roundly endorsed the King's continued collection of customs duties originally granted only during Charles II's life, asserting that 'your Majesties high Prerogative is the greatest Security of the Liberty and Property of the Subject'. By contrast, a shorter and less provocatively worded 'Humble Address and Congratulations' to the new monarch was represented as being more inclusively subscribed, by 'the Benchers, Barristers and Students, of the Society of the Middle-Temple, London'.[16]

In this new world of endemic Tory–Whig conflict, the Middle Temple had plainly not been captured by either party. It was indeed the house of the Tory lawyers Roger and Francis North, Edmund Saunders and Francis Wythens, but also of their Whig antagonists and counterparts John

---

[12]   *London Gazette*, 5–9 July 1683, 1; HAC Sturgess (ed), *Register of Admissions to the Honourable Society of the Middle Temple, from the Fifteenth Century to the year 1944* (London, Middle Temple, 1949) i., 185; [J Bernard], *To the King's Most Excellent Majesty. The Humble Address of the Society of the Middle Temple* (London, J Tonson, 1683).

[13]   *Ibid.*

[14]   CH Hopwood and CT Martin (eds), *Minutes of the Parliament of the Middle Temple* (London, Middle Temple, 1904–5) (hereafter *MTR*), iii.,1356–57.

[15]   *London Gazette*, 25 Jan 1683, 2 (emphasis added).

[16]   *London Gazette*, 9–13 June 1687, 9–12 March 1685, 12–16 Feb 1685. Cf T Harris, *Revolution: The Great Crisis of the British Monarchy 1685–1720* (London, Penguin, 2006), 50, 221.

Maynard, Henry Pollexfen, John Somers, George Treby, Richard Wallop and Francis Winnington.[17] So if the spurt in the growth of the society after 1660 had something to do with its royalist connections and image, the sustained demand for Middle Temple membership from the 1690s onwards can scarcely be explained in similar terms, especially given the marked improvement in the Whigs' political fortunes after 1688, and even more so from the outset of George I's reign in 1714.

One obvious physical attraction which the house possessed over the other three Inns was its virtual reconstruction and refurbishment after the 1679 fire. Roger North recounts how the collapse of an initial project devised by one Mr Fitch, a bricklayer-relative of the then treasurer, enabled the former physician turned speculative developer Nicholas Barbon, who 'was certainly cut out for the business of the Temple, for he converst much with those of the society, being a neighbour, and full of law', to secure agreement for his own large-scale rebuilding scheme. North termed this outcome 'the happiest resolution of a perplext touchy affair, that I have knowne, *and the present prosperity of the Temple is owing to the fortunate circumstances of it*'.[18] Associated beautification and embellishment of the Middle Temple's public buildings and spaces in the later seventeenth and early eighteenth centuries also helped send a positive message to potential entrants.

But if the Middle Temple still accounted for more than 45 per cent of all recorded Inns of Court admissions during the first five years after George III's accession, the lion's share of overall expansion which set in from that point onwards went to Lincoln's Inn, with the Middle's intake dropping back to second place from the late 1770s. A careers' handbook first published in 1747 and reissued ten years later claimed that Lincoln's Inn was 'held in best repute at present, as it is inhabited by the most eminent Men in the Profession'. According to the author, 'a common Saying, which expresses the Notion the Town has of these Inns' and 'may be either true or false', ran as follows: 'The Temple for Beaus, Lincoln's Inn for Lawyers, and Gray's Inn for Whore[r]s'.[19] Professor Lemmings tells us that by the

---

[17] M Landon, *The Triumph of the Lawyers: Their Role in English Politics 1678–1689* (University AL, University of Alabama Press, 1970), ch 2. The adoption early in 1688 of a 'scrutiny or balloting box' to record votes in Parliament may have been intended to reduce party-political friction: *MTR*, iii., 1382–83.

[18] *Notes of Me*, above n 1, at 122–23, 126–27, 128–29 (emphasis added); *MTR*, iii., 1318. While only a quarter of entrants between 1688 and 1714 appear in the chamber admissions records, informal sub-letting doubtless swelled the total of on-site residents: Lemmings, above n 6, at 3–9.

[19] R Campbell, *The London Tradesman* (London, T Gardner, 1747), 74. Yet in March 1755 Lloyd Kenyon was informed that 'the society of the Middle Temple is esteemed equal, if not preferable, to any other': Historical Manuscripts Commission, 14th Report, appendix iv, *The Manuscripts of Lord Kenyon* (London, HMSO, 1894), 494.

1740s, 'the bench of Lincoln's Inn seems to have included the cream of the bar'.[20] As for the profession's most glittering prizes, after two Lord Chancellors (Somers and Cowper) at the beginning of the century, it was not until 1801 that another Middle Templar (John Scott, Lord Eldon) held this highest titular legal office—although Scott was also a member of Lincoln's Inn. Sir Peter King had been called to the Bar at the Middle Temple in 1698, but transferred to the Inner house before he became Chief Justice of Common Pleas in 1714, then Chancellor from 1725. Philip Yorke, Lord Hardwicke, likewise called at the Middle Temple, migrated to Lincoln's Inn where he served as a bencher for nine years before his promotion as Chief Justice of King's Bench in 1733 and Chancellor shortly thereafter; Hardwicke's short-lived successor on King's Bench, Dudley Ryder, followed a similar course. Lloyd Kenyon, who presided over King's Bench for fourteen years from 1788, was a barrister and bencher of the Middle Temple; but he also joined Lincoln's Inn in 1779, five years before becoming Master of the Rolls. Middle Templars were even less prominent as heads of the quieter Common Pleas jurisdiction, where Thomas Reeve served for one year only in 1736, although William de Grey held the place for the better part of a decade from 1771. On the other hand, while Lincoln's Inn was the only house whose output of barristers steadily increased between 1700 and 1800, the Middle Temple still accounted for more than a third of all new Bar calls over the whole century, compared to just over a quarter from Lincoln's Inn.[21]

Yet only a minority of those who joined the later Stuart and Hanoverian Inns of Court ever became barristers. The Middle Temple admitted more than 6,000 new members during the eighteenth century, while some 1,450 Middle Templars were called to the Bar during that same period. The proportion of entrants who would eventually be called varied considerably from year to year, but rose only quite gradually, from around one in five to about one in four, between the later seventeenth and early nineteenth centuries. All sorts of personal circumstances might explain why someone admitted to membership did not go on to obtain this basic professional qualification. But one general reason was identified by the bencher Charles Worsley, who in 1734 organised the compilation of a set of 'Observations Historicall and Chronologicall, on the Constitution, Customs, and Usage of the Middle Temple'. Worsley insisted that the Inns were then still regarded as 'places designed for the education of

---

[20] DF Lemmings, *Professors of the Law: Barristers and English Legal Culture in the Eighteenth Century* (Oxford, Oxford University Press, 2000), 64. Lincoln's Inn doubtless gained a further competitive edge from 1768 by dropping its previous requirement that each entrant must have two members of that house as 'manucaptors' or sureties; my thanks to Guy Holborn for this suggestion.

[21] *Ibid*, at 63–64.

the sons of the nobility and gentry', rather than solely 'seminaries of law-learning'. Many gentlemen believed their sons not

> duly educated till they have passed some time in some Society of Law; though they never design to practise it; as seems to be evident from the many who commence Students, and never are, and probably never designed to be Called to the Bar; and many others who take upon them the degree of an Utter-Barrister without any design to practise the law.[22]

Needless to say, parental ambition and the inclinations of offspring were not inevitably as one; Henry Fielding's comedy *The Temple Beau*, first performed in 1730, features a young man sent to study at the Temple, whose horrified father later discovers his son wholly engaged in 'being a Beau, when I thought you a Lawyer'. (Fielding wrote this play, drawing on a well-worn literary stereotype, before he himself had joined the Middle Temple.[23]) If some originally intended for the Bar did not become barristers, it was also possible for a non-barrister to practise the law as conveyancer, special pleader, equity draftsman or official in the legal bureaucracy. Conversely, many barristers never practised as such, mainly because they found the law uncongenial, or came into money, or both. (One among numerous possible exemplars was William Blackstone's Oxford contemporary Thomas Tyers, who migrated from the Middle to the Inner Temple in 1753 and was 'bred to the law', yet 'having a handsome fortune, vivacity of temper, and eccentricity of mind ... could not confine himself to the regularity of practice'.[24])

If the notion of the Inns of Court as liberal academies, or finishing schools where sons of the landed gentry might acquire some metropolitan polish, had not died out entirely by the 1730s, it was allegedly in serious trouble twenty years later. For by 1758, according to Blackstone's inaugural lecture as Professor of English Law at Oxford University (he himself was admitted to the Middle Temple in 1741, called to the Bar five years later, and an occasional resident until 1753), 'few gentlemen now resort to the inns of court, but such for whom the knowledge of practice is absolutely necessary; such, I mean, as are intended for the profession'.[25] Promoting the common law as an academic discipline, a fit

---

[22] AR Ingpen (ed), *Master Worsley's Book on the History and Constitution of the Honourable Society of the Middle Temple* (London, Middle Temple, 1910), 117.

[23] H Fielding, *Plays, Volume I, 1728–1731*, ed T Lockwood (Oxford, Oxford University Press, 2004), 141; see the editor's remarks on the 'formula character of the Temple beau', *ibid*, at 100–01; Prest, *Inns of Court*, above n 7, at 137–42; MC Battestin and RB Battestin, *Henry Fielding A Life* (London, Routledge, 1989), 237–45.

[24] RW Chapman (ed), *Boswell's Life of Johnson* (London, Oxford University Press, 1953), at 960.

[25] W Blackstone, *Commentaries on the Laws of England. Book the First* (Oxford, Clarendon Press, 1765), 'On the Study of the Law', 26.

subject for 'persons of birth and fortune' to study at university, Dr Blackstone undoubtedly exaggerated the extent to which the Inns were now monopolised by budding practitioners, and correspondingly deserted by sons of the political and ruling elite. Modern historians broadly agree with contemporaries like Sir Henry Chauncy, treasurer of the Middle Temple in 1685, that the social status of the Inns' membership was declining between the later seventeenth and mid-eighteenth centuries. But it seems that two-thirds of entrants between 1688 and 1714 were drawn from the landed aristocracy and gentry.[26] Moreover, complaints about the invasion of the lower orders go back to Tudor times, while inflation of status titles and wide inconsistencies in their application make it very difficult to map long-term changes in members' social origins from the meagre and stylised information provided by the Inns' own admissions records. In any case, Blackstone's claim is contradicted by the fact that in the year it was made, 52 persons were admitted to the Middle Temple, of whom only seven were ever called to the Bar. During the following decade a mere 100 out of 551 new members became barristers, while in the 1780s the ratio was even lower, with 97 future barristers among a total of 601 incoming students. Not until the first decade of the nineteenth century did the ratio of those admitted who gained (sooner or later) the right to don a barrister's robes increase to slightly more than one in four (100 out of 363, or 27.5 per cent). These figures scarcely corroborate Blackstone's depiction of the Inns as a near-exclusive preserve of would-be practitioners, even if they are quite compatible with a mounting influx of less well-born entrants.

Closer scrutiny of Middle Temple entrants at different points in the eighteenth century may help to clarify these complexities. The tables below summarise data about the recorded birth order, parental rank and geographical origin of members admitted during five three-year periods between 1699 and 1801.

---

[26] Lemmings, above n 6, at 12–13; Lucas, above n 7, at 231–32; H Chauncy, *The Historical Antiquities of Hertfordshire* (London, 1700), 529; cf Anon, *The Laws of Honour* (London, R Gosling, 1714), 289–90.

Birth Order of Middle Temple Entrants

Triennium	First, elder, or only son	Younger son	Unknown	Total
1699–1701	144 (68%)	63	5	212
1719–21	172 (71%)	69	2	243
1739–41	127 (66%)	56	11	194
1779–81	113 (58%)	70	13	196
1799–1801	44 (55%)	35	0	79

Paternal Rank/Status of Middle Temple Entrants

Triennium	Peer, Baronet, Knight	Esquire	Professional/ Bourgeois	Gent	Unknown	Total
1699–1701	17	94	42	57	2	212
1719–21	13	118	60	49	3	243
1739–41	6	101	49	34	4	194
1779–81	5	121	37	30	3	196
1799–1801	2	45	25	7	0	79

Geographical Origins of Middle Temple Entrants

Triennium	England & Wales	America & W Indies	Scotland	Ireland	Unknown	Total
1699–1701	166	9	—	28	9	212
1719–21	160	11	1	67	4	243
1739–41	124	8	2	51	9	194
1779–81	70	13	—	108	5	196
1799–1801	48	9	—	22	0	79

Three main points emerge. First, the proportion of first-born, elder or only sons (those likely to inherit the bulk of a paternal landed estate) declined by some ten percentage points in the last two sampling periods, consistent with a trend away from use of the Inn as a non-vocational academy by the upper classes. Secondly, the very small minority whose fathers were peers, baronets or knights continued to shrink throughout the century, from 8 per cent at its start to 2.5 per cent by its end; while such parental titles were by no means the sole preserve of landed families, this seems strong evidence of a dilution in social status. The same conclusion is supported by an apparent increase in the proportion of sons from mercantile and professional backgrounds over the period as a whole, even if the admission registers are not a wholly reliable source of information on the social quality of members. Lastly, the proportion of non-English or Welsh entrants—overwhelmingly Irish, but also North Americans, West Indians and Scots—rose from about one-fifth at the beginning of the century to nearly two-fifths by the 1779–81 triennium.

When he stated in 1758 that 'few gentlemen' then attended the Inns of Court for other than professional purposes, Blackstone may have been generalising from his knowledge of the situation at the Middle Temple in relation to its *English* membership. While relatively few Irishmen sought to be called to the Bar in England, many if not most of those enrolled at the Inns of Court were there to keep eight terms in commons as a necessary prerequisite for qualifying to practise at the Irish Bar. Treasurer Worsley had noted that 'a great many gentlemen of Ireland pursue the study of the law in this house', despite the fact that 'a native of Ireland pays Five pounds for his Admission', rather than the standard £4 fee charged everyone else.[27] This premium was fixed by Parliament in 1684, together with the proviso that Irish entrants must provide two English guarantors to the bond which all entrants were required to lodge as security for payment of their debts to the house.[28] But these discriminatory provisions—albeit much diluted from the blanket prohibition which had once prevailed— were no effective deterrent. In the first decade of the new century, 121 Irishmen were admitted to membership of the Middle Temple, comprising 17 per cent of the total cohort entering the house; by way of comparison, during that same period no more than three of their compatriots appear to have joined Lincoln's Inn. The Middle Temple is well known to have been particularly favoured by North American colonists during the eighteenth century. But fewer than 150 Americans were admitted over the entire century, substantially fewer than the 224 from the West Indies, and a tiny fraction of the Irish contingent, which numbered some 1,782 persons, or just over 29 per cent of the entire student body admitted between 1700 and 1799.[29] (See Fig 2 below.)

---

[27] Ingpen (ed), above n 22, at, 131, 137. On Irish students at the Inns of Court generally, see T Barnard, *A New Anatomy of Ireland: the Irish Protestants, 1649–1770* (New Haven CT, Yale University Press, 2003), 117–22.

[28] *MTR*, iii., 1359; JB Williamson, *The History of the Temple*, 2nd edn (London, John Murray, 1925), 491–92.

[29] Figures from L Whitelaw, 'Appendix' to J Colyer, 'Middle Temple's Connections with the United States', ts, 2000; *MTAdmR*, i–ii; Lucas, above n 7, at 245; *Records of the Honourable Society of Lincoln's Inn. Vol I. Admissions from AD 1420 to AD 1799*, ed WP Baildon (London, Lincoln's Inn, 1896); CEA Bedwell, 'Irishmen at the Inns of Court' (1911–12) 37 *Law Magazine and Review* 275; CEA Bedwell, 'Scottish Middle Templars 1608–1869' (1919–20) 17 *Scottish Historical Review* 100.

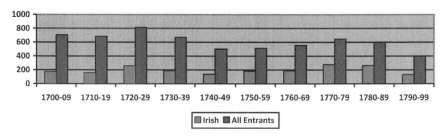

Figure 2

So significant a presence were the Irish at the Middle Temple that, according to an early 19th-century biographer of the politician and judge John Philpot Curran, when his subject—'[l]ike the rest of his countrymen'—entered the house in 1773, 'the seats extending from left of the benchers' table to the noble screen of high-wrought wainscot, have long been known by the appellation of the "Irish side"'.[30] At the Temple, Curran reportedly mixed 'almost exclusively' with Irishmen, or other non-English, such as 'a Frenchman, Dr Du Garreau' and 'a German, Mr Skell'. The Grecian coffee-house in Devereux Street was 'the favoured resort of Irish Templars'. A satirical chapter of advice addressed in 1792 'To the Irish Students of the Law in London', asserted that whether walking down the Strand, lounging in coffee-shops, at the theatre or at the tavern, 'you must associate with men of your own country and description only'. Indeed:

> You must learn to abuse the English. Nay, when you dine in Commons you should not only exclude Englishmen from your mess, but from the same side of the hall that you sit in. You ought to look upon them all as a set of stupid phlegmatical John Bulls, and not suffer their dull pedantry to break in on your spirited conversations ...

which supposedly covered

> the fine women of the town, theatres, boxing-schools, gambling houses, or any other subject equally fashionable, ornamenting the whole with those elegant expletives, vulgarly called oaths.[31]

Although a founding father of Anglo-Irish colonial nationalism, William Molyneux, had been a Middle Temple student as early as 1675, such

---

[30] Anon, *A Memoir of the Life of the Right Honourable John Philpot Curran* (1817), quoted in C Kenny, *King's Inns and the Kingdom of Ireland* (Dublin, Irish Academic Press, 1992), 180. Cf (1788) 3 *The Templar* 302–03.

[31] WH Curran, *The Life of the Right Honourable John Philpot Curran* (London, Longman, 1819), vol. i., 69, 75; EB Day, *Mr Justice Day of Kerry, 1745–1841* (Exeter, Pollard, 1938), 53; Anon, *Advice to a certain Lord High Chancellor ...* (Dublin, 1792), 23, 28–29.

attitudes and behaviour probably become more prevalent towards the end of the eighteenth century, as political differences between Britain and Ireland widened. For when either colonial-patriot Dubliners, or men 'from the wilds of Connaught, well furnished with a rich brogue' encountered the English in 'the metropolis of the British Empire', mutual misunderstandings were all but inevitable. Notwithstanding Dr Johnson's belief that 'Irish mix better with the English than the Scotch do', the stereotypical 'spirited' behaviour of the Anglo-Irish abroad generally elicited a negative response. After 1660, we are told, 'English attitudes towards Ireland were settling into a more-or-less permanent sneer', as 'Irish' became 'a by-word for the second rate'.[32] During George III's reign the growing popularity of Lincoln's Inn also saw a considerable expansion of its Irish intake, which reached a quarter of the total during the last two decades of the century. Yet from the 1720s onwards there was never less than that proportion of Irishmen among the Middle Temple's entrants. By the 1750s over one-third of newly-enrolled Middle Templars came from Ireland, while during the two decades after 1770 Irishmen comprised well over 40 per cent of all entrants to the house. It would be surprising if the public image and reputation of the Middle Temple in its domestic catchment area remained entirely unaffected by such a massive invasion.

II. Equilibrium

Mutual avoidance strategies in and out of Hall may have minimised outright conflict between English and Irish Middle Templars. But tensions between the self-perpetuating oligarchs who governed the society and the barristers and student members whom they ruled were overt and institutionalised. Roger North, who anatomised the relationship, described the 'humor of the gentlemen' as 'pert ... and tenacious in the fancy of priviledg, and aping of prevailing powers', prone to 'partys and combinations' and 'very averse to any thing that seems to be imposed'. The 'supercilious' benchers, on the other hand, were 'apt to use their authority in pinching the gentlemen, which they will not take, but oppose in the forme of what they call a rebellion'. While the benchers held their parliaments on the first and last Friday of every term, the gentlemen

---

[32] Anon, above n 31, at 23; Chapman (ed), above n 24, at 531; D Hayton, 'From Barbarian to Burlesque: English Images of the Irish, *c.* 1660–1760' (1998) 15 *Irish Economic and Social History* 15; T Bartlett, '"A People Made rather for Copies than Originals": the Anglo-Irish, 1760–1800' (1990) 12 *International History Review* 12; Lucas, above n 7, at 234.

that is the barristers, and those under the bar, pretend to a subordinate authority, and that allowing the benchers to govern in terme, they have the swaye in the vacation. And on occasion of greevances, they make a parliament of themselves, even in terme time ...[33]

North observed that

yong fellows got together in this manner ... by aping the nationall Parliament (for they choose a speaker, and keep to the orders of the Hous) together with jesting upon, and abusing their superiors, make excellent sport. And as it was ever a custome to do thus, so it will be, and the wiser sort make a jest of it ... But the ill bredd sour part of the bench will be as rediculously in earnest, and like state polititians argue for their owne gove[rn]ment ...[34]

On the eve of the Temple fire,

a formidable rebellion was depending; the gentlemen were more united than had bin knowne; even the gravest of the barristers engaged with them, which was rare, and spoke their caus just.[35]

Further, the rebels had attended on the judges at Serjeants' Inn,

soe numerously in the hall there, filling all the benches, and windoes, and making such noise, that the benchers durst not come amongst them ...[36]

while in response to the statement of their grievances, 'the judges mediated accomodation'. According to North, by having thus 'mortified the benchers, so they were to submitt to reason', the rebellion made possible a mutually satisfactory solution to 'a work so intricate and perplext' as the rebuilding project turned out to be.[37]

North was a remarkably frank and perceptive observer-participant. Notwithstanding his own later experience as a member of the governing body, to which he was elected in 1682 on becoming Queen's Solicitor-General, he entertained no illusions about the benchers' propensity to 'impose upon us ... under colour of acting for the good of the society'.[38] As for the 'obstinate, pert, and opiniative individualls' who typically made up the body of discontented 'gentlemen', the next major outburst of dissension well illustrated the manner in which their expression of complaints replicated—at least in part—the forms of Westminster politics.

Following a 'Representation' against excessive rates charged for commons during term time, signed in June 1694 by some 80 barristers and students, two barristers and two students under the Bar were expelled for

---

[33] *Notes of Me*, above n 1, at.117.
[34] *Ibid*, at 117–18.
[35] *Ibid*, at 118
[36] *Ibid*, at 118.
[37] *Ibid*, at 118–20.
[38] *Ibid*, at 120.

insubordination (having 'in mutinous and disorderly manner not only disobeyed but torne down from the Skreene severall orders of Parliament' and 'in riotous manner affronted & Assaulted the masters of the Bench in the Hall and Parliament Chamber assembled').[39] In November 45 barristers addressed a formal petition of complaint to Sir George Treby, Chief Justice of Common Pleas, and his judicial colleague Sir Nicholas Lechmere, both one-time Middle Temple benchers.[40] This document drew in turn upon a set of 'Resolutions' compiled by a 'Committee of Grievances', which joined to the unexceptionable proposition that 'The Society of the middle Temple is a voluntary Socyety' the potentially subversive claim that the benchers' rule was 'enlivened and enspirited by the general concurrence, submission, and consent of the Socyety'. A series of specific complaints followed, against actions variously represented as 'illegal', 'against the fundamentall rules of the Socyety' and 'an invading of Liberty'. The benchers were accused of self-interested inconsistency with respect to calls to the Bar made 'out of favour' and contrary to their own repeated orders setting out the minimum qualifications for call. The recent call of one 'Mr Nowis at the special instance of Sir W. W. and some scores before that have always practised as Attornys and Sollicitours' seems to have been particularly resented. Hence 'the putting by several Gentlemen the term before that had done several exercises and calling Mr Nowis that had done no exercises and not at all under those qualifications' was denounced as 'an arbitrary and partial proceeding'.[41] The 'extravagant eating and drinking on Parliament nights' was also condemned, together with the benchers' poor example in requiring other members who held chambers to be in commons at least two weeks in every term, while 'sometimes there is but two, sometimes one, and sometimes nere a Bencher in the Hall'. Lastly the Committee claimed to have 'particulariz'd but a few', since to 'enumerate all the circumstances of thire partial and arbitrary gouernment, and call to Assize' all the under-treasurer's embezzlements and extortions demanded

> such volumes of Paper that ... would so enhaunce the revenue of the Stamp office that thire Majestys would not want a further supply of Taxes for the subsequent yeare.[42]

---

[39] *MTR*, iii., 1426; Historical Manuscripts Commission, *Fifth Report*, 385; MT.1/MPA/6, 409 (31 Oct 1694); Williamson, above n 28, at 559–60.

[40] MT.3/MEM, 19 Dec 1694, 'To the Right Honble. Sr George Treby ...'.

[41] HB Box 122, Bundle 6, No 31. Charles Nowes, admitted in 1677, was called to the Bar on 18 May 1694: *MTAdmR*, i., 196; *MTR*, iii., 1423. 'Sir W. W.' is presumably William Whitelock, a bencher from 1671 to his death *c* 1718: *The Middle Temple Bench Book*, JB Williamson (ed) (London, Middle Temple 1937) 134; BD Henning (ed), *The House of Commons 1660–1690* (London, HMSO, 1983), vol. iii., 712–713.

[42] HB Box 122, Bundle 6, No 31.

The subsequent barristers' petition dropped the complaint about irregular Bar calls, and the facetious final paragraph, but specifically accused the veteran under-treasurer James Buck of exacting excessive fees, 'encouraged by long continuance in his office ... which officer ought to be annually elected'. It also demanded that 'according to the Antient constitutions of the House' the accounts should be audited by 'the Gent at the Barr joyntly with the Bench'. For good measure the petitioners attacked the discontinuance of readings (with the claim that although some benchers had offered to read, 'they have not been permitted, whereby the Ancient Dignity of the said society is fallen'), finally asserting that the benchers' failure to add to their number John Conyers and William Cowper (a future Lord Chancellor), who had recently taken silk, was an act disrespectful to the new monarchs William and Mary 'and soe resented by this Society'.[43]

The benchers met this comprehensive challenge to their authority with a detailed refutation over three broadsheet pages of the 'Mutineers' Articles of Complaint'. Not the least interesting aspect of this document is its claim that since the decision to discontinue readings, more than £3,000 had been spent on improving the public buildings and amenities of the Middle Temple. All these works 'in building the Temple Gate, in Paveing the Church, in new Pews, the Organ, the Fountain, the Garden' had been carried out without imposing any financial burden on the membership in general, thanks to the payments made to house funds by benchers who would otherwise have delivered a reading (and thereby spent much larger sums of food and drink).[44] Lechmere and Treby formally considered both documents and heard accompanying verbal submissions in the Middle Temple Parliament Chamber on 1 March 1695. Their adjudication was not delivered until the beginning of May, a leisurely pace presumably intended to cool passions on both sides. The same goal is apparent in the terms of the eventual ruling, which firmly rejected all the junior members' complaints and fully endorsed the prerogatives of the Bench, but also recommended that the four expelled members be restored, on apologising for their offences.

Subsequent confrontations were more restrained. While the benchers might contest, deny or ignore specific claims and complaints from the bar and student body, they never questioned the legitimacy of vacation parliaments, nor their right to present petitions or 'representations' on a wide range of issues. So vacation parliaments continued to meet at irregular intervals until the mid-1770s, and successive generations of

---

[43] MT.3/MEM, 19 Dec 1694: 'Articles of Complaint against the Trer & other Masters of the Bench of the Honble Society of the Middle Temple', broadsheet, endorsed 'Mutineers Articles of Complaint to the Judges agst the Bench with the Trers anser. Copy'; *MTR*, iii., 1431–32.

[44] *MTR*, iii., 1432–38.

benchers showed themselves prepared to listen with at least half an ear to complaints and grievances raised there. Thus in 1731, criticism of the lack of a library catalogue and the 'Practice of Monopolizing Chambers' (held by trustees) seem to have prompted some action, despite a Bench ruling that claims to hold a parliament after vacation commons had ended, together with 'Authority to Command the use of the Publick Hall and attendance of the officers and servants' were contrary to 'Usage and Custome', and 'tending to the disturbance of the Peace and good Government'.[45] Calls to extend the library's opening hours also eventually elicited a positive response. While unsuccessful in 1730, a further request twenty years later that the library keeper should attend between five and eight in the evenings during term, 'as otherwise the Library is of no use or advantage to the Gentlemen of this society who attend Westminster Hall', saw parliament make an order precisely to that effect.[46]

The quality of food in hall and the manner of its service became a significant issue from mid-century onwards. Despite congratulating the Bench in 1750 on the Middle Temple's 'flourishing Condition', the 'Number and Worth of its Members' and its 'established Reputation, which continually brings in a Supply of Students ready to join themselves to a Body distinguished by its Harmony, Order and Learning', the vacationers expressed 'great concern' that

> several Gentlemen enter themselves in Lincoln's Inn and other societies who would have entered in, and greatly increased the Number of this Society, but that there is a general Complaint of our Term's Commons which we beg leave to inform your Masterships are in themselves very indifferent ...[47]

A vacation parliament repeated these claims in 1754, asserting that 'Commons which are far inferior to those of any other Inn of Court' deterred many potential entrants; in response the benchers appointed a committee to consider what change, if any, was needed.[48] Perhaps there was some improvement, since when a vacation parliament next met in February 1756 it dissolved itself after two days, 'there being no real grievances to redress'.[49] But five years later a lengthy 'Humble Representation' combined deferential (and doubtless ironic) reference to the benchers' 'Truly Paternal Care' with a litany of complaints about the neglected state of the library, the need for a night watchman to attend the gate at

[45] MT.1/MPA/7, 49, 182, 218, 358, 360, 362, 372, 379, 434, 499. Box LVI, Bundle III, No 5.

[46] Box LVI, Bundle III, No 5.. MT.7/BUB/1, 8 Dec 1750; MT.1/MPA/6, 72–3, 77. Library access remained a problem: cf MT.7/BUB/2, 29 Nov 1761, 16 Feb 1766.

[47] MT.7/BUB/1, 8 Dec 1750, report of Committee of Grievances and 'Representation'; MT.1/MPA/7, 72–5, 77.

[48] MT.7/BUB/1, 8 Feb 1754; MT.1/MPA/7, 142.

[49] MT.7/BUB/1, 18 Feb 1756.

Devereux Court and the 'bad Oeconomy of the Hall'.[50] The same theme recurred in 1766, when the Bench was further informed that commons compared particularly unfavourably, both in quality and quantity, with the Lincoln's Inn equivalent. Three years on the cook was accused of serving far worse provisions than his predecessors, and was further complained against in 1771.[51] These criticisms may well have reflected problems stemming from a major administrative and financial restructuring which had occurred in 1747, when the post of steward was abolished and the cook given sole responsibility both for providing meals and collecting payments from members in commons.[52]

Unlike earlier manifestations of discontent, most eighteenth-century airings of grievance involved no overt challenge to the authority exercised by the Masters of the Bench. That authority was now so secure as to be virtually unquestionable. But there are signs of increasing frustration with the lack of response to representations from below: thus a vacation parliament summoned by the Bar mess in 1766 resolved that

> many successive Parliaments have addressed the Masters of the Bench in the most Decent & dutiful terms in order to obtain a redress of Grievances ... [and] no such Redress has ever been Obtained though the existence of such Grievances has never been disputed.[53]

This was something of an overstatement, but the failure of campaigns by vacation parliaments in the 1760s and early 1770s against both the cook and the under-treasurer Charles Hopkins may explain why no further meetings are recorded in the buttery books after 1774.[54]

The decline of communal life at the early eighteenth-century Inns of Court, with particular reference to membership, residence and legal education, has been comprehensively mapped by Professor Lemmings. The Tudor and Stuart Inns were jealous of their individual autonomy and identity; as late as 1694, a person who had been admitted to another (unspecified) Inn before joining the Middle Temple had his admission monies returned and his admission cancelled when that fact was discovered, while in 1712 the under-treasurer was deputed to enquire 'whether Mr Caldecott J a member of this Society be admitted to Gray's Inn and called to the degree of the Utter Bar there', in which case he was to appear before the next parliament.[55] But the old corporate exclusiveness was weakening; a few years later parliament accepted Mr Fortescue's petition for the return of his bond, subject to 'producing a Certificate or otherwise

50   MT.7/BUB/2; MT.3/MEM; MT.1/MPA/8, 281, 284, 287.
51   MT.7/BUB/2,16 Feb, 22 June 1766, 3 Dec 1769, 23 June 1771.
52   MT.1/MPA/7, 551–2, 564.
53   MT.7/BUB/2, 16 Feb 1766.
54   MT.7/BUB/3, 26 June 1774.
55   *MTR*, iii., 1425; MT.1/MPA/7, 49.

making it appear that he is admitted of the Society of the Inner Temple', and the payment of 'what is due to this Society from him for Commons and other duties'.[56] Such transfers became increasingly frequent. Thus William Hay, a reformist politician and writer, although no practitioner, kept a chamber all his life at the Middle Temple, having been admitted in 1715, a year after joining Lincoln's Inn; shortly afterwards John Bridges, a veteran Middle Temple barrister, better known as the historian of North-amptonshire, moved in the opposite direction, departing in 1716 for Lincoln's Inn, where he became a bencher three years later. At the age of 12 years, Charles Yorke, son of the future Lord Chancellor Hardwicke, joined the Middle Temple (as his father had originally done); but after a stint at Cambridge Charles again retraced his father's footsteps by transferring to Lincoln's Inn, where the Court of Chancery held its out-of-term sittings. The same connection helps explain the move of Philip Carteret Webb, a former attorney turned barrister, antiquary, MP and treasury solicitor, who had been admitted to the Middle Temple in 1727 but transferred to Lincoln's Inn 18 years later, doubtless following his patron Lord Hard-wicke. Practitioner migrants were also often motivated by the acquisition of a set of chambers in another house, as when William Blackstone petitioned for the return of his bond in 1759, having 'purchased chambers in the Inner Temple and paid all Duties due and obtained a Certificate from this Society in order to transfer himself and be admitted to his said Chambers'. However, Blackstone subsequently failed to collect the bond, and two years later petitioned successfully to reverse the process, 'being desirous of returning to his own Society', perhaps because his earlier move had entailed some loss of acquired seniority.[57]

The 'revenue and support of this Society', according to Charles Worsley, 'doth principally consist in fines upon Admittances into Chambers'.[58] Individual proprietors were admitted to their chambers for life, on pay-ment of a fine; sometimes (especially in the case of new or significantly renovated buildings), admissions were for life with one or more assign-ments of additional lives thereafter, creating valuable reversionary interests which could be inherited or sold.[59] This system had the undeniable

---

[56] MT.1/MPA/7, 49 at 97.

[57] *Ibid*, at 241–42, 265.

[58] Ingpen (ed), above n 22, at 144.

[59] North (*Notes of Me*, above n 1, at 116–117 notes that purchasers have no 'title, but an *admissus est* by the Treasurer, whereupon they pay a fine'. He goes on to explain: 'This is for the life of the person admitted. If he purchase or obtain by favour an assignment, it is a power reserved to his executors, to sell, and nominate another life, which shall have right to be admitted paying an usuall fine, which is small in respect to the value. And so for 2 and 3 assignments which import so many lives successively to be named upon the falling of any, until all are expired.' When all these interests expire, the chambers revert to the Inn. Thus the assignees were nominated only when the tenant's interest fell on his demise, although the number of such assignments was fixed at the time of the initial grant.

TWENTY POUNDS
REWARD.

WHEREAS a Male Child, fuppofed to be about Eighteen Months old, having a Burn or Scald on the Left Leg, dreffed in a White Dimity Cloak, White Bedgown, Flannel Petticoat, and Night-Cap, was found deferted on Friday Evening laft, at about Eight o'Clock on the Ground-Floor of the Paffage, No. 5, *Effex-Court, Middle-Temple.*

A REWARD OF TWENTY POUNDS

Will be paid by the Treafurer of the *Middle Temple* to any Perfon who fhall give such Information at the Treafurer's Office, as may be the Means of bringing to Juftice the Perfon or Perfons who were concerned in deferting the above-mentioned Child.

March 16, 1801.

Carpenter and Son, Printers, Fleet-Street.

Foundling's Reward Poster

advantage of minimising the administration and maintenance burdens borne by the house as landlord, but at the cost of devolving responsibility for its most valuable capital assets to individual proprietor-lessees. While they, and any person to whom they might sub-let their chambers, were required to be members, not 'strangers', this restriction was difficult to enforce, despite occasional efforts to eject non-members, women and children.[60] Thus in June 1718, parliament ordered the removal of 'one Hodder', living with his wife and family in an Elm Court upper chamber, under threat of the chambers being 'padlocked' or sequestered by the house; the order had to be repeated four months later. Early next year there were 'many complaints of very great disturbances' in another Elm Court garret,

> occasioned by severall women residing in the said chambers contrary to and in contempt of many good orders made to prevent strangers from inhabiting in Chambers belonging to this Society.[61]

The extra-parochial status of both Temple societies meant that each society had a potential liability to maintain babies born, and an actual liability to maintain babies abandoned, within its limits. Thus pregnant females were particularly unwelcome. When in April 1722 a woman 'big with child' was reportedly living in a chamber in Essex Court, and there appeared 'ground to suspect that the Child may become chargeable to the Society', the under-treasurer was charged to take 'the porter and any other officers of the house along with him as he shall think fitt' and enquire 'concerning the said Woman, and wither she be delivered of a child, and what is become of the same'.[62] On the other hand, the benchers were quite prepared to accommodate members seeking call to the Bar who lacked the formal requirement of chamber ownership in their own right, by selling three-year leases of 'house' chambers. Thus the Bar ledger described William Blackstone after his call in 1746 as having house chambers 'four pair of stairs and a half back' on staircase number 2 in Garden Court, while noting that he actually 'Lives in Pump court No 3'.[63] Chambers belonging to the house were also occupied by various officers and servants as part of their remuneration, and supposedly leased out only with the treasurer's permission. In May 1785, Elizabeth Horsfall, widow of the late under-treasurer, who 'had been an Officer of this Honourable Society during a period of 50 years and upwards', sought permission to continue to occupy the Lamb Building chambers where she had evidently lived for the past 16 years with

[60] Eg *MTR*, iii., 1441, 1451–52. In 1715 the under-treasurer was deputed to 'inquire who are proprietors of the Chambers in the Society let to Gent[lemen] who are not of the house; and especially of those who have families': MT.1/MPA/7, 73.

[61] MT.1/MPA/7, 109, 112, 113, 117–18.

[62] *Ibid*, at 176; FD Mackinnon, 'The Temple Family'(1946) 62 *LQR* 152. See generally MT.18/FOU (papers relating to Temple foundlings).

[63] Ingpen (ed), above n 22, at, 30; MT.3/BAL/1, 49.

her husband and their six children. Although granted an annual pension of £25 (once James Horsfall's accounts with the society were settled), Mrs Horsfall was told she must vacate by Christmas.[64] Parliament's concern in this instance was probably to ensure that the chamber in question became available for Horsfall's successor, rather than to prevent it falling into the hands of a female tenant (although this latter principle would be explicitly avowed in 1816).[65] While the benchers were evidently resigned to tolerating the residence of women and children within what had once been exclusively male habitations, the occupation of chambers by non-members and non-lawyers remained a long-standing grievance among their juniors. In 1769 a vacation parliament deplored the presence of the

> Lowest Handicrafts of various kinds, who nestle here to escape the payment of parochial rates ... Milliners, Mantua makers, Laundresses, Gamesters, Prostitutes ...[66]

The residential character of the Hanoverian Middle Temple was diluted as much by the absence of members as the presence of non-members. While the proportion of entrants without chambers in the house continued to grow after 1700, so did the difficulty of ensuring that those who possessed chambers came into commons.[67] The discovery in 1730 that the Chief Butler had been 'admitting Gentlemen into Commons upon notice given or sent ... by Letter or Message for that purpose (they themselves not appearing in the hall to Eat or take such commons)' caused parliament to order that henceforth appearance in person at commons twice each week for two weeks of every term was necessary to fulfil the requirements for call to the Bar. Similar resistance to what had become the residual corporate activity of the society is suggested by an order of 1783 requiring those keeping commons to remain in Hall until grace was said after dinner; a later amendment prescribed that they must also be present for the pre-prandial grace.[68] That the problem was not confined to junior members is apparent from the complaints of the 1694 Committee of Grievances, and Parliament's own attempts at self-regulation, which in 1690 and 1697 stipulated that all benchers must be in commons for at least one week, or two half-weeks, every term. The ineffectiveness of this provision is suggested by a subsequent decision to debar from the influential and lucrative office of treasurer all benchers who had not been 'actually' in

---

[64]   MT.1/MPA/7, 570–1; MT.1/MPA/9, 153.
[65]   *Rules and Orders of the Honourable Society of the Middle Temple* (London, Middle Temple, 1882), 24.
[66]   Cf MT.1/MPA/8, 226: Elizabeth Finch, widow of late Robert, panierman, 'had resided in the Society above Fifty years and for about thirty years had been Tenant to this Honble Society'; MT.7/BUB/2, 3 Dec 1769.
[67]   Lemmings, above n 6, at 38–39.
[68]   MT.1/MPA/9, 126.

commons for one week at least during the two terms preceding election.[69] By 1777 the quorum for parliament meetings had shrunk to five.[70]

As with the required wearing of gowns in Hall (in 1722 it was found necessary to specify 'decent and Compleat Gowns whole and untorne'[71]), there were numerous attempts, especially in the half-century following the Glorious Revolution, to maintain at least the formal protocols of the old learning exercises. But it was a losing battle. Thus, after research by Treasurer Viney into 'the antient use of the house', and 'takeing notice of the neglect in performing Mootes & Exercises in the Hall to the decay of learning within this Society', parliament ordered in January 1714

> that the antient usage ... be revived & duly observed for the future. And no Exercise upon Assignment in Terme time shall be allowed ... unless in every assignment performed by Gentlemen of the Barr the Moote be in assise or other reall action & the pleadings be drawn at large & performed memoriter without Reading ...

While this edict was duly 'screened' (that is, published to the membership by being posted on the screen at the entrance to Hall), its requirements were evidently so unrealistic that the very next parliament decided to drop the words 'memoriter without Reading'.[72] Similar compromises and concessions affected New Inn readings,[73] which continued throughout our period to provide a setting where the exercises required of all would-be barristers were performed, while entailing neither the effort nor the expense associated with now defunct house readings. We have the text of a 'Reading on the Law of Uses' purportedly given at New Inn by the Cornish barrister and future serjeant Thomas Carthew in Michaelmas term 1691.[74] This brief document takes the form of an initial statement of the reader's case (an hypothetical set of facts, with points or questions in law arising), followed by discussion of the general nature of conveyances, the law of marriage and the statute of uses, all leading to the reader's own opinion by way of conclusion. Although presented in a clear and straightforward manner that might well have been appreciated by novice law students, the fact that no other such readings survive from our period suggests that

---

[69] See above p 219; *MTR*, iii.,1305, 1451; MT.1/MPA/7, 149.

[70] MT.1/MPA/9, 19.

[71] *MTR*, iii., 1422; MT.1/MPA/7, 177.

[72] MT.1/MPA/7, 66, 68. Cf *MTR*, iii., 1418–19, 1439, 1457.

[73] Originally all the Inns of Chancery conducted learning exercises, including readings, for law students. But by the later 17th century the prime function of these readings was, it seems, to provide the occasion for moots required as part of the qualifications for call to the Bar.

[74] Beinecke Library, Lee Papers, Box 18, folder 4, which appears to be the source of the text printed by F Hargrave, *Collectanea Juridica* (London, E and R Brooke, 1791–2), i., 369–77. However, it should be noted that Carthew was a barrister of the Inner Temple: J. H. Baker, *The Order of Serjeants At Law*(1984) 5 Selden Society Supplementary Series, 203, 452.

Carthew's was an exceptional production. Like many if not most New Inn readings, moreover, it was evidently delivered by Carthew on behalf of the appointed reader, despite earlier and later orders specifying that barristers chosen to read at New Inn must serve in person and not by deputy.[75]

By the 1730s it was possible to detail the 'expence in this Society attending any Gentleman in the prosecution of his studyes to and attainment of the degree of the Utter Barr'. Fees and 'Commons eaten or not' amounted in all to £25 14s 8d, with additional fines payable for 'every exercise not performed'. While barristers had further obligations in terms of commons-keeping and exercises, it was 'customary for gentlemen immediately after their Call to surrender their Chambers and compound their Vacations and Assignments which is done for £19/19/6'.[76] In short, all requirements, other than 'actually [to] keep commons in the Hall' by the formal act of dining three times each term over three years, were commutable for cash payments. This may well have been true from the beginning of our period. Roger North was doubtless drawing on personal experience as a Middle Temple student and barrister in describing the elaborate provisions of the medieval learning exercise system as

> shrunk into mere form, and that preserved only for conformity to rules, that gentlemen by appearance in exercises, rather than any sort of performance, might be entitled to be called to the bar.[77]

Nothing had changed by the 1790s, when the young Daniel O'Connell undertook to inform his Irish uncle from London

> what the study of the law is. There are no public lessons given in it. No professors of it. In short all that is necessary for being called to the bar is to be inscribed in the Books of the Temple or other Inn of Court, to dine there three times each term, and to attend the King's Bench during 12 terms. The study depends on the will only of each individual who may reside and act where and how he pleases (provided he attends the terms) for the rest of the year.[78]

While Middle Temple readers continued to be elected throughout our period, their main duty (apart from paying £200) was to give a dinner for their fellow benchers. Whereas the reader's dinner had traditionally included the high-status feasting fare of venison, from 1779 even this link with the past was broken; instead each reader was required to 'pay the sum of Twenty Guineas into the Treasury before his Reading is allowed'.[79]

---

[75]   *MTR*, iii.,1281, 1444.

[76]   Ingpen (ed), above n 22, at 209–12.

[77]   R North, *A Discourse on the Study of the Laws* (London, Baldwin, 1824), 1.

[78]   MR O'Connell (ed), *The Correspondence of Daniel O'Connell* (Dublin, Irish Manuscripts Commission, 1972–80), vol. i., 10–11 (O'Connell was mistaken in supposing attendance at King's Bench to be obligatory).

[79]   MT.1/MPA/9, 53. MT.3/MEM, Stephen Ram to William Eldred, 24 Sept 1801.

Like some other institutional survivals from the Middle Ages, the eighteenth-century Inns of Court had lost much of their former purpose and vitality. The men who governed the Hanoverian Middle Temple were, with a few exceptions, not among the leading practitioners of their day, because the Inn's membership structure now bore little direct relation to the professional hierarchy of the Bar. Nevertheless, thanks to generally buoyant enrolments, the rulers of the Middle Temple continued to garner a substantial income from fees and fines paid by both students and barristers. They also drew investment earnings from a small but growing portfolio of annuities (£6,000 in old South Sea annuities by 1747), equities and other financial instruments, as well as rents paid for 'house' chambers and retail outlets; Lemmings tells us that by 1733, 'this most commercial of inns contained no fewer than 22 shops, including several booksellers, stationers, barbers, a hatter and a shoemaker'.[80] Notwithstanding occasional cash-flow problems and difficulties in collecting arrears of commons, on a year-to-year basis income almost always exceeded expenditure throughout the eighteenth century.[81] This comfortable surplus supported a considerable body of officers and servants (although they relied largely on fees and perquisites, not just their salaries or wages). Under the titular headship of annually-elected treasurers, responsibility for everyday administration of the society's affairs rested in the hands of the under-treasurer. His salaried post was sufficiently lucrative and respectable to attract barristers to compete in what was often a hotly-contested election, with the successful candidate required to lodge substantial securities for the

> monies ... Plate Linnen Books Rolls Bonds writings goods and other things belonging to this Society and wherewith he hath been intrusted by virtue of his said Office ...[82]

Besides butlers, cooks, gardeners, porters, watchmen and other such servants, whose places seem to have been in the treasurer's gift, the benchers reserved the collective right to endorse the nomination of certain artisans and professional men as 'by appointment'; thus in 1780 they confirmed the treasurer's proposal that one Anne Robinson should succeed her late husband 'as Painter to this Society'.[83] Other patronage opportunities arose from the numerous petitions considered at each parliament meeting. These related mainly to chambers and qualifications for call, but also begged charitable

---

[80]   Lemmings, above n 6, at 57; MT.1/MPA/7, 564.

[81]   MT.2/TAV/1–6 (Treasurer's Accounts, 1658–1826). Cf Lemmings, above n 6, at 48–49.

[82]   MT.1/MPA/7, 94. BL MS Additional 35585, fo 40 (a canvassing letter addressed on 27 May 1726 by the bencher Archibald Hutcheson to Sir Joseph Jekyll about a vacancy in 'the place of Under Treasurer of the Middle Temple', seeking 'the favour of your vote and interest on the day of Election').

[83]   MT.1/MPA/9, 66; cf MT.1/MPA/8, 273 ('Mistress Deane ... dismissed from her business of Plaisterer to this Society').

relief for destitute members, foundlings brought up by the Society, former servants and their widows. They also sought, usually without much success, cash compositions for members who had long since left the society without taking their names off the books, so remaining liable for dues which continued to accumulate in their absence. All calls to the Bar followed nominations by individual benchers, who were supposed 'able to give some account to their Masterships (if required) of the Character and Qualification of the Gentleman he proposes'.[84] More material and visible benchers' perquisites included reserved seats in the Temple Church, food and wine consumed both at the Bench table in Hall and in their private Parliament Chamber, opportunities to extend hospitality and participate in royal visits and those of other distinguished guests, borrowing rights from the house library, and concessional admissions for their sons—all this in addition to a partly-furnished Bench chamber which could be either occupied in person, or rented out, at the proprietor's discretion.[85]

It is tempting to dismiss the eighteenth-century rulers of the Middle Temple as a self-perpetuating coterie of second-rate rent-seekers, whose main interest lay in exploiting the substantial material advantages which had fallen into their laps largely by effluxion of time. In 1758, William Blackstone, who would himself join the Middle Temple Bench three years later, noted that at the Inns 'all forms of regimen, or academical superintendence, either with regard to morals or studies, are found impractical, and therefore entirely neglected'.[86] If Blackstone did not expressly indict the governing bodies for failing to supply what Samuel Paterson later termed 'the want of a proper system of juridical education in the inns of court ... this gross deficiency', others showed less restraint.[87] For their part the benchers seemingly felt no compulsion to defend themselves, or the societies over which they presided, against these stirrings. Having suffered a similar earlier decline in student enrolments and educational activity, the two universities experienced a marked revival in both during the closing decades of the eighteenth century. But the Inns shared only in the numerical increase (which, as noted in section I. above, largely bypassed the Middle Temple). The continued migration of fashionable society to London's West End did nothing to improve their public image; in her last

---

[84] MT.1/MPA/7, 342.

[85] MT.1/MPA/7, 155 (reference to 'Goods, furniture & Necessaries in their respective Bench Chambers purchased by or belonging to the house'). North, *Notes of Me*, 117.

[86] *Commentaries*, i. 25: 'Introduction ... On the Study of the Law'.

[87] [S Paterson], 'An Essay on Debating Societies' (1788) iii *The Templar* 164; cf [J Rayner?], *The History and Antiquities of the Four Inns of Court ... published by Desire of some Members of Parliament, in order to point out the Abuses in the Government of the Inns of Court and Chancery* (London, G Kearsly, 1780), v–vi, xi, xiii; RW Bridgman, *Reflections on the Study of the Law* (London, Brooke and Clarke, 1804), 5, 7–8.

novel, *Persuasion*, Jane Austen has Mr Elliot's formerly straitened condition depicted as 'inferior in circumstances, he was then the poor one; he
had chambers in the Temple, and it was as much as he could do to support
the appearance of a gentleman'.[88] Indeed, a knowledgeable contemporary
described 'the ancient seminaries of juridical learning established in London' as 'almost forgotten', or at all events 'not known to common
observers as places set apart for profound study and patriotic erudition'.[89]

Yet other than James I's grant of the Temple to both societies 'for the
accommodation and education of those studying and following the profession of the laws', the Inns lacked any formally constituted commitment to
learning and teaching, let alone endowments dedicated to those ends. Their
critics also tended to exaggerate the educational efficacy of the old aural
learning exercises. Further, in the absence of consensus as to what, if
anything, might best replace that pre-Gutenburg relic, the Middle Temple
did continue to provide some minimal level of support for those attempting
to learn the law, even if only as a consequence of its more mundane
function in providing lawyers' chambers and apartments. In 1740, the poet
Thomas Gray cautioned his young friend Richard West, following the
latter's announcement that he had just moved to Bond Street because he
could study law as well there as at the Middle Temple, in the following
terms:

> ... is it not putting yourself a little out of the way of a people, with whom it is
> necessary to keep up some sort of intercourse and conversation, though but little
> for your pleasure and entertainment (yet there are, I believe such among them as
> might give you both) at least for your information in that study ... ?[90]

More than half a century before, a future Lord Chancellor of Ireland and
barrister of the house informed a correspondent in London that 'I hold
myself so very little obliged by the Middle Temple that I owe the society no
service'.[91] Notwithstanding the later Lord Kenyon's claim that 'Within
these walls I have spent my better days, and formed my dearest friendships;
and if I possess any knowledge or abilities ... I readily confess that I am
wholly indebted for them to the discipline of this Inn of Court', the
Hanoverian Middle Temple may not to have evoked strong feelings of
attachment from the bulk of its members.[92] Yet some individual benchers
did present the house with gifts or legacies of silver plate and cash, while
various authors donated books; the library's list of benefactors is empty

---

[88] J Austen, *Persuasion* (London, John Murray, 1818), ch 21.
[89] Bridgman, above n 87, at 7–8.
[90] *The Works of Thomas Gray*, 3rd edn (London, 1807), vol, i, at 253.
[91] Lemmings, above n 6, at 42. Brodrick nevertheless had his son St John admitted to the
Middle Temple in 1700: *MTAdmR*, i., 247.
[92] (1788) iii *The Templar* 304.

from 1711 until the nineteenth century, but this primarily reflects administrative shortcomings rather than missing benefactions.[93] Neither should we entirely discount the 1771 vacation parliament's protestation of their 'Serious concern for the Reputation and Welfare of this Antient Seat of Legal Learning'.[94] For the unreformed Middle Temple still provided its members with something more than board and lodging.

The house library re-established by Robert Ashley's legacy in the early seventeenth century was maintained thereafter by a succession of salaried library keepers, including Henry Carey, better known as the musician sometimes credited with composing 'God Save the King'. Early in George I's reign, Carey claimed to have

> employed myself in regulating and reducing to decency and order a place which, through long neglect, was become a perfect chaos of paper and a wilderness of books.

One fruit of his labours was 'a new Catalogue ... of all the tracts contained in the Library'. This listing of the society's collection of 'Miscellaneos Libellos (vulgo Anglice Pamphlets)' ran to more than 100 pages when printed in 1734 as an appendix to the alphabetical catalogue of the library published that year during the treasurership of Charles Worsley, following a request by the 1731 vacation parliament.[95] The first printed catalogue of the Middle Temple library had appeared in 1700 with the support of an earlier treasurer, Sir Bartholomew Shower. Arranged by subject, it listed works of theology, history, geography, medicine, mathematics, politics, 'English Affairs' and saints' lives, in addition to books of canon, civil and common law. According to an early eighteenth-century topographer, this 'good Library near the Back Steps of the Hall, to which Sir Bartholomew Sho[wer] and several others have contributed Books', was open to readers about six hours a day.[96] While a printed list of additions to the collection between 1734 and 1766 is dominated by law books, it also includes Thomas Broughton's *Bibliotheca Historico Sacra*, Ephraim Chambers's

[93] Cf *Middle Temple Bench Book*, 155 (Avery), 160 (Worsley), 163 (Onslow), 173 (Norton), 177 (Cust), 185 (Champion), 190 (Popham), 191 (Hatsell), 194 (Scott): MT Library MS 137. Gifts to the library by members included a newly-published set of House of Commons journals from Francis Fane, member for Petersham (1747), the first edition of William Blackstone's *Commentaries on the Laws of England* (1765–69) as well as his 'most correct Edition' of Magna Carta (1759), and 'An Introduction to the History of the principal States of Europe, begun by Baron Puffendorf, continued by Mr De La Martiniere, improved by Joseph Sayer Serjeant at Law' (1764): MT.1/MPA/7, 572; 8/244, 325.

[94] MT7/BUB/2.

[95] Historical Manuscripts Commission, *The Manuscripts of His Grace the Duke of Portland, preserved at Welbeck Abbey* (London, HMSO, 1899–1931), vol v., 552. *Catalogus Librorum Bibliothecae Honorabilis Societatis Medii Templi Londini Ordine Dictionarii Dispositus* (London, Middle Temple, 1734), 447–54. Box LVI, Bundle III, No 5.

[96] J Hatton, *A New View of London* (London, R Chiswell, 1708), vol ii., 103.

Cyclopaedia, the 24-volume *Universal History*, Maitland's *History of London*, Robertson's *History of Scotland* and Temple Henry Croker's *Experimental Magnetism* (1761).[97]

On entering the Middle Temple from South Carolina in 1769, young Edward Rutledge was advised by his somewhat overbearing older brother that

> There is generally a good preacher at the Temple Church, and it will be more to your credit to spend a few hours ... there, than as it is usually spent, in London especially, by the Templars.[98]

This fraternal admonition was strictly superfluous, since the penal bond signed by each new member obliged him to

> usually resort to the Service and Sermon, in the Temple Church, and communicate there, so often as by the Laws of this Land he ought to do.[99]

Yet there is no evidence that these notably vague requirements were ever enforced. During the early eighteenth century, candidates for the Bar were still required to receive communion 'in some Protestant congregation' before call, but even that diluted provision was repealed in 1748.[100] If Templars were not generally reputed to be assiduous church-goers, services at the Temple Church evidently attracted sufficiently large congregations for junior members to complain that their assigned pews behind the benchers' seats on the north (Middle Temple) side of the church were taken up by 'strangers', eliciting orders to the 'pew-openers' that non-members should be admitted only after the reading of the first lesson.[101]

The two Temple societies shared joint responsibility for the ancient fabric of the Temple Church and its clerical establishment, headed by the master of the Temple, although presentations to this benefice remained in the gift of the Crown. There was occasional conflict, most notably the celebrated 1680s 'battle of the organs', when two instruments were installed in the church by rival organ builders (see 'The Temple Church' by John Toulmin above, at p 15); that of the protestant Bernard Smith (Bernhardt Schmidt), favoured by the Middle Temple's benchers, was eventually chosen over that of the Inner Temple's preferred candidate, the Catholic Renatus Harris.[102] A more cooperative atmosphere characterised the extensive works on and around the church fabric itself, following a

---

[97]   *Catalogus Librorum*, above n 95, at 1–17.

[98]   JB O'Neall, *Biographical Sketches of the Bench and Bar of South Carolina* (Charleston SC, SG Courtenay, 1859), vol i, 121.

[99]   Eg MT.3/CBB, Francis Plowden, 25 Nov 1796.

[100]   *MTR*, iii., 1416, 1417, 1421; MT.1/MPA/8, 1–3.

[101]   MT7/BUB/1, Feb 1754; 2 (29 Nov 1761, 17 Feb 1766); MT.1/MPA/8, 357.

[102]   D Knight, 'The Battle of the Organs: the Smith Organ at the Temple and its Organist' (1997) 21 *Journal of the British Institute of Organ Studies* 76.

report commissioned from Sir Christopher Wren in 1682.[103] Gradual acceptance of the principle that each society would appoint in turn to even the most minor posts (including 'the office of Sexton and Cleaner' as well as that of organist)[104] minimised tensions previously associated with the appointment of Temple Church readers or lecturers, as did the gradual easing of both sectarian passions and neighbourly contentions for precedence.

While the scholar Thomas Broughton, the controversialist John Eachard and the miscellaneous writer Temple Henry Croker were prominent among the Middle Temple's readers, their influence hardly matched that of the masters of the Temple. Dr Richard Ball, who held office from 1661 to 1684, was followed by the remarkable father-and-son team of William and Thomas Sherlock, who consecutively managed to clock up nearly 70 years in post. During the second half of the eighteenth century the Sherlocks' successors included Thomas Thurlow, brother of the Lord Chancellor, who resigned on becoming Bishop of Durham in 1787, and Thomas Rennell, Dean of Winchester, who served from 1798 to 1826.

When Thomas Sherlock was translated from the bishopric of Salisbury to the see of London in 1748, it was expected that he would resign the mastership of the Temple. Lord Chancellor Hardwicke accordingly pressed the claims of his own candidate for what he termed 'a Director of the Conscience of the Lawyers. It is a Preferment of more consequence' (Hardwicke claimed) than its monetary value might suggest, with 'an influence amongst the Members of the two Societies, & particularly the young Gentlemen who are sent thither for education'.[105] Sherlock eventually decided that he could not afford to relinquish the mastership, especially the house which went with it. When 'age and infirmities' at last forced his resignation in 1753, just two years short of a full half-century as master, Sherlock addressed the benchers of both the Inner and Middle Temples with his heartfelt thanks for 'the greatest happiness of my life', having enjoyed 'the acquaintance of some of the greatest men of the age', while 'living and conversing with gentlemen of a liberal education and of great learning and experience'.[106]

These sentiments possibly embodied an element of hyperbole. But they cannot be discounted altogether, even with reference to the Middle Temple

---

[103] See R Griffith-Jones, 'An Enrichment of Cherubims: Christopher Wren's Refurbishment of the Temple Church' in D Park and R Griffith-Jones (eds), *The Temple Church in London: History, Architecture, Art* (Woodbridge, Boydell and Brewer, 2010).

[104] MT.1/MPA/8, 213; *ODNB*, sv Jones, John (1728?–1796).

[105] British Library, Additional MS 32717, fo 74, quoted by E Carpenter, *Thomas Sherlock 1678–1761* (London, SPCK, 1936), 145–46. Sherlock's letter was copied into the Middle Temple's Parliament Book of Orders, together with the benchers' response: MT.1/MPA/8, 133–4.

[106] Carpenter, above n 105, at 147.

alone, although according to a barrister of the other house, 'The Inner Temple stands upon a much larger site than the Middle, and contains nearly 100 sets of chambers more than the sister society.'[107] While the moral tone of the plays and verse of Congreve, Shadwell, Burnaby, Higden and some of their less well-known colleagues might not have met with Bishop Sherlock's entire approval, the Middle Temple's literary tradition certainly continued to flourish from the Restoration onwards.[108] Among the more respectable later dramatists and poets who had at least enrolled at the Inn were George I's poet laureate Nicholas Rowe (1674–1718), Richard Gwinnett (1675–1717), John Hoadly (1711–76), Morgan Macnamara (*c* 1720–62), James Murphy (1725–59), Richard Brinsley Sheridan (1751–1816) and Anthony Champion (1725–1801), who bequeathed £1,000 to the society where he had lived as a bencher. Oliver Goldsmith also famously resided in the Inn, as a non-member of the house, in the closing years of his life, and was buried from the Temple Church, while his prosperous near-contemporary, the novelist and playwright Henry Fielding, was a Middle Temple barrister.

The pseudonym 'A Gentleman of the Middle Temple' disguised the authorship of many political pamphlets, as it did the barrister Matthew Bacon's *Compleat Arbitrator* (1731) and *New Abridgment of the Law* (1736).[109] Less inhibited Middle Temple law reporters and legal writers included Thomas Barnardiston, William Blackstone, William Bohun, James Burrow, Henry Boult Cay, Richard Francis, Richard Hemsworth, William ('Oriental') Jones, William Nelson, and Thomas Vernon. Closely related to the law, antiquarian, heraldic and historical studies were strongly represented, notably by Anthony Allen (the bencher who proposed Blackstone for call to the Bar), John Anstis, Elias Ashmole (who in 1686 politely refused Henry Chauncy's invitation to join the Bench),[110] Blackstone again, Chauncy himself, James Hill, Stephen Leake, Thomas Madox, Peter Le Neve, Antony Norris, Thomas Rawlinson and James Wright. But authors and scholars with Middle Temple connections covered a vast range of subjects: William Gwavas researched the Cornish language, George Lewis Scott tutored the young George III in mathematics, the polymath Roger

---

[107] 'A Letter from the Hon Daines Barrington to the Rev Dr Lort ...', *Archaeologia*, ix (1789), 132.

[108] Cf 'Literary Associations of the Middle Temple', by Jessica Winston, above at p 147, with an Appendix by Lesley Whitelaw, 'Men of Letters Associated with the Middle Temple'. I am grateful to Prof Winston for allowing me to read her article in draft.

[109] Eg *The Grounds of Unity in Religion* (London, John Hodges, 1679); [J Banks], *A Short Critical Review of the Political Life of Oliver Cromwell* (London, 1739); *A Critical Review of the Liberties of British Subjects* (London, R Watkins, 1750); *An Introduction to the Knowledge of the Laws and Constitution of England* (London, J Worrall, 1763); *The Out-of-Door Parliament* (London, J Almon, 1780).

[110] Bodleian Library, MS Ashmole 1136, fos 170–71.

North investigated the mechanics of musical organs and much else,[111] while John Asgill (co-founder with the speculative developer Nicholas Barbon of the first land bank) advocated the registration of land titles and wrote on other economic issues, as did his near-contemporary Henry Martyn. Philosophical and theological themes were addressed by the free-thinker Anthony Collins, the bibliophile Benjamin Heath and the deist bencher Henry Dodwell; in 1704, George Hickes expressed his gratitude to 'the honourable Society of the Middle Temple' and the bencher Sir Bartholomew Shower for their 'great encouragement in my undertaking', presumably a reference to their support for his *Linguarum Veterum Septentrionalium Thesaurus Grammatico-Criticus et Archaelogicus* (1703– 5).[112] Bibliographical interests of a less desirable kind saw the barrister Henry Justice sentenced to seven years' transportation in 1736 for stealing numerous books, discovered in his Elm Court chambers, from Trinity College, Cambridge.[113]

Of course the nature of the association between these individuals and the Middle Temple varied considerably, and sometimes may have been little more than casual or nominal. Yet the Inn clearly could and did provide a point of contact for persons with serious intellectual, literary, scholarly and scientific interests, as well as for beaux and gallants. And these were not mutually exclusive roles; the barrister Edward Capell, a 'professed beau' as a youthful Middle Templar, later published a pioneering ten-volume edition of Shakespeare's plays from his Brick Court chambers. Capell's neighbours included the physician and astronomer John Bevis, who died in his rooms while observing the sun's meridian altitude; Bevis's executor was the under-treasurer James Horsfall, FRS. In an earlier generation the Middle Temple had played host not only to Tradescant's famous collection of antiquities and curiosities, but also to that of William Charleton, which in the 1680s and 1690s attracted fashionable society, natural philosophers and virtuosi to view what John Evelyn thought 'one of the most perfect assemblys of rarities that can be anywhere seen'.[114] Yet in 1694 the barrister Samuel Travers, barred from conducting chemical experiments in his chamber with a former assistant to Robert Boyle, complained that he was not allowed to 'receive visits from one of the most learned and

---

[111] JM Kassler, *The Beginnings of the Modern Philosophy of Music in England* (Burlington VT, Ashgate, 2004), 114–15; JM Kassler, *The Honourable Roger North (1651–1734)* (Farnham, Ashgate, 2009).

[112] BL, MS Stowe 750, fo 2.

[113] P Gaskell, 'Henry Justice, A Cambridge Book Thief' (1952) 1 *Transactions of the Cambridge Bibliographical Society* 398.

[114] ES de Beer (ed), *The Diary of John Evelyn* (Oxford, Oxford University Press, 1955) vol v, 13; RD Altick, *The Shows of London* (Cambridge MA, Belknap Press, 1978), 13–14.

ingenious mathematicians and philosophers in England', although 'the very staircase where the dispute lies, has for many years harboured wives, misses and costermongers'.[115]

As one of the court painter Peter Lely's executors, Roger North stored the artist's drawings and portraits in his Middle Temple chambers (part of the new gatehouse fronting on the Strand which still stands as he designed it[116] following the 1679 fire). The recently-founded Society for the Propagation of Christian Knowledge maintained its offices at the other end of Middle Temple Lane from 1714 to 1728, notwithstanding various 'Lewd women and other Idle persons' then 'Sculking about the house', or the noisy oaths and obscenities of the Thames watermen who plied nearby.[117] The German scholar Zacharias von Uffenbach, visiting London in Queen Anne's reign, was impressed more by the size than by the amenity of the Middle Temple hall, for 'they dine here as in slovenly a fashion as they do in the colleges of Oxford', on tables set with wooden platters and green earthenware pots; there were 'no napkins, and the table cloth looked as though a sow had just had a litter on it'.[118] Newly arrived in London in 1763, James Boswell rhapsodised (somewhat unoriginally) on the tranquillity of the Temple's courtyards, 'a pleasant academical retreat'. A very different impression was conveyed by the Old Bailey trial that same year of one James Brown, sentenced to death as a highway robber for a theft with menaces in Middle Temple Lane.[119] Such contrasts were entirely characteristic of the unreformed Middle Temple, a diverse and loosely-structured institution whose complex human realities defy easy generalisation.

[115]   Lemmings, above n 6, at 54.
[116]   That Roger North was the designer of the gatehouse appears from his own manuscript account; see HM Colvin and J Newman (eds), *Of Building: Roger North's Writings on Architecture* (Oxford, Oxford University Press, 1981), 42, 51–52; see also *ibid*, at xiii–xiv and 156.
[117]   WOB Allen and E McClure, *Two Hundred Years: the History of the Society for Promoting Christian Knowledge 1698–1898* (London, SPCK, 1898), 129; LW Cowie, *Henry Newman: an American in London 1708–43* (London, Church Historical Society,1956), 30, 41, 45; MT.1/MPA/7, 68, 72. House servants who attempted to prevent members bringing in women after 'Twelve a clock at night' risked physical assault: *ibid*, at 148.
[118]   WH Quarrell and M Mare, *London in 1710 from the travels of Zacharias Conrad von Uffenbach* (London, Faber, 1934), 57.
[119]   FA Pottle (ed), *Boswell's London Journal 1762–1763* (London, Heinemann, 1950), 234; see also <www.oldbaileyonline.org/browse.jspd?id=t1763091452>.

The American Connection

JOHN COLYER

I. WHY MIDDLE TEMPLE?

THAT MIDDLE TEMPLE has been and still is the Inn of Court with the closest connections with the United States is clear. What is not clear is *why* Middle Temple has had that close relationship. The purpose of this article is to trace the involvement of members of the Inn with the New World and to see whether even a tentative answer to the question 'Why Middle Temple?' can be given.

The Inn's connections with America can conveniently be dealt with in three parts, as follows:

a) 1584 to about 1720: see 'II. Voyagers and Charters', also considered in 'The Maritime Connection'.[1]

b) Approximately 1720–89, but with its results lingering for another 25 years: see 'III. Students, Revolutionaries and Constitutions'.

c) From then until the present day the connection of friendship which we can appropriately entitle 'IV. Ambassadors and Friends'.

II. VOYAGERS AND CHARTERS

It has already been noted[2] that from the beginning the Middle Temple had a strong west-country bias in its admissions, and it is reasonable to assume that this made it natural for the mainly west-country mariners of the Elizabethan age to join the Inn, attracting some of their other maritime compatriots to the same Inn. Maritime and legal members interacted and

---

[1] See Richard Hill's 'The Maritime Connection' at p 111.
[2] See ch 1, p 41.

collaborated in promoting exploration and colonisation. The roles of Raleigh,[3] Hakluyt[4] and Popham[5] are noted elsewhere.

Sir John Popham was the principal promoter of the Virginia Company; himself a west-country man, he managed to persuade the merchants of London to combine with those of the west-country ports—Bristol, Exeter and Plymouth—to subscribe to the venture. Fifty-five City Livery Companies subscribed, and the venture pioneered the concept of the joint stock company: but that is another story. Some of the foundation meetings of the Virginia Company were held in the then new Middle Temple Hall. Eventually the Royal Charter of 1606 provided for two companies—the 'London' and the 'Plymouth' Companies.

Another Middle Templar who was active on behalf of the colonists but was working in London in the early eighteenth century was Abel Ketelbey.[6] He acted as the agent in London for the colony of South Carolina and was a bencher of the Inn. That may have inspired members of the Inn to go to South Carolina, planting the seeds of awareness of Middle Temple in that colony.[7]

There was a legacy of ideas of liberty and good government, the seeds of which were sown in part by the early Virginia charters of Sir Edwin Sandys.[8] In the history of ideas Sandys is an important and also a symbolic

---

[3]   See Hill, p 114 ff.

[4]   *Ibid.*

[5]   *Ibid.* Sir John Popham (1531–1617); treasurer, Middle Temple 1580–87; Speaker of the House of Commons 1577; Chief Justice QB, 1592. Technically, Popham should be described as an 'ex-Middle Templar' by the time he promoted the Virginia Company, for the judges were not then members of the Inn; like all barristers then they would have begun their careers at an Inn of Chancery—a legal preparatory school, and then joined one of the 'four great Inns of Court' to be called to the Bar within one of those four Inns of Court; but they left that Inn if and when they became serjeants, either to practise as a serjeant or in order to be 'made up' as a serjeant and become a member of Serjeants' Inn as an essential preliminary to taking up their appointment to the Bench. There was a ceremony when the senior barrister would leave the Hall as a bell was rung, and he was said to have been 'rung out' of his Inn and he would walk across to Serjeant's Inn. However, former members of the Inn who were upon the Bench were frequently entertained by their original Inn, and doubtless retained a connection with and a warm affection for it. So we count Popham as still a Middle Templar, albeit he had become Chief Justice of the Queen's Bench in 1592.

[6]   Admitted 1693, called 1699, bencher 1724, treasurer 1735, and an MP., (sometimes spelt) Kettleby.

[7]   Specifically, one wonders whether Andrew Rutledge (see p 243 below), when studying in the Temple from 1726 to about 1730, had any contact with Ketelbey before he chose South Carolina.

[8]   Sir Edwin Sandys (1561–1629). The Sandyses were a Middle Temple family. Sir Edwin and his brother George were both sons of Edwin Sandys, Archbishop of York 1577–88. George (admitted to Middle Temple 1596) was treasurer of the Virginia Company and resided in Virginia 1621–31, and later was agent in England for the colony, dying in 1644. Despite his official position he was zealous in defending the rights of the colonists against the Crown, quarrelling with the Colonial Council and the Royal Governor (Sir Francis Wyatt, a Gray's Inn man).

figure—the first English lawyer, and a Middle Templar, to use his legal skills not merely in organising colonisation but in devising *government*. Born in 1561, by the reign of James I he was emerging as a leader of Parliamentarian thought. He it was who in Parliament advocated the truly avant garde suggestion that prisoners—*prisoners*—should have the right—*the right*—to be represented by counsel. Four centuries ago that was a startling proposition. Sandys also asserted that the King's authority rested upon the mutual obligations of subject and sovereign which neither party could violate with impunity, which led him to be arraigned before the Star Chamber; but he was so popular a figure that it dared to do nothing beyond binding him over.

Sandys' Virginia Charters gave to the colonists, 'all the liberties, franchises and immunities of English subjects'. The first seed of constitutional liberty for the English colonists could be said to be contained in that first charter, or certainly in his later charter, the so-called 'Great Charter' of 1618, which led to there being established the first legislature in a British colony and which recognised free speech, equality before the law and trial by jury. Under it the first elected legislature in the New World met in Jamestown in August 1619. Although James I rescinded the Virginia Company's charter in 1624 and made the colony a Royal Colony,[9] so that in one sense Sandys' charters were a false start, but their notions survived: the charters were good precedents.

Sandys did rescue the Virginia Company's projects, if not its fortunes, by insisting that the highest calibre of emigrants be sent out to the colony and by establishing responsible local government, ie a regime answerable to the settlers. He opposed the practices of exiling the lowest elements of society to the colonies, or even of allowing such folk to emigrate. Sandys, at home in London, also helped out the early Pilgrim Fathers by using his influence to obtain a patent to permit them to settle on land then claimed by the Virginia Company. The Honourable James M Beck, sometime Solicitor General of the United States of America and an honorary bencher of Gray's Inn, expressed the view in his book *The Constitution of the United States of America*[10] that 'these Charters were the beginning of constitutionalism in America and the germ of the constitution of The United States of America' and that Sandys might not too fancifully be called 'the Father of American Constitutionalism'.[11]

---

[9] King James took this step because the Company was in acute financial difficulties, Sandys having finally failed to turn its fortunes around, despite the venture being propped up by a lottery—nothing is new!

[10] JM Beck, *The Constitution of the United States* (London, Oxford University Press, 1924) 28, 29.

[11] Ibid, p 29. Even in a book on Middle Temple it would be churlish not also to add (as Beck further recalls) the fact that the Charters were put into legal form for Royal approval by Lord Chancellor Bacon himself, the treasurer of Gray's Inn.

So Middle Templars sowed many of the seeds of American constitutional development, fusing their legal expertise, radical opinions and mercantile aspirations.[12]

III.   STUDENTS, REVOLUTIONARIES AND CONSTITUTIONS

A.   Students

Middle Templars, mainly non-lawyer members of the Inn, were prominent in the exploration and early colonisation of the American colonies, and one at least (Sandys, a lawyer) left a legacy of ideas. But until the late seventeenth century it was inevitably British-born members of the Inn who visited the colonies or emigrated who constituted the connection. In section III. of the Appendix I have assembled a list of the most noteworthy of the emigrants; but it is far from complete. In the first place, no record was (or is) kept by the Inn of its members' locations after their admission or (if relevant) their call to the Bar. So there are certainly some 'undetected' emigrants. Secondly, there are deliberately omitted from the list those early explorers whose activities were confined to short visits, but who feature in the discussion of our maritime connections.[13]

The next development in the evolution of the Inn's special relationship with America began when colonists started to come to England for education—usually as young men in their early twenties, necessarily coming from the more prosperous colonial families who could afford to send a student son to England. Much research has been done on this connection starting notably with E Alfred Jones's book in 1924.[14] Most researchers have relied upon lists, compiled from the admissions registers of the four Inns of Court, of those students whose admission records demonstrate an American origin,[15] but the writer's more recent research

---

[12] It is outwith the scope of this article to consider the other 'seeds', notably the 'covenants' and 'compacts' or collective agreements between the early settlers (mainly in New England), as to which see DS Lutz, *Documents of Political Foundation by Colonial Americans* (Philadelphia, PA, Institute for the Study of Human Issues, 1986).

[13] There are 'borderline cases' such as Governor Lane (see Hill, 'The Maritime Connection' above, p 118). I have taken the view that all who came to *settle* in the colonies, however brief their actual stay, should be included in the list appended.

[14] EA Jones, *American Members of the Inns of Court* (London, The Saint Catherine Press, 1924) (out of print). It is an encyclopaedic work of reference. The writer has noted only two plain errors in that magisterial assembly of data: (1) making Sir Edwin Sandys (above n 8) son of the Archbishop of Canterbury, and (2) giving Middle Temple an eighth signatory of the Constitution of 1789, when in fact there were seven. The book was prepared in connection with the occasions when the American Bar Association held their annual conference in London, a visit now usually repeated at approximately fifteen-year intervals (see below p 265, n 137).

[15] All the Inns' admissions data recorded the student's father's address.

suggests that in fact there were a number of students who should reasonably be regarded as American colonists but whose fathers still owned property in Britain, and whose British address was recorded in the admissions register.[16] This frustrates attempts to make wholly inclusive lists, or to calculate the precise percentages of American students of the Inns who were Middle Templars. All figures which are extracted from the records are likely to be below the true totals. Furthermore, should one regard a man[17] born in England who is taken by his parents at an early age to America, but who returns to study for a few years in England, as 'English' or 'Colonial'? Surely 'Colonial'. I have expanded earlier lists so as to include such men (see the Appendix, section I.), but I emphasise that men on both lists would have lived and worked together as lawyers without distinction as to their place of birth.

It is fascinating to see the same surname crop up in both lists. Thus Andrew Rutledge from Ireland was admitted to the Middle Temple in 1726, although never called to the English Bar. He emigrated to Charleston, South Carolina, where he flourished as an attorney[18] and married the widow of a wealthy planter. His brother John, a physician, followed him to South Carolina four or five years later and married Sarah Boone Hext, probably the richest heiress in the colony, who was Andrew's stepdaughter. Edward, John[19] (of whom more later) and Hugh Rutledge were all sons of this union.[20]

We really do not know why Middle Temple as opposed to the other Inns of Court initially attracted the great majority of the colonial students. It may be something as mundane as the fact that one of the earliest colonial students came here and the others followed.[21] Perhaps the servant of the Inn who then fulfilled the Students Officer's role was as welcoming as is

[16] An English (or British) address simplified the formalities of a bond and may have made a student more welcome.

[17] All Bar students had to be male until 1919.

[18] There was no distinction drawn between barristers and attorneys in the American colonies.

[19] John Rutledge (1739–1800) admitted to Middle Temple 1754, called to the Bar 1760. See below at pp 256, 258.

[20] Private correspondence (2007) with the Rev Benjamin Bosworth Smith of South Carolina, a Rutledge descendant. Andrew Rutledge, by his will proved in 1755, left the residue of his estate to his brother John's children, John, Thomas, Andrew and Sarah Rutledge.

[21] The very first American-born Bar student in London in fact went to Gray's Inn (Stephen Lake from Massachusetts) in 1668. Jones, above n 13, at xxviii, gives the number of American-born members of an Inn of Court prior to 1815 as Middle Temple 146 (62%), Inner Temple 43 (18%), Lincoln's Inn 32 (14%), with only 9 going to Gray's Inn (4%) (percentages added). Six students (or 2%) joined more than one Inn. (Mostly these were students joining Middle Temple after starting in another Inn.) I also point out that over half of Middle Temple's recruits joined between 1750 and 1775. If we include loyalist refugees, admitted after 1776, Middle Temple's figure becomes even higher.

our present Students Officer. We do not know; but for some reason they started coming here rather than to the other Inns.

By 1700, seven colonial students had become members of an Inn of Court. Five of them came to Middle Temple. Middle Temple lost ground a little as the century went on. By 1815 we find that 148 out of the 238[22] colonial students who had come to the four Inns of Court were Middle Templars, still a healthy 62 per cent, although for reasons already stated[23] the figures and the percentages cannot be too precise. Furthermore, should one regard loyalist exiles who joined the Inn after the Revolution as part of the American student connection; and what of those who were not so much colonists as 'Britons in America' whose American addresses disguised their Britishness?[24] I have included both groups in section I. of the Appendix to this chapter, and have separately noted in section II. of the Appendix all known loyalist refugees who did not give an American address, for what matters, surely, is the extent of the connection—whether created by colonial students coming to *domus*[25] and returning or staying, or by Middle Templars emigrating to become American, even if later they returned, voluntarily or otherwise.

There were of the order of 350[26] lawyers in the colonies who had been trained in England when the Revolution or War of Independence broke out in 1776. There is no means of ascertaining precisely how many members of *domus* had emigrated, but about half (and if many undetected Middle Templars did emigrate, then maybe even more) of the 350 were Middle Templars. Scottish and Irish lawyers and English attorneys made up the

---

[22]   But see my caveat above as to exact figures.

[23]   Above, p 241.

[24]   Eg Jonathan Belcher, admitted 14 March 1730 and 'second son of the Hon Jonathan Belcher, Esq, Governor of New England in America' and Thomas Child, Esq, 'Attorney General to HM King George II in the province of Carolina, North America', admitted 22 April 1746. It should be noted that including both these gentlemen, 145 American students had been admitted by Middle Temple by 1800; three more were admitted (1804, 1807 and 1808) before the intake dried up. Of the total of 148, no fewer than 28 (including loyalists in exile, some of whom returned to the new republic) came to Middle Temple after the signing of the Declaration of Independence, further proof, some may say, that the War of 1812 did greater harm to the relations between the ex-Colonists and the Mother Country than the War of Independence itself.

[25]   Middle Temple is known as 'domus' to its members

[26]   Andrew Rutledge exemplifies the numerous Irish Middle Templars who emigrated to the colonies after being called. He escaped Alfred Jones's researches. In the view of the writer there must be more such 'untraced' emigrant sons of Middle Temple. Jones (above p 242, n 14) estimated there were of the order of 340 English-trained lawyers in the colonies in 1776. As noted, this is the *minimum* number, ie all who had then been traced, and we have added several more to the lists in the Appendix of members of the Middle Temple. Andrew Rutledge also exemplifies the tendency of some students who intended to emigrate and some American students who knew they would be returning home to practise, to complete their studies but avoid the necessity to pay the call fee, so that they were not formally called to the English Bar. To have studied at an Inn of Court in itself seems to have enabled one to practise in most of the American colonies in the early 18th century.

difference between the 238 members of an English Inn of Court and the estimated total of 350 lawyers. Again, there are as yet untraced emigrants to be added.

The first American-born Bar student[27] to come to any Inn of Court was Stephen Lake of Boston, admitted to Gray's Inn in 1668. There was then a thirteen-year gap before William Wharton, also from Boston, joined Middle Temple, to be called in 1686. William Spencer (son of a member of Lincoln's Inn), though born in Virginia, was educated in England and inherited his family's English estates. He was admitted to Inner Temple in 1685. All the next four American-born students[28] to be admitted to an Inn of Court came to Middle Temple, although one[29] later joined Lincoln's Inn too.[30]

The lists and the records of the Inn show that there were several notable clusters of support from which most of the students who came from the colonies emanated. These varied somewhat in the course of the eighteenth century, so that the proportion of young American students from, say, Charleston, was not constant. The main such clusters for Middle Temple recruitment (not all of which have previously been identified) included the following:

a) South Carolina (in effect Charleston). Here Andrew Rutledge[31] appears to have been the main originator of what became a fashion to send young men from South Carolina to Middle Temple. William Drayton,[32] its first American-born student from South Carolina, was admitted to Middle Temple in 1750. He was destined to be a judge both before the Revolution in Florida and after the Revolution in South Carolina, becoming in 1789 the first federal judge in that state.

---

[27] Always assuming no earlier colonial son was admitted to an Inn using an English address of his family: see text pp 242–243 nn 15 and 16.

[28] Benjamin Lynde (Boston 1692), William Byrd (Virginia 1692), Paul Dudley (Massachusetts 1697) and Benjamin Harrison (Virginia 1697; forebear of two Presidents of the US, William Harrison (1841) and Benjamin Harrison (1889–93)).

[29] William Byrd, Virginia, above n 28, called Middle Temple 1695, admitted Lincoln's Inn 1697.

[30] If he be counted equally to each of his Inns, the 'score' by 1700 was therefore Middle Temple 4½, Inner Temple and Gray's Inn 1 each, and Lincoln's Inn 1½.

[31] Above p 243.

[32] Admitted 1750, called June 1755. It is interesting that he chose to come to Middle Temple when his uncle, Stephen Fox Drayton, had been admitted to Inner Temple in 1733; it suggests that Drayton was attracted in 1750 by Middle Temple's already established Whig reputation.

There were eventually to be at least 65 South Carolinian Middle Templars,[33] who were to divide bitterly in the Revolution.[34]

b)   Philadelphia and its environs, and after 1740 the College of Philadelphia. There was both a geographical and an educational link here. The College, now matured into the University of Pennsylvania, was founded in 1740 by Benjamin Franklin. Whilst resident in England, Franklin placed his own son William[35] at Middle Temple. Philadelphia immediately before the War of Independence had recently (and briefly) overtaken Dublin as the second largest city of the English-speaking world, and Franklin's College rapidly attracted students not only from Philadelphia but beyond, including the British West Indies.[36] Whilst the very wealthy colonists early in the century would send sons to Eton or other English schools, and thence to Cambridge or Oxford and finally an Inn of Court, rapidly as the century progressed more local colleges became the training ground for the intended Bar student who would go direct therefrom to London and an Inn of Court, usually Middle Temple. If we examine the records[37] we find the 'Colleges of origin' (to coin a phrase) of the American students who came to London and who had previously attended an American College were:

[33]   People did not always stay in one state, and in some cases attribution is arguable; eg, Drayton himself could be 'shared' as Florida and South Carolina. Five of the South Carolinians came from one distinguished family, the Pinckneys, some of whom were to play an important role in the Revolution.

[34]   See below, p 254. See below p 259 for Middle Templars' contribution to South Carolina as a new state.

[35]   William Franklin (1731–1813) admitted 17 February 1751–52, and described in the Admissions Register as 'William Franklin, son and heir of Benjamin F of Philadelphia, America'. William was called to the Bar in Middle Temple on 25 November 1758. See below, p 251.

[36]   Eg Isaac Hunt from Barbados, admitted to Middle Temple 1760, practised Philadelphia Bar 1760–65, fled to exile in England 1776, eventually taking holy orders. He was the father of the poet Leigh Hunt.

[37]   For most of the research into these data I am indebted to Alfred Jones, above p 242, n 14. There were 36 American students with American degrees, and 17 (47%) were from the College of Philadelphia. Having taught at the University of Pennsylvania Law School, the writer is not surprised at this primacy. Some American students came to England for a degree before being admitted, including 27 who went to Cambridge, 11 to Oxford, 6 to Scottish universities, 2 to Trinity College, Dublin.

College of Philadelphia	17[38]
Harvard	9
William & Mary, Virginia	4
Yale	3
Princeton	2
King's College New York (Columbia)	1

That 17 Philadelphia students came to London is not surprising, as the city was one of the legal centres of the colonies[39] as well as then being capital of the Commonwealth of Pennsylvania. The Philadelphia connection with Middle Temple was strong even before the College was founded, there having been Philadelphians in *domus* by 1718. There were to be 24 Pennsylvanian members of Middle Temple, plus two from Delaware; and perhaps five New Jersey students should also be regarded as part of this 'cluster'.

c) Virginia, starting with the earliest American students,[40] sent 46 sons to Middle Temple, including four Lees and three Randolphs. Some of these we shall meet shortly.

d) Massachusetts: three of the first four American Middle Templars came from Boston; but in contrast to South Carolina, here the Inn's share of recruitment dried up later in the century.

e) Maryland: George Calvert, Lord Baltimore, had been a stockholder in the Virginia Company. He was also a convert to Roman Catholicism. He persuaded Charles I to grant him that part of Virginia which lay north of the Potomac, but died before this was formalised, and the patent was issued in 1632 to his son Cecilius, the second Lord Baltimore. The new colony was named 'Maryland' after Charles I's Catholic queen, Henrietta Maria, and settlement began in 1634. The first Lord Baltimore's intention that the colony should be a refuge for Roman Catholics led to religious toleration in Maryland and attracted many émigré Roman Catholics seeking to escape the religious oppression which they suffered in Britain. So there were many Irish settlers, and these included the founders of the Maryland 'dynasties' of the

---

[38] Jones, above p 242, in his Introduction at xxix incorrectly says 16 (but records all 17 in separate entries). The 17 (with the Inns of the five who were not Middle Templars noted) were: Andrew Allen, James Allen, Phineas Bond, John L Bozman, Benjamin Chew Jr, Peter De Lancy (Lincoln's Inn), William Hamilton, Isaac Hunt (above n 36), Alexander Lawson, Josiah Martin (Inner Temple), John Morris, William Paca (Inner Temple), Joseph Reade (Inner Temple), William Roberts, Edward Tilghman, Henry Waddell (Lincoln's Inn) and Jasper Yeates.

[39] 'A Philadelphia lawyer' was (and I hope still is) a by-word in the United States for an efficient and well-informed advocate, who may be described by a layman with a hint of mild hostility as 'As sharp as a Philadelphia lawyer'.

[40] Byrd and Harrison, above p 245 nn 29, 28.

Dulany and Carroll[41] families, both of which were to be associated with Middle Temple. It was certainly a natural thing for American students of Irish ancestry[42] to choose Middle Temple of the four Inns of Court, with its combination of strong Irish and American connections and strong Whig politics. There were 21 Marylanders who came to Middle Temple.[43]

About half of Middle Temple's pre-revolutionary American students were admitted between 1750 and 1776, and there were several years in the 1750s when the numbers of the American and the Irish students admitted, if added together, outnumbered the new English students. Whilst we can only conjecture how Middle Temple achieved this situation, there can be no doubt as to the reason why it continued through the last twenty-five years or so prior to the Declaration of Independence; for Middle Temple at that time was increasingly a hot-bed of whiggery, ie of those who in politics were opposed to the expansion of royal power. It was therefore a congenial dining and debating place for the Irish and American students. Edmund Burke[44] and John Dunning[45] were both members of the Inn, and parliamentarians. It is interesting to speculate whether their pro-colonist stance in the run-up to the American Revolution was created or nurtured by their contact with the young American students they met in Hall. Certain it is that they became the colonists' great protagonists in the House of Commons, where the incomparable orator and parliamentarian Burke in 1775 thundered against the use of force against the colonists. Force, he

---

[41] An interesting examination of these two families is to be found in E Stockdale and RJ Holland, *Middle Temple Lawyers and the American Revolution* (Eagan, MN, Thomson West, 2007), ch 7, at 217–18.

[42] The Maryland Carrolls descended from Charles Carroll (or O'Carroll); born in Ireland, he studied law at the Inner Temple and emigrated in 1688 to take up the office of attorney-general in Maryland, only to arrive just as his appointor, James II, was dethroned in the 'Glorious Revolution' of 1688 which was parallelled by a protestant *coup* in Maryland. He stayed on in the New World. It is not surprising that such an Irish American family should have sided against the English Crown in the Revolution. This first Charles Carroll was of a Gaelic chiefly family and a direct descendant of King Tadh (Thaddeus) of Eile (Ely), an ancient Irish petty kingdom. As to his lineage, see P Berresford Ellis, *Erin's Blood Royal* (London, Palgrave, 2002), 134–35.

[43] If purely being born in Maryland counts, there was also one of Middle Temple's most distinguished revolutionary lawyers, John Dickinson; but he is more appropriately ascribed to Pennsylvania.

[44] Edmund Burke (1729–97) was, of course, one of Middle Temple's Irish students and was admitted in 1747.

[45] John Dunning (1731–83), later (1782) Lord Ashburton, admitted 1752, called 1756, bencher 1768, treasurer 1782. His portrait hangs in the library; there is another in the benchers' apartments. Dunning moved and secured the passing of the famous parliamentary resolution in 1780 that 'The influence of the Crown has increased, is increasing and ought to be diminished.'

said, could subdue for a moment but did not remove the necessity of subduing again, and a nation is not governed which is perpetually to be conquered:[46]

> This fierce spirit of liberty is stronger in the English colonies probably than in any other people of the earth [because] the people of the colonies are descendants of Englishmen . . . they are therefore not only devoted to liberty, but to liberty according to English ideas and English principles.[47]

So by the eve of the American Revolution, Middle Temple's position as the congenial place for colonial students to go was well established.

Those young American students did not settle in Middle Temple. They returned to the colonies filled with the stirring ideas which the 18th century produced, a formidable combination of English legal training and French political theory. So it was inevitable that the government, law and constitutional evolution of the colonies into the United States of America should be heavily influenced if not shaped by Middle Templars, who drew upon the legal training that they had absorbed here, especially as so many of them were pre-eminent in the pre-revolutionary American colonies as lawyers, as political leaders or as politicians, or a combination of these roles.[48]

B. The Revolution (the American War of Independence)

In September 1774 the first Continental Congress convened. The representatives of twelve colonies (all except Georgia) met together, in itself a landmark event. They elected a Middle Templar, Peyton Randolph of Virginia, as President.[49] Peyton Randolph had drawn up the remonstrance of the Virginia House of Burgesses in 1764 against the then proposed Stamp Act, and became Speaker of the Virginian House of Burgesses. He was a moderate who strove to avoid a conflict. He was chairman of the Committee of Correspondence between the Colonies in 1773 and President of the Virginia Convention, and it was natural that he preside over the Continental Congress. Later the last President of the Continental Congress was Cyrus Griffin (1748–1810)[50] of Virginia, another Middle Templar.

---

[46] E Burke *Speeches and Letters on American Affairs* (1908), 89.

[47] Ibid, 91; Prior, Memoir of Edmund Burke, H&E Sheffield, London (1839), 170–171.

[48] There is not space here to set out in detail the accomplishments of all the revolutionary Middle Templars, but the author has tried to indicate the most important in the brief annotations to the lists in the Appendix to this article where the text does not mention them.

[49] Peyton Randolph (1721–75) admitted 1739, called 1744, and the brother of John Randolph (1727–84), admitted 1745, called 1750. John Randolph was a loyalist and the last royalist Attorney-General of Virginia. His son Edmund (Peyton's nephew) was the first Attorney-General of the state after the Revolution.

[50] Cyrus Griffin, Admitted 1771.

The Second Continental Congress convened in May 1775. They again elected Peyton Randolph as President, although he soon withdrew (dying the same year), to be succeeded by John Hancock. Meanwhile serious hostilities now commenced, with the battle of Bunker Hill[51] on 17 June 1775.

That moderate revolutionary, the Philadelphia lawyer and Middle Templar John Dickinson,[52] drafted and carried in Congress his Olive Branch Petition, and the very next day (6 July 1775) a 'Declaration of the Causes & Necessities of Taking up Arms'. The latter resolution rejected the notion of separate independence and severance from the Crown but asserted that the colonists would rather die than be enslaved. Dickinson was the leading pamphleteer of the Revolution, draftsman of the *Resolutions in relation to the Stamp Act* of the Pennsylvanian Assembly in 1765, the *Declaration of Rights & Petition to the King* of the Stamp Act Congress in 1765[53] and in 1767–68 his influential *Letters from a Farmer in Pennsylvania*. His moderation and anxiety to achieve a just settlement of the conflict cost him popularity and aroused distrust, so that at one stage he was excluded from Congress and forced to resign his commission, later re-enlisting as a private, from which rank he was promoted (October 1777) to brigadier general.[54]

By spring 1776 the mood of the colonists had swung in favour of complete separation. In July, Congress met in the Pennsylvania State House in Philadelphia to draft and sign the Declaration of Independence. There is a copy in Middle Temple library (see Plate 3–1). The Declaration was signed on 4 July 1776. Middle Templars played quite a part in the stirring events of that hot Philadelphia summer. John Dickinson, the 'Penman of the Revolution', now played a part in drafting the Declaration, although it was Thomas Jefferson who created it.

The final vote, by states, was twelve for, none against. This unanimity was achieved at the eleventh hour only by a change of decision by South Carolina, the arrival of another delegate who swung Delaware's vote and the deliberate absence of John Dickinson, John Morris[55] and Andrew

---

[51] The British victory was pyrrhic, for they suffered 1,054 casualties (many officers) as compared to the 397 suffered by the rebels.

[52] 1732–1808. Admitted 1753, called 1757; a reluctant rebel whose earlier correspondence shows his affection for the mother country.

[53] The Stamp Act provoked the crisis which led to the American War of Independence by imposing direct taxation upon the colonists for the first time.

[54] After the war Dickinson was Governor of Delaware (1781) and Governor of Pennsylvania (1782–85).

[55] See above, p 247 n 38 and below, p 253 n 69.

Allen.[56] Their absence had left the Pennsylvania vote in favour of independence, albeit by less than a majority of all the Pennsylvania delegates
entitled to vote. When the 55 delegates of the 13 colonies signed, five were
Middle Templars.[57]

C.   Loyalists and revolutionaries

It is fashionable to idealise the heroes of the Revolution and take pride in
Middle Templars' remarkable contributions to the new republic, but it
should not be forgotten that perhaps a third of the population of the
colonies, and more specifically at least half—maybe more—of the lawyers
in the colonies, did not support the Revolution. Lawyers are naturally
people who recognise authority and are reluctant revolutionaries. So let it
not be forgotten that many of the Middle Templars conscientiously
objected to severance from the Crown. Some were to suffer for that stand.
Many ended in exile, as United Empire loyalists in Canada, or back in the
Mother country as refugees. Two 'cameos' will serve to illustrate this, both
relevant to persons already mentioned in this article:

a)   William Franklin,[58] Benjamin Franklin's son, had lived with his father
     in London[59] and had in 1762 been appointed a rather youthful
     Governor of the Colony of New Jersey, where prior to the Revolution
     he had been energetic and successful. He had upon appointment as
     Governor of course taken an oath of allegiance to the Crown, and he
     was unwilling to break it. So he was hounded out of America, ending
     as a refugee in England. He was not to see his father again, beyond a
     brief meeting in 1785, although they did correspond minimally in later
     years, and he died in exile in England in 1813.

b)   Reference has been made to the large number (seventeen) of students
     from Benjamin Franklin's foundation, the College of Philadelphia, who

---

[56]   See above, p 247 n 38 and below, p 253 n 67.

[57]   Three of these five Middle Templars were destined later to occupy high positions in the
new republic. The signatories were Edward Rutledge (1749–1800), who in 1798 became
Governor of South Carolina; Thomas Heyward, jun (1746–1809), appointed in 1778 Judge
of the High Court of South Carolina; Thomas McKean (1734–1817), President of Delaware
in 1777 and first Chief Justice of Pennsylvania in 1799; Thomas Lynch, jun (1749–79), of
South Carolina; and Arthur Middleton (1743–87), of South Carolina. (Another signatory,
William Paca, afterwards Chief Judge and later Governor of Maryland, was a member of the
Inner Temple.)

[58]   Above, p 246. For a biography of William Franklin, see SL Skemp, *William Franklin
'Son of a Patriot, Servant of a King'* (Oxford, Oxford University Press, 1990).

[59]   When the University of Oxford gave Benjamin a doctorate for his scientific discoveries
in relation to electricity, William was given an honorary MA in recognition of his work as his
father's assistant.

came to the Inns of Court, twelve of them to Middle Temple.[60] Philadelphia was perhaps the least solidly revolutionary city in a State which itself had not been originally of extremist views and whose delegates' vote, as we have seen, had only just tipped in favour of the Declaration of Independence. So it is no surprise to find that if we take our twelve College of Philadelphia and Middle Temple students,[61] they end up very much divided in the Revolution, as were in some cases their families.[62]

The colonial lawyers with Middle Temple training (if not call) who were alive at the time of the Declaration of Independence numbered about 150, of whom at least 41 can reasonably be described as loyalists of various shades of opinion. It is interesting to see what happened to those 41:

— 16 became political refugees in England (where two soon died, one in a duel)
— 1 died en route to exile
— 1 died as a consequence of the war
— 1 died in the service of the Crown
— 3 took jobs elsewhere from the Crown
— 3 emigrated to Canada, ending up with judicial appointments
— 1 only[63] returned not to London but to Dublin, to be called to the Bar by King's Inn, and thence, again uniquely among his fellow refugees, went to practise in India
— 1 returned home to pose as a loyalist and to have his audacious claim for compensation rejected.[64]

So 27 loyalist lawyers from Middle Temple left the colonies by reason of the war: others left as refugees and then were admitted to the Inn. Of fourteen (mainly fairly mildly) loyalist Middle Templars, 10 remained in

---

[60]   See above, p 247 n 38.
[61]   *Ibid.* See further below p 253 for the loyalties and fates of these twelve.
[62]   Eg Benjamin and William Franklin, above; and Alexander Harvey (admitted 1765), who returned home to Charleston, SC, to practise. On the outbreak of hostilities he enlisted in a loyalist regiment, the Colleton County Loyal Militia, but was captured and held prisoner in Charleston. The conditions of his incarceration were so bad as to wreck his health—after the war he came as a refugee to England, became insane and died in 1806, a late casualty of the war; but his father, William Harvey, was an ardent revolutionary who disinherited his son because of their conflicting political views.
[63]   Richard Tilghman (1746–96). He went to India in 1777, and died on his second voyage en route to India in 1796.
[64]   Elias [Ely] Wrixon, a cashiered Irish Officer, went to America in 1774 and created a great impression, being described by John Adams as a great friend of liberty and of the American cause, whom Adams hoped would be employed by Congress. Wrixon claimed to have been offered high offices in the revolutionary forces which he declined, and returned to Europe after 10 months only. He joined Middle Temple (but was never called) *after* returning to England (July 1775).

their home states, 3 of them to become US or State Judges, one a politician; 1 came home after a period in exile; and 3 had died before the war ended.

And what of our College of Philadelphia 'sample'? It will be recalled[65] that 17 graduates of Franklin's College of Philadelphia had come to an Inn of Court, twelve of them to Middle Temple.[66] Those twelve comprised six loyalists,[67] one moderate Whig,[68] three definite revolutionaries[69] one whose ambivalence kept him out of trouble[70] and one post-revolutionary student who cannot fairly be allocated to either side.[71]

So our sample was indeed divided in its loyalties; but it is important to note that it is not a representative sample overall of the lawyers in America in 1776, for Philadelphia was a conservative enclave and some of the College's students came to the College from the West Indies anyway.[72]

Let us now turn to see what those Middle Templars who supported the Revolution were doing, as the war progressed. The British having occupied New York, Congress looked abroad for help, and in September 1776 appointed three Commissioners to negotiate with European powers—Silas Deane, Benjamin Franklin and Thomas Jefferson. The last-mentioned

---

[65] See p 247.

[66] See list above, p 247 n 38.

[67] (1) Andrew Allen (a Whig who became a loyalist alarmed by the Declaration of Independence); he was one of the founders of the First Troop of Philadelphia Cavalry and had been a member of the first Continental Congress, but resigned from the First Troop and then absented himself from the crucial vote by the Pennsylvania delegates on the Declaration of Independence and took the oath of allegiance to the Crown. The Allens were large landed proprietors, and Phineas Bond (below) testified to the Commission for Loyalist Claims that they and the Penn family 'thought that if they could be independent of England they should be petty princes, but when they saw that the rebels confiscated their estates, they turned about and became very loyal'; (2) Phineas Bond himself (see section III.F. below, p 261 n 115); (3) William Hamilton (who had raised a regiment for the Continental Army, but changed sides upon the Declaration of Independence); (4) Isaac Hunt (above p 246 n 36); (5) Alexander Lawson, a passive loyalist who avoided participation in the conflict; (6) William Roberts (called in 1787 when a loyalist exile).

[68] James Allen, brother of Andrew Allen. (Both were sons of William Allen (admitted 1720, Chief Justice of Pennsylvania 1750–74, when he left as a loyalist refugee for England).)

[69] (1) John Leeds Bozman (served a legal apprenticeship from 1777, in America), admitted to Middle Temple in 1785 when already 28, he became a highly successful Maryland lawyer; (2) John Morris (*c* 1737–85), a moderate revolutionary, appointed 1776 Judge of Common Pleas and Quartermaster of Pennsylvania troops; and (3) Jasper Yeates (who became an Associate Judge of the Commonwealth of Pennsylvania and a member of the Constitutional Convention).

[70] Edward Tilghman had been admitted in 1772. He became a Trustee of the College of Philadelphia (now University of Pennsylvania), and in 1806 declined to become Chief Justice of Pennsylvania.

[71] Benjamin Chew Jr, (admitted 1785, when 27). His father, also a Middle Templar, had been Chief Justice of Pennsylvania 1774–77, but was accused by each side of supporting the other, and did not return to judicial office until 1790 as President of the High Court of Errors and Appeals. The Chews 'trimmed' somewhat, but young Benjamin came to his father's old Inn for two years' study in 1785.

[72] Eg Hunt, in our 'sample'.

declined the appointment, and so a Middle Templar, Arthur Lee,[73] was appointed and proceeded to Europe, the beginning of a successful diplomatic campaign by the colonists, in which he was to be joined by other Middle Templars. His cousin Henry Lee[74] chose a more energetic war, as a daring cavalry leader, 'Light Horse Harry'. On the whole the young American members of Middle Temple favoured the Revolution more than their parents (not always, of course, as noted in relation to the Franklins and the Harveys).[75]

One especially was to see service at the very centre of events: John Laurens[76] arrived to study in London in 1772, aged but 17. He was no stranger, having in part been educated in London and then Geneva. His father, Henry Laurens (not a Middle Templar) was later to become President of the Continental Congress and be captured by the British when en route to Europe on a diplomatic mission, and spend 15 months confined in the Tower. The young Laurens married in haste in October 1776 the daughter of an old friend and business associate of his father, and hurried home to join the revolutionary forces despite his father trying to dissuade him. He was never to see his new bride again, nor ever see his posthumous daughter. A young man of immensely attractive character and great abilities, he was posted to the Commander in Chief's (Washington's) staff, where his knowledge of French proved useful in dealing with the American's new allies, and he fought gallantly in the bitter South Carolina conflicts. By the age of 26 he was a Lieutenant Colonel, and it was he who negotiated the terms of Cornwallis's surrender and was then placed in charge of all prisoners (which led to the eventual exchange of Cornwallis for Laurens's father, who was then able to take his place in the negotiations for peace which brought the war to an end).[77] Sadly, young Colonel Laurens fell to a sniper's bullet only weeks before the cessation of hostilities. In Middle Temple, opposite the door to the American Library, there hangs a splendid copy of a portrait of him dressed in his uniform.[78]

South Carolina was a bitterly divided state, scene of sanguinary fighting in the War of Independence. The loyalist dragoons of Colonel (later Sir)

---

[73]   Arthur Lee (1740–92), admitted first to Lincoln's Inn 1770 and then to Middle Temple (1773) where he was called to the Bar in 1775. Unusually, he had studied medicine at Edinburgh, qualified and practised as a physician in Charleston, South Carolina, before taking up the law.

[74]   Henry Lee (1756–1818) admitted 1773, but probably did not get to London to begin his studies; Captain in the Virginia Dragoons; Governor of Virginia 1792–95. He gave the oration at George Washington's funeral.

[75]   Above, p 252 n 62.

[76]   John Laurens (1755–82), admitted 1772.

[77]   Colonel Henry Laurens was one of the American Commissioners who signed the Articles of Peace.

[78]   See p 265 below as to the American Library. The painting is after Charles Fraser and was the gift of one of Henry Laurens's descendants, Thomas Ashe Lockhart, in 2004.

Banastre Tarleton were much feared and hated by the supporters of independence. Tarleton scored a number of successes[79] and almost captured Thomas Jefferson.[80] His escapades are mentioned here only because Tarleton too was a Middle Templar.[81]

Many combatants could be listed, but one other certainly merits mention: Joseph Reed,[82] a Philadelphia lawyer who was Lieutenant-Colonel of the Pennsylvania Associated Militia and became military secretary to George Washington. So two Middle Templars were on the 'staff'. Reed was promoted to Colonel and Adjutant-General, but soon felt his lack of military experience and preferred to become a voluntary *aide-de-camp* to Washington. Attorney-General of Pennsylvania (1778–80), he was elected President of that state's Executive Council in December 1778 but returned to practice at the Bar in 1781. In summer 1778, belatedly Lord North attempted unsuccessfully to make peace before the French joined in the conflict and sent commissioners, headed by the Earl of Carlisle, to negotiate, only to be rebuffed by Congress, who took up the position that they would only negotiate for the withdrawal of British troops and independence. One of the British group unsuccessfully attempted to bribe Reed and two other congressmen, all of whom repudiated this attempt. Reed, when President of Pennsylvania's Executive Council also in January 1781, had the unenviable task of negotiating with the mutinous Pennsylvania troops.

---

[79] Eg Waxhaw Creek, May 1780, destroying a Virginia regiment, and Camden, South Carolina, 16 August 1780, capturing 1,000 and killing 800 to 900 of the insurgents; but suffering a great defeat near Cowpens, South Carolina 17 January 1781.

[80] At Charlottesville, VA, 4 June 1781.

[81] Banastre Tarleton (1754–1833). This colourful but dissolute member of the Inn was admitted in 1770. He never studied in the Temple but went to University College, Oxford and then purchased a commission in the army, where he volunteered for service in the American conflict and was involved in almost all of the major battles. As the English commander of the 'British Legion' (that name had indeed been used before the 20th century) he led or permitted extremely harsh measures against the civilian population in South Carolina. After the war he returned to England, briefly to be hailed as a dashing cavalry officer and national hero: his portrait was painted by Sir Joshua Reynolds in the green uniform of the legion. He became a full general (1812), and was made a baronet in 1816. Intermittently he was an MP for Liverpool, sometimes losing elections for his home city. A friend of the Prince of Wales, Tarleton scandalised society by a 15-year affair with the Prince's former mistress, Mrs Mary ('Perdita') Robinson, his gambling and extravagance, allegedly spending £2,500 a year. The family fortune derived from Liverpool shipping and trade, especially the slave trade which Tarleton energetically defended in Parliament. Among several biographies is RD Bass, *The Green Dragoon: the lives of Banestre Tarleton and Mary Robinson* (New York, 1957). As a mere (and very unwelcome) visitor to America, he is not included in any of the lists in the Appendix to this article.

[82] Joseph Reed (1741–85), admitted 1763.

D.   After the war

Britain lost the war, unable to take on its energetic and distant kinsmen in America, plus France and Spain. Negotiations for peace began in June 1782 in Paris. Preliminary Articles of Peace were signed on 30 November 1782, but were not to become effective until peace was agreed by Britain with France and Spain. That was achieved in January 1783 and Britain proclaimed the cessation of hostilities on 4 February. Such was the pace of communications in 1783 that Congress received the text of the Articles only on 13 March, ratifying them a month later. Finally the treaty itself was signed in Paris on 3 September 1783, and was ratified by Congress on 14 January 1784; ratifications were exchanged on 12 May 1784.

So peace (and independence) ensued at last. But the cessation of hostilities did not immediately produce prosperity or orderly government for the former colonies, where there were lawlessness and minor rebellions from time to time.[83] It soon became obvious that the Articles of Confederation provided too loose an association to enable firm leadership of the nation; the confederation really only worked when in time of crisis there was unanimity of view.[84]

It was a Middle Templar who brought the problem to a head and set in motion the enacting of the world's most durable modern constitution, and another who was responsible more than anyone else for drafting it (and all lawyers know that 'the devil is in the detail' of such a task, and that the drafting often becomes as important as deciding the policy to be adopted).

Those two Middle Templars were Charles Pinckney[85] and John Rutledge.[86] It was Pinckney who in 1786 brought forward a motion in Congress (ie the Congress of the Confederation) for the reorganisation of the Government, and this triggered much debate and committee work. Virginia had in January 1786 invited all the other states to a Convention at Annapolis to consider inter-state commerce. It was held in September 1786 with only nine of the 13 states represented. John Dickinson, by now of Delaware, was elected to preside. The delegates concluded that with so poor a response from the states it would be futile to consider commerce,

---

[83] Eg Shays's Rebellion in 1787. Two States—Pennsylvania and Connecticut—even fought a minor war over conflicting claims to the Wyoming Valley in Northern Pennsylvania, arising from overlapping land grants made by Charles II.

[84] The Articles of Confederation were wholly unsuited for the constitution of a great but varied nation, even if communications had been speedier than they were in the eighteenth century; eg, in relation to the exercise of Congress's power of peace and war, and the conduct of foreign affairs, nine states had to agree before any important action could be taken.

[85] Charles Pinckney (1757–1824), admitted 1773. A delegate to Congress and to the Constitutional Convention, Governor South Carolina 1789–92 and 1806–08, US Senator 1798–1801. Minister to Spain, he negotiated the Louisiana purchase. Possibly the most significant Middle Temple 'contributor' to the new republic.

[86] John Rutledge – see above p 243.

and instead they adopted a resolution drafted by Alexander Hamilton (not a Middle Templar) calling for a Constitutional Convention.

The Constitutional Convention opened on 25 May 1787 meeting in the State House, Philadelphia (Independence Hall). Of the 55 delegates from 12 states (for Rhode Island did not send any), half at least had some legal training and Middle Temple was there in force. The Convention immediately elected George Washington as President, and then proceeded to debate the conflicting Virginia plan (promoted by the large states) and New Jersey plan (promoted by the small states).[87] At last, on 16 July 1787, unexpectedly and dramatically, the well-known compromise was effected, namely, representation proportionate to the population of each state in the House of Representatives, and equal representation for all states in the Senate. The latter equality of representation cannot be altered by any amendment of the Constitution.

After this compromise came the really crucial work, and history attributes to John Rutledge much of the credit for its ultimate success. The decisions of the Convention had to be embodied in the formal draft of a Constitution, and on 24 July 1787, a drafting committee of five persons was appointed. Without doubt, that committee would have fallen a long way short of its purpose but for the impressive personality of John Rutledge (1739–1800)[88] of South Carolina, its chairman. Rutledge had already served as Governor and Commander in Chief of his home state as the war began; later he was to be one of the first justices of the Supreme Court (1789–91), resigning to become Chief Justice of South Carolina. In 1795 he returned to the Supreme Court briefly to act as the second Chief Justice of the United States of America[89]. He was a man of immense constitutional knowledge, of great personal influence and power, a finished orator, and of outstanding ability and amazing versatility. He himself prepared the main draft of the Constitution, embodying much of Charles Pinckney's work, and thereafter the drafting committee completed its great task in ten days of intensive labour. It handed its draft to the Convention on 6 August 1787. The Convention made certain additions and amendments to the draft, approved it as so amended, and then appointed a 'Committee on Detail' to revise the style and arrange the articles. That committee reported on 12 September. On 15 September the Convention finally adopted the draft, which had thereafter to be ratified by nine states before coming into effect.[90]

---

[87] The text of what follows, to the end of this section III.D, is taken substantially from *Middle Templars' Association with America* (London, Middle Temple, 1957), 2nd edn (ed Colyer) (London Middle Temple, 1998). The original booklet derived from readings given by Sir Lynden Macassey to the Middle Temple on 13 November 1930 and to the American Bar Association on 18 September 1931.

[88] See above p 243 n 19.

[89] 'Briefly' because the Senate refused to ratify the appointment, angered by a speech Routledge had made criticising the treaty of peace with England negotiated by John Jay (the first Chief Jusice) in 1794.

[90] The ninth ratification was secured by June 1788 (Maryland); Rhode Island held aloof until May 1790, and then only voted in its state convention 34 to 32 in favour.

E.   Seven Middle Templars sign the completed Constitution

On 17 September 1787, the draft Constitution was signed by 39 members of the Convention, these being all who remained of the original 55. This immortal document bears the signatures of no fewer than seven members of the Middle Temple.[91] Listed in the order of their dates of admission to the Society they were:

a)   William Livingstone (1723–90), admitted 1742, not called by Middle Temple but called to the state bar in 1748), the first Governor of New Jersey, 1776. (His bookplate is inscribed 'William Livingston of the Middle Temple'.)

b)   John Blair (1732–1800), admitted 1753, called 1757, Chancellor and Chief Justice of Virginia and Associate Justice of the Supreme Court 1789–96.

c)   John Dickinson, already mentioned.[92]

d)   John Rutledge, already mentioned.[93]

e)   Charles Cotesworth Pinckney.[94] He declined appointment to the initial Supreme Court Bench.

f)   (Charles) Jared Ingersoll,[95] first Attorney-General of Pennsylvania after the signing of the Constitution.[96]

g)   Charles Pinckney[97] (admitted 1773 to Middle Temple, but never in fact studied law in England).

The importance of the work of those who participated in the Constitutional Convention in 1787 cannot be over-emphasised. Master Burger[98] has commented:

> In the last quarter of the 18th century, there was no country in the world that governed with separated and divided powers providing checks and balances on the exercise of authority by those who governed. A first step toward such a result was taken with the Declaration of Independence in 1776, which was followed by

---

[91]   The bicentennial of the drafting and signing of the Constitution of the United States of America was appropriately celebrated by a dinner on 30 November 1987 in Middle Temple Hall, by the Society of English & American Lawyers.

[92]   Above, p 250.

[93]   Above, p 243.

[94]   (1746–1825), admitted to Middle Temple 1764, called to the Bar 1769. Educated in England, he had attended Blackstone's lectures as an undergraduate at Oxford. He was the unsuccessful Federalist candidate for the presidency in 1804 and 1808.

[95]   (1749–1822), admitted to Middle Temple 1773, not called to the Bar.

[96]   He served from 1790 to 1799 and in 1809. His father, who had fled as a loyalist, had been the last royalist Attorney-General of the state.

[97]   Not to be confused with Charles Cotesworth Pinckney. Both were sons of 'Charles Pinckney of Charleston', South Carolina, but their fathers were different Charles Pinckneys.

[98]   Masters of the Bench (or 'benchers') of Middle Temple are referred to within the Inn and in documents relevant to the Inn as 'Master —'. Master Burger was Warren Burger, Chief Justice of the United States, 1969–86. He made this observation in his capacity as Chairman of the Commission on the Bicentennial of the United States Constitution in his Foreword to the Commission's printed booklet of the Constitution.

the Constitution drafted in Philadelphia in 1787; and in 1791 the Bill of Rights was added. Each had antecedents back to Magna Carta and beyond.

The work of 55 men at Philadelphia in 1787 marked the beginning of the end of the concept of the divine right of kings.[99] In place of the absolutism of monarchy, the freedoms flowing from this document created a land of opportunities. Ever since then discouraged and oppressed people from every part of the world have made a beaten path to our shores. This is the meaning of our Constitution.

The Constitution was soon fortified by the Bill of Rights.[100] It has worked well, and has been the model of many other schemes of government. The country now embarked upon a period of growth and settling down into its new institutions. Still a few students came to Middle Temple from the now independent United States, although for political reasons those who were returning home could not be called to the English Bar. Mostly the American students were following the steps of fathers who had been there.[101] It is interesting to speculate how they mixed with the loyalist refugees; did the 'patriots' and the exiles share a mess?[102]

The repudiation of royal (and in the proprietary colonies proprietorial) authority had already led to each state drafting its own constitution, some as early as 1776. Again Middle Templars played a major part: thus in South Carolina a majority, six out of eleven, of the members who were appointed to this task were members of Middle Temple[103]; and Thomas McKean[104] drafted that of Delaware.

Over the next quarter century, in state and national government Middle Templars continued to play a significant part. Some of their contributions have been noted; others can be seen in the annotations in the lists in the Appendix to this article. One group should be mentioned specifically, for Middle Templars seem to have enjoyed almost a temporary monopoly of the critical diplomatic posts of the new republic. Thomas Pinckney[105] was the first Ambassador to Britain sent by the federal government. Charles

---

[99] Some would date this to 1649 in Britain [Ed.].

[100] 1789; ratifications brought these amendments into operation in 1791.

[101] Eg the Chews.

[102] Then, as now, tradition requires students dining in Hall to do so in 'messes' of four, and to converse until coffee time only within their mess.

[103] Thomas Lynch, admitted 1767(see above, p 251 n 57); Arthur Middleton, admitted 1757 (see above p 251 n 57); Thomas Pinckney (see below, p xxx); Charles Cotesworth Pinckney (see above, p 258 n 94); John Rutledge (see above, p 243) and Thomas Heyward, admitted 1764/65, called 1770 (see above, p 251 n 57).

[104] Admitted 1758 (see above, p 251 n 57). Thomas McKean had already practised law for at least four years in America before joining Middle Temple.

[105] Thomas Pinckney (1750–1828), admitted 1768, called 1774. Governor South Carolina 1789, Minister to the Court of St James (London) 1792–96, appointed a Major-General when war broke out in 1812.

Cotesworth Pinckney[106] was sent to Paris, Charles Pinckney[107] to Madrid, William Loughton Smith[108] to Lisbon and then Madrid, and William Vans Murray[109] to The Hague. At home in the US, two of the first Supreme Court Judges were Middle Templars—John Rutledge,[110] from 1789 to 1791 (and briefly in 1795 as Acting Chief Justice), and John Blair,[111] from 1789–96.

F.   After the war: the loyalists

What about our Loyalist members, once the war was over? How did they fare whilst their revolutionary friends had been creating the new republic and its constitution? A hundred thousand loyalists were forced to emigrate. The British, whatever the crassness of their treatment of the colonists inducing them to rebel, had sought to protect the loyalists, and Congress (which had no power to compel the thirteen now independent states to do anything[112]) was committed by the Articles of Peace to 'earnestly recommend' to each state a full restoration of loyalists' rights and property, which would have been a reversal of policy, since Congress had earlier, in 1777, recommended to the states that they appropriate the property of residents who 'had forfeited the right to protection', and by 1782 all the states had indeed passed confiscation acts. The pious promise in the Articles of Peace was ignored, and the loyalists—many wealthy—faced ruin. The British Government in July 1783 recognised the loyalists' predicament and established a Commission to assess compensation to be paid to the loyal émigrés. The Commissioners of Loyalist Claims heard no fewer than 4,118 claims, and continued their work until 1790, authorising payment by the British Government of over £3,200,000 in compensation.[113] Awards were discretionary and had regard to the amount of the

---

[106] See above, p 258 n 94. Charles Cotesworth Pinckney was Federalist Candidate (unsuccessful) for the Vice-Presidency in 1800, and the Presidency in 1804 and 1808 (losing to Thomas Jefferson and James Madison).

[107] See above, p 256 n 85.

[108] William Loughton Smith, admitted 1774. Came back after the war for three years (1779–82) to study, although never called to the English Bar. In Middle Temple's Records and in the Appendix he is called 'William Smith'. He added his mother's maiden name about 1800.

[109] William Vans Murray, admitted 1774 and studied in the Temple for about three years.

[110] See above p 257.

[111] John Blair (1732–1800), admitted 1753, called 1757. Chief Justice of Virginia, Justice, US Supreme Court 1789–96.

[112] See p 256 n 84 above, and text to that footnote.

[113] £3,292,452, which applying a multiplier of 55 to approximate to current (2010) values equates to over £180 million. Some life pensions granted to loyalists ceased to be payable only in the 1830s as the last claimants died.

loss and the behaviour of the claimant: so an owner of vast estates who had blown hot or cold, or been but a passive loyalist, would have his losses scaled down.[114]

The records of the Commission's proceedings introduce us to one very attractive Middle Templar: Phineas Bond.[115] Bond was the son of a Philadelphia doctor and was one of those moderate whigs who were propelled into being loyalists by the Declaration of Independence. But although a loyalist, he firmly refused to take up arms against the insurgents and thus to fight his friends. He thereby earned a certain respect from the eventual victors in the war, although he felt constrained to quit the city with the British when they evacuated to New York. From New York he returned to London to resume his studies, staying until 1786 when he was appointed to the delicate post of British Consul in his home city. Bond was a much-respected and influential witness before the Commission, a man who projected an aura of truthful respectability and fair reporting. He became an admirable consul, but was forced again to flee his country in 1812 when anti-British feelings became extreme there by reason of the war of that year. In England he attracted sympathy and admiration, and was showered with honours: bencher of Middle Temple 1812, reader 1815, honorary Doctorate of Civil Law from Oxford, and Fellow of the Royal Society 1815.[116] It is often thought that he was Middle Temple's first American bencher: but this depends upon how one defines 'American'. On one view Middle Temple had indeed already had an 'American' treasurer in 1761, Thomas Mompesson.[117]

---

[114]   This happened to the Penn and Allen families of Pennsylvania.

[115]   Phineas Bond (1749–1816), admitted 1771, returned to Philadelphia when his father died in 1773; called 1779, bencher 1812, reader 1815, died (and buried in the Temple Church) 1816. He is mentioned at p 253 n 67 above.

[116]   His compatriots perhaps relented when he died, and the *American Daily Advertiser* for 14 March 1816 ran an obituary notice *inter alia* recording that 'he was bred to the Bar where he was rising into celebrity, when the Revolution commenced. Uniform and undeviating in his adherence to principles which he believed to be correct, he avowed himself as a Loyalist, but though he maintained his opinions with steadiness, he determined to take no part against his fellow citizens, and quitted his country, bearing with him the attachment and esteem of the most respectable of those with whose political feelings and conduct he was at variance. After the War of the Revolution he returned to America in a public character, and was received with the respect and affection due to his acknowledged worth. He was faithful, zealous, and indefatigable in the discharge of his official duties.'

[117]   Thomas Mompesson, admitted 1714, called 1720, bencher 1750, treasurer 1761. Son of Roger Mompesson of Lincoln's Inn who had emigrated in or about 1703 (when Thomas Mompesson was a small child), so that he grew up in America, where his father died in 1715.

Other loyalists stayed or came to England. Between 1776 (the Declaration of Independence) and 1812 (the War of 1812) some 36 American students were admitted—perhaps more.[118] It is estimated that at least 11 of these were refugees.[119]

G.   The war of 1812

The war of 1812 brought an end to the already dwindling stream of American students who came to the Inn. It is not generally realised in Britain that this unnecessary war was declared by the United States and was very unpopular there. Basically, the conflict arose because the British sought to blockade Napoleonic France. The French had been landing cargo destined for France in US ports, passing it through customs and securing fresh clearance for the cargo to be delivered by a US vessel to what (in the British view) was a belligerent port. At first this device was upheld by decisions of the British Admiralty Courts,[120] and American vessels as neutrals plied between the French West Indies and France with near impunity. But in 1805 Sir William Scott,[121] the Admiralty Judge (and a distinguished Middle Templar), declared in the *Essex* case[122] that American cargo was subject to seizure and condemnation unless the shipper could prove that he had originally intended to terminate the voyage in an American port; otherwise the voyage could be regarded as a 'continuous' one between enemy ports. As a result, many American vessels were seized. Worse still, American seamen were pressed into service in the Royal Navy. Britain and France then began reciprocal blockades, the British blockade especially damaging the American shipping trade. The *Chesapeake* incident in 1809 (when the British warship *Leopard* demanded of the US warship *Chesapeake*, just outside territorial waters, that it yield up four alleged deserters; and upon refusal opened fire, killing three US sailors, wounding 18, seizing the alleged deserters and crippling the *Chesapeake*) further inflamed relations, as did the US retaliation by the Embargo Act, prohibiting trade with most foreign

---

[118] Perhaps more, because some refugees gave their or their parents' English addresses and may be undetected.

[119] Some, eg John Saunders (1753–1834), admitted 1783, called 1789, identified in the lists in the Appendix to this chapter as American, had had distinguished and honourable careers in the loyalist forces. Saunders was awarded £4,850 compensation and half-pay as an officer of the British army. After being called to the Bar he emigrated to Canada, ending up as Chief Justice of New Brunswick.

[120] See Hill 'The Maritime Connection' above pp 142m 143 as to the blockade leading to the war of 1812.

[121] William Scott (1745–1836), admitted 1777, called 1780, bencher 1794, reader 1799, treasurer 1807, created Lord Stowell 1821.

[122] See Richard B Morris, *Encyclopedia of American History* (New York, Harper and Bros, 1953), 134.

nations. Eventually, not realising that Britain had partially given way by revoking the most offending orders in Council, on 19 June 1812 the US declared war. The Senate votes of the New England states (save non-maritime Vermont), New York, New Jersey and Delaware all supported peace.[123] In Massachusetts the Governor declared a public fast in view of the war 'against the nation from which we are descended', and the legislature objected to enlistment, 'save for defensive war'. Both Connecticut and Massachusetts refused to furnish militia for the war. Nevertheless, in December 1812 President Madison was re-elected, defeating De Witt Clinton and Vice-Presidential candidate Middle Templar Jared Ingersoll.[124]

This is not the place to discuss the campaigns of the war. Suffice it to say that the Americans tried and failed to seize Canada, and that once the British were able to move troops from Europe after Napoleon's first abdication and exile to Elba, they startled the Americans with the vigour and ruthlessness of their response. Especially the Americans resented the British expedition[125] which captured and then burned the main government buildings in the then newly-built capital city of Washington. The Peace of Ghent concluded the war in 1815,[126] but although restoring both sides territorially to their pre-war positions, the peace terms were silent as to the matters which had caused the war, and did nothing to quell the wave of anti- British emotion which swept even the states which had opposed the war. This unfortunate conflict soured Anglo-American relations for generations, and 1812 marked the end of the English Inns of Court's role as a training ground for American lawyers. There were only two admissions from America between 1812 and the 1860s, and only fifteen in the period 1860–1900.

The departure of so many loyalist lawyers created a shortage of legally-trained men, especially of those trained in London, but it did not reduce the effect of English law upon American jurisprudence. Blackstone's *Commentaries on the Laws of England* had been published at Oxford and Dublin between 1765 and 1769, and a Philadelphia edition followed in 1771–72, destined for repeated revision through many editions and to have a greater influence on the law than any other textbook in the USA. Sir William Blackstone[127] was, of course, a Middle Templar. He did not

---

[123] Peace lost by 19 to13 votes.

[124] Above, p 258 n 95. He tended not to use his first name (Charles).

[125] Sent as a diversionary tactic, to draw off the American invasion of Canada.

[126] News of the signing of the peace terms did not reach America in time to avoid the battle of New Orleans two weeks later, a striking victory by Andrew Jackson, which in itself restored the Americans' national pride.

[127] William Blackstone (1723–80), admitted 1741, called 1746, bencher 1761. The *Commentaries* were based upon the lectures he had given as Professor of English Law at Oxford.

emigrate, but perhaps he had a greater effect upon law in the United States than any other British-trained lawyer.

IV. AMBASSADORS AND FRIENDS

So came an interval. No more came the young American students to the Middle Temple. The ghosts of Burke and Dunning, who had both fought so manfully (though verbally) for the colonists in the House of Commons, fell silent.

And yet all was not forgotten. When the parent and the child had been reconciled, when the two nations achieved an amicable relationship, some old ties were still cherished and recalled. Very rarely in those days were honorary benchers elected, and never before one who was not a British citizen, but in 1899 there came to the Court of St James an American Ambassador who was a very distinguished lawyer. Joseph Choate had been the President of the American Bar Association the year before he came to London. Before he ceased to be Ambassador in 1905, he was elected an honorary bencher of the Middle Temple. He was the first foreigner to be so elected by any Inn of Court.

The custom then grew up of electing as an honorary bencher each US Ambassador who was also a lawyer. Almost half of them were lawyers. They included John Davis,[128] said to have been the finest trial lawyer in the US in the twentieth century, who argued 140 cases before the US Supreme Court. In addition, in 1922 Chief Justice William H Taft[129] was elected, the only man ever to serve both as President (1909–13) and as Chief Justice (1921–30). In 1924 a future Chief Justice, Charles Evans Hughes,[130] and in 1930 General Dawes (US Vice-President), were elected as honorary benchers.

Then came the Second World War. The pictures, the armour, the shields of our former readers and treasurers, the stained glass windows, even the ornamentally carved gates to the screen with their ferocious iron spikes (which had been hung there in the late seventeenth century 'to keep unruly students out of dinner'—our forebears meant business) were all removed to safety in the country, except, alas, by oversight Drake's Lantern.[131] Then

---

[128] John William Davis (1873–1955), Solicitor-General of the US 1913–18, Ambassador to Court of St James 1918–21, unsuccessful Democratic candidate for President 1924. See William H Harbaugh, *Lawyer's Lawyer: the Life of John W Davis* (New York, OUD, 1973). Davis was a prominent campaigner for the repeal of prohibition.

[129] Taft's great ambition had always been to be Chief Justice, rather than President. He was a federal judge at age 34.

[130] Chief Justice 1930–41.

[131] Drake's Lantern was destroyed in the Blitz. A replica containing a fragment from the original now hangs in the ante room to Middle Temple Hall.

came the Blitz. The Treasury Offices and Bench apartments were damaged, with widespread damage to windows (1–2 January 1941). Two incendiaries landed on the Hall roof on the night of 14–15 July 1941, destroying the cupola, though most of the roof was saved by the Inn's firefighters. Then V-1 explosions (24 July and 3 December) damaged the temporary glazing—the windows kept getting blown out. The Library suffered damage, rendering it unsafe and necessitating its demolition.

After the Second World War Middle Temple faced a truly daunting task repairing the Hall and rebuilding the Inn. War damage payments from Her Majesty's Government went so far, but not far enough. With magnificent generosity our 'offspring' rallied. In the ante-room to the Hall today two panels honour and commemorate the contributions of the American Bar Association and the Canadian Bar Association to the restoration.

It was in this era of reconstruction that our American friends by a series of donations gave us the books which comprise the American Library, making it then the largest collection of hardback American Law reports outside the United States.[132] All these fill the upper 'American' floor of our post-war library.[133]

So it is fitting that since the Second World War every US Ambassador has been elected as an Honorary Master of the Bench, a custom which will surely continue. In addition, other distinguished Americans, including Masters Burger,[134] Rehnquist[135] and Roberts,[136] have been elected (thus creating a custom of electing each Chief Justice of the US Supreme Court).

Constantly the legal professions of the USA and Britain have become more aware of each other, and as time goes on, more and more links are being forged between them. Middle Templars are proud of their transatlantic connections, and were represented in the celebrations for the 400th anniversary in 2007 of the foundation of Jamestown in the Colony of Virginia, and the ensuing conference on the Rule of Law at Richmond, Virginia. The anniversary of the Virginia Charter of 1606 had been celebrated in Middle Temple Hall by two gala dinners on 10 and 11 April 2006. Whenever the American Bar Association (ABA) meets in London[137] it is always the pleasure and privilege of Middle Temple to entertain them,

---

[132] Many donors gave, notably the Carnegie Endowment for International Peace (2,042 volumes), Ambassador Aldrich (540) and many by the US Government itself.

[133] The Inn's problems are now of space: there is a total of about 80 series to continue. The Inn is having to switch to CD roms.

[134] Above p 258. Master Burger was elected in 1971.

[135] Chief Justice Rehnquist (elected in 1995).

[136] Chief Justice Roberts (elected in 2006).

[137] Such meetings (being part of the American Bar Association's annual conference) have taken place in London in 1924, 1957, 1971, 1985 and 2000.

a custom which began with the great dinner held in 1924 on the occasion of the ABA's first London conference.[138]

---

[138] To that conference we owe E Alfred Jones's work *American Members of the Inns of Court*, already much cited (see above p 242 n 14). The genesis of this article was the talk by the writer to Middle Temple's ABA guests after dinner in Hall on 17 July 2000. That talk in turn owed much to the booklet written by Sir Lynden Macassey as a memento of the dinners held in Hall for the ABA in 1957 (and which the writer had revised in 1998; see above p 257 n 87). Sir Lynden in turn owed much to Jones. The Appendix was compiled for the 2000 talk, but enlarged and revised by the writer when that talk was reprinted in 2008 by the Luzerne County Bar Association on the occasion of its meeting in New York with the NY City Bar Association in September 2008, with annotations and several further names added for this publication.

Appendix
The American Connection[*]

I. STUDENTS COMING FROM AMERICA

Date admitted to Middle Temple

1692

25 April   William Byrd II, son of William Byrd of Virginia, called 1695. By his death in 1744 he had established an estate of over 180,000 acres. His candid and entertaining accounts of the escapades of the Virginia Commission of which he was the leader, which set out in 1728 to settle the boundary dispute with North Carolina, can be read in W Martin (ed), *Colonial American Travel Narratives* (New York, Penguin Books USA Inc, 1994).

18 Oct   Benjamin Lynde, son of Simon Lynde, of Boston Mass. Called 22 November 1695. Chief Justice of Massachusetts, died 1745.

1697

18 Oct   Benjamin Harrison, son and heir of Benjamin Harrison of Surrey County, Va. Attorney-General (1702) and then (1705) Speaker of the Virginia House of Burgesses, died young in 1710. (His grandson Benjamin Harrison signed the Declaration of Independence, and Presidents William Henry Harrison and Benjamin Harrison were direct descendents. Carter Henry Harrison (qv) was his grandson).

10 Nov   Paul Dudley, eldest son of Joseph Dudley, Governor of Massachusetts. Called 1700. CJ, Massachusetts and a distinguished naturalist.

---

[*] Members' names and description of parents' names are as recorded in the Middle Temple Admisions Register.

1706

11 Feb   William Dudley, second son of Joseph Dudley, of New England, America, esq. Judge of Court of Common Pleas, Massachusetts.

7 Nov   Robert Livingston, third son of Robert Livingston; of New York, America, merchant.

1713

30 Apr   John Carter, son and heir of Robert Carter of Virginia, in America, esq. Called 27 May 1720. Became Secretary of State for the Colony of Virginia.

1714

26 Apr   Thomas Mompesson, oldest son of Roger Mompesson, of New York and New Jersey. Called 27 May 1720, bencher 4 May 1750, reader 1760, treasurer 1761, died 1767. (Not born in America, but came from there to London and stayed). See p 261.

1718

24 Jan   James Trent, son and heir of William Trent, of Philadelphia, Pennsylvania, merchant. Briefly CJ of New Jersey.

1719

13 May   Richard Lee, son and heir of Philip Lee, of the Colony of Maryland, merchant. A loyalist.

5 Nov   Robert Beverly, only son of Harry Beverly, of Urbannia, Virginia, esq. Called 26 October 1722.

1720

15 Mar   Antony Palmer, second son of Antony Palmer, of Philadelphia, Pennsylvania, America, merchant. Called 11 February 1726.

24 Aug   William Allen, second son of William Allen, of Philadelphia in Pennsylvania, merchant. Chief Justice of Pennsylvania. Died a loyalist exile in London, 1780.

1721

23 June   Wilson Cary, son and heir of Miles Cary, late of York River, in the county of Warwick, Virginia, America, gent, deceased.

1722

8 Sep   Beverley Whiting, son and heir of Henry Whiting, of the colony of Virginia, esq. Godfather of George Washington.

8 Sep   Henry Fitzhugh, only son of William Fitzhugh, late of Stafford, colony of Virginia, esq, deceased. Called 10 February 1726.

1725

13 May   William Wragg, son of Samuel Wragg of London and Charlestown, South Carolina. Called 1733, a loyalist who was shipwrecked and drowned en route to Europe as a political refugee in 1777.

1727

16 May   Christopher Robinson, son and heir of Christopher Robinson of Virginia. Member Virginia House of Burgesses, died 1768.

1729

6 Sep   Andrew Hamilton, second son of Andrew Hamilton of Philadelphia, Pensilvania, esq. Called 24 November 1732.

1730

14 Mar   Jonathan Belcher, esq, second son of the Hon. Jonathan Belcher, esq. Called 1734. Practised in Dublin 1742–54. Chief Justice Nova Scotia 1754–1776. His father, described in the Admissions Register as 'Governor of New England in America', was Governor of Massachusetts 1729–34, and of New Jersey 1747–57.

1731

3 May   John Chambers (father's name not recorded in the Admissions Register, but stated to be of New York, America, gent). A judge in colonial New York 1751–60.

1733

2 Feb   Joseph Jekyll, third son of John Jekyll, late of New England, America, esq, deceased. Called 1 June 1739.

5 July   George Carter, youngest son of Robert Carter, of Virginia, in America, esq. Called 24 November 1738.

27 Nov   Thomas Elde, only son of Thomas Elde, late of New York, America, gent, deceased.

1739

13 Oct   Peyton Randolph, second son of John Randolph, of Virginia, America, knight. Called 10 February 1744. See p 249.

1742

16 Mar   Daniel Dulany, son and heir of Daniel Dulany, of the province of Maryland, America, esq. Loyalist who died in exile.

29 Oct   William Burnett, youngest son of William Burnett, esq, deceased, late of New York, America, Governor.

29 Oct   William Livingstone, son of Colonel Philip Livingstone, of New York, America, esq. See p 258.

1743

27 Oct   Benjamin Chew, son and heir of Samuel Chew, of Pensylvania, North America, esq. Chief Justice of Pennsylvania until 1777; after the Revolution, President, High Court of Errors and Appeals, Pennsylvania.

1744

2 Nov   Edward Shippen, only son of Edward Shippen, of Philadelphia, Pensilvania, North America, merchant. Called 9 February 1750. A judge before the Revolution and CJ, Pennsylvania 1799.

15 Dec   Thomas Bordley, fourth son of Thomas Bordley, late of the province of Maryland, America, esq, deceased.

1745

8 Apr   John Randolph, third son of John Randolph, late of the island of Virginia, America, knight, deceased. Called 9 February 1750. See p 269. Died a loyalist in exile.

1747

6 Jan   William Byrd, son and heir of William Byrd, late of the island of Virginia, America, esq, deceased. A loyalist.

1750

29 Jun   Phileman Hemsley, son and heir of William Hemsley, of Queen Anne's County, Maryland, esq, deceased.

6 Oct   William Drayton, eldest son of Thomas Drayton, of South Carolina, esq. Called 13 June 1755.

9 Oct   Henry Churchill, third son of Armistead Churchill, of Virginia, America, esq. Called 24 May 1754.

1751

11 Feb   William Franklin, son and heir of Benjamin Franklin, of Philadelphia, America. Called 10 November 1758. See p 246.

2 May   Joseph Jones (admitted to Inner Temple 7 December 1749), son and heir of James Jones, late of Virginia, gent, deceased. Called

21 June 1751. Briefly a judge; in the War of Independence a Major-General. Great friend of George Washington.

14 Aug   Thomson Mason, third son of George Mason, of Virginia, America, esq. Called 22 November 1754. Judge of the General Court of Virginia.

19 Oct   Charles Carroll, eldest son of Charles Carroll of the city of Anapolis, Maryland, America, MD. Called 22 November 1754. Prominent Maryland revolutionary.

1752

2 Dec   Ryland Randolph, third son of Richard Randolph, late of Virginia, America, esq, deceased.

2 Dec   Robert Goldsborough, eldest son of Charles Goldsborough, of Dorset, Maryland, esq. Called 8 February 1757.

1753

2 Jan   John Wilcox, eldest son of John Wilcox, of Urbanna, Middlesex in Virginia, gent.

17 Feb   John Hammond, second son of Philip Hammond of Severnhead, Anne Arundel, Maryland, America, esq. Called 9 February 1760.

25 May   David Graeme, 2nd son of Dr William Graeme of Charlestown, South Carolina.

2 Jun   John Blair, eldest son of John Blair of the county of York, Virginia, America, esq. Called 20 May 1747. See p 258. Chief Justice of Virginia, Justice US Supreme Court 1789.

18 Jun   William Hicks, eldest son of Edward Hicks, of Philadelphia, America, esq.

9 July   James Michie, eldest son of John Michie, of South Carolina, esq.

27 Sep   John Banister, eldest son of John Banister, of Dinwiddie, Virginia, America, esq. Prominent Virginia revolutionary. Jones (see above p 242), describes him incorrectly as 'This signer of the Constitution of the United States'.

6 Nov   Robert Mackenzie, only son of Kenneth Mackenzie, esq, of Surrey, Virginia, America. Wounded at Bunker Hill when serving in the 43rd Foot.

21 Dec   John Dickinson, second son of Samuel Dickinson, of Delaware, Kent, Pensylvania, America, esq, Called 8 Feb 1757. See p 250.

1754

1 Jan   Carter Henry Harrison, second son of Benjamin Harrison, of Barkley, Charles City, Virginia, esq.

28 May   Cornelius Low, second son of Cornelius Low, of New Jersey, America, merchant.

11 Oct   John Rutledge, son and heir of John Rutledge, of Charlestown, South Carolina, America, esq. Called 9 February 1760. See p 243.

20 Nov   John Mackenzie, son and heir of William Mackenzie, of South Carolina, esq. Called 29 June 1759.

21 Nov   John Ambler (admitted Inner Temple 27 November 1752), second son of Richard Ambler, of Virginia, esq. Called 28 January 1757.

3 Dec   James Hollyday, eldest son of the Hon James Hollyday, of Queen Anne's County, Maryland, esq, deceased. Prominent revolutionary.

25 Dec   John Morris, eldest son of Samuel Morris, of the city of Philadelphia, America. See p 250.

1755

31 Dec   Robert Bolling, sixth son of John Bolling, of Cobbs, Chesterfield, Virginia, America, esq.

1756

17 Jan   Ralph Peters of Platbridge, near Wiggan, Lancashire, eldest son of William Peters, of Philadelphia, America esq. Called 25 November 1757 and settled in England.

11 Feb   Gawen Corbin, eldest son of Richard Corbin, of King's and Queen's County, Virginia, America, esq. Called 23 January 1761.

24 Feb   Philip Thomas Lee, son of Richard Lee, of Charles County, Maryland, America, esq. Called 10 February 1764. A loyalist so distressed by the Revolution that he is said to have died of a broken heart in 1778.

1757

5 Jan   Robert Beverley, only son of William Beverley, of Blandfield, Essex, Virginia, America, esq, deceased. Called 6 February 1761. A passive loyalist.

14 Apr   Arthur Middleton, eldest son of Henry Middleton, of South Carolina, America, esq. See p 251.

27 Jun   Henry Eustace McCulloch, only son of Henry McCulloch of Turnham Green, Middlesex (but who was Surveyor, Inspector and Controller of the Revenue of North Carolina) emigrated as a child in 1740. Agent in England for North Carolina 1773. A staunch loyalist, he was expropriated by the state of North

Carolina and was awarded £17,234 compensation as a loyalist refugee by the Royal Commission on Loyalists' claims.

11 Nov   John Brice, eldest son of John Brice, of Anapolis, Maryland, America, esq. A keen Maryland revolutionary.

1758

9 May   Thomas McKean, son of William McKean, of Cheshire, Pennsylvania, America, esq. See p 251. McKean had already practised law for at least four years in America before joining Middle Temple.

1759

12 Jul   Joshua Ward, second son of John Ward, late of Charlestown, South Carolina, gent, deceased.

6 Aug   Andrew Allen, second son of William Allen, of Philadelphia, Pennsylvania, America, esq.

6 Aug   James Allen, third son of William Allen, of Philadelphia, Pennsylvania, America, esq.

30 Nov   Edmund Key, sixth son of Philip Key, of St Mary's County, Maryland, America, esq.

18 Dec   Alexander Lawson, only son of Alexander Lawson, of Baltimore County, Maryland, America, esq. A passive loyalist. See p 247.

1760

25 Sep   William Fauntleroy, eldest son of William Fauntleroy, of Essex County, Virginia, America, esq.

1761

9 Jan   Walter Livingston, second son of Robert Livingston, of New York, North America, esq.

9 Jan   Robert Livingston, third son of Robert Livingston, of New York, North America, esq.

14 Oct   Lloyd Dulany, fourth son of Daniel Dulany, late of Anne Arundel County, Maryland, America, esq, deceased. A loyalist, in exile in London he was killed in a duel with another loyalist émigré, the Rev Bennet Allen.

1762

3 Aug   Jasper Yeates, second son of Jasper Yeates, of Philadelphia, Pennsylvania, esq. See p 247. Justice of Pennsylvania. Supreme Court 1791–1817.

1763

14 May   Gabriel Cathcart, only son of William Cathcart, of Roanoak, North Carolina, America, esq.

16 Dec   Nicholas Waln, second son of Nicholas Waln, late of Philadelphia, America, gent, deceased. A Quaker loyalist.

16 Dec   Joseph Reed, eldest son of Andrew Reed, of Trenton, Hunterdon, New Jersey, America, esq. See p 255.

1764

23 Jan   William Hamilton, second son of Andrew Hamilton, of the City of Philadelphia, America, esq, deceased. See p 247. A revolutionary who became a loyalist.

24 Jan   Charles Cotesworth Pinckney, eldest son of Charles Pinckney, late of Charlestown, South Carolina, in America, esq, deceased. Called 27 January 1769. See p 258.

27 Oct   John Matthews, only son of John Matthews, late of South Carolina, America, esq, deceased. Governor South Carolina, Chancery Judge in South Carolina.

1765

10 Jan   Thomas Hayward, eldest son of Daniel Hayward, of Charlestown, South Carolina, America, esq. Called 25 May 1770. See p 251 sub nom. Heyward.

15 Feb   Isaac Hunt, son of the Rev Isaac Hunt of Barbados. After practice at the Bar in Philadelphia he became a loyalist refugee in England and took holy orders.

19 Jun   James Wright, second son of James Wright, esq, of Georgia, in America, governor. Called 27 November 1772. Loyalist combatant.

28 Jun   Hugh Rutledge, son of John Rutledge, late of Charlestown, South Carolina, America, esq, deceased. See p 243. Became Chancellor of the Court of Equity, South Carolina.

2 Jul   Alexander Harvey, eldest son of William Harvey, of Charlestown, South Carolina, America, esq. See p 252.

1766

6 Feb   Henry Yonge, eldest son of Henry Yonge, of Georgia, America, esq. A loyalist, in exile he became Secretary and Registrar of the colony of the Bahamas.

1767

12 Jan   Edward Rutledge, fifth son of John Rutledge, late of Charlestown, South Carolina, America, esq, deceased. Called 3 July 1772. See p 251.

17 Feb   Paul Trapier, only son of Paul Trapier of Winayah, South Carolina. A captain in the (revolutionary) Artillery of South Carolina.

6 Mar   Thomas Lynch, only son of Thomas Lynch, of Charles Town, South Carolina, America, esq. See p 251.

17 Nov   Gustavus Scott, eldest son of the Rev James Scott, of Prince William's County, Virginia, America, clergyman. Called 27 November 1772.

1768

29 Sep   Alexander Moultrie, youngest son of John Moultrie, of Charlestown, South Carolina, America, esq. Attorney-General, South Carolina, 1776.

4 Oct   Richard Shubrick, eldest son of Thomas Shubrick, of Charlestown, South Carolina, America, esq.

6 Oct   Philip Neyle, only son of Samson Neyle of Charlestown, South Carolina. Called 1773. Lieut in South Carolina revolutionary forces, killed 1780.

16 Dec   Thomas Pinckney, second son of Charles Pinckney, late of South Carolina, esq, deceased. Called 25 November 1774. See p 259. Governor SC, 1789. Minister, London 1792.

23 Dec   James Peronneau, fourth son of Henry Peronneau, late of Charlestown, South Carolina, America, esq, deceased.

1769

2 Jan   William Oliphant, eldest son of David Oliphant, of Charlestown, South Carolina, America. Fought first for the rebels, later for the Crown, ending as a captain in the Duke of Cumberland's regiment. Unsurprisingly, he did not return to South Carolina after the Revolution.

7 Jan   John Fauchereaud Grimke, son and heir of John Paul Grimke, of Charlestown, South Carolina, America, esq. A revolutionary but fought a duel with Henry Laurens, father of John Laurens.

18 Jan   Henry Lee Ball, eldest son of William Ball, of Lancaster County, Province of Virginia, America, esq.

15 July   Richard Tilghman, second son of James Tilghman, of the City of Philadelphia, America, esq. See p 252.

1770

8 Nov   Daniel Dulany, son and heir of Walter Dulany, of Maryland, America, esq. Loyalist.

1771

15 Apr   Phineas Bond, only son of Phineas Bond, of the City of Philadelphia, America, doctor of medicine. Called 18 June 1779, bencher 24 January 1812, autumn reader 1815. See p 247.

3 May   Walter Aitchison, son and heir of William Aitchison, of Virginia, America, merchant. A loyalist, he was killed in a naval battle with an American privateer.

31 May   Cyrus Griffin, sixth son of Le Roy Griffin, late of Virginia, in America, esq, deceased. See p 249.

1772

25 May   William Ward Burrows, son and heir of William Burrows, of Charlestown, South Carolina, America, esq. First Commanding Officer, US Corps of Marines.

10 Jun   William Heyward, third son of Daniel Heyward, of Charlestown, South Carolina, America, esq.

24 Jun   Edward Tilghman, eldest son of Edward Tilghman, of Queen Anne's County, Maryland, America, esq. Declined to become CJ of Pennsylvania in 1806.

16 Sep   John Laurens, son and heir of Henry Laurens, of Charlestown, South Carolina, America, esq. See p 254.

1773

13 Jan   Henry Lee, eldest son of Henry Lee, of Lee-Sylvania, Prince William County, Virginia, America, esq. See p 254. ('Light Horse Harry").

1 May   Richard Beresford, eldest son of Richard Beresford, late of South Carolina, America, esq, deceased. Lieut Governor South Carolina.

4 May   Charles Pinckney, eldest son of Charles Pinckney, of Charlestown, South Carolina, America, esq. See p 256.

14 May   Nicholas Maccubbin, eldest son of Nicholas Maccubbin, of Annapolis, Maryland, America, esq.

28 Jun   Thomas Shubrick, second son of Thomas Shubrick, of Charles, South Carolina, America, esq. Distinguished Revolutionary soldier.

16 Jul   Jared Ingersoll, only son of Jared Ingersoll, of the City of Philadelphia, America, esq. See p 258. Politician and lawyer.

Briefly President, District Court of Philadelphia. A Pennsylvania delegate to the Constitutional Convention, 1787.

31 Jul   Henry Nicholes, second son of Isaac Nicholes, late of St Paul's Parish, South Carolina, America, esq, deceased.

31 Jul   John Pringle, eldest son of Robert Pringle, of Charlestown, South Carolina, America, esq. A-G, South Carolina, 1792–1808, he declined in 1805 to become A-G of the US.

29 Sep   Joseph Ball Downman, eldest son of Rawleigh Downman, of Virginia, America, esq. Stayed in England throughout the War.

15 Nov   Arthur Lee (admitted to Lincoln's Inn 1 March 1770), youngest son of the Hon Thomas Lee, late of Virginia, America, esq, deceased. Called 5 May 1775. See p 254.

1774

28 Jan   Moses Franks, second son of David Franks, of the City of Philadelphia, America, esq. Called 23 November 1781. A loyalist who served in a loyalist militia, he returned to his studies in England before being called to the Bar.

30 Mar   Benjamin Smith, son of Thomas Smith, of Charlestown, South Carolina, America, esq. *Aide-de-camp* to George Washington; Governor of North Carolina 1810–12.

12 May   William Smith, eldest son of Benjamin Smith, late of Charlestown, South Carolina, America, esq. See p 260. *Chargé d'affaires* Portugal and Minister to Spain. He changed his name to (and is referred to in the text as) William Loughton Smith.

25 Oct   Robert Milligan, only son of George Milligan of Cecil County, Maryland, America, esq.

1775

13 May   William Simpson, eldest son of James Simpson, of Charlestown, South Carolina, America, esq. Called 26 May 1786.

31 May   John Parker, eldest son of John Parker, of Goose Creek, South Carolina, America, esq.

31 May   Hext McCall, son of John McCall, of Charlestown, South Carolina, America, esq.

1776

24 Jan   William Dummer Powell, son and heir of John Powell, of Boston, New England, America, esq. Called 6 February 1784. Loyalist, after fighting for the Crown, he ultimately became CJ of Upper Canada.

15 Nov   Charles Pryce, only son of Charles Pryce esq. Attorney-General of the Province of Georgia, America.

1777

14 Nov   James Simpson, esq. Attorney-General of the Province of South Carolina, eldest son of William Simpson, late of Georgia, America, Chief Justice. Called 4 July 1783. Very active and respected loyalist, awarded over £10,000 compensation and a pension of £860 per annum. Buried in Temple Church graveyard.

1781

15 Feb   William Roberts, eldest son of Humphrey Roberts, of the Province of Virginia, America, esq. Called 18 May 1787. Loyalist exile. See p 247.

4 Jun   James Smith, fourth son of Thomas Smith, of Charlestown, South Carolina, America, esq.

17 Aug   William Rawle, only son of Francis Rawle, late of the City of Philadelphia, America, merchant, deceased. A Quaker loyalist, he returned to the US in 1783. He declined an offer from George Washington to be made US Attorney-General.

6 Sep   Joseph Manigault, second son of Peter Manigault, late of Charlestown, South Carolina, America, esq, deceased.

25 Oct   Daniel Horry, eldest son of Daniel Horry, of Charlestown, South Carolina, America, esq. He changed his name to Daniel Lucas Pinckney Horry and settled in Europe.

1782

28 Jun   Peter Porcher, second son of Philip Porcher, of Charlestown, South Carolina, America, esq.

15 Jul   John Gaillard, eldest son of John Gaillard, of Charlestown, South Carolina, America, esq.

15 Jul   Theodore Gaillard, second son of John Gaillard, of Charlestown, South Carolina, America, esq. Speaker, South Carolina Assembly and later a South Carolina judge.

22 Jul   Archibald Young, eldest son of Benjamin Young, late of Georgetown, South Carolina, America, esq, deceased.

1783

10 Feb   Thomas Simons, eldest son of Maurice Simons, of Charlestown, South Carolina, North America, esq.

3 Jun   William Mazyck, eldest son of William Mazyck, late of Charlestown, South Carolina, America, esq, deceased.

1784

7 Jan   Benjamin Chew, only son of Benjamin Chew, of the City of Philadelphia, America, esq. See p 247.

13 Jan John Saunders, eldest son of Jonathan Saunders, late of Virginia, esq, deceased. Called 6 February 1789. Loyalist, ultimately became CJ of New Brunswick.

2 Feb Phillip Barton Key, son of Francis Key of Cecil County, Maryland. Fought on both sides in the War of Independence. He was admitted to Middle Temple while a loyalist refugee. Awarded £1,496 compensation as a loyalist; nevertheless he returned to Maryland and successfully practised law, becoming Chief Judge of the Fourth Circuit (but he held office for only 14 months). He was a Federalist Congressman 1806–13.

28 Apr William Vans Murray, eldest son of Henry Murray, of Maryland, America, doctor of medicine. See p 260.

1785

12 Jan John Leeds Bozman, only son of John Bozman, late of Maryland, America, esq, deceased. See p 253.

14 Jan Robert Alexander, second son of William Alexander, of Richmond, Virginia, America, esq.

22 Apr George Boon Roupell, only son of George Roupell, of Charlestown, South Carolina, America, esq. Called 4 June 1790. Loyalist.

29 Apr Henry Gibbes, second son of William Gibbes, of Charlestown, South Carolina, America.

1786

18 May John Gaillard, second son of Theodore Gaillard, of Charlestown, South Carolina, America, esq. Loyalist officer in the War.

4 Nov William Allen Deas, second son of John Deas, of Charlestown, South Carolina, America, esq.

9 Nov William Boyd, second son of George Boyd, of Low Layton, Essex, England, and Portsmouth, near Boston, in America, esq. A loyalist exile, he died on the way home in 1787, having been refused compensation in view of his ambivalent attitude during the hostilities and since he had not lost his vast estates.

1787

1 Feb Miles Brewton Pinckney, third son of Charles Pinckney, late of Charlestown, South Carolina, America, esq, deceased.

27 Apr Roger Pinckney, eldest son of Roger Pinckney, late of South Carolina, America, esq, deceased.

1793

28 Mar Henry Izard, eldest son of Ralph Izard, of Charlestown, South Carolina, America, esq.

1794

16 Sep   James Edmund Houston, eldest son of James Houston, of Savannah, Georgia, America, doctor of medicine.

1796

20 July   Jonathan Perrie Coffin, esq, (had been admitted to the Inner Temple 23 May 1788), fifth son of Nathaniel Coffin, late of Boston, America, esq, deceased. Loyalist.

1804

15 Mar   Clement Simpson, only son of Jacob Simpson, late of Georgia, in America, esq, deceased.

1807

23 Apr   Samuel Gordon, eldest son of Robert Gordon, late of Farrerin, Sligo, Ireland, and Johnville, Abbeville, South Carolina, esq.

1808

Nov 17   Jacob Shoemaker Wain, youngest son of Nicholas Wain, of Philadelphia, America, esq.

II.   SOME REFUGEE LOYALISTS WHO WERE ADMITTED

(Others of the 31 Americans admitted 1777–1808 were loyalists; these four gave English addresses and asserted their refugee status.)

1786

20 May   Samuel Phephoe, only son of Thomas Phephoe an Irish lawyer of Charlestown, South Carolina, living in 1786 as a loyalist refugee in Bristol.

1790

25 Nov   John Izard Wright, 2nd son of James Alexander Wright of London, formerly of Charlestown, South Carolina.

1792

2 July   Thomas Hutchinson, eldest son of Thomas Hutchinson of Boston, Massachusetts (and a loyalist refugee in England from 1776).

1793

28 Jan   Peter Oliver, youngest son of Peter Oliver, a loyalist refugee then living in England.

III. MIDDLE TEMPLARS RESIDENT IN GREAT BRITAIN OR IRELAND WHO
EMIGRATED FROM GREAT BRITAIN TO THE AMERICAN COLONIES
(SOME OF WHOM RETURNED)

1554

3 Dec   Ralph Lane, second son of Ralph Lane of Hogshawe, Bucks, knight. First Governor of Virginia (see above, 'The Maritime Connection', section II.B.).

1597

12 May   George Percy, seventh son of Henry, late Earl of Northumberland, and brother of Henry, now Earl. Deputy Governor of Virginia (and one of the incorporators of the second Virginia Company). He returned to England in 1612.

1610

10 May   William Ferrar, third son of Nicholas Ferrar, of London, gent. Died in Virginia before 1637.

1620

24 Oct   George Evelyn, son and heir of Robert Evelyn, of Godstone, Surrey, esq, deceased. Capt George Evelyn spent 1636–49 in Maryland and latterly Virginia, returning to England.

1624

3 May   William Berkley, fourth son of Maurice Berkley, of Bruton, Somerset, knight, deceased. Sir William Berkeley (modern spelling) was Governor of Virginia 1641–51, remaining in Virginia during the Commonwealth, again Governor 1660–65. Died (in England) 1677.

1663

17 Jul   John Bridges, son and heir of John Bridges of Grayes Inn, Middlesex, esq. Chief Justice of New York 1702, died 1704.

1664

21 May   Thomas Lawrence (or Laurence), esq, son and heir of John L, of Chelsey, Middlesex, baronet. Sir Thomas Lawrence had emigrated to Maryland by 1691 (and had a colourful political career), dying 1714.

1671

13 Feb   Sampson Shelton Broughton, son and heir of Richard Broughton, one of the a Masters of the Utter Bar, deceased. Called 1677, Keeper of Middle Temple Library 1696–1700. Attorney-General New York 1700, died 1704 and succeeded by his son Samson Broughton (*qv*)

1688

12 Jun   Stevens Thomson, son and heir of William Thomson, one of the Masters of the Utter Bar. Stephens Thompson (as it was then spelt) became Attorney-General of Virginia, and died 1739.

1691

25 Nov   William Stephens, esq, son and heir of William Stephens, of the Isle of Wight, knight. Col William Stephens, an English MP, was appointed Secretary to the Trustees of the Colony of Georgia in 1737 and emigrated there, becoming the first President of Georgia in 1743. Died 1753.

1694

13 Apr   Edward Chilton, son and heir of Edward Chilton of Wilbra-ham, Cambridgeshire, esq, deceased. Called of grace 22 May 1696. He had been educated in Ireland and Cambridge, emigrated and was Clerk to the General Assembly of Virginia in 1683. He held various legal offices before his death.

1697

23 Jun   Sampson Broughton, son and heir of Sampson Shelton Broughton, esq, one of the Masters of the Utter Bar. Called of grace 22 November, 1700. He emigrated to New York with his father (*qv*, above). Also appointed Attorney-General of New York, but prevented from acting in that office.

1697

10 Nov   Paul Dudley, son and heir of Joseph Dudley, of the Isle of Wight, Hants, esq. Called of grace 22 November, 1700. His father Joseph Dudley was Governor of Massachusetts, who had already returned to England when his son was admitted. Paul Dudley returned to Massachusetts, 1707, and died in 1751 when Chief Justice of Massachusetts.

1704

3 July   William Keith, esq, son and heir of William Keith, of Ludwharne, Scotland, baronet. Called 28 November 1729. Lieut-Governor of Pennsylvania 1716–26; died 1749.

1705

5 Apr   Robert Auchmuty, 3rd son of John Auchmuty of Newton, Co Longford, Ireland. Called 1711, emigrated to Boston, Mass; Judge of the Vice-Admiralty Court for New England 1733–47. Died 1750.

1706

11 Feb   William Dudley, second son of Joseph Dudley, of New England, America, esq. Brother to Paul Dudley, above; Judge of the Court of Common Pleas of Massachusetts. Died 1743.

1711

26 Mar   William Burnett, esq, son and heir of Guilbert Burnett, late bishop of Salisbury. Governor New York 1720–28; of Massachusetts and New Hampshire 1728–29 (when he died).

1713

18 Jun   Thomas Kimberley, 3rd son of the Dean of Lichfield; emigrated to become an eminently successful lawyer in South Carolina.

1717

26 Nov   Robert Johnston, 2nd son of the Rev Gideon Johnston, Bishop of London's Commissary in South Carolina. Emigrated with his parents circa 1707. Called 1724, returned to South Carolina, assuming the surname of Ketelbey.

1721

20 May   Daniel Horsmanden, son and heir of the Rev Daniel H of Purleigh, Essex. Joined Inner Temple 1724, Chief Justice New York, died 1778.

1725

12 May   Joseph Murray, of New York, America, esq. Son of Thomas Murray, Queen's County, Ireland; he had emigrated *before* his admission.

1726

1 Feb   Andrew Rutledge, son and heir of Thomas Rutledge, late of Callan, County Kilkenny, Ireland. See p 243, 245.

1730

11 Jun   Nathaniel Jones (admitted Inner Temple 15 June 1723). Son and heir of Thomas Jones. Appointed Chief Justice of New Jersey in 1759 but prevented on his arrival from fulfilling that office.

1733

22 Oct   Francis Bernard. Called 1737. Sir Francis Bernard, Bt, was Governor New Jersey 1758–60, of Massachusetts 1760–68. Bencher 1770, elected reader and died 1779.

1734

22 Oct   Robert Lightfoot, second son of the Rev Robert Lightfoot. Judge of the Vice-Admiralty Court in the Southern District of North America, residing in Virginia. Retired to Rhode Island, later Connecticut, died 1794.

1735

19 July   William Kemp, son and heir of Edward Kemp of Lewes, Sussex. Called 1737. Appointed Attorney-General of New York 1753, where he died in 1759.

1739

1 May   William Gregory, son of the Rev Benjamin Gregory of Maynooth, Ireland. Chief Justice of Quebec 1764–66 but dismissed; assistant judge, South Carolina 1774. Imprisoned for his loyalist views and died 1781.

1743

1 Nov   William Lyttleton, fourth son of Thomas Lyttleton, baronet. Called 29 January 1748. Lord Lyttleton of Frankley was Governor of South Carolina 1755–60, thereafter of Jamaica.

1746

22 Apr   Thomas Child, youngest son of Richard Child of Lavenham, Suffolk. Called 1746, upon his appointment as Attorney-General of North Carolina.

1772

18 Jun   Peter Livius, esq, eldest son of Peter Lewis Livius, merchant late of Lisbon, Portugal. He had already had a varied judicial career before admission to the Inn. Called 1775. Briefly Chief Justice of Quebec.

1775

14 July   Ely Wrixon, 2nd son of Henry Wrixon of Cork, Ireland, emigrated 1774, returning in 1775. He briefly managed to get a loyalist pension until his pretensions were detected. In his brief stay in the US, where he was known as Elias Wrixon, he greatly impressed John Adams. Wrixon claimed to have been offered and refused high appointments in the rebel forces. He joined Middle Temple after his return and seems to have disappeared after losing his pension.

1777

14 Nov   James Johnston, eldest son of Robert Johnston of Irvine, Scotland. Called 1783. He practised at the South Carolina bar 1764–77, when he was banished as a loyalist.

4

The Middle Temple in the 19th Century

THREE PROMINENT MEMBERS of the Inn reflect the phases of its history during the nineteenth century. The Chancery lawyer, Lord Eldon (John Scott) was called by the Inn in 1776 and died in 1838. His long career saw a time of comparative continuity in the life of the Middle Temple, with the number of admissions steadily increasing and an absence of radical reforms. It was as if he was the link between the eighteenth and nineteenth centuries. Certainly, for the first four decades of the new century contemporary members of the Inn could usually take its old ways for granted, and Lord Eldon's well-known distrust of innovation was of a piece with this. He and the Inn of these years stood for continuity.[1]

---

* I should like to thank Lesley Whitelaw, the Archivist at the Middle Temple, for assistance with the use of sources; Rachel Cox for her response to a draft; and the Editor for useful observations.

[1] See RA Melikan, *John Scott, Lord Eldon, 1751 – 1838: The Duty of Loyalty*, (Cambridge, Cambridge University Press, 1999); *Oxford Dictionary of National Biography* [hereafter '*ODNB*'] (Oxford, Oxford University Press, 2005), contribution by EA Smith;. In the footnotes below this is referred to as *ODNB*. H. A. C. Sturgess, *Register of Admissions to the Honourable Society of the Middle Temple, From the Fifteenth Century to the Year 1944* [hereafter '*ROA*'], (London, Butterworths, 1949), vol 1: Eldon was admitted in 1773 and called in 1776. In the footnotes below this Register is referred to as *ROA*. J Hutchinson, *A Catalogue of Notable Middle Templars: with Brief Biographical Notes* (London, Butterworths, 1902), p 218. In the footnotes below this is referred to as Hutchinson, *CNMT*. Until the creation of the High Court in 1875 upon appointment to the bench a new judge had to take the coif and become a member of Serjeants' Inn. This did not prevent him having a strong association with his 'old' Inn (which might well contain portraits of him wearing judicial robes) but he would not be on its governing body. His role within the life of the Inn was symbolic in form, and powerful in terms of general influence. On serjeants, see JH Baker, *An Introduction to English Legal History*, 4th edn (London, Butterworths, Fourth Edition, 2002), pp 157–159, and JH Baker, 'Serjeants at Law', *Selden Society Supplementary Series*, v, (1984); for a Victorian study, see Serjeant Pulling, *The Order Of the Coif* (London, William Clowes and Son, 1884).

Called in 1823, Lord Westbury (Richard Bethell) became a leading critic of all four Inns of Court and, as a Lord Chancellor, contemplated the abolition of the common law and its replacement with codes. He believed that codification would make the law more accessible and transform its substance. He was part of a restless movement for reform in the central Victorian years which threatened the ways of the Inns and even questioned their existence. Westbury wanted change at the Middle Temple, and he and others at the Inn brought about significant educational reforms in the 1850s. Like many of the mid-Victorian generation, he never allowed old ways to be taken for granted as they had been at the start of the century.[2]

Lord Reading (Rufus Isaacs) was called in 1887 and died in 1935. The late-Victorian years provided a foundation for his remarkable early career as a commercial advocate and he took Silk in 1898. His rapid success was a reflection of an Inn, and more generally of a profession, which had collectively recovered its confidence after the criticisms of the mid-Victorian years. In the final decades of the century criticism of the legal profession was no longer so fashionable, and the common law and the traditions of the Inns of Court were held in higher esteem. By 1900 few questioned the existence of the Middle Temple. It and the other Inns had survived, and despite some contentious debates (not least over legal education) in many respects the Inn was flourishing.[3] Most significant of all, the Inn was looking outwards, in the sense that its membership had increasingly strong links across the world.

I.   The First Phase: Continuity between 1800 and 1845

In visualising the Inn of the early nineteenth century it is important to remember that the Victoria embankment had not been built, and the Thames was wider and came much closer to the buildings of the Middle Temple than it does today. This would have made for an attractive prospect on a bright spring day if the river was not playing its role as London's chief open sewer. In the first half of the century the condition of the Thames steadily worsened, because many of London's cess-pits were being replaced by sewers and the latter discharged untreated effluent into the river. On a hot day its smell offended citizens and would have

---

[2] See TA Nash, *The Life of Richard, Lord Westbury*, 2 vols (London, R Bentley and Son,1888); *ROA*, admitted 1819, called 1823; *ODNB*, contribution by RCJ Cocks; Hutchinson, above n 1, at 20. A major lawyer of his day, his reputation was somewhat eclipsed after his death by a generation less sympathetic to reformers.

[3] See *ODNB*, contribution by A Lentin; book-length biographies include Marquess of Reading (GR Isaacs), *Rufus Isaacs, First Marquess of Reading*, 2 vols (London, 1942–45); HM Hyde, *Lord Reading: the Life of Rufus Isaacs, First Marquess of Reading* (London, Heineman, 1967); D Judd, *Lord Reading* (London, Weidenfeld and Nicolson, 1982); *ROA*, admitted 1885, called 1887.

combined with other odours from open drains, privies and horse manure. Anyone with a romantic view of these years also needs to remember that throughout the metropolis cholera was a constant threat, and the first significant public health legislation appeared as late as the 1840s.[4] In 1800 the Middle Temple was part of an expanding and busy city, and with this came numerous dangers to health.

Against this somewhat uncongenial background a programme of rebuilding was discussed within the Inn. After preliminary difficulties, the requisite money for construction was found in the 1820s. Between them, the architects Henry Hakewill and James Savage were responsible for what is now the Parliament Chamber and the Queen's Room, a new Hall cupola, the entrance tower and 1–2 Plowden Buildings. But the money could not be found to take on the systematic rebuilding of chambers, many of which were known to be in deplorable condition. After 1838 the Temple Church was subject to radical work under the direction of James Savage. In later years there was discontent over what had been done within the church, including the removal of the reredos which had been designed by Wren and carved by William Emmett. The changes to the church proved to be wildly expensive. Savage's initial estimate of £4,215 turned into actual expenditure of £51,896, an over-run which cost him his job.[5]

The benchers of course continued to control the Inn, and at this time they had to come to terms with a number of novelties, including the introduction of new government taxes to pay for the Napoleonic wars. They regarded the new 'income tax' as a tedious problem on top of their duty to 'balance the books', maintain the buildings, rent chambers, manage the servants of the Inn, ensure that admissions and calls were properly organised, and, at times, exercise disciplinary powers.[6] The

---

[4] See the despairingly entitled 'An Act for the Prevention, as Far as May be Possible, of the Disease Called the Cholera' (2 and 3 Will c 10). The first major reform was the Public Health Act 1848 (11 and 12 Vict c 63). For the Thames at this time, see J White, *London in the Nineteenth Century* (London, Jonathan Cape, 2007), esp at 48–55.

[5] There is a valuable guide to these architectural changes in *The Middle Temple: a Guide* (2008), prepared by the Middle Temple Archivist, Lesley Whitelaw, her assistant Hannah Baker, and others); see, in particular, *ibid*, at 29–33. For more detail, see *Notes on the Middle Temple in the Nineteenth Century: Chiefly with Reference to the Buildings in the Inn* (printed anonymously but in fact by JB Williamson, 1936), at 1–27, available from the Archivist. See also above p 67 Richard Havery, *Buildings of the Middle Temple*. The Inn's archives contain extensive records relating to the work on the Church: MT.15/TAM/264–306. More generally, the Archivist has referred me to D Lewer and R Dark, *The Temple Church, London* (Historical Publications, 1997), esp at 94–95.

[6] On the benchers generally, see JB Williamson, *The Middle Temple Bench Book: Being a Register of Benchers of the Middle Temple from the Earliest Records to the Present Time with Historical Introduction*, 2nd edn (London, Chancery Lane Press, 1937). For recent comment on the benchers of all four Inns, see W Cornish, S Anderson, R Cocks, M Lobban, P Polden and K Smith, *The Oxford History of the Laws of England* (Oxford, Oxford

actions taken by the benchers shed light on the everyday life of the Inn. In 1800 there was concern about the expense of the cutlery, with the butlers pointing out that they were now

> required to furnish the Messes in the Hall with clean knives upon a change of dishes which obliged them to keep a larger number of knives than their predecessors ever did and the expense of cleaning them was greatly increased.[7]

Ten months later the benchers were exasperated at inaction, and at a meeting of their parliament it was

> peremptorily ordered that the Bar and Puisne Butlers do provide clean knives and forks, for the members of this Society dining in the Hall, when wanted and not wiped ones.[8]

Cleanliness was slowly becoming a contentious issue.

Beyond the Hall there were times when the benchers faced problems of order. In 1808 the people living in Brick Court petitioned the benchers saying that

> their peace quiet and comfort are materially interrupted by idle boys who at certain hours of the day are suffered to collect in considerable numbers in that Court and to create therein frequent noises and disturbances (and) that the Watchman is so inattentive in his duty that in the night time nuisances of the most offensive description (are) very often committed even upon the stairs as well as in the Court by mischievous and disorderly persons who also break lamps (to) steal oil and that the applicants finding themselves seriously annoyed by such practices respectively solicit ... their masterships to take such steps as they might deem most proper to prevent the repetition of similar outrages in the future ...[9]

In the light of this sort of behaviour it was predictable that the Inn had to expend money on a system of watchmen, which was time-consuming and expensive given the propensity of the latter to get ill or hurt, or simply to retire worn-out and in need of financial support.[10]

On a more cheerful note, as before, the Inn continued to have regard for orphans left within its boundaries. The unruly nature of the place, particularly at night, made it easy discreetly to leave an infant on a stair-way.[11] There were also times when minds were concentrated on

University Press, 2010), vol XI, *1820–1914: English Legal System*, at 1078–87 (P Polden). For concern about the new income tax, see MT 1/MPA, 10 and 13 December 1799, at 64, 15 May 1801, at 115.

[7] MT 1/MPA, 4 January 1800, at 66–67.
[8] MT 1/MPA, 28 November 1800, at 93.
[9] MT 1/MPA, 5 November 1808, at 388. The benchers adjourned the matter, presumably informally instructing the watchmen to address the problem.
[10] See eg MT 1/MPA, 23 May 1800, at 80.
[11] See generally, Middle Temple Archive: Records Relating to Middle Temple Foundlings.

celebration. Crabb Robinson the diarist gives an account of a call ceremony on 9 May 1813. The occasion involved, amongst other things, a fair amount of drink: 'After drinking about six bottles of humble port, claret was brought in …'[12] It seems, too, that people wanted clean air in the Hall; later, in 1831, it was decided that 'in future all smoking of tobacco of any sort, in the Hall, with cigars or otherwise, be absolutely forbidden'.[13] A recent study has argued that the Middle Temple was perhaps the most sociable of the Inns.[14] The evidence for this lies in the way that when dining in Hall there was a general mixing in the 'Side-Messes' for barristers and students. In the words of WG Thorpe,

> barristers and students mess together; in the other Inns they not only dine at separate tables, but sit in order of seniority—a system under which sociality and friends dining together, even for one day, is impossible.[15]

More generally there is evidence to suggest that in the early part of the century it was quite common for families to live in chambers and that this saved the Inn from being dominated by professional work.[16] The Temple could bring relaxation as well as effort. Along with family life came the fact that it appears to have been common for barristers to set up in practice in an independent way as individuals rather than as part of a set of chambers containing other barristers. But again, nobody was flattering about the condition of chambers. Thackeray, the novelist and member of the Inn, wrote in *Pendennis* that 'freedom stands in lieu of sunshine in Chambers; and Templars grumble, but take their ease in their Inn'.[17] We shall see below that as late as 1854 the treasurer of the day was questioned about the state of chambers and found it difficult to respond in positive terms. Looked at as a whole, the Inn of these years was sometimes restful, but more often noisy, smelly, not very well ordered and in places poorly constructed. Charles Lamb's famous essay on the old benchers of the Inner Temple is set at about this time and has a strong sense of nostalgia for eccentric characters living

---

[12] T Sadler (ed), *Diary, Reminiscences, and Correspondence* (London, Macmillan, 1869), at 414. The experience left Crabb Robinson somewhat nervous.

[13] *Rules and Orders of the Honourable Society of the Middle Temple for the Conduct of Business at their Parliaments and Committees and Generally for the Good Government of the House*, 2nd edn (London, 1896) 11 June 1831, at 76.

[14] Cornish *et al*, above n 6, at 1087 (P Polden), referring to WG Thorpe *The Still Life of the Middle Temple* (London, Hutchinson,1892), 331.

[15] Thorpe, above n 14, at 352. But there is some danger in using Thorpe as an authority for the early years since his experience was of later decades; and in *Pendennis* (London, 1848), ch XXX, Thackeray gives a mid-century account of barristers and students dining apart, and is probably referring to the Middle Temple.

[16] *Royal Commission on the Inns of Court*, Parliamentary Papers, 1854–55 (1998), Report at 9; JC Jeaffreson, *A Book About Lawyers*, 2 vols (London, Hurst and Blackett, 1867), at 161–77.

[17] Thackeray, above n 15, ch XXXI. For Thackeray (1811–63), see *ROA*, admitted 1831, called 1848; *ODNB*, PL Shillingsburg; Hutchinson, above n 1, at 241.

out a pleasant life-style.[18] Eccentrics were, no doubt, to be found at any Inn, but the evidence relating to the Middle Temple of these years suggests little scope for sentimentality. It was lively and at times not altogether pleasant, to the extent that it drew adverse comments from contemporaries. This was to change radically in the course of the century.

A.   The underlying strength of the Inn

The Middle Temple of the eighteenth century, described by Wilfrid Prest in the preceding chapter three, was lively but did not go on to experience major shocks during the decades following 1800. After the War of Independence the decline in American admissions could be expected to continue, and it did so. (See Colyer's 'The American Connection' at pp 262, 264). But in other respects admissions increased at a steady rate for 50 years. We know that the numbers of admissions for the decades between 1800 and 1850 were, respectively, 364, 512, 548, 787, and 855.[19] As a proportion of the totals admitted to all four Inns these numbers hovered around a quarter of the intake, being, respectively for those decades, 23.2, 24.7, 20.5, 25.3 and 31.2 per cent of admissions to all the Inns.[20] In other words, in comparison with the other Inns of Court, the Middle Temple had, as one might expect, about a quarter of the intake at a time of gradually increasing numbers for the Bar as a whole.[21]

It is striking that the ratio between those admitted to the Inns and those who went further and were called to the Bar changed over the years. At the

---

[18]   C Lamb, 'Essays of Elia: Old Benchers of the Inner Temple', in *Prose Works of Charles Lamb* (London, E Moxon,1838), 188–207.

[19]   D Duman, *The English and Colonial Bars in the Nineteenth Century* (London and Canberra, Croom Helm, 1983), at 25, Table 1.10. Generally on the nineteenth-century Bar, see Cornish *et al*, above n 6, at 1017–1107, 1175–1222 (Polden and Lobban); R Cocks, *Foundations of the Modern Bar* (London, Sweet and Maxwell, 1983); WC Richardson, *A History of the Inns of Court* (Baton Rouge, Claitor 1975); M Burrage, *Revolution and the Making of the Contemporary Legal Profession* (Oxford, 2006); R Abel, *The Legal Profession in England and Wales* (Oxford, Oxford University Press, 1988); B Abel-Smith and RB Stevens, *Lawyers and the Courts, 1750–1965* (London, Heineman,1967); D Lemmings, *Professors of the Law* (Oxford, Oxford University Press, 2000); JR Lewis, *The Victorian Bar* (London, Hale,1982); WW Pue, 'Lawyers and Modern Political Liberalism in Eighteenth and Nineteenth Century England' in TC Halliday and L Karpik (eds), *Lawyers and the Rise of Modern Political Liberalism* (Oxford, 1997); WW Pue, 'Rebels at the Bar: English Barristers and the County Courts in the 1850s' (1987) 16 *Anglo-American Law Review* 308. For comparison with solicitors, see the study by D Sugarman, 'Bourgeois Collectivism, Professional Power and the Boundaries of the State. The Private and Public Life of the Law Society, 1825–1914' (1996) 3(1/2) *International Journal of the Legal Profession* 81; WW Pue and D Sugarman (eds), *Lawyers and Vampires: Cultural Histories of Legal Professions* (Oxford, Hart Publishing, 2003): for the extensive literature on the legal professions, see *ibid*, Introduction.

[20]   Duman, above n 19, at 25, Table 1.10.

[21]   True, this was a lower percentage in comparison with what had been experienced for parts of the late 18th century when the Middle Temple was somewhat 'ahead' in recruitment, although not markedly so. See ch 3, where Wilfrid Prest considers this.

start of the nineteenth century only about a quarter of the intake went on to being called, whereas by the 1840s this had risen significantly to about 60 per cent. This change has yet to be fully explained but, obviously, it looks as if the increased number of admissions came from people hoping to make a living from the Bar, and this, in turn, probably reflected increasing social respect for professional work generally.[22]

The geographical links of members for the first four decades followed a fairly consistent pattern. The Register of Admissions does not give places of birth; in most cases it refers to the current address of the applicant and the current address of his father, with references to the employment either may have held, if any.[23] It follows that at its most complete it reveals links with places which were, perhaps, likely to be a transient London address for the son and another address, likely to be more enduring, for the family home under the father's name. In 1800, 24 were admitted and, at the risk of using parental addresses as a guide, 18 were from England, 5 from Ireland, 1 from Tobago, and none from Wales or Scotland. In 1801, 31 were admitted, of whom 14 were from England, 8 from Ireland, 1 from Wales, none from Scotland, 3 from Barbados, 4 from St Christopher and 1 from Nassau. As numbers increased during the first decade the ratios between the different places remained approximately the same, with the external representation being strongest from Ireland and the West Indies, the last being, presumably, European colonists. Strikingly, something a bit like this pattern continued through the next three decades with the increase in numbers. For example, in 1840, 102 were admitted, with 76 coming from England, 13 from Ireland, 1 from Wales and 2 from Scotland. The remaining 10 for 1840 came from a diverse mix of places: 1 from Upper Canada, 1 from Nova Scotia, 2 from Trinidad, 1 from Antigua, 1 from Demerara, 1 from Boston (USA), 1 from Calais, 1 from Mauritius and 1 from Barbados.[24]

In short, there was a regular and comparatively large intake from England, very few from Wales or Scotland, and, from across the sea, a sustained and significant Irish presence, as well as some West Indian representation. The extent of the Irish presence merits special attention: it was almost as predictable as the English given the pattern established in the past. The Irish came because until the 1880s, keeping terms at one of the

---

[22]   Duman, above n 19, at 28, Table 1.12, and at 29; on the professions at this time, see WJ Reader, *Professional Men* (London, Routledge, 1966).

[23]   For the *ROA*, see above n 1.

[24]   By way of examples from earlier decades, in 1810, 41 were admitted with 26 coming from England, 11 from Ireland, 1 from Wales, none from Scotland, 1 from Jamaica, and two from India. If names are a guide (and they may not be), the 2 from India were from European families living on the sub-continent. In 1820, 45 were admitted, including 37 from England, 7 from Ireland and 1 from Scotland. In 1830, 62 were admitted, with 39 coming from England, 17 from Ireland, 3 from Wales, 1 from St Vincent, 1 from New Providence Island and 1 from Antigua.

Inns of Court in London was a prerequisite to being called to the Irish Bar.[25] Prest points to its importance in the life of the Inn, with the Irish often sitting together at dinner on one side of the Hall.[26]

Further research needs to be done on the social origins of members, but we know enough to hazard an estimate that here too there was approximate continuity in the nature of the intake during the first half of the nineteenth century. There had been a significant decline in the eighteenth century in the number of entrants who were peers, baronets or knights: Prest points out that by the end of the century this category had fallen to 2.5 per cent of the intake, and there was 'a marked increase in the proportion of sons from mercantile and professional backgrounds'.[27] As a matter of impression, there is every indication that this continued into the nineteenth century, but Duman, writing about admissions to all four Inns, points out that it did not follow from this that the presence of the landed gentry as a whole also declined. In fact Duman concludes that the number of gentry at the Bar rose slightly after 1800 and reached 28 per cent in 1835.[28] Thereafter the middle classes further strengthened their preponderance: 'Between 1835 and 1885 the representation of the middle classes at the Bar rose from 61 per cent to 73 per cent.'[29]

Beyond all the statistics on membership one simple fact stands out. For the whole of the nineteenth century it remained impossible for a woman to become a Member of the Inn. When reform came in 1919, it took legislation to force through the change. During the nineteenth century no woman could call herself a Middle Templar.[30]

B.   The membership for the early years of the nineteenthth century: professional work

A number of Middle Templars became distinguished lawyers in the course of the early decades of the nineteenth century. Eldon has already been mentioned. John Bell was one of the few people of the time to rival Eldon as a Chancery lawyer. Unlike Eldon, Bell remained at the Bar, but like

---

[25] D Hogan, *The Legal Profession in Ireland, 1789–1922* (The Incorporated Law Society of Ireland), 5. The reform of 1885 gave rise to a fractious debate in the House of Commons: *Hansard*, 3rd Series, vol 297, col 426, 22 April 1885. Examples of Irish lawyers attending the Inn (and in some cases working in England) are considered below and include Egan, Phillips and Carson. Also see Cornish *et al*, Vol XI above n 6, at 1020 (Polden).

[26] See ch 3, p 216.

[27] See ch 3, p 214.

[28] Duman, above n 19, at 16.

[29] *Ibid*.

[30] The Law Society defeated an attempt to have women admitted as solicitors in 1914: see *Bebb v Law Society* [1914] 1 Ch 286, 294 (CA). Statutory change came for solicitors and barristers with the Sex Disqualification (Removal) Act 1919.

Eldon he was instinctively conservative in legal matters and disparaged critics of established equity practice. His distrust of change rose to a climax in 1824 when he gave evidence to an inquiry into Chancery. Described as 'short, stout, and round-shouldered, with a prominent mouth and large teeth', Bell addressed the inquiry for no fewer than eight days, pouring cold water on reforming ideas.[31]

John de Grenier Fonblanque, descended from a Huguenot family in Languedoc, was called to the Bar in 1783. He developed an equity practice and was well-known for his edition of the *Treatise on Equity* ascribed to Henry Ballow. He became a bencher in 1804 and treasurer in 1815. Somewhat vain, he lived above his means and in 1809 was imprisoned 'within the rules' (in other words, was confined to an area of London) for debt, which was no bar to being appointed treasurer subsequently. His body is buried in the Temple Church and his book lived on, having an impact at 'home' and in the colonies, not least on the evolving law of contract.[32]

In respect of criminal law, Charles Phillips was one of the major criminal advocates of his day. Born in Ireland, he graduated from Trinity College Dublin in 1806 and was admitted to the Middle Temple in 1807. Called to the Irish Bar in 1812, he went on the Connaught Circuit and developed a reputation for a grand style of eloquence with explosive pace. In 1821 he was called to the English Bar and was formidably successful in criminal work. Outside the courts he was actively engaged in many of the reforming debates of the day, and had a sustained correspondence with the great law reformer and advocate Lord Brougham. His handling of the defence in 'The Corvoisier Case' aroused controversy over the permissible role of an advocate whose client has privately admitted his guilt to counsel. Was it possible to attack prosecution evidence without at least implicitly asserting the innocence of one's client?[33]

Work on private Bills in Parliament was particularly important during these years of industrial activity. Charles Austin (a brother of John Austin, the distinguished jurist) developed a national reputation as an advocate, and was said to have made a fortune out of representing 'railway entrepreneurs' seeking to extract private Acts from Parliament with a view to obtaining the

---

[31] 1764–1836; *ROA*, admitted 1787, called 1792; *ODNB*, JM Rigg, rev BF Wood; Hutchinson, above n 1, at 16–17. Bell was also admitted to Gray's Inn and Lincoln's Inn.

[32] 1759–1837; *ROA*, admitted 1777, called 1783; *ODNB*, M Lobban; Williamson, above n 6, at 199; Hutchinson, above n 1, at 94. For the impact of the book on contract law, see, eg, W Swain, 'The Classical Model of Contract: the Product of a Revolution in Legal Thought', *Legal Studies*, vol 30, no 4, December 2010, at 517–18, 520, 525, 526 fn 121. His son, John Samuel, was also a barrister and became an authority on medical jurisprudence.

[33] 1786 or 1787–1859; *ROA*, admitted 1807, called 1821; *ODNB*, DJ Cairns; extensive correspondence with Lord Brougham is preserved in the archives of University College, London; he is buried in Highgate cemetery; for the context of his advocacy see DJ Cairns, *Advocacy and the Making of the Adversarial Criminal Trial, 1800–1865* (Oxford, Oxford University Press,1998).

necessary land. It was said that in one year during the 1840s he had earned £40,000 which, to give some idea of its value at the time, was about the sum that the benchers of Lincoln's Inn had to borrow to construct their new Hall and Library. He was sometimes thought of as a future Lord Chancellor, but he had other ideas and chose instead to retire early to the Suffolk country-side. Some Victorians, emphasising duty, thought this was irresponsible; others saw it as sensible and rather more fun.[34]

Of course many successful barristers went on to become judges. Judicial appointment entailed leaving the Inn and joining Serjeants' Inn, but this did not prevent the judges identifying themselves with their 'old' Inn.[35] Sir William Bolland was notable for being able to combine success in both Old Bailey work and commercial cases. Beyond legal versatility, he was also an enthusiastic book collector with a passion for early English literature. A founder of the Roxburghe Club, he went on to support its literary publica-tions. He was a Baron of the Exchequer between 1829 and 1839.[36] A rather different character, William Draper Best, later first Baron Wynford, devel-oped an extensive practice in Common Pleas, becoming a Serjeant-at-Law in 1799. He combined this work with strong political interests, being a Whig Member of Parliament for Petersfield in 1802 and the Tory Member for Bridport in 1812. In 1818 he was appointed a Puisne Judge in King's Bench. He resigned through ill health in 1829 with the consolation of a peerage. He had severe critics who regarded him as biased (even in a judicial capacity) and self-interested. He was certainly controversial; at one time during his political career he opposed reform of the franchise in his role as a Deputy Speaker.[37]

The son of a hairdresser in Canterbury, Charles Abbott, later First Baron Tenterden, rose through a successful practice to become a judge of Common Pleas and, later, King's Bench. A high Tory in politics, his intellectual strengths were recognised, albeit that they were sometimes distorted by a bad temper. For a long time he was remembered for his dying words: he sat up in bed and said 'Gentlemen of the Jury, you are discharged'. He had never been convivial, and it may be that the members of the Middle Temple were not too distressed at the fact that he had also joined the Inner Temple in his

[34] 1799–1874; *ROA*, admitted 1823, called 1827; *ODNB*, W Rumble; Williamson, above n 6, at 219; Hutchinson, above n 1, at 9; *Fortnightly Review*, vol 23 (os) 17 (ns), March 1875, at 321–38. For the context of his Parliamentary work, see RW Kostal, *Law and English Railway Capitalism, 1825–1875* (Oxford, Oxford University Press, 1997).

[35] See above, n 1.

[36] 1771 or 1772–1840; *ROA*, admitted 1792, called 1801; *ODNB*, GFR Barker, rev Hugh Mooney; Hutchinson, above n 1, at 24.

[37] 1767–1845; *ROA*, admitted 1784, called 1789; *ODNB*, GFR Barker, rev Hugh Mooney; Hutchinson, above n 1, at 20.

youth.[38] Charles Abbott should not be confused with another member of the Inn, Charles Abbot, First Baron Colchester, who was notable for his activities as a Member of Parliament. A man of broad views and with an academic background which included a Doctorate in Civil Law from Geneva, he had a passion for historical records and administrative reform. Both interests came together when he promoted a Population Bill which established the first national census in 1801. In respect of legislation he created a rational system of annual tables so that no time-limited Act expired unnoticed.[39]

Many other judges could be mentioned. John Egan, described as a 'judge and duellist', entered the Middle Temple in 1776 and, when engaged in a case at Waterford, was involved in a duel over a point of law. At the time of the debates over the Act of Union almost all his income came from a government appointment. In his capacity as a Member of the Irish Parliament it was made clear to him that a vote in favour of the Act would be rewarded, whereas a vote against would be to his long-term detriment. This pitched him into a state of inner turmoil which he eventually resolved by condemning the proposed Act in a lively speech. He sat down knowing that his future was not assured, and indeed at his death it was said that his estate was worth 3 shillings.[40] Sir Jonathan Frederick Pollock was admitted to the Middle Temple in 1802 and called in 1807. Successful in practice at Westminster and on the Northern Circuit, he turned to politics, becoming a Tory MP. In 1844 he was appointed Lord Chief Baron of Exchequer. In the words of Rigg and Polden, 'he presided with distinction for nearly quarter of a century'. They add that 'Pollock scarcely suffered a day's illness and remained indefatigable, if sometimes sleepy, on the bench'.[41]

C. Beyond professional work: Middle Templars, reform and the written word

In addition to those who devoted themselves to professional work in the early decades of the nineteenth century, there were numerous examples of members of the Inn with an interest in reform. William Eden, First Baron

---

[38] 1762–1832; *ROA*, admitted 1787; *ODNB*, M Lobban: '... he was said to have associated less with his fellow lawyers than any man of his day'; WC Townsend, *The Lives of Twelve Eminent Judges* (London, Longman, 1846), 2, at 234–78; Hutchinson, above n 1, at 1.

[39] 1757–1829; *ROA*, admitted 1768 (*sic*), called 1783; *ODNB*, C Wilkinson; Williamson, above n 6, at 197; Hutchinson, above n 1, at 1.

[40] 1754 or 1755–1810; *ROA*, admitted 1776, thence call to the Irish Bar in 1778; *ODNB*, N Wells. Egan fought a number of duels, 'however, his warm-heartedness ensured that they were never very serious affairs'; bencher of King's Inn, 1787.

[41] 1783–1870; *ROA*, admitted 1802, called 1807; *ODNB*, JM Rigg and P Polden; Hutchinson, above n 1, at 194.

Auckland, was a penal reformer and diplomat. Deeply influenced by Blackstone's Lectures, he was the author of *The Principles of Penal Law*.[42] The book had a reflective quality and he argued that

> lenity should be the guardian of moderate government: severe penalties, the instruments of despotism, may give a sudden check to temporary evils; but they have a tendency to extend themselves to every class of crimes, and their frequency hardens the sentiment of the people.[43]

In 1799 Eden tried and failed to reform the law of adultery so as to ensure that those engaged in an act of adultery could never marry each other. He combined all this with controversial roles in Irish politics and effective initiatives in European diplomacy, and he carried his views into the early nineteenth century, being President of the Board of Trade in 1806–07.[44]

Others were direct in their response to suffering. A conveyancer with a sustained commitment to charitable work for the poor, Sir Thomas Bernard sought improvements in conditions for chimney sweeps and factory workers. As an active Governor of the London Foundling Hospital, he had striking ideas for improving the welfare of those in poverty through, amongst other projects, altering diets (more fish) and encouraging the use of allotments. The breadth of his interests may have reflected early years in America, where his father had been the colonial governor of Massachusetts and Thomas had attended Harvard University. A book of 1819 suggests in its chapter headings that he was called by Lincoln's Inn, but the text gets it right when it says

> he was called to the Bar in 1780, by the Honourable Society of the Middle Temple, but an impediment in his speech while young which the greatest care could never entirely rectify induced him to decline that line of his profession which required the constant practice of public speaking and devote himself to the more retired business of Conveyancing, in which he rapidly rose to a high degree of reputation and practice.[45]

Some linked charitable interests to campaigning work. Edward Strutt Abdy was admitted in 1813 and did not practise because of poor health. His mother's father, James Hayes, had been a bencher. Edward went to the United States of America to investigate prison reform, and became passionately involved in attacking slavery as well as the bad treatment of black people in the non slave-owning states. He developed close links with American abolitionists, played a role in the formation of the Anti-Slavery

---

[42] 1744–1814; *ROA*, admitted 1765, called 1768; *ODNB*, SM Lee.

[43] W Eden, *The Principles of Penal Law* (London, B White and Others 1771), 2 and 12.

[44] *ODNB*, SM Lee; Hutchinson, above n 1, at 82.

[45] 1750–1818; *ROA*, admitted 1772, called 1780; *ODNB*, RD Sheldon; Hutchinson, above n 1, at 19; for the book, see J Baker, *Sir Thomas Bernard* (London, John Murray, 1819), 5. Bernard also has a place in legal history as a supporter of reforms for the education of the poor.

League and was the author of the forceful social study, *Journal of a Residence and Tour in the United States of North America* (1835). It ranges widely over social problems in the USA and, by way of comparison, makes frequent references to Britain and Europe.[46] In contrast, as a politician who looked at local issues, Benjamin Bond Cabbell developed political and charitable work as a Tory MP, and was particularly involved in poor law reform. He worked with charitable organisations, including the Royal Literary Fund and the Artists' Benevolent Fund.[47]

A vivid example of those who joined the Inn at this time with little interest in legal practice and a much stronger feeling for the written word, Eaton Stannard Barrett was a poet, novelist and satirist. He was popular in his day and Jane Austen was said to read his works with pleasure. He had no respect for powerful politicians and thought that

> Men who have the courage to propagate their own praises with a solemn unblushing face, are the finest subjects for ridicule on earth …[48]

Recently there has been a revival of interest in his parodies of 'gothic' novels. His book *The Heroine* explored contemporary attitudes to law and women at the cost of fashionable romantic thought. The law has a central role in this narrative, which turned on the interpretation of fragments of a lease. There are passages where the book reaches absurdity by today's standards, but it was, to repeat the point, very popular at the time. The romantic 'Heroine' changes her name from Cherry to Cherubina, and on one occasion sets fire to a ruin leading to the possibility of a prosecution. Inevitably, given the expectations of the day, she turns to a man for rescue:

> On my pleading the prescriptive immunity of heroines, and asserting that the law could never lay its fangs on so ethereal a name as Cherubina, he solemnly swore to me, that he once knew a golden-haired, azure-eyed heroine, called Angelica Angela Angelina, who was hanged at the Old Bailey for stealing a broken lute out of a haunted chamber; and while my blood was running cold at the recital, he pressed me so cordially to take refuge in his house, that at length, I threw myself on the protection of the best of men.[49]

---

[46] 1791–1846; *ROA*, admitted 1813, not called by reason of ill health; *ODNB*, E Baigent; Hutchinson, above n 1, at 2; Abdy's *Journal of a Residence* was published in 3 vols in 1835. (London, John Murray).

[47] 1782 or 1783–1874; *ROA*, admitted 1803, called 1816; *ODNB*, GC Boase; Williamson, above n 6, at 223.

[48] *All the Talents* (London, Stockdale, 1807), Preface. His life was brief: 1786–1820; *ROA*, admitted 1805, not called; *ODNB*, JD Haigh.

[49] *The Heroine*, 3 vols (London, Henry Colburn, 1815), at 77. Generally, his work may be compared with that of Sir John Carr; *ROA*, admitted 1806, not called; Carr gave up on law for health reasons, took to travel and wrote books which many regarded as superficial. But *The Stranger in France: or a Tour from Devonshire to Paris* (London, J Johnson, 1803 and 1806) is readable and full of lively remarks on French responses to revolution. There is an electronic collection of his many poems, a lot of them devoted to fashionable ladies: *Poems of Sir John Carr*, the Project Gutenberg E Book of Poems.

It was as if some members of the Inn never stopped writing and indulging an enthusiasm for books. One treasurer of the Inn, Thomas Caldecott, left a library of such extent that on his death it took Sotheby's six days to dispose of it at auction.[50] James Boaden remained a member for 33 years without being called. He produced melodramas and musicals, and, after the loss of his private income, he also took to writing theatrical biographies, including a *Life of John Philip Kemble* in two volumes and a *Life of Mrs Siddons* in two volumes.[51] As in the case of Barrett, there has been a revival of interest in his work because, beyond biographies, some of it had gothic themes set against a background of dark castles containing romantic and much-wronged ladies.[52] A man of a very different sort, Stanley Lees Giffard was born in Ireland and became a newspaper editor in London, opposing Catholic emancipation and later the repeal of the corn laws. He was editor of the *Standard* and under his hand it became known as 'London's most reactionary voice'.[53]

Some of those who looked beyond the law defy conventional description. Thomas Reed Kemp was a daring property developer. He came from a wealthy Sussex family and was MP for Lewes at various times and Arundel once. He began the development of Kemp Town as part of the eastward expansion of Brighton, and donated the site of the Sussex County Hospital. After numerous financial difficulties, Thomas gradually declined into debt and his final years were spent in France. He died in Paris and was buried in the cemetery of Père Lachaise. His project became commercially viable at about the time of his death.[54]

D. Looking abroad: the achievement of William Wentworth

The loss of the American colonies did nothing to diminish the interest of Middle Templars in looking abroad for legal work. Sir Robert Chambers was both a judge and a jurist, with a record for innovation and achievement during his time in Bengal. He became a bencher and is buried in the

---

[50] 1744–1833; *ROA*, admitted 1767, called 1771; *ODNB*, M Spevack; Williamson, above n 6, at 199; Hutchinson, above n 1, at 41. In addition to being a barrister he was a literary editor with a strong interest in Shakespeare and a reputation for vituperative attacks on those who did not agree with views. He became treasurer of the Inn in 1814.

[51] 1762–1839; *ROA*, admitted 1793, not called; *ODNB*, JR Stephens; Hutchinson, above n 1, at 16. See J Boaden, *Life of John Philip Kemble*, 2 vols (Philadelphia, PA, Robert Small, 1825); J Boaden, *Memoirs of Mrs Siddons*, 2 vols (London, Henry Colburn, 1827).

[52] See *Dictionary of Literary Biography*, 3rd series (University of Rochester, 1989), vol 39, at 25–37.

[53] 1788–1858; *ROA*, admitted 1807, called 1811; *ODNB*, DM Griffiths; Hutchinson, above n 1, at 100. His third son became the Earl of Halsbury, lawyer, politician, Lord Chancellor and editor of *Halsbury's Laws* (but the son was not a member of the Middle Temple).

[54] 1782–1844; *ROA*, admitted 1804, not called; *ODNB*, JH Farrant.

Temple Church.[55] Active as an advocate in Calcutta in the mid-1790s, Sir Codrington Edmund Carrington was at one time junior counsel for the East India Company. After the collapse of Dutch power in Sri Lanka (then Ceylon) he was sent to the island to draw up a legal code and advise on the creation of a new judicial system. In 1801 he became Chief Justice of the Supreme Court of Judicature in Sri Lanka, but had to retire in 1805 on health grounds.[56]

Given that the British presence in Australia was very recent, it is noticeable that the Middle Temple was already becoming linked to its colonial life. The illegitimate son of a convict mother, William Charles Wentworth was born amidst all the misery of a penal transport ship. His father remained in England where he was thrice acquitted of highway robbery. Ignoring a somewhat unpromising start in life, in May 1813 William Wentworth accompanied William Lawson and Gregory Blaxland in the first notable feat of inland exploration in Australia, the crossing of the Blue Mountains. He then turned his attention to being 'the instrument of procuring a free constitution for my country' and took himself to London, where he was admitted to the Middle Temple in 1817. He engaged in numerous political debates and in 1824 was back in the colony of New South Wales. There he worked as a successful lawyer with an instinct for business and the pursuit of robust colonial politics. Arguments about the reform of the franchise in Britain, as well as current discussions about the future colonial status of Canada, made for lively ideas in an Australian context. Wentworth wanted reform, seeking an extended franchise, trial by jury and free emigration. But there were limits to his ideas about change, and 'he identified political capacity with the ownership of property and poverty with ignorance'. His chief intellectual guide was another Middle Templar, Edmund Burke, and he followed the latter's respect for the guidance afforded by history. At one time Wentworth was in negotiations for land in New Zealand, and these discussions had the potential to make him (in conjunction with his Australian properties) perhaps the world's most extensive landowner. To his frustration, the Administration in New South Wales ensured the transaction was not finalised. But his political legacy was secure. The *Australian Dictionary of Biography* points out that

> With all his apparent contradictions, more than any other man he secured our fundamental liberties and nationhood. He looked backward in many things to

---

[55]   1769–1849; *ROA*, admitted 1754, called 1761; *ODNB*, TH Bowyer: '... he was learned, virtuous, and amiable'; Williamson, above n 6, at 196; Hutchinson, above n 1, at 47–48; TM Curley, *Sir Robert Chambers: Law, Literature, and Empire in the Age of Johnson* (Madison, WI, University of Wisconsin Press,1998).

[56]   1769–1849; *ROA*, admitted 1787, called 1792; *ODNB*, TF Henderson, rev RT Stearn; Williamson, above n 6, at 212; Hutchinson, above n 1, at 45–46.

the seventeenth and eighteenth centuries; yet he built, with the strength that his sense of history gave him, for the future.[57]

Admitted to the Middle Temple in 1829 and called in 1834, Richard Windeyer became a journalist in his early years. He sailed for Sydney in 1835 and was very successful at the Bar. Elected to the first representative legislative Council in the Colony, along with William Wentworth and, later, Robert Lowe (who became Viscount Sherbrooke and a famous Victorian politician), he provided an opposition to the government of Sir George Gipps. Introducing agricultural improvements to the Hunter River area, he was one of the first to engage in the wine industry. He died insolvent but his widow managed to retain 'Tomago', his Hunter Valley residence. Through diligent work on the part of his widow, wine from the estate won a Certificate of Merit in Paris in 1855. Surely this was one of the early triumphs of the Australian grape.[58]

For these men the Middle Temple was an integral part of their determined attempt to enhance Australian autonomy through constitutional means. In one sense there was nothing new in this. They were responding to a tradition of debates about the status of the American colonies in the eighteenth century or arguments about the Act of Union and Ireland at the start of the nineteenth century. The Middle Temple was part of a system which could engender innovation at home and abroad, and, again and again, its membership had numerous interests outside practice at the Bar. At a time of rapid economic, social, and political change, Middle Templars had an active role in national and, to some extent, international life. At first sight it is paradoxical that continuity in the life of the Inn itself was combined with so much 'outside' activity on the part of its members. The paradox is resolved when one realizes the latitude which membership of the Inn provided for young men: for so long as they kept within the bounds of the Inn's not very onerous requirements, they could take their lives and their ideas in any number of directions.

---

[57] 1790–1872; *ROA*, admitted 1817, called 1822; *ODNB*, M Persse and J Ritchie; *Australian Dictionary of Biography*, M Persse. See also R Hughes, *The Fatal Shore* (London, Vintage, 1986), 461–67. After his call to the Bar, Wentworth spent some terms at Cambridge and produced a poem which is still remembered. In responding to Britain he wrote: 'May all thy glories in another sphere / Relume, and shine more brightly still than here; / May this, thy last born infant, then arise, / To glad thy heart and greet thy parent eyes; / And Australasia float, with flag unfurled, / A new Britannia in another world.'

[58] 1806–1847; *ROA*, admitted 1829, called 1834; *ODNB*, JB Windeyer; *Australian Dictionary of Biography*, James B Windeyer. Note too James Ebenezer Bicheno (1785–1851); *ROA*, admitted 1816, called 1822; *ODNB*, AGL Shaw; *Australian Dictionary of Biography*, Anon. He had an intellectual interest in the law, writing on criminal jurisprudence. His commitments went beyond this into research on botany and the Irish economy, and in 1827 he became a Fellow of the Royal Society. In 1842 he was made Colonial Secretary for Van Dieman's Land (Tasmania) and proved to be an efficient conservative. In 1848 he presided over the first public exhibition of pictures in Australia. On his death he left about 2,500 books to the Tasmanian Public Library.

II. THE SECOND PHASE: THE DEMAND FOR REFORM—1845–75

Writing in 1870, the constitutional authority Walter Bagehot commented that in the last twenty years 'A vague feeling ran through society that the Inns of Court did not "look right"'. He added that 'if you wanted to prove their usefulness the argument was difficult'.[59]

The problem lay in the reference to 'usefulness'. The idea that an Inn had to account for itself in terms of its utility to public opinion came as a shock to many barristers used to thinking that the role of the Inn was self-evident. The demands of utility, linked to the whole philosophy of utilitarianism, raised awkward questions. Could the Inn regard itself as a private club and simply ignore criticism about its professional role? This was never a possibility, because some barristers were themselves interested in reform and sought to justify their profession to the public at large. For them an organisation which was one of the routes to professional qualification could claim to have private activities but it could not be regarded as exclusively private. Yet to concede the latter point was to invite sustained and detailed questions about the public role of the Inn.[60]

Informed criticism was inescapable. Charles Dickens, admitted to the Middle Temple in 1839, remained an uncalled member until he had his name taken off the books in 1855.[61] *Bleak House* appeared in parts in 1852, was published as a book in 1853 and has often been seen as a sustained attack on the legal profession as a whole. Dickens could write with charm about, say, the beauties of Fountain Court, but he never relented in his criticism of some of the ways of the Bar, and he had scant regard for the process of qualification. In the *Uncommercial Traveller* he wrote of

> preparing for the Bar—which is done, as everybody knows, by having a frayed old gown put on in a pantry by an old woman in a chronic state of St Anthony's Fire and dropsy, and, so decorated, bolting a bad dinner in a party of four, whereof each individual mistrusts the other three ...[62]

Grievances within the profession made this a difficult time for the Bar as a whole. Statistics on those who qualified as barristers have to be treated

---

[59] W Bagehot, (1870) 7 *Fortnightly Review* 687.

[60] For the difficult context in which the Inns of these years were working, see R Cocks, *Foundations of the Modern Bar* (London, Sweet & Maxwell, 1983), chs 4 and 5.

[61] *ROA* and HHL Bellot, *The Temple*, 3rd edn (London, Methuen, 1925), at195: 'He does not appear ever to have occupied chambers in the Temple, of which he has displayed such intimate knowledge in his works. He was never called to the Bar, and in 1855 he withdrew his name from the books of the Inn.'

[62] C Dickens, *The Uncommercial Traveller* (London, 1860), ch XIV, 'Chambers'. Dickens was particularly critical of Gray's Inn. In the same essay he remarked on 'having occasion to transact some business with a solicitor who occupies a highly suicidal set of chambers in Gray's Inn, I afterwards took a turn in the large square of that stronghold of Melancholy'.

with caution when used as a guide to the realities of practice; we have seen that a fair number of early Victorian admissions never intended to make a livelihood out of the profession and that this had changed by the 1840s. Given that the total number of barristers from all the Inns increased from about 2,500 in 1835 to about 7,250 in 1885, it is likely that the number of working barristers also increased considerably.[63] According to one contemporary observer there was a particularly sudden change between 1835 and 1845 when the qualified numbers at the Bar went, he argues, from 1,300 to 2,317.[64] At about the same time there were pressures on the volume of work available. The creation of the county courts in 1846 opened up opportunities for solicitors and thereby deprived barristers at the start of their career of much of the type of work that their predecessors had enjoyed.[65] *Punch* made jokes at the expense of 'Mr Briefless'.[66] The new *Law Times* was pessimistic about the long-term prospects of the profession.[67] Such a context was likely to breed criticism of the Inns whether or not they were at fault, and helps to account for views such as those of Walter Bagehot. If the Inns were not protecting the Bar and the provision of justice, what were they for? Certainly, the pessimism had an impact on admissions in the 1850s. We have seen that between 1840 and 1849 the intake for the Inn was 855. This slumped to 410 between 1850 and 1859.[68] Thereafter it picked up sharply to 1,018 and 1,141 respectively for the 1860s and 1870s.[69] In short, within the Inn the focal point of pessimism and alarm was the 1850s.

In addition to a lack of work for barristers, legal education became a point of concern. It was widely believed in Parliament and elsewhere that the Inns of the day had forsaken their duty to educate. For many barristers, too, the present educational arrangements were an embarrassment. The era when the Inns could be regarded as the 'Third University of England' was long over.[70] Now it was argued that the country could hardly stand comparison with the achievements of legal education on the Continent and in America. In the course of the 1830s and early 1840s there were increasing demands for reform, with discomforting references being made

---

[63] The size of the working Bar is a perplexing problem, not least because the Victorians did not agree on the numbers amongst themselves: see Duman, above n 19, at 6–9.

[64] S Warren, *A Popular and Practical Introduction to Law Studies*, 3rd edn (Edinburgh and London, William Blackwood, 1863), vol 1, at 2.

[65] On the importance of the county courts generally to the Victorians, see P Polden, *A History of the County Court, 184 –1971* (Cambridge, Cambridge University Press, 1999).

[66] July–December 1851, at 65.

[67] (1852) 19 LT 57; and see (1853) 22 LT 61.

[68] *ROA*, above n 1.

[69] *Ibid.*

[70] JH Baker, *The Third University of England: the Inns of Court and the Common-Law Tradition* (London, Selden Society, 1990), 21: 'By the eighteenth century no one could seriously compare the inns of court with a university ...'

to improved arrangements for prospective lawyers elsewhere. In response, initiatives took place at, for example, the new University College in London and the Inner Temple, where at one time lectureships were established. But these reforms failed to produce major change.[71]

In the mid-1840s reformers within the Inns became more forceful. It was well-known that some of these men, such as Brougham (Lincoln's Inn) and Bethell (later, as we saw at the start of this chapter, Lord Westbury and a member of the Middle Temple), were successful in practice and politically influential, and had to be taken seriously. In 1845 an anonymous article attributed to Brougham called for the creation of a Law University.[72] In the same year Bethell ensured that the Middle Temple set up a committee to consider the provision of lectures in civil law and jurisprudence. Subsequently he received unanimous support from his fellow benchers of the Middle Temple for the creation of a lectureship, and took the proposal to a joint committee of three of the Inns. By January of 1846 the Middle Temple was committed to appointing a reader in civil law and jurisprudence, and making attendance at lectures a prerequisite for call. This approach did not endure across all four Inns (chiefly because of resistance at that time from Lincoln's Inn). But the reformers, and in particular Bethell from his base in the Middle Temple, did not give up and were soon to have external support. In 1846 there was talk of setting up a Parliamentary Select Committee to consider Irish legal education in Dublin which had run into funding difficulties. This gave a platform to the radical politician Henry Warburton, who succeeded in broadening its remit to include England.[73] Before the end of 1846 the reformers were making strong representations to the Committee and receiving a sympathetic response. The Committee concluded that there was an urgent need for the reform of English legal education.

New teaching appointments were made but, as before, with mixed results in terms of general coordination across the Inns. In 1851 the Solicitor General of the day convened a meeting of all four Inns of Court. This produced the Council of Legal Education, which was to be administered by eight members made up of two from each Inn selected by their respective benchers. Attendance at the lectures was compulsory unless candidates took a voluntary examination. The reform produced a notable

---

[71] See CW Brooks and M Lobban, 'Apprenticeship or Academy? The Idea of a Law University, 1830–1860' in J Bush and A Wijffels (eds), *Learning the Law* (London, Hambledon Press, 1999), 353; and JH Baker, *Legal Education in London: 1250–1850* (London, Selden Society, 2007).

[72] (1844) 1 *Law Review* 345.

[73] Select Committee on Legal Education, *Parliamentary Papers*, 1846 (686). See B Abel-Smith and R Stevens, *Lawyers and the Courts* (London, Heinemann, 1967), 63–76; Cocks, above n 60, chs 2 and 3; generally on the reform of legal education see Cornish *et al*, above n 6, at 1175–1222 (M Lobban).

result at the Middle Temple, where a new reader in jurisprudence was to be attached to the Inn. The position went to the young Henry Maine.[74] After a brilliant career at Cambridge both as an undergraduate and (at the age of 26) the Professor of Civil Law, Maine had engaged in limited forms of practice at the Bar (both common law and chancery) and was increasingly active in writing for the 'quality' press of the day. After his appointment he went on to give lectures which had a famous literary result. Grant Duff, later a senior administrator, was present and wrote:

> The public lectures were given in the beautiful hall of the Middle Temple, one of the noblest rooms in London … Maine was a most admirable lecturer; his voice was exceptionally powerful, his style like crystal and every sentence perfectly finished. As to the scientific value of the lectures which he read, it is enough to say that the expressed essence of several courses was afterwards given to the world in Ancient Law.[75]

Maine's book, *Ancient Law, its Connection with the Early History of the Society and its Relation to Modern Ideas*, published by Murray in 1861, has an important place in the history of the Inn. The book was to sell very well, not least in pirated editions. It has been argued that Maine 'wrote the only legal best seller of that, or perhaps any other century'.[76] History, particularly when it was understood in evolutionary terms, had a strong resonance with a Victorian audience. Maine was not significantly influenced by Darwin's work. But for a reader looking for an analysis of social and legal change he provided numerous explanations in broadly evolutionary terms. In particular this applied to his identification of progressive change as a movement from status to contract. Using the language of today, one might say that Maine explained law in social terms and gave guidance to a generation worried by the incessant changes produced by economic and social upheaval. There is a case for saying that the Middle Temple Hall was of particular importance because his audience probably had an impact on what he wrote. The lectures gave an opportunity for questions and the students—their minds fortified by the attendance of a waiter serving wine—would surely have asked questions. In particular

---

[74] R Cocks, 'That Exalted and Noble Science of Jurisprudence': The Recruitment of Jurists with "Superior Qualifications' by the Middle Temple in the Mid-Nineteenth Century' (1999) 20(2) *The Journal of Legal History* 62. There had been previous appointments for three other people but they had not 'lasted'. Discussions about legal education by the benchers include those recorded at: MT 1/MPA, 16 April 1847, at 13, 7 May 1847, at 16, 28 May 1847, at 23, 19 November 1847, at 34–35. Lincoln's Inn objecting to the provision of compulsory lecturers was noted at: MT 1/MPA, 20 April 1849, at 71. A concern for achieving a uniform approach from all the Inns may be seen at MT 1/MPA, 9 February 1852, at 175–80.

[75] Sir ME Grant Duff, *Life and Speeches of Sir Henry Maine: a Brief Memoir* (New York, Henry Holt, 1892), 13–14.

[76] AWB Simpson, 'Contract: the Twitching Corpse' (1981) 1 *Oxford Journal of Legal Studies* 265, at 268.

Maine had things to say about what law could and could not do to encourage or hold back social change. He could be particularly incisive in considering law in India, and this would be interesting to those in his audience who had strong links with the sub-continent as prospective civil servants and judges. At this time these people were Europeans—we shall see that indigenous Indian membership 'came through' towards the end of the century. It might be said that he was providing an intellectual context for an Inn with increasingly strong overseas links. Viewed in an international perspective these lectures were, surely, the most distinguished cultural achievement of the nineteenth- century Middle Temple. In their day they were to have a world-wide resonance, and the quality of Maine's prose still has few rivals in legal literature.[77]

Maine was exceptional. In general terms the achievements of the new Council of Legal Education were not sufficient to satisfy critics of the Inns. In the House of Commons it was pointed out that the old Universities had been investigated and now it was time for the Inns to be given 'the same process of purification'.[78] The result was a Royal Commission on the Inns.[79] Appointed in 1854, its membership included a number of radicals such as Bethell. The Commissioners soon made it clear that they were in no mood to avoid painful issues. Charged to 'inquire into the arrangements of the Inns of Court and Inns of Chancery for promoting the study of the law and jurisprudence', and a number of associated issues, they were not much impressed by arguments about barristers learning exclusively through work, although they saw that pupillage was important. Equally, they were not persuaded that eating dinners in the company of other lawyers was a substitute for education, although, as with pupillage, they saw that it was important. After due deliberation they also did not think that the new requirements at the Council of Legal Education were going to be sufficient.

Exploring these issues led the Commissioners to the belief that the Inns had diverted funds from educational purposes. But when it came to details, witnesses pointed out that the notion that the Inns were under some fiduciary or other duty to provide an education was open to argument.

---

[77] On Maine's lectures, see R Cocks, 'Who Attended the Lectures of Sir Henry Maine: and Does it Matter?' in Bush and Wijffels (eds), above n 71, at 383–96. On Maine generally, see G Feaver, *From Status to Contract* ((London, Longmans,1969); R Cocks, *Sir Henry Maine* (Cambridge, Cambridge University Press, 1988 and 2004); N O'Brien, '"Something Older then Law itself": Sir Henry Maine, Niebuhr, and "the path not chosen"' (2005) 26(3) *Journal of Legal History* 229; N O'Brien, 'In Vino Veritas: Truth and Method in Vinogradoff's Historical Jurisprudence', (2008) 29(1) *Journal of Legal History* 39.

[78] *Hansard*, 1 March 1854, 3rd Series, col 150.

[79] The Royal Commissioners were appointed 'to inquire into the arrangements in the Inns of Court for promoting the Study of the Law and Jurisprudence, the Revenues properly applicable, and the means most likely to secure a systematic and sound education for Students of Law, and provide satisfactory Tests of fitness for Admission to the Bar': *Royal Commission on the Inns of Court and Inns of Chancery, PP 1854–55* (1998).

Gray's Inn and Lincoln's Inn had no binding obligation in this regard, and at best it applied to only part of the income for the Inner and Middle Temples. It was in this setting that on 21 June 1854 Charles Whitehurst, QC, then treasurer of the Middle Temple, was examined at length by the Commissioners. In considering income he first pointed to the 'Chambers and Buildings, a considerable part of which were purchased by the Society, and the remainder they hold under a grant of James I'. The property which came with the latter grant was, he thought, already in the possession of the Inn before the grant. Matters were made more intricate by reason of the fact that at first this property was held by both the Inner and Middle Temples when it was owned jointly, with particular portions appropriated to each Inn. In his own words, in 1732 all the Real Property

> with the exception of a very small portion (in fact out of the Temple) was conveyed to trustees upon the same uses and trusts as are specified in the grant of James. They vary, indeed, a little, though I think only in one word. The Trusts of that Deed of partition, which is in English, were 'to serve, and be employed for the entertaining, education, and habitation of the Students and Professors of the Law residing within the Temple'.

He went on to say:

> The words of the Grant of James are for 'the habitation and education,' the difference being in the introduction of the word 'entertaining'.[80]

At its most extreme, these and other references to education could have opened up arguments which might force the Inn into a dispute in Chancery, but the Commissioners did not press these arguments very far. In their final report they founded the obligations of all the Inns on two principles: 'The Student is compelled to have recourse (to an Inn of Court) before he can practise at the Bar'; which led inevitably to a 'duty which the Inns of Court owe to the community whilst conferring on individuals the right of practising at the Bar'.[81]

At the end of the day the precise arguments about a duty to educate were unlikely to be of primary importance. At this time enough people within all four of the Inns believed that whatever the law on the matter, more should be done by way of legal education. For such people the central question was how rich were the Inns? Did they have enough money to fund a legal University? Certainly, the Commissioners were insistent in inquiring after the wealth of the Middle Temple. For example, they wanted to know about the letting of chambers. Whitehurst pointed out that income from chambers could vary from year to year and was restricted by the entitlement of

---

[80] *Ibid*, Evidence of Charles Whitehurst, Esq, QC, at 64, question 456.
[81] *Ibid*, at 13.

some occupiers to enjoy their rooms for life. In respect of the latter, no more such arrangements were being permitted and

> when those lives fall in, all the Chambers in the Inn will become the property of the Society, except 26 sets of Chambers, which are called the Benchers' Chambers, and are appropriated to the Benchers.[82]

Whitehurst was challenged specifically on the possibility that chambers in general were let out at below a market rate. He responded saying what was well-known:

> The Chambers in the Middle Temple are in a very wretched condition; they are very old, and must almost all come down; ... every year we are merely delaying it to seek the most convenient opportunity of taking them down, and also for getting funds for the purpose; they are almost all of them in a very bad state.[83]

Questions then shifted to the role of the benchers. The mode of election was given as being 'by open election, by a majority'.[84] The substantial fees they paid the Inn were explored.[85] Lesser sums were paid by those 'who were not silk gowns'. (In an incidental aside the treasurer remarked that 'the Stuff gowns at our Inn' were 'seldom called to the Bench much under forty years standing after admission to the Inn, or before approaching seventy years of age'.[86]) The other charges required by the Inn had an intricate history at this time, but in 1854 it could be said that

> Each person when admitted to the Society, pays £7 10s for fines and fees, and £2 10s to the Library, making £10 which includes all payments.

Beyond these sums a

> student pays one guinea per Term when dining, which entitles him to dine six times, and he pays 2s 6d for each day he dines beyond the six.[87]

Looking beyond fees, the Commissioners wanted to know about 'funded property'. They were told that it then consisted of '£44,755, 5s, 3 per cent Consols, and £15,000 Consols'.[88] As soon as he had said this the treasurer stressed the inadequacy of these sources for the Inn's needs and returned to the challenge presented by the condition of chambers:

---

[82] *Ibid*, at 65, question 468.
[83] *Ibid*, at 65, question 470.
[84] *Ibid*, at 65, question 473.
[85] 'The Queen's Counsel pay upon admission £352; those who are not Queen's Counsel £252; they pay £331 and £231 respectively upon their being made Benchers; then, when they are made Readers, which is always shortly afterwards, they each pay £21 more; of these sums, respectively £10 is paid towards the Library, £42 for Entertainments, and the remainder in Fines'; *ibid*, at 65–66, question 474.
[86] *Ibid*, at 66, question 477.
[87] *Ibid*, at 67, question 491; and at 70, question 517.
[88] *Ibid*, at 66, question 478.

GOLDSMITH'S TOMB IN 1860

Goldsmith's Tomb, showing the dilapidated state of buildings in the Temple in 1860

[W]e are rather lying by till we can get entire stacks of Chambers at our disposal, and until we have accumulated quite sufficient to make ourselves safe, in case that in pulling one stack down, another should come down with it. In all probability, if we were now to take a stack down upon an estimate of £20,000, £30,000, or £40,000, we should find that two or three other stacks would come down also, being merely kept standing by supporting each other, and these must be rebuilt.[89]

[89]   *Ibid.*

In substance the Treasurer was arguing that the Inn had little capacity for any novel initiatives because of the likely need to spend large sums on rebuilding chambers. The condition of chambers comes through again and again as a theme to Victorian debates about the Inn.

When the questions moved from income to everyday 'disbursements' the Treasurer was able to point in a gloomy way to one inescapable source of expenditure after another. In 1850, for example, the librarian and his assistant were paid a total of £217 12s 8d, and book purchases amounted to £215 18s 11d. Provision for the church was complicated, involving both the Temples and requiring additional resource because 'Mr Rowlett, the late Reader, retired upon rather more than his full pension …'. From the Middle Temple the organist had £80 a year, plus an extra payment of £25, and the marble polisher £35; and many other liabilities arose, including those for 'dusting the columns', to say nothing of major repairs. The officers' salaries, not including the librarian or reader or preacher, amounted to £2,795. The sub-treasurer received £600 a year and chambers, the treasurer £100. A long list of those in receipt of lesser sums included annual payments to a laundress (£22), eleven watchmen (£330 in total), fourteen waiters (£280 in total) and a rubbish carter (£30). More generally there were rates and taxes, some of which were regarded as unfair:. 'Last year the Police rate was £433 6s 8d. We derive no benefit from that. We do not admit the Police to come in.'[90] Beyond this there were repairs to the knives and forks in the Hall.

Whitehurst spoke for the conservatives at the Inn:

> Some of the very best, and first advocates of the English Bar, were no lawyers; they were very ignorant of Law. The Profession must be looked at, not as a mere profession of jurisconsults, to advise. The Inns of Court are rather considered as places where people are educated to be Advocates.[91]

He saw a need for some changes, but in his view there was no need for radical educational reform. Given the standing of other witnesses (which included Henry Maine) the treasurer's educational views were unlikely to be decisive, but what he had done was emphatically to disappoint anyone who thought that the Middle Temple was in a position to support change with a large amount of money. For the most part this view was supported by the information from the other Inns. In their final report the Commissioners used the accounts for 1854, and they do not reveal the wealth some of the reformers had hoped for. In respect of income the situation was not promising: Middle Temple, £10,192 10s 7d (with outgoings of £10,191 13s 9d); Inner Temple, £21,168 16s 0d (with outgoings of £15,945 0s 10d); Lincoln's Inn, £18,242 12s 3d (with outgoings of £14,345 8s 2d); and

---

[90] *Ibid*, at 68, questions 499, 500, 502; and at 69, question 505.
[91] *Ibid*, at 70, question 524.

Gray's Inn, £8,343 4s 8d (with outgoings of £8,717 9s 3d).[92] The tables did not claim to be wholly accurate. Gray's Inn, for instance, had an additional income of £773 from the renewal of certain leases. Even in so far as they were correct, they had to be read with an awareness of other outgoings; we saw above that Lincoln's Inn had to repay a debt which then stood at £40,000 incurred when building the new Hall and Library. Taking all in all, those in search of radical change had not discovered a pot of gold to support novel educational initiatives.

In part the Commissioners responded by expressing the hope that over the years the Inns would extract themselves from uneconomic arrangements, particularly in the letting of chambers. After all, the Commissioners observed, the Inns did occupy very valuable sites. Despite their failure to unearth wealth, in regard to education the final recommendation at the end of their Report was adventurous. The Commissioners deemed

> it advisable that there shall be established a preliminary Examination for Admission to the Inns of Court of persons who have not taken a University Degree; and that there shall be Examinations, the passing of which shall be requisite for the Call to the Bar; and that the four Inns of Court shall be united in one University for the purpose of these Examinations, and of conferring Degrees.[93]

In more detail, the constituent members were to be 'The Chancellor, Barristers-at-Law, and Masters of Laws', and there would be a Senate with 32 members. In respect of the latter, eight members would be elected by each Inn, with five being benchers and elected by benchers and three being barristers elected by barristers (exclusive of the benchers) of the Inn to which they belonged.[94]

The proposal for a 'legal' university remained a part of Victorian debate but it never came near to fruition:

> For sixty years after the Inns of Court Commission there was an ongoing debate about the professional education of lawyers, punctuated by proposals to give it a more 'scientific' basis.[95]

The demand for innovation nevertheless did something to ensure that the Council of Legal Education was sustained, because so many saw a clear need for some organised form of instruction. The Council did put on some novel courses, including those on the laws of the Indian sub-continent. But its comparative weakness was revealed in the way that it was possible for a prospective barrister to avoid any examination in law until 1872; and when the examinations did become compulsory, contemporaries were at pains to emphasise that they were not very demanding. For traditionalists

---

[92]   Ibid, at 6.
[93]   Ibid, at 17.
[94]   Ibid, at 17.
[95]   Cornish *et al*, Vol. XI, above n 6, at 1186 (Lobban).

it was the least objectionable response to the demands for change. But the reformers never gave up, and there were some lively debates in Parliament. In 1872 Lord Selborne renewed the attack on the Inns by seeking the establishment of a new, large and powerful law school in London which would be outside the control of the Inns and more effective than any of the country's existing law schools:

> We have been going on a great deal too long upon the system of allowing this matter to take care of itself, leaving it in the hands of irresponsible bodies who acknowledge no public trust, who are under no public constitution, who are not even incorporated; and who, if they had been much better organized than they are, have not shown themselves in past times capable of doing the necessary work in this respect.[96]

In short, a number of well-known Victorian lawyers remained unrelenting in their criticisms of the Inns.

A.   Sustaining the Inn in an era of reform

Having condemned the state of chambers, the novelist Thackeray went on to give a brighter account of dining in Hall, although in doing so he also revealed the chasm between those barristers who had money and those who were poor.[97] In general terms his account of dining is corroborated by at least one professional source.[98] In any event, the barristers of these years were not wholly obsessed with issues of reform. In the mid-1860s they were as happy to discuss wine, as they had been when Crabb Robinson had been called to the Bar in 1813. On 19 May 1865 the Inn established a rule with a view to calming passions, whereby

> the selection of wine to be used by any Mess, be decided by the Majority of the votes of the members, and in case of equal numbers of votes, the senior of the Mess to have a double or second vote.[99]

The 1850s saw a dramatic architectural initiative with the construction of a new library. Under the direction of HR Abraham, it was built on a space to the south of the Hall and proved to be an adventure in gothic revival. On its south side the new building had an oriel window which, it

---

[96]   *Hansard*, HC Deb, vol CCIX, ser 3, col 1230 (1 March 1872). For similar examples of attempts at reform, see Abel-Smith and Stevens, above n 73, at 63–76. Although the strength of the reformers waned in the final decades of the century, they never gave up.

[97]   Thackeray, above n 15, ch XXX. For Thackeray see also above n 17.

[98]   WG Thorpe, *Middle Temple Table Talk* (London, Hutchinson, 1894). For a possible difference of view on how Messes were constituted, see fn. 15.

[99]   *Rules and Orders of the Honourable Society of the Middle Temple for the Conduct of Business at their Parliaments and Committees and Generally for the Good Government of the House*, 2nd edn (London, 1896), 19 May 1865, 154.

was said, jutted out above the Thames, then taking its wide pre-embankment course through London. The library was opened in 1861 by the Prince of Wales, whose appearance was a reminder of the Inn's long association with royalty. In later years it was not regarded as the most efficient of buildings but it was certainly distinctive. For the Inn it was, surely, the most notable building of the nineteenth century. Unfortunately, it was so badly bombed in the early years of the Second World War that it became unsafe and the ruins were removed after the end of hostilities.[100]

In a less dramatic way, it was in the 1850s that barristers also became interested in the installation of water closets. The existing arrangements had their own rules. For example, the Inn's gardener had had various duties under a rule of 27 November 1818, and these included the requirement that

> he do also keep clean the privy belonging to the Barristers and Students of the Society, and as much as possible prevent improper persons from entering into and using the same.[101]

This sort of arrangement was hardly satisfactory for the modern age. Mr Hurrell and Mr Heath of No 1 Pump Court told the benchers that they 'suffer very great inconvenience and annoyance from the want of a Water Closet in or near their Chambers'.[102] Permission to construct one was given, albeit at the considerable cost of £25. Later, decisions on the construction of water closets were delegated to a Chambers Committee, with the restriction that the occupant or tenant had to pay at least 10 per cent of the expense.[103] The building of lavatories around the Inn surely had an influence on everyday living conditions.

On occasion the benchers were driven to manifest annoyance. In 1850 they had to consider allegations of fraud against a member of the Inn in relation to the discharge of a judgment debt:

> The Masters of the Bench are desirous of finding something in the previous conduct of the said Augustus Newton which could justify them in taking a milder course on the present occasion but considering that he was in the year 1845 subjected to the animadversions of the Bench for malpractice and punished by a lenient sentence on that occasion which does not seem to have had the desired effect and that his defence on the present occasion is rather an aggravation than an exculpation the Masters of the Bench here assembled in

---

[100] See *Middle Temple: A Guide*, above n 5, at 31–37.
[101] *Rules and Orders of the Honourable Society of the Middle Temple for the Conduct of Business at their Parliaments and Committees and Generally for the Good Government of the House*, 2nd edn (London, 1896).
[102] MT 1/MPA, 10 June, 1853, at 242. See, too, MT 1/MPA, 28 January 1853, at 218.
[103] MT 1/MPA, 21 January 1859, at 140.

Parliament consider it is their bounded duty to determine and adjudge that the Call to the Bar of the said Augustus Newton in this House be forthwith vacated ...[104]

This was not the last the Inn heard of Mr Newton. Between 1861 and 1863, Digby Seymour QC, MP had his professional conduct reviewed by the benchers. Three allegations involved business transactions, and in a fourth it was suggested that he had taken briefs for an attorney as a way of repaying money he owed to the attorney. The latter, it was pointed out, was likely to deprive the attorney's clients of the freedom they were entitled to expect in the choice of counsel. The benchers could not agree on the first three issues and only the last one 'stuck', but this did not lead to the withdrawal of his call to the Bar. The case became a national issue, with allegations of professional jealousy and inappropriate political behaviour in his constituency of Southampton. The issues have been looked at in detail by W Wesley Pue. He reveals that one of Digby's champions in the press was an A Newton, and it seems fair to assume that the latter was Augustus and that he was out to embarrass the benchers.[105]

One difficulty encountered by the benchers was to increase in the decades to come. In the course of these years they had to deal with more applications from members living abroad who were seeking modifications to their attendance requirements. For example, there was a slight adjustment allowed for John David Bell who was at the Calcutta Bar.[106] After some difficulty, Paul Francois Osrar, 'a colonist from the Island of Mauritius', was allowed a similar request.[107] And so on. In an *ad hoc* fashion, the Middle Temple was taking on an increasingly international role.

B.   The mid-Victorian membership: intellectual commitments

The reforming barristers of these years often went on to distinguished careers. Hugh McCalmont Cairns, First Earl Cairns (1819–85), was a law student in Dublin in 1839. Admitted to Lincoln's Inn in 1841, he moved to the Middle Temple in 1844 and was called in the same year. He had to cope with being a life-long asthmatic. A Tory and devout low-churchman with strong Irish Protestant links, he was a successful lawyer and Chair of the Judicature Commission of 1867–69 on appellate jurisdictions. He sought major changes in legal education and was unusual in wanting to

---

[104]   MT 1/MPA, 6 May 1850, 17 May 1850, at 102–10. See further below, Woolley's 'The Inn as a Disciplinary Body', at p 357.

[105]   WW Pue, 'Moral Panic at the English Bar: Paternal vs Commercial Ideologies of Legal Practice in the 1860s' (1990) 15(1) *Law and Social Enquiry, Journal of the American Bar Foundation* 49, particularly at 96–102.

[106]   MT 1/MPA, 20 April 1848, at 48.

[107]   MT 1/MPA, 3 November 1848, at 59.

focus on giving the existing Universities a greater role. As a Member of Parliament he was heavily involved in debates about India, Ireland and extensions of the franchise. He became Lord Chancellor twice (holding office in 1868 and between 1874 and 1880). Viscount Bryce thought he was the greatest of Victorian judges.[108] He was a clear example of a reforming lawyer who was both practical and strongly intellectual.

Given the extent of the concern about legal education, it was predictable that the Inn would produce experts in this area. Andrew Amos was admitted to the Inn in 1832. Born in Calcutta, with a father in the East India Company and a Swiss mother, he had an international outlook. At Eton he was quaintly remarkable for being 'Shelley's only friend'. He developed a practice on the Midland Circuit, but his heart was in education and law reform. In 1832 he was appointed the first Professor of English Law at University College London. In the 1830s he served on Criminal Law Commissions and in 1837 he succeeded Macaulay as a member of the Governor-General's Council in India. Active as President of the Indian Law Commission, on his return he was appointed one of the new county court judges and elected Downing Professor of the Laws of England at Cambridge in 1848.

There was an equally intellectual quality to the lives of many other barristers at this time. James Hannen attended the University of Heidelberg and became a 'lifelong Germanophile with a taste for philosophy'.[109] His reputation survives to this day as a lawyer who developed a strong commercial practice. Appointed a judge of Queen's Bench in 1868, he became President of 'Probate, Divorce and Admiralty' in 1875 and a 'Law Lord' in 1891. Patrick Polden has pointed out that when presiding over the divorce court,

> he imposed his notions of rules and practice with unarguable decisiveness and maintained an evenness of temper (the product of self-discipline rather than a natural gift) which made him, for many, the embodiment of the judicial ideal.[110]

He was elected a Bencher in 1878, and a portrait may be found in the Middle Temple.[111]

In terms of intellectual energy, few could rival Sir Robert Joseph Phillimore. Admitted an Advocate of Doctors' Commons in 1839 and called to the Bar at the Middle Temple in 1841, he became a QC and a bencher in 1858. In the words of Williamson

---

[108] 1819–85; *ROA*, admitted 1844, called 1844 having already been a member of Lincoln's Inn but not called by Lincoln's Inn; *ODNB*, D Steele; Hutchinson, above n 1, at 40.

[109] 1821–94; *ROA*, admitted 1841, called 1848; *ODNB*, P Polden.

[110] *ODNB*, P Polden.

[111] Hutchinson, above n 1, at 108. Picture in Middle Temple: TB Wirgman, oils, 1890; Williamson, above n 6, at 245.

as Lent Reader 1861 on 29 January he read in Hall a paper on 'The Laws of Different States respecting Majority and Minority, and the patria potestas'; and again on the expiration of his office as Reader in May 1861 he read in Hall a paper on 'Jurisdiction', founded on the early part of Donellus. Although different from the ancient public readings, being merely lectures not followed by discussion, he thus revived an interest in the ancient custom of reading and set a precedent which has been followed by later Readers in the twentieth century.

The last judge of the High Court of Admiralty, in 1875 Robert Phillimore was appointed to what was then the Probate Divorce and Admiralty Division of the High Court, with Hannen (above) as its President. A Liberal conservative, as a Member of Parliament he was frequently involved in debates on church law. With CF Jemmett he published a monumental work of 2,466 pages on the latter subject.[112]

His relative, John George Phillimore (1808–65), was well-known for intellectual combativeness. Admitted to Lincoln's Inn in 1828, he became linked to the Middle Temple when, in 1851, he was appointed its Reader in Civil Law and Jurisprudence. A highly controversial figure in his day, with a commitment to codification and an emotional distrust of the common law, he was much involved in educational debates in the middle of the century. His hostile view of the common law was sometimes expressed in terms which were almost insulting, and it is not surprising that he was replaced by Henry Maine when the post was re-advertised.[113] An altogether more moderate man with intellectual interests, Sir John Richard Quain was admitted to the Inn in 1837, and from 1841 was working as a special pleader in the Chambers of Thomas Chitty before being called in 1851. Irish born, and educated at University College London and Göttingen, he had an international outlook. After developing a successful practice on the Northern Circuit, he became a bencher of the Middle Temple in 1866 and a judge of Queen's Bench in 1871. He died in 1876 and left a substantial bequest for legal education.[114]

It is possible to mention others with similar cerebral interests, and by themselves these mid-Victorian barristers reveal the extent to which a member of the Inn at this time could feel at ease in developing theoretical views on contentious legal topics. The Inn was playing a leading role in an era of legal reform and adventurous thought. If everyone had explored ideas like these people, the Inn could hardly have continued to administer itself. The dedication of members such as Whitehurst, with his defence of

[112] 1810–85; *ROA*, admitted 1837, called 1841; *ODNB*, N Doe; Hutchinson, above n 1, at 190; Williamson, above n 6, at 227.

[113] See generally Cocks, above n 74.

[114] 1816–76; *ROA*, admitted 1837, called 1851; *ODNB*, JA Hamilton, rev P Polden; Hutchinson, above n 1, at 281; Williamson, above n 6, at 234.

the Inn before the Royal Commissioners, produced the sort of work that was essential to the Inn's survival at this time. It is as if there were two types of mid-Victorian members: those with a commitment to law as a form of intellectual enquiry, and those whose almost exclusive focus was on everyday professional activity.

C.   Mid-Victorian members and national life

This era of reform could have a sharp edge, with radical ideas going far beyond arguments about the education of barristers. Edmund Beales was called to the Bar by the Inn in 1830, and developed a practice as an equity draftsman and conveyancer. He combined his professional work with a commitment to supporting movements promoting European and American democracy. He also supported the earliest demonstrations on behalf of refugees from Poland. By the middle of the century he had a national political reputation and was an obvious choice for membership of the committee which organised the welcome of the republican Garibaldi on his visit to London. When enlargement of the franchise was a major political issue in the 1860s, Beales became President of the Reform League which was dedicated to seeking universal male suffrage. He was central to the organisation of the large demonstrations, which caused major problems for the preservation of order in London and which culminated in a confrontation in Hyde Park at a meeting that got out of control. Soon afterwards the Home Secretary of the day felt obliged to resign. Many Victorians feared an insurrection. Beales, having done much to cause the problem, subsequently assisted with the restoration of more orderly forms of debate; and after Disraeli's Reform Bill of 1867 he dissolved the League, having achieved much of what he sought. It is a striking fact that his participation in what was possibly the most notable example of disorder in the history of Victorian London did not damage Beales's career. In 1870, Hatherley, the Lord Chancellor of the day, appointed him to the county court bench. It was possible for successful professional work to be combined with very robust and controversial political engagement on the part of a member of the Inn.[115]

---

[115] 1803–81; *ROA*, admitted 1824, called 1830; *ODNB*, T Cooper, rev M Lee; Hutchinson, above n 1, at 16. Beales's career might be compared with that of John Humffreys Parry (1816–80): called in 1843, he went on the Home Circuit, serjeant-at-law 1856, bencher 1878. He appeared in famous trials, including those arising out of the collapse of the bank, Overend and Gurney. An advanced Liberal who supported the more moderate commitments of Chartism, he was a founder of the Complete Suffrage Association in 1842. He was father of the judge and author Sir Edward Abbott Parry (1863–1943), also a member of the Middle Temple.

Some were more conventional in their approach but also addressed issues of pressing economic and political concern. Sir Rupert Alfred Kettle was admitted in 1842 and, coming from a Birmingham family, he developed a practice on the Oxford Circuit and became a county court judge in 1859. He was well-known for his creation of a system of arbitration for the building trades and, more generally, for his personal success as an arbitrator in industrial disputes. He became known as 'The Prince of Arbitrators' and gave advice at national level on trade union reforms.[116]

Others were devoted to causes which have long passed out of fashion. Sir Thomas Chambers, a bencher in 1861 and treasurer in 1872, was described as being '[u]nder middle height, with an apple rosy face and Victorian side whiskers'.[117] In 1878 he was appointed Recorder of the City of London in preference to the favoured candidate, Fitzjames Stephen. As a Liberal MP he tried and failed to legalise marriage to a deceased wife's sister, and had no more luck in his quest to ensure that convents were subject to inspection. William Francis Finlason was called in 1851 after working as a special pleader under the Bar. An active journalist, he held unorthodox views on legal history, thinking that the institutions of the common law had been derived from the Roman occupation. Michael Lobban notes that

> for nearly half a century, he was the chief legal reporter for *The Times*, reporting nearly all the major cases in the Queen's Bench, albeit in a manner sometimes too florid for the liking of the legal profession.[118]

Interestingly, 'although only a stuff-gown barrister, on 10th May 1887 he was appointed one of the Masters of the Bench of the Middle Temple'.[119]

The work of one Middle Templar of these years was of importance to the legal profession as a whole. Edward Cox combined legal work with Tory politics, an interest in spiritualism and publishing. His efforts with politics and spiritualism did not, for the most part, prosper. But publishing was another matter. His popular magazines included *Exchange and Mart* and fashionable productions of the day, such as *Queen*. His wealth from these enterprises was such that on the effective dissolution of the Order of Serjeants in 1877, he was able to purchase the site of Serjeants' Inn. His personal publications included the *The Advocate, His Training, Practice, Rights and Duties* (1852) and a useful series of law reports which appeared

---

[116] 1817–94; *ROA*, admitted 1842, called 1845; *ODNB*, EI Carlyle, rev MC Curthoys. Hutchinson, above n 1, at 137; Williamson, above n 6, at 248.

[117] 1814–91; *ROA*, admitted 1837, called 1840; *ODNB*, JM Rigg, rev P Polden; Williamson, above n 6, at 228; Hutchinson, above n 1, at 48. For his description, see JHB Browne, *Forty Years at the Bar* (1916), at 141.

[118] *ODNB*, M Lobban.

[119] 1818–95; *ROA* admitted 1841, called 1851; *ODNB*, M Lobban; Williamson, above n 6, at 252; Hutchinson, above n 1, at 91.

as *Reports of Cases in Criminal Law Determined in All the Courts of England and Wales, 1846–1878*, known thereafter as *Cox's Criminal Cases*. But for the profession it was his publication of *The Law Times* in 1843 which was of most significance. Appearing each week, it could be distributed nationally by the new railway network. It frequently combined legal news with comment on public issues and social events, and in doing so it could give the impression that the legal profession was not serving the interests of litigants and others. At times it was particularly critical of the Bar, not least through recording practices which angered Victorians, such as the late return of briefs. Over time, the new periodical presented the Bar with a dangerous shift in power. The way the profession worked could be looked at regularly and in detail by a national audience, many of whom were solicitors. It was as if the periodical put the Bar in a vulnerable position during the difficult mid-Victorian years. It is perhaps unsurprising that Cox was never to receive any 'honour' or title other than that of serjeant-at-law. With the advantage of hindsight there is a case for wondering if any other Middle Templar had a comparable impact on debates about the profession. Cox often put into print words which probably had previously only been spoken.[120]

D.   Mid-Victorians looking abroad

In 1867 Thomas M Chester was admitted to the Inn. A black American born in Virginia, he had an unusual career behind him, having combined education in Vermont with visits to Liberia. Always seeking to advance the interests of black Americans, he had an important role in the American Civil War, both as a journalist and as the person who, more than anyone else, was responsible for raising two black regiments. Recognising the need to give his causes an international resonance he visited Britain, and whilst here he qualified for the Bar. He was briefed for at least one trial, but was soon working again in Africa and the United States. He qualified as a lawyer in America and his reputation went from strength to strength. This remarkable man was almost certainly the first black citizen from America to become a barrister in England.[121]

The Inn of these years produced a number of men who went on to major colonial careers as lawyers. It was as if some of them treated the world as the setting for their work. Henry Samuel Chapman was called in 1840. As

---

[120] 1809–79; *ROA*, admitted 1840, called 1843; *ODNB*, RCJ Cocks; Hutchinson, above n 1, at 61. His book *The Advocate, His Training, Practice, Rights and Duties* (London, J Crockford,1852) sometimes attempts to put oral conventions into written form. On serjeants, see JH Baker, 'Serjeants at Law' *Selden Society Supplementary Series*, v (1984).

[121] *ROA*, admitted 1867, called 1870; HL Gates and EB Higginbotham (eds), *African American Lives* (Oxford, Oxford University Press, 2004), entry by RJM Blackett.

a young man he emigrated to Canada and founded the country's first daily paper, *The Daily Advertiser*, which collapsed. He returned to England in 1835 and developed an interest in law. Within three years of call he was appointed a judge for the Supreme Court of the Southern District in New Zealand. In 1852 he became Colonial Secretary for Van Dieman's Land (Tasmania), but was dismissed soon afterwards for opposing convict transportation. In 1854 he practised law in Melbourne and a year later was elected to the legislative assembly. On two occasions he was Attorney-General for Victoria. He also held a Chair of Law at Melbourne University and was appointed an equity judge. In 1864 he was reappointed to the judicial position he had held in New Zealand. He settled in Dunedin and became Chancellor of the University of Otago, 1876–79.[122]

Another 'colonial' had an instinct for controversy. After an early education in Australia, Thomas Chisholm Anstey came to England to study at University College London. As a Member of Parliament he supported the repeal of the Union with both Ireland and Scotland. In 1854 he became Attorney-General for Hong Kong, where he rapidly became unpopular amongst Europeans. He attributed this to his persistent attacks on colonial abuses, but others found him intemperate and lacking in judgment. In 1858 he 'withdrew' to India, only to fall out with colonial officials once again. Thereafter he returned to England and became committed to arguing for universal manhood suffrage. By 1868 he was back in India where he was as controversial as ever. He died in 1873, and a recent biographer has observed that 'his aims were invariably legitimate enough, but he rarely took rational measures to attain their fulfilment'.[123]

A different personality, John Elliot Drinkwater Bethune was called in 1827 and established a personal reputation as a draftsman of Acts, which was not an easy thing to do before the Office of Parliamentary Counsel was created. His strength in this area led to his appointment to the Supreme Council of India in 1848. In India he angered certain Europeans by supporting legal reforms which would have made it possible for Indian judges to try British subjects. Working in Calcutta (as it was then called), he did not confine himself to law and to this day he is remembered as a pioneer of female education in India.[124]

Cricket was an interest of Sir Joseph Arnold (sometimes known as 'Arnould'), who was admitted in 1836. After a 'glittering academic career at Oxford' he worked as a special pleader and joined the Home Circuit. In

---

[122] 1803–81; *ROA* admitted 1837, called 1840; *ODNB*, GC Boase, rev J Tucker; Hutchinson, above n 1, at 49.

[123] 1816–73; *ROA*, admitted 1835, called 1839; *ODNB*, S Lee, rev KD Reynolds; Hutchinson, above n 1, at 4.

[124] 1801–51; *ROA*, admitted 1821, called 1827 (then with Drinkwater as a surname); *ODNB*, K Prior; Hutchinson, above n 1, at 21.

1848 he published his *Treatise on the Law of Marine Insurance and Average*, the sixteenth edition of which appeared in 1997. In 1859 he was made a Puisne Judge of the Supreme Court of Bombay (as it was then called), and retained this position across the revolutionary legal changes of 1859–62 in India, becoming a judge of the new High Court in 1862. He had a reputation for ability, scholarship and 'an openness to reform'. He also has a small place in the history of Indian cricket, in that in a non-judicial capacity he supported the Parsees in Bombay who faced opposition when seeking to use a public park as a cricket pitch. Some have seen this dispute as the start of Indian cricket, at least in Bombay.[125]

Others went on to major foreign roles. Sir Edward Clive Bayley studied law at the Middle Temple when on furlough in England in 1857. A distinguished administrator and antiquary, in India he became an authority on numismatics, and was Vice-Chancellor of Calcutta University between 1870 and 1875. He designed and built at Allahabad a court waiting room in traditional Mughal style, and also wrote papers on Asiatic subjects.[126] Another orientalist, Edward Backhouse Eastwick, was a diplomatist coming from a family with long-standing links to the East India Company.[127] Proficient in numerous languages, he was at one time a Professor of Urdu at the college for the East India Company at Haileybury. He wrote various books, including *Journal of a Diplomat's Three Years in Persia*. Middle Templars with interests such as these were increasingly common during these years. They were part of an Inn which was looking outwards across the globe.[128]

III.   THE RETURN OF CONFIDENCE: 1875–1900

In the last decades of the century the professional press could still be critical of the Inns of Court and the Bar, with the *Law Journal*, for example, remarking on the 'apathy of the Bar' and pointing to 'the lotus-eating influence of the Long Vacation'.[129] In some respects this was less than fair, because there were debates within the profession during these years. At times it was fashionable to demand fusion between the Bar and solicitors, and this obviously had the potential to raise long-term questions about the role of the Inns.[130] These were also the years when the Bar Committee, later the Bar Council, came into existence, and there were

---

[125] 1813–86; *ROA*, admitted 1836, called 1841; *ODNB*, K Prior; Hutchinson, above n1, at 6; See B Majumdar, *Battles Off the Pitch* (Abingdon, Routledge, 2006), 2–4.
[126] 1821–84; *ROA*, admitted 1855, called 1857; *ODNB*, S Lane-Poole, rev K Prior; Hutchinson, above n 1, at 15.
[127] 1814–83; *ROA*, admitted 1858, called 1860.
[128] *ODNB*, S Lane Poole, rev P Loloi; Hutchinson, above n 1, at 82. The book was published in two volumes in 1864.
[129] (1899) 34 *Law Journal* 564.
[130] See, eg, (1884–5) 78 *The Law Times* 233 and 324.

occasional skirmishes over how these novelties would work in conjunction with the Inns of Court. Criticism of the provision of legal education continued with a Lord Chief Justice of the day, Lord Russell, being particularly firm in talking of its 'discreditable' state.[131] As before, the benchers were never immune from public criticism, or indeed from independent thought within their own ranks.[132]

What changed during these years was, it seems, a sense on the part of many of the benchers that they could pay less attention to criticism. In any event, whatever their thoughts, they *did* pay less attention to criticism. This was made easier by the criticism being more restrained than it had been. It was public knowledge that teachers of law at London University saw the possibility of a new legal university based on the Inns of Court as a threat to their own efforts, and that this served to limit academic demands for change.[133] The benchers could use moderate changes at the Council of Legal Education as an answer to those who demanded further educational reforms. They could point to considerable activity in sustaining and developing the Council, albeit still leaving it with a role which reformers found unsatisfactory. They spent time resolving routine problems associated with, say, the provision of rooms for teaching. In short, although criticism of the standard for passing examinations continued, they could always claim to be doing something.[134] More generally, they would have known that public criticism of legal services had been somewhat satisfied by the reforms introduced by the Judicature Acts of the 1870s. Doubts about the wisdom of further change had ensured the survival of the House of Lords as a judicial body. In intellectual terms, there was now an open and modern-sounding commitment to the common law in Dicey's *Law of the Constitution*.[135] In national politics, sweeping utilitarian demands were no longer so significant. Instead there was a fear of enhanced powers of reforming governments responding to a widening franchise. From looking like expensive and inefficient anachronisms for an industrial age, both the common law and the Inns of Court could now be seen as valuable legacies from the past which could counter-balance dangerous developments in national politics. *The Law Times* had some truth in it when it spoke of Lord Russell as 'a voice crying in the wilderness'.[136] In short, legal reform was no longer so fashionable.

---

[131] (1897) *The Law Times* 103. It was 'about as discreditable as it could well be'.

[132] See, eg, (1892–3) 94 *The Law Times* 454.

[133] For an analysis of the Bar's educational developments between 1860 and 1914, see Cornish *et al*, above, Vol XI, n 6, at 1186–97 (M Lobban).

[134] For educational discussions on the part of the benchers, see MT 1/MPA 20, at for example 8 November 1889: on 31 January 1890 it was recognised that there was a need to set up a joint committee to consider 'the present state of legal education'. For problems in finding room space, see 6 February 1893, at ibid, 229, 230.

[135] AV Dicey, *Introduction to the Study of the Law of the Constitution*, (London, Macmillan, 1885). For the professional context, see Cocks, above n 60, chs 7, 8 and 9.

[136] (1898) 105 *The Law Times* 1.

The Inns were also helped by a concern with what was happening in the informal side of professional life. Something sociable had been lost when the law courts moved in 1883 from Westminster to the Strand, for the simple reason that lawyers did not share a walk from the Temple and back again in the course of a day's business. More important, there was a strong belief that life on circuit was not what it had been. The railways made it easy to visit an assize town as and when a man was briefed, and he had no good working reason for staying on over-night and attending the Mess dinner when his work was done. With a decline in attendance, the Circuit Messes were losing some of their authority. In the retrospective words of the *Solicitors' Journal* for 1905–06, 'the changes which have taken place in the life of barristers in the last thirty years have certainly tended to withdraw them from each others society'.[137] Now, tradition and the maintenance of corporate life were more fashionable topics than reform. Because of problems elsewhere in the profession, the Inns had acquired a more assured place in professional life through providing opportunities to be sociable.

The benchers' position was all the stronger because they had no worries at this time about the level of admissions. We have seen (section I.A. above) that after the sharp drop in the 1850s there was an intake of 1,018 in the 1860s. This was followed in the last 30 years of the century by intakes of 1,141 for the 1870s, 1,268 for the 1880s and 1,102 for the 1890s. It is impossible to express these intakes as a percentage of the total intake for all four Inns because the statistics for the Inner Temple are missing for some years.[138] But the intakes for Lincoln's Inn and Gray's Inn suggest that the Middle Temple was popular.

Given this setting, it was predictable that many of the issues facing the benchers of these years were trivial in comparison with the problems which arose in the mid-Victorian decades. In 1891 it was decided not to grant barristers and students the privilege of playing golf in the gardens.[139] Later in the same year, as the darkness of winter approached, Hume Williams of 2 Pump Court sought the benchers' permission to introduce the 'Electric Light' into his chambers, and was informed that any application on his behalf by the Electric Lighting Company would be considered.[140] As always, there were disciplinary matters. For example, in respect of a particular student it was ordered

> that having removed books from the Library without permission and returned them surreptitiously he is hereby severely censured. And that this order be screened in the Hall and Library until the end of Trinity Term next.[141]

---

[137] (1905–06) 50 *Solicitors Journal* 166. Generally, see Cocks, above n 60, ch 10.
[138] *ROA*; and Duman, above n 19, at 25.
[139] MT 1/MPA, 17 April 1891, at 109.
[140] MT 1/MPA, 11 November 1891, at 150.
[141] MT 1/MPA, 27 April 1894, at 316.

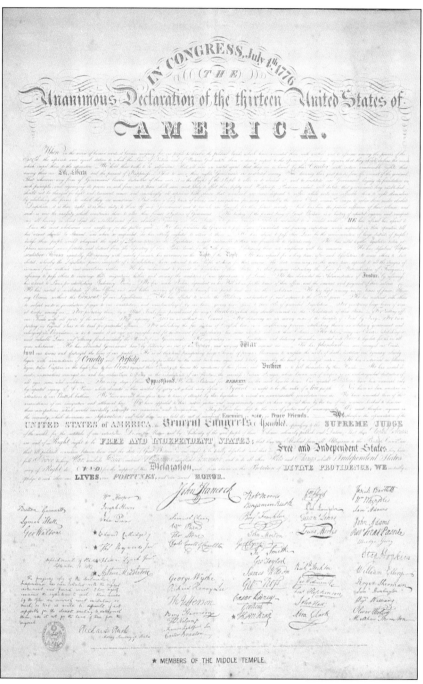

3 – 1 US Declaration of Independence. 1817 facsimile subscribed by Richard Rush, Acting Secretary of State. The names of Middle Templar signatories are identified by red stars.

3 – 2   *Middle Temple Library: Henry R Abraham, architect.*

3 – 3   *'Fountain in the Temple' 1738 by Joseph Nicholls*

3 – 4   William Blackstone, after Gainsborough   3 – 5   Master Sherrard, by Israel Zohar

3 – 6   Arms of Sir Walter Raleigh in the windows of Middle Temple Hall. A volume in the College of Arms shows these were in Hall in 1602. By the time Middle Temple commissioned its own illuminated volume of armorial glass in 1630 Raleigh's window had been removed following his conviction and eventual execution. In the 19th century his arms, copied from the 1602 depiction in the College of Arms volume, were restored to Middle Temple Hall where they can be seen adjacent to those of Sir John Popham, Chief Justice of the King's Bench by whom Raleigh had been sentenced to death.

3 – 7   Pump Court showing bomb damage, 1941

*3 – 8   The Call to the Bench of John Roberts, Chief Justice of the United States, 2007.
John Roberts is standing behind the table known as the cupboard.*

3 – 9   Lamb Building before the Second World War

3 – 10 *Middle Temple Garden from the Embankment*

3 – 11 *The Princess of Wales meeting students and Master Babington after dining at the Inn as a Royal Bencher in 1990*

3 – 12 Middle Temple Hall, circa 1800, showing the open hearth removed in the 1830s

3 – 13 Taking commons 1840

3 – 14 Masters of the Bench, including the Prince of Wales, in the Parliament Chamber, 1880. This is a photograph of a painting which hung in the Library and was destroyed in the Blitz.

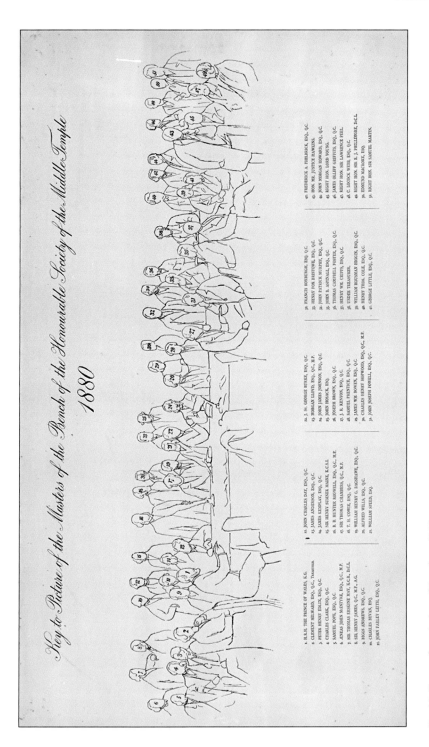

3 – 15 Key to the painting of Benchers 1880

3 – 16 Wren's Cloisters before the War

3 – 17 Cloisters as rebuilt by Edward Maufe after the war

3 – 18 '*Armistice Day 1940' by Frank Beresford*

3 – 19 Call to the Bar in the bombed Hall, Trinity Term, 1941

3 – 20 Damage to Brick Court, 12th May 1941

3 – 21 The Temple after the first Blitz in 1941, showing Crown Office Row, Elm Court, Lamb Building and the Wren Cloisters, all subsequently demolished in successive air raids

3 – 22 Joint dinner of Inner and Middle Templars in Middle Temple Hall presided over by their respective Treasurers, King George VI and Queen Elizabeth, 1949. By Terence Cuneo

3 – 23 Sir Banastre Tarleton, by Sir Joshua Reynolds

3 – 24 Copy of a posthumous portrait of Colonel John Laurens

3 – 25 John Scott, first Earl of Eldon by Henry Perronet Briggs RA

3 – 26 Richard Bethell, Lord Westbury by Sir Francis Grant PRA

3 – 27 Rufus Isaacs, first Marquess of Reading in the robes of Viceroy of India by Oswald Birley (Detail)

The prohibition on smoking was relaxed for some occasions in Hall.[143] There was a certain calmness about the proceedings.

One issue which was not trivial related to the judiciary. The judges presented all four Inns with what could have been a major problem at this time. We have seen that after the effective abolition of Serjeants' Inn, barristers who became judges did not leave their respective Inns.[144] They remained within the Inn, and it seems that this gave some members of the Inn pause for thought. If the judges in question were made benchers, or were already benchers (and in reality they often would be), what sort of a role would they have? To some Victorian barristers the Inn was one thing and the judiciary another. It was fine for eminent judges such as Eldon or Westbury to have a social connection with the Inn after their elevation, but letting them take part in everyday business was another matter. The debates at the Middle Temple make it clear that all the Inns were involved in considering this.[145] At the Middle Temple there was at first a restriction imposed on judges taking part in business, but after four years (in 1880) this was repealed.[146] In 1890 Lord Coleridge proudly pointed out that 'I am the first Lord Chief Justice who, while holding that office, was also Treasurer of the Middle Temple'.[147] It is difficult to be precise about the importance of this change, but it was now a fact that judges had a direct influence on *everyday* professional life.

In respect of the social life of the Inn two changes require further research. We saw that at the start of the century it was common for a young barrister to set himself up for practice in his own chambers. In the final decades there were still some who took this course, but there were now a number of 'sets' of chambers and the importance of this fact is apparent from most legal biographies. Becoming a member of a good set was often seen as the foundation for success; it brought with it the prospect of guidance and support during the early years of practice. At the same time it introduced a new form of control into the life of the Bar. If a young man in search of a practice needed to find chambers, he obviously had to satisfy established barristers that he was worthy of joining their ranks. An older generation was gaining more power over a younger generation.

---

[143] *Rules and Orders of the Honourable Society of the Middle Temple for the Conduct of Business at their Parliaments and Committees and Generally for the Good Government of the House*, 2nd edn (London, 1896), 12 November 1880, at 204.

[144] See above, n 1.

[145] MT 1/MPA, 22 November 1895, at 417–18.

[146] 30 April 1880: repeal of the order of 5 May 1876. See *Rules and Orders of the Honourable Society of the Middle Temple for the Conduct of Business at their Parliaments and Committees and Generally for the Good Government of the House*, 2nd edn (London, 1896), 12 November 1880, at 199.

[147] MT 1/MPA, 4 November, 1890 at 204.

Perhaps this does something to explain the decline in reforming activity within the profession as a whole. It may have been that the profession was becoming more hierarchical.

Another possible change in the social life of the Temple is even more difficult to assess. We have seen that by 1854 it was being remarked that increasingly barristers lived elsewhere and came to work at the Inns: they came to what was becoming more exclusively a place of work.[148] As a consequence of this, fewer families were to be found living within the Temple, and this may have been linked to a further development. If two authors are to be believed, at some time in the course of the century prostitutes began to use the Temple in fairly large numbers. This is considered by John Cordy Jeaffreson, who is clear that it happened but is not consistent in dating it.[149] It is also a matter of comment for the author George Moore. At the least, it looks as if it had become a sufficient embarrassment to make it undesirable for a respectable mid- or late-Victorian lady to be seen unescorted in the Temple.[150] It is, perhaps, understandable that other authors might choose to ignore this change, particularly if they were writing in praise of the Inns, but the general lack of comment makes it difficult to measure the extent of what was happening.

An increasingly important matter for the benchers was the large number of applicants from abroad, in particular from the Indian sub-continent. This had two aspects. The first was inward-looking: how was the Inn to administer the change? The other was outward-looking: the Inn was establishing links with other parts of the world which went far beyond its old eighteenth-century association with the West Indies and the American colonies. Concern about what examinations were appropriate surfaced as an issue, and there were problems of administering admissions at a distance.[151] It was fine, say, to donate 100 guineas to the Indian Famine Fund.[152] But in the following month the benchers had to consider a protest

---

[148] *Royal Commission*, above n 79, at 9: '[O]wing to a change in the habits of the times, the members of the Inns of Court have to a great degree ceased to reside in their precincts or vicinity'.

[149] JC Jeaffreson, *A Book About Lawyers* (London, Hunt and Blackett, 1867), vol I, at 161–64, cf 164–77. The author at first emphasises that the change was of long-standing, but then implies that it was fairly recent.

[150] J Hone, *The Life of George Moore* (London, Gollancz, 1936), at 150, remarks of one of Moore's pieces that 'It was a tale of London in the 'eighties, young lawyers in the Temple, and a great many prostitutes'. In another work, set about the year 1894, a lady visitor of George Moore reproaches him for bringing her to the Temple ('I realized that she was right; the Temple is too rough and too public a place for a lady'): see G Moore, *Hail and Farewell: Ave* (London, Heineman, 1911), at 88. For a comment suggesting that there was a problem with prostitution in the Temple, see K Chesney, *The Victorian Underworld* (Harmondsworth, Penguin, 1976), 401–02.

[151] In MT 1/MPA for 29 May 1891, at 118; and 27 October 1892, at 201–02.

[152] *Ibid*, 26 March, 1897, at 514.

by the Calcutta Bar on what was essentially an internal Indian matter.[153] The Indian issues were only the largest in an increasing number of overseas problems: difficult points arose from across the globe involving, say, in the month of January 1896, Ceylon (as it was), Queensland and New South Wales.[154] In some cases being disbarred abroad was followed by the same penalty in England. In one instance the Supreme Court of the Straits Settlement (Singapore) ordered that Charles Grant Logan be struck off the list of advocates and solicitors of that court: 'After an opportunity to present his case—which he did not do—he was disbarred by the Inn.'[155] What is noticeable is the way in which the benchers dealt with the issues 'one by one'. There seems to have been no sustained attempt to consider the implications of what was happening as a whole. The reason for this surely lies in the simple fact that the big change in intake was for the most part manageable within the normal course of business. The students were admitted, there were more people dining in Hall and being taught at the Council of Legal Education, and, of course, there were also more fees being paid to support the change. We shall see below that this adaptability was to prove to be one of the major achievements of the nineteenth-century Middle Temple. It was to give its membership a global reach.

A.   Late-Victorian Middle Templars: politicians, scholars, and eccentrics

The Inn of these years was never far from politics, not least because it had members from Ireland, Scotland and Wales. Edward Carson had developed a substantial practice at the Irish Bar by the mid-1880s and was already well-known for being an active opponent of the nationalist interest. Solicitor-General for Ireland in 1892, in the same year he was elected the Unionist Member for Dublin University. In 1894 he was called to the English Bar by the Middle Temple, and was soon a QC and Solicitor-General for England. Busy as both a lawyer and a politician, in 1910 he became the leader of Irish Unionist MPs at Westminster and continued in later years to play a decisive role in the crises over Home Rule. An advocate of commanding presence, he was particularly formidable in cross-examination. He became a Lord of Appeal in Ordinary in 1921. A striking individual, he has a place in the legal and political history of both

---

[153]   Ibid, 6 April 1897, at 517.
[154]   Ibid, 17 January 1896, at 426.
[155]   Ibid, 12 January 1894, at 288.

Ireland and England, and the merits of his actions are debated down to the present day.[156]

Laurence Ginnell had views which stood in contrast. In Ireland he had been active in the anti-landlord 'Plan of Campaign', and in 1887 he started the Irish Press agency. In London he helped to establish the Irish Literary Society, and in 1894, a year after his call to the English Bar, he published an analysis of the ancient Irish Brehon laws. By 1899 he was secretary of William O'Brien's United Irish League, and was to become more and more active politically, not least during the First World War. For various reasons and at various times he served sentences of imprisonment and internment. Ultimately he became involved in a bitter dispute with the 'treatyite government' of the Free State and was sent by De Valera to the USA to lead an occupation of the Irish Free State Consulate in New York. He died in the United States in 1923.[157]

A successful advocate in Scotland, George Young had a reputation for a coercive style of advocacy. Appointed Lord Advocate in 1869, as a Member of Parliament he also had a major role in introducing a national system for education in Scotland in 1872. He was well-regarded in English legal circles and became a bencher of the Inn.[158]

> What were described as his bleak, inscrutable face and his thin compressed lips were said to be familiar to students at the Middle Temple, as he dined there during term time on regular visits to London ...[159]

He had a gift for sarcasm. When an enemy of his, James Baird, gave half a million pounds to the Church of Scotland, Young described it as 'the heaviest insurance against fire on record'. Young died after a fall at the Middle Temple.[160]

Robert Bannatyne Finlay was born in Scotland and educated at Edinburgh University, but worked in London from the start of his career. Called by the Middle Temple in 1867, he was a successful advocate from an early age, and became a bencher in 1884 and Treasurer in 1902. In 1885 he was elected a Liberal Unionist MP, but later became part of a Conservative administration, being Solicitor-General in 1895 and Attorney-General in

---

[156] 1854–1935; *ROA*, admitted first in 1875 and then again in 1893, and called in the same year; *ODNB*, DG Boyce; Williamson, above n 6, at 263. A bencher in 1900, he was treasurer in 1922. Various books on Carson include E Marjoribanks, *The Life of Lord Carson* (London, Gollanz, 1932); I Colvin, *The Life of Lord Carson* (London, Victor Gollanz, 1934); HM Hyde, *Carson: The Life of Sir Edward Carson, Lord Carson of Duncairn* (London, Heinemann, 1953); A Jackson, *Sir Edward Carson* (Dublin, Dundalgan, 1993).

[157] 1852 (bap)–1923; *ROA*, admitted 1890, called 1893; *ODNB*, DR O'Connor Lysaght; J Sheehan, *Worthies of Westmeath: a Biographical Dictionary, with brief lives of famous Westmeath people* (Westmeath, Wellbrook Press, 1907).

[158] 1819–1907; *ROA*, admitted and called 1869; *ODNB*, GF Millar.

[159] *ODNB*, GF Millar.

[160] Williamson, above n 6, at 238.

1900, holding the latter position until 1905. When out of office, he sustained a strong reputation in appellate cases and international law. At times he attracted wide public attention, as when he represented the White Star Line at the inquiry into the sinking of the *Titanic*. He was appointed Lord Chancellor in 1916 at the age of 74, and did not try to develop a high political profile or take an active part in administration. In 1919 he was content to be replaced by Lord Birkenhead. Between 1921 and 1928 he was a judge of the Permanent Court of International Justice at the Hague. In England there were those who thought that in his later years the quality of his judgments declined significantly.[161]

Sir Samuel Thomas Evans was born in Glamorgan in 1859. He read Law at London University and began practice as a solicitor in South Wales. In 1890 he was elected MP for mid-Glamorgan, which constituency he represented as a Liberal for twenty years. Called to the Bar by the Middle Temple in 1891, he soon developed a strong reputation in South Wales and became a QC in 1901. In 1908 Asquith made him Solicitor-General and, rather surprisingly, in 1910 he accepted an appointment to a judicial position involving an area of law in which he had hardly worked. As President of the Probate, Divorce and Admiralty Division he was not welcomed by the Bar, but he proved to be hard-working and attentive to detail. His judicial reputation was made during the First World War with his judgments in prize cases; here it was recognised that he built effectively on Lord Stowell's decisions. In retrospect one has an impression of a man who never quite felt at one with the metropolitan legal world. It was as if he always had to prove himself.[162]

Another contemporary member of the Inn also began life as a solicitor in South Wales. Sir Clement Meacher Bailhache came from a Huguenot and Baptist background, went to London University and was called in 1889.[163] He developed a strong commercial practice and had a public reputation for being a firm teetotaller. As a judge

> he saw no reason why swift and businesslike methods should be confined to the commercial court and was known, for example, to ask counsel whether there was really any defence to the charge.[164]

He became a bencher in 1912.[165]

---

[161] 1842–1929; *ROA*, admitted 1865, called 1867; *ODNB*, GR Rubin; Williamson, above n 6, at 250, where the author points out that 'The Society possesses an admirable portrait of Viscount Finlay by G. Fiddes Watt, R.S.A.'; bencher 1884, treasurer 1902.

[162] 1859–1918; *ROA*, admitted 1891 and called in the same year; *ODNB*, JL Brierly, rev H Mooney; Williamson, above n 6, at 270, where the author points out that the Society has his portrait in oil by Christopher Williams.

[163] 1856–1924; *ROA*, admitted 1888, called 1889; *ODNB*, T Mathew, rev H Mooney.

[164] *ODNB*, T Mathew, rev H Mooney.

[165] Williamson, above n 6, at 274.

Sir James George Frazer, the social anthropologist and author of the famous book *The Golden Bough* (published in 1890), was called in 1882 but never took a brief.[166] In his time he was an important secularist, who was well-known for explaining religion as a phase of history which was now, in his view, being replaced by rationality and positive science. In 1908 he was appointed to the first Chair in Social Anthropology. In retrospect it may be argued that he 'placed on record an array of facts of even greater value than his theories'.[167] In his day he had a major reputation, and the Inn made him an honorary bencher on 18 June 1931. This may have reflected his award of the Order of Merit in 1925.

The Near East attracted Middle Templars. Sir Edwin Pears, called in 1870, became a General Secretary of the Social Science Association and an Editor of the *Law Magazine*. In the words of Chandrika Kaul:

> When in January 1873, he heard that the practice of Sir Charles Parker Butt at the Constantinople Bar was vacant, he decided to try his hand at the job. ... Settling as a permanent resident in Turkey, he rose to become President of the European Bar in Constantinople in 1881 and made a name for himself as a newspaper correspondent and historian of the city.[168]

In 1876 his reports on atrocities in Bulgaria became a part of Gladstone's campaign on the issue. He is remembered as the author of books (some of them very controversial) on Turkish history.[169] Pears's career might be contrasted with that of the epigraphist and classical scholar William Paton. Admitted to the Inn in 1878, he chose not to work but used a private income to wander around Greek islands looking for classical inscriptions. A visitor observed that

> Paton spoke Greek and French to his wife, German to the children's governess, English to me, Turkish to the servants, Latin and Gaelic to the children.[170]

Ernest Belfort Bax, an uncle of Sir Arnold Bax the composer, was called in 1894 and went on to practise at the Bar. At the same time he became a Marxist theoretician and activist, and published various books, including *Outlooks for the New Standpoint* (1891). He formed the Socialist League with William Morris, and attacked imperialism, the legal system and (most

---

[166] 1854–1941; *ROA*, admitted 1878, called 1882; *ODNB*, R Ackerman; Williamson, above n 6, at 293–94.

[167] *ODNB*, R Ackerman.

[168] *ODNB*, C Kaul.

[169] 1835–1919; *ROA*, admitted 1867, called 1870; *ODNB*, C Kaul; E Pears, *Forty Years in Constantinople* (London, Herbert Jenkins, 1916).

[170] 1857–1921; *ROA*, admitted 1878, never called; *ODNB*, D Gill, who points out that he kept terms to 1884.

of all) the middle-class family. He was unusual in believing that the moral and legal conventions of the day enabled the female to dominate the male.[171]

John Evelyn Barlas, admitted in 1882, was the son of a merchant based in Rangoon and went on to be a poet, anarchist and communist. As an early Marxist he was brave enough to start a socialist society in Chelmsford. A gifted linguist, and arguably a seriously underestimated poet, he suffered mentally in later years. It was said that his mental difficulties arose after being hit by a truncheon at a demonstration in Trafalgar Square, at the end of which he collapsed at the feet of Eleanor Marx.[172]

B. The world-wide reach of the late-Victorian Middle Temple

Woomes Chunder Bonnerjee came from a Calcutta family and began his career in that city, being articled to a local solicitor in 1861. He won a government scholarship to study law in England and was admitted to the Middle Temple in 1864. On his return to India he was enrolled as a barrister in the Calcutta High Court. Thereafter he succeeded in developing both a legal practice and a political career. He mixed being an anglophile with roles designed to create representative government in India. In 1885 he had the distinction of being the first President of the Indian National Congress. Throughout his life he retained British links, and in his later years he had a large house in Croydon and engaged in a considerable amount of Privy Council work.[173]

For a brief time Prime Minister of New Zealand, Sir Francis Henry Dillon Bell was born in New Zealand and educated at local schools before he went to Cambridge. Called to the Bar in 1874, he worked in England before returning to establish himself as a successful lawyer in his country of birth. Amongst other areas of expertise he developed a knowledge in the law relating to Maori resources, and he was also active in supporting the creation of the first series of local law reports. After 1893 he developed a lively and sometimes controversial political career. He was the first native-born person to hold the post of Prime Minister. He had a reputation for success before the Judicial Committee of the Privy Council and took on

---

[171] 1854–1926; *ROA*, admitted 1890, called 1894; *ODNB*, S Pierson; EB Bax, *Reminiscences and Reflections of a Mid and Late Victorian* (New York, Seltzer, 1920); EP Thompson, *William Morris, Romantic Revolutionary* (London, Merlin Press, 1955). Sir Arnold Bax's father, Alfred Ridley Bax (1844–1918), was a Middle Templar; *ROA*, admitted 9 January 1891, not called.

[172] 1860–1914; *ROA*, admitted 1882; *ODNB*, G Krishnamurti.

[173] 1844–1906; *ROA*, admitted 1864, called 1867; *ODNB*, RT Stearn.

numerous roles, including being involved in the creation of the International Court of Justice at The Hague.[174]

Rufus Isaacs, mentioned at the start of this chapter, became Lord Chief Justice of England, Ambassador to the USA and Viceroy of India. He had entered his family's business as a fruit merchant at the age of fifteen, and subsequently went to sea as a ship's boy and then tried various lines of work, including jobber on the Stock Exchange. Called to the Bar in 1887, he took silk in 1898 and, in the next century, was remarkable for both his legal and political career, not least in respect of his work in India between 1921 and 1926. For romantics there is the true story of him first visiting Calcutta as a ship's boy and then, on his second visit, returning as Viceroy.[175]

In considering the international dimension of the Inn for the last half of the century, there comes a point where individual biography breaks down and has to be replaced by a broader perspective reflecting a shift in the pattern of admissions. Unfortunately, in this context the statistics can only be presented as being likely to be broadly accurate. It has been pointed out above that the *Register of Admissions* does not record the birth-place of applicants. Instead it supplies the addresses of the applicant and his father, together with information about the father's type of work and (sometimes) indications of any positions already held by the applicant. In many cases it looks as if applicants from abroad gave a temporary address in London, with the father's address being the guide to the whereabouts of the family home. It seems reasonable to conclude that this information enables the reader to track the extent to which the Inn was developing international links, even if one has to be cautious in allocating a permanent home address to any particular admission.[176]

Using the registers with these qualifications in mind, it is possible to say that for the period 1850–75 there were a significant number of applicants with English links (total 1,036); the Irish numbers were important (total 514) and there was a mild increase in Scottish representation (total 102), with a weak Welsh presence (total 43). There is the start of a change in respect of those who had links to the Indian sub-continent, which begins to

---

[174]   1851–1936; *ROA*, admitted,1871, called 1874; *ODNB*, R Hill.

[175]   See above, n 3.

[176]   So, for instance, what should be made of, say, Thomas McClatchie, of Her Majesty's Consular Service Japan, and of the Beaconsfield Club, Pall Mall, SW, fourth son of the Rev Thomas McClatchie, MA, of Shanghai China, Canon of Holy Trinity Cathedral, Shangai, and St John's Cathedral, Hong Kong? Some do not even supply a London address. We are simply told that Le Do Frederick Mathews, of Van Dieman's Land, Australia, was the second son of the late John M Mathews, of Port Louis, Mauritius, admitted 26 April 1870. Problematical examples of 'where people belonged' could be repeated many times over but, it is suggested, the proliferation of external links of one sort or another is clear. It has to be added that there is an element of subjectivity in deciding in any particular case what foreign links count, so the statistics quoted here paint with a broad brush.

be a significant part of the overseas intake with Indian numbers for each year usually reaching double figures after 1862 (total 170). In the last 25 years of the century there was a fair measure of stability for those with English links; there was a very sharp dip in Irish links after barristers from that country could qualify without attending an English Inn; and there are mild increases for Scotland and Wales. In contrast, the total from India more than doubles (424) and there is a great increase in the number of people from a wide range of other overseas countries (total 436). The total with foreign links in the second half of the century amounted to 1,234.

Taken together, the applicants had links with 67 places: using the spelling of the day, they came from England, Ireland, Wales, Scotland, Jamaica, St Vincent, St Bartholemew in the East Indies, India, France, Mauritius, Trinidad, Australia, Hong Kong, St Petersberg Russia, Hayti, Sierra Leone, Penang, Grenada, Cape of Good Hope, Burma, Canada, Gibraltar, Barbadoes, USA, British Guiana, New Zealand, Antigua, Smyrna Asia Minor, Nassau, St Lucia, Monrovia Republic of Liberia, St Helena, South Africa, Saint Kitts, Japan, Dominica, Portugal, Germany, Ceylon, Constantinople, Singapore, China, British Honduras, Italy, Formosa, Brazil, Denmark, Malta, Lagos, Egypt, Madeira, Gold Coast Colony, Siam, Behamas, Nevis, Phillipines, Argentina, Accra, Goa, Spain, Greece, Warsaw, Vienna, Rhodesia, Fiji and Cyprus. Given that the second half of the century saw admissions from well over a thousand people with links to a wide variety of countries, it may be said that the Inn was developing a strong international dimension, with obvious potential for the future.

C. What we still do not know about the 19th-century Middle Temple

This chapter is a slender response to the depth of the Inn's archive material for the nineteenth century. The Archivist has under her care very extensive records relating to generations of benchers, barristers and servants of the Inn. The sources relate to numerous aspects of life within the Inn, from the provision of food to the care of servants. These in turn interlock with the Inn's records concerning admissions, calls, discipline and many other activities. Some of the records relate in one way or another to the world beyond the Inn. Towards the end of the century this is increasingly the case in a literal way, in that they point to the overseas links mentioned above. Neither has it been possible to consider all significant Middle Templars; for example, there has been only fleeting reference to the lawyers in the Coleridge family.

Certain remaining issues are particularly challenging. What was the full significance of the life of the Inn for legal thought? Law is more than what is written down in statutes and cases. In part it is what is accepted as good practice, and this may evolve through discussion, or even informal observations, in the course of professional social life. What of professional understandings evolving in the course of conversation? Possible topics include the fundamental change from a focus on the forms of action to a focus on the development of substantive law. Of course the acute problem with this is that conversations were not recorded, and the research would have to be done obliquely through a range of printed and manuscript sources. In short, one wonders, can anything be done to recreate the conversational history of the Middle Temple?

IV.   CONCLUSION

Over 8,000 new members of the Inn passed through Middle Temple Hall between 1800 and 1900. In the course of the century the Inn more than 'held its own' against the recruitment of the other Inns of Court. At the same time, it produced famous lawyers, competent lawyers and a few whose standards were frankly questionable. And it was not just a matter of legal work. Members often looked far beyond the law and became involved in politics or literary pursuits, or travel or charitable work, or any number of other activities. It was as if the Middle Temple always stood for more than the sum of its purely professional roles.

The appearance of the Inn changed. There were improvements to the condition of chambers, many of which had begun the century with a reputation for being dark, cramped and poorly-built. Two specific building programmes were of major importance. A new library in neo-gothic style was constructed on land to the south side of the Hall. We have seen that it was rather grand and had a much publicised opening ceremony in the presence of the Prince of Wales in 1861, thereby reminding the public of the Inn's long-standing links with royalty. About 80 years later the library was badly damaged in the Blitz, and shortly after the end of the War it had to be taken down. Presumably it is now passing out of personal memory; anyone who used it is likely to be at least 90 years old. The second major nineteenth-century project proved to be more enduring. The construction of the new embankment ensured that the Thames no longer lapped the southern-most walls of the Inn. The new arrangement provided the Inn with a more spacious setting and the opportunity to construct new sets of chambers. Beyond construction work there was a radical improvement in the sanitary condition of the Inn. The Thames was not only further away; from about the mid-1860s it had ceased to be London's chief way of disposing of untreated sewage. Like other parts of London, the Inn benefited from improved drainage and standards of public health. If epidemics were still feared, at least the threat of cholera had diminished. The Inn was a larger, more open and healthier place in which to work.

In terms of its institutional life the major changes came during the mid-Victorian years. Between the 1840s and the 1870s the Middle Temple and the other Inns of Court were shaken by sustained criticism from barristers and the public at large. In 1846 a Parliamentary Select Committee castigated the Inns for their failure to provide legal education. In 1854 the treasurers of the day had to answer to abrasive Royal Commissioners in search of detailed financial and other information on all the Inns. Many eminent lawyers now doubted the merits of the common law. They looked forward to modern and efficient programmes of codification, and this questioning outlook could easily spill over into doubts about the Inns. People wondered about the usefulness of the Inns: were they merely social clubs? How could they justify their role in regulating a profession concerned with the provision of justice? Part of the answer to the criticism lay in responding to the radicals within the Inns. Here the benchers of the Middle Temple played a leading role in listening to the ideas of Westbury and other restless reformers within the Inn. His fellow benchers did not go as far as Westbury would have wished, but at least the Council of Legal Education was established in the 1850s and examinations became compulsory in 1872. Reformers continued to question the Inns and their ways, not least through the creation of the Bar Committee, later the Bar Council, but in the last two decades it became clear that the Inns had survived an era of reform. In the 1880s and 1890s the Inns were more fashionable than they had been during the mid-Victorian years. There was less talk of legal change, and, at a time when many were worried about political developments, the independent Inns of Court and the common law could be seen increasingly as valuable bulwarks against the excesses of executive power. The context of legal thought had altered, and this gave the Middle Temple (and the other Inns) a more assured role.

Towards the end of the century the focus of change lay in the nature of the Inn's intake. Irish lawyers no longer appeared in substantial numbers. Now there was a large increase in applicants with distant overseas links, including strong links to the Indian sub-continent. This change was such that by the end of the nineteenth century the Inn could be said to be part of a world-wide community of lawyers. Looking to the future, this had the potential to encourage lawyer-politicians from overseas to use their legal skills in the same way as earlier generations of Middle Templars had used them when they supported American independence, or had become involved in passionate debates about Ireland or Australia. There was now a clear possibility that overseas members of the Inn would play a central role in bringing to a close Britain's imperial experience. It was equally clear that in doing this they might sustain a shared interest in legal ideas which would do much to turn the empire into a Commonwealth of nations. In

1900 the Middle Temple was both a national and an international organisation, and its membership had the potential to play on a global stage.

The Inn as a Disciplinary Body

DAVID WOOLLEY[*]

I. Introduction

THE INN'S FUNCTION as a body responsible for the professional conduct of its members goes back as far as the records which still exist. The sources are of two kinds. First, there are the Minutes of Parliament, the earliest of which recording disciplinary proceedings dates from 1512.[1] These cover, in varying degrees of detail, the essence of the matters complained of by the Bench against members or servants of the Inn. In the early years, and for many centuries thereafter, they tended to reflect the Inn's collegiate functions. Indeed, much of the disciplinary business transacted would seem familiar to the Senior Tutor of an unusually intemperate and unruly Oxbridge college today. Yet the writ of the Masters of the Bench ran considerably wider than that. For many years after the Reformation they enforced attendance by members at church, and acted as thought police to ensure that there was no straying from orthodox religious belief, or at least the appearance of it, as laid down by the government of the day. Less explicably, there was continuing concern to enforce sumptuary rules, drawn up by reference to no discernible criteria. This leaves the suspicion that the intense, almost neurotic preoccupation with ensuring that the members of the Inn complied with the rules regulating dress and costume was no more than the instinctive reaction of age to the sartorial flights of fancy of the young, comparable to the responses of the more apoplectic judges to the appearance of the first female trouser suits in their courtrooms in the twentieth century. The

[*] The author is greatly indebted to the Middle Temple Archivist, Lesley Whitelaw, for her help throughout the research for and writing of this chapter, and for correcting a number of grievous errors in the first draft. He was also much assisted over a period of many months by the staff of the Archivist's department. Thanks are also due to Masters Sir Louis Blom-Cooper QC and Richard Havery QC, for valuable suggestions and the prevention of more errors, almost as grievous as the others.

[1] The earliest recorded Minute is dated 1501. Except where otherwise stated, the Minutes are the sources for this account of the proceedings. All dates of years are here given in New Style.

origins of the functions of the Inn as a local authority are also discernible in the Minutes. Much time was spent in apparently futile attempts to prevent the domestic servants of members and tenants from emptying chamber pots out of upper windows, to the understandable dismay of those living or passing below. Because of the difficulty in making complete records of proceedings in Parliament, however, and the fact that the diligence of successive Under-Treasurers over the centuries in making those records was variable, it is necessary to supplement the written word with strenuous exercise of the imagination.

Following the invention of Pitman's shorthand in the middle of the nineteenth century, there came about a sea-change in the documentation. From that time until enforcement of the Bar's professional Code of Conduct passed from the Inns of Court to the Bar Council in the 1960s (it later passed to the Bar Standards Board), there are transcripts of the major disciplinary hearings. These bring vivid life to the cases, many of them dramatic. The practice was that hearings took place in Parliament Chamber. This must have been daunting even to the most stout-hearted defendant, who would face a ring of as many as a dozen or more benchers holding his professional reputation and future in their hands. This was combined with procedures that strike the modern mind as at least strange, or possibly worse.

Usually, proceedings would begin at 5.00 pm, presumably after many of the participants had already had a full working day. This, as repeated experiments with evening court sittings in later years have conclusively demonstrated, almost guarantees that the outcome would be unsatisfactory, even in ideal conditions. In more robust times, before the Human Rights Act passed into law, a Master of the Bench would invariably assume the role of prosecutor, with his brother benchers acting as judges. The transcripts do not reveal that the prosecuting bencher ever left Parliament Chamber while the others considered their verdicts. On the other hand, the transcripts make it clear that when, as often happened, the proceedings occupied two or more hearing days, the Committee was not made up of the same individuals every day on each occasion. It was therefore common-place for the professional future of a member of the Inn to be determined by a bencher who had not heard all the evidence in the case, even though he (never a she in those days) might have read the transcripts, assuming them to have been available in time. Yet there is no record of a defendant ever complaining about what would now be thought to be the demonstrable unfairness of the process, perhaps reflecting the fact that past generations were not only more robust, but also more deferential than today's.

II.   THE VIOLENCE

An unattractive feature of many early disciplinary proceedings before the Bench was the readiness of members of the Inn to attack and insult each other and anyone who tried to remonstrate. The first record of this sort of violence dates from 1512. On 18 May, Bray Cornwall appeared before the Bench charged with assaulting a fellow member, Trowte, and with using 'unsuiting words' in that 'by cause, Master Portman having rehearsed him thereof, he spake unsuiting words unto him sitting at high board.' The nature of the assault was not recorded, but, as will be seen, the use of weapons was, or became, commonplace. 'Unsuiting' words were also used frequently. Bray Cornwall got off fairly lightly in the circumstances. He was fined 5 marks (£3.30, equivalent to about £1,250 in 2010 values), expelled from commons, meaning that he was unable to use Hall, postponing his call to the Bar if he was a student, and sentence was deferred in respect of the assault on the luckless Trowte. One can only speculate, since the Minutes do not record, whether Cornwall was full of supper and distempered draughts at the time, as so many others in similar case seem to have been. He began[2] an ignoble tradition.

Eleven years later, on 12 May 1523, several Masters complained that Holte had used defamatory and seditious words. He was fined 20s (£375 today) and, in effect, warned as to his future conduct. Unfortunately, the Under-Treasurer of the day omitted to record what the words complained of were. There follows a gap in the records until 1552. On 17 November of that year, however, an anonymous member was expelled for causing disturbance, scandalous behaviour to the Treasurer and disobedience, but inexplicably was pardoned at the instance of the Chief Justice[3] and one other. In the absence of any particulars of the grounds on which the Chief Justice and his colleague successfully urged leniency on the Bench, the suspicion of nepotism arises. This is not merely fanciful, since it was the custom for the sons of benchers or others who were spoken for in the same way to be admitted to membership without paying the levies imposed on the less privileged.

A recurring feature of the jurisprudence exercised by the Bench in the sixteenth and seventeenth centuries was the readiness of the Masters to impose severe punishment, only to relent once an apology, with or without financial recompense, had been offered. In 1566, for example, a Mr Piende was fined 20s, by this time equivalent to about £275, for wounding Mr Hennerford, ordered to satisfy his victim for the wound given him and

---

[2] So far as the surviving records reveal.
[3] This was, apparently, Sir Edward Montagu CJCP, who had been Autumn Reader in 1524 and again in 1531 (see *Oxford Dictionary of National Biography* [hereafter 'ODNB']).

readmitted to the Inn. One year later the same order was made, presumably because Piende had done nothing in the meantime, with the proviso that if attacker and attacked could not agree on the damages to be paid, the Masters of the Bench would settle them. To modern eyes this looks merciful. Willingness on the part of the Bench to forgive and forget was not in short supply.

In the latter part of the sixteenth century a Mr Snagge was a conspicuous member of the awkward squad. He first came to the notice of the benchers in November 1570, when he was put out of commons, or banned from Hall until the Parliament after Candlemas (2 February, so the suspension would last three months or so) for using English in a suit at the Guildhall before the Chief Justice; additionally, the Bench deferred a decision whether Snagge should be expelled from the Inn. Evidently, he was not, because he was back in front of the Bench again in 1573. In June of that year, he having been previously barred from commons until All Saints' Day (1 November), not for using English but for the different offence of contumacy, Parliament decided to restore him to Hall at his humble petition. Unabashed by his previous scrapes, the unblushing Snagge was again put out of commons in February 1579 for insolence to Mr Smythe, one of the Masters of the Bench. Next year, he was on the mat yet again. It was resolved at the June Parliament that he should be readmitted to commons, on condition of behaving quietly and moderately. Unfortunately, there is no record of the transgression which caused him to be put out of commons, but it is easy to guess at it. Snagge, however, was not the only offender. Three years earlier Mr Bayliffe, having been expelled from the Inn, not merely put out of commons for contumacy, was restored at his humble petition and submission, another example of the tendency of the Bench to oscillate between what now looks like unnecessary severity and inexplicable readiness to let bygones be bygones. Eventually, even the quarrelsome Snagge benefited from this disposition to mercy, for he was elected Lent Reader, no less, in February 1582. By then, he must have become a reformed character, because the May 1581 Parliament resolved that

> As the last Lent reading was performed by the industry of Messrs Snagge and Blancher ... the same shall be to them both sufficient for their first lectures.

This will have come as a relief to Snagge and Blancher, because the duties of reader included not only the giving of lectures, as they do still, but also standing drinks and food to all and sundry, a custom commemorated, of course, in Reader's Feasts. Exemption from the obligation to give a lecture or lectures would therefore result in substantial saving of expenditure, so the rehabilitation of Snagge may be taken to have been complete by this time. This respite was, however, to be only temporary.

Misbehaviour continued, almost without interruption. Two members, Smith and Ingraham, were expelled for contumacy and disgraceful conduct in 1584; and Snagge met his final nemesis in November 1585. Then, Parliament confirmed the order for his sequestration from the Fellowship of the Masters of the Bench and from all governance of the Inn, adding, confusingly, that the order was in the pantry book and not here. Again, and again unhappily, there is no record of the wrongdoing which finally exhausted the patience of the Bench. Perhaps this was thought to be superfluous in view of Snagge's long and well-documented history of transgression.

In the following year there occurred the first in a long series of incidents in which members beat up the Inn's servants. At the May Parliament the Bench readmitted to the Society 'with his antiquitie' a Mr Bacon, lately put out of the House for certain ill-usage of the steward, on paying 10s to Mr Philip Cole, the Under-Treasurer. One wonders why the steward was not to receive some sort of compensation. Perhaps the unwritten assumption was that the Under-Treasurer, after his kind, would do the decent thing and at least share the 10s with the wronged steward.

The dignity of the Bench continued to offer no safeguard from outrage by hot-tempered members. February 1590 saw Mr Philippes put out of commons and fined 10*l*, the equivalent of £1,250, for his open misdemeanours towards Mr Harris of the Bench at the Chancery Bar, and for his private speeches before the Bench in the Parliament House [*sic*]. Philippes was also ordered to reconcile himself with Master Harris as a prerequisite to being readmitted to commons, and in default he was to be evicted from his chambers. More than a year later, in May 1591, Parliament remitted the fine and revoked the eviction from his chambers which Philippes had evidently suffered as the result of his failure or refusal to make it up with Master Harris. Once more, however, the Minutes give no hint of why this leniency was exercised. All was not forgiven, because he was not to be allowed into commons until the following term.

Occasionally the disorder went too far. In February 1598 there was an ugly incident, 'while the Masters of the Bench and other fellows were quietly dining publicly in the Hall'. John Davyes, a Master of the Bar (see above, p 89), came into Hall, in cap and gown, and girt with a dagger, his servant and another with him, being armed with swords. It is hard to tell whether the most serious element in the behaviour complained of was the fact that all three men were armed, or whether it was because Davyes was wearing his cap and gown. Parliament sometimes seemed to take an equally serious view of each solecism. Davyes then left his accomplices at the bottom of the Hall, next to the screen, and walked up to the second table where the Masters of the Bar, including Richard Martyn, were 'quietly dining'. Davyes then took a stick, 'which is commonly called a Bastianado', from under his gown and struck Martyn over the head until the Bastianado broke. He added insult to injury by running back down the Hall, taking the servant's sword and shaking it over his own head, before running down to the water steps (at the bottom of Middle Temple Lane, there being no Embankment until the eighteenth century) and jumping into a boat. 'He is expelled never to return.' This account leaves intriguing questions unanswered. There was clearly careful premeditation and planning beforehand, even to the point of laying on the escape boat. Was there a grudge between Davyes and Martyn, and why the waving of the sword after the attack? Why should the Under-Treasurer, if it was he, take the trouble to record this apparently unimportant detail? Understandably, Davyes's expulsion was confirmed at Parliament in February 1599. Astonishingly, he was readmitted in 1601, after apologising to his victim and going through some sort of penitential ritual at the Cupboard in Hall, just before dinner and in the presence of a bevy of grandees, including the Chief Justice of the Queen's Bench, the Chief Baron of the Exchequer, and assorted judges, Barons and Serjeants-at-Law. GBH[4] was apparently more acceptable in Tudor times than it is now.

Mr Hugh Boscawen followed Davyes's lead in 1600, by striking William Boughton in the Hall with his dagger on Saturday night, giving him two wounds on the head, and earning a fine of 10*l* and expulsion from the Inn. With characteristic inconsistency this punishment was remitted in May 1601, Boscawen was allowed back into the Society and ordered to pay 26s 8d, in addition to the 40s which he had already paid. His eventual fine was therefore £3.33, or £410 in 2010 values, instead of the original equivalent of £1,250.

This unedifying pattern of thuggery lasted down the centuries. The Minutes record a knifing in Hall in 1610, the threat of a duel after a quarrel in 1612, a punch up in 1613, a mini-riot with broken windows in 1614, another attack on the steward by a barrister in 1631 and attacks on the watch in Fleet Street. The dreary catalogue stretches down the years until about the middle of the eighteenth century. Thereafter standards of behaviour in the Inn seem to have improved, and violent incidents became rare. Between 1745 and 1761 no disciplinary proceedings of any kind were minuted as having taken place in Parliament. Violence became very much the exception. In 1721 Parliament evicted the tenant of a wine shop in the passage leading out of Garden Court into Middle Temple Lane, whose customers got drunk and generated many complaints. In June 1741 the Bench received a complaint from a watchman that he had been attacked by a member of the Inn late at night, although nothing apparently came of the matter, because the member was served with a copy of the complaint and no further action was taken. Sixty-five years were to pass before the next

---

[4] Grievous bodily harm.

similar complaint was made, this time not against a member but against a tenant of chambers in Elm Court, John Brady. The Inn's Gardener came upon two small boys fighting in the Garden and turfed them out when they refused to leave. The father of one of the boys later fell upon the Gardener, and was threatened with prosecution, but apologised and the matter was allowed to drop. For reasons which will become clear, Brady turned out to be the original neighbour from hell, who was to attract the attention of the Bench again.

The last incident took place in August 1819, when George Price, a barrister of the Inn, got drunk and beat an Inn watchman with a stick, putting him on the sick list for 10 days and causing him to lose wages. Having originally agreed to pay 3*l* damages to the watchman, Price then resiled from this, and was threatened with indictment in the courts and with eviction from his chambers. The affair dragged on until 1822 when a Master of the Bench managed to broker a settlement, whereupon unsullied decorum within the Inn and its neighbourhood broke out, and not before time.

III. Unseemly Merriment and Other Misbehaviour

Domestic discipline extended not only to the criminal or near-criminal conduct already described, but also to lapses from what were seen by the authorities as normal good behaviour. This was another aspect of the supervision which the Inn had to exercise over large numbers of young men who were in essence undergraduates, without any sense of vocation to Holy Orders which had to be assumed in those who chose to go to Oxford or Cambridge. The Inns of Court were the alternative for those whose aspirations were avowedly secular—the Court, politics, or the armed services being their intended destinations, as well as the law. Much and recurring trouble arose from the prolonged drinking bouts associated with the creation and tenure of office by Lords of Misrule.

The Lords of Misrule were beings to be found not only in the Inns of Court. They had their origins in the Festival of Saturnalia of classical antiquity, when, over the period of the winter solstice, there was general merrymaking, with the usual order of things reversed; slaves became temporary freemen, and were at liberty to command and require their masters to wait upon them. One slave would be made King of the Saturnalia and lead the revels. There is some evidence that he was required to cut his own throat at the end of proceedings, or be executed.[5] By the Middle Ages the King had evolved into the Abbot of Unreason, the King of the Bean or the Bishop of Fools; and by the sixteenth century he was the

---

[5] See Sir James Frazer, *The Golden Bough* (London, Macmillan, 1995), ch 58.

Lord of Misrule at the Court, at the City Guildhall in London and in the houses of the great. If his existence was seen to pose at least a latent threat to the authority of the Bench, this might explain the severity which was exercised in a number of ways towards those who over-indulged.[6]

The earliest record of the problem dates from 1590. Parliament met on 5 February, three days after Candlemas. The Minutes recall that in 1584 Parliament had forbidden playing at dice or cards, outcries in the night, breaking open chambers, as by the Lord of Candlemas night, and that on Candlemas night 1589 divers gentlemen had set up a Lord of Misrule and were punished therefor. On the anniversary in 1590 the Masters of the Bench caused a general admonition and reminder of the prohibitions against outcries in the night and so on to be given in the midst of supper (ie in Hall). Nevertheless, eight named miscreants and others 'not yet known' broke the embargo by making outcries, forcibly breaking open chambers in the night, levying money as the Lord of Misrule's rent, and 'contemptuously refused to declare the names of the others; and Mr Lower abused Mr Johnson, a Master of the Bench'. Mr Lower was therefore expelled, and the others fined 20*l* (£2,500 or so now), to be paid before the end of term, with expulsion in default of payment. The fines look savage, for what seems to have been little more than a drinks party that got out of hand. There may have been more to this than appears on the surface, because two years later the same transgressors were back again.

On 11 February 1593 (note the proximity to Candlemas) Parliament noted that in spite of the past history,

> divers gentlemen of the House on last Candlemas night joined with ... Mr Lower who [was] expelled for breaking the said orders [prohibiting outcries, etc] and broke open chamber doors and abused many gentlemen of the House, and some of the Fellowship knew them notwithstanding their disguised attire.

The result was six more expulsions from the Inn and three suspensions from commons. It looks as if there was something more than a rowdy evening involved, since Lower, a disgraced former member of the Inn, took the trouble to come back and either lead or join in a re-run of the behaviour which had got him expelled two years before. This, together with the harshness of the punishments consistently handed out, suggests that there was a concerted attack on the benchers' authority, with the Lord of Misrule festivities used only as a pretext for what amounted to rebellion. This may also explain the unusual speed with which Parliament dealt with the offenders on each occasion.

A century later the problem had not gone away. Following similar disturbances in 1640, on 27 January 1641 eight gentlemen were fined 20*l* each. By this time, because of the fall in the value of money, the fine was

---

[6] *Ibid.*

the equivalent of £1,500 in 2010 values. The offence was to have broken open the doors to the Hall, Parliament Chamber and kitchen at Christmas, and setting up a 'gaming Christmas', persisting after Mr Treasurer's admonition and continuing the disorders until a week after Twelfth Day. The Bench also ordered that 20*l* was to be given to the butlers and officers who obeyed orders and did not attend on them. This shows that the culprits had done more than set up a poker school lasting the twelve days of Christmas, for there is no need for butlers and other officers for that. It looks rather as if there was unauthorised roistering, which is what had taken place in the past. Almost identical disorders took place at Christmas 1671, ending only on the Monday after Twelfth Day, and leading to four more expulsions and 20*l* fines on different individuals at Parliament on 26 January 1673. A new feature was that the ringleaders had got a locksmith to open the doors, and a cook and a waiter to serve them in the buttery. These, not being members of the Inn, were to have informations laid against them in the Crown Office, which is another indication of the gravity of the offences. One of the band got himself restored to membership on payment of a 20s (£75) fine in February 1674, but the heavy fine imposed on him the year before was to be reconsidered at the next Parliament.

IV. DRESS CODES

The Bench showed itself, consistently and down the years, sensitive to the sartorial extravagances of the young. The first record of concern dates from May 1557, when Parliament ordered that

> none of the Company after the end of May shall wear breeches of any light colour nor use coifs of any English lawn, velvet caps, scarfs, or 'whynges' in their study gowns.

Those indulgences look harmless enough, with the possible exception of the coifs, which were the distinguishing mark of the serjeants-at-law, and about which the Bench might have had legitimate concern.[7]

Parliament returned to the matter in the next month, June 1557, and ordered that

---

[7] A coif is a headdress, usually white and framing the face, worn now by some orders of nuns. The serjeants-at-law were a *corps d'élite* of barristers and judges, the leaders of the profession. They had their own Inn, Serjeants' Inn, which is now represented by an architecturally non-committal office block off Fleet Street, just outside the Inner Temple. The influence and importance of the serjeants waned slowly and progressively after the establishment of King's and Queen's Counsel in the 17th century. The last English serjeant was appointed in 1877. See, further, EH Warren 'Serjeants-at-Law: The Order of the Coif' (1942) *Virginia Law Review* 911.

> None of the Companies, except Knights or Benchers ... shall wear in their doublets or hose any light colour except scarlet or crimson, or wear any upper velvet cap, or any scarf or wing in their gowns ...

on pain of a fine for a first offence, and expulsion for a second. The issue of dress seems to have come down to a battle of wills between the Bench and the rebels, as often as not.

On 9 May 1617 four members of the Inn appeared before Parliament to answer a variety of charges. In the first place, they petitioned to be allowed to wear hats in Hall, not a matter, it might be thought, of any great consequence. Permission was refused, but the defendants then went into Hall and the church wearing hats. The ringleader, a John Dowle, was also charged with keeping a catalogue of those who had resolved with him to continue wearing hats, boots and spurs in the church and in Hall. Dowle's conduct of his own defence was such that the Bench 'saw good cause to suspect him for a chief stirrer of mutiny' and expelled him. The other defendants appeared wearing hats, boots and spurs, refused to pay the fines which had been imposed on them earlier and were put out of commons. They nevertheless reappeared in Hall wearing hats, and continued to insist that they would go on wearing hats in Hall. For this they were also expelled, unless they agreed to toe the line by next Tuesday. Seen from the twenty-first century, this looks much like a storm in a wine-glass, comparable to contemporary Hall members or students refusing to wear ties at dinner. As social conventions relax themselves, it may yet come to that.

The proceedings of 9 May set off a conflagration. On 30 May Parliament put out no fewer than 46 members from commons. Their offence was to have taken part in a great conspiracy to 'break up' [*sic*] the ancient custom of wearing caps in the Hall at dinners, suppers and breakfasts, and in the church at prayer and sermon times. The transgressors were not to be readmitted to commons until they had obeyed the rules and ceased to wear hats in Hall and the Church, in default of which they would be evicted from their chambers. Thereafter, there was to be a fine of 3s 4d (one quarter of a mark, or about £15 in 2010) for each breach of the rule, and further punishment if the Bench thought fit. By 1668 the fine had gone up to 10s (£36), which the Bench fined John Hanham for coming into Hall in a white hat, 'being an indecent habit'.

By the eighteenth century the furore had blown over, and in 1722 Parliament had to do no more than order that no member should eat in Hall unless he was wearing 'a decent and complete gown whole and untorn'. This proved not to be controversial because there were no subsequent proceedings for breach of this decree.

The oddest rule of dress and behaviour which can ever have applied in any learned society concerned pattens, the wooden supports worn under the sole of an ordinary shoe, so as to lift the wearer out of the mud and protect a lady's long dress. This produced an indignant petition to Parliament from a solicitor, a Mr John Izard, in February 1829. Mr Izard did not use one word where ten would do, but the essence of his complaint was that he was on his way to Elm Court with a lady client in November 1828 to do business with another attorney. Because there had been heavy rain, the lady was wearing pattens. As solicitor and client were on their way to Elm Court, in Mr Izard's words, 'a voice was heard exclaiming in a rude manner "Pull off your pattens"'. Mr Izard seeing no one but a porter standing a few yards off, it was considered unnecessary to take any notice. The order was repeated, and Mr Izard asked the porter 'Who are you?', receiving the ungracious reply 'What's that to you?' There followed an undignified but mildly ridiculous scuffle, which ended with the porter seizing Izard

> by the Neckerchief and planting his knuckles into the side of his throat and in this situation held your Petitioner until he was nearly choked.

When released, Izard showed the porter his business card and was told that the latter's orders were that no person was to be permitted to go through the Inn with pattens on. By this time the inevitable small crowd had gathered, from which a voice called, rather officiously it might be thought, 'Now Officer, you have done your duty.' Thus emboldened, the porter then gripped Izard by his coat collar and frog-marched him out of the Inn. As if that was not enough, the subject of the petition to Parliament was that the indictment brought against him, presumably for assaulting the porter and at the instigation of the Inn, should be stayed. The reason given was, understandably, that he had no idea that it was forbidden to wear pattens within the Inn. The Bench graciously ordered that the prosecution should be stayed and granted the petition. Had he lived 150 years later that porter would have been one of the great traffic wardens. Whatever, the reader may ask, could have been the justification for the prohibition on wearing pattens in the first place? It was an entirely reasonable precaution for a lady to take to protect her dress at a time when many—if not most—streets and courts in London were not paved, and when those streets were thronged with horses. Further, it is worth recalling that the practice of wearing pattens was sufficiently widespread for there to be a City of London Livery Company, the Patten Makers, devoted to the craft of their manufacture—a Company which still exists, as it happens.

V. THE BENCH AS THOUGHT POLICE

In 1570, for reasons partly religious and partly *realpolitikisch*, Pope Pius V issued a Bull excommunicating Queen Elizabeth I, declaring her deposed and anathematising all who continued to obey her laws.[8] This provoked a flurry of legislation, which made it treasonable to call the Queen a heretic, to bring Papal Bulls into the country or to import rosaries, and made it an offence for Catholics to leave the country or to be trained for ordination. Until then, in a very English way, the Government had turned a largely blind eye to the observance of the Catholic religion, but the Catholic community in general, and the legal profession in particular, now faced heavy pressure. Prominent on both counts was Master Edmund Plowden, whose family home was at Shiplake in what is now Oxfordshire. That is less than ten miles from Stonor Park, the home of the Stonor family, one of the country's great Catholic dynasties, then as now. There were other prominent Catholic families not far away at Buckland, near Faringdon, and at Ashbury in the Vale of the White Horse. Predictably, Catholics who faced the threat of prosecution or worse tended to profess undying loyalty to the Protestant religion by law—or at least by Act of Parliament—established, and to protest vehement detestation of popery, while continuing to hear Mass in secret. It is likely that some, at least, of the Catholic Middle Templars against whom no action was taken were not above such dissembling, for which it is hard to blame them.

The year of the Spanish Armada, 1588, marks the first appearance of the Middle Temple Bench as the enforcer of religious observance. This may not be accidental. The naval Battle of Gravelines, off Calais on 27 July, had begun the process of destroying the Armada, which continued throughout August 1588. The maritime manoeuvring which preceded this had been going on for months. Against this background, on 21 June 1588 Parliament took its first recorded disciplinary action associated with religion. It is easy to infer that this was inspired either by fear that the Inn might be harbouring popish spies or plotters, or by pressure from government. Whatever the explanation, on that date the Bench expelled no fewer than eight members of the Inn for failure to take Holy Communion in the Temple Church, despite their having been ordered to do so earlier.

The matter came up again at Parliament three months later on 25 October. Sibthorpe, one of the eight expelled in June, was found to have been the object of a wrong information by the butler, and was restored to membership and his 'antiquitie' on his petition showing his detestation of the popish religion. Another of the suspected Papists, Richard Walter, was treated somewhat less leniently on the same occasion. He was ordered to have conference touching his religion with Mr Hoker, whose identity is not revealed in the Minutes. He was, however, Richard Hooker, as he is known now, Master of the Temple and one of the great English theologians.

---

[8]   JB Black (ed), *Oxford History of England—The Reign of Elizabeth*, 2nd edn (Oxford, Oxford University Press 1959), 168.

Hooker had been Master of the Temple since 1585, and, with his deserved reputation, would have been well able to vouch for the sincerity of any claim to detest the popish religion. At all events, the Masters of the Bench resolved to restore Richard Walter to membership at the next Parliament if he produced a certificate, presumably from Mr Hoker, touching his reformation, and also on showing that he had taken communion.

By the time Parliament met in February 1590, the matter was resolved. Richard Walter made suit to be restored to membership, which was granted, provided he first made detestation in writing under his hand of all popish religion, and delivered this to the treasurer. This he did, and there is no more mention of popery in the Minutes. Presumably, memories of the Armada grew dim, and the need to enforce communion with the new Church of England became correspondingly faint. A hundred and fifty years were to pass before Parliament next concerned itself with religion.

The circumstances of that case were curious, and so far as the Inn's records go, unique. William Bohun was the Deputy Reader at New Inn, the Inn of Chancery owned by and most closely associated with the Middle Temple. On 28 November 1738 he was brought before the Bench accused of blasphemy, having drawn up a paper for discussion at a moot or similar event at New Inn. The question to be discussed was whether a defendant was guilty of blasphemy if he denied that Christ was God, relying on, among other things, texts from the *Book of Common Prayer* and the *Epistle of Paul to Timothy*, 1 Tim c2, v5.[9] To modern eyes this looks more like a debate among medieval schoolmen than a discussion between law students in the age of Gibbon, Rousseau and Voltaire. Moreover, Bohun had done no more than raise a hypothetical and academic question, without apparently expressing any opinion as to whether Christ was or was not God. He, unwisely as it turned out, did not appear to answer the complaint, and was expelled, Parliament having declared the Case as drafted to be highly profane 'and altogether improper to be Read upon at New Inn'. In order to guard against any repetition of such scandal, the Bench further ordered that all Cases to be presented in future should be submitted to the Bar Mess six days in advance, for scrutiny and censorhip if appropriate. To modern eyes, Bohun looks to have been hard done by, but it is difficult to escape the conclusion that by not appearing to answer what would have been, even in the eighteenth century, a serious charge, he had only himself to blame.

---

[9] 'For there is one God, and one mediator between God and men, the man Christ Jesus.'

VI.   THE INN AS LOCAL AUTHORITY

One of the quirks of local government administration is that for many years the Middle and Inner Temples, although not the other two Inns, have been local authorities for many purposes. The reason, although it is hardly a satisfying explanation, may be that the two Temples are within the City of London, while the other two Inns are not. For example, section 180 of the Local Government Act 1972, the principal statute currently regulating local authorities, establishes the Temples as public health and sanitation authorities for their respective areas. The origins of this are probably to be found in the frequent exercise over the centuries of Parliament's jurisdiction over chamber pots and other aspects of good neighbourliness within the Inn. This derived from the Inns' succession to the land and some of the privileges of the Knights Templar and Knights Hospitaller. These orders had been answerable only to the Pope, by virtue of a medieval Bull,[10] and they were exempt from all civil and ecclesiastical jurisdiction. Having dissolved the religious orders, Henry VIII preserved the Inns' tenancies of the Temple. Their continued immunity from the jurisdiction of the Mayor and Corporation of London was a matter occasionally in dispute until the twentieth century.[11]

This independence survives in part. In 1598 Parliament noted that

> Divers grievances are daily committed by reason of water, chamber pots, and other annoyances cast out of gentlemen's chambers to the great offence of gentlemen of good worth passing by, as well as [*sic*] of the House as others; in future the owner of a chamber where such an offence is committed, shall be fined 40s [£250 in 2010].

This proved to be no deterrent. In 1612, following a complaint, it was ordered that windows in Temple Churchyard should be wired up so as to prevent the emptying of chamber pots, and the gutters of some penthouses below cleansed. The condition of those gutters is all too imaginable. This was followed up in 1620 by a second order repeating that of 1598, and adding that laundresses or other servants emptying chamber pots in unseemly or unbefitting places were to be dismissed and their employers fined. This was equally ineffective, for a Mr Hawkey had his chambers repossessed in November 1663, following complaint by an utter-barrister of damage from strangers lodging in the chambers pouring down filthy water. Paradoxically, the order was suspended two weeks later, without explanation. In 1689 some benchers themselves were incommoded by water and filth thrown out of an upper window by a laundress. That cost

---

[10]   *Omne Datum Optimum* (1163), by Alexander III.
[11]   Under an Act of 1540. See Silsoe Lord, The *Peculiarities of the Temple*', (London, The Estates Gazette 1972), at 18–20.

the tenant a fine of 40s. The fine was by then the equivalent of £150 in 2010. The passage of time seems to have brought about no greater refinement in behaviour, because the same difficulties arose in 1714, 1717, 1718, 1721 and 1807, and even as late as 1831.

The governance of the Inn extended into other fields as well. The Bench, acting as a sort of licensing authority, was concerned from time to time to put a stop to gambling. In 1584 it decreed that playing with dice or cards within the Inn was to be prohibited, on pain of expulsion, and followed this up by expelling Mr George Cane in November 1587 for making divers matches and bargaining with Mr Richard Calthorpe. The latter escaped with being put out of commons, and the Bench later relented in Cane's case, ordering that he should be readmitted if he agreed to submit his bargains and agreements with Calthorpe to arbitration. It seems as if the disapproval of gambling was more a matter of form than genuine disapproval. Attitudes were to become progressively less stern. In 1611 a member who had been put out of commons for playing at tables in his chambers and fined, petitioned to be restored to commons and to have the fine remitted. He failed, in part at least. The fine was to be paid publicly during dinner, whereupon the Masters of the Bench were prepared to review the question of his coming back into commons.

The Bench was also concerned with various consequences of other frailties of the flesh. The first hint of this comes in 1640, when the January Parliament expelled the treasurer of the Bar, a senior Hall member responsible for the behaviour of the Bar, put his under-treasurer out of commons, and sacked the steward. Their offences lay in having allowed or conspired in activities deemed to amount to insufferable enormities. These were related to the Christmas revels, a matter, as has already been seen, of serious enough concern. This was compounded at Christmas 1638 by admitting

> base, lewd, and unworthy persons into the Hall and other places of the House under pretence of gaming, and also continuing play and excess of diet almost a fortnight beyond the time limited by order, notwithstanding.

Since the 'gaming'—presumably meaning plays and feasting rather than gambling—was apparently intended to give an air of respectability to the base, lewd and unworthy persons, one can only infer that they were ladies of easy virtue.

The first incident of the Inn discharging poor relief functions linked to its disciplinary jurisdiction dates from 1642, when a bastard child was brought into the House and laid at the chamber door of Mr Richard Dewes, charged to have begotten it in his said chamber. The Masters of the Bench, by reason of Mr Dewes's absence, were forced to take care of it; and to remove so great a scandal, were driven in his behalf to deposit 5*l* towards the keeping of the child. In order, no doubt, to remove any opportunity for Mr Dewes to repeat his behaviour, his chambers were repossessed. The suspicions of the Bench were apparently aroused again in 1657, because in April it required one of the most ancient of the Utter Bar to show cause to Master Treasurer what woman it was that lodged in his chamber. This seems to have been a case of 'once bitten, twice shy', the Bench not wishing to have to support the offspring of a succession of unsanctified unions taking place within the Inn.

The Inn, in common with conventional Poor Law Guardians, was responsible for the upbringing of abandoned babies or foundlings, and the Minutes of Parliament record several instances of this liability extending over many years. In each case the baby was given the surname Temple, and generally ended up being apprenticed to a trade or put into service. There is a Petition to Parliament of June 1797 which is at once entertaining and moving. Daniel and Mary Doran, who were not members of the Inn, petitioned the Bench to call off a prosecution begun against them. They had, as they said, been

> concerned with deserting a child at the entrance to the staircase No 1 Middle Temple Lane ... they had no premeditated design in giving their Masterships the trouble any further than the impulse of the Moment and most wretched Indigence. That the Petitioners had suffered more already by pecuniary embarrassments than they would be able to recover by the strictest economy in a considerable length of time. That if the Petitioners were compelled to endure any further the rigour of the law they would be driven into a Gulph of indigence from whence it would be impossible for them to recover.

And so on for several pages. It worked, however, because the Bench relented and agreed to stay the prosecution, on terms.

The Brady family from hell has already been met (see section II. above). The Bench had to concern itself not only with the father's assault on the Inn's gardener, but also with the rest of the brood. In May 1806 a member of the society, Mr Hedron, who had the misfortune to live on the same staircase in Elm Court, applied for what was in effect an anti-social behaviour order against the whole family. He complained that they made so much noise and occasioned so much filth as exceeded all endurance. On his complaining about the children's noise to the mother, she loaded him with abuse, in which example she was followed by the children who railed after him in the street. Hedron had then got his servant to warn Brady's eldest boy about his behaviour. The response was a physical attack on the servant. Hedron's neighbours in Elm Court came to his support, and at the Parliament in January 1807 the Bradys were threatened with eviction unless they reformed. It is uncertain whether the Bench was being exceptionally tolerant, or whether it did not wish to be put to the trouble of finding new tenants. Poor Hedron made further complaints in November 1807 and May 1808, ending with a rent strike. Even this did not galvanise the Bench into taking action against, rather than threatening, the Bradys. Elm Court had, in short, become a sink estate, and the Bench seems to have been as powerless, or perhaps unwilling, to deal with it as are many contemporary local authorities in such cases.

VII. THE CRIMINALS

On 2 July 1571, John Hunt jun and John Yate were expelled because they had been imprisoned by the (Privy) Council for attempts touching the state of the Kingdom. Nothing more is known about what they had done, and nothing at all is known about Hunt. Yate, however, has the same surname as one of the recusant families who were notable for their heretical and presumed treasonable beliefs, and this may explain the punishments visited upon the two. That, however, is speculation.

Less heinous, one might have thought, was the offence of killing a tame stag of the King's, for which three members were expelled in 1609. One of the three was noted in the Minutes as being in prison in 'the Marshalsy', and the other two had 'absented themselves', no doubt to avoid a similar fate. Historically, it had been a capital offence to poach in the royal deer forests, but the fact that the stag had been tame points to the killing having been a mistake or an accident rather than a deliberate act of poaching. There is some support for that, since later in the same year the prisoner in the Marshalsy ' . . . was desired to obtain the Prince's hand to his petition for reinstatement to membership, signifying the Prince's pleasure that he (the offender) shall be restored to membership of the Inn'. It looks as if cordial relations between Sovereign and subject had resumed, and that bygones were to be bygones. In May 1610, having obtained the Prince's favour to pardon and remit the offence, two of the three malefactors were restored to the Fellowship. That could hardly have happened if there had been deliberate poaching.

Mysteriously, Mr Anthony Gearing was expelled in 1624, being of lewd life and behaviour, and having been several times indicted of felony. He had never before come before Parliament, and on a strict reading of the Minute had merely been accused of felony and never convicted. If so, the presumption of innocence counted for little. Gearing was, on the other hand, never restored to membership, and did not even petition to be readmitted. Perhaps he was a black sheep, after all.

The year 1630 saw a domestic but ugly incident, which had repercussions outside the Inn. There was something not far short of overt mutiny against the authority of the Bench. In January Parliament fined three ringleaders for refusing to leave Hall when required, 'on pretence of their liberties [as they termed it] being infringed'. By February 1632 they were back. The same three, named Dyer, Lisle and Oglander, had set up what they called a 'parliament' and fined the Inn steward and forcibly put him in the stocks, for refusing to provide them with commons. When summoned to explain themselves by the Bench, they advanced on the High Table during Hall, and demanded that the earlier fines should be remitted.

> Being fairly treated by the Masters of the Bench, they went down to their places, but towards the end of supper came up again, telling the Bench they had given them time to consider, and with many insolent speeches peremptorily pressed to have the order repealed. This being denied them, they hasted down tumultuously, and calling for pots, threw them at random towards the Bench table, and struck divers Masters of the Bench as they were walking, being risen from the board.

The benchers complained to the Lord Chief Justice 'of this notorious outrage, the like of which had not formerly been known in any other Inn of Court'. The Chief Justice with two puisnes heard the complaint, sent two of the rebels to the King's Bench prison and bound two more to be of good behaviour. This looks like the origin of the jurisdiction of the Judges as Visitors of the Inns of Court, a function which they still exercise, sitting to hear appeals against orders of the Inns of Court Disciplinary Tribunals. Parliament Minutes go on to record that the Bench had intended to expel all four offenders, but relented in view of the orders of the Judges, and went so far as to be merciful and not only remit the fines but also receive all four back into commons. The Bench had the last word, though:

> They damn their order and doom their book to the fire, ordering it be hereafter *ipso facto* expulsion for anyone to claim any power to govern within the House otherwise than as subordinate to Masters of the Bench.

And quite right too, as any bencher would say.

Yet within the year, with characteristic inconsistency, and in spite of what must have been a disagreeable experience, Parliament changed tack. Christmas 1631 had brought the by now familiar disorders to Hall. A fresh group of hotheads set up a parliament and 'assembled with the young gentlemen, and made an order to drink healths in Hall with loud music expressly against the said orders' (made after the *evenements* of February 1630). The perpetrators were, however, merely fined 20s and put out of commons until the fines were paid. At this time the fine was the equivalent of £80, a surprisingly modest sum when compared with others levied before and after, as has been seen (in section III. above).

The most spectacular of the Inn's criminals were Messrs Goodenough, Wade and West, expelled in October 1683 after being charged with high treason and fleeing. The Minute of Parliament does no more than record those facts. It conceals the involvement of the three in the Rye House Plot. This was a plan drawn up at the house after which it is named, located near Waltham Abbey in the Lea Valley. It was fomented by supporters of

Charles II's illegitimate son, James Duke of Monmouth, with the aim of assassinating the King and James, Duke of York (later King James II), as they were on their way back to London from a visit to the races at Newmarket, where the Rowley Mile course is named after Charles himself.[12] Monmouth, like the three conspirators, was a member of the Inn, admitted in 1664. His sympathies were Protestant and Whig, while those of the royal brothers were Tory and Catholic.[13] After the Plot was betrayed, Wade escaped by way of Scarborough to Holland and later joined Monmouth's Rebellion in 1685, fighting at the Battle of Sedgemoor after which he was captured. Goodenough's subsequent career was similar, since he too joined Monmouth's Rebellion and was captured after its collapse at Sedgemoor. The later history of the two was unedifying. After their capture they turned informers and perjurers, and were used by the Government as witnesses against rich and powerful Whigs in the City of London, who had long been marked out for punishment for their politics, and who were duly convicted and executed. Wade and Goodenough both received pardons for their pains, the former ending up as Town Clerk of Bristol.[14]

The three were continuing an unedifying tradition. Two brothers, Robert and Thomas Winter, had been hanged, drawn and quartered at the beginning of the century for their parts, which had been significant, in the Gunpowder Plot. There is no evidence of their having been disciplined by the Inn. Perhaps the Government got to them before the Bench was in a position to act, and it was thought superfluous to expel them in the circumstances.

Another criminal, although on a less spectacular scale, surfaced in 1735. In August 1734 the Librarian reported that some half dozen books had been stolen from the Library, and another damaged by the removal of single pages, evidently including prints. The stolen books turned up at a bookbinder's in Covent Garden without covers, brought there by Henry Justice, a member of the Inn. The books were bound, and Justice then asked a bookseller in Drury Lane to sell them for him, except for one which was found in Justice's chambers in the Inn, as were the missing prints. The Bench therefore unanimously declared that Justice was guilty of stealing the books and prints, a conclusion which it cannot have hesitated long in reaching. It then transpired that Justice was in Newgate Prison, likely to be prosecuted by Cambridge University for similar offences, so the benchers stayed their hands. By May 1736 Justice had been convicted at

[12]   Charles II's nickname was 'Old Rowley': JP Kenyon, *The Stuarts* (London, Batsford, 1958), 153.

[13]   Feiling, *History of England* (London, Macmillan, 1950), V, ch II.

[14]   Macaulay, *History of England*, (London, Longmans, Green, Reader & Dyer, 1877) ch V.

the Old Bailey of stealing books from the Wren Library at Trinity College, Cambridge, and pleaded guilty to stealing more books from the University Library there. He was expelled, and no more was heard of him.

The last entry in the Minutes made before the introduction of the practice of making transcripts of disciplinary proceedings was, as it happened, a complaint unprecedented in all the years since records began. In November 1847 a solicitor complained that Ernest Charles Jones, a non-practising barrister member, was giving legal advice without instructions from an attorney, and was acting as a sham attorney in the conduct of legal proceedings. The complainant went on to opine that such proceedings were highly derogatory to the dignity of the Bar, 'to say nothing of being a direct invasion of the rights and privileges of my profession as an Attorney and Solicitor'. That, perhaps, was the real thrust of the complaint.

Ernest Charles Jones was a radical firebrand and supporter of the Chartist movement. He edited a number of more or less revolutionary newspapers, and at some stage after the complaint of misconduct was lodged got two years at the Old Bailey for sedition, having made inflammatory speeches at public meetings. Jones made a habit of offering legal advice to poor people and of refusing payment, initially at least. By his own account he became swamped with requests for advice, and began to charge a five shilling fee in order to discourage unnecessary correspondence and to cover his costs and postage, and so on. He even claimed to have ended up out of pocket. His reason was that his clients, if that is what they were, had been the victims of knavish legal practitioners in Mr Halsall's (the complainant's) branch of the legal profession, and he unblushingly asserted that he intended pursuing the same course in future.

The matter had to be adjourned repeatedly, because Jones kept failing to appear to answer the charge, probably because he was unavoidably detained elsewhere by Her Majesty. Finally, however, on 27 November 1850, three years after the complaint, Parliament was able to deal with it, and informed Jones that his conduct had been most irregular and unprofessional, as no doubt it had. The Bench expressed its severest censure, but because Jones had discontinued the practices imputed to him, even if he had no choice in the matter while inside, and because of his assurance of not renewing them, it took no more severe course. This looks to have been merciful in the circumstances—perhaps Parliament had sympathy with one who was obviously sincere and had not profited personally from his breaches of professional propriety.

A. Augustus Newton

No such mitigation was available to the next member of the Inn to come to the attention of the Bench, in 1850. Augustus Newton had been the unsuccessful defendant in an action for damages in which a John Harrison was plaintiff. Harrison was awarded £104 11s (£5,025 in 2010 values). Newton did not pay and was imprisoned for debt. He was charged before Parliament by the Attorney-General (later Chief Justice), Sir John Jervis, with having fraudulently procured his release from prison and absolution from paying the judgment debt by persuading the plaintiff to sign a release the meaning and effect of which Newton had misrepresented. When he first appeared before Parliament Newton objected to the proceedings on the ground that the Attorney-General should not be appearing as prosecutor and deliberating on the case with his fellow benchers. One might think that he had a point, but the objection failed, the Attorney arguing that he was only there to present the facts.

The exasperated shorthand writer recorded that Mr Newton ultimately proceeded at great length on the merits of his defence. This was that the document signed by Harrison was not an unconditional discharge of the judgment debt and release from the debtors' prison, and that notwithstanding this the entire debt had been paid off. The Bench was not impressed, disbarred Newton and expelled him from the society.

This was not the first time that Newton had been in trouble. Although nothing came of it in the end, there had been suggestions that he was in the habit of appearing for defendants at Petty Sessions in the Cheltenham area and at Gloucester Quarter Sessions without being instructed by solicitors, with interviewing witnesses at his own home, and negotiating his own fees directly with the friends and relatives of the prisoners for whom he was acting. While Parliament plainly could not be seen to take account of these unproved allegations, it would hardly have been unaware of them, and human frailty might have made it impossible for the benchers, or some of them, to put them wholly to one side. Even if they fell into that error, they reached a decision with which a strong Bench of Visitors, to whom Newton appealed, agreed.

Newton acted for himself before the Visitors, as he had before Parliament. The transcript shows that he did himself no favours. He had an unfailing penchant for the irrelevant. At one point Chief Justice Campbell, who presided, had to stop him in the middle of a rambling submission to the effect that his appeal should succeed because there was parliamentary privilege which protected MPs from the execution of warrants for debt. Newton was not and had never been an MP. He went on to repeat the submission that his conviction by Parliament was wrong because he had since repaid the debt in full. He even made the elementary mistake of introducing before the Judges the matters of his having been said to have appeared before courts in Gloucestershire without proper instructions and to have acted improperly there. He had to be stopped from doing so not only by Chief Justice Campbell, but also by Chief Baron Pollock who sat on the case as well. It comes as no surprise that the Visitors took little time to dismiss the appeal, saying that they saw no reason to reverse the judgment of Parliament.

B.   William Digby Seymour QC MP

Seymour was, as the initials after his name indicate, an established practitioner and also a long-serving MP. By his account, he had at least a respectable practice on the Northern Circuit in the north-east, which he tended when his parliamentary duties allowed. However, he got involved, as Chairman, in Waller Mining, a company set up to mine gold in the United States, of the kind which figures frequently in nineteenth-century law reports. One of the shareholders was a Mr Parker, who met Seymour either through the Waller Mining Company, or through a member of the Home Circuit, who dropped out of the story almost immediately.

Seymour did not confine his dubious speculations to gold mines. In 1855 he also had a scheme to buy and develop a printing patent, in which he contrived to interest Parker, although the latter was not prepared to commit himself immediately. According to him, the purchase was to be financed by each contributing £500, which was to be put on deposit while Parker decided whether to go ahead with the venture. Parker put up his £500, giving Seymour a cheque for the amount in August 1855. Almost predictably, the money disappeared. There followed a long correspondence between Parker and Seymour, in which Seymour put forward a variety of explanations of the fate of Parker's £500. With considerable forbearance, Parker stayed his hand until February 1858, when he issued a writ in the courts for the recovery of the money.

One feature of the case which later became significant was that Seymour relied in part on the evidence of a Mr Hudson, a fellow director of the Waller Mining Company, who was said to have been either present or at least in the offing when Parker made out and handed over his cheque, and who also attended later meetings of the parties. Parker and his witnesses strongly denied that Hudson had anything to do with any of these transactions. In the end Seymour in effect submitted to judgment, and attempted to persuade Parker to agree that the debt should be paid off in easy instalments. Later, he offered to insure his life, with Parker, as judgment creditor, to be entitled to any proceeds from the transaction. Eventually, in December 1856, he wrote to Parker's solicitor admitting that he was deeply in debt, and that his only way of paying his numerous creditors was by means of his practice at the Bar. He went on to offer payment of 2s in the pound, with the interesting suggestion that he would pay the solicitor's costs by holding a brief or briefs on his instructions in any court of his choosing (the insurance policy on his life had lapsed due to his failure to keep up the premiums). This was to get Seymour into more trouble.

His dealings with the mining company were going equally badly. Almost inevitably, it got into financial difficulties. As commonly happens with such ventures, there was much negotiating of bank loans and lodging of shares as securities. One of these became the subject of another complaint before Parliament. A Colonel Robertson, another director of Waller Mining, had deposited a large number of shares with the company's bankers as security for a loan. Like Mr Parker's £500, these shares disappeared, and, the Colonel having died, his brother complained to the Inn that Seymour had improperly appropriated them for his own purposes. The answer was that the shares had indeed been taken, but that they had been dealt with only in accord with the wishes of the late Colonel Robertson. Seymour's account, supported by the evidence to Parliament of the same Mr Hudson who corroborated his version of the dealings with Parker, was that Seymour had had to lay out large amounts of his own money in order to save the company from insolvency. This came about because the Waller Mining Board, with the knowledge and agreement of both Robertson and Seymour, had attempted to rig the stock market and drive up the shares, with a view to taking a profit when their value increased. However, one of the conspirators, if that is what they were, had unloaded a large number of shares at the top of the market, leaving the others with losses. Hence Seymour's subvention of the company out of his own pocket, and his subsequent dealing in the shares deposited at the bank.

In the face of that conflict of evidence, the credibility of the evidence of Seymour and Hudson was important, if not crucial to the charge. The bencher charged with presenting the case therefore cross-examined Hudson about other transactions in which he had been concerned. He had written to the resident agent of the mine in Virginia, asking him to send accounts, adding that these were needed for the purpose of declaring a dividend, that the alleged profit for the year was to be 'let out by degrees ... keeping the best thing for a climax'. The letter was one of a bundle which had been produced by the solicitor who had eventually wound up the company. Subsequently, as was common ground, a fictitious dividend was declared, and paid, not out of the trading profits of the mine, but out of money raised from a bank by pledging the company's shares. These matters emerged towards the end of one hearing, which Parliament then adjourned until a later date.

Hudson returned to the witness box on the resumption. The benchers were moving on to other matters when he interrupted and asked to see the bundle of letters which contained the one about the accounts and the dividend. The bundle was handed to him, and he then said that he was going to keep the letters, and refused to return them, saying to the Under-Treasurer, who had gone to take them from him, 'Don't touch me or I shall knock you down. Go away, sir.' Repeated requests from a number of benchers, and from Seymour himself, were in vain, and eventually the porter and another servant of the Inn were summoned. They attempted, again unsuccessfully, to recover the letters from Hudson by force, and an unseemly scuffle seems to have occurred. In the end the police were called, and Hudson, two benchers and the Inn servants ended up in the police station. No arrests were made, but Hudson later brought an action against the Inn for assault and malicious prosecution.

In the meantime, the proceedings against Seymour dragged on. Following the events just described, he had the wisdom to instruct Lush QC (later Lush J) to represent him. By this time the Bench was meeting for the twelfth session—there were to be sixteen in all. The arrival of an advocate who was not a party to the case brought shape and direction to the arguments which had been notably lacking until then. Finally, Parliament gave judgment on 21 February 1862, nearly seven years after Mr Parker gave Seymour the cheque for £500, five and a half years after the dealings in the Waller Mining shares and eighteen months after it began the inquiries into the allegations of professional misconduct. The language of the judgment was stern. The benchers found that

> they have the painful duty to perform of stating to you that they find much worthy of severe condemnation, even on the most favourable construction of your actions ... [they] are also under the painful necessity of declaring their opinion that [your conduct] was an arrangement to which a right-minded man, even in the hour of heavy pecuniary distress, would not have submitted ... Your proposal [to pay off the judgment debt by appearing on the instructions of the creditor's solicitor] was one most improper from a barrister to an attorney, and invited a breach of duty on the part of the attorney.

Yet, in spite of these strictures, Seymour was not disbarred nor, so far as the records tell, punished at all. Curiously, Parliament records do not state what verdict the Bench reached. The sequel has to be found in the columns of *The Times* for February 1862.

Days before the formal pronouncement of the judgment, Seymour was addressing his political supporters in his constituency of Southampton, trumpeting his 'acquittal' to loud acclaim and complaining about the fairness of the procedure adopted. This the paper reported on 19 February 1862, with a leading article criticising the Bench for refusing to release the record of the hearings and a copy of its judgment. On 22 February the paper published a letter from the Under-Treasurer pointing out that Seymour had been given a copy of the judgment before he addressed his constituents, and *The Times* printed a copy of that, supplied by Seymour, on 24 February. It also took the opportunity to print a second leader, again taking the Bench to task for keeping the proceedings confidential. Finally, Seymour again wrote to the paper, enclosing a copy of his 'protest', sent to the Bench after it had issued its judgment, in which he rehearsed the arguments on the merits of the verdict.

In view of the severity of the language which was used to describe Seymour's conduct of his commercial affairs, it is hard to escape the conclusion that his hide must have been unusually thick. Many would have been glad to skulk away, rather than parading the case before the general public as he did. That, however, was the last of the matter of Seymour.

This did not bring the sorry story to an end, for there remained Hudson's action against the Inn. This was tried before Cockburn CJ and a jury over five days in December 1862. The summing-up identified the main issue as being whether the letters were, as he asserted, Hudson's private property, which he was entitled to obtain, even by chicanery, and to keep. Alternatively, if they were company documents, they were lawfully in the possession of the Bench, because they had been handed over voluntarily by the company solicitor. On this, the summing-up was strongly in favour of the defendant benchers, but the jury, as it explained when called back into court, was irredeemably divided, seven to five. By agreement with counsel for both sides, the judge discharged the jury, and there is no record of a retrial. The case must have settled, and not before time.

C. Charles Edward Moore

While William Digby Seymour was undoubtedly an embarrassment to his profession and the Inn, worse was to come. In March 1888 a member ended up in Holloway Prison, committed for contempt of court by Kay J, sitting in the Chancery Division. Charles Edward Moore was junior in a case brought by a young man who had been abducted by a father and son, with a view to taking him to America. The motive for this never emerged, but was probably an attempt to relieve him of money. The plaintiff, a Mr Linwood, brought an action against his aunt, a Miss Andrews, who seems to have been a party to the attempted kidnap. One claim was that Miss Andrews had made off with some valuable bearer securities belonging to the plaintiff. The next ingredient in this Victorian melodrama was that Miss Andrews instructed a dishonest solicitor to act for her in the proceedings, who in turn instructed Moore. Moore and the solicitor were personal friends and members of the same clubs. Moore settled an affidavit in the action on behalf of Miss Andrews, in which she swore that she did not know what had become of the missing securities, and that no one was holding them on her behalf. In reality, as Moore knew, because he personally had given the securities to his instructing solicitor, this was, as the solicitor described it to Moore, an 'ingenious' affidavit, or, as others would say, perjury. As could have been foreseen, the solicitor then sold the securities and pocketed the proceeds. Moore had a leader in the case, and allowed him to read the affidavit to Kay J and to conduct the case on the footing that the affidavit was the truth. When the truth emerged, the plaintiff moved to commit Moore for contempt of court before a by now sympathetic judge. Moore went into the witness box and, in the words of Kay J, made a 'laboured attempt' to persuade him that he had never read the affidavit. Moore's counsel made a valiant but faint attempt to argue that while the conduct might be a matter for his benchers, it did not amount to contempt of court. Without calling on counsel for the plaintiff at the end of the evidence, Kay J sent Moore to prison until further order. Moore reappeared before the judge in May of the same year. By this time the dishonest solicitor had died, and those concerned had decided, rightly or wrongly, that he alone was responsible for the misappropriation of the plaintiff's holdings. This enabled the judge to discharge Moore, on terms that he returned his fees and paid the costs of the committal proceedings.

The *Daily Telegraph* reported the proceedings at length, and naturally the matter came before Parliament in due course. Peremptorily, the Bench had the press reports of the case read to Moore, asked if he admitted their accuracy, and when he did so, giving explanations described in the Minutes as 'wholly unsatisfactory', disbarred him. Nothing more was said, and Moore then disappears from the records.

D.   Samuel Hawkins

Samuel Hawkins ran the family tobacco wholesaling firm in Cardiff in the 1890s. In 1896 he employed a young woman in the business, and in 1898 joined the Inn as a student. He claimed later that on deciding to be called to the Bar he sold the business to a Mr James Davies, but it later transpired that this might not have been so. What became clear beyond argument was that in 1899 the firm of Lambert & Butler, later well known for their cigarettes, but at the time also tobacco manufacturers, sued Hawkins's firm for damages and an injunction, claiming that he and his wife had been opening packets of tobacco supplied by Lambert & Butlers, pilfering some of the contents, re-sealing the envelopes and selling them on. The girl employee gave evidence before Channel J and a jury at Cardiff Assizes that she had herself seen Hawkins and his wife steaming open the envelopes and removing the contents. At that stage the defence was that Hawkins had done nothing of the sort alleged against him. When cross-examined by counsel for the plaintiffs, Hawkins accepted that if any of the packets were tampered with he would have known of it, and that if they had been opened he could not explain why. Hawkins also contended, as a second line of defence, that if the packets had been opened, this was done only in order to show the contents to customers or to test the condition of the tobacco. Given the implausibility of the defence case, the jury took less than an hour to find for the plaintiffs. Hawkins did not appeal, because, as he was later to tell the Bench, he could not afford to. These events occurred in 1900.

In 1909, having apparently succeeded in keeping his membership of the Inn, Hawkins voluntarily resigned that membership. The explanation he gave when Parliament considered his application to be re-called to the Bar in 1913, was that he had been advised by a member of the Bar known to him that the business of the action would have to be dealt with and that this would cost him more money. There was also a faint suggestion that he had the offer of a job in Australia, which did not materialise. As his friend had forecast, the story of the action and the verdict came out in front of Parliament, in spite of considerable evasion by Hawkins under firm, almost hostile questioning by Master Tindal Atkinson. This time round, Hawkins's case was that he did not own the tobacco business at the time when the frauds were said to have taken place; but after implacable demands from the Bench, the instructions to counsel who appeared for him at the hearing were produced and found to contain no suggestion that he was unconnected with the firm at the relevant times.

The denouement came towards the end of the second hearing. Master Terrell interrupted when questions about the conduct of the action were being put, to ask if he could put a question. Master Atkinson's reaction was that 'The understanding was that questions should be put at the end.' This provoked Master Terrell to say

> It is rather difficult. Mr Hawkins said just now that he had taken no steps to be called. He came to me and asked me to propose him to be called.

Sensation. It turned out that after being told that the question of his fitness to be called would have to be investigated, Hawkins approached Master Terrell, in a great hurry to get the nomination papers signed. The Master had become aware that Hawkins knew both junior counsel who had appeared in the Cardiff trial, and asked why he had not asked them to propose him for call. Master Terrell was due to meet both counsel at lunch, and told Hawkins that he would speak to them then, but was urged to sign the papers before lunch. At lunch the barristers told Master Terrell that the reasons given by Hawkins for not approaching them were wholly untrue, with the result that the Master refused outright to propose him. Hawkins tried to deny this, but his application for re-call was by now, of course, doomed, and was rejected unanimously. In his closing address Hawkins's counsel did not even try to deal with the episode of the abortive attempt to find a proposer for call, but instead applied himself to discrediting the witnesses who had given evidence at the Cardiff trial and whom the jury had believed thirteen years before.

E.   ARV Dimmer and SH Riza

The cases of these two members, which took place on 9 March 1915 and 24 November 1917, had much in common, and show the attitude of the benchers to one type of professional misconduct which would be treated much more leniently today. This is partly due to a relaxation of the rules governing the relations of members of the Bar and those who instruct them in the age of direct professional access and Bar Direct.[15] In addition, it is interesting to compare the severity of the punishments delivered in the early twentieth century with those thought appropriate for similar misconduct at the beginning of the twenty-first. There is also a marked difference of approach to the confidentiality of the proceedings. The contemporary Code of Conduct of the Bar provides that disciplinary proceedings shall take place in public unless there is good reason for them not to, and that findings shall be made available to news agencies and posted on the Bar Council website. Ninety years ago, during the First World War, the word 'transparency' was little more than a technical term used by photographers.

The details of the case of Dimmer are relatively unimportant. He falsely pretended to a number of prisoners at Marlborough Street magistrates' court that he had been instructed by solicitors, so as to get instructions to appear at their trials. On one occasion he had sent a faked telegram to a prisoner in custody, suggesting that a solicitor should be instructed to defend him. The solicitor was of course to instruct Dimmer in turn. He also made an arrangement with an inquiry agent, in return for payment, so as to get introduced to many prisoners awaiting trial. Finally, he forged a backsheet with the name of a solicitor who had not instructed him, for the purpose of its being used as instructions to himself. The combination of greed and dishonesty which informed this behaviour was thoroughly reprehensible, and Dimmer was disbarred, as he probably would be had he behaved in the same way today, given that he had behaved dishonestly. As contemporary Bar Council records show, on the other hand, lesser irregularities involving backsheets and accepting instructions from unqualified

---

[15] In recent years the Bar Standards Board, which now regulates the professional conduct of the Bar, has permitted barristers to accept instructions from some professions other than solicitors (DPA) and, in strictly limited circumstances, from lay clients (Bar Direct).

persons in dubious circumstances generally attract lighter penalties, of which the most serious tend to be no more than reprimands or, in bad cases, fines.

Riza had done much the same as Dimmer. The details of the transactions differed, but the final result was much the same. Riza went into effective partnership with more than one solicitor, of whom one had provided Riza with his business cards for the purpose of his procuring work for the solicitor. The solicitor was a cipher, who was doing no more than give spurious respectability to Riza's acting for the lay clients with no proper instructions. Described by the treasurer, Master RA McCall QC, as 'a most vicious and dangerous system', and compounded by Riza having given an account of himself which the Bench thought was deliberately misleading, the misconduct led to twelve months' suspension from practice. Again, in view of the element of dishonesty in the course of conduct, this sentence is not surprising.

At the end of the hearing, after conveying the Bench's findings to the victim of the malpractices of which Riza was convicted, the Treasurer went on to warn him that he was not entitled to publish anything which had taken place. The right to give this direction was questionable, as the Inn had discovered when it defended Hudson's action in 1862 (see above, section VII.B.). Then, it will be remembered, much distasteful linen had been washed over several hearing days in the Court of Queen's Bench, with no suggestion by the Inn or the court that the disciplinary hearing was confidential. The insistence on confidentiality in 1917 contrasts sharply with the publicity given to disciplinary proceedings now.

F. Samuel Beach Chester

Samuel Beach Chester contrived to unite within himself most of the defects which had brought Middle Templars before the benchers down the centuries—these included lust, greed, a tenuous contact with reality and a profound misunderstanding of the legal process. The only failings characteristic of those who preceded him before the Bench to which he does not seem to have been in thrall were drunkenness and a propensity to physical violence. Chester was admitted to the Inn in 1902 and called in 1907. He never practised. In 1912 he was in his early thirties and a bachelor. He had met and fallen in love or become infatuated with a Miss Bertha Soames, a lady whom he described as 'a very worldly person, 28 years of age, whose private life had been somewhat chequered in its sexual aspects'. In April of that year he received a telegram from her, telling him to meet her at Paddington Station that evening. Knowing that she was going to stay with her sister in Ireland he obeyed, thinking, according to him, that he was required to do no more than see her off on her train. As the Irish Express was about to leave he started to say his goodbyes, but Miss Soames stopped him and said 'You're coming too, Beach.' He was apparently thunderstruck, but not too appalled to go along with the suggestion and arrive at Fishguard with the lady. On the ferry she booked a private sleeping cabin for both, which they shared. They travelled on and parted affectionately at Fermoy, where the sister lived.

Then the idyll turned sour. The Soames family strongly opposed the idea that the two should marry, as Chester wished. In any case, the lady had by the month of May decided to get engaged to a previous flame, whom Chester believed she had abandoned on meeting him. He thereupon wrote a series of letters to the family, threatening to tell the world what had happened on the Irish ferry and threatening to do so in the course of legal proceedings. The response was a letter from the Soames family solicitors threatening Chester with prosecution for criminal libel. He riposted by suing Bertha Soames for breach of promise, claiming damages only. The flavour of the letters comes from one written to Bertha Soames herself, in which Chester wrote:

> If you play up and try marrying anyone else, I will make every detail of our story and your letters public. You have acted with such perfidy recently that I am quite determined to marry you, or disclose the infinite force of my case.

He seems to have missed the inherent contradiction in the sentiments expressed there. The writ was issued in June 1913, and Bertha Soames was married in August of that year. The case was listed for 20 January 1914.

On the evening of 19 January 1914 Chester gave notice that he was discontinuing the action. The next day Marshall Hall KC and a junior appeared before Darling J for Miss Soames, and Chester was not represented. The judge required his counsel and solicitors to appear after lunch, and when the moment arrived Chester appeared in person. The judge then ordered letters written by Miss Soames to Chester to be returned to her legal representative, and gave judgment for her. Marshall Hall reported the matter to Chester's benchers, and the newspapers swooped. Chester appeared before the Bench in February 1914.

His defence was that he was not himself when he wrote the letters in May 1913 in essence blackmailing the Soames family into allowing him to marry Bertha Soames. That failed to impress the Bench and he was disbarred, having been questioned by the Treasurer with some vigour. There was, even so, a sharp division of opinion among the benchers as to whether he should be disbarred. The minority seem to have taken the view that, no matter how disgraceful his behaviour, what he had done had no bearing on his status as a barrister. He appealed to the Lord Chancellor and the Judges, who dismissed the appeal in February 1915. The Lord Chancellor presided at the hearing, and the tribunal included no fewer than seven High Court judges. They dealt with the argument which had swayed the minority of the Middle Temple Bench and was pressed upon them by concluding that Chester had been morally wrong in threatening to reveal the night of illicit passion to the world, and morally wrong to carry on with the breach of promise action after she had married someone else, this amounting to blackmail. The appeal failed.

Chester was not done, even then. Twenty years later he petitioned for readmission. He wrote a short letter acknowledging that his action had been very irresponsible and committed while he was in a very unbalanced state, and going on to claim that he had been bitterly, overwhelmingly punished. This was enough, he argued, adding that he had claims to leniency, being now decorated with the Gold Cross of Officer and Knight of the Order of the Redeemer by the Greek Government, it seems because he had written a biography of the Greek statesman Venizelos.

The Minutes do not record what occurred in debate about the application. Chester was not invited to appear. In the end the application was rejected, by 17 votes to 6. The continuing division of opinion is suggestive, bearing in mind that the Lord Chancellor and the Judges had unanimously endorsed the sentence of disbarment in 1914. Although the majority was nearly three to one, the existence of a sizable minority in favour of leniency perpetuates the feeling of unease that events which were to a considerable extent part of the man's private life should impinge so heavily on his professional career.

The case raises several questions, of which some are still material. The current Bar Code of Practice lays down that a barrister must not engage in conduct, whether in pursuit of his profession *or otherwise*, which is dishonest *or otherwise* discreditable to a barrister.[16] Plainly that leaves room for the Code to apply to some activities taking place in a barrister's private life away from professional practice. But where does the boundary run? It is difficult to deny that Chester was on the wrong side of it, if only because he was guilty of blackmail, and had invoked the processes of law as part of his project. Yet in giving judgment on the appeal, the Lord Chancellor identified the test as being one applicable to men of honour and gentlemen. This raises difficult questions as to how far behind the closed bedroom door, or even the front door, the Inns formerly (and now the Bar Council or Bar Standards Board) were (and are) entitled to pry. As yet, the guidelines have not been clearly drawn. What power did the judge have to order the return of the letters, rather than warning Chester that unauthorised publication might be a breach of copyright? And if Marshall Hall had not known that Chester was a barrister, would the disciplinary proceedings have happened at all? One doubts it.

---

[16] Code of Conduct, para 301(a).

On the one hand, the contemporary Code of Conduct of the Bar, following the lead given by the majority of the benchers in Chester's case, makes it professional misconduct to engage in dishonesty or other impropriety, whether or not in pursuit of the profession. There must, therefore, be some room for intrusion into a barrister's non-professional life. By going to law at all, when by virtue of his experience he should have foreseen the consequences of discontinuing the action, Chester arguably fell over the boundary separating professional misconduct from private indiscretion. By contrast, even if in 1913—and even more so in the early twenty-first century—a barrister made an attempt on the virtue of another member of the Bar (of whichever sex), a client or a passing stranger in the Temple, many would say that this was no concern of an Inn or the Bar Standards Board, provided there was no criminal offence. Disciplinary bodies are not, or should not be, courts of morals, still less act as thought police, the argument runs.

G.   Harold Eaden

After the drama of actions for breach of promise the world of building arbitrations appears mundane, but it was from this that Harold Eaden emerged to face the benchers in 1934. He was reported to them by Scrutton LJ as the result of an appeal from the award of a building arbitration in Birmingham about a house in West Bromwich. Eaden had been a solicitor for many years before he went to the Bar, and had built up a busy practice in the West Midlands. He was instructed to appear in a building arbitration by an old friend, who asked him to suggest an arbitrator. Innocently, as he was to tell the Bench, who believed him, he suggested his pupil, who duly sat for three days. To make matters worse, another man who was later to become a pupil of Eaden was appointed and acted as Umpire in the case, although he did not begin pupillage until after the hearing was over. In the 1930s the Birmingham Bar seems to have been small and the numbers of practitioners available for this sort of case limited. As corroboration of this Eaden assured the Bench that his opponent was aware that the arbitrator was his pupil and took no point on this. Indeed, the practice of having arbitrator and advocate out of the same set of chambers in the City was commonplace. This did not deter the other side in the arbitration alleging, quite wrongly, that Eaden and his pupil had visited the site together and in the absence of any other party.

Although they met virtually every day, with the pupil-arbitrator working on Eaden's papers in other matters and doing some of his small returns,[17]

---

[17]   A return is work returned by another barrister who is not available to do it.

the two, according to Eaden, scrupulously refrained from discussing the case. It was never suggested that the arbitration had been in fact tainted by the relationship of Eaden and his pupil. In fact, nobody saw anything amiss until Scrutton LJ took the point during argument on the appeal, adding that it was easy to be wise after the event.

As a footnote, two other members resigned from Eaden's chambers without warning after the row about the case broke out, claiming that this was in part the reason for their departure. This had distressed Eaden a good deal, but he was at least able to console himself with the ruling of the Disciplinary Committee, which was that a letter was to be sent to Eaden expressing their disapproval of what he had done, while taking no further action. Most people would agree that it was right to take no further action, while doubting that there was any need to disapprove at all.

H.   Cuthbert John Thomas Pensotti

Cuthbert John Thomas Pensotti must have been a nice man. He was an established member of the South-Eastern Circuit, much liked and respected within the profession before the Second World War. At some stage in that war he joined the RAF and became a Squadron Leader in the Judge Advocate General's Department of the service. In 1943 he was serving in North Africa, under the immediate command of a Wing Commander Trounson. The two, to put it mildly, detested each other. An Aircraftman by the name of Lynch was charged with a relatively minor motoring offence for which he was court martialled, with Trounson responsible for drafting the charge or charges. For reasons which will emerge, that alternative was highly material. When Aircraftman Lynch faced his court martial, Pensotti in his capacity as Judge Advocate advised the tribunal that the charge which Trounson had framed was void for duplicity. One suspects that advice to have been given with more than a little satisfaction. The court martial accordingly found the charge to be bad and adjourned for the Convening Officer to decide whether to halt the prosecution or to frame fresh charges. Pensotti made a manuscript note of what happened, and gave this to a clerk to type up.

In the course of the next two weeks or so a number of versions of the manuscript note were produced, typed both by the clerk who undertook the original typing and by one other. One at least contained a few words which emphasised that Trounson was wrong to have drafted the charge in the way which he did. The essential dispute which led to Pensotti himself facing a court martial was whether he had fraudulently inserted those words in a later draft of the record of Lynch's first court martial, or whether they had appeared in his original manuscript notes, which by then had been lost or destroyed. In fact it would have made little difference whether they were properly included or not. They merely added to the emphasis of the summary, without changing the substance. The thrust of the charges against Pensotti before the benchers was the finding of perjury by the court martial. The story was made still more complicated by the fact that what turned out to have been the first typed version was taken out of the file in which it should have been more than once, was put back in the correct file more than once, and was for a time mislaid by Pensotti, to the knowledge of Trounson. When he found it again Pensotti put it back in the right file, without telling Trounson. This minor subterfuge so enraged Trounson that he initiated an inquiry which led to Pensotti being court martialled. At that trial Pensotti gave evidence on oath in which he denied that he had fabricated any summary note of the Lynch court martial. His advocate ran the defence, foolishly as it turned out, on the footing that the first typist was an honest witness, and that if his account of the affair was right then Pensotti must be wrong and not telling the truth deliberately. Importantly, the advocate, a Flight Lieutenant Ormerod, did not allow for the possibility of a genuine mistake by Pensotti or any other witness as to the identity of the clerk who typed up the original version of the summary. Pensotti's court martial had therefore to decide which of the two central witnesses it believed, and it preferred the evidence of the clerk typist. The inescapable inference was that Pensotti had perjured himself, which led to his being reported to the Inn.

In the meantime, ironically, Trounson had overruled Pensotti's advice as to the validity of the charge against Aircraftman Lynch, and ordered that the latter should be retried on the original charge. The second court martial, amid general hilarity, convicted him of one offence and entered a special verdict on the second, one of 'Not Guilty'. This was described by Serjeant Sullivan KC, who as treasurer presided over the disciplinary proceedings against Pensotti, as a 'fiasco, with perhaps a little touch of malice in it, which resulted in exposing [Trounson] to a great deal of ridicule'. Suspicion falls on Pensotti, who acted as Advocate General again at Aircraftman Lynch's second court martial, of having had something to do with the result(s).

When the case came on before Parliament, Pensotti was represented by two distinguished members of his circuit, which testifies to the regard in which he was held. The leader was Sir Walter Monckton KC, famous as the adviser to King Edward VIII at the time of his abdication, and as the chief conciliator or appeaser, according to one's standpoint, of organised labour under Sir Winston Churchill's post-war administrations. He led Mr Geoffrey Lawrence, a future High Court judge, and the leader for the defence in a *cause célèbre* of the 1950s, *R v John Bodkin Adams*. No other party was represented, as was usual. Having heard the case for Pensotti, the Bench took the unusual course of adjourning and asking the Air Ministry for its comments on the case.

The result must have been disconcerting. At the resumed hearing not only was the Air Ministry represented, but it had instructed the Solicitor General, Sir David Maxwell Fyfe KC, MP, the future Lord Kilmuir and Lord Chancellor, and the Treasury Devil and future Lord Chief Justice, The Hon Hubert Parker. Their instructions, which they loyally discharged, were to resist the suggestion that Pensotti's court martial had reached the wrong conclusion as vigorously as possible. To this end, the Solicitor General submitted to the Bench at some length that there was sufficient corroboration of the evidence of the first clerk typist who had claimed, honestly but mistakenly as it turned out, to have typed the summary which first Wing Commander Trounson and later the Air Ministry itself claimed was forged.

By the end of the Solicitor General's submissions, it had become common ground that if the second clerk typist had, as he said he had, typed the alleged forgery from Pensotti's original manuscript summary of Lynch's first court martial, then that was the end of the case and Pensotti was innocent. Sir Walter when he replied demonstrated from the transcripts of the court martial that Pensotti had quite simply forgotten that the second clerk had done the typing, with the result that the Bench was unanimous in finding him not guilty.

This vindication enabled Pensotti to give up driving a London bus for a living and resume practice at the Bar, which he had felt unable to do while the charges of professional misconduct were pending. It had no effect on the Air Ministry, however. When Pensotti petitioned the King for a free pardon, the Ministry replied that the Secretary of State was unable to advise the King to issue any special directions in the matter. A second petition went unanswered.[18] The departmental attitude is inexplicable. Why spend public money on sending heavy ordnance such as the Solicitor General and the Treasury Junior to a domestic disciplinary hearing in which the Ministry had no direct interest, Pensotti having been dismissed from the RAF after the findings of guilt against him? Why instruct counsel actively to support the verdict of the court martial rather than take a neutral stance and abide by the Bench's verdict? Why, when the mistake made by the court martial had been demonstrated to the complete satisfaction of a distinguished tribunal, twice refuse redress to Pensotti, almost peremptorily? The Committee which acquitted Pensotti consisted, in addition to Serjeant Sullivan, of one sitting and one future Lord of Appeal, a High Court Judge, county court judges, senior and junior Treasury Counsel at the Old Bailey, and distinguished silks, including Sir Patrick Hastings KC. The Ministry's attitude was as much a discourtesy to

---

[18]   Front page main report in *The Evening News*, 17 September 1946.

them as an injustice to Pensotti. Was it because the civil service mind could not encompass the possibility that a mistake had been made, or was it too much trouble?

I.   DN Pritt KC, MP

After a colourful left-wing political career in the 1930s, DN Pritt KC MP was instructed to defend the Mau Mau insurrectionary Jomo Kenyatta on a charge of sedition in 1952. The brief must have been as much due to his anti-colonial sympathies as to his forensic abilities, which by all accounts were considerable.[19] He came to the notice of the benchers in 1953, when reported by the Attorney-General of Kenya for his behaviour when defending Kenyatta. The Attorney-General sent the transcripts of the trial to the Under-Treasurer to support the complaint. These showed that Pritt had been guilty of at least gross discourtesy to the prosecuting counsel and the trial judge by making disparaging stage-whispered comments on the quality and conduct of the prosecution case, and of the trial in general. There had been several deliberately audible rows between the prosecutor and Pritt, with the judge making ineffectual efforts to intervene. For no very clear reason, but presumably because of Pritt's prominence in public life and the fact that he was well-known to the general public, the Treasurer took the unusual step of consulting a former Lord Chancellor as to what should be done. Viscount Jowitt, not only a bencher of the Inn but also a member of the political party which had expelled Pritt, wrote from the House of Lords in June 1953 that since the trial had taken place abroad and, more importantly, that it was a matter for the trial judge to keep order in his own court, no action should follow. The hint was taken. Previously, on the other hand, the Inn had always been ready to investigate the professional conduct of Indian, Malayan and African members in matters arising in their own countries. It has also for many years been normal for judges who take exception to the conduct of barristers in court to report them to their Inns, or to the Bar Council or Standards Board. Lord Jowitt's reasoning is therefore unpersuasive, and looks very much like what would come to be known 50 years later as an old-fashioned fudge. At all events, Pritt died shortly afterwards in retirement, with his reputation untarnished, at least in this respect.

---

[19]   Master Louis Blom-Cooper QC, who knew Pritt, attests this.

5

The Middle Temple Since 1900

ERIC STOCKDALE

I. THE PERIOD BEFORE WORLD WAR II

THE TWENTIETH CENTURY started in an ominous manner, even though the Inn was little affected by the omen in question: the South African War, which left few traces in the records of the Inn. Early in 1900 the commanding officer of the Inns of Court Rifle Volunteers thought the Inn might care to supply some of his men with horses and equipment, but he withdrew his request. In November 1902, Colonel J Reeves, who owed £6 for six past annual dues, wrote to say that having been on active service during the war and having lost his health, he would have to withdraw from the Inn. The Finance Committee decided that a single payment of £5 would be sufficient to wipe out the arrears and to cover all future annual duties. That sum was paid before the December meeting.

In December 1903 the committee heard from the surety of a South African student member of the Inn, who had also been on active service— but on the enemy side. The surety paid the student's arrears of duty amounting to £6, adding in his covering letter that he had reason to believe he had no intention of being called to the Bar, or indeed of recognising the Inn in any way. The surety had misjudged the student, for in June 1904 he personally sent £6 to the Inn. He was informed that the arrears had already been paid and that his name would be restored to the list of members on payment of the current year's duty of £1, which he paid. In 1906 he came to England to speak to the junior Minister for the Colonies, Winston Churchill, about the future of his country, and they became the closest of friends.[1] In 1917, by then a British general, our student was made an honorary bencher on the nomination of the treasurer, seconded by Master Reading, the Lord Chief Justice, in the absence of Master Finlay, the Lord Chancellor. The student was not only a brilliant lawyer but also one of the

---

[1] MT./MPA/21; MT.1/CFM/4; R Jenkins, *Churchill* (London, Macmillan, 2001), 93.

most distinguished men ever to grace the Bench. He was, of course, Jan Christian Smuts, the man who led South Africa on to the British side in both World Wars, despite the opposition of a considerable number of his compatriots, who would have preferred to join the Germans.

The Inn had one other link with South Africa, albeit a tenuous one. On 4 December 1900, the City of London Electric Lighting Company wrote to ask the under-treasurer if he could confirm that one of the Inn's students was financially sound enough to pay his electricity bills. He intended moving from 4 Brick Court to his new chambers at 3 Temple Gardens and wished to be connected to the electric supply there.[2] The student was John Buchan, who was called to the Bar by the Inn in June 1901 and then spent the next two years as assistant private secretary to Lord Milner, the High Commissioner for South Africa. Thereafter he followed a career in journalism and politics, but is best remembered as a highly successful author, whose novels included *The Thirty-Nine Steps* and *Greenmantle*. From 1935 to 1940 he served as Governor-General of Canada as Baron Tweedsmuir, and in January 1936 was elected a bencher.

On the death of Queen Victoria in January 1901, the Prince of Wales succeeded as Edward VII but remained a bencher of the Inn: the first reigning monarch ever to be a bencher of an Inn. Apart from that, the years before World War I were fairly unremarkable for the Inn, save for various improvements to the facilities in the Hall and two other events with financial consequences. The London County Council obtained powers under an Act of 1899 to widen the Strand and to acquire land in connection with the works. One of the properties duly acquired was New Inn, on the present site of Australia House,[3] the freehold of which was vested in the Middle Temple. The Inn had granted a lease for 300 years in 1745 to the Society of New Inn at a rental of £4 a year. After complicated negotiations, which were concluded in 1902, the Inn eventually received £45,500 for its interest.[4]

The second event was the speedy demolition of No 1, the south side of Brick Court, in 1908, after it had shown signs of imminent collapse. On 19 May, Master Phillimore, the treasurer, pointed out in a memorandum that those premises were not the only ones to cause concern. The surveyor had warned that New Court would probably have to come down within a few years. Master Phillimore, who clearly knew his colleagues well, warned them:

---

[2] MT.6/RBW/206.

[3] At the junction of the Strand and Aldwych.

[4] MT.1/MPA/21; MT.12/LCC. In 1961 the Inn was able to buy a souvenir of its former property: a pair of silver porter's badges, dated 1833 and bearing the emblem of New Inn: MT.1/CEM/4.

When it does, during the period of rebuilding and the possible longer period in which the Bench is making up its mind whether to rebuild and how to rebuild, the loss of accommodation, if 1 Brick Court has not been rebuilt, will be very great.[5]

Somewhat surprisingly, on 20 May the treasurer was the only member of the Building Committee to vote in favour of rebuilding. Some of his colleagues probably enjoyed the new unobstructed view of the Hall on walking down Middle Temple Lane. Fortunately, Parliament decided, by a large majority, to seek the advice of one of the country's leading architects, Sir Aston Webb, not only on Brick Court, but also on the other old buildings.[6] Webb was the architect of the main entrance of the Victoria and Albert Museum, of the Admiralty Arch, and of the improvements[7] to Buckingham Palace and The Mall. His report, dated 14 October 1908, was alarming:

> First, with regard to the probable life of the present blocks of old buildings, they appear to be built of poorly bonded brickwork, the mortar and the surface of the brickwork is perished in places, while judging from No 1 Brick Court, the walls stand on the ground without concrete or footings; further the roofs and floors are very unscientifically constructed so that when they begin to sag, as they have done in several cases, a thrust is thrown on the outer walls causing them to bulge in places.
>
> Some of the old buildings such as New Court, show cracks in them from the cellar upwards, these cracks I understand are recent and are increasing. In fact most of the buildings, including the Hall, appear to be slightly on the move and require watching, the principal cause I am informed being the withdrawal of the water from the subsoil, through the piercing of the soil for the underground railways. How far this may be the case I have not sufficient local knowledge to speak of with certainty, but on the face of it, it appears probable. Certain it is that movement is going on, and this, taken in conjunction with the poor construction of the buildings, must make the length of their lives uncertain. It is true that, in spite of their defective construction, these buildings have stood for some two centuries, but they are now nearly worn out and require all the care your Surveyor bestows upon them to maintain them.[8]

Webb recommended the reconstruction of 1 Brick Court, with significant improvements, the main one being the provision, at the eastern end of the

---

[5] MT.6/RBW/213.

[6] MT.1/MPA/21.

[7] A new front to Buckingham Palace, and the architectural settings in front of the palace for the Victoria Memorial and the Mall: D Yarwood, *The Architecture of England*, 2nd edn (London, Batsford, 1976), 535.

[8] MT.6/RBW/214.

new building, of an arcade as a ground floor passageway for the pedestrians, who in the past had been forced out into the carriageway of Middle Temple Lane by the original solid building. His suggestions were duly implemented.

Technological changes caused the benchers problems from time to time. Having earlier refused the Postmaster-General permission to lay a telegraph line in the Inn, in August 1902 the benchers allowed him to introduce the telephone. Water closets were gradually introduced, with increases in rent to cover the cost of improvements, and eventually gas, electricity and telephones became universal. The Inn did not always receive the cooperation it was entitled to expect. For example, in January 1900 the Finance Committee considered a letter from Mark Knowles of 1 Elm Court, refusing to pay 30 shillings (360 old pence) a year extra rent for a new water closet, despite the fact that he was only being asked, in effect, to spend a penny a day. He stated firmly that 'if an epidemic breaks out in the Temple, the Bench may look out for consequences.' The committee members ordered a notice to quit to be served. After an order for possession had been obtained, Knowles apologised and petitioned for another chance. The Committee could see no mitigation and resolved

> That in view of the course Mr Mark Knowles had thought fit to adopt before presenting this petition, the Masters of the Bench feel that they cannot interfere.[9]

Motorcars repeatedly caused problems for the Inn, both those belonging to members and those of strangers. Parking caused the greatest problem from early on in the century, but speeding also disturbed the Bench from time to time. In January 1913 the House Committee considered the complaint from a tenant about the dangerous driving of taxis in Middle Temple Lane, most of them taking a shortcut through the Inn. The Committee resolved that a notice, 'Drive slowly', should be placed at each of the three entrances to the Lane, but one member was not satisfied with that proposed solution. The documents of the Inn over the years record a number of instances when expert advice was sought, sometimes when the question was essentially one for the jury of benchers. No request for expert advice was quite as bizarre as that suggested by Master McCall, who was to be treasurer four years later. Possibly influenced by the fact that the new Automobile Association had its first office just outside the Fleet Street gate, he seriously suggested that the Inn should write to the Association, 'for them to advise upon the best type of notice warning motors to drive slowly'.[10] In July 1921 Parliament ordered:

---

[9]   MT.1/CFM/3 and 4.

[10]   MT.1/CHM/1. To be fair to Master McCall, no *effective* notice has ever been devised anywhere.

That the owners be informed that the Bench disapproves of the precincts of the Middle Temple being used as a garage or yard for motor cars and that the owners be requested to abstain from doing so.[11]

In May 1923, clearly still concerned about danger to life and limb, 'The Treasurer gave instructions that no bicycles might be ridden in the Lane.'

Some of the entries in the Minutes of Parliament relate to very minor matters indeed, which scarcely needed to be put before two dozen or so of the country's leading lawyers. For example, in August 1901 consideration was given to a letter from a member called Cock, who reported his decision to change the spelling of his name. He gave the dubious explanation that he had reverted to the old form of his name, Coke, and asked that the Inn books might record the change. Master Badcock, who had attended both July meetings, absented himself from the August parliament, but unashamedly retained his name without any amendment.

There was one unusual way in which the years before World War I stand out: they saw what the Inn's Archivist, Lesley Whitelaw, described to the Library Review Committee in August 2004 as 'a flurry of scholarly activity'.[12] That productive period saw the publication of the Minutes of Parliament from 1501 to 1703, a further volume of *Middle Temple Records* and the first edition of the *Bench Book*, giving particulars about all the Inn's benchers.

There is one possible explanation for the relative dearth in the records of signs of activity before 1913, other than the matters already discussed: there may indeed have been little activity. If his successor is to be believed (and there is no reason to doubt him) the under-treasurer of the time, James Waldron (from 1886 to 1912), ignored many problems and the benchers seem not to have noticed, save possibly in his last few months, when he was clearly a dying man. His successor, Major Henry Beresford-Peirse, who had served in the South African War, earning a DSO, was appointed under-treasurer on 1 January 1913 and proved to be a very efficient new broom. After some two years in office he reported on the progress he had made:

> My main objects in all departments have been to eliminate discontent and staleness, to rectify any legitimate grievance, which I think has been accomplished by the readjustment of wages, which the Finance Committee have already approved, and to insist upon honest and efficient work.[13]

His detailed comments on the different departments made it clear that he had uncovered and rectified some serious problems. He reported finding 'great discontent and dissatisfaction' in all departments:

[11] MT.1/MPA/23.
[12] 'The Records of the Inn: A History of the Middle Temple Archive'.
[13] MT.8/SMP/183.

There were grievances which had never been brought to the notice of the Finance Committee, in some cases applications for a rise of wages dating back as far as seven years.

His report on the porters began:

This department I found in a condition of complete chaos, the head porter an habitual drunkard, with the natural result that the warders and messengers under his direct control were in a permanent condition of insubordination.

As to the office,

This I found in a considerable state of confusion. There was no arrangement of the routine work, no up to date system of filing letters or documents, no timetable of work, all work very much in arrears, including the accounts, and a mass of unsorted letters, documents and papers, both in the outer office and the Under-Treasurer's room. The second clerk, owing to ill-health, was entirely incapable of dealing with even the routine work, still less of adapting himself to any new methods.

Beresford-Peirse was, however, able to praise Thomas Hewlett, a chartered accountant, who had been appointed assistant clerk in 1913. Beresford-Peirse managed to get a good team together for the treasury: by the time he resigned in January 1930, his staff included both Hewlett, who succeeded him, and Robert Williams, Hewlett's successor in due course.

The outbreak of World War I on 4 August 1914 was speedily followed by the enemy occupation of 'plucky little Belgium'. As early as 5 November the benchers resolved that any members of the Belgian Bar present in England should be invited to become honorary members, 'with all the privileges of the use of the Hall, Library and Common Room during the continuation of the War'.[14] At the same meeting of Parliament, the Bench had to consider the first of the many deaths of members of the Inn in Belgium, France and elsewhere. The circumstances were particularly poignant.

On 26 October, Master Erskine Pollock presented a piece of silver. He had written on 14 October, 'I am a complete invalid and shall never do any more work at the Bar.' He added:

I should like to give it to the Inn in memory of the connection with the Inn of the Pollock family, which begins with my grandfather (the Lord Chief Baron) and ends with my younger son (the fourth generation).

He expressed the wish that the gift should bear the inscription: 'In grateful recollection of what the Honourable Society of the Middle Temple have done for the Pollocks, November 1914.' On 5 November the Bench

---

[14]   MT.1/MPA/22.

resolved to send a letter of condolence to Master Erskine Pollock on the death in action of Lieutenant FR Pollock.

The Inn, like virtually every other male institution, sustained heavy losses during the next four years among its various servicemen. At least 78 barristers died, together with some students, a number of staff members and six members of the Temple Church choir. It was not only the death of actual and potential students that affected the intake after the war. The death or maiming of barrister fathers, coupled with similar disasters in non-legal families, obviously also had an effect on the number of students able to contemplate a career at the Bar. Although a few scholarships had been made available for students since 1877, awards on a significant scale were still in the future. Fortunately, in World War I the only physical damage done to the Inn was caused by what is now inappropriately called 'friendly fire': two anti-aircraft shells damaged the Queen's Room.

One file in the Inn records illustrates both the sadness that the war could cause any family, and the concern of the Inn, particularly of the under-treasurer.[15] Charles Hunt, who had worked for the Inn since 1908 and had looked after the silver, served in England in the Machine Gun Corps as a sergeant instructor. In June 1918 he wrote to the under-treasurer, who had encouraged him to apply for a commission:

> There is some rumour about the formation of three more service battalions, and I expect I shall find myself among one of them. *However one must be thankful to be allowed to live in these days.*[16]

In September, a mere two months before the Armistice, Mrs Hunt informed the Inn that her husband, 'my Charlie', had been wounded in France and was missing.

The under-treasurer wrote to Hunt's unit for further information and learned that he had in fact been killed in action at Hill 63. He went to see the widow and noted her needs: she was worried about the mortgage, which still had five years to run, but was principally concerned for her two sons, aged eight and three. The Inn, which had earlier decided 'that any permanent member of the staff called up on active service should be paid his ordinary salary, less all government pay and allowances',[17] decided to pay a regular sum, equal to half pay, to the widow and undertook to help with education. Mrs Hunt kept in touch and eventually was proud to announce that her elder son, who had been at Christ's Hospital and the University of London, had obtained a first class degree; and that the younger boy, who had attended Dulwich College, was at the Royal Academy School.

---

[15]   MT.8/SMP/193.
[16]   Emphasis provided.
[17]   MT.1/CFM/5.

After the war the names of the Inn's fatal casualties were recorded in an illuminated Roll of Honour, and a memorial for the dead of both Inns was approved for the Temple Church. Somewhat surprisingly, no such Roll was prepared after the 1939–45 War. The fact that the casualties had been a little lighter may provide some explanation for the failure to compile a record of the fallen. Fortunately, the omission was eventually repaired by the remarkable initiative of Terry Parratt, the Library porter. He had seen action as a Regular in the Army, albeit some years after the end of World War II, and was shocked by the apparent indifference of the Inn. He diligently went through the records to find the names of those members who had lost contact during the war years, or who had not reappeared after the war. Using the Internet, he then checked those names against the lists kept by the Commonwealth War Graves Commission. The outcome of Parratt's initiative was a proper record and the unveiling, in the Temple Church in 2003, of new plaques bearing the names of the fallen he had traced.

Throughout the 1914–18 War the Hall remained open for members, even though term keeping was suspended. The question of saving food was tackled on several occasions by the House Committee: first in November 1914, when the treasurer expressed his concern about the length of the Sunday dinners at the Ancients' Table. Eight courses were served to those eight worthies, who were charged only two shillings each, despite the fact that their meal cost the Inn five shillings a head. A week later the committee resolved that in future the Ancients' Table should be served with one turkey only in place of the customary two, and that the solitary turkey should be carved off the table by a staff member. The Inn records do not include any protest from the Ancients, but some of them will doubtless have felt that the Committee was taking the war rather too seriously. One can almost hear the cry, 'Are there no limits to the sacrifices we are expected to make?' Later in the war the Inn was able to assure the Ministry of Food that it was complying with the spirit of the Order relating to the provision of food in hotels, restaurants and clubs.[18]

Over the years the Inn documents reveal a number of occasions when a member, whether student or barrister, who had received a scholarship or other financial assistance without any obligation to repay, insisted on returning some or all of his grant when able to do so. An early instance occurred after the war, in 1922:

> During the war the chairman of the Bar Council collected privately certain money to help the families of some of the barristers called up. One barrister who received £300 in this way wrote recently that he was doing well and desired to

---

[18] MT.1/CHM/1. Even after the losses caused by the Ancients had been staunched, catering chronically showed a deficit.

return the sum to the Bar Council. The Bar Council had no claim to receive the money and so it was suggested he should send it to the Barristers' Benevolent Association.[19]

When the guns fell silent many survivors, some of them wounded, came back determined to continue or to embark on a career at the Bar. The Bench regularly considered and granted requests for a dispensation of terms, or a relaxation of the requirements for certain examinations, helping whenever possible. In February 1918, Captain EJ Davis was permitted to sit certain examination papers in Salonika. One of the dispensation cases is of particular interest to the present writer, as it concerned his pupil-master, Captain HG Garland, who, after being seriously injured by a shell in France, had joined the Inn as a student in February 1918. On 15 April 1920 he was let off four terms and on 28 April he was called to the Bar, eventually becoming a head of chambers at 1 Essex Court. Garland was one of 16 students called on the same day. One of the others was Richard Doake, DSO, MC, Croix de Guerre; another was also a Companion of the Distinguished Service Order, while two more had the Military Cross. Some of the rest had doubtless been equally courageous, though not decorated. A number of the veterans who came to the Inn, such as Master Sachs, who had been wounded in France, were young enough to serve in uniform again in the next war.

In January 1921, Captain Paul Bennett, who had been awarded both the Victoria Cross and the Military Cross during the war, was given leave to omit the Part I examinations. He eventually became a London Metropolitan magistrate. Second Lieutenant James Leach won the Victoria Cross in the war, but he chose to earn a living in the City. He was admitted to the Inn only in January 1936, but seems to have withdrawn after two years. When he applied for readmission he was, somewhat surprisingly, turned down.[20] Ironically, that was in the middle of World War II, in October 1943, a year before Tasker Watkins earned his Victoria Cross at Falaise in Normandy. In 1988 Master Watkins was appointed Deputy Chief Justice and also Autumn Reader.

Other survivors—some of them doubtless post-war Regulars—took their time, like Leach, before applying for admission. For example, Major Archibald Church, DSO, MC, was admitted only in April 1935, naming Master Jowitt as a referee, as they had been fellow Members of Parliament. Captain JKA Robertson, MC, waited until the following February before joining the Inn.

---

[19] *Daily Mail*, 3 April 1922. It was perhaps this item of news that started the proprietor of the newspaper, Lord Rothermere, thinking about a fund for members of his father's Inn.
[20] MT.1/MPA/25. The Inn may fairly be described as ambivalent about Leach, as it now proudly displays his name as that of one of its VC holders.

Jumping ahead for the moment, it should be added that after World War II, the Inn once more received a number of requests from men serving in the armed forces for exemptions. In October 1942, on the recommendation of the Council of Legal Education, Captain Airey Neave, MC, who had recently returned from captivity in Germany, was granted exemption from the whole of the Bar finals, so he could be called in January 1943. He is best remembered as the first British prisoner of war to get home after escaping from Colditz Castle, disguised as a German officer. Having survived all the attempts of the uniformed enemy to kill him, he served a lengthy spell as a Member of Parliament, and was then[21] assassinated by a terrorist bomb in the precincts of the Palace of Westminster. In January 1943 the Inn also received an application from a prisoner of war camp from Captain Frederick Corfield, who asked for admission without the necessary entry qualifications. His request was granted. In due course he was a political colleague of Neave's in the House of Commons and became a Minister and a bencher. In May 1944, JG Rogers was allowed to rely on the Roman Law examination he had passed in a prisoner of war camp before his admission to the Inn.[22]

One student, who had been absent for some time, made an unusual request in July 1923. He had been admitted to the Inn 44 years earlier, had kept only four terms and asked to be readmitted as a student. His explanation proved satisfactory: he had been at the Irish Bar and had served as Attorney-General and then as the war-time Lord Chancellor of Ireland. He had been admitted in June 1879 as Ignatius John O'Brien; the benchers decided that they could safely waive all further formalities and examinations, and so he was called to the Bar, as Lord Shandon, in November 1923. He had certainly been more successful with his studies than a student called Marsh, whose 60 years as such was marked, in April 1936, by the indulgence that he need not pay the annual duty of £1 in future.[23]

One of the few good things to come out of World War I was the increased friendship with American lawyers, especially after the United States joined the exhausted Allies in 1917. In 1905, Hon Joseph H Choate, an attorney, had been the first American Ambassador—and the first non-Briton—to be made an honorary bencher. He must have appreciated the link with *Domus*, as according to one account he considered himself to be homeless in London:

> At a time when his government owned few embassies and forced its representatives to find quarters at their own expense, a London bobby stopped him on a

---

[21]   30 March 1979.

[22]   MT.1/MPA/25. Lawyers in some prisoner of war camps gave law lectures, benefiting both student and teacher.

[23]   MT.1/CEM/2.

late evening stroll and inquired why he was not at home, where he belonged. 'I have no home,' replied Mr Choate, 'I am the American ambassador.'[24]

During the war Master Reading was Lord Chief Justice and Ambassador in Washington, and helped to cement the traditional links of the Inn with the former North American colonies. In July 1918 the Inn gave a dinner to some 50 American lawyers and law students serving with the US Army in England. In the following year Hon John W Davis, the Ambassador and former Solicitor-General of the United States, was called to the Bench. In 1922, the Chief Justice of the United States, William Howard Taft, who had been President just before the war, was made an honorary bencher. When waiting to take his place at the High Table, he was visibly affected, explaining to his neighbour: 'I feel strangely moved, finding myself sitting here in the home of Blackstone, in the very cradle of the Common Law of England and of America.'

The war had two other beneficial after-effects: the admission of women and, later, the setting up of the first major scholarship funds. The essential part that women had played in the war, working in munitions factories, as well as in the more traditional professions such as teaching and nursing, coupled with the efforts of the Suffragettes, gained women the vote and the opportunity to join the Inns of Court. The first women students arrived in the Inn immediately after the Sex Disqualification (Removal) Act 1919 received the Royal Assent, but their numbers were small for many years and their problems large. The Fleet Street Press kept a careful eye on its neighbouring profession in the Temple and happily printed any account indicating that the hide-bound males were slow to adapt to the arrival of members of the opposite sex. On 16 January 1920, the benchers ruled that women members should lunch and dine at separate tables, doubtless feeling that was kinder to them than forcing them to mix with the men, some of whom were likely to be less than welcoming. On the next day the *Daily News* asked:

> Are the Benchers of the Middle Temple, after all, a little frightened of the women law students they have admitted? It seems rather like it. Five ladies had sat with men friends ten days ago.

The *Evening Standard* on 22 January stated that the ladies had a table at right angles to the Ancients' table, adding: 'One evening this week a solitary lady student had the table to herself.' On 27 January a correspondent in the *Daily News* referred to the 'ridiculous attempt to make women sit at separate tables', and added some valid points:

---

[24] LE Ellis, *A Short History of American Diplomacy* (New York, Harper & Brothers, 1951), 6.

It appears to me a very pettifogging way of trying to hold back the prize after the race has been honestly won. Women have struggled to their present position in the law through the splendid efforts of a small band of pioneers. The least the men can do is to admit them heartily into comradeship. The whole thing seems to me directly against the spirit of the Sex Disqualification (Removal) Act.

To modern eyes, there were some remarkably chauvinist male opponents of women in the law. One correspondent wrote to the *Pall Mall Gazette* of 1 January, signing himself 'M.T.' and so presumably a member of the Inn:

Is it really necessary that they should be required or allowed to invade the halls for the purpose of keeping terms. If it be in the public interest that there should be female barristers in these days, why not institute a special Inn for them, a kind of London Girton?

Another man, who also seems to have believed in the doctrine of Separate and Unequal, suggested in an article in the *Evening Standard* of 13 January, that perhaps Gray's Inn could organise separate dinners for women in Staple Inn or Clifford's Inn.

The *Manchester Guardian* on 31 January, in an attempt to live up to its reputation for fairness and common sense, came up with what a Mancunian might have called a 'daft suggestion, namely, that each Inn should have a 'responsible woman official' to look after its female members: 'The simplest and most graceful solution would be for the Benchers of each Inn to call to the Bar and the Bench a woman of distinction.'

Helena Normanton, who was to be the first woman to take Silk in due course, was the first to join the Inn, and the publicity that she received may well have brought other women in too. On 14 August the *Morning Post* made the point:

The majority of would-be feminine barristers have chosen the same Inn, with the result that now there are over twenty of them at the Middle Temple, whereas there are only about half-a-dozen scattered among the other three Inns.

When Mrs Normanton was called to the Bar with nine other women on 18 November 1922, they still had to sit at a separate table. Mrs Normanton was not the first woman to be called, as a distinguished academic, Dr Ivy Williams, had beaten her to that honour by obtaining an exemption of two terms from the Inner Temple. In May 1923 the Middle Temple parliament took a decision that was doubtless both welcomed and found offensive by the women members: in future they could bring guests to dinner on Guest Night, but only if they were female. Progress towards equality was very slow. Even by May 1933 Parliament was prepared to go only so far as change Standing Order 85 to read:

> Women students shall sit either at the table set apart for the exclusive use of women members, or at a table set apart for the use of men and women members desiring to sit together.[25]

While the women had a hard time getting work, much the same could be said about the men attempting to practise in the depressed inter-war years, years that were hard and saw little prosperity, in the law or elsewhere. One point that emerges from the Inn records is that it was often difficult for heads of chambers to pay their rent. The Executive Committee regularly instructed solicitors to serve a notice to quit and to take proceedings for possession. Fortunately, many cases were settled with an arrangement for the payment of arrears, but the benchers of the 1920s and 1930s were regularly faced with this sad and unpleasant problem on a scale never matched after World War II.

A minor indication of the difficulty of meeting the standard rent demand is to be found in an application made in January 1932 by a barrister of Lincoln's Inn, AT Denning, for a tenancy of professional chambers at 4 Brick Court. The tenancy had been screened at £200 a year and he offered to take it on for £170. Somewhat unusually, the benchers were prepared to haggle and resolved to let him have it at an inclusive rental of £187 10s.[26] He was admitted to the Inn *ad eundem*, and in 1972, by then Master of the Rolls, was elected as an honorary bencher, to the great delight of his many admirers.

There was one exceptional case of rent arrears, which could hardly be blamed on lack of work or late payment of fees by solicitor clients. On 22 February 1922 the Collector wrote to a tenant in Elm Court, who was a member of Gray's Inn:

> I am directed to ask you to be good enough to have the demands for three quarters' rent, £140.12.6, due Christmas last, put forward for settlement. The repeated applications have received no attention.[27]

The tenant ignored this letter as well, so on 28 March 1922 the Finance Committee directed:

> That the Lord Chancellor be written to and asked to pay his arrears of rent due at Lady Day 1922, amounting to £187.10.0 and that a copy of Rule 62 be also sent to him.[28]

[25] MT.1/MPA/24.
[26] MT.1/CEM/1. It was a busy and expensive year for Tom Denning: he also got married and moved into a residential flat on 'the top floor of no 1 Brick Court; light and airy rooms overlooking the Middle Temple Hall': Lord Denning, *The Family Story* (London, Butterworths, 1981), 87.
[27] MT.1/LBO/26.
[28] MT.1/CFM5.

The unsatisfactory tenant was none other than FE Smith, Lord Birkenhead. One of his biographers has recently written, with unconscious irony:

> But his greatest moment as a law reformer was carrying a vast and complicated Law of Property Act (1922), bringing the law of property into the twentieth century.

He added:

> In October 1928 Birkenhead left the government, pleading poverty. He could not support his family on a cabinet minister's salary.[29]

Master Sachs, in his article on the Inn's first two great benefactors of the twentieth century, Lord Rothermere and Master Astbury (who was treasurer in 1925), stated:

> The day that Lord Rothermere first came to lunch in the Benchers' Rooms proved to be fortunate for the Middle Temple. Whatever may have been the initial cause of his warm feelings for the Inn to which his father had been called in 1869, it is clear that his interest and affection grew rapidly.[30]

The Alfred Harmsworth Memorial Fund was established in June 1924 by Lord Rothermere, together with his mother, in memory of his father. Lord Rothermere, like both his father and his brother, Lord Northcliffe, was a highly successful newspaper proprietor and had served as Air Minister during the war. His initial gift was of £60,000, the income of which he wished to be used for two purposes. The first was the relief of members' wives, widows and children in indigent circumstances. The second was for scholarships for members of the Universities of Oxford and Cambridge who were also Middle Templars. The Vice-Chancellors were to be asked to nominate suitable candidates, bearing in mind

> their studious habits, their disposition to follow loyally the traditions of the English Bar, and the necessity or probable necessity for financial assistance to enable them to become practising barristers.

The greater part of the income was to be used for scholarships: only the first £1,500 was to be set aside for relief.[31]

In 1927 Lord Rothermere topped the Memorial Fund up with a further £40,000. From then until his death in 1940, in addition to his financial gifts he regularly presented fine pieces of plate made between 1557 and 1658. The account of Master Sachs continued:

---

[29] John Campbell, entry for FE Smith in the *Oxford Dictionary of National Biography*.
[30] 'Two Great Benefactors of the Middle Temple', *The Lawyer*, 1963 6: 3, reprinted as a pamphlet.
[31] MT.10/HMM/1. The requirement for a Vice-Chancellor's recommendation was later dropped.

Some of the senior officials of the Inn retain to this day [1963] vivid memories of the arrival of these splendid items. Lord Rothermere would walk rapidly into the Under-Treasurer's office, abruptly deposit on the desk an object roughly wrapped in crumpled newspaper, and depart with no less speed than he came. It was left to the Under-Treasurer to unwrap the parcel, find a superb 1569 rosewater dish, rush it to the strong room, and attempt to discover its insurance value. On no single occasion was there a formal presentation.[32]

The Inn set up a committee of benchers to administer the Memorial Fund, and on 12 October 1925 they interviewed the first five candidates, awarding three of them £100 per annum for three years. The committee made similar awards in the next two years, and then Lord Rothermere increased the capital of the Fund once more. On that occasion he not only gave a further £70,000, but promised to keep the income from that capital sum topped up. On 4 May 1928 he wrote to the under-treasurer, who was also secretary to the Fund, enclosing a list of the securities he was giving, then worth £70,200:

> The present gross annual income therefrom is approximately £2800 and it is my intention to make up this sum to a 5 per cent gross income on the amount of the fund, *viz*, £3500, by payments from my bank. Will you please apply to them at the end of each full year from the date of the commencement of the fund, for the difference between £3500 and the gross income you will have received from the above securities.

For administrative purposes the relief fund was then allocated £50,000 and the scholarship fund the balance of £120,000, but thereafter the division was changed from time to time.

One of Lord Rothermere's reasons for increasing the Fund was that he wished the scholarships to be for three years, as before, but for them to be increased to £200 per annum. He was approached about the possibility of extending the scholarships to women, but his letter to Master Reading made it clear that he wished to 'confine the scholarships to male members of the Universities mentioned'.[33] In 1953, thirteen years after Lord Rothermere's death, the treasurer, Master Needham, raised the issue of a change to the scheme so as to cover women and non-Oxford or Cambridge graduates. During the discussions Master Needham, who had helped to set up the original scheme, made a comment which gave a further insight into the donor's wishes:

---

[32]   Sachs, above n 30. These gifts, together with other post-Civil War acquisitions, ensured that the Inn had, and has, a fine collection, the responsibility of the Master of the Silver, who is usually an expert on the subject.

[33]   MT.1/MPA/23.

What Lord Rothermere wanted was (I personally know this) to encourage those who would, apart from the scholarship, not have a sure chance of getting through the doubtful and costly preliminary stages.[34]

Lord Rothermere's son Esmond wrote to Master Needham on 31 January 1953:

I am perfectly sure that my father himself would have approved the proposed alterations. Few people knew him as well as you did and as you know he would have been the first person to appreciate the new demands resulting from rapidly changing conditions. Moreover, he would in a matter of this kind have been only too happy to leave the whole situation to the judgment of the Benchers. The proposal has my blessing.[35]

There may well have been more than one explanation for Lord Rothermere's additional generosity in 1928. From 1926 on, concern had been expressed about the large number of students from overseas, and particularly from the Indian sub-continent, coupled with a shortage of students intending to practise in England. On 19 May 1927 a motion was placed before Parliament that the Inn should restrict its annual entry to 150 students, of whom no more than one-third should be of non-European origin.

The motion was adjourned to a Special Parliament, held on 26 May. The Inn was fortunate that one of the most distinguished benchers of all time was present. Master Reading had been Lord Chief Justice from 1913 to 1921. During that time he had also served for a while, with the concurrence of his judicial colleagues, as a war-time Ambassador to the United States. From 1921 to 1926 he served as Viceroy of India, so that he was both well-equipped to discuss the legal education of Indian students sympathetically and conscious of the sensitive nature of the questions being discussed.

Master Reading proposed an amendment to make it clear that the principal concern was not with the fact that the Inn was educating a large number of overseas students, but rather with the troubling fact that too few students were coming forward with the intention of practising in England and Wales. His proposal, which was carried unanimously, read:

(a) That it is imperative in the interests of each of the four Inns of Court and their good government that there should be an adequate supply of barristers of each Inn who practise, or have practised, in England, and (b) That the Masters of the Bench of the Middle Temple have serious ground for apprehension that there will not in the future be a sufficient number of members of their Inn to provide suitable candidates for election to the Bench by reason of the admission of a disproportionately large number of students who intend to practise outside England and do not intend to reside in this country.

---

[34]   MT.10/HMM/2.
[35]   MT.1/MPA/26.

The Inn suggested a conference to the other Inns, but nothing came of the idea. The other Inns were not so concerned, as they usually had a smaller proportion of overseas students and as moves were afoot in India to provide for legal studies to be completed here. On 1 January 1928 Master Reading took office as Master Treasurer for the year. On 19 April Lord Rothermere became an honorary bencher, and a week later he made his gift of the additional £70,000. It is distinctly possible that the two peers had discussed how best to encourage more suitable candidates to practise at the Bar in England, and that they had agreed that scholarships of £200 per annum would be twice as attractive as the earlier ones of £100.

The relief fund over the subsequent years dealt sympathetically with many appeals for help, and at times helped even though no request had been made by the eventual recipient. Benchers or members of Hall sometimes drew the attention of the committee to an elderly barrister or a deserving widow, too proud or too ill to approach the Inn for help. The committee had a good working relationship with the Barristers' Benevolent Fund: sometimes the two bodies would share the grant made to a Middle Temple beneficiary, at other times a case would be transferred from one charitable body to the other. Inevitably, some recipients were more deserving than others, and some of the less meritorious applicants could cause the most work.

In March 1925 the committee agreed to pay for the fare of Mr S to Singapore, where, it was hoped, all his problems would be solved. Unfortunately, the Passport Office refused to issue him with a passport unless the Inn was prepared to guarantee the cost of repatriation, should the occasion arise. That was not an unreasonable condition, as Mr S had already been twice repatriated to England at public expense. As there was no time for a committee meeting, the treasurer felt able to give the guarantee, so the applicant set sail for the East. He never made it, for he jumped ship at Cape Town. He later demanded that the committee pay for his fare to Tanganyika and complained of the treatment he had received. He eventually returned to England and was supported by the Fund until 1942, when he qualified for his old age pension.[36]

A crisis relating to the Inn's estate occurred soon after World War I. Sir Frank Baines, the Director of Works at the Office of Works, was invited to comment on the state of the Hall roof, after insects had fallen onto the new women students' table. (It is possible that the male members of the Inn had become accustomed to the bugs and no longer bothered to report their presence.) Baines eventually presented an interim report on 15 August 1922, containing some disturbing findings[37]:

---

[36]   MT.10/HMM/1.
[37]   MT.6/RBW 225.

Some of the modern timber used for strengthening the hammer beams on trusses No 5 and 6 South side were apparently unseasoned and are decaying rapidly, the timber is rotten and can easily be removed by means of a chisel.

Fortunately, the death watch beetle was not as serious as that which he had found in the hall of Hampton Court Palace and in Westminster Hall. Nevertheless, Baines suggested very extensive remedial work at a cost of £28,000.

The Bench ruled out expenditure of that order and sought the advice of Sir Aston Webb once more, together with that of Basil Mott, a consultant engineer, and they suggested a far cheaper solution. Their report of 8 November 1923 gave a detailed account of the construction of the roof. On one view of it, the Inn's claim to have one of the finest hammer-beam roofs has to be modified, for this is what the report stated[38]:

Although we are of opinion that this insect [Xestobium tessellatum, death-watch beetle] attack forms the principal danger to the roof, there are also matters of construction that require our attention. As has been pointed out, the roof appears to have shown signs of spreading soon after its erection, caused chiefly, in our opinion, by the faulty hammer-beam construction.

The purpose of a hammer-beam is to give support to the principal rafter at its weakest point 'A' where the collar-beam is tenoned into it, and to carry the weight by means of a curved brace down the wall.[39] In this case, however, the supporting post from 'A' to 'B' has been omitted; and the post itself [sc below B], , instead of resting on the hammer-beam, is carried past it, and, as a consequence, the hammer-beam is useless as a means of support for the principal rafter, which is some 35ft long and has to carry the whole weight of the roof, with the result that these rafters sagged some 4 inches at the point 'A' where the collar-beam is tenoned into them and has pushed out the walls some 10 inches.

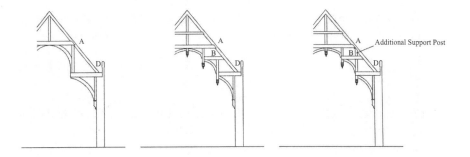

Figure 1   Figure 2   Figure 3

Diagram showing repairs to Hall roof

---

[38] MT.6/RBW 226.

[39] See Figs 1, 2 and 3. Figs 1 and 2 substantially reproduce drawings included in the report. Fig 3 shows how the original structure should have been built.

The architect and engineer added that very enterprising means had been used in the past to strengthen the hammer-beams,

> by means of heavy timbers bolted on either side of them, and an ingenious wedge for stiffening the angle formed by the junction of the principal rafter and hammer-beam at 'D' [the top of the wall].

They recommended the chemical treatment of the timbers suggested by Professor Lefroy, and steelwork to reinforce the roof: 'steel plates, angles and tie bars', as shown on their drawings. They were confident that

> When this has been done the structural part of the truss will have been made secure, the double hammer-beams etc, owing to their design, being merely ornaments hanging on to the constructive members of the truss.[40]

The work was executed by Dove Brothers in 1924 and 1925, and cost only some £9,000 in all, as opposed to the £28,000 that Baines had recommended. However, that was not the end of the pre-war troubles of the Hall. Ten years after the completion of the roof works, the foundations of the Hall—or the absence thereof—caused great concern, and Maurice Webb (Sir Aston's son, who was continuing his late father's practice) was called in to advise. He was assisted by the structural engineer BL Hunt.

On 16 March 1936, Webb reported that the south end of the west, gable-end wall was still moving towards the River Thames.[41] He listed the main sources of the weakness of the west wall. First, the initial ten feet below the base of the wall were found to comprise nothing more substantial than vegetable matter, earth and other material of poor quality. Secondly, the four buttresses were useless as supports: they were not bonded into the wall but were in the nature of separate pillars resting against the wall for their own support. Thirdly, when the two-storey houses and shops attached to the wall had been demolished in 1758, the new outer face of the wall had been badly built. Webb found that the outer skin comprised courses of brickwork varying between nine inches and half that width, together with a partial backing of tiles. That eighteenth-century facing was 'entirely unbonded to the body of the wall and is bulged away from it at some points to two inches'.

When the underpinning that Webb and Hunt had recommended was commenced under the southernmost buttress, more weakness was revealed:

> We found that there was a clear space between the base of the buttress and the ground. This ground, for several feet of depth below the space, consisted of soft mud and silt, which had apparently settled and shrunk away from the base of the buttress, leaving the buttress itself hanging as a dead load from the wall.

---

[40] See also, *Middle Temple Hall—An Architectural Appreciation*, written by Michael G Murray, the Inn's Surveyor from 1977 to 1988, and published as a pamphlet by the Inn in 2000.

[41] MT.6/RBW 248.

They also discovered that the Hall privies had at one time emptied straight into the subsoil, as they found four pipes built into the body of the buttress, leading to the ground directly under it, which still had such an offensive smell that 'large quantities of disinfectant' were hastily sent for and used.

Once the work had been executed during the Long Vacation in 1936, Webb and his colleague were able to advise that the newly-strengthened wall 'should stand for a very long period of time'. It seems likely that it was the effect of his work on the wall, coupled with his father's earlier reinforcement of the roof, that made the Hall strong enough to withstand the blast of the land-mine which was to test it before long.[42]

In between these two major improvements to the strength of the Hall, various chambers blocks had also had work done, which was similarly to stand them in good stead in wartime. The strengthening of some buildings probably enabled them to survive serious blast damage, while the provision of proper fire escapes over various roofs was to assist the Air Raid Wardens and fire-watchers to deal with the large number of incendiary bombs that were to hit the Inn.

The promotion of CG Swanson, the under-surveyor since 1919, to surveyor in 1926, marked the end of what was clearly a long period of disagreement between his predecessor and the under-treasurer, Beresford-Peirse. The under-treasurer had from time to time expressed his concern about the dubious manner in which the previous surveyor ran his department, but in February 1926 he prepared a forceful report for the Master Treasurer in which he recommended a reorganisation, pulling no punches. His comments included the following:

> I am certain that my suggested reorganisation would not be carried out either honestly or loyally by the present Surveyor. [Swanson, the Under-Surveyor] has done well since he came into the service of the Inn, in spite of the Surveyor, who has deliberately made his position very difficult and has withheld as much information in connection with the working of the department as he could contrive to keep from him. This attitude of disloyalty caused me to duplicate every order sent to the Surveyor, the duplicate being sent to the Under-Surveyor, in some cases even to his private address.[43]

During the Long Vacation in 1932 an amazing amount of repair and maintenance was done in the Inn, quite apart from essential fire escape improvements. The architect, Clyde Young, concluded his report on this work by pointing out:

---

[42]   That was Surveyor Murray's later professional opinion; see, above n 39, at 10.
[43]   MT.8/SMP/183.

The foregoing list of works were carried out during a very bad trade depression and provided employment for at least 600 men for a period of ten weeks.[44]

The achievement, which involved work on Pump Court, the Cloisters and the old Lamb Building by the Temple Church, was possible in the time available only because of good organisation. Despite the time constraints, great care was taken, as is shown by Young's report on one building:

> The Cloisters roof was found to be in an advanced state of decay. All the old roof timbers were taken out and an entirely new roof constructed. The old tiles were carefully preserved, cleaned and relaid—only 25 per cent new tiles were needed to complete the new roof, these were on the internal slopes where they are not seen.

II. WORLD WAR II

Middle Temple Ordeal was the very apt title given to an excellent pamphlet published by the Inn after the war in 1948. It was based on the reports of bomb damage prepared contemporaneously by CG Swanson, the Inn's surveyor, with Thomas Hewlett, the under-treasurer, coupled with the reminiscences of residents, staff and others who had played their part in minimising the damage, principally by dealing with the many incendiary bombs. The author was a woman member who lived in the Temple throughout the war but chose to remain anonymous. The present writer has drawn heavily on her pamphlet.

By 1937 it was fairly clear that war could not be far off and that the greatest danger would come from the skies.[45] The Inn began to make preparations and in 1938 built eight air raid shelters in the basements considered best able to survive bombing. They proved to be invaluable from 1940 to the end of the war. George Kingham[46] was in charge of the Air Raid Precautions for both Temple Inns, and various training sessions were undergone by Inn employees, barristers, their clerks and residents. The Middle Temple Librarian, HAC Sturgess, specialised in first aid training and the problem of how best to cope with a gas attack. The spirit of the times may be gauged from two letters.

The first, dated 14 December 1939, was from SG Newland, who was to become the first chairman of the Barrister's Clerks' Association. He sent Sturgess the names of twelve clerks, including his own,

---

[44] MT.6/RBW 245.

[45] There had been bombing of London in the earlier war by Zeppelins and Gotha bombers, leading to the serious suggestion then by a bencher that steel netting might perhaps be placed over the Hall and Church as protection against bombs.

[46] George Kingham became a bencher of Middle Temple in 1942.

who have expressed their willingness to form a first aid squad and act as stretcher-bearers. All are trained in some form of Air Raid Precautions work and therefore will need little further training. I can and will get more, but this is a good number to start with. There are three teams and sufficient fully trained first aiders to include at least one in each team.[47]

The Librarian added a number of other names to the list later.

The second was a letter that Master Kingham received in October 1939 from a barrister's wife, who had successfully taken the first aid course shortly before the war:

I should very much like to help at the First Aid Post in the Temple but am afraid that I cannot undertake any regular service as my husband has very little sight and has to have somebody always with him. If I could be of any use at the times when he is at court or in chambers I should be very pleased and will get in touch with Mr Sturgess.

It was signed by Kathleen Mortimer, the wife of Clifford Mortimer, a practising Inner Templar. Their son, later Sir John Mortimer QC, immortalised his parents in his play *A Voyage Round my Father*.

Once it became clear that war was inevitable, the Inn sent off some of its collection of documents to the Montgomeryshire home of Master Stable for safe-keeping. The 1608 Charter followed on 31 July 1939, in a chest surrounded by asbestos and escorted by the Inn's carpenter.[48] The paintings and stained glass windows of the Hall were also evacuated.

The first eight months of the hostilities, sometimes called the Phoney War, passed without any enemy attack, but the Inn was affected by them in many ways. Barrister tenants and staff alike went off to the armed services or other war work, as did many barrister's clerks and students. Parliament was able to help members of the staff who were called up by resolving, on 18 September 1939, to make their service pay up to their salary on departure.[49] The financial problems of the barristers were not so easily resolved. The Inn's resources were clearly going to be stretched to the limit at a time when its income was severely reduced. As a result, a number of tenants who applied to be relieved of rent because of their impending or actual departure for war service were turned down, even though the benchers did their level best to help members already in the forces. As early as 1 January 1940 the Special War Committee[50] reported that an adverse balance of £10,000 would be accrued by the end of the year. The Committee added that its 'most difficult work' had been the great number

---

[47]   MT.1/WAR/2.
[48]   MT.4/JAS/3 and 4.
[49]   MT.1/MPA/24.
[50]   The Special War Committee consisted of Master Treasurer and two other benchers: Parliament decision 18 September 1939: MT.1/MPA/24.

of applications for reduction of rents. Incidentally, that Committee, comprising Master Henn Collins (the treasurer), Master Gregory (treasurer in 1933) and Master Hunter, had ample work, as it was authorised not only to act for Parliament, but also to undertake *all* its committee work.

Master Rothermere had already been made aware of the difficulties. On 19 September 1939, sixteen days after war was declared, he wrote to the treasurer with typical generosity:

> Your letter does not in any way surprise me. From my correspondence I find there is already much hardship, in fact as much as there was in the last years of the Great War. There are very difficult times ahead, but the only thing we can do is to stand shoulder to shoulder and meet them as far as is in our power. For my part I wish you would accept the accompanying cheque for £2500 which I hope I may supplement by a further contribution perhaps before the end of the year. I hope you will apply this money in any direction you think proper, whether in relief of rents or in assistance to the senior members of the Inn who will, if the war is a prolonged one, suffer very grievously. Will you let me know from time to time how you are getting along so that I may be ready to lay my hands on any funds upon which I can draw? I am afraid the war will leave all of us quite poor, but this is a contingency which personally will in no way perturb me because I started life without anything and will probably be meeting only my deserts if I end without anything.[51]

A second cheque for £2,500 was sent by Master Rothermere in November.

The first bombs fell on the Inn on the night of 24 September 1940. One of them demolished 1 Elm Court, opposite the Hall, narrowly missing the three men on duty at the look-out post on the roof of 4 Elm Court. They managed to get down and smelt escaping gas, so hastily moved the occupants of the shelter under 3 Elm Court to the one under Goldsmith Building. The force of the Elm Court explosion may be gauged from the fact that two cornice stones, each weighing a ton and a half, were blown clean over the roof of the adjoining Pump Court.

One high-explosive bomb fortunately failed to explode. It was found, in the basement of 6 Pump Court, by JL Manquet (later Head Porter) and H Collison, the Inn's fireman. They were joined by a resident barrister, PH Sée, and a police sergeant. According to the report of the incident, 'On the advice of Mr Sée, who considered it reasonably safe to do so, it was removed to the garden'. The four men who carried the bomb were lucky not to be killed. Quite why three of them felt able to rely on the opinion of counsel, even if he was a former Harmsworth scholar, is not clear.

Hitler seemed determined to demolish Elm Court, and with his second raid on the Temple he succeeded. A mine, attached to a parachute, not only destroyed the remainder of Elm Court on the night of 15 October, but also

---

[51] Cf Job i 21 [Ed.].

damaged many nearby chambers. The under-treasurer and surveyor described the serious damage caused by that same mine to the Hall, in their report of 14 November:

> The explosion blew a large hole in the east gable, at the same time partly demolishing the clock tower. The falling masonry together with large stones from the explosion in Elm Court, smashed the gallery floor, throwing the screen onto the Hall floor, where at the moment it is buried more or less under the gallery timbers. The blast going through the Hall found its chief outlet through the Chancellor's window in the south bay and the opposite window in the north bay.[52]

Once the rubble was cleared away it was clear that the carved screen was damaged but, possibly, not beyond repair. All the pieces were placed in some 200 sacks and sent to the country for eventual, highly successful reassembly.

The report added that only one air raid shelter had received minor damage: the one under 6 Middle Temple Lane:

> Fortunately, two members of the staff and the Inn's fireman happened to be in the shelter at the time and they managed to extricate both themselves and the other occupants without injury to anyone.

The fireman, Collison, led a charmed life: he had been one of the three men on the roof look-out post at Elm Court during the first raid, had helped to carry the unexploded bomb and, according to a later treasurer, Master Cassels, 'was never absent during a major raid'.[53] The fireman was not the only one who seems to have had a guardian angel. One of the most extraordinary facts to emerge from the history of the bombing is that there was not a single fatality in the Temple. The reinforced basement shelters provide a part of the answer only, for staff members like Collison and residents such as William Latey (treasurer in 1966) often spurned shelter when on look-out duty—which was usually known as 'fire-watching'—or when tackling incendiary bombs.[54]

One of the first benchers to learn of the damage to the Hall was Master Jowitt, then Solicitor-General. On 16 October he wrote to the treasurer, Master Hurst, from his chambers in the Royal Courts of Justice:

> My deepest sympathy with you that in your year of office this awful catastrophe should have happened to Domus. I would urge you to try and get communal life of the Bench resumed as soon as may be. It doesn't matter what we eat but it does matter that we should eat it together and in this way preserve our mutual

---

[52] MT.1/WAR/2.
[53] In his Foreword to *Middle Temple Ordeal*.
[54] Both Cassels and Latey had been journalists before joining the Inn; there were many successful members who, like them, had first had another occupation.

interests. Bread and cheese—or cold ham—in the Library common room and an oil stove to warm up coffee would encourage us all.[55]

Another parachute mine floated down on the night of 8 December and landed about 20 feet from the south-east corner of the library. The explosion left a crater some 40 feet wide and 18 feet deep. Two of the Royal Air Force men in charge of the barrage balloon, located in the garden nearby (with its cable to discourage low flying by the bombers), were seriously injured by the blast but recovered. The blast also demolished the large oriel window of the Library facing the river. The windows and roof tiles were all affected: no fewer than 48,000 tiles were found piled behind the roof parapets of the east and west walls. At that time the building was considered to be stable enough for repairs to be considered, but there was more to come.[56] Fortunately, the Library had not caught fire, so most of the books were salvaged by a team made up of

> the Librarian and his staff, now only two men, the Librarian from Lincoln's Inn and his assistant, and a Bencher from that Inn dressed in a boiler suit, together with a woman barrister, a West African student and a Bencher of our own Inn.[57]

On 2 January 1941 a skeleton library was opened in the Common Room in the building, but most of the rescued books were evacuated to the country.

The Call ceremony, thanks to the bombers, became a movable feast. On 18 November 1940 Call Night was in the Library, as the Hall had been damaged. The Call ceremony on 27 January 1941 was in the old Parliament chamber as the Library had by then been put out of action. One of the many photographs in the Inn's possession shows the ceremony being conducted back in the Hall, once the damaged east end had been sealed off. One of the students being called was in military uniform, the rest in wig and gown. (See plate 3-19, 'Call to the Bar in the Bombed Hall').

The Inn's greatly reduced team of workmen executed first-aid repairs to damaged buildings as speedily as possible, but must have felt disheartened whenever a later raid undid their work. The report of the under-treasurer and surveyor about the repeated damage to the Hall is revealing:

> The whole of the damage done on 15/16 October had been temporarily made good. The Hall had been shut off from the Parliament Chamber and plumbers and fitters were busy disconnecting the hot water pipes to Hall and service rooms, reconnecting cold water services to kitchen and Benchers' rooms and carrying out other necessary repairs, when the land-mine of 8 December destroyed everything that had been done, including work to the roof of Hall. The

---

[55] MT.6/RBW/295.
[56] MT.6/WAR/8.
[57] *Middle Temple Ordeal*, at 22. The helpful 'woman barrister' was perhaps the anonymous female author of *Middle Temple Ordeal*.

work was started once again and by 27 December was ready for Benchers' and barristers' lunches etc, even to a temporary service of electric light. On the evening of 1 January another land-mine struck a partly demolished building in Crown Office Row and again all the repair work was smashed and, for the third time, the necessary repairs were put in hand.

Not only the Hall, but also the Library was damaged by this third mine.

In January and March 1941 many incendiary bombs rained down on the Temple, but most of them were tackled successfully. In June 1941 Hitler made his greatest mistake, when he attacked the Soviet Union. That diverted his bombers from the west. However, shortly before that, he ordered another attack on London. On the night of 10 May, according to the under-treasurer and the surveyor, the Inn experienced 'the worst raid yet with more damage done than in all previous raids'.[58]

The Temple Church and Master's House, both owned jointly with the Inner Temple, were burnt out. The bombers dropped high explosives first and then incendiary bombs, which inflicted terrible damage. A bomb in the garden smashed the water main, flooding shelters and the first aid post in 3 and 4 Temple Gardens. The Fire Brigade and other fire-fighters were seriously hampered in their work by the 'almost entire lack of water', and as a result, 'many of the fires were not finally extinguished for three or four days'.

The old Lamb Building, the southern half of Pump Court, Nos 2 and 3 Brick Court and 3–6 Plowden Buildings were all destroyed. As Master Cassels mentioned in his Foreword to *Middle Temple Ordeal*,

> No. 2 Brick Court, where Oliver Goldsmith lived and entertained Dr Johnson and other celebrities of the eighteenth century and where Blackstone wrote his Commentaries and Thackeray had chambers, is no more. Gone is Lamb Building, where Judah Philip Benjamin, the Attorney-General of the Confederate States under President Davis, practised successfully at the English Bar during seventeen years of the last century.[59]

Many of the remaining buildings sustained serious damage, including those in Brick Court and Essex Court. First-aid repairs were commenced at once and steps were taken to increase the amount of water supplies for fire-fighting. Pipes were laid from the Thames, high enough over the Embankment to clear the buses and trams, and into the Temple. The former basements of 2 and 3 Brick Court were made waterproof and an emergency water supply tank was built there by the London County

---

[58]　MT.1/WAR/12.
[59]　He also found time to write *Benjamin on Sale*, still a standard work.

Council.[60] A similar tank was built in Pump Court and the Inn's fountain basin was built up to provide a third reservoir.

Fortunately, there was a respite period of almost three years before the next attack. However, during that time the Inn could not afford to lower its guard:

> Throughout those years the inmates slept like cats with one ear open, ready to distinguish the 'alert' from the many other sounds to be heard—the trams on the Embankment, the river craft hooting down the Thames, five clocks striking, never in unison, the screech of an owl evidently evacuated from the country, the cable in the garden winding the balloon either up or down, and from daylight several local cockerels, then the trumpet sounding Reveille on the training ships, the *President* and the *Chrysanthemum*.[61]

The absence of any major air raids, and therefore of any substantial noise from enemy aircraft or bombs, led to what may perhaps be called the resumption of normal peacetime hostilities. In July 1942 Parliament resolved:

> That notice to quit his chambers at 6 Pump Court be served on Mr Norman Platt in consequence of complaints received of the disturbance caused by his singing and piano-playing.[62]

The bombers returned to London on 25 March 1944, when some 140 incendiaries fell on the Inn. The Hall cupola was burnt out, but the roof, though badly burned, was saved by the joint efforts of various fire fighters. The report of the incident stated:

> Thanks to the efforts of Collison, the Inn's fireman, assisted by other fire guards and the prompt arrival of the National Fire Service, the Hall was saved from being entirely gutted. The other fires were all effectively dealt with by the fire guards and other helpers.[63]

The Allied invasion of Normandy on 6 June 1944 was followed, a week later, by the unleashing of the V1 flying bombs on to London, to be followed by the larger and more dangerous V2 rockets, which could not be intercepted. Fortunately, none of them landed on the Inn, although further blast damage was done to the Hall, Library and other buildings by near misses, which landed outside its precincts.

Apart from the damage to the Hall, Library and Temple Church,[64] all the bombing cost the Inn 122 of its 285 sets of chambers. Repairs and

---

[60] Thanks to the bombing and the removal of debris, London was able to use many waterproofed basements, marked 'EWS', to store water for fire-fighting, as the author recalls.

[61] *Middle Temple Ordeal*, at 44.

[62] MT.1/MPA/25.

[63] MT.1/WAR/23.

[64] See Toulmin's 'The Temple Church' above at p 22.

rebuilding were to take many years to effect, as there was a national shortage of building materials and strict government control of supplies.

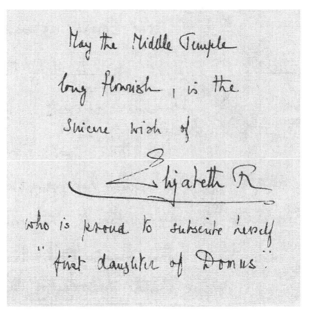

Excerpt from letter from Queen Elizabeth to Serjeant Sullivan

Much has been written about the spirit of the Londoners who lived with the bombs. On 12 December 1944 the Queen was called to the Bench by the Inn, her visit being bracketed by explosions of flying bombs and rockets. Her Majesty's letter of thanks to Master Treasurer reflected the feelings of many residents of the capital:

> Dear Serjeant Sullivan, I write to say with what pleasure I look back upon my visit to the Middle Temple, and to send you a personal word of appreciation and gratitude for having arranged such a delightful evening. In the midst of the crashing and banging and the discomfort which was our life in this dear London, it was an inspiring thing to step into the peace and beauty of Domus, and I assure you that I shall never forget that night, or the kindly welcome I received from my fellow Benchers. It was most agreeable to be able to defy the Germans as well—they did their best to destroy us with terrifying weapons, and though they hurt the Great Hall, they could not destroy the spirit of our brave and gentle people, amongst whom I count my fellow Benchers. May the Middle Temple long flourish, is the sincere wish of
>
> *Elizabeth R*
>
> who is proud to subscribe herself 'first daughter of Domus'.

Immediately after the ending of the war in 1945, the Special War Committee asked Masters Holman Gregory and Carpmael to look at the salary structure of the Inn's employees. In their report they made a point that could only really be made by those who had both experienced the bombing of London and witnessed what the staff had undergone and achieved. Their comment speaks volumes:

> During the period of the war, the work and conduct of each individual has been loyal, brave and disinterested on all occasions, both by day and night and during the periods of extreme danger to life or limb.

Unfortunately, the Inn could not afford to meet all the demands for increases of pay then made by those deserving employees—including the Librarian, who pointed out that he had not had any increase since 1928—but did what it could to meet the strongest claims.

III.   POST-WAR RECONSTRUCTION

As early as 16 April 1942, Parliament agreed unanimously that the Special War Committee should confer with the Inner Temple about the reconstruction of the Temple after the war. By 18 June the Committee was able to report that the 'closest collaboration between the two Inns had been decided on'. On 11 December 1946 Parliament appointed a Special Reconstruction Committee with executive powers, subject to sufficiently important matters being referred back to it and subject to the requirement of regular reports. The Committee was authorised to negotiate terms with any architects to be engaged, and also to discuss and agree with the Inner Temple an exchange of parcels of land to facilitate reconstruction. That such an agreement was reached in 1944 is shown by the letter that Master Montgomery, the Inner Temple treasurer, wrote to Master Sullivan, his Middle Temple opposite number, on 6 July 1944:

> I am pleased to tell you that the Inner Temple Bench last night approved the proposal you made to us to convey to the Middle Temple land, roughly plotted on the plan which your architect kindly forwarded to me, for the purpose of building a Lamb Court.[65] They also approved the grant of a three-foot strip on the east side of the Cloisters, to give the proposed new building a better width. All this in exchange for the site of the old Lamb Building, on which of course we are not to build. The details of the new scheme to be worked out by the two architects and submitted to our two Benches. As to the recommendation for an opening some 33 feet in width from Middle Temple Lane to the new Crown Office Row, my Bench approved this also and agreed we should increase

---

[65] In practice, a new Carpmael Building and Arch, early on referred to as 'the bridge site'.

(southwards) the amount of ground to be conveyed to your Inn to enable your Inn to carry out the recommendation without loss of building land.

The extra width for the Cloisters made it possible for the architect to provide for two internal rows of columns in the open ground-floor area, in place of the single row provided by Sir Christopher Wren for the destroyed building. Wren had specified on 24 September 1680: 'A middle row of Dorick pillars of stone set upon good foundations to divide the Cloyster belowe into a double walke and to support the floors and partitions.'[66] Edward Maufe's double row of internal columns enabled him to provide a larger and even better proportioned Cloisters than Wren's, complete with a triple 'walke'.

Master Sullivan was one of the Inn's great characters. He was the last lawyer to be appointed a King's Serjeant in Ireland, but felt obliged to leave his homeland on the painful partitioning of the island. He inscribed the copy of his memoirs, which he gave to the Inn, with the touching dedication:

> To Domus, within whose fold a broken exile found happiness in the companionship of great gentlemen. From the son of her adoption, AM Sullivan.

However, he sometimes failed to keep the under-treasurer informed of steps he had taken as treasurer. Unfortunately, he seems to have got into a muddle over the agreement with the Inner Temple and overlooked the fact that the cardinal terms relating to the exchange of land had been agreed. He dismayed the 1945 treasurer of the Inner, Master MacKinnon, by suggesting that the exchange agreement was conditional on the higher rate of War Damage compensation being received by the Middle.

On 22 June 1945 Master MacKinnon justifiably wrote to protest. The benchers of the Middle Temple were appalled by their past treasurer's lapse of memory, and speedily resolved:

> That this Parliament deplores the fact that any misunderstanding should have arisen and wishes the Treasurer of the Inner Temple to be assured that the Middle Temple does not regard the agreement entered into in relation to Lamb Building as to an exchange of sites as subject to any condition as to compensation on a cost of works basis being received, but recognises it as a concluded agreement subject only to the settlement of details.[67]

A copy of the resolution was sent by Master Scholefield, Sullivan's successor as treasurer, to the treasurer of the Inner Temple, who replied on 19 July 1945 in inspiring terms:

> I received this afternoon, with profound satisfaction, your letter of today's date. I very cordially echo your own words— 'I am personally much gratified by this happy issue.' That the two Honourable Societies should have existed side by side for more than 500 years, without any fences between them, and with never a

---

[66]   MT.1/CMM/8.
[67]   MT.6/RBW/260.

serious disagreement, might well seem incredible to outsiders. But it has been so, and happily it is so. I trust it may so continue for a 1000 years to come. I know it will give great pleasure to all my colleagues if you and your fellow Benchers will dine with us in the Niblett Hall at an early date in Michaelmas Term.

After the misunderstanding had been cleared up so amicably, both Inns were content to deal informally with the exchanges of land suggested by the architects, and did not feel the need to execute the formal documents required until 7 December 1959. Apart from the alterations to the boundary already mentioned, the plans attached showed the tidying up of the ownership of different parts of Elm Court.[68]

The moving spirit of the Inn's Reconstruction Committee was Master Carpmael, whose untiring efforts to get the Inn rebuilt, with the help of appropriate public funds, were eventually successful. His hard work was acknowledged by Parliament's decision to give his name to the new archway from Middle Temple Lane and to the adjoining building.[69] In May 1948 Edward Maufe, the architect of Guildford Cathedral, who had already been consulted, became the sole architect for the Inn. The Inner Temple recognised his worth, and later asked him to design and supervise the rebuilding of Crown Office Row and Francis Taylor Building.[70]

Both Inns made a policy decision at an early stage that not all the destroyed buildings should be rebuilt on their original sites. The Middle Temple did not wish to rebuild 2–3 Brick Court, as that block had been awkwardly sited too close to its neighbours: a mere seven or eight feet away, so as to interfere with the light of 16 other sets of chambers. The Inner Temple was concerned that the Middle Temple should not rebuild Lamb Building, which had been similarly awkwardly sited between the church and the Inner Temple Hall. The Inner Temple also wished to ensure that the north side of a new Crown Office Row should not be spoilt by the Middle Temple rebuilding Elm Court close to it, and was prepared to abandon any idea of rebuilding the adjoining Fig Tree Court for the same reason. The Middle Temple held similar views about a new south side of Pump Court, and was content not to rebuild the destroyed Elm Court buildings.

As it happened, the town planning authorities insisted on some such improvements:

The replanning of Elm Court and new Lamb Court and the re-siting by Inner Temple of Crown Office Row, will eliminate the confined courts and narrow

---

[69] MT.1/CRR/2. His report on the work of the Committee has been drawn on heavily by the present writer.
[70] Gray's Inn also appointed him as the architect for its reconstruction. In 1954 he was knighted for his many achievements.

passageways which were disagreeable features of this area as it was. Their elimination was specifically required by the Town Planning authorities and the Royal Fine Arts Commission.[71]

Middle Temple decided that it would be better if the new Library were to be built on Middle Temple Lane, on the vacant site of 3–4 Plowden Buildings and the adjoining site of 4 Temple Gardens. It would then adjoin the Treasury and Hall, while the pre-war Library site could be used for replacement chambers.[72] The Inn had decided to build 4 Temple Gardens only in 1926—as cheaply as possible and without the expensive stonework of Nos 1–3, so that the building looked like a poor relation of the massive white stone block. It had survived the bombing, but in April 1954 the tenants were transferred into the new Lamb Building so that No 4 could be demolished.[73]

All these ideas were to be implemented in the fullness of time. Numbers 1–5 Essex Court and 1 and 4 Brick Court (the two surviving buildings of that court) were left with an open space in the centre and ample light. A grassed square would have been an asset, but the Inn, unlike the Inner Temple, was desperate for parking space and in due course turned the site of 2–3 Brick Court into a small car park, which was always inadequate for the needs of the tenants. There was a delay because the site was first occupied by the temporary Library, built by the Inn's own workforce and opened by the Queen in November 1946. However, the word 'temporary' had a fairly elastic meaning in the immediate post-war days: the Librarian and a very small staff managed to run a reasonable service there for twelve years.

Inner Temple achieved its goal of a large open space between its new Hall and the church, now known as Church Court. Both Inns benefited when Pump Court and Crown Office Row were rebuilt without Elm Court or Fig Tree Court buildings crammed in between them. Finally, Middle Temple built its Library with access to the Treasury and Hall. These desirable ends were not achieved without a long-running dispute about the construction to be placed on the War Damage Act. On 25 July 1945 the War Damage Commission expressed the view that all the buildings designed to be and in fact occupied by the Inn itself, should be treated as a single unit. The Temple Church and Master's House were also to be regarded similarly: each as a single unit. However, when it came to

---

[71]   MT.6/RBW/312.

[72]   MT.1/CRR. The Inn had considered building a joint library with the Inner Temple, which showed little enthusiasm for the idea. On 22 February 1945 the Middle Temple's Reconstruction Committee resolved that 'owing to lack of a suitable site, it was not practicable for a joint library for the use of both Inns to be erected after the war': MT.1/CMM/8. The possibility of sharing a library was discussed again during the financial crisis of 2009, but once more was ruled out.

[73]   MT.1/CEM/1 and 3.

chambers buildings, the Commission's view was that each staircase should be treated as a separate unit. It declined to accept the argument that the Inns were like Oxford and Cambridge colleges, pointing out that the Inn chambers were let out for professional purposes and that some of the lettings were to non-lawyers.

The Inn argued forcefully that that its 'headquarters' buildings and chambers blocks should be treated as one unit, but got nowhere with the Commission on this point for some five years. The point at issue was of great importance. If the Commission was correct then the full compensation could be paid only for each unit rebuilt on its original site—even though the planning authorities were not prepared to allow such rebuilding, for example, in Elm Court. If the Inn chose, voluntarily or otherwise, to rebuild 2 and 3 Brick Court, or Lamb Building or Elm Court elsewhere, there would then be a significant financial loss.

Five years later, in a letter dated 22 May 1950, the War Damage Commission still stuck to its guns:

> It is impossible for the Commission to regard the erection of a new building on a different site from that of a destroyed building as making good the damage to the hereditament. In such a case, therefore, the Commission cannot pay a cost of works payment but only a value payment under the provisions of Section 13 of the War Damage Act.

A meeting of all interested parties was called by the Commission for 30 June. Master Carpmael told his Inner Temple colleagues that he was going to argue the unit point once again; they had clearly given up all hope of obtaining a reasonable response from the Commission and told him he had no chance of success. The meeting gave no cause for optimism, but by letter dated 20 July 1950 the Commission finally gave way and agreed that all the lands of the Middle Temple were to be regarded as one unit; the same applied to the Inner Temple.

In his later report to Parliament, Master Carpmael wrote:

> The reason for the change of view on the part of the Commission is not known. The only specific claim to credit which can be claimed by the representative of the Middle Temple is obstinacy.

However, the Inn records relating to another crisis, brought about by the refusal of licences for the necessary reconstruction work, may possibly provide an explanation for the change of mind.

On 4 December 1947, Master Carpmael and Master Craig Henderson (the previous year's treasurer) reported on a meeting they had attended at the Ministry of Works on 21 November, accompanied by the architects and Inn surveyor. They had received a pleasant surprise. The meeting was attended by representatives of all the Inns and the Law Society, as well as of the Ministry of Town and Country Planning and the War Damage

Commission. The chairman was Major RL Brokenshire of the Ministry of Works, who explained that Working Party No 3 was concerned with the demands made on the building trades in the City of London by professional bodies such as the Inns of Court. He very helpfully suggested that the Inns had not sufficiently pushed their strong claim for priorities on educational grounds, and recommended them to submit a concerted plan on that basis, together with other information needed by his Ministry. The Inn representatives concluded:

> It was obvious that the attitude of the chairman and of his Ministry towards the claims of the Inns of Court is very sympathetic and that Major Brokenshire is anxious to have his hands strengthened in supporting our claims for priorities.

The four Inns immediately sent in a joint memorandum on their education functions.

On 7 June 1948, representatives of the four Inns met at the Middle Temple and agreed that once the Minister of Town and Country Planning had approved their reconstruction plans, they would submit a further joint memorandum to the Ministry of Works, setting out each Inn's programme of work and their need for priority in the grant of licences for work and materials. On 31 January 1949, Maufe reported that the drawings for the reconstruction of the Inn were complete and ready for submission to the appropriate Ministry. His scheme had been prepared in agreement with Sir Hubert Worthington, the architect working on the rebuilding of the Inner Temple.

The Inns had little difficulty in getting licences for first-aid repair work on surviving buildings, especially where there was a danger of deterioration in the absence of such work, and the War Damage Commission paid for such essential works fairly speedily. The really important question in 1949 was when work on the replacement buildings could be commenced.

The substantial repairs required for the Temple Church were a matter of joint responsibility for the two Inns, but on 13 April 1949, Master MacGeagh, the Middle Temple deputy treasurer (for the Queen was treasurer in that year), wrote to Master Jowitt, by then Lord Chancellor, to ask for his help. He reminded Master Jowitt that the Temple Church had been classified by the Commission as a building of special architectural and historic importance, justifying a cost of works payment. Although the cost was estimated to be no less than £120,000, a licence for only £5,000 for preliminary works had been granted. Unfortunately, the work was proceeding 'painfully slowly', as Dove Brothers had only one mason on the site. If more masons could be obtained, the work could make better progress.[74]

---

[74] MT.6/RBW/298.

The Lord Chancellor wasted no time and wrote to the responsible Minister, Charles Key, on the next day. Key replied on 29 April, pointing out that Dove Brothers had another four banker masons working in their own yard, preparing the stone, but added that the Ministries of Works and Labour were making every effort to find more masons, including possibly some from Italy. On 4 August the Lord Chancellor wrote to the deputy treasurer to inform him that the Minister of Works had found four additional masons for the church and that another three were being sought. He added the cheering remark: 'He promises to keep this job under continuous review until the major labour demands are satisfied.'

The deputy treasurer thanked the Lord Chancellor by letter of 4 August and raised the really important issue:

> As you will appreciate I am most anxious to get chambers rehabilitated and in use again with as little delay as possible, so that our rental revenue may be to some extent restored. As you know, we are at present labouring under a very heavy loss of annual revenue as the result of over one hundred sets of chambers being blitzed. We are now starting as soon as possible with the reconstruction of Cloisters and Pump Court.

A week later he stated that the application for the requisite licence was about to be sent in, adding: 'I should be very grateful if you could lend a helping hand with the Ministers towards expediting the granting of permission.' On 12 August the under-treasurer sent the Lord Chancellor a copy of the earlier joint memorandum of the four Inns on the importance of their educational work, 'for possible use as ammunition with the Minister'. On the same day the Lord Chancellor wrote to the deputy treasurer, promising, 'I will certainly send a note to the Minister which at least secures that this matter receives prompt consideration.'

On 30 August Swanson submitted the application for a licence for the rebuilding of Cloisters and the south side of Pump Court at a cost of £197,000. With its answer of 13 September 1949 the Ministry of Works dropped a bombshell (perhaps 'land-mine' would be more appropriate in all the circumstances):

> A comprehensive programme of work for 1950 for the rebuilding of Central London is at present being considered in conjunction with the requirements of other war damaged cities and until a decision on the general programme has been arrived at, it will not be possible to approve specific schemes.

The Inns agreed that they had to challenge that decision, although all the benchers must have been aware that the country had for some time been facing a balance of payments crisis. On 18 September 1949 the devaluation of the pound sterling was announced. The Lord Chancellor nobly approached Key again, but cannot have been surprised by the reply from his ministerial colleague:

As you know, the whole question of the level of capital invested is at present under discussion. It may well be that we shall have to be even more restrictive for the next year or two than we have been of late.

On 30 September the Lord Chancellor wrote to the deputy treasurer:

Frankly, in view of the emergency which has hit us, I do not think that at the present moment he can say any more than he says. I have asked him to keep the matter under his constant and personal review, and this I think he will do.

The only progress that was made during the winter of 1949–50 was in February, when the Inn received a licence permitting the expenditure of some £3,000 for demolition work on the ruins of Cloisters and 1–3 Pump Court. The work was to start at the end of March and last for some weeks.[75] On 6 March 1950, the Chief Inspector of Ancient Monuments at the Ministry of Works, BH St J O'Neil, wrote a letter to Maufe, the architect, which contained both an interesting rebuke and a compliment. He thanked him for letting him see the ruins of those two seventeenth-century buildings and added:

We have no official standing in the matter. During the war we came into the picture in an endeavour to stop total demolition, but were rather late in the day. The Cloisters had by then been demolished, quite unnecessarily of course, and the same remarks apply to the south side of Pump Court. I agitated for and saved that which still remains standing, not because I aimed to have them retained, but as a pointer to a rebuilding in keeping with the remainder of the court. Now that I know who is to design the rebuilding, I am quite content.

On 4 April the Ministry of Works blocked the rebuilding of the Cloisters for the rest of the year:

It has not been possible to include the work to the above site in the programme for the current year and I regret therefore that this work must be deferred for the time being.

The Lord Chancellor was asked if it would be proper for a direct approach to be made to his colleague, the new Minister of Works, Richard Stokes, to discuss the whole matter. Master Jowitt agreed to Master Carpmael seeing the Minister, who turned out to be very sympathetic on the licence issue. Although Master Carpmael was acting for the Inn only, he felt it proper to put the case for all four Inns when he saw the Minister on 30 April 1950. The Minister told him to come back three weeks later with an agreement of the four Inns on the amounts each needed for rebuilding. On 23 May the four Inns sent in their agreed requirements. The two Temple Inns asked

---

[75] MT.6/RBW/306.

to be allowed to spend £90,000 a year each and Gray's Inn £120,000. Lincoln's Inn had suffered relatively little damage from bombing and so could be treated differently.

On 12 June the Minister sent a most welcome reply:

> I agree entirely that far and away the most satisfactory arrangement will be for us to settle a yearly figure to which the architects can work and which we know will have to be reserved out of our quota of work for London. But I am afraid that bearing in mind the appalling amount of reconstruction which there is to be done in London generally, I should find it extremely difficult to mortgage as much as £300,000 a year for the three Inns of Court, at any rate in the next year or two. You will, I am sure, appreciate that I must try to maintain some balance between the various types of reconstruction work which I allow, and I am very severely restricted in the amount of building work which I can licence in the country as a whole and in London particularly. I would like, therefore, to suggest that we might agree on a somewhat lower figure for the first two years with the hope, and the intention on my part if things improve, as I trust they will, that we may be able to increase the quota thereafter—certainly we will undertake not to decrease it, ie, £400,000 between now and 31 December 1951. The figure I have in mind is £200,000 a year for the first two years—ie two-thirds of the figure stated by the architects to be the desirable sum.

On 22 June Master Carpmael accepted the Minister's offer on behalf of the Inns.

Between 22 May and 20 July 1950 the War Damage Commission[76] changed its mind on the unit issue and at last agreed with the submissions made by Master Carpmael. However, the Commission gave no reason for the sudden departure from the opinion it had held for five years. Master Carpmael does not anywhere suggest that he discussed the unit point with the Minister, or that the Lord Chancellor was asked to intercede. Happily, common sense prevailed by 20 July, both on the unit issue and on the licence question. On 26 February 1953, Parliament resolved to name the new arch over Crown Office Row the Carpmael Arch. Master Carpmael ended his letter of thanks for that honour to the treasurer:

> I would also like to say that the negotiations with the War Damage Commission could not have been carried through without the cordial cooperation of the Inner Temple Bench and in particular of Sir Malcolm Eve.[77]

The rebuilding of the Inn at last became possible on 27 September 1950, almost 10 years to the day after the first bomb had demolished 1 Elm Court. On that day a licence was granted for work costing £60,000: £45,000 for the Cloisters and the balance for Pump Court, up to first-floor

---

[76] Sir Malcolm Trustram Eve (a future treasurer of the Inner Temple, as Lord Silsoe) was the chairman of the War Damage Commission.

[77] MT.6/RBW/306.

level. Dove Brothers, who had worked in the Inn for many years, submitted the lowest tender, and started work on rebuilding those chambers on 4 December.

The Pump Court work also included a new underground heating chamber in Elm Court, to be covered in due course by the new Lamb Building. It was to provide hot water and central heating not only for the Cloisters, the rebuilt south side of Pump Court and the new Lamb Building, but also for the Carpmael Building and Arch, to be built on land provided by the Inner Temple, by the western end of Crown Office Row. This central provision, apart from the obvious benefits, saved the large amount of labour, materials and costs which would have been needed to reconstruct all former chimney stacks, fireplaces and coal cellars. This point was to be made to the War Damage Commission in due course, when settlement figures were being discussed.

On 27 April 1951 the Inn was granted a licence for £60,000 for the remainder of the work on Pump Court. In the summer the tenants of surviving No 4 moved out so that the new work at No 3 and No 4, south side, could be tied into it. Work proceeded smoothly, and the architect, Edward Maufe, advised the Reconstruction Committee in November that he hoped for completion of the Cloisters in mid-summer of 1952, with a possibility that the neighbouring No 1 Pump Court, which shared its staircase, would be sufficiently completed by then for it to be occupied too. He also was able to announce: 'The work of reconstruction of the Hall is complete.'

The restoration of the east end of the Hall had been a labour of love, involving craftsmen of many trades. The painstaking reassembly of the many pieces of the screen was commemorated by a plaque recording the names of the men who had executed that remarkable piece of work. The financial help given by members of the American and the Canadian Bar Associations, who had been appalled by the destruction in the Inns, was similarly recorded. The Hall had been reopened for some time, but there had been a number of finishing touches to be seen to before Maufe was completely satisfied and prepared to issue his final certificate to the builders. As a final touch he donated to the Inn a replica[78] of the 'Drake' lantern. The glazing of the replica was carried out by Moira Forsyth, who had undertaken other stained glass repairs for the Hall.[79]

On 10 June Maufe pointed out that the cost of the some of the work on the Hall, totalling some £6,300, had been correctly disallowed by the

---

[78]   The replica incorporates what metal could be retrieved from the smashed original: LA Whitelaw, *The Molyneux Globes and the Middle Temple* (London, Middle Temple, 2003), 23.

[79]   MT.6/RBW/300. Fortunately, the stained glass windows of the Hall had been removed to the country before the bombing started.

Commission, as it was for improvements rather than war-damage repairs. That work included greatly improved access to the roof space by means of trap doors, ladders and a bridge to the cupola. He added: 'I feel that it is most satisfactory that they were done at such a comparatively small cost.' The same comment could be applied to other works of improvement, paid for by the Inn and prudently included in the war-damage rebuilding.

On 15 April 1953 Maufe informed the under-treasurer that Pump Court would be completely rebuilt by the end of July. That completion marked the end of the first, laborious stage of the new chambers buildings: the continuous block running east to west. The new Lamb Building, Carpmael Building and Arch followed more smoothly to provide the next block, running north to south down Middle Temple Lane from the corner of Pump Court. Once that work was completed, the last new chambers building could be constructed on the site of the old Library on the western edge of the garden. With the consent of The Queen Mother it was named Queen Elizabeth Building and opened by her on 5 November 1957.[80]

In the following year the Plowden Buildings gap was filled by Maufe's beautiful new Library, conveniently linked with the Treasury, benchers' rooms and the Hall. Following his precedent of the Elm Court heating chamber, the boiler house in the Library was designed by Maufe to provide some heating and hot water for the range of buildings up to and including the Hall, which benefited from losing its own cumbersome heating provision. The Library heating plant also fed the new Queen Elizabeth Building, via a tunnel under the garden. Nearly 50 years later a branch was taken off that tunnel so that Garden Court could be supplied as well.

The partner of Wetherall, Green and Smith, the surveyors dealing with the matter (GJ MacDonald), put forward the Inn's claim for a final settlement figure to the War Damage Commission during 1953 and 1954, while the work was still in progress. At first, the Commission argued that it was liable to pay only about £350,000. It took MacDonald's 'patient arguments' until 3 September 1954 to get the concession from the Commission that it would accept the claimed figure of £518,000 as the permissible amount for all the built and planned new buildings.[81]

The rebuilding of the Temple Church took rather longer. As mentioned earlier, a shortage of masons initially held the work up. Also, the two Inns could scarcely claim that speedy rebuilding was needed for either educational or professional accommodation purposes. However, the time taken for the repair work was well spent: the church when completed was a significant improvement on the earlier edifice. The Temple Inns were lucky

---

[80] It was built with one staircase serving five floors. The Inn had considered erecting a larger building with two such staircases, but decided in favour of the smaller version because of the lack of funding.

[81] MT.6/RBW/315.

in that they had another enthusiastic and highly skilled architect, Walter Godfrey, for the work, coupled with the workforce of Dove Brothers once again. There were many technical problems to be overcome, such as the need to replace all[82] the Purbeck marble pillars of the chancel, which had split in the intense heat of the fires started by incendiary bombs. Godfrey later described the minor miracle needed to rebuild the pillars:

> The Purbeck quarries, in spite of discouragement, had never fully died away in Dorsetshire, although their great days of prosperity were six or seven centuries ago; and, with the help of Mr WJ Hayson, of St Aldhelm's Head Quarry, new workings were opened up. I had the pleasure of getting marble of beautiful colour and texture and of seeing the drums, capitals and bases cut and dressed with a skill as good as that of any ancient craftsmen.[83]

During excavation work the builders uncovered the 12th-century treasury of the church underneath the south aisle; some of the remains of St Ann's Chapel, which had earlier adjoined the south side of the church; a treasury, and the tomb of John Selden, the seventeenth-century Inner Temple jurist. Godfrey made provision for these finds to become visible to visitors, by providing steps down in a new south porch and an armoured glass window above the tomb.

Three further bonuses of the reconstruction must be mentioned. The Victorian 'improvers' of the Temple Church had disposed of the beautiful wooden carved reredos designed by Christopher Wren and originally installed in 1682. It was bought for £900 from the Bowes Museum in County Durham, where it had been since 1842, and restored to its rightful home.

The second addition was the new stained-glass central triplet window at the altar end, made from more than 15,000 pieces of glass. It was the gift of the Worshipful Company of Painters and Glaziers, and designed by Carl Edwards, who had won the design competition. Godfrey described it, without exaggeration, as 'one of the finest windows of modern times'.[84] The Inns had made a sound choice of artist: Edwards went on to design the Royal Air Force Church altar windows in the nearby St Clement Danes, the new windows for the rebuilt House of Lords, and the vast west window of Liverpool Anglican Cathedral. In 1954 and 1957 he added a Middle Temple and an Inner Temple window to flank his central triplet in

---

[82] IT TEM 5/8/10: Memorandum headed 'The Temple Church. February 1949', signed and dated by the contractors 16 March 1949; letter, architect to contractors 11 August 1949; contractors' reply 12 August 1949; contractors' letter to St Aldhelm's Quarry, 29 August 1949; contractors' review of the work at the Temple Church with covering letter to architect 26 April 1950. IT TEM 5/8/8: Choir Committee minutes 14 October 1949; IT TEM 5/8/11: contractors' letter to architect 29 January 1951.

[83] *Manchester Guardian*, 24 March 1954.

[84] *Ibid.*

the Temple Church.[85] Edwards had used his elder daughter, Julia, as the model for the Virgin Mary in the altar window. In 2005 his younger daughter, Caroline Benyon, who had been repairing the stained glass windows of the church, was commissioned to design a new window for the Round, and one for the south aisle of the chancel to mark the 400th anniversary of the grant of the 1608 Charter to the two Temple Inns.

The third addition was also a gift. As a replacement for the organ built by Bernhardt Schmidt in 1685 and destroyed by his compatriots[86] in 1941, the Inn received an offer[87] from Lord Glentanar of the substantial organ, built in 1924 by Harrison and Harrison, which he had at his Scottish home. He attached two minor conditions to his offer. The first was that he might be allowed to play the instrument on his rare visits to London, and the second was that it should first be overhauled by a well-known firm. The Inns had no difficulty in accepting his generous gift with those conditions.

This is perhaps an appropriate place to mention the Temple Church choir, which had attained world-wide fame before the war, thanks to the recordings it had made under Dr George Thalben Ball, who served as organist and choirmaster for some 60 years.[88] The men who returned after the war included Ernest Lough, whose treble voice had enchanted millions, on the radio and on gramophone records, when singing works such as 'O, For the Wings of a Dove'. After the war Lough sang as a bass, while his former role as lead treble was taken over for a while by his son, Robin—and later, by his grandson. The rebuilding could not really be considered completed until the church could once more produce the glorious sound of organ and choir combined. When the chancel of the church, which had been rebuilt before the Round, was rededicated by the Archbishop of Canterbury in March 1954, in the presence of The Queen Mother, the choirboys had not yet returned to the Temple, so the choirmen were partnered by boys from Westminster Abbey.[89]

One additional incident relating to the Temple Church deserves a mention. In 1960 the famous trial of Penguin Books, the publishers of DH Lawrence's *Lady Chatterley's Lover*, took place at the Old Bailey. The defence team was led by Gerald Gardiner QC, soon to be Lord Chancellor,

---

[85]   None of his windows bears his signature. Edwards told the author of this chapter that his medieval predecessors had not signed their windows and that he felt he should follow their precedent. See also Toulmin's 'The Temple Church', section III.A.

[86]   Bernhardt Schmidt ('Father Smith') may well have been German.

[87]   MT.15/FIL/16. I

[88]   It was Dr. Ball who had made Lord Glentanar aware of the Temple's need for an organ.

[89]   For further details, see D Lewer and R Dark, *The Temple Church in London* (London, Historical Publications, 1997). Once the boys came back, the two Inns resumed their pre-war practice of contributing to their fees at the City of London School.

and the jury acquitted the publishers of obscenity.[90] The Master of the Temple, Canon TR Milford, gave evidence at the trial for the defence on the issue of literary merit. When he entered the witness box he declined to take the oath and affirmed instead. Both these actions seem to have offended one bencher of the Middle Temple, as Canon Milford was asked for an explanation. The Canon explained by letter that he had been asked by a solicitor in the defence team, who was a friend of his, whether he had read the book. He told him that he had, and that he thought there were two or three things to be said for it. He was asked by his friend to give evidence, and explained why he had done so:

> I felt it would be cowardly to refuse to testify because of possible misunderstand-
> ings. I stand by what I actually said, which still represents my honest opinion. It
> never occurred to me that I should be thought to be committing the Temple, or
> that I was speaking for anyone other than myself.

As to not taking the oath, the letter went on to indicate that that was a decision based on religious grounds.

The Inn decided to take no further action.[91] (The Inn had normally shown a liberal approach to matters of conscience. For example, in October 1952 Parliament considered the case of a Nigerian student, who had been unable to obtain a recommendation from the Director of Colonial Scholars at the appropriate ministry, 'owing to his suspected pro-Communist activities'. Parliament resolved to inform the Director 'that it has not been the practice of this Inn to refuse an applicant otherwise qualified for admission purely on grounds of his political views'.[92])

IV.   THE INN AT WORK

In the previous pages the problems of the Inn's real estate have been discussed at length, mainly because the provision of accommodation for barristers and students in chambers, Hall and Library has always been one of the principal tasks of the Inn. It may be helpful to consider the provision of services other than accommodation by discussing briefly the benchers, together with the under-treasurers; the Library; catering; and the various provisions made for students.

---

[90] Counsel leading for the prosecution was Master Griffith-Jones, whose son Robin became the Master of the Temple in 1999 and an honorary bencher of the Inn in 2008.

[91] MT.1MPA/27.

[92] MT.1/MPA/26.

A. Treasurers and other benchers

The Inn throughout the twentieth century had three classes of Master of the Bench: royal, honorary and ordinary benchers. The ordinary benchers jointly governed the Inn and served on its various committees.

In January 1901, on the death of Queen Victoria, the Prince of Wales, the Inn's royal bencher, succeeded as King Edward VII. In June 1903 the King, who had been a bencher since 1861 and treasurer in 1886, established

> another great landmark by presiding at Grand Night both as King and as senior Bencher, no previous Sovereign having ever attended in anything but an honorary capacity.[93]

After the death of Edward VII in 1910, the Inn's efforts to call the new Prince of Wales were eventually successful in 1919, when he attained the age of 25. The Prince in due course became King Edward VIII and, after his abdication, the Duke of Windsor, but he did not participate in the Inn's life in the way that his grandfather had done, and was certainly not as actively involved with the Inn as his sister-in-law, Queen Elizabeth, was to be from 1944.

Queen Elizabeth's presence in London throughout the bombing had earned her tremendous respect, and we have seen what she had to say about the bombs in her letter to Master Sullivan in 1944 (p 400 above). On the death of her husband King George VI in 1952, the Queen became Queen Elizabeth The Queen Mother, and as such enjoyed her links with the Inn for almost another 50 years. The Queen Mother often enjoyed Grand Day and Family Dinners with the benchers, but also made a point of attending at other evening functions, as well as day-time ones, as, for example, when she formally opened both the post-war libraries and Queen Elizabeth Building.

In 1949 the Queen was elected treasurer, with Master MacGeagh as deputy treasurer. The most memorable occasion of that year was on 20 July, when Her Majesty, who had in June formally opened the rebuilt Hall, attended the unique joint dinner with the Inner Temple in the Hall, honoured also by the attendance of her husband, King George VI, the treasurer of the Inner Temple. The occasion was painted for the Inn by Terence Cuneo, an artist well known not only for his railway and war paintings, but especially for his precision and attention to detail.[94]

---

[93] L Heald, *Some Notes on the Royal Connection with the Temple and the Inns of Court 1185–1958* (Lent Reading, April 1958).
[94] He is also known for including a mouse in his paintings, but there is none to be found in his splendid painting of the dinner, as he had not started that practice by then.

On 2 February 1951 The Queen, accompanied by her younger daughter, Princess Margaret, attended a performance of *Twelfth Night*, given by Donald Wolfit and his company to celebrate the 350th anniversary[95] of the first night there, thus reviving the tradition of revels and other entertainments in Hall. Wolfit later wrote that it was his company's contribution to the 1951 Festival of Britain. The next major celebration came in 1970, when the Queen Mother attended the Ball given by the Inn to celebrate the 400th anniversary of the Hall itself, and clearly enjoyed herself. The author of this section has a fond memory of seeing her dancing the Charleston with a very skilled Master Scarman, a man of many talents.[96]

Students and barristers attending Cumberland Lodge were often invited by the Queen Mother to visit her on the Sunday morning of a weekend training session. It was because of the affection in which Her Majesty was held, that the Inn in 1984—the 40th anniversary of her arrival at the Inn—opened a scholarship fund in her name, to commemorate the link in the most suitable manner, namely, by raising money to assist students.

In 2000 the Queen Mother's 100th Birthday celebrations included a parade to which the Inn contributed a contingent, headed by Master Price. Her last visit to the Inn was to the Family Dinner held on 5 December 2001. When she dined with the benchers she fulfilled her usual task of adding the brandy to the Christmas pudding mixture brought into the Parliament Chamber by the chef, coyly pausing, after pouring in a goodly quantity, for the invariable cries of 'more' before adding a further contribution. The Middle Temple shared in the nation's mourning for her when she died in 2002. Diana, Princess of Wales, became a royal bencher in 1988, but was able to attend on only two further occasions before her sad premature death nine years later. But on those occasions she established rapport with the students by joining their messes after dinner. In July 2009 her son, Prince William of Wales, became a bencher.

Another event involving royalty occurred in November 1950, when the Foreign Secretary, Ernest Bevin, asked for the use of the Hall, as the Foreign Office had lost its own hospitality suite.[97] The Bench readily agreed, so on 22 November the Government entertained Queen Juliana of The Netherlands and Prince Bernhardt at a reception in Hall, which was also attended by the King and Queen, then immediate past treasurers of the two Inns. Another such event occurred in 1992, during the year of office of

---

[95] This was actually the 349th anniversary (ignoring the 11 days removed from the month of September in 1752). The first night was 2 February 1601 OS (2 February 1602 NS).

[96] The editor recalls a later occasion when a performance of *Iolanthe* was held in the hall in the presence of the Queen Mother, where the part of the Lord Chancellor was played by the Lord Chancellor then in office, Lord Elwyn-Jones, who danced a merry figure.

[97] MT.1/MPA/26.

the Inn's only Danish treasurer, Master Heyman. He then had the great personal pleasure of inviting Queen Margrethe II of Denmark to join the Bench as an honorary bencher.

In January 1900, Lord Robertson, the former Lord Justice-General of Scotland, was called to the Bench as an honorary bencher on his promotion to the House of Lords. This appointment created a happy double precedent. Not only were honorary benchers regularly called after that, but the Inn made a point of electing not only distinguished Scottish and Irish lawyers, but also Chief Justices from the Commonwealth.

After several years of exchange visits with the King's Inns, Dublin, the Middle Temple's good relations with the Irish Bar were further strengthened in 1991, when Mary Robinson, the President of Ireland, who had been called to the English Bar by the Middle Temple in 1973, became an honorary bencher. In 1995 Master Babington, who had arranged the successful Middle Temple exchanges with the Irish Bar, was rewarded by being made an honorary bencher of the King's Inns. In 1998 Master Ashe, also a member of the Irish and of the Northern Ireland Bar, suggested another such meeting. The Executive Committee agreed that such contact was desirable, in view of the somewhat surprising fact that 'the only three Common Law professions in the European Union have little formal contact socially or intellectually'.[98]

The Inn's traditional links with the legal profession in America, dating back to John Dickinson, John and Edward Rutledge, and others before Independence, were also cemented by a number of such elections: of Chief Justices, Ambassadors (many of them lawyers) and Chairmen of the American Bar Association. As already mentioned, the first United States Ambassador to be called to the Bench was Joseph Choate in 1905. The second, John W Davis, called in 1919, had served as Solicitor-General of the United States in the five years preceding his London appointment. Since 1947 every United States Ambassador has been elected an honorary bencher. William Howard Taft has already been referred to but deserves a further mention here, as he must rank as one of the most distinguished benchers to date. Not only had he served as President of the United States from 1909 to 1913, but at the time of his call to the Bench in 1922 he was Chief Justice of the United States. His successor as Chief Justice in 1930 was Hon Charles Evans Hughes, who had been appointed an honorary bencher in 1924, when he was both Secretary of State and Chairman of the visiting American Bar Association.[99] Chief Justice Hughes had the enviable reputation of being able to cut counsel short in the middle of the word 'if'. Chief Justice Warren Earl Burger was called to the Bench in 1971, Chief

---

[98]   MT.1/CFM/18. Scotland has many laws in common with England, but is not a Common Law country.

[99]   MT.1/MPA/23.

Justice William H Rehnquist in 1995 and his successor, Chief Justice John G Roberts Jr, in 2007. Later in that year Justice Don Lemons of the Supreme Court of Virginia was called, underlining the historic connections of his state with the Inn. In 2010 Eric Holder Jr, the Attorney-General of the United States, was invited to become an honorary bencher. Chief Justice Burger regarded his election as an honorary bencher as the greatest honour. His links with the Inn were crucial to his role as the founder of the Inns of Court of America.[100] The American Bar Association was to return to London and the Inns in 1957, 1971, 1985 and 2000, but many other smaller parties of American lawyers, as well as individual judges and attorneys, have been welcome guests as well since the 1924 meeting.

In the second half of the twentieth century, distinguished people from other walks of life were invited to become honorary benchers, for example, Bishops of London,[101] former Prime Ministers (Harold Macmillan and John Major), a future Prime Minister (David Cameron), retired senior civil servants and representatives of the arts, such as Dame Veronica Wedgwood, the historian. Dame Veronica was elected in 1978 and became President of the Middle Temple Historical Society—and its first speaker—when it was formed in 1981. In 1993, Alfred Brendel, the distinguished pianist, who had performed in Hall and appreciated its acoustic, was made an honorary bencher. A number of academic lawyers were also appointed, both to help the Inn with advice on educational matters and to act as liaison officers for their universities' law schools. The Inn eventually also made a point of inviting a number of distinguished academics, who were already barristers of the Middle Temple, to join the Bench as ordinary members. Among their number was Professor Dawn Oliver, who on 1 January 2011 became the first woman treasurer of the Inn, apart from Queen Elizabeth in 1949.

Distinguished members of the business community were elected from time to time, and were able to advise the Inn on matters relating to the estate and to investments. For example, Sir Jules Thorn, the Chairman of Thorn Electrical Industries Ltd, was called to the Bench in 1970 and was a good friend of the Inn, both before and after becoming a Master. He first advised the Inn about the lighting of the Hall and Library, then generously paid for electrical improvements and finally left the Inn a substantial legacy for the scholarships. Similarly, Sir Christopher Benson, a surveyor and property company director, who was made a bencher in 1984, gave valuable advice to the Inn and particularly to the Estates Committee in connection with the major acquisitions in Essex Street and Fleet Street.

The custom of electing the treasurer annually from among their number, to head the Inn, was continued by the Bench. Each single one was, of

---

[100]   See note by Judge Peter Murphy in *The Middle Templar*, Spring 2010, at 18.
[101]   Fisher (1945), Ellison (1976), Leonard (1982), Hope (1991) and Chartres (1997).

course, a distinguished lawyer, so that it is invidious to pick out any particular individual. However, some must be mentioned, especially the father-and-son treasurers. In 1902, the Attorney-General of the day, Sir Robert Finlay, served as treasurer. He was Lord Chancellor, as Viscount Finlay, from 1916 to 1918, and was later a Judge of the Permanent Court of International Justice at The Hague. His son, the second Viscount, was a member of the Court of Appeal and treasurer in 1942.

In 1927 the first Marquess of Reading served as treasurer: his many great appointments have already been mentioned. His son, the second Marquess, who had been awarded the Military Cross and the Croix de Guerre in World War I, was treasurer in 1958. When the first Lord Reading was appointed Viceroy of India in 1921, his post as Lord Chief Justice was filled, in unedifying circumstances and for one year only, by another member of the Inn, Master Alfred Lawrence, who had been treasurer in 1914. The Attorney-General of the day was at that time, by convention, entitled to claim the post as his, once there was a vacancy. However, Sir Gordon Hewart, the Attorney, was needed in government by the Prime Minister, and so was asked to wait for his 'reversion' to fall in, with the safeguard for him that Lawrence, who was already 77 years old, signed an undated letter of resignation on appointment.[102] After a year in office, the caretaker Lord Chief Justice, by then Lord Trevethin, learned of the end of his term in office from a newspaper.

Mr Justice Hawke was treasurer in 1937, and his son, Sir Anthony Hawke, in 1962, when he was Recorder of London. While still at the Bar, Anthony Hawke once appeared in front of his father as counsel and cited a Latin tag. His father stated that he thought it was pronounced differently, but the Carthusian son insisted that his pronunciation was the correct one. 'Well you should know, Mr Hawke,' the judge conceded, with a sigh, 'You had a *very expensive* education.'

Sir George Baker was treasurer in 1976, while serving as President of the Probate, Divorce and Admiralty Division. His son, Sir Scott Baker, was to be treasurer in 2004, while a member of the Court of Appeal.

Master Edward Carson deserves a special mention. He managed the rare distinction of holding three posts as a Law Officer: as Solicitor-General in Ireland, and then as Solicitor-General and Attorney-General in England. He was the Leader of the Ulster Unionists, and in 1921 was appointed a Lord of Appeal in Ordinary without ever having served as a judge. In the following year he was elected treasurer of the Middle Temple.

Viscount Sankey was treasurer in 1935, after being Lord Chancellor for six years, and Earl Jowitt also became treasurer immediately after his term of office as Lord Chancellor, in 1952. After that date the Inn had a number

---

[102]   R Jackson, *The Chief* (London, Harrap, 1959), ch 7.

of treasurers who managed the great double: they either were in their year of office, or were later to become, Lords of Appeal in Ordinary. They were Masters Tucker, Donovan, Salmon, Diplock, Roskill, Ackner, Templeman and Nicholls. In 1972 the Inn celebrated the fact that five benchers were then Lords of Appeal in Ordinary: Masters Wilberforce (who had been promoted directly from the High Court), Diplock, Simon, Cross and Salmon. A portrait by Michael Noakes was commissioned as a memento.

Master Eustace Roskill had an extremely successful year in 1980. He was not only promoted from the Court of Appeal to the House of Lords, but was treasurer of the Inn. In the same year he became an honorary bencher of the Inner Temple. His brother, Sir Ashton Roskill QC, who had been Chairman of the Monopolies and Mergers Commission and of the Barristers' Benevolent Association, was treasurer of the Inner Temple in 1980 and was made an honorary bencher of the Middle Temple during his brother's year of office.

In 2005 the Inn scored a unique treble. Master Phillips was appointed Lord Chief Justice of England and Wales; he had been Master of the Rolls and was replaced in that office by Master Clarke. At the same time, Master Judge, the Deputy Chief Justice, was appointed to the newly-created post of President of the Queen's Bench Division. When three years later Master Phillips was appointed as the Senior Lord of Appeal in Ordinary, with a view to his becoming the first President of the new Supreme Court, Master Judge took over as Lord Chief Justice. When the Supreme Court opened in October 2009, Master Clarke joined his four fellow benchers who were already there by virtue of their membership of the Appellate Committee of the House of Lords: Masters Phillips, Saville, Brown and Mance. The twelfth seat in the Supreme Court was shortly afterwards filled by Master Dyson.

In 1981 Master Willis, who had been a bencher since 1948 and treasurer in 1969, wrote[103]:

> The late Master Sachs, who was Treasurer in 1967, was largely responsible for the introduction of a number of changes concerned with the administration of the Inn. This had not been substantially altered for many years and the Committee structure and Standing Orders were beginning to show themselves unable to cope efficiently with the ever-growing complexity of modern life, while the burden on the Treasurer was becoming almost too great for anyone still actively working. The Inn owes a great and continuing debt to Master Sachs for the improvements that he initiated and, largely, devised. The most significant was the introduction of a system of Annual Budgets, a Deputy Treasurer and a new Committee structure.[103a]

---

[103]   In his Introduction to *The Middle Temple Bench Book* (1982), vol 2, 51.

[103a] The names and responsibilities of the various committees were changed from time to time. The many changes have been omitted from the present work.

One of the most useful changes made to the committees was that the treasurer, while formally remaining the chairman, was relieved of chairing all the committees. A vice-chairman was appointed to all committees, save the Executive, and thereafter acted as its chairman. After a while the Bench acknowledged the reality of the situation by dropping the prefix 'vice'.

In 1966, the year before he was treasurer, Master Sachs was requested by his fellow benchers to respond to an attack on the Inns, contained in an article in *The Times* for 8 June. The author had written of the four Inns:

> The general feeling is that they are rapacious and inefficient landowners, ruining the profession by failing to provide accommodation for their working barrister members, refusing to disclose their accounts and holding up reforms.

Master Sachs went to see the Editor, Sir William Haley, and asked for a right to reply, which was granted. His article, entitled 'What the Inns of Court do for the Law', appeared on 16 June and included an explanation for the proposed increases in rents. Far from being rapacious, the Inns had charged low rents to assist the Bar:

> So in recent years barristers' rents have been low to the point of being somewhat out of touch with realities. Now rising costs and the need to put the Inns' finances on a reasonably firm basis, make an increase in rents essential, but because of past policy the percentage rise will seem steep and retrospective gratitude for having kept rents down is hardly to be expected.[104]

Despite the intemperance of the language used, some of the criticisms contained in the article of 6 June had some validity and were followed up. On 22 June Parliament asked the Finance Committee to consider the opening of the accounts, and during Master Sachs's year of office (1967) the Bench decided that they should be made available annually, although initially only to Heads of Chambers and 25 other representatives of the Inn.[105]

In 1968 Master Sachs produced a written report on his stewardship during the previous year, which included the following points:

> Perhaps the best tribute to all concerned with our students is to note that this year we have had 398 admissions against a recent normal average of just over 300—with a steadily increasing proportion from the United Kingdom.

He added that redeployment had produced some 60 extra rooms for barristers. He also drafted a letter appealing for contributions to the new Benefactors' Fund to provide further scholarships, and played a full part in

---

[104] MT.1/MPA/27.
[105] MT.1/MPA/28.

the discussions about the future of legal education and the restructuring of the governance of the profession in 1971. Many benchers will have echoed his lament:

> There are at present far too many committees engaging the time of far too many men, producing far too many papers on the same or overlapping subjects.[106]

At the beginning of the twentieth century there were 50 ordinary benchers; a proposal in June 1902 that the Bench should be increased gradually to 70 was lost.[107] It was not until 1954 that the number was increased to 60. The size of the practising Bar hovered around the 2,000 mark for many years, but more than doubled by 1978 and then doubled again before the end of the century. In July 1969 Master Scarman, then the first Chairman of the Law Commission, expressed his concern about the reluctance of some benchers to increase the size of the Bench. He felt strongly enough about the matter to write:

> I have no doubt that if we are to eliminate the lack of confidence which I know the Bar feels in the Benchers of the four Inns, our Middle Temple contribution should [include] widening and increasing the Bench.[108]

After that the make-up of the Inn Bench was a matter of increasing concern for many benchers, but it was not until January 1983 that Parliament accepted the recommendations of a sub-committee, headed by Master Templeman, that the number of ordinary benchers should be allowed to go up from 60 to 150. Parliament also accepted the recommendation that Masters aged over 72 should be asked to become emeritus, if necessary, to make room for newcomers. The description 'emeritus' was later changed to 'senior' and the age cap reduced to 70. Senior benchers could then attend parliament meetings and speak, but not vote. In 2009 the Inn took advice about the implications of the age discrimination entailed. Benchers attaining the age of 70 could choose whether to remain as ordinary benchers, retaining the right to vote in parliament but still having to pay commons, or to become senior benchers, losing that right and that obligation. Existing seniors were given the right to revert to ordinary bencher status.

In December 1985 Parliament considered yet another suggestion that the practising Bar was no longer adequately represented on the Bench of the Inn, and asked the Bar Selection Advisory Committee, chaired by Master Nicholls, to look into the matter. The Committee reported in October 1986 that for some time new Silks had waited for about eight years before

---

[106]   MT.1/MPA/31. Master Sachs had earlier been one of the leading architects of the civil Legal Aid Scheme.
[107]   MT.1/MPA/21.
[108]   In a letter to Master Monroe: MT.6/ESX/3.

being elected as benchers: as the average age of taking Silk was about 43, the average age at election was 51. Judicial appointments had regularly reduced the number of active benchers still in private practice, and the increasing number of such appointments was likely to reduce the proportion of practitioners still further. On 1 October 1986 the active Bench totalled 140 members, of whom 67 were still in practice, 61 were judges (most of whom were already benchers when appointed to the judicial bench) and 12 were others appointed on the various treasurers' nomination.[109]

The Committee concluded that the upper limit of 150 should remain, but added:

> We think that, in the present climate of opinion at the Bar and elsewhere, having a majority of practitioners as active Benchers on the Bench of this Inn at all times is an attractive and sensible goal. We believe that there is likely to be general agreement amongst Benchers on this.

The Committee recommended that nine practising Silks should be elected annually, so that more than half the active Bench should be practitioners by the end of 1987. The Committee, at the request of Parliament, also considered the recurring question of juniors[110] being elected to the Bench, bearing in mind the fact the bulk of the Bar consisted of juniors under 10 years' call.

The existing practice of electing a junior to the Bench only in exceptional circumstances was considered to be fair. The Committee concluded:

> Once elected, a Bencher is a Bencher for life. There are other, more appropriate ways in which (for example) the views of members of Hall of less than 10 years' standing should become known and considered when decisions are made regarding the Inn's affairs: the revised representation of Hall on committees, and the newly enlarged Hall committee, whose members are elected by Hall, provide machinery in this regard.

A further point was made:

> Recent experience is that when particularly able and suitable juniors are elected, in many instances they subsequently take Silk, so that the effect of their election as juniors is to enable them to 'jump the queue' and by-pass the 'waiting period' which equally able and suitable Silks have to suffer.

Parliament in due course adopted the principal recommendations.

In 1995 Parliament decided that the number of ordinary benchers should be allowed to rise to 170 by the year 2000 and that twelve practising members of the independent Bar should be elected annually.[111] Another

---

[109]   MT.1/MPA/38.
[110]   Counsel who have not taken Silk, ie are not QCs.
[111]   MT.1/MPA/44.

reason an increase in the size of the Bench was considered was because it was felt desirable to include more circuit judges, leading members of the Government Legal Service and respected academics.

Circuit judges, like their predecessors, the county court judges and permanent criminal court judges, had previously been elected benchers only in exceptional circumstances, as in the case of Judge Stephen Tumim, when serving as Her Majesty's Chief Inspector of Prisons. Of course, benchers who became lower-court judges remained as such and could even be elected treasurer, as was the case with two county court judges, Master Ruegg, treasurer in 1924 and Master Tobin in 1930. Some concern was raised at the time about Master Ruegg being able to carry out all his Inn duties, as he was based at Birmingham county court, but the Lord Chancellor was prepared to relieve him of some of his judicial duties in his year of office.[112] Master Tobin was well able to cope, as his court was Westminster county court, near by. By the end of the century the Bar outside London had increased greatly, as had the number of students undertaking their post-graduate studies there, so that circuit judges out on the different circuits could be useful representatives of the Inn, particularly if they were benchers.

In 2001 the number of benchers to be elected annually was increased to 24, after the treasurer, Master Alexander, had asked Master Clarke, the chairman of the Bench Selection Advisory Committee, to look at the problem once more. Master Alexander pointed out to him that each year some 75 new Silks were being appointed, of whom some 30 were Middle Templars. He personally favoured an inclusive approach to the question of numbers, adding: 'It does not matter if only a certain proportion of them are able to serve on committees or do other useful work for the Inn.'[113] Parliament accepted his proposal that there should be no fixed limit to the number of benchers.

After Master Clarke had reported back, the Inn adopted a new approach:

> The most important criterion for election should be future service to the Inn, but that the criteria should also include future service to the profession, the holding of important positions in government, politics and the Bar Council, the circuits and specialist Bar associations and particular distinction in the profession.

A new sub-category of bencher was created for members of the Inn who were academics, and who had in the past been elected as honorary benchers only. In future they were to be ordinary benchers, but relieved of the obligation to pay the usual entrance fee. The annual figure of new ordinary benchers reverted to twelve in 2005, the total number of such

---

[112]   MT.1/MPA/23.
[113]   MT.1/MPA/50.

benchers having been raised to 236 by the end of 2004, but was increased to eighteen in 2007. Parliament had become increasingly concerned about the number of highly-qualified Silks who were not being elected.

It must be conceded that, nearly a hundred years after women were first admitted to the Inn, the number of women benchers remains very small, as does the number from ethnic minorities—despite the Inn's very detailed anti-discrimination provisions. However, it will have been seen that the Bench has been largely made up of Silks of an average of eight years' seniority, and of newly-appointed High Court judges, about whose qualities there could be little dispute. The choice of appropriate members of the Inn to become Queen's Counsel or High Court judges has, of course, never been in the gift of the Inn, but was the responsibility of the Lord Chancellor until recently. Over the years, it is to be expected that the new appointment arrangements will produce a wider range of appointees and so lead to the 'widening' of the Bench, which Master Scarman thought essential as long ago as 1969. An example of that is the appointment of Master Scotland to the post of Attorney-General in 2007; she had been elected to the Bench in 1997. In 2007 exactly one-third of the 36 new benchers were women.

The work of the treasurer and his deputy, and of the various Bench committees, could not have been efficiently carried out without the continuous support provided by the under-treasurer of the day and his staff. The work of Henry Beresford-Peirse (1913–30), whose efficiency was in marked contrast to that of his predecessor, has already been discussed. His successor, Thomas Hewlett (1930–49), the son of a High Court Master, soon proved a worthy replacement. In 1934 the treasurer, past treasurer and other Masters formed a salary committee and recommended an increase for Hewlett, stating:

> It is universally acknowledged that our Under-Treasurer has been unsparing in his efforts for the advancement of the Society and that his work has been successful.[114]

Hewlett had the dubious honour of filling the post throughout World War II, and clearly had a far harder and more anxious time in office than his predecessor had from 1914 to 1918. After the war Hewlett regretted that he had not kept a diary in the early days of the bombing. One can get some idea of the uncertainty of life then, from his explanation: 'As the raids increased in intensity the chances of survival, either of the Temple or its wardens, appeared small and it hardly seemed worth while.'[115] In February 1946 the Bench recorded its appreciation of Hewlett's wartime service and

---

[114] MT.8/SMP/191.
[115] *Middle Temple Ordeal*, at 14.

mentioned that until illness had intervened, he had been on duty as an Air Raid Warden five nights a week and leader of the fire watchers.[116]

By the time he left office in April 1949, Hewlett had served the Inn faithfully for 36 years. Robert Williams had worked under him since 1921 and was appointed as his successor. He served as under-treasurer for 19 years, and so worked for the Inn for nearly 47 years. Unfortunately, he seems to have regarded himself more as a chief clerk than a chief executive. He told his successor, 'as if it were an achievement,' that he 'had hardly ever set foot in the Inner Temple or spoken to its Sub-Treasurer in all his 46 years'.[117] The benchers clearly decided to get a more highly-qualified chief executive from then on. From Williams's departure in 1968 until 2011, every under-treasurer was a retired senior officer from one of the three Armed Services, starting with Air Commodore Alastair Mackie (1968–70) and Captain JB Morison, RN (1970–84). The other Inns have made many similar choices.

The Inn was very fortunate to have two excellent under-treasurers at the time when the estate, financial turnover, membership and scholarships all increased significantly. Rear-Admiral Richard Hill filled the post in the important years 1984–94, and Brigadier Charles Wright in the following ten years. Both made excellent assessments of the problems and difficulties the Inn faced regularly, and both routinely prepared briefing papers for the treasurer and the Bench, which focused on the nub of the manifold problems and helped to concentrate minds wonderfully. Both were popular with members and with staff, and each one was elected an honorary bencher on leaving his post. Brigadier Wright was succeeded in 2004 by the Inn's second Air Commodore, Peter Hilling, a Cambridge law graduate. He did good work for the Inn, helping it to run efficiently in a time of financial stringency and playing a major part in organising the call to the bench of Prince William in 2009 and the attendance of HM the Queen at a luncheon later in the same year to celebrate the 60th anniversary of the Treasurership of the Queen Mother. He resigned his office with effect from the end of March 2011, and was succeeded by the Inn's first female Under Treasurer, Catherine Quinn.

B.   The Library

The Library will be discussed so as to cover five principal topics: the three successive Library buildings and some of their problems; the move to

---

[116]   MT.1/MPA/25.
[117]   See below, n 132.

professional staffing; the American Library and other special subject sections; the alarming problem of theft and vandalism; and lastly, the Common Room.

i. The Library buildings

The wartime damage to the Victorian Gothic Library has already been mentioned, as has its post-war demolition on safety grounds. However, it is tolerably clear that the Inn would sooner or later have needed a new library in any event, as the 1861 building was very wastefully designed, with no room for expansion. There is no record of any significant mourning for its loss.

The temporary Library in Brick Court, built in 1946 on the site of the demolished Nos 2 and 3, served the Inn very well for the twelve years preceding the opening in November 1958 of the new Library. The temporary building was constructed by the Inn's workforce, using recycled materials as much as possible, as a single-storey library, with a basement for storage. It was that basement which had been turned into one of the emergency water supply tanks in the war.[118] It had a Common Room and snacks could be obtained from a minute kitchen run by the long-serving Dawkins sisters. The first winter of the building, 1946–47, was one of the coldest in memory, and not helped by the severe shortage of fuel, but even after that the hot-air heating system regularly proved inadequate in winter, until an enterprising junior porter devised a means to improve it. As the roof was the principal recipient of the hot air, he devised a simple way, using a sheet of metal, to deflect the heat downwards onto the readers and staff. The manufacturers of the system approved the alteration, which clearly had never occurred to them, so in February 1952 the grateful Bench gave the ingenious porter a small reward.[119]

The new Library was opened by the Queen Mother in November 1958. The building work had been deferred until after that of all the chambers, but the wait was well worth it. The new Library was not only most attractive, but was suitable for the anticipated growth of materials in the next 40 years or so. However, by the end of the century it, too, was too small for all the demands made on it—and especially by the need for that building to house the Inn's archival materials—so that the possibility of expansion into the roof space had to be explored.

---

[118] When the work of resurfacing the Brick Court car park was commenced in 2005, it soon became apparent that the basement had never been properly filled in. To complicate the situation further, the City made a tree preservation order in respect of both trees in the car park.

[119] All references in this section are to MT.9/LCM unless otherwise stated.

In the meantime the Library had a number of problems, most of which had to be dealt with by the surveyor, notably problems relating to the basement: flooding, over-heating and the ingress of dust. Like all libraries it also had problems of security, but those proved harder to remedy. While architects and surveyors could provide security against unwelcome intruders, they could not provide safeguards against thefts by staff[120] or supposedly bona fide readers.

One of the most serious incidents of flooding occurred in August 1977, when some 3,300 books were damaged. The Thames Water Authority explained that torrential rain, coupled with high tide on the river, had prevented the escape of the water, some of which found its way into the basement.[121] As a technical explanation it was doubtless impeccable, but it was hardly reassuring, given the tendency for heavy rain to fall on the Inn and the continued proximity of the river. The next flooding of the basement, in January 1987, came from above, when an electrician working in the Common Room kitchen drilled through a water pipe in the floor. On that occasion over 500 books were damaged. There was a further incident of flooding in December 2001, caused by a break in a pipe in the same kitchen. Unfortunately it occurred during a weekend, so the leak was undetected for many hours. The damage, costing some £200,000, included a partial collapse of the ceiling of the basement, as well as damage to books and documents. Lisa Psarianos, the part-time paper conservator, had just finished preparing a Disaster Control Plan on the necessary first-aid measures to be taken in case of such an emergency, which included the addresses of firms able to supply specialist equipment, such as drying machines. The plan was pressed into service at once and proved most useful, thanks to the hard work of the staff.

At the end of 1991 the surveyor reported that over-heating of the Library had been caused by—of all things—the faulty operation of the newly-installed energy management computer. In the Rare Books Room the temperature had reached almost 90° F. In March 1992 a director of the antiquarian dealers, Bernard Quaritch Ltd, gave the Inn advice about its rare books, but his remarks could equally be applied to its archival materials: 'The first and most urgent need is for a clean, sympathetic environment.' That involved not only protection against fire, water, dust and excessive heat, but also the correct degree of humidity.

The end of 1992 saw further problems for the contents of the basement. The lengthy and expensive resurfacing of Middle Temple Lane, which involved the grinding of materials nearby, led to books in the basement

---

[120]   There have been occasional thefts by assistant porters.
[121]   MT.5/ESF.

being covered by unwelcome dust. The single-glazed, ill-fitting windows had proved inadequate as protection.

Throughout the twentieth century, raised standards of fire protection and health and safety requirements involved the Inn in extensive and expensive improvements. The insistence of the authorities on an additional fire escape in the Library caused some alarm for a number of reasons, of which cost was only one. The installation of a second staircase from top to bottom at the south end, incorporating the existing internal stairs, could be effected only with a great deal of disturbance and the loss of some valuable space. On the other hand, the necessity to install the staircase stimulated the Inn to think about using the roof space for the archives, and the staircase was accordingly built to access that space.

In 1997 the new stairs were duly installed in the south end of the Library, with minimal visual damage being done to Maufe's original design. Storage space in the basement was increased by the installation of rolling shelves, but the risk of flooding limited the use of the lowest shelves there. Some rudimentary protection from water from above was provided by plastic sheets.

The decision to convert the loft space into fully usable space was taken by Parliament in 2005, after it had received a report from the Library Review Committee in October 2004 emphasising that the Inn was finding great difficulty in treating its precious archival material with the care required. Apart from the storage problems, the Archivist and the part-time document conservator shared a small room, which could not be used as a laboratory or workshop for the essential conservation work on documents, made imperative by years of neglect.

The importance of the archive had been stressed by the Assistant Keeper of the Royal Commission on Historical Manuscripts and a colleague. They wrote in October 1989:

> As regards its value, it appears to be the most nearly complete archive of the four Inns of Court, and thus of outstanding importance to the history of the Inns and of the organisation and tradition of the legal profession more generally.

It was after that report that the Inn decided to appoint Lesley Whitelaw in 1990 as a full-time Archivist (see further below); before her arrival the Inn had only one part-time archivist, who had left in 1976. The new floor could also provide added security for the archive and the rare books, including non-legal ones. The Bench agreed that the idea should be implemented, despite the cost and the inevitable disturbance that would be caused. One of the factors affecting not only the cost, but also the length and amount of disruption inherent in drilling through it, was the solidity of the ceiling above the third floor of the Library, which Maufe had designed to be virtually bomb-proof.

The work of rebuilding and equipping the loft space, with modern facilities for storage and conservation, was completed in time for the new fourth floor to be opened on 19 July 2007 by Master Phillips, together with the Chief Justice of the United States, who immediately afterwards was called to the Bench as Master Roberts. As a tribute to the chairman of the Library Committee, it was named the Sir Louis Blom-Cooper QC Floor. Once the rare books had been moved to the new floor, the library staff members were able to reorganise the shelving of the books on all the three original floors—a major undertaking.

The Library Review Committee had also considered a number of other matters, including the question of whether the Inn should sell the Moly-neux Globes, which had been owned by it since some time after they were made at about the end of the reign of Elizabeth I. Any proceeds of sale would have provided a significant addition to the funds available for scholarships. The question inevitably arose: if it is appropriate to sell the Globes, what should be sold next? In March 2004 Parliament decided by a large majority to retain them.

ii.   Professional staff

For the first half of the twentieth century the Library managed with a Librarian, who had one or two assistants only, and a couple of porters. At the beginning of the century, incidentally, the porter's job was almost a hereditary one, judging by a letter received by the Bench in March 1904 from John Ing. He pointed out that he had already completed 26 years as a library porter and that his pay had risen in that time from 20 to 35 shillings a week. He continued:

> May I venture again to humbly ask for an increase of my salary. My grandfather and my father were library porters: their wages rose to 40 shillings per week. I have to pay a very high rent living in London (12 shillings per week) so as to be near my work.[122]

By the end of the century, the work of the librarians' profession had undergone major changes, some of which had been brought about by the computer and others by the additional needs of library users. The Library was eventually staffed by a highly professional group, after a number of incremental changes.

In October 1921, HAC Sturgess, who had been employed as an assistant librarian since 1909, was appointed Librarian, a post he held until his

---

[122] MT.8/SMP/168. It seems that John Ing's request was granted: this file includes a recommendation from John Hutchinson, the Librarian from 1880 to 1909, dated 28 March: 'I think the petitioner in every way deserving of any mark of favour the Committee may think proper to extend to him'.

death in 1963. In 1925 he also took over responsibility for the archive from the under-treasurer and so became Keeper of the Records as well. Included in his splendid efforts, during and immediately after World War II, was his preparation of the three-volume Admissions Registers of the Inn for publication, but he had no time, or indeed training, to deal with the records he kept.

In 1969 the Inn appointed the first professionally-qualified librarian, Charlotte Lutyens, to the post, and after a year in office she prepared an outspoken report, drawing attention to some of the shortcomings of the Library:

> The Library does not provide the normal facilities of a special library (such as bibliographical searches), and is under-productive, in that its existing reader's enquiry service is poor, its opening hours restricted, and its provision for students severely limited. In addition, its administrative records and catalogues are so confused that it is often difficult to find out whether a volume is in stock or a subject represented.

She suggested that, as a first step, the Inn should appoint a properly qualified reader's adviser, cataloguer and library trainee. Parliament agreed to those appointments being made immediately.

The computer enabled the Inn as a whole to organise its records of stock, orders, expenditure and other matters more efficiently, and the Library was able to benefit similarly, with the help of a new Librarian appointed partly because of her previous experience with computers. Janet Edgell was appointed in July 1989, and in November she advised the Library Committee that the Library should be automated and that a systems librarian should be added to the staff. That work was duly executed and 14 workstations were provided for staff and users. In February 1990, Mrs Edgell prepared a memorandum demonstrating how a distance service could work for the benefit of members outside London, using photocopies and fax machines—soon to be overtaken by e-mail. She made the point that of the Inn's 1,307 practising barristers, as many as 448 were practising in the provinces, and only the 859 with chambers in London could take advantage of the proximity of the Library. The increasing size and prosperity of some sets outside London enabled them to form a number of working chambers libraries, but there would always be a need for reference to the Inn Library for works not kept in such smaller collections. Incidentally, the excellent specialist libraries of some of the larger London sets helped to ease the pressure on the Inn's resources. The distance service scheme was implemented, but it was always hamstrung by problems of copyright—so much so that by November, the specialist practitioner who had kindly advised the Library in the past declined to give his further assistance in this particular area, 'as it is a minefield'.

The introduction of the year-long postgraduate Bar Vocational Course (renamed the Bar Professional Training Course in 2010) initially led to a concentration of students in London from 1989 on, so the Library came under considerable pressure to provide more seating, copies of recommended books, photocopying facilities and staff time. Opening hours were extended; students were given tours of the premises; information was obtained from the Inns of Court School of Law about the changing recommended texts, and extra copies of some of the more important books were obtained.

iii.   *The American Library and other special collections*

The many gifts of American books during the twentieth century came from a number of official and private sources, and were supplemented by purchases and exchanges suggested by the Librarian. Doubtless prompted by the American Bar Association meeting in London in 1924, the Assembly of Virginia in 1927 authorised the Governor to obtain and give to the Inn a set of the official state reports. In January 1928, Sturgess reported an exchange of some duplicates held by the Inn, for 237 volumes of the Michigan Reports. In April, the Chief Justice of Ohio was thanked for the gift of a set of Ohio Reports. One of the first of many American lawyers practising in London was Barnett Hollander, who regularly helped the Library. In July he was thanked for his further generosity in paying for the freight for some of the gifts. Later in the year he suggested that American lawyers should be charged for using the Inn Library, but the Committee clearly felt that such a step would amount to ingratitude:

> The Librarian was instructed to convey to Mr Hollander the thanks of the committee for the suggestion and to inform him that they cannot see their way to adopt it.

In October, Master Rothermere came forward with yet another generous proposal: he offered to supply 'anything which is wanted for the Library at any time'.

Shortly before the Wall Street crash in 1929 and the resultant slump, the Carnegie Endowment for International Peace, at the suggestion of the New York City Bar, allocated $7,000 for more reports and for textbooks. The financial crisis led to a sad entry in the Minutes in December 1931:

> In accordance with a resolution passed by the Executive Committee on 25 November, it was resolved that the order for all American reports be cancelled, until such time as the rate of exchange is more favourable for their continuance.

The Committee also cancelled the subscriptions for some periodicals permanently, and for others 'until further order'.

The fortunes of the American collection revived after World War II. In April 1954 the Committee recorded the gift from the United States Government of 550 volumes of reports, statutes and treaties, 'which, added to those already in the Library, would form the most complete working library of American Law in Europe'. In October, Winthrop Aldrich, the Ambassador, who was an honorary bencher, presented those volumes personally. Further donations and purchases by the Inn helped to fill some of the gaps in the collection, and some contributions came from two of the American universities with a campus and law students in London: Notre Dame and Pepperdine.

A fairly new addition to the American collection is a small section on 'Capital Punishment', used by members of the Inn and others who attempt to help the hundreds of prisoners kept for many years on Death Row in the United States. In May 2005 the collection was formally opened by Lord Bingham, to the obvious delight of Master Blom-Cooper, the chairman of the Library Committee, who was not only a published authority on the subject but the last surviving founder of the successful National Campaign for the Abolition of Capital Punishment.

The second important collection to be built up by the Library, after the American one, was that covering the European Community works. In 1972 the Inn, at the suggestion of Master Diplock, volunteered to house that collection as the other three libraries had run out of space. Not only did the other three Inns agree to share the cost of the collection, but so did the Law Society, on condition that solicitors could consult it. A specialist member of the staff was assigned to the task of keeping the collection up to date and answering readers' inquiries, which could be highly technical and time-consuming. In 1990 the Law Society started its own collection and withdrew from the cooperative venture. In December 2000 Gray's Inn gave notice that it also intended withdrawing, partly because it no longer wished to contribute to the salary of the specialist librarian employed by the Middle Temple for the benefit of all users. The other two Inns expressed a similar objection, so a new arrangement was made, which left the Inn paying the whole of that salary, with contributions still being made by the others toward the cost of acquisitions. Inner Temple and Lincoln's Inn specialised in different areas of the Commonwealth, while Gray's Inn concentrated on international and foreign law areas. As and when certain countries joined the Community, Gray's passed over any pertinent books to the European Community Collection.

A number of benchers also held office as chancellors of different dioceses and belonged to the Ecclesiastical Judges' Association. In 1991, when Master Newey, Commissary General of Canterbury, was chairman of the Library Committee, an agreement was reached with the Association and the Ecclesiastical Law Society that the Inn should house a small collection of relevant reports and books. The collection was formally opened by the

Archbishop of Canterbury in November 2003. To mark the occasion, the Library staff also arranged a display to celebrate its ownership of 66 books from the collection of the former Dean of St Paul's, John Donne, which the Archbishop examined with interest.

As well as having these special collections, as a result of regular discussions between representatives of the four Inn Library Committees and Librarians designed to minimise duplication (or even quadruplication), the Middle Temple additionally concentrated on certain subjects, such as the law relating to banking, health and safety, and professional negligence. In 1992, Rear-Admiral Hill, the under-treasurer, summed up the cooperation in one of his magisterial papers, 'The Role of the Inns 1993–2005'[123]:

> Coordination of the libraries' work, policy and facilities is now regulated by the Inter-Inn Library Liaison Committee, which has developed policies on matters as diverse as subject allocation for specialist books and compatibility of computers. The Inns believe that this form of coordination, while preserving four separate libraries, is the correct path the for the future.

iv.   Theft and vandalism

Libraries have always been the victims of theft and the vandalism that sometimes accompanies it; the Middle Temple has not been immune. The thefts have fallen into the usual three classes: the serious ones perpetrated by thieves targeting high-value books, illustrations or maps; thefts by assistant porters; and those committed by users.[124] It seems that many books and periodicals must have been stolen over the years by both law students and members of the profession.

The first major theft in modern times was of maps from the three-volume *Ortelius Atlas* in the Library, which the Inn had owned since 1700 at the latest. The thief, a student member of the Inner Temple, had managed to find the volumes, which were then still inadequately protected. The Inn became aware of the theft only when the student was found by the police to be in possession of some of the maps he had cut out. He was convicted and imprisoned in 1981, but the damaged atlas was forgotten. In December 1993 the Librarian reported: 'Three sorry looking volumes of obvious antiquity have been discovered at the bottom of a filing cabinet.' As the cost of repairs was estimated to be between £10,000 and £15,000, the Inn considered selling them, but in the end resolved to keep them, partly repaired.[125]

---

[123]   MT.1/MPA/43.

[124]   Failure to return books that are not signed out may involve theft, depending on the state of mind of the 'borrower'.

[125]   MT.1/MPA/44. The razor slashes were not repaired, since they were now part of the history of the volumes.

The second major theft occurred a few years later and arose, indirectly, out of a worthwhile endeavour. Early in 1993 the Inn approached Camberwell College of Art for help with conservation work. As a result, a number of students of that subject were allowed access to the Inn's collection and executed some valuable work while gaining useful experience. In view of that success, the Librarian then selected an apparently suitable, qualified graduate of the College to work part-time on paper conservation. As a member of the staff, he had unsupervised access to precious assets, but unfortunately turned out to be a heroin addict, who stole to support his habit. Once again, the police had found the thief to be in possession of items stolen from the Inn, one of which was the front page of the first Bible to be printed in Spanish. In March 2003 he was sent to prison on six counts of theft from the Inn. On this occasion the Inn was able to recover a number of the stolen items, thanks to some good detective work by the police specialist unit, assisted by Lesley Whitelaw, the Archivist.[126] After these serious thefts, the rare books of the Inn were all catalogued by outside experts, and security was improved, especially by the conversion of the loft.

There have been other problems of dishonesty affecting the Inn. Walk-in thieves and homeless trespassers caused considerable problems by day and night, until security was substantially improved in different ways. One of the principal improvements introduced was that of closing off all chambers entrances and supplying swipe or proximity cards. The provision of alarms to protect the valuable property of the Inn was another measure, as was the introduction of monitored closed circuit television.

One unusual theft occurred in 1995. The Inn drew a cheque for some £183,000 on its bank, Child & Co, in favour of Sun Alliance Insurance Ltd, its insurers. It was crossed 'Not negotiable' and marked 'Account payee only'. The cheque was stolen, probably in the post, and then presented to a bank in Turkey by a man who was not a customer. This stranger was paid some 11 billion lira in cash, presumably not in coin. The cheque purported to have been endorsed, in handwriting, by the insurance company. The Turkish bank sent the cheque to Lloyds Bank in London for collection. Lloyds paid the Turkish demand and debited the Inn's account. When the Inn asked Lloyds for reimbursement, the bank rejected the claim and maintained it had acted in good faith and non-negligently. The bank seriously claimed that there was nothing to put its staff on inquiry, and even suggested that the name, the Honourable Society of the Middle Temple, connoted a Masonic institution or a strange Middle Eastern religious sect.

---

[126] L Whitelaw, 'Theft Recovered', *The Middle Templar*, Trinity 2004, at 44.

Expensive litigation followed against both the Turkish and the English banks. The insurers had accepted the loss and sued in the Inn's name; the court inevitably found against both banks. The Inn had been advised throughout by Master Bueno, who concluded his report on the case to Parliament:

> The costs of this whole affair have been enormous, surpassing the amount of the loss several times over. Happily, Middle Temple's devotion to the welfare of the legal profession was only a nominal one.[127]

v. The Common Room

The Common Room could be considered under the head of 'catering' (see further below), but in the twentieth century it was always located in the three successive Library buildings (Victorian, temporary and the present building) and used by readers as well as others. It had always been intended by the Inn for use by both the Bar and by the students as a meeting place, where a drink and a snack were available at a reasonable price. From time to time the Common Room made a loss sufficiently large enough to trouble Parliament, but there was generally a preparedness on the part of the benchers to subsidise the facilities, especially for students, as the meeting place contributed to the collegiate atmosphere.

For many years the Common Room was run by the Dawkins sisters, who provided a very modest range of refreshments. Their family, like others, served the Inn faithfully for many years. Their father joined the Inn staff in 1897 and became the Common Room attendant in 1905, serving refreshments with the help of his wife. His appointment as attendant was probably made as a result of a committee report in April 1903, which had criticised both the poor state of the Common Room and the short opening hours.[128] His daughters started to work there in 1922, and continued for many years. The younger Miss Dawkins served in the Women's Auxiliary Air Force during World War II, but rejoined her sister after her demobilisation. In 1949, Williams, the newly-appointed under-treasurer, noted:

> Both Miss Dawkins are extremely good and loyal servants of Domus, hardworking, clean and with good manners. A type rarely met these days.[129]

By the end of the century the Common Room had been modernised in every way: more staff made more food available, and alcohol could be bought. The name was changed to 'Refreshers'. On hot days drinks could be taken down a few steps to tables in the garden. However, the losses increased to such an extent that in 2005 the food and hot drink facilities

---

[127]   MT.1/MPA/48.
[128]   MT.6/RBW/208.
[129]   MT.8/SMP/180.

had to be discontinued until a satisfactory alternative method of operating the Common Room could be found some months later. A commercial enterprise then opened a restaurant there, but felt obliged to surrender its lease at the end of 2008. Fortunately, another enterprise was able to take on the premises for a similar venture with a two-year lease. In June 2010, after the expiry of that lease, Parliament decided that the ground floor of the Library could no longer be used for refreshments, as the space was urgently needed for use by the Treasury staff housed in unsatisfactory conditions in Plowden Buildings. The space vacated was immediately let to a set of chambers. The loss of a congenial meeting place for students and barristers was regretted, so Parliament also resolved that an alternative Common Room site should be found as soon as possible.

C. Catering

Like the Library, the catering branch had some long-serving employees. In January 1911 the Bench presented Henry Darling, the Chief Butler, with 150 guineas and a silver bowl to mark his 50 years with the Inn.[130] However, arrangements for catering often left much to be desired, and many years passed before Parliament decided to tackle recurring problems by having a dedicated committee and a professional caterer to head the staff.

In 1967 Parliament decided that the time had come for a standing Catering Committee to be set up, and it met for the first time on 4 April. In July Parliament resolved:

> That in order to curtail the alarming losses which have been made in our catering operations, outside bodies of distinction (to be sponsored by a Master of the Bench) may sometimes be allowed to hold dinners in Hall.[131]

This decision was to be crucial for the future of the catering finances. One further outside source of income was similarly to prove increasingly helpful: the fees received from film and television companies for the use of the Hall and gardens. Perhaps the most appropriate filming was that which showed Judy Dench in her Oscar-winning role as Queen Elizabeth I, in the Hall for a performance of one of Shakespeare's plays in her presence, in the film *Shakespeare in Love*. To the dismay of the Master of the Gardens and his small team, their beautifully maintained garden suffered regularly from the dozens of support vehicles needed to produce even a few seconds of

---

[130] MT.8/SMP/178.
[131] MT.1/MPA/28.

film, but the reinstatement of the lawn was mostly paid for by the film-makers. The garden, incidentally, has received many prizes over the years.

Air Commodore Alastair Mackie, appointed under-treasurer in 1968, made it clear that he was not very happy either about the state of the catering arrangements, or about the fact that some of the responsibilities fell directly on his shoulders. In 1970, shortly before he decided to leave the Inn, he wrote a brilliant and—as far as one can tell many years later—largely justified appreciation of the Inn catering activities.[132] The first criticism was of the Masters:

> Benchers have evidently been anxious about catering for at least the last seven years. There have been successive reviews—by Lyons, by the auditors and most recently by the professional consultants, who in 1967 examined procedures, equipment and staffing in some depth. The feature common to all the reviews is the accuracy with which the central problems—smallness of scale and under-use of resources—have been identified. Unfortunately, the policy decisions prerequisite to dealing with these problems do not appear to have been considered. Meanwhile the cost to the Inn, as the losses since 1962 listed at Annex 1 show, has been about £177,000.

After pointing out that the most important element in the whole operation was the personnel, Mackie described the role of the two principal responsible officers, the under-treasurer and the steward. While accepting that the under-treasurer was in general charge of catering, he made the fair point: 'This, of course, he should do, as in his other areas of activity, through the head of department directly responsible.' In practice, he found himself directly involved with much of the work in detail:

> The second component of management is the Steward, to whose devotion and long experience at operating level, every review, and indeed all concerned, rightly pay tribute.

The sting was in the tail:

> But these qualities are not a substitute for the literacy, articulacy, flexibility of mind and powers of supervision that so complex a catering operation as the Inn attempts requires. It is greatly to the Steward's credit that much is successfully achieved; but the multifarious faults, the strain and uncertainty particularly associated with major functions, the excessive inroads that the need for detailed supervision make into the Under-Treasurer's time, and the all-round lack of professionalism, make it clear that management is seriously amiss.

---

[132] This and all other references in this section are to MT.1/CRR, unless otherwise stated. In his entertaining memoirs, *Some of the People all of the Time* (Sussex, Book Guild Publishing, 2006), ch 12, Alastair Mackie refers to 'the administrative mess left by my predecessor', and gives a description of the various steps he took when 'very busy mucking out the Augean stable I had landed in'. There is no reason to doubt his account.

Mackie continued:

> The unskilled kitchen staff are of a standard that can only be described as deplorable: the casual ward, indeed is the immediate source of substitutes if the regulars are too dirty or too drunk to work. But this is the best that can be expected in the horrid surroundings in which kitchen washing-up and labouring take place, and in face of the general shortage of labour of this kind.

After pointing out that permanent waiters tended to be loyal and well-behaved, he stated that they were paid a full wage for a relatively small number of days worked in a whole year. He added:

> Temporary waiters are far more flexible, but release from the obligation of paying them to do nothing is itself expensive. They are, moreover, of much lower quality: those so employed in recent months have included drunks and at least one convicted thief. An effort can be made to improve the quality of the temporary waiters by tapping other sources than the pubs from which they are traditionally drawn.

The under-treasurer's description of the facilities for the staff was undoubtedly justified:

> The fixed equipment in the kitchen is basically sound, but its layout might have been so designed as to use as many men as possible. The kitchen also suffers from other defects, notably the numerous small rooms surrounding it, which generate confusion and uneconomical movement of staff; the multiplicity of nooks and crannies which defy cleaning; the changes of floor level, which make porterage needlessly onerous and dangerous; and above all the ubiquitous squalor which suggests that, apart from the sources of power, there has been little change since the 16th Century. More generally, the whole area is an essay in wasted space.

The constant loss on lunches was noted, and the customers, almost all barristers, did not escape criticism. Despite the fact that their meals were subsidised, some of them had not cooperated fully with a self-billing system, described by consultants, 'with an irony that was doubtless unwitting, as the "honour system"'. The under-treasurer also made detailed comments on the dinner arrangements and on accounts, and concluded with a summary and recommendations. Two of the points were perhaps not valid, but many of the recommendations were later implemented. The first questionable comment was: 'The kitchen should be extensively altered and the wasted space released for letting.' It will be seen that when the rebuilding was executed, extra space was needed, and could be obtained only by excavating a new basement area. The second was his statement: 'Non-domestic catering has greatly expanded but this process is not likely to continue.' Fortunately, such valuable trade did increase further, and played an important part in the reduction of catering losses.

In response to the report, the Committee in March 1970 recommended that a catering manager should be appointed. Since that time the Inn has benefited from having a professionally-trained expert in charge of all the catering matters, although he, like other departmental heads, is required to report to the under-treasurer as well as to the Catering Committee. For a few years the catering was let out, but eventually it was brought back in house. However, nobody was able to prevent the almost constant loss on lunches, despite the various examinations of likely causes. At different times the quality of the food, the cost and other reasons were given by members for their being poor customers, but the main explanation in the last 40 years for the small numbers lunching, was that more and more people resorted to the many sandwich providers in the area. A sandwich at the desk increasingly replaced the convivial lunch in Hall—and especially for the increasing number occupying chambers at some distance from the Inn. The Committee, after ringing the changes on waiter service and self-service, on food quality, quantity and price, decided to increase the range of people permitted to lunch in Hall, so as to include not only members of other Inns, but also members of various tribunals sitting in the area and pre-booked parties escorted by official guides.

However, lunch numbers stubbornly continued to create problems. Increased student numbers meant that there were more dinners served, at any rate until the required number of dinners per student was reduced, but that did little to assist the overall financial situation, as students meals were subsidised—a measure always accepted as a proper exercise of the Inn's duty to its students. If the Inn ever has to cease providing lunches in Hall, the blame can fairly be laid at the door of the London practitioners. Master Alexander, when treasurer in 2001, pointed out:

> But when we look at the extent of the service we find that there are over 2500 barristers practising from chambers in London who are members of the Middle Temple. Yet on average only 92 lunches for barristers, 19 for Benchers is served every day. I see it as very questionable whether we are justified in losing very substantial amounts of money in serving lunch to a comparatively small number of barristers.[133]

In October 1993 Parliament considered the detailed 1992 paper by the under-treasurer,[134] mentioned above. It contained confirmation of the fact that the catering situation had improved, and that the other three Inns were also unable to manage without losses:

> In 1990, the last year for which full figures are available, the Inns had a turnover on catering in Hall of some £2.3 million. Their combined deficit on catering was about £1 million. Middle Temple had a significantly lower deficit than any other

---

[133]   MT.1/MPA/50.
[134]   MT.1/MPA/43; R. Hill, The Role of the Inns 1993–2005.

Inn (about £120,000) due partly to greater volume (some 60,000 lunches and 16,000 term dinners), partly to higher non-domestic profits and, partly, it is hoped, to greater efficiency.

Computerisation had by then time helped this department as much as the others. Rear-Admiral Hill added that there was some consolation for the Inn to be derived from the catering loss:

> Subsidised student dining is regarded as an educational activity and is a safeguard of the Inn's [charitable] status. In this context, on those rare occasions when catering nearly broke even over one year, there was some embarrassment in explaining it to the Revenue.

The problems of the kitchen outlined in the earlier under-treasurer's 1970 report were dealt with piecemeal. Some new equipment was bought (and caused problems), and retiling improved hygiene marginally, but more drastic steps were needed. Legislation brought new demands on the catering department, and at the end of 1991, Colin Davidson, the Catering Manager since 1988, pointed out that the staff required more uniforms, with attendant increased laundry bills, and more training; also that more refrigeration was essential. By the end of the century it was clear that the rebuilding of the kitchen could no longer be deferred, despite the fact that the likely cost of the proposed works, which were expected to take up to eighteen months, was first thought to be £2,260,000 and later twice that much.[135] In October 1999 the Minutes recorded:

> It was noted that most members of the committee were appalled at the state of the 'below stairs' accommodation for the Inn's staff and all agreed that the work need to be carried out.

Colin Davidson summarised the situation in October 2000:

> The kitchen is out of date in terms of its equipment, practices and layout—no significant changes have been made since the early part of the last century,[136] despite the huge increase in the use of Hall which has been seen in recent times. The equipment is generally on its last legs and costs an inordinate amount to maintain each year.

The plans for the rebuilding were prepared by the architects Carden and Godfrey, who had been in charge of the Temple Church rebuilding after the war, and were accepted by Parliament. The space beneath the old kitchen was excavated to a depth of 3.4 metres, to create a new basement with rest and eating areas for the staff, together with locker and shower rooms. Twenty mini-piles to a depth of 15 metres were inserted, and the subterranean work yielded a number of finds, including some Tudor foundation

---

[135] MT.1/CFM/21.
[136] The 20th century.

material, later displayed in the garden, and coins dating back to 1765. At the level above the new basement, a completely new kitchen was built, eliminating the objectionable features of the old one, such as the differing floor levels and 'the multiplicity of nooks and crannies'. While the work was being executed, the chef and his staff managed to continue to provide meals from a stack of cabins piled up next to the Hall.

The substantial works confirmed the soundness of the Hall structure, as did the 10-yearly inspection of its roof in 2005. The only minor defect then revealed to the consulting engineer and the Director of Estates, Ian Garwood, was the past insertion of wooden wedges into the gaps that had opened up in the timbers over the years. These wedges gave no strength to their host timbers but merely provided board and lodging for some beetles, which were evicted, together with the wedges or their remains.

D.   Students

We now turn to consider the students, who constitute a fundamental part of the raison d'être of the Inn. The initiation of the substantial scholarship schemes in the 1920s, which marked the beginning of a great success story, has already been recounted (See p 387 et seq). In 1948, when appealing for funds for the new Benefactors' Fund, Master Sachs made an interesting comment about his fellow benchers:

> There can be no doubt that high amongst the assets enjoyed by the Middle Temple was its range of scholarships, and that this was a big element in the attraction to the Inn of relatively large numbers of high quality students. As the quality of the present Bench showed, the Harmsworth Awards had done much to attract the best type of students to the Inn over the years. As but one indication, 27 of today's Benchers had been Harmsworth Scholars.[137]

From time to time, particularly when the inflation rate was high, it became clear that awards were too small. For example, in 1979 Master Sherrard drew attention to the seriousness of the problem, stating that in the past year no fewer than thirteen barristers, who had received a scholarship from the Inn, had surrendered it and taken up employment elsewhere. In October 1980 Master Bates was able to announce that the recent decision to increase most awards to £2,000 per year had already paid off: only one recipient had dropped out. Furthermore, twelve of that year's applicants for twenty-one awards had

> virtually picked themselves because, apart from their other qualifications, they all had first class degrees. Half of this number had two first class degrees.[138]

---

[137]   MT.1/MPA/29. There were still only 50 ordinary benchers at the time.
[138]   MT.1/MPA/35.

Thereafter further donations, large and small, enabled the Inn to make an increasing number of awards over the years, with the size of the awards gradually also being increased. However, once law student numbers increased substantially and government funding for a university and professional legal education diminished significantly, leaving students with massive debts on graduation, the annual income of all the schemes put together proved far too little, particularly in years when interest rates were low.[139] The Inn therefore decided to supplement that income with annual contributions from its funds, principally derived from rents.

In the year 1991–92, the scholarships awarded were worth some £300,000, most of which came from the various donors' schemes. By 1997 there were seven major funds, which provided the bulk of the scholarships, together with ten minor ones.[140] In that year Master Nicholls, the treasurer, stated:

> The purse strings of local authorities and central government are drawn more tightly than ever. Last year the Middle Temple awarded £450,000 in scholarships to students and young tenants. This is an increasingly important function if the Bar is to remain accessible to all. I myself was able to join and Inn and start to practise only because I was awarded a Blackstone Entrance scholarship and then a Harmsworth scholarship.[141]

By 2005 the Inn was making annual awards to students (including subsidised rent for 23 of them each year) amounting to over £1,000,000, nearly 80 per cent of which came from the Inn rather than from the donors' funds. Most of the awards were for one year and for £10,000.

Both the Queen Mother's Fund, which had been launched in December 1984 to celebrate the fortieth anniversary of her Majesty's wartime call to the Bench, and the Benefactors' Fund had overtaken the Harmsworth and Astbury by then in capital value, while the bequests from Masters Thorn and Diplock had caught up with them.[142] The next largest Fund was that set up by Master Booth in memory of her late husband, Master Joseph Jackson, which benefited from the royalties earned by Rayden on *Divorce*, which they had both edited.[143] Master Booth, incidentally, was the Inn's first woman bencher other than the Queen Mother.

One of the ways in which the Inn was unique was that the benchers always insisted that each applicant for a scholarship should be given the opportunity of putting his or her case in person in an interview. The other

---

[139] The information relating to scholarships is mainly to be found in MT.10/HMM and MT.1/CSM.

[140] MT1./CFM/17. Since 1975 all the funds have used a common investment fund for efficiency.

[141] MT.1/MPA/46.

[142] MT.1/CFM/20.

[143] MT.4/TRU/28.

Inns interviewed only a proportion of those applying, but the Middle Temple Bench felt that some candidates with a fairly unimpressive record on paper might well provide an explanation, given an opportunity. Sometimes comparatively poor results were attributable to the applicant having had to cope with, say, ill-health, almost insuperable problems at home, or prejudice at an important stage of his or her life. Such candidates might well score extra points for the character traits revealed by their success in overcoming obstacles that had not even been mentioned in the application papers. That point was made by Master Saville, when Chairman of the Scholarship Committee, in a letter to the Bar Council, dated 29 July 1992. He added a further important point:

> The Inn is firmly of the view that its awards do not exist for the purpose of simply assisting those who wish to become barristers, but to attract and help those who not only have that wish but can demonstrate an outstanding potential ability to provide the services for which the Bar exists. In the view of the Inn, the Bar does not exist for the purpose of providing a congenial career—but for the purpose of serving the public.[144]

The annual round of interviews always demanded a great deal of time from the members of the Inn sitting on the selection panels. By 2005, some 300 applicants were applying annually for a grant for the Bar Vocational Course and a further 39 for the Common Professional Examination for non-law graduates. (The cohort of non-law graduates, incidentally, was always very impressive and provided a number of worthy members for the Bar.) Each of the applicants was interviewed by one of four panels of three members, who made their assessments under four heads, then listed as follows:

a) *Intellectual ability*: the ability to conduct legal research and give written advice, as demonstrated by performance in school and university examinations, the interview and, where appropriate, other experience.

b) *Motivation to succeed at the Bar*: knowledge of the profession and the courts, and steps taken to acquire the personal skills of a barrister, will be taken into account.

c) *Potential as an advocate*, both in oral and written skills.

d) *Personal qualities*: those required by members of the Bar include self-reliance, independence, integrity, reliability, and the capacity to work effectively with clients, colleagues and chambers staff.

After the provision of scholarships, perhaps the Inn's main contribution to the life of all its students was the provision of a collegiate atmosphere, designed to help them to absorb the traditions of the Inn and the Bar. For

---

[144]   MT.1/CSM/5.

many years this was provided mainly by the requirement to eat a large number of (subsidised) dinners in Hall in the presence of benchers and barristers, as well as fellow-students. Students found the requirement increasingly irksome, especially those who complained that they saw relatively little of the Bench or Bar at dinner, and those with long, expensive journeys. In response to a questionnaire, they suggested that the dining experience should be enriched, with more after-dinner events.[145] The Inn responded by joining the other three in agreeing a reduction of dinners, and by providing more educational and/or entertainment functions after dinners. The term 'qualifying session' was introduced to encompass both dining and other functions. Weekend fixtures, such as those regularly run by the Inn at Cumberland Lodge (see below) or in the North, and introductory weekends at the Inn for students from outside London, counted as more than one qualifying session. The collegiate atmosphere was further enhanced by the Common Room and by subsidised accommodation,[146] both inside and outside the Inn itself.

In 1947 King George VI permitted Cumberland Lodge in Windsor Forest to be occupied as a grace-and-favour residence by St Catharine's Foundation, of which the Queen became patron. The Foundation was set up principally to provide a meeting place for university staff and students. Since 1964 the Middle Temple has been regularly invited to hold weekend seminars there for students. The trainers have been judges and barristers, together with some academics, and the subjects covered have included advocacy, sentencing exercises and other practice points. The weekends have been greatly valued by students and currently attract three qualification points each.

It should be added that Cumberland Lodge proved very popular with students, who had contributed to the success of the weekends from the very start. For example, in November 1968, the Middle Temple Students' Association suggested that students might benefit from more practical training on topics such as pleas in mitigation. Master Diplock, always a great supporter of law students, later reported that the suggestion had been implemented at the following June weekend. The 37 students attending had acted as advocates in eleven different cases, six of which involved pleas in mitigation.[147] In 1975 Master Cumming-Bruce, the treasurer, suggested that some pupils and students might benefit from acting for a short time as a marshal to a High Court or circuit judge. The idea proved very popular and gave the marshals an early opportunity to see the law in action from an ideal vantage point.

---

[145] MT.1/CSA/3.
[146] See section V. below.
[147] MT.1/CSA/1. Pleas in mitigation are submissions to the court for mitigation of sentence on behalf of defendants found guilty in criminal cases.

The Inn was also greatly assisted at other times by obtaining the views of the student body, represented as it was by its very active Association, whose fixtures further assisted with the collegiate atmosphere. The student President of the Association latterly served as a member of the Executive, Hall, Education, and Students and Pupils Committees. One such President, incidentally, later became in turn a member of the Hall Committee, a Silk and a bencher: Master Paul Darling.

Over the years the Inn gave small grants not only to the Association but also to Middle Temple students societies at different universities, which gave its members an early opportunity to meet some members of the Bench and Bar. The societies also proved to be useful sources of information on student matters; for example, in 1977 Paul Clark (later Master Clark), a great supporter of the Oxford Middle Temple students, gave the Inn an early warning that the students he met were being approached by firms of solicitors 'bearing gifts on quite a large scale'.[148]

The most important area in which the Inn was able to help the newly qualified barrister was with Advocacy Training, largely the brainchild of Master Sherrard, although the need for it had been discussed as early as 1926. The Executive Committee had then recommended:

> It will be advisable for the next five years to try the experiment of lectures in Hall, after dinner during Dining Terms, and at such other times as shall be found desirable, on 'The Art and Practice of Advocacy'.[149]

Nothing significant seems to have come from that proposal, possibly because it was appreciated, even then, that advocacy is best learned by practice under supervision, rather than an attendance at lectures; or as one bencher put it: 'You learn advocacy on your feet, not on your bottom.' In 1993 Master Sherrard suggested that an Institute of Advocacy should be set up for all pupils, but the Inns' Council preferred to leave the matter to the individual Inns. Middle Temple Advocacy, set up for the Inn by Master Sherrard in response to the rejection of his first idea, was run by him very successfully for the first ten years of the scheme, assisted by Master Simpson and a large, willing team of volunteer helpers of judges and barristers. When Master Sherrard ceased to be the Director, he was succeeded by Master Mortimer for the next five years and then by Master Whitfield, who had been treasurer in 2005.

In the period October 1995 to July 2005 the Inn provided 2,241 two-hour workshops for pupil courses, requiring the attendance by volunteer trainers for 4,482 hours, as well as time for preparation. The Bar Council insisted on a minimum of 12 hours of training for each pupil, but comparatively few pupils chose the short course provided to cover that

---

[148] MT.1/CSA/2. He clearly feared them.
[149] MT.1/MPA/23.

requirement: most of them elected to attend the two-week full-time course provided by the Inn. The training was provided by the Inn free of charge to its own members, who made up the majority of the 2,021 pupils attending one course or the other. The New Practitioners' Programme, between March 1998 and June 2005, involved the trainers in a further 1,622 hours of training. The New Practitioner's Programme was enlarged in 2009 so as to include tailor-made training for barristers in the Government Legal Service, and for those in industry and commerce.

In 2003 Master Sherrard, who had also served as treasurer in 1996, was rewarded for his sterling work by being appointed a Commander of the Order of the British Empire. The Stuart-Smith Working Party on The Future of the Inns pointed out that advocacy training schemes had done more than merely teach that subject:

> We think that it is no exaggeration to say that the involvement in teaching skills of advocacy has had a major effect on revitalising the Inns. Although those who take part in this work find it greatly rewarding in itself, we have no doubt that it is a commitment to their Inn which is a critical factor in motivating the teachers.[150]

On 31 March 2009, in a paper prepared for Parliament, Master Whitfield summarised the principal provisions of Middle Temple Advocacy and its more than 150 volunteer trainers:

> Unlike the other inns, which provide weekend courses only, Middle Temple provided five courses, each lasting two weeks. Each consists of daytime lectures and evening advocacy workshops which last for two hours, daily except for Thursdays, when court visits are arranged. At the end of each course, the Director considers the reports of the trainers which he then discusses with each pupil and, where appropriate, arranges for the Bar Standards Board to be informed that pupils have completed it satisfactorily.

> Two three days pupils' courses to 'sweep up' those who are unable to attend the longer courses.

> Three annual weekends for training new practitioners: advocacy on Saturday, ethics on Sunday. Specific courses have been arranged for employed barristers with different advocacy and ethics modules for those in public and private sectors respectively. For self-employed barristers there are separate advocacy courses for criminal, civil and family law practitioners, as well as separate ethics workshops.

One other earlier attempt to assist pre-pupillage[151] students was rather less successful. The Sponsorship Scheme, started in 1963, provided for any

---

[150] MT.1/MPA/51.
[151] Pupillage is a period of time required to be spent in barristers' chambers, under the tutelage of a particular barrister, as a condition of being allowed to practise at the Bar.

student who so wished to become a 'spondee' of a barrister, who could be approached for advice on any topic relating to practice at the Bar, or to the traditions of the profession and the Inn. Ideally, the sponsor would dine in Hall from time to time with his spondee, answer queries about the Bar and, with luck, might be able to help him find a pupillage. Thanks to some enthusiastic barristers, such as Leo Price (treasurer in 1990), the Scheme started off in a promising manner, so much so that Sponsorship Night on 1 November 1967 was attended by 279 students and barristers.[152] In April 1973 Master Milmo, the treasurer, stated:

> But perhaps the best tribute to the Scheme lies in the figures for admission to the four Inns of Court for 1972. These show that the Middle Temple had a total of 361 admissions, of which 258 were students resident in the United Kingdom. No other Inn had more than 217 admissions from the United Kingdom or total admissions exceeding 309.[153]

The Inn is currently admitting over 500 students annually.

But those figures may not have been attributable to the good reputation of the Sponsorship Scheme at all: the four Inns were constantly changing places on the recruitment leader board. Sometimes a reason is discernible, as when one Inn, in an effort to improve its own recruitment figures, dropped a requirement for Latin, or for a deposit for good behaviour; at other times there is no explanation readily to be found. Students sometimes recommend the Inn they consider to be the most generous with scholarships, but they are not necessarily correct with their rankings. One of the factors that probably affected the Scheme adversely was the insistence of the Bar Council that in the new century there should no longer be any private introduction of pupils, but that all candidate selection should follow a standard procedure.

In 1990 Parliament had considered the report of the Bar Council Committee, chaired by Master Phillips, on Funding for Entrants to the Bar, one important recommendation of which was that scholarships and other support funds should be switched from pupils to students. This was prompted by the fact that public funding for the fourth or sometimes fifth year required for professional legal education, had been discontinued, and by the view that the profession itself could and should support its pupils. The Inn had already implemented such a shift to a considerable degree, but total diversion was hampered by the terms of some of the trusts concerned. Master Phillips was soon able to report that two-thirds of the chambers approached in all four Inns, about funding for pupils, had replied to his inquiry. Some 335 funded places had been offered with a total commitment

---

[152]　MT.1/CSA/1. After a while the Sponsorship Scheme faltered, but was revived in 2009, when the Inn resolved that every student should be provided with a sponsor.
[153]　MT.1/MPA/32.

of £2,750,000.[154] Eventually, in 2001, the Bar Council ruled that each pupil must receive an award from chambers of at least £10,000: £5,000 for the first six months and a like sum, less any receipts from practice, for the second. Only in exceptional circumstances was a waiver of this rule to be permissible.

The rule requiring pupils to be funded did not help the problem of finding sufficient pupillages for the large numbers taking the Bar Vocational Course. As long ago as December 1982, the Middle Temple Pupillage Committee drew attention to the 'present crisis of numbers seeking pupillage', caused by the greatly increased numbers of law students. The Committee discussed the various alternatives suggested, but was against the proposal that a levy should be imposed on the Bar as a whole.[155] The compulsory funding of pupils is, of course, a variation on that theme. By 2005 the number taking the Bar Vocational Course had risen to nearly 2,000, but the number of pupillages available for those passing the course was likely to be down to some 500 only. The fact that a small number of pupillage awards from the most prosperous chambers were much higher than the mandatory minimum, was small comfort to the many students failing to obtain a pupillage

The Inns at different times received expressions of concern from Commonwealth governments or students about the difficulty of obtaining full, like-for-like training as a barrister. While always anxious to make adequate provision for students from the Commonwealth—who still totalled 28 per cent of the Inn's students in 2005—the press of numbers of home students at times required difficult decisions to be made. Such decisions inevitably led to criticisms of discrimination, or of making overseas students 'second-class citizens'. The first such occasion was in 1952, when the Council of Legal Education introduced a short post-final practical course for home students, many of whom were having difficulty in finding a pupil-master.[156] The problem had come about largely because of the large bulge of ex-servicemen and others in the immediate post-war years, commencing with 1946. But for the war, they would have been spread over a longer period of years.

A more important instance occurred when the Bar Vocational Course was introduced for post-graduate students intending to practise in England, with the concomitant phasing out of the old Bar Finals. Although the problems had to be tackled jointly by the four Inns, the Middle Temple always played its full part in the efforts to be fair to all students, actual and potential. For example, in June 1990, Master Price, the treasurer, confirmed the existence of 'disgruntlement' on the part of overseas students

---

[154] MT.1/MPA/40.
[155] MT.1/CEM/10.
[156] MT.1/MPA/26.

and referred to the concern of some Malaysian barristers about the new Course. At the November parliament, the dismay of Master Lee Kuan Yew, as expressed in a speech to the Singapore Academy of Law, was considered sympathetically. Master Lee bitterly observed:

> We had assumed that the British would continue to help train our lawyers. It was an unfounded assumption. The Inns of Court have made changes that clearly differentiate between their own law students and Commonwealth students. Courses conducted for their own students are not available to ours.[157]

The stricture was justified, but in fairness to the Inns, several additional points should be made. They never ceased 'to help train our lawyers'. They were faced with a vastly increased number of home students, not all of whom could be taken in by the Council of Legal Education and the Inns of Court School of Law. Additionally, they were aware of the pressing need for the English Bar to have a sufficient number of fully-trained recruits. Not only was there a need for them, but the solicitors' profession increasingly made more and more financial offers to promising law students, which they could not easily refuse.

In April 1991, the Inn's parliament considered the Report of the Bar Entry and Training Working Party, Part I (the Taylor Report), and felt obliged to agree with the proposal that the intake to the Inns of Court School of Law should be for 750–800 selected home students only. Master Gerald Darling, the treasurer, expressed his concern for the Commonwealth students, who had come with the legitimate expectation of training for the Bar, and Parliament agreed that the Inn should record that concern. How much the shortage of places, even for home students, was likely to affect the future of the Bar, may be gauged from the bad news reported by Master Hollis, the treasurer, in May 1994. He announced that of the 96 Middle Temple students thought to be good enough for a scholarship from the Inn, as many as 29 had failed to obtain a place on the course commencing that year.[158]

In 1993 a Working Party on The Future of Legal Education, chaired by Master Phillips for the Inns' Council and the Bar Council, found a solution to the problem, which was speedily implemented.[159] The Working Party pointed out in an interim report that the Taylor recommendations could not work:

> The demand for entry to the Inns of Court School of Law has outstripped the places available to an extent the Taylor Committee did not anticipate. Over 1900

---

[157] MT.1/MPA/40. Master Lee was the fifth student called to the Bar by the Inn in June 1950. The present writer was next-but-one, and recalls his colleague saying, shortly before Call Night, that he was going home to govern his country.

[158] MT.1/CFM/14.

[159] MT.1/MPA/43.

applications have been received for places on the 1993–1994 course and applications are expected to be even higher next year. An attempt to perpetuate selection is likely to meet vigorous attack from the universities, the Director General of Fair Trading and the racial minorities and will be perceived by the public as an attempt by the Bar to maintain a privileged position. The Inns of Court School of Law has not the resources to expand to provide training for all who wish to do the course. If such training is to be provided this will have to be at other institutions—and it is desirable that these should be in various parts of England. One advantage would be that overseas students could once again be offered the same vocational training as those intending to practise in this country.

The Bar Vocational Course problem was solved by the setting up of a number of approved courses in different parts of the country from October 1997 on, but the pupillage problem remained for both home and overseas students. The Council of Legal Education, which had originally been the four Inns' body responsible for the Inns of Court School of Law, became the Bar Council Education Trust, with a financial trousseau from the Inns; while the School lost its monopoly and merged with the City University, becoming merely one of a number of bodies teaching the Bar Vocational Course, albeit the largest.[160]

This is not the place for a full history of the changes made in legal education, nor of the increase of the powers of the Bar Council at the expense of the Inns, following on the Courts and Legal Services Act 1990. The former topic awaits a detailed study. The latter has been well summarised by Master Leggatt and Nicholas Lavender in *Halsbury's Laws of England*, vol 3(1), 2005, under the title 'Barristers'.[161] However, anyone considering the changes that have taken place in the past 30 years, must be conscious of the fact that nothing is immutable. Master Phillips, who before becoming Master of the Rolls and then Lord Chief Justice had devoted a great of his time to the problems of legal education, made the following chilling comment to Parliament in May 1998:

> It is not axiomatic that the Inn now has any role to play in the education and skills training of either students or barristers. The Inn should not intervene merely out of an attempt to justify its existence or nostalgia for its historical role. Insofar as the Inn plays a part in education or skills training, this should be because this can be better provided by the Inn than by any alternative source.[162]

To date the Inn has demonstrated its ability to pass on the acquired skills of its judicial and barrister trainers better than any other institution. Not

---

[160] MT.1/CFM/15.

[161] Some of the other disputes, such as that relating to rights of audience, have been discussed in great detail by R Abel, *English Lawyers between Market and State* (Oxford, Oxford University Press, 2003).

[162] MT.1/MPA/47.

only must it maintain its quality of training, but it would seem to be essential that the other Inns should be equally proficient in this field.

V.   BURSTING AT THE SEAMS

The rapid growth of the Bar after 1960 provided perhaps the greatest problem for the Inn: that of finding sufficient professional accommodation for members and barristers of other Inns. In the event, the relentless increase of the numbers being called to the Bar made it impossible to find enough accommodation, so many members were obliged, with the permission of the Bar Council, to seek it elsewhere. Fleet Street and the Strand to the north provided a few opportunities for the Inn to enlarge its estate, but only one came to anything. The small site owned by the Inn at 8 Fleet Street did not look very promising, as it comprised only a column of single rooms with no independent access or staircase of its own, but in the end it proved the key to expansion on the northern margin of the Inn.

Expansion to the west was not a new idea, as the Inn had owned various properties in Essex Street since the 19th century. A great deal of effort went into the attempted acquisition of other sites there, and into the development of such sites as were owned by the Inn. The Inn tried taking on leasehold premises but found them to be unprofitable—unless they led to the later acquisition of the freehold, as happened with the two Devereux properties off Essex Street, considered below. Inevitably, lessors made any available profit on the holding, imposed various restrictions and insisted on expensive dilapidations being attended to at the end of any lease.

Within the Inn itself there were three ways in which the accommodation available for professional use could be increased, and all three were tried over the years. The first was by the conversion of residential chambers to professional use; the second by the easing out of non-barrister tenants, mainly solicitors; the third by the conversion of cellar and roof space. The first method proved to be the most controversial and led to some heated discussions between benchers.

In October 1965, Parliament was concerned enough about accommodation to consider erecting a temporary, single-storey building in Fountain Court, to house thirteen desks in six rooms, 'with all urgency'.[163] However, the Bar showed little interest in the proposal, so that idea was abandoned. The completion of the war-damage rebuilding, combined with the conversion of some residential chambers, left the Inn with only a

---

[163]   MT.1/MPA/27. In September 1943 the possibility of 'temporary wooden and uralite huts', to accommodate up to 150 barristers, had been considered: MT.1/CMM/8.

limited demand for accommodation by the time the Estates Committee reported to Parliament at the end of March 1968. The redeployment of chambers, the Committee stated,

> has proceeded satisfactorily, and the Lord Chancellor expressed his warm appreciation of what had been done for the benefit of the Bar. Up to a comparatively recent date no application by barristers for accommodation remained unsatisfied.[164]

However, by May 1970 the shortage of chambers was such that the Minutes recorded:

> The Committee members were advised of nine outstanding applications for additional professional chambers. They noted with concern confirmation of the shortage of such accommodation.

Two possible schemes were being considered at that time.

The first was a proposal made by Child's Bank of Fleet Street, that the Inn should jointly undertake a large-scale redevelopment involving land behind the bank, together with the site of 4 Brick Court and 5 Essex Court, and some of the Brick Court car park. The second was for an ambitious redevelopment of the Inn's houses at 32–34 Essex Street. The architects Powell and Moya thought that a modern building of five or six storeys, plus a basement, might be possible there.[165] Numbers 32 and 34 had been listed by the Minister in 1958 as being of special architectural or historic interest, but No 33 had been rebuilt in the nineteenth century and so was not protected in the same way.[166] These three low buildings, together with No 35, were hemmed in between two large and undistinguished office blocks, which—together with further developments—were considered by the architects and others to have ruined the character of Essex Street beyond redemption.

The first proposal was fairly speedily abandoned, but the second ran into strong opposition from the local authority and others, notably Master Simon, anxious to preserve the few remaining houses in the street. It involved the Inn in a great deal of trouble and expense over a considerable period of time, before being replaced by a less ambitious scheme, designed and executed under the supervision of the Inn's surveyor, LS Sheppard.[167]

Early in 1972 the Council of Legal Education made it clear to the Inns that it would need more money from them, especially in view of the

---

[164] MT.5/ESF. The Lord Chancellor was Lord Gardiner, a former Chairman of the Bar Council.

[165] MT.6/ESX/3.

[166] MT.4/BOX/2.

[167] In July 1974 some £30,000, the cost of the plans, inquiry etc., was written off: MT.1/CFM/8.

recommendations of the Ormrod Committee.[168] Middle Temple promptly accepted its responsibility to pay its share of the increased cost of education. In January 1972 the new treasurer, Master Salmon, wrote a letter to all barrister tenants, pointing out the basic facts of life in the new climate. He started by informing them that Weatherall Green & Smith had made a detailed valuation of all chambers, which showed that rents were well below market rents.[169] He continued:

> The Inn has been reluctantly forced to decide that there is no alternative other than to raise our rents from 24 June 1972 to a sum equal to two-thirds of their market value as assessed. I recognise that in some instances this decision will involve massive increases on the rent now being paid. The new rent will still, however, be one-third less than current market value. For many years the rents charged have been extremely low. The Inn's financial position is now in an alarming state. We have been making very serious losses, which, if left unchecked, would quite soon lead us into insolvency. The only possible way of maintaining our Inn, which means so much to us all, is by taking the unpalatable course to which I have referred.

Master Salmon added some further important points:

> I ought, perhaps, to point out that in every other profession the rent paid for comparable accommodation (besides being one-third higher than our new rents) brings nothing to the profession except the accommodation which it provides. In our case any surplus of rent over the amount spent upon our buildings goes towards satisfying the needs of the profession for legal education and amenities such as the Library, Hall, Common Rooms and Gardens. All this expenditure is rigorously watched and controlled so as to keep it to a minimum consistent with maintaining satisfactory standards. The costs likely to be incurred on legal education even when strictly scrutinised are formidable. Unless however the Bar shoulders this burden, it will cease to exist. Without a steady and indeed increasing flow of newcomers, the Bar would not continue to provide the service which it now renders to the public and also fill from its ranks the judicial and quasi-judicial appointments which are ever increasing.

The Inns had been criticised for not disclosing their accounts, but the letter ended with an invitation to inspect not only the valuations, but also the accounts and budget of the Middle Temple.

The treasurer's letter has been quoted at length, not only for its wisdom, but because it marked a watershed. Thereafter rents and the income of the Inn went up significantly. That in turn had three important effects: first, barrister and other tenants found that the gap between rents inside and outside the Temple had narrowed, and so were prepared to contemplate

---

[168] Mr Justice Ormrod was the chairman of the Lord Chancellor's Committee on Legal Education, which made a number of important suggestions for changes, with cost implications.

[169] MT.1/CEM/8.

moving out of the Inn; secondly, the Inn had more money available for improvements; thirdly, it was able to provide more help for students. Whereas earlier scholarships had largely been provided by funds provided by donors such as Lord Rothermere and Master Astbury, after the rent increases the Inn was in a better position to top up the funds available for students—a matter of even greater importance once central government and local authorities washed their hands of the cost of professional legal education.[170]

In April 1973 only 111 sets of chambers of the 214 owned by the Inn were occupied by the Bar as professional chambers. Twenty sets were still occupied by solicitors and other outsiders, while 83 were residential, four being occupied by staff members. As many as 45 of the residential chambers were considered to be suitable for conversion to professional use.[171] As some post-war flats had already been so converted, the Estates Committee warned:

> If this policy is continued over a number of years, the result might be that all the new flats would cease to be residential and residential flats would be limited to approximately 38 old sets out of a total of 214 sets, or between one-fifth and one-sixth. These flats would also tend to be the small and inconvenient sets. We think that such a policy would be very undesirable and would very adversely affect the character of the Temple.

Parliament saw the matter differently, and resolved on 2 May:

> As long as there is a need for additional professional chambers, when residential chambers which are suitable for professional use fall vacant, so far as practicable, they should prima facie be destined for such use.[172]

In July 1973 some doubts emerged about the need for the Inn to apply for planning permission when seeking to convert chambers from residential to professional use, or vice versa. It had earlier been assumed that the Inn, like Oxford and Cambridge Universities, was entitled to make such domestic alterations without the need for permission. However, an appreciation of the fact that the Inn was not on all fours with either university, coupled with an abundance of caution, led to a request for permission being made—possibly unnecessarily—to the City of London planning authority.[173] Once the first one had been submitted, applications for permission were routinely made. That led not only to the loss of decision-making, but also to extra expense and substantial delays. In January 1978

---

[170] Public funding remained available for students on law degree courses, but gradually disappeared for those pursuing postgraduate studies for professional legal qualifications.

[171] MT.5/ESF.

[172] MT.1/MPA/32.

[173] The City was the authority for all the Inn, save for its western edge, which fell within Westminster.

the Committee reported that the delay in obtaining permission, in the five worst cases until then, amounted to no fewer than 20, 37, 58, 68 and 81 weeks.

In October 1973 the Inn was able to let the newly-converted third floor of Queen Elizabeth Building as barrister's chambers for the first time. Until then both the third and fourth floors had been residential and divided into four highly desirable flats. On 17 January 1974 the Estates Committee recorded:

> Concern was expressed by various members of the committee at the apparent lack of interest in additional accommodation being provided, despite the shortage of room for barristers who had completed their pupillage.

The truth was, of course, that newly-qualified barristers could not take on a new set: it needed a Silk or senior junior to be bold enough to leave his old set and take on the financial risks involved in setting up a new one; alternatively, for an established set to move into larger premises so as to be able to take on more tenants.

In January 1975 Master Sachs gave notice that he would be vacating his residential half of the fourth floor of Queen Elizabeth Building. The existence of sharply divided views on the issue of further conversion to professional use was underlined by what followed. After a prolonged discussion the Estates Committee agreed to recommend to Parliament that the Sachs chambers should be retained for residential use. However, on 13 March Parliament rejected that recommendation and ordered those chambers to be advertised as available for professional purposes. Permission to convert was eventually obtained, and both fourth-floor flats were let together as professional chambers.

In January 1976 Master Simon, one of the Inn members who was a Lord of Appeal in Ordinary, prepared a paper for Parliament on 'Middle Temple Accommodation Planning', expressing his strong views. He stated that he would not wish it to be thought that he held

> a belief that we have anything that could properly be called a policy. On the contrary, I believe that we have been reacting spasmodically to the results of our own mistaken actions, and then jerking further when those spasms failed to produce promised results.

He thought that the trouble originated from

> a grotesque overselling of the Bar to potential law students a few years ago, coupled with a complete failure to make any plans to cope with the resultant problems involved.

Master Simon added:

Nothing more original could be devised than the intensification of the stale and sterile attempt to get the Middle and the Inner Temple to convert residential into business accommodation.

He suggested: 'More consideration should be given to the deployment of the Bar into the Provinces (or even into Greater London).'[174]

Master Ackner, a former Chairman of the Bar Council, was always ready to take up the cudgels on behalf of barristers, whether in the Inn, the House of Lords or elsewhere. He responded with a paper on 9 February 1976, asserting that the Bar, far having been oversold, was still under-manned and therefore vulnerable. He asserted that the Inn had a very clear policy about conversions, pointing out that when the Estates Committee had recommended limiting the number of conversions of residential chambers, Parliament had disagreed, unanimously. He added that Sir Desmond Heap, the City Solicitor, who was a great authority on planning law, had told him that he and his staff had been embarrassed to get the first application relating to conversion, as they had been happy to leave the Inn to control its own affairs.

In June 1975 the Estates Committee and other committees enthusiasti-cally recommended the acquisition of the lease of Devereux Chambers, a building just outside the Inn, to the west of Essex Court, which would provide fourteen rooms for the Bar, as well as a top-floor flat and basement storage. Fortunately, the Inn was shortly afterwards able to purchase the freehold, together with that of the adjoining building, 9 Devereux Court. At about this time also, a less controversial redevelopment of 32–34 Essex Street, approved by the planning authorities, was forging ahead. Sheppard, the Inn's surveyor, had found a good way to overcome the difficulties created by the fact that both 32 and 34 were listed buildings. Number 33, in between, had been reconstructed in the previous century and so could be handled less delicately. He removed the stairs from the middle building and inserted a lift in the well, while retaining both the other staircases and opening access gaps in the party walls. This work made some 36 rooms available for the Bar, with direct access into the Inn from the back door of 33 Essex Street. The enlarged building adopted the name of the earlier central one, namely, Fountain Court. Soon after completing this project, Sheppard retired after 42 years' service with the Inn. When 35 Essex Street was acquired in due course, it was similarly linked with Fountain Court.

In November 1977, as the Inn still had a number of non-Bar professional tenants showing little disposition to move out, Master Bernstein drafted a letter appealing to their better nature and asking them to leave. As well as stating that the grant of a new lease would be opposed, he made a point about the Inn's past efforts:

[174] MT.1/MPA/33.

Although during the last five years the Inn has increased the professional accommodation available for barristers by about 32 per cent, this increase falls far short of the expansion in the size of the Bar in London during that time, which amounts to about 39 per cent.

In December 1978 Master Sheen, then chairman of the Estates Committee, was informed at a meeting with the City planners that further permissions to convert flats were unlikely to be granted:

The Planning Committee has made clear that a significant factor in their thinking was that, even if all residential chambers were converted to professional use, this would only partly solve the shortage of accommodation for the Bar.[175]

In October 1979 the damp-proof course in the basement at the back of Garden Court needed attention. Unfortunately, the Inn had no access to the exterior: access could be obtained only from 24–27 Essex Street, one of several buildings in that street owned by the British United Provident Association (BUPA). Master Bernstein, by then chairing the Estates Committee, had a good idea:

[He] suggested that a high level approach be made to BUPA to establish contact with a senior official of that organisation, the purpose of this being with an eye to the future possibility of acquiring the BUPA building as additional barristers' chambers.[176]

The idea got off to a bad start: BUPA refused the Inn access to the rear of Garden Court. But relations improved and the Inn was some years later able to acquire 24–27 Essex Street from the Association, when it moved out of the street altogether.

The Chairman and members of the Estates Committee had a great deal of work to do over the years, despite the ample help of the staff, when they were trying to satisfy the many applicants for accommodation. It would be easy to overlook the tremendous efforts of the members who were specialists in landlord and tenant work, such as Masters Bernstein, Colyer and Rich, each one of whom chaired the Committee for a while. They repeatedly spent many hours preparing helpful memoranda, schedules and proposals relating to premises that might be bought or converted. They also worked hard on a chambers re-allocation scheme, which arose because some sets had expanded into annexes spread throughout the Inn, while their tenants would have preferred to be under one roof: either in one larger set, or in two or more sets close to one another. The members of the Committee went to great pains to ascertain the wishes of the larger sets, and then to meet those wishes as far as was reasonably possible.

---

[175]   MT.5/ESF.
[176]   *Ibid.*

In December 1979 Park Nelson, the Middle Temple's solicitors, vacated 11 Essex Street, enabling the Inn to obtain a 25-year lease from June 1980 and to offer those premises to Master Alexander's Brick Court Chambers for overflow purposes, in exchange for their annexes.[177] That in turn enabled the Inn to help other chambers to move and free some more accommodation. By June 1981 the Committee noted: 'This means that Phase II of the professional chambers re-allocation scheme is currently on schedule.'

Inevitably, the various reallocation schemes could not be administered to everyone's satisfaction. In November 1990 Master Colyer produced a schedule showing the 22 possible re-allocations of chambers that best suited the requests for larger chambers, in exchange for the surrender of smaller annexes. In diagrammatic form the schedule showed possible schemes for different areas, eg Pump Court and Cloisters combined; Essex Court and Brick Court together. The preparation of the schedule clearly involved a great deal of work, as was confirmed when Master Colyer wrote:

1. To some extent this memorandum and proposed allocations reflect the views and prejudices of the exhausted Chairman of Estates! The great hopes one had of achieving rationalisation are confounded by the fact that almost no-one will move other than to acquire larger premises.

2. Thus most people's unhelpful idea of 'rationalisation' is simply to ask for more space and some of the most strident demands for help are from sets which have already been helped in the past three or four years; but there are others who have waited a decade without being helped and whose cries really must be heard.

The fact that the larger sets kept asking for more was hardly surprising, since they regularly took in a considerable number of pupils and were always anxious to accommodate the most promising ones.

In October 1980 the Professional Rents and Tenancies Sub-committee commented on the fact that the Senate Accommodation Committee had during the past three years encountered difficulties in its attempt to formulate a common rent policy for all four Inns, but agreed 'that this Inn should support the coordination of the ideas of the four Inns through the Senate.'[178] By January 1982 the Senate and the Inns had eventually reached substantial agreement on the appropriate approach, namely, that rents in the Inns should by 1984 go up to 90 per cent of market rents.

---

[177] Park Nelson had acted for the Inn, and had occupied 11 Essex Street, since before 1900.

[178] The Senate of the Four Inns of Court was set up in 1966 to act for the Inns collectively. It was replaced in 1974 by the Senate of the Inns of Court and the Bar. Since 1 January 1987 the Bar Council has acted as the governing body of the Bar, and the four Inns have cooperated through the medium of the Council of the Inns of Court (the Inns' Council for short).

In its hunt for further professional accommodation, the Estates Committee and Parliament at different times considered using a part of the Library as chambers or as annexes. Three alternative schemes were drawn up and considered in 1979–80, and a further three were put forward by the surveyor in 1983. The American Library on the third floor, the loft above it and the basement were all investigated, with various permutations. Not surprisingly, the Library Committee was unenthusiastic about the proposals, not least because the American Library had been largely built up from a large number of generous gifts and housed the principal specialist collection of American legal works outside the United States. There was a moral obligation to keep it going with proper facilities, which could scarcely be found in the basement or the loft.

During the discussions Master Sherrard, a leading proponent of the idea of using some of the library space, pointed out that the shortage of chambers was having an adverse effect on able students, who were dissuaded from coming to the Bar. Many such students were choosing the solicitors' branch of the profession, partly because of the financial incentives offered by some large firms. The shortage of accommodation point won the day, but the Inn chose the least intrusive option. The opening up and conversion of the loft was put to one side for a few years, and the structure and book contents of the American Library were left intact. However, the Inn purchased a number of carrels for erection between the bookcases in the American Library. They could be let out to individual barristers for use as outstations of chambers which had no physical room for them, but which were prepared to have them as tenants, with the use of their clerking facilities. Although the Inn was able to offer eighteen carrels for an annual licence fee of £750, later reduced to £500, very few barristers were interested in this idea and so it was soon abandoned.

Another possible place for expansion was considered in July 1983, when Master Rich prepared a report on Temple Chambers—built as a hotel in the 1880s, but always used as offices—outside the eastern boundary of the Inner Temple, immediately behind King's Bench Walk. The building contained about 54,000 square feet of office space and was owned by the City of London. The planners there thought that when the lease to a commercial tenant expired in 1991, the City might demolish and reconstruct the block itself. About eight barristers were under-lessees there at that time, but that number was to increase in the next seven years to about 170. If the Inn, with or without the help of the Inner Temple, failed to obtain the site in 1991, not only would the opportunity of expansion be lost, but any barristers then accommodated there would require rehousing. In the event, after the 1991 expiry date the existing building was retained by the City, so that exploration also came to a dead end.

In October 1983 the Committee considered the possibility of taking an assignment of the lease of 28–31 Essex Street, before rejecting the idea. The

Inn had bought three houses on that site in 1909 for £15,000, but had sold them on in 1923 for £16,000, as rebuilding then would have produced a return of only 3½ per cent.[179] In 1925 a large stone office block had been built there, and that in turn had been replaced by a very tall office block in the 1970s, comprising a basement and eight floors.[180]

The great need for further chambers to be made available may be gauged from an application from a set (using the word loosely) inadequately accommodated in an office building outside the Temple. The head of the chambers enclosed a very glossy brochure, which boasted that the dozen or so members covered no fewer than seventeen areas of specialisation. The application also revealed that the barristers had no rooms to occupy: not even a single shared one. The only accommodation was the room occupied by the sole clerk and the only telephone. The result was that there was a tendency for some members to haunt that room. When accommodation for a conference was needed, the landlord kindly made a vacant room available elsewhere in the building.

Every nook and cranny in the Inn was examined to see whether it could provide additional space for the Bar. The Inn's determination to make more accommodation available was underlined in November 1984, when the Buildings Sub-committee looked at the ground floor of 4 Essex Court. This was

> to see whether the old, bricked-up ground floor passageway leading to Palsgrave Place, which had been sealed off in the mid-nineteenth century, could provide additional space. A maximum of twenty square feet could be gained but it was considered not worth the expenditure due to the structural complications involved.[181]

A rather more ambitious scheme was considered for the rebuilding of Garden Court, so as to provide twice as much space for chambers there. One variation provided for the building of a new block to link up Garden Court with Queen Elizabeth Building, but the whole idea was eventually shelved in 1985, partly because of the cost, partly because of the opposition of Westminster City Council and the Victorian Society. The Inn was also influenced by the impending costly acquisition of the two Devereux freeholds. Incidentally, once they had been acquired, not only were those two buildings linked internally, but the first floor of 9 Devereux Court acquired a short bridge to link it with its parent chambers in 4 Essex Court, whose members paid for the work.

In October 1985 a set of chambers boldly prepared to move out of the Inn: from Carpmael Building to 49 Fleet Street (later renamed 3 Serjeant's

[179] MT.1/MPA/22 and 23.
[180] MT.6/ESX/1.
[181] MT.5/ESF.

Inn). They were the first set to move out of the Inn, and approached the Bench for help. Their proposed commercial landlord was concerned about the end of the lease, by which time most of the members of chambers might have moved on. He was concerned to have a form of guarantee, by way of a 'put option', so that the Middle Temple might be called upon to take an assignment of the lease in certain circumstances. The Inn agreed on this occasion to help, but resolved that any future such request should, as a general rule, be referred to the Senate.[182]

The Inn's next major venture into Essex Street was at the end of 1989, but netted only a lease of Nos 36–39 from the Duchy of Cornwall until 2003, which on expiry was not renewed. After extensive refurbishment the building was let by the Inn to a consortium of three chambers, whose move made more rooms available in the Inn itself. The lower ground floor was converted for use by the Bar Practising Library, an initiative of the Senate, based on a recommendation of a committee chaired by Lord Rawlinson QC. The Inn lent to the scheme the Salmon Law Library, donated to it by Master Salmon. The idea was that young barristers could be accommodated there while having a personal link with chambers elsewhere. Like the carrel experiment, this scheme did not last long, mainly, it seems, because it never found favour with the barristers' clerks.

The Inn in October 1991 decided to convert that lower ground floor into an arbitration suite, which proved to be moderately successful for a few years, but then had to be abandoned, principally because many large solicitors' and other offices by then had adequate facilities for arbitrations and mediations. When in February 1995 the Inn finished converting the basement of 1 Brick Court into two conference rooms, with access for the disabled, the administrator of the arbitration suite took charge of that too. When it was not being used for the disabled, it was available for Middle Temple Advocacy, or for tenants unable to use their chambers for conferences because of building work disruption.

The need of the Bar for chambers was again considered by the Estates Committee in 1991, when it received the report of the Accommodation Committee of the Bar Council, chaired by Master Whitfield, a future treasurer of the Inn. The profession in London alone was stated to have gone up from 3,125 members in 1979 to 4,638 in 1990, in increase of 48 per cent. Apart from increasing the amount of space available for professional accommodation in the Temple, the two Inns had succeeded 'by varying arrangements' in providing a further 46,000 square feet. The Whitfield Committee added:

---

[182] Donald Keating's chambers had moved from the Inner Temple to 10 Essex Street in December 1984. Its Middle Temple members had secured similar assistance from the Inn: MT.4/BOX/53 and 59.

Although the rise in rents inside the Inns has removed part of the deterrent to moving outside them, there is still a strong wish to remain within their precincts. On any analysis there is still reluctance to take steps to alleviate overcrowding.

Overcrowding had one consideration to commend it, especially to the younger members of any chambers: the more tenants sharing a room, the smaller each share of the rent.

In 1992 the Inn was able to buy 35 Essex Street, although vacant possession was not obtained until the following May and expensive refurbishment was completed only in November 1994. The Middle Temple then owned the four adjoining old houses, Nos 32–35, on the east side of Essex Street and south of Nos 36–39, the block then still leased by the Inn, but it still badly needed to obtain a larger building there. There were only two possibilities: Rowell House at 28–31 Essex Street, or its neighbour, Provident House at 24–27, at the south end of Essex Street. Rowell House, though not conveniently laid out, could provide as many as a hundred rooms for barristers, but when eventually put on the market, the asking price was over £7,000,000, and so those premises ceased to be of interest.

In an effort to make more accommodation available within the Inn, a number of basements were converted to professional use over the years, but only with a great deal of architects' and builders' input. For example, in the 1930s the Inn had undertaken major piling in the basement of 1 Essex Court to keep the building standing. Obviously a conversion of that and similar basements could be undertaken only with the greatest care. Apart from anything else, staircases to refurbished basements had to be redesigned and rebuilt, so that clients would no longer feel they were heading for the privy or the coal-cellar. The conversion of loft spaces was also explored, but the only feasible scheme was for the addition of fifteen new rooms for professional use, plus two studio flats, in the roof space of the post-war building erected on the south side of Pump Court, Nos 1–3. The existing tenants of Pump Court were extremely unfortunate with the timing of that work carried out over their heads, as it followed immediately on earlier essential work to remove the asbestos found in the vertical ducts of the post-war building and to improve their central heating systems. Some of them protested to the Inn and asked for a rent rebate because of the considerable disturbance, which in extreme cases had led to some tenants working and holding conferences elsewhere.

The Estates Committee responded to these justifiable complaints sympathetically, but with what may appropriately be called a dusty answer, similar to that regularly given to other tenants complaining about the disruption of their lives by building work. If the Inn were to give rebates in respect of work designed to improve the estate for the benefit of all, it would have less money available for further improvements. Another point made from time to time, was that if building work were timed to take place in vacations and at weekends only, not only would the cost of works escalate, but the Inn would be faced with longer periods of disruption and of voids in lettings, with resultant further loss of rent. In the case of the Pump Court protesters, the Committee was at least able to offer them the possibility of an increase of accommodation once the roof space work was completed. The Committee was also able to give them priority for tenancies of further premises in Pump Court: a surrendered solicitors' set and new basement space at No 6, in the old part of the Court. In July 1991, when the work was nearing completion, Master Rich undertook the difficult task of drafting a schedule of possible moves and exchanges.

The new Pump Court roof premises were not immediately snapped up—a matter that was reflected in the 1992 accounts.[183] The lack of enthusiasm for the converted premises provided a warning of the fact that large sets were increasingly looking outside the Inn for modern accommodation. As a result, in October 1993 Parliament approved the suggestion made by the Future Planning Committee, 'That high priority should be given to modernisation of professional accommodation.'

In August 1991 the largest and one of the most attractive flats owned by the Inn became available. It overlooked the Thames at 3 Temple Gardens, fourth floor south, and had three large living rooms plus four bedrooms, but it was not very suitable for conversion to professional use. The question of housing students in the Inn had been discussed from time to time and the decision was made to let it—experimentally at first—to six students, for ten months from October, that is, for their Bar Vocational Course year.

Stanley Wareing, the Head Bench waiter, who had been with the Inn for 32 years, died in December 1992, leaving his house in south London and the rest of his estate to the Inn, so that it might be used to house Middle Temple students or young barristers.[184] Master Price, his executor, later reported that Wareing had expressed a wish for a copy of his will to be exhibited in the house, as a

> lively reminder to young members, that the servants of the Inn, as well as its students and barristers, have been contributors to its heritage and tradition.

Inspired by this splendid example from one of its long-serving staff members, the Inn soon afterwards, with a legacy from the late Master Stocker and a substantial gift from the estate of Ferris Luboshez, bought another two houses for students near the Wareing house in Clapham. Ferris Luboshez was a retired captain of the United States Navy, who had been called to the Bar by the Inn in 1927. The three houses in Clapham provide a moving demonstration of the affection in which the Middle

---

[183]   MT.1/MPA/43.
[184]   MT.4/BOX/80.

Temple is held by its staff and its members, both home and overseas. The Inn then also made two newly-linked flats in Plowden Buildings available. Although the total number of those who could be accommodated in the five premises was small, 23 each year, the accommodation—particularly that within the Inn—was greatly appreciated by students as a useful adjunct to the scholarship provisions. Unfortunately, as a result of the pressing demand for accommodation in the Inn, coupled with the need for the receipt of market rents, the student accommodation in Temple Gardens and Plowden Buildings was withdrawn in 2009. In 2010 Parliament was informed that it was not economic to manage and maintain the student houses in Clapham. It noted a proposal[185] to let the houses on the open market and use the extra net income, probably in excess of £50,000 per annum, for scholarships.

In March 1992 the Inn attained a minor milestone: the last non-barrister tenant moved out of its professional chambers. He was not a solicitor but an architect, by then in his eighties, who had worked on several of the conversion projects and on the proposed Garden Court rebuilding scheme: Dr WH Marmorek, who had occupied the third floor north in New Court. The Estates Committee was able to record: 'This means that all [professional] chambers in Middle Temple are now available for barrister use.' The tenants from outside professions had initially taken on their tenancies at a time when the Inn was anxious to let vacant premises to them, and they had paid higher rents than barristers.

Ironically, the exodus from the Inn was eventually so large-scale that early in the twenty-first century Parliament had to consider a reversal of its policy and a return to the practice of letting to suitable outsiders. Not only did modern office premises outside the Inn appeal to many barristers because of their facilities, but they could sometimes be bought by their tenants, who could form a property company to own them. Such a step could form a useful means for barristers to make provision for their retirement. In 2005 the Inn was faced with a considerable loss of rental income as a number of chambers remained unlet, but by the end of 2006 they were all let once more. The credit crisis of 2009 created a number of budgeting problems, aggravated by the need to defer rent increases, but did not lead to any further voids. However, the deferment of rent increases necessitated retrenchment and led, for example, to the cancellation of the standing orders for some important legal periodicals and updates for the library.

---

[185] The proposal was made by the Finance Review Group, which had been established in November 2009 to oversee a finance review of the Inn's activities.

Middle Temple Lane was resurfaced in 1992 at great expense, brought about—as on other occasions—by the historic nature of the site. The surveyor explained that the cost of over £500,000 was attributable to the fact that

> we are now faced with having to satisfy English Heritage and the City of London Planning Authority, as the Temple is designated as a Conservation Area.

Like any other substantial property owner, the Inn repeatedly incurred significant expense when repairing the cost of unexpected damage done by, say, flooding or dry rot. One of the most expensive unexpected outlays arose when work was started in 1993 on 1–4 Middle Temple Lane. The buildings at the top of the Lane are some of the oldest in the Inn and the builders' work very quickly revealed major structural problems. Some of the floors were in danger of collapsing as the front elevations were inadequately tied to the main frame: 'In some cases floors and exterior walls did not meet.' Careful repairs, scrutinised by English Heritage and the City, consumed a great deal of time and money, but when eventually completed, received the City Heritage Award for 1998.[186] During the execution of the repair work, an opening was made in the back wall of 3 Middle Temple Lane, and then bricked up again and covered with panelling in such a manner as to make it a simple and clean operation to break through, in case the Inn should ever need direct access to 8 Fleet Street. The idea of some such work had been mooted by Sheppard, the Inn surveyor, as early as July 1960, when he suggested that when the lease of No 8 fell in 36 years later, 2 and 3 Middle Temple Lane should be rebuilt and combined with the small Fleet Street building.[187]

The repairs originally anticipated for the Lane buildings would have been expensive in any event, but with the addition of the unexpected work, the total bill came to some £2,300,000. The Estates Committee, when contemplating improvements, usually worked on the sound basis that the cost could be recovered in eight or 10 years by way of increased rents. When met by extraordinary expenditure such as this, the Committee could obviously not look for such future reimbursement. The costs overrun on this occasion led to the setting up of the Estates Review Working Group, chaired by Master Colyer. The principal conclusion of the Group's report, dated 25 June 1997, was as follows:

> We find no evidence that any significant part of these extra costs should or could have been avoided. Unfortunately the relevant buildings are all Grade 1 or Grade 2*, they abut on two highways (Fleet Street and Middle Temple Lane) and they are inalienable (being within the Charter lands). Whilst no prudent investor would incur costs and fees of £2,300,000 plus the costs of Phase III to safeguard

---

[186]   MT.1/MPA/47.
[187]   MT.1/CEM/4.

a rent roll of £68,000, the Inn unfortunately had no choice—the work *had to be done*. This is an example of how our more historic properties are of potentially negative value if significant works become necessary.

The Group also pointed out how the intervention of others had increased costs for the Inn:

> In relation to older properties we are often required by English Heritage and other authorities, faithfully to reproduce what can only be termed 'antique' construction techniques and details. Inevitably this magnifies costs. The architect wished to start with the assumption that all ceilings would have to be renewed. English Heritage demurred, and so the contractual documents provided for no new ceilings and a small cost allowance only was made. In the end 90 per cent of ceilings did have to be renewed—not just at the cost of new ceilings (a mere £85,000) but also so as significantly to disrupt and therefore delay the project.

The two largest expansion opportunities of the century came up near its end, and very close together, so that it was distinctly possible that only one could be afforded. The surveyor reported to the Estates Committee in July 1995 that an expensive refurbishment of 8 Fleet Street would only yield some 5,000 square feet gross. Developers were interested in buying the property from the Inn, and by the October meeting an offer had been made. However, having learned that BUPA was proposing to move out of its Essex Street properties, the under-treasurer and the surveyor visited Nos 24–27, then called Provident House. The premises contained nearly 17,000 square feet of lettable space and could easily have a direct entrance into the Inn provided, near the southern end of Garden Court. Although the purchase price and cost of refurbishment would be substantial, the building could both house a large number of barristers and provide a reasonable rental in return. The Committee was so impressed by this proposal and by the unattractiveness of the idea of converting 8 Fleet Street, that it recommended that the latter should be sold.

In December the Estates Committee reported to Parliament that a developer had considered building a 60-bedroom hotel on the site of 7–15 Fleet Street, less No 8. The Inn had applied for permission to develop its small site in order to enhance the value: 'This has proved to be the case as the original offer of £150,000 has now been extended to £450,000.' Fortunately, the decision to sell was put on hold.

In 1996, prompted by the Bar Council, the four Inns briefly investigated the possibility of converting the former Public Record Office in Chancery Lane to chambers.[188] In the event the Public Record Office was bought by King's College London for use as a library.

---

[188] The Library Liaison Committee of the four Inns also considered whether the library in the Public Record Office could be turned into a common library for the four Inns. The idea was not pursued.

The Middle Temple took the opportunity to purchase 24–27 Essex Street when that block became available at the end of 1996. The Inn then embarked on an expensive conversion scheme at the request of, and with a substantial financial contribution from, the proposed barrister tenants. Costs overran early estimates by a long way; but when completed, with an entrance into the Inn, the building made a splendid addition to the estate, with accommodation for some 60 barristers. Originally it was proposed to name the building after Master Wilberforce, who had been one of the Inn's five simultaneous Lords of Appeal in Ordinary, but his name was already being used by a set of chambers elsewhere, so an earlier Master's name was chosen, that of Sir William Blackstone.

Blackstone House was opened by Master Treasurer on 14 October 1998, but still required some work on the comfort cooling system that the tenants had requested rather than a full air-conditioning system.[189] On the same day the Estates Committee discussed the Fleet Street expansion idea again. Numbers 7–15, including the Inn's No 8, had been empty for some time. A Singapore company owned the site, but had not proceeded further. The Committee resolved to examine further the possibility of acquiring the site for development as chambers. It had become clear that developing No 8 on its own for occupation by students was financially out of the question, as the cost of providing thirteen or so rooms, greatly enhanced by the need to replace the staircase removed by earlier owners, would have amounted to almost £100,000 per room.

The Inn decided to go ahead with the purchase of 7–15 Fleet Street. The architects and builders were able to incorporate some of the best existing architectural features to great effect. The project turned out to be an excellent and attractive investment.[190] The existing reserves (including shares at near their peak, before a major down-turn in the City) covered the whole of the purchase price of some £4,600,000, so that borrowing was required for the building work only. The word 'only' is used loosely, as the work cost some £12,000,000. As had happened with Blackstone House, the premises were pre-let to one set of chambers at the outset. Like Blackstone House, the new Fleet Street premises, occupied by Quadrant Chambers, had a direct access provided into the Temple, albeit into Inner Temple's Hare Court, but Middle Temple made a contribution to improvements in that court. The project incorporated No 8, but not No 16, at the top of Inner Temple Lane, which was hemmed in by the site on two sides but remained in the ownership of the Inner. In acknowledgement of the

---

[189] The increasing cost of conversion caused the Finance Committee some concern: MT1/CFM/16 and 17.

[190] The City insisted on a shop being included in the redevelopment; that also produces useful income.

extensive work done by Master Burnton, the Chairman of the Estates Committee, the new acquisition was named Burnton Buildings by Parliament. It was opened in 2004.

The substantial building works described obviously involved the Director of Estates and his staff in a great deal of work. The Director for most of the time was Lyn Grenville-Mathers and his Deputy (and successor) Ian Garwood.[191] However, mention must also be made of the Inn's Clerk of the Works, Gerald Williams, who saw to it that the builders completed all those works in accordance with their contracts.[192] He received an award from his own professional body for his contribution to each of the four major projects, was formally thanked at a parliament in December 2005 and was elected President of the Institute of Clerks of Works in 2008.

The general rule that tenants of residential accommodation should be members of the Inn was waived in very happy circumstances in November 1963. John Donaldson QC, who was to become a bencher in 1966 and treasurer in 1986, asked if his wife could be made a joint tenant with him of his flat in Temple Gardens. Mary Donaldson wished to stand for election to the Court of Common Council of the City of London, but it was a condition that any candidate should be the owner or tenant of property within the City. The Executive Committee agreed to the requested change.[193] Dame Mary Donaldson served as the first female Lord Mayor in 1983–84, by which time Master Donaldson was Master of the Rolls. Master Gavyn Arthur served as Lord Mayor in 2002–03, thus cementing relations with the City further. An unusual event took place in between those two distinguished mayoralties. On 30 April 1992 the Inn invited the Lord Mayor, Sheriffs and Aldermen of the City to a dinner in Hall. The Minutes of Parliament record that many warm letters of thanks were received, 'and it had been suggested that the gap between such dinners should be reduced to under 300 years'.[194]

The allocation of flats in the Inn by the appropriate sub-committee was always the subject of the guidance contained in Standing Orders, as approved by parliament. In December 1960 the Executive Committee expressed the view that sympathetic consideration should be given to applications from young barristers for the smaller flats, but only a few succeeded in obtaining tenancies. The question of residential tenancies

---

[191] Mr Garwood discovered some old panelling in a storeroom and recognised it from a photograph, which showed it in the Parliament Chamber. It was restored to its rightful place in August 2001. It seems that it was banished from the Parliament Chamber in the 1940s at the instigation of a treasurer's wife who considered that its robust representations of the female figure were indelicate.

[192] Namely, 1–4 Middle Temple Lane, Blackstone House, the new Hall kitchens and 7–15 Fleet Street.

[193] MT.1/CEM/5.

[194] MT.1/MPA/42.

came up again in November 1999, when Master Kennedy, the treasurer, made some telling points when querying in a discussion document whether the existing system was the best:

> About a third of our accommodation is in the hands of members who have retired, in a few cases those who live abroad, and some make little or no use of their flats. Our overall duty under our Charter is to provide for the students and professionals of the law and I fear that we are not within the spirit of that injunction.

He suggested that when tenants' needs changed, perhaps they should move out in favour of someone 'with a better claim to the Inn's premises'.

VI.   A Glance Back and a Look Forward

The years 2006–08 saw the Inn celebrating three quatercentenaries, the first two of which were closely linked. In 2006 the founding of the Virginia Company in 1606, with the support of leading members of the Inn, was commemorated. Later in the year the sailing of the three ships[195] bound for Jamestown in 1606 was celebrated, particularly at an Anglo-American dinner in Hall. In the following year Master Seabrook, the treasurer, and Master Blair, the deputy treasurer, represented the Inn at the Rule of Law conference at Richmond, Virginia, which was also attended by Master Phillips, the Lord Chief Justice, and his opposite number, Chief Justice Roberts of the United States Supreme Court. At the end of the conference Master Phillips unveiled a plaque on behalf of all four Inns of Court at Jamestown, in the presence of his fellow Chief Justice. The Middle Temple figured prominently in the celebrations.

The charter granted by James I to both Temple Inns in 1608 had for many years been stored in a chest under the communion table in the Temple Church. The parchment had suffered badly from its time in the church chest, and despite the best efforts at conservation in recent years, it was in poor condition. On the initiative of Master Blair and Master May of the Inner Temple, an application was made for new Letters Patent for the two Inns, confirming the original charter. The result was that Her Majesty the Queen presented the Letters Patent at a ceremony in the church on 24 June 2008.[196] The presentation was illuminated by the light streaming through the new stained glass window in the south wall of the

---

[195] Named *Susan Constant*, *Godspeed* and *Discovery*.
[196] Master Blair described the various technicalities in *The Middle Templar*, Winter 2008 commemorative issue. One essential step was the translation of the 1608 Letters Patent by Sir John Baker QC, the author of ch 1 of this book.

chancel. It had been specially created to celebrate that 400th anniversary by Caroline Benyon, the daughter of Carl Edwards, who had designed the altar windows after the war.

Master Blair, the treasurer for 2008, and his opposite number at the Inner Temple, Master May, organised and presided over a number of celebratory events that combined to make the 400th anniversary year stand out. In January the two Inns got off to a good start by having a joint open weekend, which was attended by some 25,000 members of the public. In July a Celebration Ball, organised by Master Worsley, was attended by a thousand guests and raised £35,000 for charity. A number of musical events were held in the Temple Church throughout the year.

As mentioned earlier, on 19 July 2008 Chief Justice Roberts was called to the Bench as an honorary bencher, after he had, jointly with Master Phillips, declared open the new archive facilities built on the fourth floor of the Library, immediately above the American Library. The links between the two countries was further celebrated in October, when Justice Donald Lemons of the Virginia Supreme Court, who had been one of the principal organisers of the Richmond conference, was also called to the Bench.

Apart from cementing relation with American colleagues, during the past few years the Inn has increased its contacts with various Common-wealth jurisdictions, such as The Bahamas and Mauritius, taking advantage of the fact that such jurisdictions have members of the Inn working at different levels in their legal systems.

At home, great efforts have been made to improve the lot of students. The collegiate experience has been improved by the replacement of some dinners with other qualifying functions; and more money has been raised for scholarships. The Inn has recently been making awards worth over £1 million annually, of which over two-thirds has come from the income of the Inn (mainly rentals, which provide roughly 85 per cent of that income), with the remainder coming from the various funds provided over the years by members and others. The Inn is making great efforts to raise a significant sum for a further endowment fund for scholarships.

The Inn's contribution to the rounded education of the barrister, provided during pupillage and early years in the profession, coupled with continuing professional development courses, continues. The Middle Temple Advocacy provisions[197] remain the principal ones in the country. Master Sherrard's sterling five years as the first Director of Middle Temple Advocacy were followed by five years' service by Master Mortimer. In 2008, Master Whitfield, a former treasurer, took over as the third Director.

---

[197] See Section D. Students at p 446 et seq.

In view of the increase in student numbers, further staff had to be engaged and the search for increased accommodation continued. As long as the Middle Temple continues to make such extensive provisions for the profession, it will demonstrate its essential role. In June 2010, Parliament decided that the American Library should be remodelled, so as to provide adequate accommodation for advocacy training, while continuing to house the Inn's American collection. The total experience of the student and young barrister will help him or her to absorb not just the traditions of the profession, but its ethics. The disregard of ethics in some other walks of life recently has demonstrated how much it is in the interests of the public that each profession should have bodies that concentrate on such important matters. The Middle Temple, with the three other Inns of Court, provides an important safeguard.

Index of names

Index